· THE ·

International

ENCYCLOPEDIA OF SEXUALITY

Edited by

ROBERT T. FRANCOEUR

Preface by

TIMOTHY PERPER

Introduction by

IRA L. REISS

· THE ·

International ENCYCLOPEDIA OF SEXUALITY

VOLUME I

Argentina to Greece

CONTINUUM · NEW YORK

1998

The Continuum Publishing Company
370 Lexington Avenue
New York, NY 10017

Typography, Design Coordination, and Computer Graphics by
Ray Noonan, ParaGraphic Artists, NYC

Printed in the United States of America

Library of Congress Cataloging-in-Publication Data

The international encyclopedia of sexuality / edited by Robert T. Francoeur ; foreword by Timothy Perper ; preface by Ira L. Reiss.
v. cm.
Includes bibliographical references and index.
ISBN 0-8264-0838-9 (v. 1 : alk. paper)
1. Sex—Encyclopedias. 2. Sex customs—Encyclopedias.
I. Francoeur, Robert T.
HQ21.I68 1997
306.7'03—dc20 95-16481
CIP

3-Volume Set ISBN 0-8264-0841-9

Vol. 1 ISBN 0-8264-0838-9

CONTENTS

VOLUME ONE

VOLUME TWO

VOLUME THREE

Foreword

Robert T. Francoeur, Ph.D., A.C.S., General Editor

The International Encyclopedia of Sexuality brings together unique and invaluable information about patterns and trends in sexual attitudes and behavior in thirty-two countries around the world. Each chapter is written by a scholar or team of scholars very familiar with a particular country and its culture. Even when a chapter is written by a single author, that author has consulted with other specialists for advice and information to make sure the material in their chapter is accurate, up-to-date, balanced, and as objective as possible. In this *International Encyclopedia of Sexuality*, the reader can compare religious and ethnic factors affecting sexual behavior, gender roles, concepts of love and sexuality, sex education, masturbation, adolescent sex, courtship, marriage patterns, homosexuality and bisexuality, gender-conflicted persons, rape and incest, sexual abuse and harassment, prostitution and pornography, contraception and abortion, sexually transmitted diseases, HIV/AIDS, sexual dysfunctions and therapies, sexological research, and advanced education, as well as significant ethnic minorities in thirty-some countries around the world.

This encyclopedia began four years ago as an idea I could not resist. It seemed simple: I would recruit two dozen colleagues and friends in the Society for the Scientific Study of Sexuality (SSSS) and the World Association of Sexology (WAS) to write twenty-five-page chapters summarizing sexual attitudes and behaviors in their own countries. Twenty-five countries, twenty-five teams, twenty-five chapters, each about twenty-five pages in length. In a single volume, the reader could compare and contrast heterosexual or homosexual behavior and attitudes, sex education, contraceptive practices, or teenage sex in China, Japan, Australia, Canada, Poland, Russia, South Africa, Ireland, the United States, or other countries.

I did not anticipate the serious interest, high enthusiasm, and dedicated scholarship my invitation would provoke. The first few chapters to come in were about the expected length, because little information was available on those countries. Then China and Russia ran over fifty pages, Polynesia over sixty. When the chapter on the Netherlands arrived with over a hundred pages, I knew I had a much more massive project than originally planned. Subsequently, Finland ran one hundred ten pages, while Israel and Canada approached two hundred pages of tightly packed, fascinating information available nowhere else.

My original publisher had insisted on a single volume, but the material was obviously so unique and valuable I refused to edit and condense it. Fortunately, Jack Heidenry, a long-time friend, colleague, and editor for Continuum Publishing Company, recognized the extraordinary importance of the material. Nothing like this kind of cross-cultural comparison had ever been attempted.

The sheer volume of information contributors packed into their chapters could have turned into a chaotic mess. Fortunately, all the contributors were serious about fitting their information into my standard contents outline, which organizes their material into fourteen areas of concern. That standard outline allows the reader to draw comparisons and contrasts between specific attitudes and behaviors in whatever countries they are interested.

The common problems, concerns, and objectives experienced by all the contributors to this encyclopedia were nicely described by Drs. Ronny Shtarkshall and Judith Abrahami-Einat in an early draft of their chapter on Israel:

> The aim of this chapter is to give more than a detailed sketch of the sexual mores, attitudes, and behavior in Israeli society and a description of related issues of gender, marriage and family, fertility, and family planning. We aim to give our readers some insights as to the hows and whys of sexual issues in this society, which has many unique characteristics, and an understanding of the sexual issues within the wider context of Israeli society. Our ability to elucidate these issues may be limited by the multiplicity of influences and the formative stage of modern Israeli culture.
>
> Such an attempt may also be wrought with pitfalls, mainly because we are insiders to the society and therefore involved and possibly partially blind to some phenomena. On the other hand, we can bring to the discussion the inner understanding and the recognition of nuances that can come only from experiencing life within such an intense, sometimes baffling scene, to an outsider. Balancing the dangers of involvement is the fact that both authors are academics who also spent several years living outside Israel in Europe and the United States; one of us is also strongly involved in intercultural research and development projects. Such an experience will allow us, we hope, to avoid some of the difficulties or to overcome them.
>
> Other possible sources of biases include the fact that both of us are married (not to each other) and parents of children within traditional monogamous marriages. This may bias us toward a typical Israeli familial and heterosexual (hopefully not heterosexist) point of view, but this in itself is a central part of the Israeli scene. We are also an integral part

> of the "establishment": both of us hold academic positions, Dr. Shtarkshall is the current chairperson of the Israeli Family Planning Association (IFPA) and a long-time member of its board of directors, a consultant to the ministry of education on sexuality and sex education, and a member of the National AIDS Committee. Dr. Abrahami-Einat is the former Executive Director of the IFPA, a founding member of a rape crisis center, and a board member of the Israel Women's Network.
>
> We teamed together to write this paper because it was important for us to look at the sexual scene from both masculine and feminine points of view, synthesizing the foci where possible, or balancing them, but also pointing to differences or disagreements where they were irreconcilable.

Soon after work on the Israel chapter began, Dr. Abrahami-Einat accepted a new position, dropped out of the project, and was replaced by Minah Zemach, who brought her own expertise to the chapter. With other chapters, contributors were added or dropped out due to a variety of reasons. The author of a chapter on Egypt called to inform me that he could not deliver his chapter because religious fundamentalists had warned him not to publish it. Fortunately, I subsequently recruited a knowledgeable and courageous Egyptian Moslem woman doing graduate work at New York University in gender roles, who will produce a chapter on Egypt in the future with the unacknowledged help of friends and relatives in that country. Practical and political realities also emerged in the chapter on Bahrain, where the twenty Bahraini professionals and eight expatriates who helped an American expatriate to produce this detailed and carefully nuanced chapter could not be in any way identified. The American author sent the chapter the day she returned to the United States. Similarly, we are not free to name others who contributed to half a dozen other chapters where writing on sexuality is risky: American Iranians who provided comments on that county's chapter asked not to be named, as did persons who helped with other chapters on African, Middle Eastern, and Asian chapters.

Eusebio Rubio finished his chapter on Mexico, only to have his computer and all disk copies of his chapter taken by armed robbers as he tried to move them to a new office. He was fortunate to save a hardcopy which could be scanned. After three weeks with New York University graduate students studying cross-cultural aspects of sexuality in Copenhagen in 1992, I was particularly eager to have a chapter on Denmark. However, a priority call to work with the victims of the Bosnian crisis has kept its author, Dr. Soren Buss Jensen, preoccupied—Denmark remains for a future work. There were other surprises. There were delays due to unexpected surgery, serious automobile accidents, temporary blindness of one author, and the deaths of family members.

After a year's silence during which several inquiries to Dr. Jayaji Nath and Vishwarath Nayar went astray in the mail to Bombay, Federal Express unexpectedly delivered their chapter on India. As news of this project spread, Ted McIlvenna, founder of the Institute for the Advanced Study of Human Sexuality in San Francisco, put me in touch with Dr. Lionel Nicholas and Priscilla Daniels, at the University of the Western Cape, who were able to draw on their extensive work with black South Africans to complete the picture of South Africa provided by Dr. Mervyn Hurwitz from a white perspective. At the same professional meeting where I met Nicholas, I also recruited Drs. Tamara Gorovun and Boris Vornik who, despite the difficulties in the former Soviet Union, managed to provide a summary of sexuality in the Ukraine that complements Igor Kon's fascinating chapter on sexuality in Russia.

At times, as editor, I had to make sensitive decisions and difficult compromises. Shtarkshall and Zemach informed me that it would be premature at this time to go into any detail about Russian and Ethiopian Jews in Israel. Igor Kon's comments on the effects of a devastated infrastructure and lack of hygienic facilities on Russian sexuality are very important to understanding the situation in that country, but also are very sensitive. As a cultural anthropologist, Dr. Paula Drew reports her own observations of many years of familial customs including a strong voyeurism in Iranian families to which several male Iranian scholars took strong exception when they reviewed this chapter. The chapter on Kenya was written by an American Catholic missionary priest, Norbert Brockman, a political scientist and member of SSSS, with help from native Kenyans who could not have their names associated with the chapter because of the political situation and censorship in Kenya.

Finally, as General Editor, I would be remiss if I did not mention two major obstacles that arose just as we thought the material for the three volumes was near completion. After much consultation with colleagues to gather material, the unexpected consequences of a very serious automobile accident to David Weis, one of the co-editors of the United States chapter, nearly brought this chapter to a standstill. The co-editors, however, stuck with the project, and together we recruited two dozen friends and colleagues, members of SSSS, who recognized the importance of having a solid chapter on sexuality in the United States included in this *Encyclopedia.* Dividing up the topics we needed covered, these scholars worked diligently to prepare outstanding summaries of the different areas. In six months, we had in hand much more than a chapter on the United States. Our twenty-five contributors and thirteen consultants presented us with a manuscript of 120,000 words. This is, in many respects, a definitive study. As General Editor, I am happy to join Drs. Patricia Barthalow Koch and David Weis in thanking our friends and colleagues in SSSS for producing a truly informative and unique chapter on American sexuality. The unexpected problems we encountered with this entry resulted in a unique work.

The other problem we encountered was the decision to include an entry on the United Kingdom. For three years, I had been trying with no success to find experts to write on France, Italy, and the United Kingdom. I spent two desperate days calling colleagues, seeking leads. My search led me to two graduates of the New York University human sexuality program, Maria Bakaroudis and James Shortridge. These former students of mine are now working as health educators in the international divisions of Planned Parenthood and the Sexuality Information and Education Council of the United States (SIECUS). James and Maria quickly came to my rescue, using E-mail, fax, and the World Wide Web to find Dr. Kevan R. Wylie, a psychiatrist and specialist in sexual medicine in Sheffield, England. Dr. Wylie quickly accepted our invitation, recruited two dozen experts, and delivered to us an outstanding chapter on sexuality in the United Kingdom, all in three months' time. Only an extremely knowledgeable and dedicated sexologist could have accomplished this task, and the readers of the *Encyclopedia* will benefit greatly from the chapter Dr. Wylie and his team created on such short notice.

Although slightly over half of our contributors are male, we have a good gender balance. Admittedly, we would have preferred to have more anthropologists and sociologists contributing; psychologists and physicians are more likely to specialize in sexology, so they are more frequently found among our contributors. As editor, I strongly encouraged male contributors to obtain input on their material from knowledgeable female colleagues whenever possible. This they were often able to do. Unfortunately, it was not always possible. In the Canadian entry, Michael Barrett and his colleagues note that serious governmental efforts to obtain information from ethnic minorities that would be helpful in designing AIDS prevention programs encountered a strong reluctance, even resistance to researchers speaking about sexual issues with women in certain minorities. My own efforts to obtain comments and feedback from knowledgeable Hindu and Moslem women acquaintances for the chapters on Iran, India, and Indonesia invariably produced only embarrassed retreat and avoidance. In some cultures, women, even college graduates, do not speak about sexual issues with men, especially outsiders.

Throughout the chapters, the reader will find that attempts to describe a sexual custom or behavior in great detail leads inevitably to a loss of its context. But if one describes the context in detail, one frequently loses the character of the behavior or custom. The authors tried to keep a balance between detail and context, which we trust readers will be aware of and sensitive to as they draw comparisons and contrasts.

I must admit that I have enjoyed no other writing project as much as I have my work as editor of this *International Encyclopedia.* I must thank each and every contributor for their diligent and dedicated work, which is only rewarded by the knowledge that they have made possible a unique and herculean reference work we know will be of great use to sexologists and other professionals interested in the state of sexual attitudes, customs, and behaviors in the rich diversity of cultures around the world.

In late 1993, after it was obvious that we would end up with more than one volume, my editor Jack Heidenry and I spoke of the possibility that this project might grow beyond three volumes. In late 1996, as the manuscript neared completion, authors from additional countries had begun to inquire about contributing to an additional volume. By early 1997, entries on Nigeria, the Philippines, and Portugal were well underway, and other entries on Austria, Chile, Colombia, Denmark, Egypt, France, Italy, Lebanon, Morocco, Namibia, New Zealand, Pakistan, Peru, Portugal, Sri Lanka, Swaziland, Turkey, and Venezuela had been initiated. Two alumni of the New York University graduate program in human sexuality have joined me as Consulting Editors for this continued effort. Their regular international travels and contacts will be invaluable in recruiting new contributors, particularly in Africa, Asia, and South America. I have already acknowledged the invaluable contribution Maria Bakaroudis and James Shortridge made in coordinating the entry on the United Kingdom. Their combined expertise, energy, regular international travel, and many personal contacts with experts in human sexuality around the world will be crucial in any expansion of *The International Encyclopedia of Sexuality.*

Using This Encyclopedia

The information on each country in this encyclopedia is organized according to the following standard outline. The fourteen major headings are also listed on the first page of each chapter with the appropriate page numbers for that country. The reader interested in drawing comparisons on specific issues between different countries will find page references for specific topics and refinements beyond the major headings in the complete index at the end of third volume. Checking this index under a specific topic, such as premarital sex, teenage pregnancy, puberty rites, or sexual harassment, the reader will find page references that facilitate comparisons among the thirty-two countries covered in these three volumes.

Demographics and a Historical Perspective
  A. Demographics
  B. A brief historical perspective

1. Basic Sexological Premises
   A. Character of gender roles
   B. Sociolegal status of males and females
   C. General concepts of sexuality and love
2. Religious and Ethnic Factors Affecting Sexuality
   A. Source and character of religious values
   B. Character of ethnic values
3. Sexuality Knowledge and Education
   A. Government policies and programs
   B. Informal sources of sexual knowledge
4. Autoerotic Behaviors and Patterns
   A. Children and adolescents
   B. Adults
5. Interpersonal Heterosexual Behaviors
   A. Children
   B. Adolescents
   C. Adults
      Premarital relations, courtship, and dating
      Sexual behavior and relationships of single adults
      Marriage and family
      Cohabitation and monogamy
      Divorce, remarriage, and serial monogamy
      Extramarital sex

Sexuality and the physically disabled and aged
Incidence of oral and anal sex

6. Homoerotic, Homosexual, and Ambisexual Behaviors
   A. Children and adolescents
   B. Adults
7. Gender Conflicted Persons
8. Significant Unconventional Sexual Behaviors*
   A. Coercive sex
      Child sexual abuse, incest, and pedophilia
      Sexual harassment
      Rape
   B. Prostitution
   C. Pornography and erotica
   D. Paraphilias
9. Contraception, Abortion, and Population Planning
   A. Contraception
   B. Teenage (unmarried) pregnancies
   C. Abortion
   D. Population programs
10. Sexually Transmitted Diseases
11. HIV/AIDS
12. Sexual Dysfunctions, Counseling, and Therapies
13. Research and Advanced Education
    A. Graduate programs and sexological research
    B. Sexological organization and publications
14. Aboriginals, Important Ethnic, Racial, and/or Religious Minorities

References and Suggested Readings

---

*In Section 8, "Unconventional Sexual Behaviors," we consider a group of "other" sexual behaviors. These include sexual coercion (rape, sexual harassment, and child sexual abuse), prostitution, pornography, paraphilias, and fetishes. As a general rule, sexologists and the general public tend to view heterosexual relations between consenting adults in an ongoing relationship, such as marriage, as the norm. It is true that such sexual relations are the modal pattern in every culture. However, the earlier reviews of premarital sex, extramarital sex, alternative patterns of marriage, homosexuality, and bisexuality in Sections 5 and 6 serve to illustrate that in any country variable percentages of people engage in sexual behavior which departs from this assumed "conventional" norm. Sexologists have struggled for some time to develop acceptable terminology to describe these "other" sexual practices. "Unconventional behaviors" appears to be the least judgmental and restrictive label for "other behaviors." This is preferable to other labels, such as "sexual deviance" or "sexual variance," which convey a sense of pathology, dysfunction, or abnormality to behaviors.

The social meaning of specific incidents of "unconventional behavior" is defined by its situation. Exhibitionism, for example, has one meaning when engaged in by a couple in private, a different meaning when engaged in on the stage of a "go-go" bar for patrons of that bar, and a third meaning when engaged in on a public street. Second, some of these behaviors are, in fact, quite common. Although the number of individuals who engage in any particular form of "unconventional behavior" may be small, it seems clear that in most countries, taken together and added to the forms of non-marital sexual expression, rather large percentages of people do participate in some "other" "unconventional" form of sexual practice.

Preface

Timothy Perper, Ph.D.

What can a modern reader make of a book calling itself *The International Encyclopedia of Sexuality*? In the past, it could have been a *Baedeker's*—a *Guide Michelin*—to the sexual hotspots of the world, or a swinger's and sophisticate's tourguide to the super-sexy clubs of the international sex scene. It might well have contained addresses and ratings of brothels in far-flung places. Or perhaps it was a serio-comic autobiographical tale of a young person turned loose on the world of sex.

There was also a time that an *International Encyclopedia of Sexuality* would have recounted "the curious erotic customs" of people native to Borneo, Upper Nepal, and the tributaries of the Amazon, with a chapter (once obligatory in such works) about footbinding among the Chinese, crammed between strange stories about marriage rites among Polish villagers, African pastoralists, or Paraguayan landholders. And the illustrations—old-style black-and-white photographs—would have shown a peasant wedding in the Tyrol, a bride in Hindustan, the groom's party in Southern Russia, or anywhere else older times believed dwelt "primitive" or "simple" people.

Each of these has been a genre in sexual writing, as are dry-as-dust treatises of solemn university professors awash in jargon, incomprehensible tables of statistics, and deadly dull theorizing. Any and all could fill a book called *The International Encyclopedia of Sexuality.*

One value of the book you now hold is to reveal how much Western sexological writing has changed over two or so centuries. The essays here were each written by a person native to the land and culture described or familiar with it through years of life and study there. Each of the authors is trained in one or another academic discipline, from cultural anthropology to medical sexology. The language is international scientific English, stylistically straightforward and uncomplicated. And thanks to the Editor's foresight, the chapters all follow a common outline, covering similar topics in similar orders—which ought to facilitate comparisons among cultures. After a brief introduction, each chapter deals with a single society, discussing religious and ethnic sexual values, gender roles and the sociology of men and women, relationships between sexuality and love, sex education formal and informal, autoeroticism, heterosexuality and marriage and the family, homoeroticism, gender conflicts, and "unconventional" sexual behavior—including rape, prostitution, pornography, and erotica—followed by material on contraception, abortion, and population planning, and ending with a discussion of sexually transmitted diseases and sex counseling/therapy. It is quite a palate of topics.

And you will notice that it is a serious list of topics. Perhaps nothing else so well illustrates how Western and Westernized writing on sexuality has refocused over two centuries. Today, we "moderns"—which means only that we Westernized intellectuals proudly call ourselves modern and, by implication think others primitive—disdain older modes of sexological writing and publication. For many years, a primary form of "sexological" writing was the illustrated book—please, to be sold only to medical professionals!—with titles like *Femina Libido Sexualis,* and containing a mish-mash (to our modern eyes) of "medico-scientific" material on female anatomy, circumcision practices, phallic worship, all ostensibly published for "the advancement of knowledge," but actually printed as erotica and hidden from the censor's vigil by their Latinisms and their faux-science. But the mainstay of such works—definitions, discussions, and depictions of "female sexual beauty"—is absent in modern sexological writing, and is equally absent from this *International Encyclopedia of Sexuality.* Gone are the black-and-white photographs of nude women, steel engravings of Arab weddings, and suggestively titled but oh-so-innocent tales of life in the Turkish *seraglio.*

Today, sexuality has become the focus of intense concern, often outright anxiety. Topics that we today consider "sexologically appropriate" border more and more closely on psychological, medical, and social pathology. We are concerned with the criminality of sexual acts, their morality, their capacity to index—if not to stir up—social destruction and vehement conflict. Furious debates over pornography and deep concern about child sexual abuse illustrate how much, for us, sexuality no longer focuses on sexual beauty, be it male or female, but on sexual ugliness, disease, and crime.

To a large extent—though it varies by author—this focus on sexological pathology and problems is shared by all the chapters in the *International Encyclopedia.* No wonder, either: we live in a world of sexual change and rearrangement where politics, more than nudity, seems the proper companion of the goddess of love, Aphrodite herself. For us, sexuality represents the body in flux: not a Heraclitean flow of all things growing and waning, but embodied future shock and upheaval. Books celebrating "sexual beauty" or regaling the reader with "odd and curious marriage customs" of foreign people could be written only in days that themselves had firm and clear sexual guidelines—a sexual culture—to shape readers' behavior and assure them that they were culturally normal by the standards of their own Western societies. But—rota fortuna—things change.

There is a story told—apocryphally, I am afraid—of an Indian tourguide at the temples of Khajuraho, famed for what Westerners perceive as highly erotic sculptures. A woman ethnologist, primarily interested in these sculpted images of the most variegated forms of copulation imaginable, continued to ask to be shown those portions of the temple grounds. The guide steadfastly refused, saying only, "But they aren't interesting, miss."

The point is not the tourguide's recalcitrance. Instead, let us wonder where he obtained the phrase he used to defend his efforts at censorship: "They aren't interesting." Partly, to be sure, he expressed a personal emotion, but we can readily imagine British tourists in the days of the Indian Raj expressing dismay and anxiety by saying precisely the same—"These statues are not interesting." In those days—that is, for many years indeed—sexuality was not interesting to the normal Westerner outside the bedroom and those all-male soirees with which folklore bedecks the 1890s and similar eras of "sexual excess."

So *The International Encyclopedia of Sexuality* reveals a fascinating aspect of how our own—Western or Westernized—visions of sexuality have shifted. Today, we find sexuality much more openly important, even if public and media attention often focuses on its less pleasant sides, e.g., exploitation of women in pornography. Unlike our recent ancestors, we find sexuality interesting to extents that would have deeply shocked and troubled both the British visitors to Khajuraho and its Indian tourguide.

Over the intervening century, sexuality has slipped loose from its originally tight moorings in Western and Westernized societies. Today, it touches all aspects of life: certainly, it seems to touch everything in the media! One can plausibly argue that these are not deep social or psychological changes, but merely that previously dominating masks and disguises have fallen away to reveal what probably was always there—widespread interest in sexuality among many people indeed.

In this newly unmasked interest, we all need good, solid information—not rumor, hearsay, travelers' tales, and secret books celebrating female pulchritude across the globe—but good data, compiled with serious intent and presented with serious purpose. Such intentions and purposes *The International Encyclopedia of Sexuality* achieves. I do not perceive its seriousness of outline or topic as anti-sexual so much as I see it as anti-frivolous. We do not trivialize sexuality nowadays and we live in an era of "serious works about sex."

We cannot escape the solemnification of sexuality, not because solemnity is foisted upon us by prudes, but because we understand that sexuality is dangerous as well as pleasurable. Yet we also carry within ourselves a desire to worry about sexuality—an echo from older days when sexuality was taboo for polite discussion and a matter only of whispered gossip: something to worry about. In our modern world, sexuality is legitimated partly by surrounding it by a veil of worried concern, e.g., about pornography, child sexual abuse, sexual Satanism, and the like. Knowledge has been bought at the price of thinking that sexuality ought to be studied and worked at. Whatever instincts exist (modern sexological scholarship denies them), they do not operate easily or comfortably today. If sexuality no longer wears the obscuring masks of the past—the opaque black garb that once clothed the body—then instead it wears translucent gauze, not erotic so much as disinfectant. In modern sexology, sexuality inhabits the forums of research, and *The International Encyclopedia of Sexuality* is quite modern.

Its importance—considerable, I think—exhibits another change in sexological discourse, to use a revealing and portentous word made popular by academic sexologists. In older days, only one officially sanctioned form of discourse existed about sex: the language and meanings of moralists, churchmen typically, that upheld certain visions of how we should write about sex. Though he had predecessors, Kinsey changed all that permanently, in effect substituting technicalisms for a dying moralism in sexual language. A curious consequence is that sexology no longer speaks to the masses about matters they understand and know. As modern life fractalizes, sexology has sprouted many officially sanctioned discourses, such as postmodernist criticism, feminism, conservative rhetoric, biomedicalese, all anti-populist, all above the heads of the man and woman in the street (or bedroom). Indeed, it sometimes takes an expert to understand that the topic is sex. Nonetheless, adherents of these different discourses spend much time examining each other's prose with the officiousness of churchmen hunting out sinful thoughts. Sex remains a charged, powerful topic, and its significance will not diminish soon. Its powers radiate outwards from an embodied center to touch arenas of disagreement, like politics, that nonetheless remain more comfortable than open sexuality, at least for many people.

And so this *International Encyclopedia* raises a curious question: Will there come a time when sexuality can display itself nude? Or is nude sexuality still "not interesting"? Judging from public worry over Madonna's *Sex*, with her deliberate evocation of nudity, we still share a great deal with the Indian tourguide. However, the authors of the chapters in this book are closer kin to the woman ethnologist who wished to examine those statues. For her and her modern scholarly descendants, sexuality is interesting, even if still garmented in sociological, psychological, and biomedical gauze. Whereas we Westernized intellects still feel that Aphrodite must be partly covered, nonetheless many layers of wrapping and disguise have been removed. To the prude, it is all to the bad (even if "not interesting"). To the scholar, it is an important step towards understanding sexuality itself. To the modern reader, *The International Encyclopedia of Sexuality* will be more interesting than a *Baedeker* to the world's sex clubs or an autobiography of a reprobate or even a lusciously colored edition of the once banned *Thousand and One Nights*: it provides a thoroughly scholarly examination of what is still not fully exposed even in an enlightened modern world—or, judging from the temples at Khajuraho itself, the partly enlightened and partly interested modern world.

An Introduction to the Many Meanings of Sexological Knowledge

Ira L. Reiss, Ph.D.

Welcome to this treasure chest of sexological knowledge and understanding. You will find in these volumes a wealth of information concerning sexuality in a very wide range of human societies. To introduce this extremely rare and valuable *International Encyclopedia of Sexuality*, I will not review the fascinating reports of these authors. Instead what I shall do is to try to afford the reader some perspective on the many ways that this knowledge can be understood and used. I will focus on three controversial aspects of cross-cultural work where scientific fads and fashions have tended to limit how that knowledge is presented. Having a broader view of these three aspects of cross-cultural studies should help the reader to utilize the accounts of sexuality in this *Encyclopedia* more completely.

I will first deal with the question of how our personal values and other assumptions about the world enter into the way we do our scientific work on sexuality, and what we can do about it. Secondly I will deal with the current emphasis upon stressing the uniqueness of each society and the criticism of the search for cultural universals. And thirdly, I will deal with the important question of taking the "insider" and the "outsider" perspective when studying a society's sexual customs. By discussing these three controversial areas and suggesting possible resolutions, the reader should be better prepared to make his or her own judgments on what is valuable in sexological knowledge.

Issue One: Science, Values, and Assumptions

There are those who still perceive of science and society as properly separated by an impenetrable wall. In this "positivist" view, the scientist is protected from "bias" by his/her withdrawal from taking sides on any of the basic value disputes in a society. As a result we supposedly get a "value-free" and "pure" form of knowledge rather than a "biased" or "value-laden" point of view. That is still a popular view concerning science and society. Nevertheless, I contend that that sort of sharp separation of science and society is based upon an erroneous view of the way science really operates in society.

In my view, science cannot be separated from society, for it is an institution existing in a human society and conducted by human beings. Science, and its practitioners, can no more avoid the influences of the broader society than can the mass media, corporate business, government, religion, education, or the family. Further, the very support of science by a society depends on people's believing that science is useful to the solution of the problems of that society. The high value placed upon physical science emanates from the advances it has produced in valued areas such as health, industry, and warfare. Denying this connection to society does not produce a lack of bias in science. Instead, it may produce an inability to be explicit about one's values to others, and perhaps even to oneself.

Most obviously in the social sciences and in sexual science, where we seek to understand the way humans behave and think, there can be no meaningful separation of science from society and its values. But this does not mean that we cannot avoid bias in our scientific methods. Rather, if science is to maintain its claim to being fair, reasonable, logical, precise, and cautious, then it must acknowledge the possible values of the scientist and learn how to prevent them from overwhelming our scientific methods. Scientists cannot prevent bias in their work by simply claiming to be value-free. Rather, as I shall seek to illustrate, scientists must do it by demonstrating that they are value-aware. Let me illustrate my meaning with a research project I was involved in not long ago.

In 1988, a colleague, Robert Leik, and I set out to develop a probability model that would compare two strategies for reducing the risk of an HIV infection (Reiss and Leik 1989). The two strategies to be compared were: (1) to reduce the number of sexual partners or (2) to use condoms with all partners. Although utilizing both strategies simultaneously is clearly the safest way to reduce the risk of HIV, a great many people seem to choose to do one or the other. The model we built compared the risk in these two strategies using a very wide range of estimates of several key factors: (a) the prevalence of HIV, that is, the likelihood of picking an infected partner; (b) the infectivity of the HIV virus, that is, the likelihood of becoming infected with HIV if one picked an infected partner and had unprotected sex with that person; (c) the failure rate of condoms ranging from a low of 10 percent to a high of 75 percent; and (d) the number of partners ranging from one to twenty.

What we found was virtually unqualified support for the greater probability of avoiding HIV infection by using condoms rather than by reducing partners. In almost all cases, even if one had only one or two partners over a five-year period, if one did not use condoms with them, one had a higher risk of HIV infection than someone with twenty partners who did use condoms. This was true even if condoms were assumed to have a failure rate between 10 to 25 percent. Our conclusion was that those giving advice and counsel should recommend condom usage as the more effective tactic.

Now this project with its probability model was surely a scientific project, and the results of testing our models seemed unequivocal. Nevertheless, although the great majority of the scientific community fully endorsed and used our findings and suggestions, a few scientists did not accept our interpretation of our results. We received criticism from scientists who said that people will not use condoms to prevent HIV infection and so our findings were meaningless in the real world. There were others who said that publishing our results would encourage people to increase the number of partners and that would lead to more HIV infections. Some other critics raised the question whether having more than one partner and using condoms was worth even the very small increased risk that we described.

This difference of interpretation of our findings is not a result of the poor scientific judgment of our critics, as much as we might have liked to think that. Rather it was basically a consequence of some scientists' not sharing our values and assumptions about the world in which we live. Specifically, our critics did not accept our view that people will use condoms to protect themselves. Instead, our critics believed in a more emotional than rational view of human sexual choices. They held this view despite the evidence that gays have greatly increased their condom usage and even teenagers indicated similar dramatic increases in the late 1980s (Reiss 1990). Other critics rejected our assumption that motivations for having more sexual partners have very little to do with the publication of an article like ours. Finally, unlike some of our critics, we made no assumptions about whether condom-protected sex with several partners was worth the increased risk involved.

Our critics and we clearly had different assumptions and values regarding sexuality and that was the reason why they questioned our evaluation of the evidence from our model. They did not disagree with the results of the model, but they disagreed with our assumptions about sexuality. The reader should note that the assumptions we make about sexuality are not only factual assumptions, but they embody value judgments. For example, we valued people who learn how to protect themselves, and supported the moral right of people to make their own personal choices regarding the number of partners that they have.

We might not have become so fully aware of our assumptions if our critics had not spoken out revealing that they made different assumptions and had different values about sexual behavior. The critics would never have undertaken our study because, lacking the belief that condoms will be used to prevent HIV infection, why should one study that strategy? Also, as one scientific journal editor wrote to us, his values would stop him from publishing an article that seemed indifferent to the norms of sexual monogamy. These differences in values and assumptions do not just enter into the choice of research projects, but as is apparent here, they enter into the very interpretation of the meaning and worth of that research.

The important point here is that no scientist can undertake a research project without making some set of assumptions regarding human behavior. And those assumptions also influence how to interpret the validity and worth of the findings. As our critics demonstrate, our interpretation that recommending condoms is the safest path to take is not one that inevitably follows from our probability model's evidence. Our recommendation of condom use follows only if you also share our assumptions about human behavior. The great majority of sexual scientists do share our view and so they agreed with our interpretation. Where all scientists share the same assumptions, we are the most likely to be blind to the fact that we are even making any assumptions. Without the critical response, we would not have become so aware of our own assumptions, and of those of our critics.

To believe that science operates in a vacuum devoid of values and assumptions about human behavior is to delude ourselves as scientists. Further, unless we realize the assumptions we are making, and put them forth explicitly, we will be unable to comprehend fully one basis upon which we are judging the worth of our scientific work. Only by becoming more value- and assumption-aware will we be able to be more even handed and fair in evaluating and understanding the basis of our scientific judgments. Such awareness makes the scientist more thoughtful about what assumptions will be accepted, and more conscious of the possibility that we must be sure not to allow these assumptions to bias our gathering of evidence.

The recent findings concerning causes of homosexuality offer another illustration of the point I am making here. The 1993 work of Dean Hamer published in *Science* created a public storm of interest. Hamer and his collaborators reported that they found on the long arm of the X chromosome a possible location of a special set of genes that were present in thirty-three out of forty families with two gay brothers. The support this finding found depended in part on the background assumptions of the particular scientists. Those who, like biologist Simon LeVay (1990) stress biological factors as determinant of human behavior, are more willing to conclude that biological factors are key pieces in the homosexual puzzle. Other scientists in social science fields where nurture is stressed more than nature make assumptions about humans that lead them to be hesitant to accept Hamer's work as anything more than mostly speculative at this point.

There are also values associated with any position on nature and nurture. Whether we are a biologist or a sociologist, if we oppose the status quo in society, we are more likely to want to emphasize the plasticity of human inheritance. In addition, those scientists who feel that seeing homosexuality as strongly biologically determined would lessen societal prejudice, may also be more likely to accept biology as definitive. Conversely, those who, like myself, oppose prejudice, but who note that prejudice continues against groups with known biological differences such as blacks and women, do not feel pressure to endorse biological etiology.

One very important conclusion from these and other examples is that our assumptions and values can easily impact on our interpretation of research findings. But that does not mean that we should conclude that all sexologists are "biased" or all research on sex is "unfairly" interpreted. Rather, what it says to me is that all members of a society, including scientists, have values and make assumptions about human sexual behavior. Better than pretending that we can be neutral and value-free, we should openly assert our assumptions and values so we can check each other's scientific work and promote a clearer, and more balanced and fair-minded evaluation of the worth of our research results.

Bias or distortion of evidence is unacceptable in scientific work. We seek to use the most reliable and valid measures, to publish our results for criticism by others, and to follow rules of careful reasoning and fair gathering of evidence. Making our scientists more "value-assumption aware" will help us minimize the times when these unstated assumptions overwhelm our science. We cannot eliminate assumptions, but we can demand that they be made explicit and require scientific rigor regardless of what assumptions are made. Then we can as scientists reach consensus on which explicit assumptions we are willing to accept and thereby decide what will be accepted as knowledge in our science of sexuality. When you read the accounts in this book, try to discern the author's assumptions. Finding assumptions is not by itself an indication of a flawed account. Rather, it is a way of giving you deeper insight into the meaning of that author's account.

Issue Two: Scientific Fads about Cultural Universals

There is little question that during the past several decades, the anthropological and sociological work on different societies has stressed the uniqueness of cultures and criticized attempts to find cultural universals (Suggs and Miracle 1993). If we apply our awareness of the place of assumptions in scientific work, we may surmise that this emphasis is a result of assuming that people and societies are basically different and do not universally share any significant characteristics. Further, that assumption may be based on the value judgment that stressing how different we are builds tolerance, whereas emphasizing universal traits among different societies encourages people to criticize the society that is not like their own.

All our views are but partial views of whatever reality is out there. If we all share the exact same assumptions about the world, we will never become aware of what these assumptions are, and we will not be alert to the possible biasing of our scientific evaluations. It is in this sense that accepting but one narrow view of what is worth pursuing, and making that a compulsory position, is dangerous to the growth of sound scientific methods and to the careful evaluation of evidence.

In opposition to the current scientific fad of stressing differences, David Suggs and Andrew Miracle, in their overview on cross-cultural sex research point to the need to find commonalities in societies around the world. They say: "We need more work on sexuality from those research strategies that are specifically oriented toward seeking an explanation of 'Culture'—as opposed to 'cultures'" (1993, 490).

They cite my 1986 book, *Journey into Sexuality: An Exploratory Voyage*, as one of the few attempts to find such commonalities while not denying the importance of cultural differences. In that book, I set out to try to locate the key areas of our social life that, in any society, most directly shape our sexuality. I started with the assumption that, unless the evidence indicated otherwise, we can assume that, "with careful attention to the social context, intercultural comparisons can be made" (Reiss 1986, 7). After examining a large number of cultures, I developed my Linkage Theory, which asserted that sexual customs in all societies were most crucially linked to the power, ideology, and kinship segments of that society. This I called the (PIK) Linkage Theory.

I did not ignore differences in the way individual societies create such linkages. To be sure, a class system in America may be very different from a class system in Kenya. But that does not prevent us from saying they both have a class system and examining how that class system relates to existing sexual customs. So I would say to the reader, look for the important differences among the cultures described, but also compare societies and see if you can detect some commonalities among the cultures, such as I suggest in sexuality being linked to power, ideology, and kinship systems in every society (Reiss 1989). I believe that finding commonalities in our sexual lives can enhance our tolerance for the cultural differences that exist. We can better identify and have empathy for a people with whom we believe we share some important similarities.

Issue Three: The Insider and the Outsider Perspective

In the last few decades, the emphasis in cross-cultural work has been on what Kenneth Pike has called the Emic or "insider" approach and less on the Etic or "outsider" approach. The concepts of Emic and Etic were first put into print by Kenneth Pike in 1954 and have since become common jargon in anthropology. Some anthropologists, like Marvin Harris, have made modifications in Pike's concepts but still utilize them (Headland, Pike and Harris 1990). Let me try to clarify these very important terms and relate them to a third and final issue concerning how we view other societies.

The originator of the concepts of Emic and Etic, Kenneth Pike, indicated his current meaning in a 1990 book when he said:

> I view the emic knowledge of a person's local culture somewhat as Polanyi views bicycle riding. A person knows how to act without necessarily knowing how to analyze his action. When I act, I act as an insider; but to know, in detail, how I act (e.g., the muscle movements), I must secure help from an outside disciplinary system. To use the emics of nonverbal (or verbal) behavior I must act like an insider, to analyze my own acts, I must look at (or listen to) material as an outsider. But just

as the outsider can learn to act like an insider, so the insider can learn to analyze like an outsider. (Headland, Pike and Harris 1990, 33-34)

Although it is a bit of a simplification, Emic can be seen as the insider view constructed by people in a culture, and Etic the outsider view constructed by science seeking to understand that culture. The recent fad in social science, as I have noted in my discussion of the emphasis placed on cultural uniqueness, is to emphasize the Emic view. The possibility of an Etic view that can conceptually compare and find commonalities in different cultures is too often overlooked and/or criticized today.

I support the essential worth of both Emic and Etic approaches and I reject the notion that we must give priority to an Emic or an Etic view. Some of the support for promoting the Emic view comes from those who feel that we should not make invidious comparisons of cultures and should rather just accept them. I, of course, share the tolerance values behind such an approach. But as a social scientist, I must be allowed to compare and contrast and to develop understandings that go beyond just saying all cultures are unique. I must also add that there are societies, like the Nazi society under Hitler and many other totalitarian reigns of terror that exist today in our world, that I do not want to tolerate. I want more than the insider view of a people on which to base my understanding of a society.

Another point to be aware of in this debate is the fact that there is much that people in any society do not understand about their own culture. How many people in Western society understand enough to be able to suggest workable solutions to the many social problems they see in their society? One of the major values of any science is to afford a broader perspective on a social problem area. It is true that the outsider view that scientific explanation can provide will be based on some assumptions about human beings, but the attempt will still be to evaluate carefully and fairly the evidence relevant to that perspective. This is precisely what Robert Leik and I were trying to do when we compared the two strategies for reducing HIV infection. Our assumptions were clear and we attempted to evaluate fairly the choices in light of those assumptions.

If we opt only for the insider's views and deny the possibility of an outside scientific explanation that goes beyond the insider's views, then we are reducing ourselves to the role of stenographers writing down what people believe and stopping there. I think an Etic science perspective is far too valuable to toss away that easily. True, science has limitations in its assumptions and in its fads and fashions. But science presents us with the opportunity to arrive at a consensus as to how to understand most effectively, and perhaps change, a particular sexual problem. Such a scientific consensus will never be the total picture of reality, but it will be valuable in our search for solutions. It offers something beyond what the partisan person can offer in his or her Emic viewpoint, and I would therefore reject any postmodern, relativist attempts to play down the value of an Etic perspective in sexology or in any science.

Readers of this *International Encyclopedia* should keep in mind the Emic and Etic distinction, the relative advantages and limitations of these vantage points, and watch for efforts by the authors to balance these views. Some authors are native to the country they are writing about. Others are not natives and write from an outsider's perspective even though they may have lived in the country for many years. Being aware of the vantage point from which the individual contributors to this *Encyclopedia* speak will help the reader make the most advantageous use of the information presented.

Quo Vadis, Cross-Cultural Sexology?

Let me try to sum up the implications of my approach to cross-cultural sexual knowledge and its value to you in reading this encyclopedia. First, I would suggest that seeing how science and value assumptions interact should make us more likely to want our science of sexuality to do more than present abstract knowledge. We will want science to deal with the problem areas that mean the most to us. This sort of postpositivist view of sexual science makes science a major helper in reconstructing or reinventing ways of living that can promote the resolution of the many sexual problems that confront us.

True, there may well be conflicting solutions proposed by scientists with different value assumptions, such as I encountered with my probability model on HIV infection. But we can still examine scientifically what will best help to resolve problems from the viewpoint of the set of assumptions most of us in a community will endorse. Further, people with different assumptions can put forth different tactics to resolve social problems. We can examine the reasoning and evidence relevant to competing assumptions. We can choose based on what type of world we want to create.

The scientific search for evidence to examine our solutions can still be rigorous and will be scrutinized particularly by those who do not fully accept our assumptions. I see the future as favoring this movement towards a sexual science that helps us create the type of world we consensually agree we want. I see the problem-resolution aspect of sexology as very important, because it will promote the value of sexual science in the minds of the public, and that will help fund the important research and theory work we want to do.

On the second issue of commonalities: if you accept my position on the legitimacy of searching for cultural universals as well as for cultural variability, then we in sexology can search for common elements in our sexual lives in societies around the world. In the over two hundred societies I examined in my 1986 book, I found universal condemnation of what that society judged to be "excessive" sexual force and to what that society saw as "undue" sexual manipulation (Reiss 1986, 1990). So we have at least a minimal cross-cultural area of ethical agreement on what sexual acts ought to be prohibited: sexual force and sexual manipulation. Of course, within this area of agreement there are quite different definitions of what is "excessive" sexual force and what is "undue" sexual manipulation. But within any society, we can as sexual scientists seek to find what changes in custom would best avoid that culture's conception of "unacceptable" force and manipulation.

In Western cultures, I believe we would agree that avoiding force and manipulation is best accomplished by promoting preparation for sexuality that emphasizes honesty, equality, and responsibility between the sexual actors. I have developed the evidence and reasoning on this in a recent book (Reiss 1990). Western cultures are moving towards an ethical standard that accepts a wide range of sexual acts, providing they are honestly, equally, and responsibly negotiated. As the accounts in this encyclopedia will reveal, there surely are significant differences even within Western societies as to how to define unacceptable force and manipulation, and also on defining what is meant by honesty, equality, and responsibility in sexual relationships and how to achieve that. But at least there is some common ground for such a dialogue to take place, and I believe sexologists should take the lead in examining and researching this vast area of possible ethical agreement.

Although non-Western societies are pursuing the same goal of reducing unacceptable force and manipulation, there are many significant differences in the ways that these societies may seek to control these outcomes. Promoting honesty, equality, and responsibility in sexuality may not be so popular in some of these societies. So clearly individual attention to particular societies is needed. But I stress that it is in the search for universals here that we are led to explore cultural differences. These are not opposing goals.

Finally, in line with my position on the insider and outsider approaches, I encourage taking both an Emic and an Etic approach so as to gain more complete answers to the sexological questions that interest us. The insider view is essential for any successful resolution, because it is people that must put into action any resolution to a social problem. But we must also go beyond individual viewpoints for it may well be that in unintended ways we promote the very outcomes that we then condemn as problems. Our conflicted and negative view of sexuality in America is a cause of the very problems that our conflicted and sex-negative people then condemn (Reiss 1990).

If we who have devoted our career to the study of sexuality cannot state what our assumptions are and offer useful resolutions to our shared sexual problems, then who can? A famous American sociologist, Robert S. Lynd (1939, 186) many years ago made this very point about social science in general:

> Either the social sciences know more than do the 'hard headed' businessman, the 'practical' politician and administrator, and the other de facto leaders of the culture as to what the findings of research mean, as to the options the institutional system presents, as to what human

> personalities want, why they want them, and how desirable changes can be effected, or the vast current industry of social science is an empty facade.

The cross-cultural analysis of sexual customs in this encyclopedia should help us to understand and to cope better with the dramatic changes occurring in sexual customs in so many societies today. I have discussed elsewhere other reasons why we need to make our assumptions explicit and thereby make our sexology more problem-resolution centered (Reiss 1993). All I need add here is that the more society feels that sexology can aid in resolving our sexual problems, the more our field will be valued and will flourish. I hope we who are sexologists will resolve our internal disputes on issues like those discussed in this chapter by taking the broader and more eclectic view of science and its role in society that I have presented. While doing this we must hold to the great value of scientific method—we must reject the nihilistic and relativistic conclusions that some who would dismiss science altogether promote today. I hope that as you read the fascinating chapters in this book, the key issues and ideas I have put forth will help you to obtain a deeper insight into human sexuality. I wish you all: Bon Voyage to the many societies described herein!

References

Hammer, D. H., S. Hu, V. L. Magnuson, N. Hu, and A. M. L. Pattatucci. July 16, 1993. "A Linkage Between DNA Markers on the X Chromosome and Male Sexual Orientation." *Science.* 261:321-27.

Headland, T. N., K. L. Pike, and Marvin Harris, eds. 1990. *Emics and Etics: The Insider/Outsider Debate.* Newbury Park, California: Sage Publishers.

LeVay, S. 1993. *The Sexual Brain.* Cambridge, Massachusetts: MIT Press.

Lynd, R. S. 1939. *Knowledge for What? The Place of Social Science in American Culture.* New York: Grove Press.

Reiss, I. L. 1986. *Journey into Sexuality: An Exploratory Voyage.* Englewood Cliffs, New Jersey: Prentice-Hall.

Reiss, I. L. 1989. "Society and Sexuality: A Sociological Theory." In K. McKinney and S. Sprecher, eds. *Human Sexuality: The Societal and Interpersonal Context.* Norwood, New Jersey: Ablex Publishing Corp.

Reiss, I. L. 1990. *An End to Shame: Shaping Our Next Sexual Revolution.* Buffalo, New York: Prometheus Books.

Reiss, I. L. February 1993. "The Future of Sex Research and the Meaning of Science." *Journal of Sex Research.* 30:3-11.

Reiss, I. L. and R. K. Leik. November 1989. "Evaluating Strategies to Avoid AIDS: Number of Partners vs. Use of Condoms." *Journal of Sex Research.* 26:411-33.

Suggs, D. N. and A. W. Miracle, eds. 1993. *Culture and Human Sexuality: A Reader.* Pacific Grove, California: Books/Cole Publishing Co.

Argentina
(*República Argentina*)

Sofia Kamenetzky, M.D.

Contents

Demographics and a Historical Perspective

A. Demographics

Argentina, the second largest country in South America with 1,073,518 square miles, occupies most of the southern tip of the American continent. It extends from slightly above the Tropic of Capricorn to the Antarctica, on which it keeps a constant military and research presence. Hence, it has a variety of climates and the different natural resources associated with them, although it is best known for its fertile pampas of the temperate region. As the poet describes it:

> This miraculous indigenous America
> Made everything at a fantastic scale
> Wanting to look at the sky,

she raised herself on the Andean Mountains
And her cross, instead of wood,
is made of stars.[1]

Argentina's neighbors are Chile on the west, Bolivia and Paraguay on the north, and Brazil and Uruguay on the northeast. Argentina's 1995 population was 34,292, 742. The age distribution was 30 percent below age 15; 61 percent ages 15 to 64, and 9 percent age 65 and older. Eighty-seven percent of the population are urban dwellers. Eighty-five percent are white, mainly Spanish and Italian, with the remaining 15 percent mestizos and indigenous Indians.

Life expectancy at birth (1995) was 68 for males and 75 for females. The birth rate was 20 per 1,000 population, the death rate nine per 1,000, giving a natural annual increase of 1.1 percent. Argentina has one hospital bed per 205 persons, one physician per 326 persons, and an infant mortality rate in 1994 of 29 per 1,000 live births. Literacy in 1992 was 95 percent with education compulsory to age 14 (*1996 World Almanac*). The 1993 per capita gross domestic product was $5,500.

B. A Brief Historical Perspective

Nomadic indigenous tribes roamed the pampas when the Spaniards arrived in 1515 and 1516. The land quickly became a part of the Spanish empire. By the late nineteenth century, nearly all the native peoples had been killed.

The long period of disorder that followed the colonists' declaration of independence in 1816 ended only when a strong centralized government developed. Large-scale Italian, German, and Spanish immigration after 1880 spurred modernization, and major social reforms were instituted in the 1920s. Military coups were common from 1930 on to the 1946 election of General Juan Perón as president. Perón and his wife, Eva Duarte (died 1952), effected labor reforms, but suppressed freedom of speech and the press, closed religious schools, and ran the country into serious debt. A series of military and civilian regimes followed Perón's ouster in 1955. After an eighteen-year exile, Perón returned in 1973 and was elected president. When he died ten months later, his second wife, Isabel, who had been elected vice president, succeeded him, becoming the first woman head of state in the western hemisphere. Mrs. Perón was oustered in 1976, amid charges of curruption.

The military junta that followed existed in a state of siege with guerrillas and leftists. An estimated 5,000 people were killed and thousands jailed and tortured. Democratic rule returned in 1983 after Great Britain successful defended the Falkland Islands in 1982. In 1985, five former junta members were found guity of murder and human rights violations. By 1989, the nation suffered as severe hyperinflation and political problems sparked looting and rioting in several large cities. Perónist President Carlos Saúl Menem, elected in 1989 and again in 1995, has introduced harsh but necessary economic measures to curtail hyperinflation, control government spending, and restructure the foreign debt.

1. Basic Sexological Premises

A/B. Gender Roles and Sociolegal Status of Males and Females

In Latin American societies, the sexual behavior of women is always much more conditioned by norms, rules, regulations, and taboos than the sexual behavior of men. Argentina is no exception. Women were supposed to reach marriage in a virginal state, and then take care of the home, go to church, bear and educate children, and support their men in political, professional, and economic activities.

For a long time, this double standard was accepted without open criticism. But since the late 1940s, women have taken steps towards equal rights and independence from parents, spouses, and lovers. Of course, the first steps were taken by women with college degrees and businesswomen. They started painfully opening spaces in Argentina's political, economic, legal, and educational arenas. The governments have also opened opportunities for them in political and administrative positions. Today we see women in university chairs, legal benches, large corporations, research laboratories, journalism, medicine, and all fields of art. However, it is still possible to observe discrimination against women and privileges given to men not because of their excelling in a job or profession, but simply because they are males.

C. General Concepts of Love and Sexuality

Virginity is no longer a condition for marriage. On the contrary, before deciding to engage in a permanent relationship, most women want to know their future spouse in bed. Argentine women are exercising their new roles in markets and societies with a flexible mental attitude that tries to integrate all aspects of their complex new situation. They know that it is not easy to balance their responsibility as mothers and lovers with their workplace obligations; they need to walk a tightrope and compromise, giving when needed more visibility to their men. They do not want to renounce breast feeding their babies because they know its importance for healthy development, hence they are fighting to increase the availability of day care facilities close to their workplace. Accepting now their share of responsibility in maintaining a healthy sexual life, they take initiative in foreplay and learn techniques to introduce variety in sexual intercourse, while at the same time they try to increase both depth and scope in the emotional and intellectual communications within the couple.

For males, it is sometimes difficult to internalize these changes in the patterns of family life. However, most are starting to perceive that they enrich the relationship and are beneficial for both partners. The advantages of sharing two incomes, and participating in the rearing and education of the children awakens emotions and provides a joy never felt before. Men are also learning to relax when making love, enjoying alternate passive and active roles, and accepting the fact that they can also be seduced and excited.

Women's liberation from submission to parents, brothers, and spouses is slowly harmonizing male and female energies and leading to a win/win situation for both, although the way to this end is not yet free of obstacles that will take pain to remove. Most of the population still believes in a double standard, but increased dissatisfaction with their sexual lives show that their rigid positions of the past are cracking.

2. *Religious and Ethnic Factors Affecting Sexuality*

A. Source and Character of Religious Values

The influence of the Catholic Church was and is hegemonic. Ninety percent of Argentina's population identify themselves as Roman Catholic, although the percentage of active churchgoers is much less.

A very conservative interpretation of Catholic dogma shaped life during colonial times. The powerful grip of the Church in Argentina's life was not relaxed after independence from Spain in 1810, nor when the country was finally organized as a modern state towards the end of the nineteenth century. Throughout the history of Argentina, secular powers have had to battle against a Church determined to maintain its hold on the institutions of civil life like education, the availability of contraception and abortion, and even the registration of major events in the lives of the people like births, marriages, and deaths.

The values and beliefs of Catholic doctrine have been inscribed in the minds of the Argentine people in a way that has proven difficult to delete. Outstanding among these are the Church's views on the social roles of males and females, its insistence on seeing the body as a root of evil, the need to free the spirit from the urges of the flesh, and sexual intercourse viewed as a curse brought upon humans with no other objective or justification than the preservation of the human species.

The influence of this dogma has led, as one might expect, to a dichotomous, often schizophrenic pattern of behavior. Recently, three Catholic women in Uruguay, Argentina's neighboring country, investigated Catholic women's ideas on and practices of sexuality and maternity. Their sample included hundreds of women from Argentina, Uruguay, and Paraguay, countries which share a similar historical and cultural evolution. The women commonly expressed dissatisfaction with their sexual lives, and had developed the strategy of "not feeling" or "getting used to putting up with it." Others were oppressed by the idea that sex is sinful and felt badly after each sexual encounter. While many of the women interviewed felt

God as a close friend, they viewed the Church as distant, disciplinary, and controlling.[2]

B. Source and Character of Ethnic Values

Before the arrival of the Spaniards in 1516, Argentina was inhabited by fierce, indomitable tribes that valued their freedom and had learned to survive by adapting to the climate and resources of the different regions of the country. Except for the Northwest, which was conquered by the Peruvian Incas, the indigenous populations of Argentina did not develop the complex, and, in some aspects, advanced civilizations whose remains can still been seen in Mexico and Peru. The indigenous people who inhabited the pampas were mercilessly condemned to extinction by the thirst for land of the Spanish conquerors first, and the new South American nation later on. A few still survive in small reserves, especially in the Northeast where the Jesuits had organized them in productive communities that were destroyed after the expulsion of the order in 1767 from Spain and all her colonies.

This, and the fact that Argentina never had a very active slave trade, explains the predominance of a population of European origin. Between 1850 and 1940, some 6.6 million Europeans joined the 1.1 million people already living in the country in 1850.[3] In 1991, Argentina's population was 32.7 million, having grown in the previous decade at the rate of 1.3 percent per year.[4]

From 1810, when the links with Spain were severed, to 1853 when a unified nation started its organizational development, Argentina was a field of constant quarrels among feudal provincial warlords and between these caudillos and the two aristocracies of money and of culture based in the port city of Buenos Aires. The two aristocracies were trying to control the chaos, often for their own benefit and neglecting the needs of the rural population.

From 1853 on, Argentina moved solidly on the roads of social and economic development until it ranked in the early decades of the twentieth century among the ten most developed countries of the world. In his study of Argentine history, David Rock comments:

> By the outbreak of World War I, per capita income equaled that in Germany and the Low Countries, and was higher than in Spain, Italy, Sweden, and Switzerland. Having grown at an average annual rate of 6.5 percent since 1869, Buenos Aires had become the second largest city of the Atlantic seaboard, after New York, and by far the largest city in Latin America. . . . By 1911, Argentina's foreign trade was larger than Canada's and a quarter of that of the United States. Argentina was the world's largest producer of corn and linseed, second in wool, and third in live cattle and horses. Though it ranked only sixth as a wheat

> producer, it was third, and in some years the second, largest exporter. Despite the competition for land from cattle and forage crops, the expansion of wheat farming after 1900 outpaced Canada's. . . . By and large, working-class conditions in Buenos Aires were much the same as in Western European cities. . . . By comparison with American [U.S.A.] cities in this period, Buenos Aires was relatively free of ethnic ghettoes, and its highly mobile labor force made it also a city with little permanent unemployment.[5]

However, the brightness of these figures hides the shadows and contradictions of the Argentine society and economy of that time. As the same historian points out:

> By 1914 Argentina had . . . evolved into an extremely mixed and diverse society. Across the regions extreme modernity and immutable backwardness coexisted. Expectations remained high that the imbalances would steadily recede as the present wave of growth continued, for there was still much to accomplish.[6]

In 1930, with the global economic crises and the first local military coup, the development trend stopped and reversed. Instead of being included among the high-income economies in the World Bank tables, Argentina is now among the upper-middle-income countries where it shares positions with Brazil, Uruguay, Mexico, and Venezuela from the American continent, Gabon and Botswana from Africa, and Latvia, Lithuania, Portugal, and Greece from Europe.[7]

The economic and cultural mismanagement of the country could not however destroy one of the main achievements of the organizational period of the country: the establishment of a gratuitous, compulsory, tax-sustained, and public education. Although the quality of education suffered from all those years of regressive, and sometimes fascist attacks, quantitatively it still is reaching the whole of the country, allowing everybody at least to read and write, and with these instruments giving the vast majority of Argentines access to information offered by a large market of diverse publications. In 1990, the pupil/teacher ration in the primary schools was 19 students per teacher; 1970 data put the ratio in secondary schools at 44:1, and for colleges at 22:1.[8]

Argentina can be seen as a large tapestry woven with different threads, each thread representing the diverse nationalities and cultures that came to the country from different regions of the world, among them Spaniards, Italian, British, French, Germans, Polish, as well as Jews and Moslems of different ethnic origins. The basic canvas on which this tapestry is woven is the native Argentines, themselves, descendants of the early *conquistadors,* and the populations that inhabited the land when the *conquistadors* arrived in the fifteen century. While a few represent a pure white or native lineage, most are products of hybridization. The result is a tapestry without a clear-cut design, a tapestry whose lines twist and appear as a *sfumato.*

Because the plantation economy never was important in Argentina, the introduction of African slaves never reached large proportions. The few slaves that were in the country at the time of its independence from Spain (1810) were freed immediately after in 1813. They gathered in the suburbs of Buenos Aires, mixed quickly with the remaining population, and gave birth to a cultural group, the mulattos, who have produced their own artistic expressions. From their music evolved the tango of which I will say more later.

Jorge Luis Borges, a great Argentine poet and writer, saw Argentina seesawing between the search of progress through mimicking foreign cultures, especially the European and North American cultures, and a deep-seated provincialism that refused to change inherited colonial patterns. Borges sought to transcend these trends by developing an ability to understand and talk with both the universal and the local.[9]

The period of accelerated economic development and social transformation (1860-1930) was a period of mimetism promoted in the school system and marketplace. During this period, provincialism found refuge among limited social groups at both ends of the economic spectrum. At the bottom level, it translated into the crude behavior of the persecuted *gauchos*, the mestizo cowboys of the Argentine pampas, and of the *compadritos* of the suburbs of the large cities, whom Richard Powers, a dance historian at Stanford University, defines as "a folk antihero somewhere between a bully, a thief and a pimp."[10] At the upper economic scale, some large land owners and church members remained nostalgic of bygone days when they were masters of the country and kept the mind of the people restrained by dogmas and myths.

Paradoxically, the provincialism of the lumpen-proletariat engendered a form of music, the tango, that would acquire universal acceptance and soon invade the salons of the sophisticated outer-oriented aristocracy. The tango expresses the sadness of displacement: from rural fields to crowded suburbs for the natives and for the immigrants from their many diverse landscapes of Europe. It also mixes instruments from the natives, the guitar, and the immigrants, the fiddle and the bandoneùn, a concertina-like German instrument. The words often speak of crude, brothel-oriented sex and of betrayal and revenge, but there is also tender romance and the longing for stable relationships. Some tangos shift from individual feelings to social criticism and become vitriolic pictures of a face that Argentina hides under its economic and cultural exploits.[11] A few examples in Table 1 illustrate this. Somehow the chronology of these examples reflects a parallel slow zigzagging movement of Argentine society towards more gentleness.

The tango was created by males for males. It reflected well the traits of the social structures among the poor urban population and those immigrants who decided to join them. The tango muses about the hybridization, the resentment, the sadness, and the longing for women that were scarce,

Table 1

Sexual Implications of Tango Music

Tango	Spanish Text	Translation
(1905) *La Morocha* Words: Angel Villoldo Music: Enrique Saborido Subject: feelings of a woman from Buenos Aires (as seen and written by a man of course!)	Soy la morocha argentina, la que no siente pesares y alegre pasa la vida con sus cantares, Soy la gentil compañera del noble gaucho porteño, la que conserva el cariño para su dueño.	I am the dark Argentine, who never has sorrows and happily goes through life singing her songs. I am the gentle companion of the noble "gaucho porteño," who keeps her love for her master.
(1924) *Griseta* Words: José González Castillo Music: Enrique Delfino Subject: prostitution	Mezcla rara de Museta y de Mimí con caricias de Rodolfo y de Schaunard, era la flor de París que un sueño de novela trajo al arrabal. Y en el loco divagar del cabaret, al arrullo de algún tango compadrón, alentaba una ilusión: soñaba con Des Grieux, quería ser Manon.	Strange mixture of Museta and Mimi with strokes from Rodolfo and Schaunard,[12] she was the flower of Paris that a romantic dream brought to the suburb [of Buenos Aires]. In the crazy rambling of the cabaret, with bully tangos for lullabies, she was cherishing an illusion: she was dreaming with Des Grieux, wanting to be Manon.[13]
(1926) *Íntimas* Words: Ricardo Luis Vignolo Music: Alfonso Lacueva Subject: romantic	Hace tiempo que te noto que estás triste, mujercita juguetona pizpireta Que te pasa? Desengaños que has sufrido? Hay recuerdos de amor inolvidables . . . Y hay vacíos imposibles de llenar!	Since long I see you sad, little playful and lively woman. What happens? Disappointments that hurt? There are memories of love that are unforgettable . . . And there are voids impossible to fill!
(1928) *Silbando* Words: José Gonzalez Castillo Music: Sebastián Piana y Cátulo Castillo Subject: betrayal and punishment.	Una calle . . . Un farol . . . Ella y él . . . y, llegando sigilosa, la sombra del hombre aquel a quien lo traicionó una vez la ingrata moza . . . Un quejido y un grito mortal y, brillando entre la sombra, el relumbrón con que un facón da su tajo fatal.	A street . . . A street light . . . She and he . . . and, silently approaching, the shadow of the man that she once unmindfully betrayed . . . A whine, a deathly scream, and shining from under the shadows, the flash of bright light of a knife piercing its fatal stab.

continued

Table 1 continued

Tango	Spanish Text	Translation
(1933) *Si Volviera Jesús* Words: Dante A. Linyera Music: Joaquín M. Mora Subject: cultural criticism	Veinte siglos hace, pálido Jesús, que miras al mundo clavado en tu cruz; veinte siglos hace que en tu triste tierra los locos mortales juegan a la guerra. Sangre de odio y hambre vierte el egoismo.	For twenty centuries, pale Jesus, you are looking at the world nailed to your cross; for twenty centuries in your sad land crazy mortals play war. Egoism is shedding blood of hatred and hunger.
(1968) *Balada Para Un Loco* Words: Horacio Ferrer Music: Astor Piazzolla Subject: modern, pure poetry.	Quereme así, piantao, piantao, piantao . . . Abrite a los amores que vamos a intentar la mágica locura total de revivir . . . Vení, volá, vení!	Love me as I am, wild, wild, wild . . . Open up to love, we will attempt the magic insanity of a total renovation . . . Come, fly with me, come!

because most of the immigrants who stayed in the city were single while those who came with families looked for a piece of land in the countryside. The hybridization in the poor neighborhoods of Buenos Aires produced insecure males who resorted to macho postures when observed or ridiculed by their peers.[14]

[*Note*: In addition to the value of *machismo* mentioned above, Argentine sexual attitudes and behaviors are strongly influenced by three other values—*marianismo, ediquetta,* and *pronatalism*—which are commonly shared with some minor variations across the Latino world of South and Central America. To avoid duplication in several chapters, these four basic values are described in detail in Section 1A, Basic Sexological Premises, in the chapter on Puerto Rico. The reader is referred to this material in Volume 2 of this *Encyclopedia.* (Editor)]

Since 1953, provincialism has made repeated attempts to regain the dominant position it held before 1853, but it was often infiltrated by foreign fascist and Nazi influences. These attempts, beside damaging the country's cultural and economic development, succeeded in drastically changing the image of Argentina in the rest of the world. David Rock's seminal book on Argentina summarizes this change in two beautiful paragraphs.[15] Before 1930:

> Indeed, for many decades many Europeans believed that Argentina offered an opportunity equal to, if not greater than, North America. The *pampas estancieros* enjoyed the reputation that Texas or Arab oil magnates have today, and the expression *riche comme un Argentin* remained a commonplace among the French until the 1930s. In 1907,

> George Clemenceau perceived the genesis of a great new national community originating from a spirit he equated with Manifest Destiny in the United States. "The real Argentino [sic]," he commented, "seems to me convinced there is a magic elixir of youth which springs from his soil and makes of him a new man, descendant of none, but ancestor of endless generations to come." The Spanish philosopher José Ortega y Gasset issued a similar pronouncement in 1929. The Argentine people, he declared, "do not content themselves with being one nation among others: they hunger for an overarching destiny, they demand of themselves a proud future. They would not know a history without triumph."

In his second paragraph, David Rock reflects on the Argentina of 1987:

> Such copious expectations and laudatory reflections form a stark and bitter contrast with more recent judgments. For at least the past two decades economists have classified Argentina in the underdeveloped or "third" world, and by the 1960s Argentina was becoming a byword for political instability, inflation, and labor unrest. During the 1970s a sudden procession of horror stories emanated from Argentina–unbridled popular riots, guerrilla warfare, assassinations, abductions, imprisonment of dissidents, institutionalized torture, and eventually mass murder. For a time Argentina elicited a single association: los desaparecidos, the thousands of students, workers, writers, lawyers, architects, and journalists, men and women alike, who had "disappeared," simply vanished without trace. At this time too, Rio de Janeiro, Mexico City, Los Angeles, Paris, New York, London, and Rome became refuges for a vast Diaspora of political and economic exiles from Argentina.

David Rock asks: What went wrong? My response, based on my own and my husband's studies of the socioeconomic evolution of Argentina, and our existential experience there, is that the 1930 regressive coup stopped the process by which Argentina, inspired by Jeffersonian philosophy, was constantly redesigning her coat of laws and regulations in order to adjust to changes in her growing physical and economic body, these changes being in turn induced by changes in the global economy and by the scientific and technological advances that humankind was achieving. That coup pushed Argentine society into the seesawing mentioned above, and from 1930 to 1983, with successive coups, the regressive forces became increasingly powerful.

Since 1983, Argentina is slowly and painfully regaining its democratic structures and its ideals of constant progress of both economies and minds. Will she be able to go beyond mimetism and provincialism and realize the synthesis that Borges and many others were longing for?

This summary of Argentine evolution as an independent nation should help readers to see Argentine sexual mores as the result of a complex mix of influences from the regressive and progressive periods of Argentine history. More details on Argentine history and sociology will be given in the following sections of this chapter when required for a better understanding of a particular subject.

3. Sexual Knowledge and Education

A. Historical Perspectives

Argentina started really its life as a modern country in 1853, when a generation of progressive politicians organized the country, promoted public education, and produced a radical transformation in the economy and society.

A census in 1869 reveals that:

> four-fifths of the population was illiterate and housed in mud and straw shacks. Twenty years later, although conditions varied greatly among the regions, in some areas education, housing, and consumption standards bore comparison with the most advanced parts of the world. By the late 1880s the nation's population was increasing by threefold every thirty years.[16]

Outstanding among those new politicians is Sarmiento, an Argentine educator who was president of the republic between 1868 and 1874. In his inaugural address he said: "We need to transform the poor 'gauchos' into people useful to society. For this purpose, the whole country should become a school."[17]

In 1847, Sarmiento had traveled through Europe to learn of the successes and failures of educational systems. Nothing of what he saw satisfied him. He wanted to know of a school system capable of developing reasoning power in the magical and mythical minds of poor peasants.

Then, one of his friends suggested that he visit the United States and get acquainted with the work that Horace Mann was doing in the school system of Massachusetts. He crossed the Atlantic and visited not only with Horace Mann, but also with other brilliant Bostonian Unitarians who were meeting at the Divinity School of Harvard, among others Henry W. Longfellow and Ralph W. Emerson.

The friendships he established then were further cultivated during his second sojourn as Argentine Ambassador to the United States, from 1864 through 1868. When Sarmiento assumed the presidency of Argentina, Mary Mann, the widow of Horace Mann, was instrumental in sending to Argentina a group of sixty five American schoolteachers with whom Sarmiento and his Ministry of Education, Nicolás Avellaneda, who succeeded Sarmiento as president of Argentina, began to organize the country's educational system. Primary schooling was free and compulsory for all. The number of well-furnished schools constantly increased, and teachers, who were quickly formed by their American counterparts in normal schools, were conferred high social status and adequate monetary rewards.

Prior to this, the monopoly of the Catholic Church over education kept the common people ignorant of the advances in science, technology, and political organizations that were taking place in the world. The education of people of certain rank and fortune was a little better, but ineffective for the development of the country. Only a small number of young men, and even fewer young women, managed to break the fences that an education based on theology created in their minds. However, these few opened the doors to the outside world, other cultures, and great foreign thinkers. Even if they were studying in a church-managed university, they would smuggle in, often with the help of prominent and open-minded priests, books from Jefferson and the great philosophers of the French Revolution, which they secretly read and discussed with friendly priests.

All this changed when Sarmiento and Avellaneda decided to organize the new school system to provide an education for life in the here and now. It is for this reason that Sarmiento and Mrs. Mann agreed that all the school teachers sent from the United States would be females so as to serve as role models for Argentine households. Sarmiento and Mrs. Mann wanted them to bring new knowledge through words, and a new vision of life through the example of their lives. Since then, the children of poor and uneducated native peasants and of equally poor and uneducated immigrants had access to scientific knowledge and learned about their own nature, about what it meant to be human. They would learn how babies are born, how to cut their umbilical cords, how to change and clean their diapers, and how to take care of babies and their own bodies.

In the years of political freedom, social progress, and economic growth that followed, issues on sexuality and the status of women began to be discussed. They were introduced mainly by female politicians of the Socialist party, and by the youth who by 1918 had achieved success in their fight to change the university system that resisted Sarmiento's reform and, although no longer managed by the Catholic Church, had remained scholastic. It is interesting to observe that while the socialists were bringing a message of sexual liberation, the communists, when they split from the democratic socialists, adopted a moral code based on strict monogamy.

Sarmiento's progressive work on the schools affected many other aspects of Argentine life. One of these aspects was a surge in bookstores that would offer writings of the most varied orientation, writings to which youth had access, and which often supplemented and amplified the information they were given at school.

The 1930 military coup started a slow process of reversing Sarmiento's ideas on education. The purpose of education now focused on keeping pace with the advances in the natural sciences and technology while preventing students from acquiring a vision of life that would contradict the obsolete moral codes of a narrow theology. However, the alliance of the most reactionary members of the Catholic hierarchy with the military never managed to take the schools completely backwards. Argentina's life had irreversibly changed, and what was not taught in the classrooms, the students would learn in their households and in the streets, although sometimes the information would reach them distorted or incomplete. For quite a while after the first military coup, books on sexuality could still be freely obtained in the bookstores. Later on, more reactionary military coups would censor even this source of information.

B. The Situation Today

Currently there are no sexual education programs at the primary school level. It is left to the teachers to give some information as part of the classes on biology. In the few cases in which a teacher decides to do so, it is no more than a description of the reproductive organs in plants and animals, and some references to the role of ovaries and testes in human reproduction, with no explicit mention or even less showing of pictures of the genitals.

It would be easy, however, to introduce full courses on sexual education in all Argentine public schools. All that is needed is an order of the National Educational Council, which by law decides on the nature and extension of primary school programs. The members of the council are appointed by the president of the country following advice of the ministry of education. Once decided at the level of the central government, there are no elective local educational boards where parents could either oppose or suggest the idea of providing sexual education to the students. The provincial educational councils have jurisdiction only over provincial schools, not on those established by the national government. Although a few sophisticated private schools have developed advanced programs of sexual education, these schools reach only a tiny minority of children of rich urban households.

The same possibilities of organizing national programs of sex education are open for secondary schools (high schools), because they too report to the authority of the central government. But here again, the situation changes from one school to the other, depends on its director (principal), and is in general well behind the demands of the present. Neither primary nor secondary schools have recovered yet from the regressive trend imposed on them by decades of regressive military coups and brief civilian intervals.

For further information about sex education, see Section 5 below.

4. Autoerotic Behaviors and Patterns

In Argentine society, despite official Catholic negative views of sex outside the marital union, it is usually seen as normal for preteenage boys to play exploratory games with other boys, and girls with other girls. These games are seen by most parents as part of the process of growing up. It allows the child to reassure him/herself of the normality of his/her body by comparing it with the body of a friend, relative, or schoolmate, although sometimes instead of being a reassurance it could generate anxieties as when girls compare the size of their breasts and boys the size of their penises. It is also a source of anxiety when a boy feels sexually excited by another boy and fears he is becoming gay.

Freedom for these kinds of exploratory games was greater in bygone days when Argentine society had less violence, and drugs were not as common. In the past, boys would gather in parks and compete to see who threw their semen further while masturbating. Parks were also a place where couples would meet for sexual encounters and teenagers would peep on their activities without disturbing the partners.

5. *Interpersonal Heterosexual Behaviors*

A. Children

See Section 4 immediately above.

B. Adolescents

What is known about the sexuality of Argentine adolescents is limited to anecdotal reports, most of which deal with middle- and upper-class urban teenagers rather than with rural poor and urban street children. In this limited context, my personal experience in the 1970s in developing a sexual education program for students, ages 13 through 17, of middle-class households may be informative. This program was for a prestigious coed secondary school of suburban Buenos Aires, the *Colegio Nacional San Isidro.* After a dialogue with the parents aimed at interesting them in the sexual education of their sons and daughters, an integrated approach led the students to discuss biological and social aspects of sexual behavior in relation to their personal development and the establishment of interpersonal relations.

Although the students were offered the possibility of presenting their questions anonymously in writing, they preferred to come out openly with their questions. Their greater concerns were with the emotional and spiritual aspects involved in a sexual relationship. One vividly remembered example is typical of the concerns and perspective these youth had. A 15-year-old male student asked: "Can you know when your partner is pregnant without performing a lab test?" I left the student to share first his own views, and his answer was: "I think that when one is deep in love, one can detect subtle changes in mood and behavior of his lover that indicate a potential pregnancy."

Among the biological issues, girls were more interested in knowing more about the physiology of menstruation, pregnancy, and delivery, while boys wanted to reassure themselves that masturbation and nocturnal involuntary ejaculations were normal and could be enjoyed free of guilt and shame. Both sexes converged in expressing that they were facing the awakening of their sexual potential with anguish and feelings of being all alone in this experience. They all needed to be reassured that there was nothing abnormal in their bodily sensations, and in the fantasies and feelings these sensations often evoked.

In 1931, when Argentina's freedom to experiment with and discuss these subjects was not yet fully eroded, an Argentine scholar, Anibal Ponce, studied the problems of growing up in Argentine society in a book titled *Ambition and Anguish Among Adolescents.* Regarding the common feelings of being isolated and alone, he said:

> With a personality not yet formed, and while trying to awkwardly build the structures of his ego, the adolescent suffers more than anybody else, the anguish of solitude, because he or she needs more than anybody else the support of the others.[18]

Unfortunately, since my experience in 1970, the situation has deteriorated for Argentine adolescents, who find in their society less and less support for their existential anguish. In 1993, while researching this paper, this deterioration was obvious in my talks with adolescents. In a meeting with a group of them, ages 15 to 17, they told me about the typical pattern of a course on sexual education in a school that chooses to implement it. The teacher does not allow questions from the students during the presentations. At the end, he agrees to receive a few. Sensing that the instructor is insecure and unable to facilitate a dialogue in depth, the students then prefer to end the class quickly declaring they have nothing to ask.

The teenagers confessed that it is attitudes like this, repeated in their homes, that make them view society and family cynically. Surrounded by injustice and hypocrisy, they feel they can do little to get the adults to change. They were, for instance, very disturbed by the expulsion of two students from their schools when they became pregnant.

The situation is no better at the college level. There are no courses of sexual education in Argentine universities, except, and this only since the 1960s, at their schools of medicine (see Section 12 below).

Premarital Sexual Activities

Sexual behavior differs from one group of Argentine youth to another depending on their social class and place of residence. Social belonging and location determine different levels of knowledge, repressions, and attitudes towards life in general and sex in particular.

In the larger cities, like Buenos Aires, Cordoba, Mendoza, Rosario, and Santa Fe, youth are exposed to a cosmopolitan vision of life and receive more information on sex and sexuality. They are also freer to experiment with this vision and information than youth living in smaller towns where family control is strong and where cultural patterns are rather narrow.

For rural youth, it is quite different. On the one hand, they receive information on sex and sexual behavior just from observing nature in which they are totally immersed, and from the relation between genders in the family where members enjoy little privacy, if any. On the other hand, the prevailing Catholic Church writes deep into the unconscious of every boy and girl, but especially of the latter, ideas of guilt and sin that trouble the pleasure that the early awakening of the senses in the rural milieu can bring. Neither boys nor girls are taught about the relational and recreational aspects of sex, and the possibilities offered by modern technology for keeping under control the reproductive aspects. Hence the purely instinctive sex leads to pregnancy, confronting the boy with the responsibility of an early marriage that he is not yet ready to assume, and the girl with the responsibility of an unwanted motherhood for which she also is not prepared.

Youngsters in the big cities have easy access to magazines where sexuality is soberly analyzed, even if their parents and the Church hide such information from the youngsters. They know about contraceptive techniques and can acquire contraceptives in the pharmacies without problem. However, the guilt and shame associated with sex are also present here and, as usual, instead of promoting either safe sex or abstinence, these only lead to quick sexual contacts. Under the uncontrollable pressure of a hormonal flood released in a hurry and in the most unromantic places, boys and girls neglect prevention of pregnancy and disease. For youth in the poverty belts around the big cities, the situation is compounded by the lack of money. Even if they would prefer to use contraceptives, they cannot buy them and there are no places where they can get these free. Only the army distributes free condoms to the soldiers when they leave the barracks on their weekly leave days. Knowing the limited budget for health care within the army, the church has not complained to the military with which they keep good relations, pretending instead to ignore a practice that otherwise they could not openly accept.

First Sexual Experiences

In late 1993, the author had long conversations with different groups of young people in Buenos Aires. These mainly middle-class youth, ages 18 to 24, were encouraged to bring to the meetings problems related to their sexual life and development.

One subject recurrent in these meetings was their difficulty in establishing a fruitful dialog with their parents. Repeatedly they expressed regret that aspects of their lives that engender so many anguishes and fears could not be explicitly discussed in the intimacy of their households.

Contrasting the information gathered in these meetings with my previous experience in medical private practice in Argentina, it became clear that sexual activities are initiated at increasingly earlier ages. Most of the interviewed youth defined their first experiences as disappointing. Asked why, they always responded that it was so because of a lack of romance. Most boys had been initiated in whorehouses, under the pressure of the fathers who would arrange the visit, and this happened without a previous intimate talk that could soothe the anxiety of the teenager by discussing what he may expect to happen and how to protect himself from diseases, mainly AIDS, about which the teenager had already heard at school. Such experiences, they said, left bitter memories, which for some disappeared when they fell in love and discovered the ingredient they were longing for: romance. The boys all agreed that the experience at the whorehouse was felt as an obligation to fulfill in order to affirm their virility.

Among girls, the memories of their being deflowered were somewhat different from the boys. Some did not bother to get prior information about the meaning and the possible consequences of their first sexual encounter. They perceived their first intercourse as the fulfillment of a strongly felt desire that at the same time would transgress a social taboo. Hence they reached the situation with many expectations, and as much anxiety as boys said they did. For other, more entrepreneurial-type female students, it was a calculated action to get rid of their virginity, which they perceived as an obstacle to enter into a more mature and fulfilling sexual life. These girls sought information from doctors in private gynecological practice and acquired the necessary contraceptive technology to protect themselves.

Reflections about Sex Policies and Politics from Meetings with Youth

The young's perception is that society is not providing appropriate responses to their needs of knowing more about sexuality and sensuality. The information they get at home, school, and church is incomplete and biased by the prejudices of the adults. Although short articles dispersed in different magazines are useful, they cannot fully fill the gap. They would prefer an honest, open, uninhibited dialogue with parents, teachers, and priests.[19] They see the AIDS epidemic slowly changing the situation, although they consider that their survival is in danger because society is reacting too slowly and is still not assuming full responsibility, preferring to stick to old patterns of thought and behavior rather than save lives.

The more enlightened youth perceive many deficiencies in the information process, deficiencies that they say may risk the future of a stable relationship. For instance, they are not told that although syphilis and gonorrhea can still be easily cured, these diseases may make it easier for the AIDS virus to invade the immune system. Girls are not told that chronic or repeated inflammation of the genital tissues may lead to infertility and ectopic pregnancies.

A generalized opinion among youth is that it is necessary to invest in improving and updating education and information to secure the future of the country. The impression left on me by my meetings in Buenos Aires is that middle- and upper-class youth are slowly evolving from a macho behavior, which still is deeply programmed into their minds by their acculturation, to an attitude of better understanding of their own and the opposite sex's sexuality. They are learning to integrate male and female traits in their own personality, and to harmonize the roles of males and females in the marketplace, households, and political arenas. They are also starting to understand and respect those who show preferences for intimate relationships with persons of their own sex.

However, the majority of the Argentine population is unchanged. It is unclear at this time whether the elite youth of the urban middle- and upper-class, as they mature, will influence the democratic process that reopened in 1983 to introduce changes in the educational and legal systems that could usher larger groups into a new vision of their sexual life.

C. Adults

Marriage and the Family

Mature people, who married before the recent shift in sexual behavior towards more openness and gender equity acquired the intensity and spread they now have, are being bombarded by the mass media and performing arts with messages that carry a heavy sexual and sensual content, telling about new techniques for love making, new roles within the couple, new risks in extramarital relationships, etc. These issues are also conversation matter among friends and families, and at business meetings and almost any social gatherings.

Inevitably, mature couples start imitating the open and direct language of their younger counterparts. This, and the perceived risks of extramarital affairs since the AIDS epidemic, is leading them to recreate their sexual life and expand their erotic horizon. They are discovering that fantasy and playfulness within the couple are the best antidotes of boredom. Men are learning to ask their spouses to use new forms of stimulation with them; they are learning that it is more important for them and their partners to be mutually tender and understanding than it is to count their performance points. Oral sex and anal intercourse are losing their status, especially among younger Argentines, as techniques practiced only with prostitutes. Masturbation is increasingly viewed not only as a form of self-satisfaction, but also as a means of sharing sensual and orgasmic experiences without penetration.

Extramarital Sex

We still find married men who maintain a long-standing relationship with a second woman, sometimes with the knowledge and approval from his spouse, and even of his grown-up children. For some couples, it is a solution that keeps their marriage alive: the man is free to express sexual needs that he does not dare to reveal to his wife, and the woman is relieved from pressures to change her sexual behavior, a task that for her heavily structured personality may be so painful that she prefers to share her partner with another woman. These are generally women with limited horizons in their lives and a very low sexual appetite.

Fewer are the number of couples where the man and woman both have temporary extramarital relationships under mutual knowledge and agreement. This is the most risky modality in today's Argentina, because many of the men resist the use of condoms and ignore whether their occasional partners may be HIV positive.

Older Adults

The new ways of thinking and making love are also resounding among couples over age 55. Often it is their own children and grandchildren who awaken them to the new sexual behavioral patterns. In Argentina, there is still strong interaction among the generations and the oldest easily perceive the freedom that the new generations have won. Nowadays, a granddaughter moving from home to the apartment of her boyfriend is not grounds for scandal. And grandparents do not stay away from a wedding where the bride in a long white gown shows signs of pregnancy.

Indeed these are open-minded elderly who keep their own sensuality and vitality alive; they are not ashamed to show tenderness between them through hugging and kissing. These are people who consult the urologist at the first signs of impotence in the man, or the gynecologist when the woman's sex drive declines. Most elderly couples, however, have not reached this openness. They let their sexual drive disappear without seeking remedies. Many drift into depression and develop hypochondriac behavior.

Incidence of Oral and Anal Sex

In Argentine society, both oral and anal sex carry a negative connotation, especially for older persons and among the traditional middle- and upper-class families. Argentine youth, however, seems to be taking a new look at these sexual expressions, according to what they said at the meetings.

Girls were divided in their responses. One group accepts and practices oral sex as a way of avoiding the risk of pregnancy and maintaining their virginity until marriage. For another group, it was a more intimate form of sexual relationship, somehow more romantic than intercourse. Youth holding this latter view believed that oral sex should only be engaged in with a stable partner, and not in the first exploratory encounters. Some other girls joined some boys in rejecting this way of expressing love to a partner, and thought that only prostitutes could practice fellatio on boys. The older the boys are, the more easily they accept oral sex as a normal part of dating and within marriage.

Prejudices against anal sex are even stronger among older adults, and even the younger set. A minority of the youths in the groups I spoke with accepted anal sex, and then only for fully committed couples and not as part of dating. The boys agree that: "A woman will never ask for it." The old injunction against sodomy is still well alive in their subconscious.

6. Homoerotic, Homosexual, and Ambisexual Behaviors

Argentina still is to a large extent a macho society, and machos detest gays, whom they see as effeminate. For a majority of the population, including physicians and psychologists, homosexuality is felt to be a perversion and a disease. Teenagers who feel a strong attraction to members of their same sex experience first extreme confusion about their feelings. When the picture becomes clear in their mind, they awake to the unpleasant reality of belonging to a group that society marginalizes.

Gayness however is increasingly being tolerated and a gay movement is gaining increased strength and fighting for its rights, which ten years ago was impossible even to think of. The scorn for gays is higher among lower- and middle-class men than among members of the upper-class. There always were artists and writers whose homosexuality was known among the elites, but carefully kept out of scrutiny from the media and the masses.

Lesbians are still not too visible in Argentine society, in keeping with the Victorian tradition, which never wanted to think about sexual activities in a relationship between two females.

Contrasting the social attitude that openly scorns gays, although sheltering them when they belong to special groups, we see Argentines as quite uninhibited in publicly expressing tenderness and affection among people of the same or different sex. Men of all ages will embrace and kiss each other when meeting, and there are also exchanges of kisses among men and women who are relatives or friends, and, of course, among women themselves. The increased publicity about the spread of AIDS has not acted as a deterrent of these affectionate expressions.[20] (See the discussion of same-gender sex rehearsal play in Section 5.)

To be gay or lesbian in a repressive environment whose stereotypes are the macho man and the submissive reproductive woman is not an easy task indeed. Anyone who deviates from a strict heterosexual behavior is ridiculed: a gay is not a man, a lesbian is a degenerate woman. However, to be bisexual is not so annoying, as long as one's same-gender behavior is kept very private.

The young gay faces the hostility of society by withdrawing from his heterosexual circles to a subculture where he can find both lovers and understanding study and sport mates. Successful professionals have solved their problems by choosing to retreat into more accepting cultures where they can be openly gay without jeopardizing their future. In private discussions, young gays report that their most traumatizing experience is when they decide to open up to their families and are rejected.

With a population of 12 million in Buenos Aires, one would expect a larger number of gay and lesbians than the numbers one can estimate from the few who have left the closet. These few, however, are very active in promoting the rights of the whole community. They speak for the visible and the invisible, helping the latter to openly assume their identities. They have formed organizations that have been given legal status, they have an official meeting and business place, and they publish and distribute documents to the press and public. In these documents they tell of their suffering, explain their lifestyles, and ask support for their fight for more legal freedom to be themselves and for equal rights with people of other sexual orientations. There is a whole gay and lesbian culture that is emerging with gay masseurs who announce their services in the most important papers and gay bars and discos. (I have not heard of any lesbian bar).

I also did not find neighborhoods exclusively or predominantly homosexual. Most mix with the mainstream population of their own social class. Those who have a well-defined and highly visible economic or political role are still in the closet. The same is true for members of the armed forces and the Church. To confess their lifestyle and orientation would be suicidal. On the other hand, among artists, writers, moviemakers, actors, dancers, and university professors, to admit openly they are gay may bring rejection from the most conservative members of society, but they end up being accepted, and sometimes even see their popularity increase.

Who are those conservative members of the Argentine society?

First, of course, are the orthodox Catholics who still believe that sexuality and sensuality ought to be repressed to achieve a spiritual development. If all sexual and sensual manifestations are sinful except in marriage, homosexuality is particularly so. It is unnatural, a perversion of nature.

Second, the orthodox Jews who still follow the Torah's abomination of this kind of relationship that in the past deserved capital punishment.

Third, in the domain of medical science, many have not yet evolved to a humanist, integrative, harmonizing approach. Orthodox psychoanalysts still consider consistency in the male or female physical and mental development as essential to a normal personality. They believe homosexuality originates in conflicts and traumas that therapy can face and resolve. In the chairs of sexuality of the schools of medicine, complex biological schemes are used to disguise the view among traditional physicians that homosexuality violates the laws of nature.

The irrational fear of physical love between partners of the same sex still pervades Argentine society. The overall situation can be described with the same words that Erwin J. Haeberle used to describe the prevalent attitude of society in the United States twenty years ago:

> Typically, they do not know any homosexuals, do not want to meet them, but would like them to be controlled, contained, put away, locked up or eliminated.[21]

Argentine society still is far from taking seriously the role of sexuality in the physical, emotional, and spiritual life of men and women. It still has to reflect on other words of Haeberle:

> The ultimate liberation of both homosexuals and heterosexuals can lie only in the abandonment of all labels and in everyone's freedom to explore his own sexual potential, whatever it may be.[22]

7. *Gender Conflicted Persons*

Argentina was always a male-dominated society where those who do not behave in the macho way were scorned by men and women alike. However, with the return to democratic freedom and TV messages from foreign countries penetrating into the intimacy of households, attitudes are slowly changing. Thus, the erotic minorities have had a chance to come out of the closet and express themselves. For the moment, the masses react to them with neither violence nor acceptance, rather with curiosity. In the world of the performing arts, cases are well known of transvestism, and because these persons are celebrities, the public accepts them with smiles and gentle jokes.

If things are not easy for noneffeminate gays or nonmasculine lesbians, they are even more difficult for those who identify themselves with the opposite sex in manners and clothing, and even more so for those who want to see their bodies change towards the features of the other sex.

Some heterosexual transvestites have acceptance from their mates, and sometimes from their children, to cross-dress in the intimacy of their homes. In this way, men, who seem to outnumber women in practicing this sexual behavior, can safely express the feminine part of their personalities. In their work and social environment, these men usually return to macho stereotypes.

Those who desire to change their sex physically and be socially recognized as a member of the other sex should seek legal authorization for both procedures, the surgical acts and biochemical treatments needed, and the right to change names and status. Usually the authorization is denied on the basis of Article 91 of the criminal code that considers them as mutilations that would affect the capacity of women to engender children, which is considered as their primary social role. The law punishes with jail the patient who has changed sex and the doctor who performed the operation; the medical license of the latter is also revoked.

Change of sex in Argentina has a tragic history. In 1958, a prestigious physician, Dr. Defacio, went into self-imposed exile after suffering several years in prison because he had changed the sex of a man, Mauro Fernandez Vega, who, in turn, was never able to get new identity documents. Now another man, Javier Alberto Urbina, who claims to feel uncomfortable with his sexual identity and desires to be transformed into a woman, has started a public campaign for the right of any person to own his/her body. For this purpose, he has challenged government and society alike, standing before the doors of the Argentine Congress with billboards asking the abolition of Article 91. The Permanent Assembly for Human Rights is supporting his actions according to a letter he proudly exhibits. In the letter, the President of the Assembly acknowledges Mr. Urbina's contributions to the cause of civil rights and individual freedom. The letter says that Mr. Urbina's actions may result in the legal recognition of the right to decide freely on matters that concern one's own body. However, legislators seem insensitive to this claim.

8. Unconventional Sexual Behaviors

A. Coercive Sexual Behaviors

Sexual Abuse and Incest

There are no statistics on incest. Professionals in the medical and legal fields who deal with family violence and abuse encounter cases at all social levels, but they seem to be more frequent in rural areas and among poor people.

Adolescent girls are often raped by the older males of the family and fathers often use them as sexual objects after the death of the mother, or when the spouse's work keeps her for long periods outside the home. Abusive males are usually unemployed people with a past of family violence, high consumption of alcohol, social inadequacy, and impulsive behavior. However, although less frequent, cases are also known in which the male is the head of a well-to-do household and respected by his community.

Lawyers at the Office for the Protection of Minors who mainly deal with cases of incest among the lower classes are surprised at how often they find that the abuser has no perception of having committed a crime. This office is now working with a multidisciplinary team of professionals. This and the recent institution of oral court hearings is increasing knowledge about the extent and motivations of this unconventional sexual behavior.[23]

It is in private medical practice that cases of incest within middle- and upper-class families surface. Young females acknowledge the trauma of an early unwanted incestuous relationship when coming for treatment of sexual dysfunction in their marriages.

Sexual Harassment

On December 19, 1993, a decree of Argentina's federal government introduced the legal concept of sexual harassment in its administrative procedures and criminal code. The decree was prepared by the Secretariat of the Civil Service, with the help of the Women's National Council.

The decree punishes sexual harassment independently of the hierarchical levels occupied by aggressor and assaulted, and regardless of their respective sex. Sexual harassment is defined as:

> Any reiterative activity, whether this be a behavior, a purpose, a gesture, or a bodily contact, that is not accepted and reciprocated by the person to whom it is aimed, that humiliates her or him, and that involves a threat against the stability of employment or the opportunities for advancement.

This action by the administration was promoted by the Secretariat for Women of the civil servants labor union (*Uniùn del Personal Civil de la Naciùn*) that provided information on the increase of this type of behavior in different government organizations: the Ministry of Public Health and Social Action, the Secretariat of Tourism, the National Atomic Energy Commission, the National Institute of Technology, the Ministry of Economy, Customs, National Parks Service and many others. After the decree was issued, more than seven hundred cases were initiated in the city of Buenos Aires alone.

Sexual harassment is punished through an administrative indictment that may end with a dismissal from public service. The administrative procedure however does not preclude legal action by the offended person because the same decree introduces in the criminal code Article 124B that reads as follows:

> Those who use their hierarchical position or any other situation of employment to induce another to satisfy his or her sexual requirements, be this or not carnal intercourse, will be punished with two to four years of prison.

This decree is important because it shows that Argentine women are expanding their political presence and are winning the collaboration of men who know, from well inside the system, the injustices perpetrated against women. Men and women both hope that the new legal situation will not be spuriously used to either accomplish personal vengeance or obtain undue economic gains.

Rape and Family Violence

Despite these aspects of sexual violence in Argentine society, such behaviors have been affected by the educational reforms instituted at the end of the last century, producing a more genteel society. However, violence within the household is still considerable, especially from husband to wife. Abuses of this kind are seldom reported to police, because women know that the members of the latter usually behave in the same manner in their homes.

Among the poorest households, since their early infancy, girls observe the violent behavior of their fathers, particularly when they return home intoxicated with alcohol. The mother is beaten and bruised, and a sexual encounter may follow that amounts to a rape. Faced with a society that until recently did not recognize female rights, the woman capitulates, represses her feelings, closes herself within her taciturn dreams, and continues laboring for the survival of her family, especially her offspring. Even then, if she does not manage to hide at least some of her earnings, the male may spend them with another woman and with friends imbibing alcohol.

Once more the tango draws on this popular behavior. A male songwriter puts on the lips of a female protagonist who falls in love with a hoodlum the following words:

> Now, even if he beats me
> my boy from the shanties
> knows that I love him
> with all my passion
> that I am all his
> that for him is my fond attention
> and that it will be ours the child
> product of this love sickness.[24]

The lawyers at the judicial branch that deals with family violence estimate that there has been recently an increase of some 40 percent in the cases of women beaten and practically raped. However, rape in public places of the large cities or by intruders in private homes is not as frequent as in other countries, although with an increase in unemployment, especially among youth, this violent behavior is also starting to increase.

Lawyers admit that when a girl or young woman is raped, the experience of going through the legal procedures and crude and insensitive examinations by forensic doctors could be more traumatic than the rape itself. The Argentine Criminal Code punishes with four years of prison the culprit of an incest with or rape of a minor.

A new brand of young lawyers, judges, psychologists, and sociologists are trying to uncover the economic and social roots of this violent behavior. As Martha Mercader, an Argentine writer of whom I will write more later, says, "Rape is not an animal act. Because it is a denial of human rights, it is an aberrant product of human culture."[25]

B. Prostitution

The Past

The *gauchos,* the native inhabitants of the country, themselves products of the heavy breeding between the early *conquistadors* and the indigenous population, and of the lower class Spaniards who arrived in the wake of those *conquistadors,* seldom commercialized the sexual favors of women. A *gaucho* would take a woman as his sexual partner and could abandon her after some time without remorse. His mind was not programmed into thinking marriage, nor seeking stability, but neither did it contain programs that would make it acceptable, even less desirable, to make profits by exploiting his or any other woman. The *gauchos* were fearless, quarrelsome, but honest *machos,* skilled in the use of knives and *boleadoras,*[26] who wandered on their horses through the vast expanses of flat land that are the Argentine pampas.

After the efforts by Sarmiento and Avellaneda to build more rational structures on the magical and mythic mind of the Argentine population (see Section 3A), the situation changed for both the *gauchos* and their women. In 1880, the image of a country that would develop following European models was well set in the minds of the country's leaders. The *gauchos* had to transform themselves from vagrant free hunters who lived with women practicing subsistence gardening and husbandry into a rural labor force for the large ranches the wealthy started to organize, or find a place in the smaller agricultural undertakings of the immigrants that started to flock to the Argentine pampas. The new generations were prepared by Sarmiento's schools to assume the new role, but they were betrayed by the large landowners who did not treat them as salaried labor within a capitalist system, but rather as peasants attached to the lord's land who rendered services to the lord in exchange for a place where they could build their shacks and where their wives could tender a garden and raise some chickens in addition to work as maids or cooks in the landlord's house. The older *gauchos,* not enough acculturated into the new system or economic and social relationships, would often rebel. The police would then seize them and send them to the armies that were battling the remaining southern indigenous populations and expanding the agricultural frontiers for the "civilized" land-based entrepreneurs. In brief, the displaced *gauchos* were making room for the *estancias* of the old native oligarchy and the settlements of the newly arrived middle-class Europeans.

The women of the older *gauchos* sent to the frontiers as cannon fodder were left without support and would often join the wives of the settled laborers as servants and sexual objects of the landowners families. They also became prostitutes in the small villages of the rural areas with their population of single rural laborers and traveling salesmen. An Argentine writer, José Hernandez, who knew well the mind-sets and lifestyles of the *gauchos,* wrote an epic poem about their suffering because of their inability to adjust to the transformational process, and the often rough way in which this process took place. It was a process that sacrificed the human dignity of the lower classes to the purpose of building a modern, productive nation. And the women suffered the most from this process.[27]

Most of the immigrants came seeking possibilities for earning their livelihood through hard work, risky but honest investments, and the use of the best available technologies. However, as in any migratory inflow, some elements came with the idea of making money quickly by exploiting native people and land. A few used prostitution as the means to accumulate wealth and wield power.

Argentina would soon become one of the most active centers of the so-called white slave traffic. In Buenos Aires, Rosario, Mendoza, and other cities of the country, powerful entrepreneurial organizations affiliated with even more powerful European organizations enslaved an unbelievable number of young women lured or forced to leave their European villages to become the merchandise of a very profitable trade in a wide variety of brothels.[28]

Just one of the organizations, known as the *Zwi Migdal,* owned 2,000 brothels where 30,000 women were each producing monthly an average of 3,000 Argentine pesos for their pimps.[29] To put this amount in due perspective, I should remind the reader that at that time the peso had the same value as the dollar, and that a sales clerk in a department store would earn less than 100 pesos per month. This gave the exploiters a tremendous financial power, and they used it to buy cooperation and loyalty from police, city and immigration officers, judges, ministers, medical doctors, and congressmen.

Who sustained such a large demand? Although for different reasons, all social classes made their contributions. The rich were looking for the merriment and diversity of sexual practices that they would never dare to ask from their wives, the respectable matrons whose aim was only to bear and raise children, manage households, and organize social activities. The poor came to brothels because either they had to prove to themselves every day by using many women that they were machos, or because they were feeling lonely. Loneliness was particularly harsh on the immigrants to the large cities who initially were without family or social groups with which to relate. But the poor native *porteño machos*[30] also often felt lonely, frustrated, and sad. They put these feelings into music and created the tango. One of the tangos declares: "In my life I had many, many chicks, but never a loving woman."[31]

Bully *porteños* would mix in the brothels with longshoremen, sailors, farmers seeking city fun, employees of government offices, banks, and large stores, small businessmen taking a break from their shops, and youth having their first experiences. Brothels varied in size and amenities according to the class they were catering to. Most were just a succession of small rooms that barely accommodated a double-size bed. In the remaining space, a chair would provide a place for the customer's clothes, and a washbowl would be the only available means for the customer's and prostitute's hygiene. A typical construction would be two rows of ten rooms, each with a latrine at the end of each row. In the more expensive brothels, there would be a grand receiving hall with sofas, vases, and paintings on the walls. There rooms were more spacious and some would have mirrors on walls and ceilings. They were the places for the rich who could afford to pay from five to fifteen pesos.[32]

The white-slave traffic to Argentina continued growing during the last two decades of the nineteenth century and the first three decades of the twentieth century. Already in 1892, a German magazine, *Das Echos*, commented on a trial that took place in Lemberg, Austria, where twenty-two persons were condemned for sending young women to different parts of the world under the pretext that they would be employed as maids, cooks, and nursemaids. Because the defendants were Jews, the magazine, in addition to denouncing an abominable trade, uses the case to encourage anti-Semitic undercurrents of German politics that would open up in the German political arena some decades later.[33]

Between 1920 and 1930, Albert Londres, an officer of the French Sureté Genérale investigating the ramifications of the international white-slave traffic, decided to mix himself in the life of the small Polish villages where many of the women were bought or seduced. He finally published a book, *Le Chemin de Buenos Aires* (The Way to Buenos Aires) whose influence among Argentines who were fighting to stop the traffic proved to be decisive.[34]

Meanwhile, homosexuals, outcasts of Argentine society until recently, were, on the one hand, persecuted by the police, and, on the other hand, using some prostitutes and their madams for their own purposes. In Buenos Aires, for instance, a group of wealthy and influential but closeted homosexuals organized young prostitutes to lure handsome young men into luxurious orgies in specially arranged places. They would be unwittingly photographed and the pictures would be used to blackmail them into providing sexual favors to the hosts of the orgies.[35]

Finally the empire built by the traffickers, which was facilitated by the regulation of the exercise of prostitution, was destroyed when the government moved to the opposite behavior and made organized prostitution illegal. Never was the Argentine market really a free market for sexual services, meaning by this, a market where the suppliers choose the profession out of their own free will, exercise it on their own and for their own benefit, and can enter and exit the market freely. Only very recently is it possible to see a type of prostitution that can be assimilated to small businesses.

From Regulation to Prohibition

The Argentine empire of whoredom was born and grew up sheltered by the regulated status of the brothels under laws and decrees whose declared purpose was to protect both suppliers and consumers of sexual services. In fact it protected neither and only served to replace risky capitalistic forms of exploitation of sexual services with a capitalism of political patronage that benefited bureaucrats and scoundrels.

Regulation of prostitution is always based on the premise that prostitution is an inevitable evil, hence, it should be regulated in order to minimize the damages to society from its practice. Some of the regulatory decrees dictated by city councils in Argentina were quite detailed in their requirements. One included the following rules:[36]

- To establish a brothel it was necessary to file an application with the municipality indicating the location. A tax was required.
- The buildings had to be placed in a given zone, and not display any particular sign that would identify it as a brothel. They also had to have a bedroom for each woman working in the brothel. Prostitutes could not reside anywhere other than at the brothel which was her official domicile. The women could not show themselves at the balconies or through the windows of the building nor could they solicit in the streets.
- To work in a given brothel each woman had to be registered with the sanitary authorities who during the registration process had to establish when the woman arrived to the city, from where she came and how, who was with her during the trip, and how she decided to join the brothel. If from the interrogatory it was established that the woman was a victim of deceit or coercion she had to be advised that she could sue the offender and be offered assistance to do so.
- Each prostitute was then given a "sanitary notebook" with her picture, personal data, registration number, and the main articles of the decree that concerned her rights as provider of a service, among which were the following:

  Whatever commitments she might undertake, she was free to stay or quit the brothel in which she lived and worked.

  The woman who managed the brothel could not compel them to buy given clothes or other objects.

  Debts were no reason to compel them to stay in a given brothel.

  Nobody could exert violence of any kind on them, or submit them to abuse and punishments.

Later on, at the request of the Argentine Association Against White Slave Traffic, a page was added to the "sanitary notebook," stating in Spanish, German, French, Yiddish, English, and Italian:

> This is a free country. Nobody can be compelled to work as a prostitute. Whoever wants to exit from the profession can contact [here the name and address of the organization was given] that will see to her defense and help her.

In this notebook, the City Sanitary Services recorded the results of the mandatory periodical medical examinations. If the woman was found to be infected with a disease, she was to be taken to a hospital and remain there until dismissal. The sanitary notebook had to be shown to any customer that would request it to attest to her health condition.

The madam managing a brothel could not leave the brothel for more than twenty-four hours without notifying the sanitary authorities, who had to authorize leaves in writing and never for more than fifteen days. She also could not accept any prostitute in the brothel who had not first registered and passed a medical examination. She had to take her pupils personally to the periodical medical examination at a hospital or have them ready if the examination was done on the site, in which case the brothel had to have a special room equipped with all the furniture and instruments the sanitary authorities requested. The madam also had to report immediately to the sanitary authorities whenever a prostitute felt ill, whether it be from a sexually transmitted or any other type of disease. If the woman could not be taken to the sanitary authority, a doctor would examine her at the brothel and decide whether to send her to a hospital.

It is easy to imagine the gigantic corruption that this naive attempt to protect customers and suppliers generated. The big trade organizations mentioned above bought the protection of the police, who were in charge of enforcing the regulations, and bribed justices and politicians, who all ignored the transgressions in favor of concentrating on the humanitarian provisions aimed at avoiding deceit and violence, and at protecting at least partially the free exercise of the profession. In reality, this approach did little to protect the health of the women and their clients, as elementary mathematics show.

With an average of ten daily services per woman and two examinations per week, and accepting that the examinations were thoroughly performed, which often was not the case, only the first client after the examination could be considered free from contracting a venereal disease. The women had no protection from customers already infected. Hence the chances of safe sex for the other thirty or forty clients that would visit the same woman before she went to the next examination were constantly decreasing. We should remember that the customers were not subject to compulsory medical control, and that many might not have shown any symptom for some time, while others would suffer in silence and continue practicing sex with prostitutes, lovers, and wives.

Although there are no official statistics from that period, we know from studies made by some concerned physicians, and from the clamor in the press that the number of cases of gonorrhea and syphilis kept increasing. From a study by the director of the sanitary services of Rosario, Dr. José M. Fernandez, we learn that the examinations practiced during one year—October 1, 1930, through September 30, 1931—revealed that 73 percent of the prostitutes had a positive serological reaction to syphilis and close to 100 percent of them were carriers of gonococcus.[37]

Finally, a law was promulgated by the federal Government on December 30, 1935, ordering the closure of all brothels throughout the nation. It even criminalized the provision of sexual services by a single person in her own home.

Anticipating this abrupt policy change, several measures were taken by public institutions and grassroots organizations to protect the women that the law would leave without job and home.

The Situation Today

The 1935 law ended the corrupting empire of large organizations involved in the white-slave traffic, but it could not end the exercise of individual prostitution. The application of the law to individual prostitution was even declared unconstitutional because Article 19 of the Argentine Constitution says: "Private activities that do not affect public order and morality and do not harm other people are reserved to the judgment of God and off-limits to the authority of magistrates."

Hence, an adult person who by spontaneous decision engages in sex with other consenting adults, for money or otherwise, cannot be penalized unless the practice takes place in such a way that it offends or harms third parties.

On the other hand, the change in mores that took place in the world after World War II was strongly felt in Argentina. Internally, the Perónist movement drastically elevated the status of the working class, including rural labor, and Eva Perón's action sped the recognition of women's political, economic, and social rights. The large masses of single immigrants, to whom the brothel provided a recreational and physiological outlet, are pictures from a distant past. The machos of the suburbs of Buenos Aires and other big cities are drowned by a wave of proud blue collar workers who may have consenting lovers in addition to their official spouses, but would never exploit one or the other. Contraceptives and information about them reach women and men of all social classes. For quite a while, penicillin brought control over venereal diseases. All this allowed women to consent to premarital and extramarital sexual relations.

However, prostitution has not disappeared. Teenagers, sometimes by their own initiative, but more often under the pressure of peers or their fathers, seek prostitutes for their sexual initiation. Then there are the handicapped and those who do not dare to share with lovers and spouses their need for special sexual practices. And as always, sailors and other single travelers from the countryside and abroad. Single women and married men with hidden homosexual or bisexual tendencies are also asking for sexual services. Hence, male prostitutes have made their appearance in the market.

The modern Argentine male and female prostitutes advertise their services through newspapers. A typical announcement reads: FIRST NAME; Your place or mine from Monday to Sunday; Telephone number. Some include the price. In one single issue of a popular newspaper, I found eight advertisements with prices ranging from 15 pesos to 40 pesos, which equaled the same amount of dollars in 1993 exchange.

Another form of advertising is the use of taxi drivers and hotel bell captains as intermediaries. These agents receive part of the price in exchange for referring clients. In the large hotels, the bell captains may have an album with pictures of different prostitutes from which the guest may choose.

Sex titillation by phone is also making its inroads. It is being introduced by representatives of foreign organizations. Romance through the line, as one of the announcements reads, is offered by calling a number in the United States, Hong Kong, or Mexico.

The spread of AIDS has further reduced direct trade of services and have made room for these telephone and other electronic alternatives. They are used for those who do not find a way to create romance and introduce fantasy in their relationships. Most of the well informed youth are now seeking to satisfy all their sexual needs through a committed relationship that may or may not end in marriage. Usually they contract marriage when they decide to have children. Among homosexuals, who are now more accepted by society, there is also a trend toward less promiscuity and more stable monogamous relations.

Prostitution is still a topic of discussion in the news media and for journalists. It is becoming clear that prostitution is a cultural as well as an economic problem. A morality that denies and represses bodily needs will never solve the problem. It can only increase the demand for commercial providers of sexual services. And a society where greed on one side creates poverty on the other will inevitably create greedy profiteers and needy prostitutes.

C. Sex in Argentine Mass Media: Erotica and Pornography

Literature

A review of the Argentine literature of the last few decades shows that Argentine writers often describe in detail heterosexual, gay, and lesbian sexual encounters in their novels. The practice of sprinkling some sexual spices to add flavor to the narration is not limited to romantic novels; it occurs also in historical novels, and indeed in psychological novels that delve deep into the feelings of their characters.

This literature has led middle-class urban readers to rethink their own attitude towards sexuality and sensuality. It helps in lifting the last traces of machismo, of seeing love and sex as two separate things that are practiced with different women, and of perceiving homosexuality as a perversity. In a historical novel set between 1851 and 1862, for instance, Martha Mercader, a famous novelist, defines in just one sentence the most common mind-set among young military men in the first armies of the equally young Republic: "He [the protagonist of the novel, an adjutant in the recently organized National Guard] must always be on top; on top of Indians, of the blacks, of the *gauchos,* of the peasants, and of the females."[38]

This same novelist dared to reveal her own sensual and sexual life in an autobiography in which she describes her puberty within a family and a society hampered by a multitude of taboos, the fantasies of her adolescence fueled by the movies that Hollywood sent to Argentina in the 1940s, the difficulties women had to choose freely and assume responsibilities, her conflicts with the rigid mind-set of an intellectual husband that was progressive in his ideology and conservative in his social and sexual behavior, and conflicts that ended in a sour divorce. Her personal history illustrates the limitations to which women were, and, to some extent, are still often subjected. For some, the limitations amounted to a veritable enslavement.[39]

When we compare the historical novels published in the 1980s by this writer with the books of the same genre published in the 1970s by another famous Argentine writer, Beatriz Guido, we perceive the advances made in language openness and in acknowledging women's feelings, their desires, their erotic fantasies, and their voluptuous carnality.

For instance, in one of her books,[40] Beatriz Guido describes the initiation of two young men with prostitutes. It is a description almost devoid of emotions, the two adolescents do not even ask one another about how they performed, they leave the brothel in silence and walk through the streets talking economics. The scene reflects what was then acceptable in Argentine society.

By contrast, Martha Mercader, in another of her novels,[41] talking through a heroine of the time of the war among provincial *caudillos* recounts the sufferings of innumerable Argentine women of the past and reveals things that today's Argentine women are still longing for. The main character questions, already in the 1830s, the role of reproductive machines that the Church has assigned to women. She is a woman that is consumed by passion for life and yearns for opportunities to share with her husband both her sensual desires and her intellectual potential, her abilities to perceive the social, political, and even military situation in which they live. By insisting on doing so, she destroys her relationship that cannot survive a destabilization of the macho role of her husband. Through Juana Manuela, her character, Martha is calling for further changes in a society that still is repressive and castrating.

It is worth mentioning a rare book discovered while browsing in an old bookstore of a provincial city. Its title is *Textos Eróticos del Rio de la Plata* (Erotic Texts from the River Plate) by Robert Lehmann Nitsche, a German anthropologist.[42] It was published originally in Leipzig, Germany, in 1923, under the pen name of Victor Borde, and includes an exhaustive collection of popular songs, poems, proverbs, riddles, sentences, and remarks with a high sexual, sensual, and erotic content. In 1956, after Julian Caceres Freyre, an Argentine scholar, obtained a copy of the German original from a bibliophile friend, a group of entrepreneurial editors undertook the task of translating it into Spanish. The 1981 Spanish edition contains the full original text plus an article anonymously published by Lehmann in the journal *Kryptadia* in 1901.[43]

Lehmann, arrived in Buenos Aires in 1897 to work at the Anthropological Museum of La Plata, the capital of the province of Buenos Aires, when he was only 25 years old, and resided there until 1930. Compelled by his curiosity and animated by a truly scientific passion for honest and forthright research, Lehmann did not hesitate to survey all sources from ordinary rural folks to prostitutes and pimps. He questioned his students at the University of La Plata and gathered graffiti from public latrines, rest rooms, and from prison walls. His work has rescued from oblivion popular customs and traditions that progress would consign to burial without a trace, because Argentine scholars considered them too vulgar and embarrassing to be scientifically studied.

Lehmann used the material he compiled to compare popular myths, prejudices, and stereotypes, some of which are still part of the collective Argentine subconscious. He dared to undertake this task at a point in the evolution of humankind when sexuality was still a bad word even in Europe, where he had to publish the result of his work either anonymously or under a false name.

After 1933, the Nazis tried to use Lehmann in their intelligence network about Argentina, given the deep knowledge the scientist had of the country, but he refused and was ostracized from the scientific community until his death in 1938.

To give the readers a flavor of this collector's work, I provide translations of one each of its riddles, sayings, and limericks. Riddles are usually innocent, but the solution is sexually charged (see Table 2).

Popular Magazines

It is through popular magazines that we can see more clearly the changes taking place in Argentine society. The numerous, so-called magazines for women are found everywhere: homes, hairdressers, doctor's offices, almost any place there is a waiting room. And in almost every issue, there are articles about sex and eroticism, some signed by respected local and foreign professionals. Articles cover a variety of subjects, such as contraception, the

Table 2

Riddles Are Usually Innocent, But the Solution Is Sexually Charged

Type of Erotic Text	Original Text	English Free Translation	Comments
Riddle	En un campo monterano Hay un pájaro francés, Tiene huevos y no pone, Tiene un ojo y no ve.	In a hunting field There is a French Bird, It has eggs, but doesn't lay It has an eye, but doesn't see	The solution is the penis. Popularly, the testicles are called eggs.
Saying	A toro viejo le gusta el pasto tierno.	Old bulls like tender pastures.	
Limerick	¡Puta que soy desgraciada!, Dice la parda Loreta; ¡Todos me meten por el culo Y ninguno por la cajeta!	Shit! I am so depresserd, says the mulatto Loreta; It is always my ass that is holed, never my cunt.	

influence of a healthy sexual life on the physical and mental well being of women, or how to improve marital relationships. Three other types of magazines deal with sexuality and eroticism:

- Magazines that deal with sexual issues avoiding pornographic images, shying away of even full frontal nudity. They are rather expensive, exhibit a good quality of printing, and aim at informing a public that accepts a scientific, although popular rather than academic language. One such magazine claims the collaboration of professionals from the Master & Johnson Institute and the American Association of Sex Educators, Counselors, and Therapists to produce illustrative videos that are distributed together with some of the issues. One such issue included the following subjects: best techniques to enjoy an intense sexuality; the skin: an ally of eroticism; how to make of your bedroom the most erotic place; your way of kissing reveals how you make love; techniques to renew sexual passion without changing partners; initiation to anal sex without traumas; the art of undressing to seduce your partner; the importance of oral sex during pregnancy; safe sex: condoms, a way of taking care of yourself without handicapping your pleasure.
- Magazines of sexual humor with pornographic texts and cartoons, but no pictures.
- Clearly pornographic magazines, devoid of any artistic quality, some with scatological content.

Foreign magazines like *Playboy* and *Penthouse* can also be bought in some newsstands.

Television and the Video Industry

With the return of democracy in 1983, it became possible to openly discuss and present sexual issues on television. Well-known physicians, psychiatrists, psychologists, sexologists, and writers are invited by popular anchor persons and questioned on all kind of sexual matters.

This situation contrasts with an experience I had in the early seventies. As medical advisor to an Argentine enterprise, I was helping to design a strategy to introduce the first tampon manufactured in Argentina, a task of which I felt very proud because it would allow Argentine professional and working class women to feel more comfortable at their workplace. However, I soon discovered that the word "menstruation" could not be used in advertising the product on television or in newspapers and magazines.

Argentine television programs are now following on the line of pioneer shows in the United States and Europe that favor participation of the public and encourage them to share in discussion of intimate problems. Argentines who know the languages can now receive these American programs and also European programs directly in their screens through satellite and cable.

The videotape industry is partially handicapped by the fact that Argentine television uses the so called PAL system that cannot play either VHS or Betamax recorded cassettes. The market is composed mainly of foreign video pornography converted to the PAL system and subtitled in Spanish. It is a new market where a fast growing demand is allowing businesses to make good profits. X-rated material is displayed in a separate room limited to adults who pay the store fees and deposit.

However, legislative revisions have not kept pace with changing public attitudes, and the old laws are used from time to time to crack down on the video pornography business. In 1994, for instance, more than three hundred titles were sequestered from one establishment and the store closed on the grounds that Article 128 of the Criminal Code considers obscene exhibitions as assaults against public morality. Some politicians and judges seem to still be under the grip of a repressive mentality, but many of them, and certainly the public in the large cities are reacting and fighting for their freedom to see and read what pleases them. Despite obstructions from conservative forces, the public's preferences are being respected. The higher courts are also reversing conservative decisions from lower courts, although desperately slowly.

Movies, Theater, and the Arts

Most of the erotic films shown in Argentina, films that would be rated R or X in the U.S.A. come from European countries, particularly France,

Italy, Sweden, and lately Spain. Picaresque films, many based on classics of literature such as Boccacio's *Decameron* or Chaucer's *Canterbury Tales*, are shown without censoring their most realistic details, which may include frontal nudity. The United States is the source of all the violent pornography and thrillers imported.

After the return of democracy, the Argentine cinema industry has itself produced many risqué films. One describes a famous historical case of a young Argentine priest and a young lady of the Argentine aristocracy who fell desperately in love in the years just before the organization of the Republic. They leave family and Church to escape from Buenos Aires to the countryside. However the combined powers of Church, money, and state persecute them implacably until they are detained and executed without trial. Because she is pregnant, the executioners gave her to drink a liter of holy water before facing the squad, so as to make sure that her child would die baptized. The film describes the tragedy in beautiful and poignant images, without sparing the torrid love scenes of the distressed lovers when they find themselves for the first time alone and far from their asphyxiating social environment.

There is also a mild censorship in the theater. A play called *La Lección de Anatomia* (The Anatomy Lesson) in which the actors play their role in the nude was playing for a long time in Buenos Aires night after night for nearly ten years.

In galleries of art, nudes are shown without hesitation or shyness. However, in the contradictory society that Argentina is, with regressive forces battling for survival and power, isolated episodes of censorship still happen, although a slowly operating judicial system repairs the damages in the end. For instance, in 1986, three photographic artists who were exhibiting their work at a cultural center found their pictures of nude people sequestered. The judge who issued the order resisted pressure from colleagues and public opinion and the appeal of the lawyers of the defendants for almost a year before returning the material to its owners.

Finally, the popular tango, whether danced in private salons or presented as part of a theatrical show, is often a display of eroticism at its purest macho style, the male proudly exhibiting his skills, his strength, and his power over women.

9. Contraception, Abortion, and Population Planning

A/B. Contraception and Population Planning

It is estimated that the population of what is today Latin America was around 50 million at the start of its conquest by Spain and Portugal.[44] Wars, brutal exploitation in mines and fields, and new diseases acquired from the conquerors because a lack of antibodies among the indigenous populations soon depopulated the continent. The conquerors then resorted to two policies: in some colonies they started importing Africans as slave labor and in all colonies they promoted maximum use of women's fertility, whether they be Spanish, native, or African. Every child, whether from wedlock or not, was welcomed.

Pronatalist policies were maintained after independence. The new countries needed people, first to sustain the wars of independence, then feed the armies of local warring lords, and later to develop the empty lands. More recently, it was believed that a large population would keep salaries low, neglecting the fact that impoverished masses do not make good consumer markets for the products and services that enterprises generate. Despite the influence of Catholicism, the concept of family has remained very lax. This explains why the number of illegitimate children has continued to run high. In some countries, it averages, even recently, 70 percent of all newborns.[45]

Argentina has not been an exception to these pronatalist policies and the use of women as reproductive machines. However, its population did not grow as fast as in other Latin American countries. This is due to the formation of a well-informed large middle-class that could not support families of the size that was usual among the upper-class, and at the same time, did not share the loose idea about family ties expressed by the lower-class. Middle-class couples quickly learned to use contraceptives acquired through private channels. In Argentina, contraceptives never were distributed or subsidized by the government, except for the army draftees who were giving condoms for prophylactic reasons rather than population concerns.

During a relatively recent period, 1975-83, during which the country was governed by repressive military juntas, there was an attempt to encourage larger families by giving monetary awards for each newborn and by paralyzing the activity of the clinics privately supported by the Argentine Association for the Protection of the Family. Besides the fact that the amount of money was ridiculously small, the military ignored the real feelings of the women of the urban working class. They had a different program in mind than to have a lot of children. From my own work as a gynecologist at a union-supported hospital, I know their reasoning. They wanted to save from their salaries and buy a sewing machine or other equipment that would allow them to do some market work at home, postponing maternity until the couple's joint income would allow them to raise one or two children decently.

In the year 1972, the Argentine Association for the Protection of the Family managed fifty-eight clinics around the country. That year, the number of new users of contraceptives was 23,000. Of these, 66 percent preferred the pill and 33 percent chose an IUD. The clinics were also offering services for the early detection of genital cancer and the treatment of infertility.

Nowadays, in the large cities, contraceptives of all kinds—pills, condoms, diaphragms, IUDs, and vaginal spermicides—are available. Condoms, pills, and vaginal spermicides can be freely bought in pharmacies. Women who can afford to pay, can use the services of private physicians to help them acquire the right diaphragm or to insert an IUD. Hospitals and clinics supported by the labor unions provide similar services to working women and spouses of workers.

The situation is more difficult for women who live in scarcely populated distant rural areas. There, both birthrate and infant mortality are still high when compared with urban figures or those in the more-developed rural areas close to the large cities. In the less-developed areas, the government is now trying to organize family planning services as part of its program of mother-child care.

C. Abortion

Everybody who practices gynecology in Argentina knows that abortion is widely used by women of all social classes to end unwanted pregnancies. This happens despite the injunction against abortion in the Argentine criminal code that penalizes with prison women who have abortions and the professionals who perform this service, with the sole exception of a pregnant woman who is mentally deranged. Abortions are common despite the strong influence on personal lives and politics of the dominant Catholic Church.

Abortion is a practice that everybody knows of and practices when needed, but nobody talks about. Argentina is a society that, instead of fighting against the powerful forces that arrogate to themselves control over women's bodies, prefers to tolerate the officially condemned practice with a mischievous twinkle of tacit agreement among professionals and citizens. Criminal processes and denunciation of abortion practices are rare, and the police only intervene when a woman dies as a consequence of an abortion practiced by a nonprofessional.

Given these conditions, there are no figures for abortion in Argentina, but it is believed that its practice is widespread in all Latin America. In 1974, the International Planned Parenthood Federation estimated that some five million abortions were performed each year in the region. This corresponds to a rate of sixty-five abortions for each thousand women of reproductive age, and to five hundred abortions for each thousand live births.[46]

In the cities, women who typically seek medical help for abortions are either married, mature women who already have several children or very young single women, high school and college students. That women resort to abortion mainly to put a stop to the increase of family size was confirmed by surveys organized by the *Centro Latinoamericano de Demografia (CELADE).*[47] In Buenos Aires, women with two children reported 39.6 abortions per 1,000 women in their lifetimes, while women with three children reported 93.5 per 1,000.

Studies on the relationship between abortion and socioeconomic position suggested that middle-class women resorted to abortion more frequently than upper- or lower-class women. More recent studies, in Buenos Aires during the 1960s and 1970s, revealed that the highest rate of abortion was among women with college educations. These studies tells us two things: one, that women of the upper-classes can afford to raise more children than they would really want, hence avoiding inner conflicts with their deep-seated religious programming as well as outer conflicts with their social Catholic environment; second, that abortions among the lower classes leave no written or oral record because they are not performed by professionals and the women deny having them to avoid problems for themselves and for those who help them in the procedure.

When abortion is performed by obstetricians in clinics or their offices following state-of-the-art procedures, with instruments duly sterilized, use of anesthesia, and postoperation care to avoid hemorrhages and infections, it seldom leads to complications. It is quite different when abortion is practiced by folk healers and unregistered midwives, with neither asepsis nor anesthesia and using primitive instruments. It is even worse when rural women in despair resort to pouring chemicals inside their vaginas, ingest toxic substances they have heard induce abortion, or use wires and the like to destroy the fetus. The end results are hemorrhages that lead to death if the woman cannot reach a hospital for a transfusion, or infections that may also lead to death if untreated. Other frequent ailments produced by these crude abortion procedures are the destruction of the vaginal walls, and the production of adhesions on the uterine endometrium.

In the end, many of these women who provoke an abortion by themselves or with inexperienced help end up in obstetric and gynecological wards of national and provincial hospitals, overloading an already tight supply of beds, blood, drugs, and medical time. Again, there are no statistics for Argentina, but it is estimated that one of every five beds in those wards are occupied with women suffering complications from self-induced or poorly performed abortions, and statistics for Latin America disclose that up to 41 percent of all blood used in hospitals is consumed by those cases.[48]

This picture of individual suffering and high social costs indicates a need to change policies. Abortion rates and morbidity and mortality from their complications can only be reduced by:

- providing appropriate sexual education and stimulating the use of contraceptives;
- legalizing abortion to take the procedure out of inexperienced or desperate hands, making it, instead, easily available from well-trained professionals; and
- increasing accessibility to well-equipped medical centers in case of complications.

10. Sexually Transmitted Diseases

In Argentina, the most frequently reported sexually transmitted diseases (STDs) are trichomoniasis, genital chlamydia, gonorrhea, genital herpes, syphilis, genital papilloma virus, chancroid, and indeed AIDS. There is a worrisome increase in the number of cases of the traditional STDs, particularly syphilis, gonorrhea, and herpes papilloma. Risky as they are on their own, they also increase the susceptibility to acquire genital cancer and HIV infections.

In the field of STDs, Argentina is a prime example of a global trend that took the total number of cases in the world to 250 millions in 1990, at a rate of 685 thousand new cases each day.[49] From 1987 through 1991, the number of cases of gonorrhea decreased in fifteen Latin American countries, but not those of primary or secondary syphilis. Twelve of these countries also saw an increase in congenital syphilis. Although most of these figures are only approximate, they tell us that there is an urgent need to mobilize all the available technologies to check the spread of these diseases,

The real numbers are difficult to obtain. Some diseases that present undramatic symptoms are initially ignored. A case in point is chlamydia, which is only detected in 70 percent of the cases when women come for other reasons for a gynecological examination. Once detected, the cases are only reported to the health care authorities if the examination took place in a public hospital; private medical offices are not required to report this disease.

The lack of an appropriate sexual education among all social classes, an attitude of indifference and/or shame in relation to prophylactic measures, and a medical system that is not well prepared for early detection and treatment all combine to increase the rate at which STDs are growing. Exceptions are the detection and treatment of syphilis and gonorrhea. The pronatalist policies of Argentina since the organization of the country has meant that doctors were trained and medical services organized to take special care of the health of pregnant mothers and newborns.

This occurs in three different medical environments. The most advanced environment is provided by private medical practices in doctors' offices and *sanatorios*.[50] In this privileged environment, only prejudice or ignorance can prevent doctors from providing timely prophylactic advice, early diagnosis, and appropriate treatment of STDs.

Another environment is made up of the *sanatorios* organized and supported by the labor unions. The number and size of medical institutions of this type increased steadily from 1946 through 1955, during the populist administration of Juan Domingo Perón, and his activist wife Evita. Some, like the one owned by the Association of Metal Workers in Buenos Aires, were well equipped and responded to the needs of the working class, supplying information on STDs and providing early detection and advanced treatment services. In others, equipment and services had to adjust to lesser resources. Neither individual labor unions nor their confederation ever issued policies related to the kind of services to be provided in their *sanatorios* for STDs. It all depended on the caliber and convictions of the medical personnel who were hired as management and staff. However, the wards of dermatology, urology, gynecology, and obstetrics of these union-supported medical services have helped large numbers of workers and their families to become aware of the risks of STDs and induced them to seek early detection and treatment.

The last environment is provided by the hospitals supported by the federal and provincial governments and the municipalities. They are entrusted with two missions: one is to provide medical services to the poorest sectors of the population, those who do not have access to either private nor union-supported medical services, the other is to serve as training grounds to the students of medicine from the public universities, which in Argentina are the most prestigious. Initially, services provided at hospitals were totally gratuitous, but the disastrous management of Argentina's economy for more than fifty years slowly eroded their physical and human assets. Recently these facilities have been charging a small fee as a contribution to the huge recurrent and investment costs involved in their maintenance.

This small fee may further discourage the population from the shantytowns in the poverty belts around the large cities from seeking early diagnosis and treatment for STDs. Although public transportation is relatively cheap and efficient, they are already discouraged by having to make more than one trip to the hospital before being given their diagnosis, and by being unable to obtain the necessary medications once the diagnosis is made.

Prostitutes form another segment of the population of the large cities that requires special consideration. In Buenos Aires, children of both sexes from the shantytowns pour into the city and become prey of drug traffickers and pimps. Through shared needles and sexual intercourse they are infected with all kinds of STDs, further contributing to their spread in their original milieus and the city at large.

The picture of three levels of medical services describes properly the situation in Buenos Aires, the other large cities, such as Rosario and Bahia Blanca, and most of the provincial capitals. In the rural areas, we may only find small infirmaries where doctors struggle to help the poor people without having at their disposal either laboratory services or appropriate equipment, such as colposcopes and stocks of drugs for early diagnosis and treatment of STDs. To make things even worse, poor rural people are more easily programmed than their urban counterparts to feel shame and guilt when affected with an STD. This prevents them from asking for medical help even from those elementary health-care facilities, even at the cost of suffering crucial pain and loss of income, and of spreading STDs to other members of their impoverished societies.

The conditions in which the very poor rural and urban people live may require a different medical approach when dealing with STDs than the now standard scientific approach of first investigating the etiology of the disease and then establishing the appropriate treatment. If the physician tells a poor sick person that he should come again to find out the results of clinical tests and only then get the prescription and go to the nearest pharmacy for the medication, this person may never return. Meanwhile the disease may be spread to others. Hence, a syndrome approach has been developed in which the physician examines the person and immediately gives the patient the appropriate medication during the first office visit and at no cost.

It may sound nonsensical to propose this approach, which is widely used in the poorest countries of the world, for use in a country like Argentina that has 2.99 doctors per 1,000 population compared with only 0.03 in Tanzania and 2.38 in the United States, 5 hospital beds per 1,000 population compared again with only 0.9 in Tanzania and 5.3 in United States, but we should realize that there are poverty spots where medical services are well below the average for the country, and that the inhabitants of these poverty spots contribute greatly to the incidence and fast growing rate of STDs.[51] In poverty-stricken areas, the dilemma for the physician is whether to act quickly on the basis of what he/she sees without waiting for accurate tests, or to wait and in the process turn the untreated STD carrier into an uncontrolled spreader.

I could not obtain precise information on the incidence of STDs at the different social levels of Argentine society, but my own experience, from the mid-1950s to the mid-1970s, and the experience of physicians I interviewed while preparing this report, show that a large number of women that come to a medical office or the outpatient services of a hospital for gynecological problems, pregnancy controls, or advice on family planning are infected with STDs.

Consider just one of these diseases, the genital papilloma virus, which, with 30 million new cases worldwide in 1992, ranks third among STDs.[52] The corresponding increase in the number of cases in Argentina has led to research work and the organization of seminars on the subject. Prominent among these is the work in three hospitals of Buenos Aires under the direction of Dr. Angélica Teyssie, who also acted as vice president of the Third Argentine Congress of Virology. In one of the hospitals, the work centers around the influence of hormones on the development of the disease in pregnant women with lesions in the uterine cervix. A team at another hospital works instead with young men with penile and urethral warts, while the third hospital concentrates on young women with vulvar lesions. The latter are followed to confirm the suspicion that the papilloma virus may be responsible for the onset of cervical cancer as late as five to thirty years after the primary infection.[53]

STDs are having a very negative impact on Argentine economy. This impact cannot be measured solely in terms of the number of deaths caused by STDs, because many nonfatal conditions are responsible for a great loss of healthy life and significant demands on the health-care system. A better indicator is the one jointly developed by the World Bank and the World Health Organization, which is the number of disability-adjusted life years (DALYs) lost due to a particular disease or group of diseases in a given time period.

The DALY indicator is obtained through a rather complex statistical process. First, for each death, the number of years of life lost is calculated as the difference between the actual age of death and the expectation of life at that age in a low-mortality population. Then the disability losses are calculated by multiplying the expected duration of a disease (to remission or to death) by a weight factor that measures the severity of the disability in comparison with loss of life — for example a weight factor of 0.22 was assigned to pelvic inflammatory disease, while dementia carries a weight factor of 0.6. Then the combined death and disability losses are further corrected by discounting them at a rate of 3 percent so that future years of healthy life are valued at progressively lower levels, and by an age weight so that years of life lost at different ages are given different relative values. By multiplying these indicators by the total number of deaths for each age and disease and summing up across all ages and conditions, it is possible to figure out the global burden of disease for a given demographic area in millions of DALYs lost in a given year. From these, two other indicators can be derived: the equivalent number of infant deaths that would produce the same effect, and the number of DALYs lost per 1,000 population.

The World Bank and the World Health Organization have estimated that in 1990, Latin America and the Caribbean area was burdened with a loss of 103 million DALYs which is equivalent to the death of 3.2 million infants and represents an incidence of 233 DALYs per 1,000 population. STDs and HIV accounted for 6.6 percent of the total, ranking third, after perinatal causes (9.1 percent) and neuropsychiatric diseases (8 percent), among the different diseases included in the study. STDs and HIV contribute more to the burden of disease than cancer (5.2 percent), and cerebrovascular or ischemic heart disease (2.6 and 2.7 respectively), but less than injuries which amount to 15 percent of the total.[54]

Unfortunately, I could not find specific statistics for Argentina, but what I have heard and observed leads me to estimate that the relative contributions of STDs and HIV to the burden of disease is not too different from that for the whole of Latin America. The high burden calls for active intervention by the governments, but a solution is hampered by a lack of information about STDs across all sectors of the population, and by a lack of resources for preventing and curing the disease among the poorest sectors. The latter problem could be solved if the government reallocated its expenditures to provide financial support for essential clinical services. However, government should limit its direct involvement in the provision of the services because it generates an expensive and inefficient bureaucracy; the government should instead promote the participation of grassroots nongovernmental organizations (NGOs) in the task.

Although government and NGOs should also work together in the delivery of information, the government's role in this should be more prominent than in the delivery of services, because the structure of the Argentine educational system makes it easy and cost effective for the government to include sexual education at all levels of the system. Most of the schools are under the authority of either the federal or the provincial governments. There are no local city or county educational boards to interfere with the decisions of what should be taught, and the largest part of Argentine households send their children to the state-supported public schools. Certainly this is the case for the poorest sectors in both rural and urban areas.

Schools should find the language that is most appropriate for conveying information on STDs to each population group and each geographical area. It should be language able to overcome deep-rooted and long-established feelings of shame and guilt. Schools can be used to teach these subjects not only to children, but also to their parents and the public at large, including the elderly whose sexuality should not be discounted, and who by becoming better informed could play a more positive role in reinforcing appropriate behavioral patterns among the younger members of the households to which they belong.

Information useful to counteract the spread of STDs should not be limited to the causes of the disease, its symptoms, and ways of preventing and curing them. Information provided at schools, by social workers, and by NGOs should go well beyond this to develop a positive attitude towards the body, a shame- and guilt-free recognition of instinctive drive, and an ability to establish trade-offs between the instinctual urges and the constraints imposed to the satisfaction of these urges by the need to build healthy households and societies. Poor peasants and sophisticated urbanites can both understand a well-phrased and well-delivered message that these trade-offs do not mean a repression of one's erotic life, but rather its enhancement by seeking to make it free of disease.

In the schools of medicine, which are all state-supported, doctors, nurses, and other paramedicals should be enabled to discuss STDs openly and clearly with their clients, avoiding scientific jargon and making them feel at ease when uncovering their bodies and their feelings. Young doctors, nurses, and paramedicals so trained could in turn facilitate in-service seminars for older physicians, nurses, and paramedicals who have not received any information on human sexuality.

The task of fighting STDs does not, however, stop with the schools, physician offices, clinics, hospitals, and rural first-aid rooms. It is a task that should involve all social organizations. Private businesses can also play an important role. The traditional Sunday soccer games that attract huge crowds could be used to distribute witty messages on the use of prophylactic measures and the high personal and social costs that result from neglecting them.

Argentina is a society that has to come to terms with the spread of STDs and the factors that contribute to this spread, such as the existence of poverty spots, male and female prostitution, and the consignment of persons with sexual preferences that do not conform with what is considered traditional behavior to a closeted sexual life that becomes much more healthy when it is integrated into all walks of a country's life. Argentina should learn that open discussion is more cost-effective than denial when facing problems.

11. HIV/AIDS

In Latin America, Argentina ranks fourth, after Brazil, Mexico, and Colombia, in the number of people affected with HIV. In December 1993, the Argentine government approved a new plan to fight against the disease that had already afflicted 2,897 persons, while there was an estimated 100,000 other people infected with the virus but not yet showing signs of disease. In the first nine months of 1993, 411 cases were recorded by the Ministry of Public Health and Social Action. It was expected that the total number of cases for that year would reach the thousand mark.[55]

Marcelo del Castillo, physician at the *Hospital de Clinicas* of Buenos Aires believes that 30 to 50 percent of the people infected with HIV or suffering from AIDS are not recorded in the official statistics.[56]

A study by three pediatric hospitals of Buenos Aires, Garrahan, Pedro Elizalde, and Ricardo Gutierrez, found four hundred children infected with HIV who were being treated. Of these, 63 percent lived in suburban areas, 30 percent within the city limits, and 7 percent came from other parts of the nation.[57]

Eduardo Lopez, the chief of the department of infectious diseases at the Hospital Gutierrez told a journalist that most of the treated children die before their third year, and that the earlier the symptoms appear the worse is the prognosis. Lopez, who received a prize from the National Academy of Medicine for his studies on AIDS, pointed out that 90 percent of the children are infected by their mothers during pregnancy and delivery.[58]

According to Lopez's studies, 20 percent of the HIV-positive mothers are 15 to 19 years old, and those below 24 years of age amount to 70 percent of the total number. Most of them, 59.4 percent, are addicted to intravenous drugs, while from the remaining 35.9 percent have partners who are HIV positive and 90 percent are drug addicts.[59]

These statistics show that the fight against AIDS should be integrated with the fight against the ravages of drug addiction, and that both fights require improved education and delivery of information to the youngest segments of the population. This has been recognized in the governmental plan that proposes to introduce information on these subjects in the high schools and universities starting with the school year 1994.[60] The plan will evaluate the possibility of extending its action to the primary level, and the Ministries of Education, Labor, and Interior will work together with the Youth Institute in forming community leaders who are prepared to deal with the subjects of AIDS and drugs. The plan is quite ambitious. In addition to the already mentioned educational and community work, it includes medical action aimed at providing medical care and medicines to those who do not have any coverage, a better knowledge of the situation through improved statistics on the epidemics, and increased controls on the blood banks.

While the government expects these to accomplish their objectives with an investment of only 10 millions dollars for the year 1994, the private sector is experimenting with interesting initiatives. One such private sector experiment was designed and undertaken by the Foundation for Quality and Participation, in the small town of Rojas in the Province of Buenos Aires, where children ages 10 to 13 attending a primary school are being led by a volunteer medical doctor with full support of the principal and teachers of the school.[61] Students in this project focus on the following tasks:

- Search in the library and study material about AIDS, to learn how the disease is contracted, its symptoms, the work of HIV in the human body, and social aspects of the AIDS epidemics.
- Discuss the subject among themselves, with their families, the teachers and the principal.
- Visit the local hospital, get acquainted with people hospitalized with AIDS, talk with the physicians in charge of them and with the hospital's director.
- Poll people in the street about their level of information on AIDS, the measures they were taking for their own protection, and their attitude towards people already suffering from the disease.

At the point I learned about this initiative, the children had drawn a declaration defining their own feelings and the results of their learning process. Their declaration exposed their understanding of the complexity of this problem, the difficulties doctors face in treating the disease, the high cost to individuals, families, and our community resulting from dealing with the disease and trying to prevent its dissemination, and the complications that educational authorities face in bringing appropriate information to the schools. Recognizing these key aspects of AIDS, the children then said they were willing to assume their role in the fight against the AIDS epidemic with responsibility, "engaging ourselves in contributing our grain of sand."

This experiment shows that every segment of the population can respond creatively to a well organized stimulus to promote their participation in solving social problems. The success of the Foundation for Quality and Participation project in getting young children to assume their responsibility in dealing with AIDS raises a serious question about what is not being done in a similar way to engage the adults?

Many male heterosexual adults still believe that AIDS is a disease of homosexuals. Many married women think they will be spared until they get the disease from a bisexual or drug-addict spouse. It is true that in Buenos Aires, three fourths of the all AIDS cases are either homosexuals or heterosexuals who got the disease through sharing needles, but the other one in four cases involves nonaddicted married women, some of whose partners are neither bisexuals, nor drug addicts.

It is clear that any plan to decrease the social and economic impact of AIDS in Argentina, as in any society, requires an emotional engagement that facilitates an important paradigmatic change of beliefs and behavior. This paradigmatic change is essential to increasing the use of condoms, decreasing promiscuity, promoting the use of disposable needles among drug addicts, understanding and respecting those who suffer, and helping individuals everywhere to enjoy sex while minimizing the risks for oneself and society. In addition to emotional engagement, such changes in individual attitudes require the support of the social groups to which the individuals belong, namely, families, schools, private businesses, and churches.

12. Sexual Dysfunction, Counseling, and Therapies

A. Concepts of Sexual Dysfunction and Treatment

Until the 1960s, physicians had no better knowledge of human sexuality than the average Argentine citizen. And even after some education was introduced into the medical training, the information they received was prejudiced, biased, and antiscientific. In an interview with a physician and psychoanalyst, I was told that in the year 1963 the chair of hygiene at the School of Medicine of the University of Buenos Aires was still telling the students that "Women experience sexual needs after reaching 25 years of age and only during their ovulatory period," and "During infancy, adolescence, and first years of youth, women have no sexual needs."

The chairs of gynecology, genitourinary diseases, and hygiene studied and taught the pathogenic aspects of the sexual organs and reproductive mechanisms, but refused to consider with the same objective scientific approach the sexual behavior of healthy females and males. In my interviews with medical doctors during 1993, I perceived they still do not feel comfortable in discussing these issues, especially in relation with the erotic minorities, the group that Erwin Haeberle calls "the sexually oppressed," which include the aging, the homosexuals, the handicapped and disabled, people with specialized sexual interests, and persons committed to mental hospitals or imprisoned.

Young and old physicians know that prestigious institutions, such as the American Psychiatric Association, have made clear that they do not consider homosexuality, whether masculine or feminine, a disease. However, they still feel that it is a perversion, a degeneration. I know of one male teenager who was subjected to electroshock treatment when his parents discovered his gay tendencies and put him under treatment with a psychologist. However, even in those cases in which counseling seeks to soothe the patient rather than to cure him or her, the prejudices of the therapists are perceived by their customers, making it difficult for them to assert their sexual preferences and seek a healthy insertion in a hostile society.

This is true not only for homosexuality, but also for many aspects in the sexual life of heterosexual people. When people come for advice on sexual problems—like frigidity, impotence, fast ejaculation or difficulties in ejaculating, painful sex, sex during pregnancy and after delivery, consequences on sexual life of drugs and surgical procedures, sex among the aging, etc.—gynecologists, obstetricians, urologists, and the general practitioner find that they all are confused. Although their scientific formation in the field of sexuality is incomplete, from the little they know, they perceive that science and common sense run against their ideologies and beliefs. The internal battles between these two opposing patterns of thinking and behaving only adds confusion and distress to ignorance.

Every time I talked with people suffering from sexual problems, they told me how much they would benefit from sound advice and support. They think that medical schools should not only give their students advanced training in human sexuality, but also should organize courses on human sexuality open to the population at large. My experience with a seminar on sexuality that I facilitated for aging people confirms this need. The group of elder women and men unanimously expressed their gratitude for having been allowed, at least for a few hours, to open up their feelings and show that they still are sexual beings with their own particular needs and desires.

For the moment, this seems rather difficult to accomplish. When a program in a school of medicine goes beyond the biological subjects of sexual differentiation and human reproduction, it is to cover technological subjects like contraception and abortion, or mainstream approaches to sexuality in infancy and adolescence, masturbation, and sexual inadequacy. The move beyond conventional teaching never reaches the subject of the sexually oppressed. Argentina however is changing fast, and the day may be not too far away in which these subjects, and the broader implications of sexuality for our personal lives, our societies and our economies, will be freely, honestly, and humanly discussed in all classrooms, and in all walks of Argentine life.

B. Impact of the Psychoanalytic School

Escaping from persecution and war, some professionals and scholars in the field of psychoanalysis left Europe and found refuge in Argentina. Here, they organized the first college-level studies on psychoanalysis in all Latin America. They planted these seeds in fertile ground. The terrain was already fertilized by brilliant psychiatrists, such as José Maria Ramos Mejia and José Ingenieros, and a self-taught psychologist, Anibal Ponce. They reflected the state-of-the-art of a science that was trying to apply to its domain the same positivistic, mechanistic approach that was yielding dramatic results in the hard sciences. Their problem was—and still is for many scientists who have not yet evolved from those stages of development of our rational mind—that instead of creating new theories around newly observed facts, they tried to bend facts into accommodating existing theories and classifications. Some of the statements of these forerunners in the field of sexuality now make us smile. Seeking a cause-effect relationship between biology and sexual behavior, they thought that all gay men were hairless, and all lesbians were bearded women.[62]

However, they deserve recognition for having brought the subject to academic circles and college teachings from which they were previously excluded. They also deserve recognition for their open-mindedness; they never thought that their teachings were cast in stone or steel forever. With Renan, one of their French masters, they thought that "the greatest progress brought about by modern rationality was its replacing the condition of being with the condition of becoming, replacing the concept of the absolute with the concept of the relative, and immovability with movement."[63]

The disciples of the pioneers became the first disciples of the European psychoanalysts and the work of both found their ideas and their practice spreading quickly among the upper and middle classes of Argentina, who were suffering the stress of fast-changing social mores, an unstable economy, and cycles of stifling and fostering political freedom. The country has now one of the largest per capita ratios of psychoanalysts and psychologists, and the highest number of people who have been psychoanalyzed.

The influence of Freudian psychology reaches even those who cannot afford to pay the high price of psychoanalytic treatment. Psychologists and psychiatrists are writing informative, easy-to-read, popular books and articles that propagate the main ideas and findings of modern psychology on sexuality and sexual behavior among a literate population. At all levels, they are helping Argentines to come to grips with their ambivalent heritage of an officially repressed sexuality, a society where the male is the active performer and the women the passive comptroller, both hiding their deepest feelings, and an intrinsically hedonistic way of life.

To take this movement one step further, Argentina will need to promote formal and informal sexual education that:

> goes beyond the narrow subject of reproduction to include a discussion of sexual feelings and fantasies, pleasures, beliefs, superstitions, and dysfunctions. It must further discuss sexual attitudes in different societies and historic periods, erotic art, sex legislation, and indeed "sexual politics." Finally it can't be restricted to children, but must address itself to the whole population.[64]

13. Sexual Research and Advanced Education

Some limited research is being currently conducted on aspects of human sexuality in Argentina. These include:

- Contraception, focusing on investigations of the effectiveness of different contraceptive methods, their side effects, and the number of users, as well as surgical procedures for sterilization.
- Sexually transmitted diseases.
- Sexual behavior. Schools of psychology are currently supporting dissertation research on male, female, and child prostitution, sexual violence (rape, incest, and spousal abuse), and homosexuality. Because the results of these studies seldom reach large masses and have little impact on the population's attitudes toward diverse sexual behaviors, popular magazines and journals regularly support surveys of their own.
- Sexual dysfunctions such as impotence, premature ejaculation, lack of orgasmic response, and aversion to sexual intercourse. Such studies usually follow the approach proposed by William Masters, Virginia Johnson, and Helen Singer Kaplan. Unfortuately, few urologists and gynecologists are informed or prepared to assist in these types of problems.

As mentioned in the section of education, very little is being done in Argentina at the university level to meet the needs of an increasingly sophisticated population with an advanced formation of professionals and technicians. Medical and paramedical personnel, along with judges, lawyers, and teachers, are increasingly aware of their need for advanced education on sexual issues and topics. They frequently feel at a loss when asked to render a judgment or verdict, or to provide guidance or information on sexual issues.

Professionals interested in advancing their own sexological knowledge as well as contributing to sexological research can now voice their interests and convey their suggestions to the public and to government officials and agencies through the *Sociedad Argentina de Sexualidad Humana.* Address: Dr. León Guimdim, Director, Darragueira 2247, P.B. "B", 1425 Buenos Aires, Argentina

Epilogue

Argentina is a society in transition. The rigid and hypocritical sexual mores of her past have created a double standard for males and females in Argentine society and a double standard for women themselves that separated the virgin vestals of the households from the pleasure providers. Slowly women and youngsters are creating more equitable, honest, and open relationships between and within the two genres. They are also seeking a difficult balance between the need to give free expression to their sexual drive and keep it alive during the whole life span, and the need to build responsible, stable, and healthy households. Men are slowly joining the efforts and starting to perceive the benefits that the changes are bringing to them too.

Will these changes end all traces of a repressive, unjust, and often violent past? Will they finally bring integration and harmony to the sexual field, and contribute to pacifying and developing the entire Argentine society? Only the future will tell.

Acknowledgments

There are a good many friends, colleagues, and young people who, in one way or another, have contributed to this work. I am beholden to all of them. In particular I would like to express my heartfelt gratitude to the following:

Dra. Bacigalupo, a University lawyer who specializes in family violence, for sharing his views on the situation of males and females in Argentine households.

Licentiate Isabel Garcia, from the Argentine Council of Women, for information on sexual harassment.

Licentiate Mariana Iurcovich, from the Argentine Center for Prevention of AIDS and the International Society for AIDS Education, for orienting me to sources of data on this disease.

Dr. Alberto Woscoff, Chair of Dermatology, National University of Buenos Aires, for information on herpes.

Dr. Enrique Copolillo, the Chair of Gynecology at the National University of Buenos Aires and a dear friend, for supplying information on STDs.

Dr. Carlos Martinez Vidal, Professor Emeritus of the National University of Buenos Aires, an old friend, an early dreamer of social justice, and a proficient tango dancer, for sharing sexual memories of his youth.

Hernán Federico, a young friend, for organizing my encounters with teenagers and youth.

Dr. Kutznezoff, sexologist and sexual educator, for his observations on sexual education at the University level.

Martha Mercader, writer and Congresswoman, for the many talks in which she conveyed her views of the situation of Argentine women that she feels from the depth of her heart and the breadth of a rich experience.

Last but not least I must express my beholdeness to my husband Mario, a learned scholar in the field of human consciousness, with whom I share dreams and realities, and who translated and typed this report from my Spanish manuscript. Without his help, his love, and unflinching support this work would have never been accomplished.

Endnotes and References

1. A reference to the constellation The Southern Cross that can be seen from under Southern skies. The verses on a free translation and arrangement by the translator are from a long poem by an Argentine poet, Horacio G. Rava, *The Son of America.* Tucuman (Argentina): Sociedad Sarmiento, 1961.
2. Mariella Mazzotti, Graciela Pujol, and Carmen Terra, *Una Realidad Silenciada. Sexualidad y Maternidad en Mujeres Catolicas.* Montevideo: Editorial Trilice, 1944.
3. Data on immigrants taken from the article on Argentina in *Funk & Wagnalls's New Encyclopedia,* vol. 2 (Funk & Wagnalls's, New York, 1979), p. 234. Data on population by 1850 is from David Rock, *Argentina 1516-1987: From Spanish Colonization to Alfonsin.* Berkeley and Los Angeles: University of California Press, 1987, p. 132.
4. World Bank. *World Development Report 1993.* New York: Oxford University Press, 1993, p. 289.
5. Rock, *Argentina 1516-1987.* p. 172. Note between brackets by the author.
6. *Ibid.*, p. 182.
7. World Bank, *World Development Report 1993,* p. 239.
8. Data is from the World Bank, *World Development Report 1993,* p. 295. Figures for primary education are expressed as the ratio of pupils to the population of school age children. The gross enrollment ratio exceeds 100 percent because some pupils are younger or older than the country's standard primary school age. The data on secondary school enrollment are calculated in the same manner. For Argentina, the secondary school age is considered to be 12 to 17 years. The tertiary enrollment ratio is calculated by dividing the number of pupils enrolled in all postsecondary schools and universities by the population in the 20 to 24 age group.
9. See Jorge Luis Borges. *El Tamaño de Mi Esperanza.* Buenos Aires: Seix Barral, 1993.
10. As quoted in Chiori Santiago, "The Tango Is More Than a Dance—It Is a Moment of Truth." *Smithsonian.* November 1993, p. 152.
11. All the examples are taken from Jose Gobello and Jorge A. Bossio. eds. *Tangos, Letras y Letristas.* Buenos Aires: Plus Ultra, 1979.
12. Museta, Mimi, Rodolfo, and Schaunard are characters in the novel *Scénes la Vie de Boheme,* written in 1851 by Henry Murger.
13. Des Grieux and Manon are characters in the novel *Manon Lescaut* written in 1733 by Antoine François Prévost D'Exiles. This reference and the previous show the

strong influence of French culture in Argentina, a culture that spilled over from the upper class to the middle classes and reached the suburbs through the tango.

14. Carlos A. Floria and César A. Garcia Belsunce. *Historia de los Argentinos*, vol 2. Buenos Aires: Editorial Larousse, 1992, p. 271.
15. Rock, *Argentina 1516-1987*, p. xxi.
16. *Ibid.*, p. 118.
17. Floria and Garcia Belsunce, *Historia de los Argentinos*, p. 140.
18. Anibal Ponce, *Ambición y Angustia de los Adolescentes.* Vol II, p. 537, in Hector P Agosti, ed., *Obras-Completas de Anibal Ponce.* Buenos Aires: Editorial Cartago, 1974.
19. Teenagers from Jewish families trust a little more their rabbis than teenagers of Catholic families trust their priests. The main reason they give is that priests are not married and have more trouble with their own sexuality than they do.
20. It is even more surprising to see that the tradition of the *mate* is kept in this time of AIDS. *Mate* is a traditional beverage prepared with the herb *Yerba Mate* (*Ibex Paraguarensis*) which is native of the Southeast part of South America, a region that includes the northeast of Argentina, Paraguay, and the south of Brazil. The herb is staffed in a dried and hollowed gourd, covered with water just at its boiling point, and sipped through a metallic straw. The *mate* circulates among people who are socializing, each taking a full gourd of the beverage by turns. Many diseases of the mouth and teeth have been blamed on this custom, which some fear could also transmit AIDS from a person who ignores his or her being a carrier of the virus. *Mate* can indeed be taken also as a tea, but the traditional way in Argentina, Paraguay and Brazil is as described.
21. Erwin J. Haeberle, *The Sex Atlas.* New York: Seabury Press, 1978, p. 452.
22. *Ibid.*, p. 453.
23. In trying cases in which the sexual rights of a minor have been violated, some legal districts have decided to hold actual court proceedings with oral testimony. Prior to this, all legal proceedings were transacted through written reports and depositions to the judge, a procedure that placed serious limits and a heavy burden on the judge and the judge's staff. Oral testimony in court allows for elaborations, explanations, and cross-examinations that are not possible with written depositions. Oral testimony can also provide a better understanding of the nature of the crime, its motivations, and its consequences in the life of the minor.
24. From the tango *Arrabalero*, words by Eduardo Calvo and music by Osvaldo Fresedo, as quoted in Gobello and Bossio, *Tangos, Letras y Letristas*, p. 24.
25. Martha Mercader, *Para Ser Una Mujer.* Buenos Aires: Planeta, 1992, p. 286.
26. A weapon consisting of two or more heavy balls secured to the end of one or more strong cords, hurled to entangle the legs of cattle and other animals.
27. Hernandez has his *gaucho* hero Martin Fierro condoning the attitude of a woman who became prostitute. Knowing the desperate situation she went through when her partner was sent to the southern armies, he says about her commerce: "What else could the poor woman do to avoid starving to death!"
28. There is no doubt that the women were considered slaves of the brothel owners, part of their chattel. I will cite just one of the innumerable stories recorded in the literature. This has been taken from Ramón Cortés Conde and E. H. Cortés Conde, *Historia Negra de la Prostitución.* Buenos Aires: Editorial Plus Ultra, 1978, pp. 135-6. A prostitute in a brothel of Tucumán is sold to another pimp by the pimp who was exploiting her since she was thirteen. During the transfer, she manages to circumvent the vigilance of her new owner and escapes hidden in a freight train to Buenos Aires where she finds work at a factory. Four years after her flight, the two old pimps

find out where she is, wait for her one early morning when she is walking to the factory, beat her savagely, and permanently disfigure her face with a knife.

29. Rafael Ielpi and Hector Zinni, *Prostitución y Rufianismo.* Buenos Aires: Editorial de la Bandera, 1986, p. 191.
30. The inhabitants of Buenos Aires are also known as *porteûos,* which means those who live at the port. *Machismo* is a Spanish expression for male chauvinism and *macho* means a male with exalted physical and cultural manhood attributes.
31. Words from the tango "El Patotero Sentimental" (The Sentimental Brawler) written by Manuel Romero (1891-1954) and taken from José Gobello & Jorge Bossio, *Tangos, Letras y Letristas,* p. 168). The words in Spanish are: *En mi vida tuve muchas, muchas minas, pero nunca una mujer.* The word *Nina,* which is a slang expression, could mean a lover or a prostitute; it is a woman with whom one dates or lives, who is part of one's possessions, and whom one may even exploit.
32. The description of the brothels and the prices paid are taken from Ielpi and Zinni, *Prostitución y Rufianismo.*
33. The article is reproduced in *La Nación,* which still is one of Buenos Aires' largest newspapers, of December 30, 1982. During all the decades of the infamous traffic, responsible Argentine newspapers kept denouncing the situation and the corruption of Argentine politicians and bureaucrats who were benefiting of it.
34. Ielpi and Zinni (*Prostitución y Rufianismo,* p. 18) reproduce a typical story included in Londres's book. It describes how traffickers sitting around the family table were discussing with the parents a contract that would guarantee their daughter a job (nature not disclosed) and the family a monthly stipend for three years. The young woman solemnly promises not to shame the family by breaking the contract!
35. Ramón Cortés Conde and E. H. Cortés Conde, *Historia Negra de la Prostitución.* Buenos Aires: Editorial Plus Ultra, 1978, pp. 145-46.
36. This is a summary of the rules that Ielpi and Zinni, (*Prostitución y Rufianismo,* pp. 29-32) quote from the ordinance Number 27 approved by the city council of Rosario on November 16, 1900.
37. From a report written in 1932 by Dr. Juan Carlos Alvarez for the City Council of Rosario that was considering a shift from regulatory policies that made of Rosario a hotbed of organized prostitution to a policy that would end by closing all the brothels.
38. Martha Mercader, *Belisario en Son de Guerra.* Buenos Aires: Editorial Planeta, 1984.
39. Martha Mercader, *Para Ser Una Mujer.* Buenos Aires: Editorial Planeta, 1992.
40. Beatriz Guido, *Escandalos y Soledades.* Buenos Aires: Editorial Losada, 1970, pp. 63-65.
41. Martha Mercader, *Juana Manuela, Mucha Mujer.* Buenos Aires: Editorial Planeta, 1983.
42. Robert Lehmann-Nitsche (Victor Borde), *Textos Eróticos del Rio de la Plata.* Buenos Aires: Libreria Clásica, 1981.
43. Anónimo. *Chistes y Desvergüenzas del Rio de la Plata,* from *Kryptádia,* recueil de documents pour servir a Étude des traditions populaires, vol 7. Paris: H. Wolter, Éditeur, 4 rue Bernard Palissy, pp. 394-399).
44. Benjamin Viel and Sofia Kamenetzky, "La Crisis Poblacional en América Latina." *Population Reports, Serie J. Numero 18.* Washington, DC: The George Washington University Medical Center, 1978, p. J-1.
45. *Ibid.,* J-4.
46. "Population Information Program, Complications of Abortion in Developing Countries." *Population Reports, Series F. Number 7.* Baltimore: The John Hopkins University, July 1980, p. F-144.

47. *Ibid.*, p. F-148.
48. *Ibid.*, p. F-118.
49. World Bank, *Investing in Health, World Development. Report 1993.* New York: Oxford University Press, p. 115.
50. In Argentina, an institution where sick people or injured persons are given medical or surgical treatment is called a hospital when it is organized and sustained by the state, it is called a *sanatorio* when it is a private undertaking.
51. The statistics have been taken from World Bank, *Investing in Health,* pp. 208 and 209.
52. *Issues in World Health, Population Reports. Series L; Number 9.* Baltimore: John Hopkins School of Hygiene and Public Health, June 1993, p. 3.
53. *Ibid.*
54. For more details on calculations and statistics that use DALYs, see World Bank, *Investing in Health,* pp. 26-27 and 213-25.
55. Lucio A. Mansilla. "Rige el Nuevo Plan de Lucha Contra el SIDA." *La Nación* (Buenos Aires), December 1, 1993, p. 1.
56. James Brooke, "In Deception and Denial, an Epidemic Looms: AIDS in Latin America." *New York Times,* January 24, C 1993, p. Al.
57. Lucio A. Mansilla, "Crece el Numero de Niûos con SIDA." *La Nación,* (Buenos Aires), November 25, 1993, p. 18.
58. *Ibid.*
59. *Ibid.*
60. In Argentina, the school year goes from March to November.
61. *Fundación por la Calidad y la Participación.* Buenos Aires, Argentina: Ciudad de la Paz 2944, 1429. Tel. 544-3535.
62. José Ingenieros, *La Psicopatologia en el Arte.* Buenos Aires: Ramon J. Roggero y Cia, 1950, p. 152.
63. José Ingenieros, *Las Fuerzas Morales.* Buenos Aires: or Editorial Futuro, 1947, p. 11.
64. Haeberle, E. *The Sex Atlas,* p. 478.

Australia

Rosemary Coates, Ph.D.

Contents

Always there, blood hanging above the clans of the barramundi:
Always there, people with moving buttocks.

Song 16: Ross River Cycle
(Translated by Berndt 1976)

Demographics and a Historical Perspective

A. Demographics

Australia occupies an island continent of 2,966,200 square miles (7,682,300 square kilometers), almost as large as the continental United States, southeast of Asia. It is surrounded on the west and south by the Indian Ocean, the Pacific Ocean on the east, and the Timor Sea and Arafura Seas on the north. The nearest land neighbors are New Guinea and Indonesia on the north, the islands of New Caldonia, Vanuatu, and Solomon across the Coral Sea in the northeast, New Zealand and Fiji across the Tasman Sea in the southeast, and Tasmania 150 miles to the south. Along the coast, east of the Great Dividing Range, the rainfall is heavy with jungles in the Cape York Peninsula reaching north toward New Guinea. The interior lands and western plateau are arid desert; the northwest and northern territories arid and hot.

Eighty-five percent of the 18.3 million Australians live in cities scattered along the widely separated coastlines. The southeastern region includes the cities of Sydney, Melbourne, and Brisbane; a smaller, southwestern region includes the cities of Perth and Adelaide (Castles 1992). The population density is 6 per square mile. The ethnic composition is 94 percent European, 4 percent Asian, and 1.9 percent Aboriginals. The population density is 5.8 per square mile. Life expectancy at birth in 1991 was 75 for males and 81 for females. The 1991 birth rate was 14 per 1,000 and the death rate 7 per 1,000, with an annual natural increase of 0.7 percent. The age distribution is 21.9 percent for those under age 15; 62.6 percent, age 15 to 59; and 15.5 percent, age 60 and older. Australia has one hospital bed per 199 persons, one physician per 438 persons, and an infant mortality rate in 1995 of 7 per 1,000 live births. Literacy in 1993 was 99 percent, with 94 percent attending fifteen years of compulsory schooling. The 1993 per capita income was $19,100.

Despite the concentration of people in the capital cities, Australia is not a homogeneous society, having an indigenous population, a history of European settlement, and, more recently, of immigration from Asia and Africa.

The indigenous people of Australia, known collectively as Australian Aborigines, constitute 1.95 percent of the population; about 50,000 are full-blooded and 150,000 part-aboriginal. The majority, mostly of mixed descent, live in urban areas. Most full-blooded Aborigines live in rural and remote areas of the interior and the north of the continent and maintain important aspects of the traditional culture. There are significant regional variations: generalizations cannot be made. There is a wide range of living conditions and adaptation to Western pressures; however, most Aborigines remain socioeconomically disadvantaged despite compensatory legislation.

Of the nonindigenous people, the longest family history of residence in Australia can be traced back eight generations. This population comprises people from all over the world, although the majority are European in origin.

B. A Brief Historical Perspective

When the British Captain James Cook explored the eastern coast of the Australian continent in 1770, it was inhabited by a variety of different tribal peoples. The first settlers, mostly convicts, soldiers, and British government officials, began arriving in 1788. By 1830, when Britain claimed the whole continent, the immigration of free settlers began to accelerate. Australia was proclaimed as a Commonwealth of the British Empire in 1901.

Racially discriminatory policies were abandoned in 1973, after three million Europeans, half of them British, had entered the country since 1945. In 1993, the Prime Minister announced a plan to make Australia a republic, independent of the British Commonwealth by the year 2001.

NON-ABORIGINAL AUSTRALIA

1. Basic Sexological Premises

A. Gender Roles

In common with many other countries, Australia is struggling with changing gender roles. Although one of the first countries in the Western world to introduce women's suffrage, other aspects of gender equality have been slower to develop. It was not until the early 1970s, through the activities of well-organized women's groups, that successive legislation has been introduced in support of women's rights. These include laws governing equal opportunity, antidiscrimination, and family law issues.

It has been claimed that, although Australia is one of the most advanced industrial democracies in the world, it is nevertheless a sexist society where women are valued only in terms of being a commodity (Dixson 1976; Mercer 1975). This legacy from the original white settlement is gradually changing, although manifestations continue to be expressed in the phenomena of "mail-order brides" and "sex tours." Both of these customs tend to exploit neighboring Asian countries where poverty forces young women (and some young boys) into bargaining with their bodies.

From the time of initial white settlement up to the early 1960s, women have been "brought" to the country to fulfill the needs of men. The transportation of British convicts to the colonies of Australia is well documented. Female convicts were transported to become servants for the administrators and to meet the sexual needs of both free men and convicts. The first governor of the early colony was instructed by the British government "to keep the female convicts separate till they can be properly distributed among the inhabitants" (Clark 1950, 117). These women were used to serve the needs of men but were not deemed suitable as wives for the free settlers. As the number of single, free male settlers increased, the British government began to offer young, single, healthy women free passage to Australia. A not dissimilar attitude persisted through to the early 1960s where successive Australian governments gave a high priority to the immigration of young, single, healthy women.

The history of white, female settlement in Australia is one of the antecedents of the nature of male-female roles and relationships in contemporary Australia. Another significant antecedent was the nature of the pioneering activities undertaken by men in the early decades of white settlement. The concept of "mateship" is a legend of male-to-male relationships, to the extent that it has a place as a literary genre in its own right. The "typical" Australian male has been, until very recently, portrayed as a "good bloke," and a real "mate." In the early years of settlement, the harshness of the country and the nature of pioneering, gold exploration, and farming led men to work in pairs or small groups, often isolated for months at a time from other people. There was an unspoken pact of mutual protection and reliance. Folklore is rich with stories of self-sacrificing "mates." Historical accounts have continued to emphasize masculine activities and associations, and ignored the role of women in pioneering the country, thus helping to reinforce the image of an Australian man who relates to other men, with women being generally ignored. Australian participation in World Wars I and II re-emphasized masculine bonding, and the stories, fact or fiction, of "mateship" and sacrifice continue to be celebrated annually with the commemoration of Anzac Day on April 25. In the view of some, it is on this day that the divide between the white men and women of Australia is most emphasized.

The emphasis on male sporting activities and the associated icons are current manifestations of traditional "mateship."

Social conventions, however, are undergoing change, albeit too slowly for supporters of the women's movement. Experiences in Australia are similar to those reported from America, Britain, and some of the European countries, in that the majority of women are in paid employment but continue to take the major responsibility for home management (Baxter 1992; Chisholm and Burbank 1991). The concept of the "glass ceiling" is well documented and the proportion of women in senior executive positions in all areas is very low. For example of the thirty-five universities in Australia, only two have women as their vice chancellors, less than 13 percent of federal politicians are women, and a similar percentage of senior positions in the federal public service are held by women, with one woman judge of the high court.

There is evidence to suggest that younger men do not have the same expectations of clearly defined gender roles as their fathers, although this does not translate into equal sharing of domestic duties (Edgar and Glezer 1992).

B. Sociolegal Status of Men and Women

In adulthood, men and women are treated equally under the law. Anomalies exist in the status of male children vis-à-vis female children. For example, the age of consent to sexual acts is 16 years; however, the age of consent for males to have sex with other males is 21 years. There is no recognition in the law for female-to-female sexual acts.

Women's social status, while being protected by various laws, remains, in fact, inhibited by misogyny and more subtle cultural factors.

C. General Concepts of Sexuality and Love

Sex is generally viewed as a recreational activity, serving purposes that go beyond procreative ones. It is customary for individuals to couple for reasons of love, with conventional concepts being promoted in European romantic terms. The media, including films, books, television, popular music, and advertising, promotes physical and emotional attraction and idealistic pairing.

Arranged marriage is not an acknowledged practice, however, it does occur in those ethnic groups that follow a particular cultural tradition.

2. Religious and Ethnic Factors Affecting Sexuality

The dominant culture from the early days of European settlement was Anglo-Saxon and Gaelic, with strong Catholic and Anglican religious influences. Later large-scale migration attracted significant numbers of Italian and Greek people, thus enriching the culture and strengthening the Catholic religious traditions. More recent migration has increased the ethnic diversity, with people from many of the African countries, the Middle East, South East Asia, and India. This has resulted in an increase in the number of people who follow non-Christian traditions such as Islam and Buddhism.

Recent data from the Commonwealth Bureau of Statistics show that 26.1 percent of the population describe themselves as Roman Catholic, 23.9 percent Anglican, and 23 percent follow other Christian movements. Twenty-five percent declare themselves as having no religion. Two percent of the population are classified as non-Christian, with 0.7 percent being Muslim, 0.5 percent Buddhist, and 0.4 percent Jewish (Castles 1992). Public sexual mores are influenced by traditional Judeo-Christian teachings, although there is an active, fundamentalist minority.

The legal system is unequivocally British in origin and practice. The criminal and other pertinent legislative codes in all states and territories have as their foundation British law. Modifications have occurred over the ensuing period, resulting in variations between different states and territories.

3. Sexual Knowledge and Education

Each state and territory, through their respective education authority, has a curriculum that provides for personal development and education in sexuality. These have been developed by experienced educators and offer well-rounded, age-related programs for both primary and secondary education. The implementation of such programs, however, is variable and no child in Australia is guaranteed a consistent and continuing sexuality education. Curricula packages are available, through the educational authorities, to both public and private schools. To date there is no education authority that has made sexuality and relationship education a required subject. Teachers and parents have the option of deciding what, if anything, is presented to children.

Today's young parents are more prepared to provide their children with sexual information and are offering a wider range of information than their own parents did. The result of this form of education is also variable and young people report that they would prefer to receive a comprehensive and consistent formal education by properly trained teachers (Coates 1992). No education department offers preservice or in-service training to meet this need.

Typically, the curriculum packages often deal with a variety of health and personal development issues and integrate the sexuality elements at appropriate stages. For example, concept of self and one's position within a family structure are included in the syllabus designed for the early years of primary school, as is nutrition and personal hygiene. Biology and reproductive sexuality is generally offered before the emotional aspects of human sexuality, although personal safety and the concept of invasion of private "space" is suggested for the 6- and 7-year-olds. Information on gender identity and sexual orientation is suggested for secondary school students at about 15 and 16 years of age.

Thus, the deficiencies within the system are the facts that the curriculum is optional and that teachers are not trained specifically to teach human sexuality, and in some areas teachers are instructed not to answer questions posed by students on certain topics.

4. Autoerotic Behavior

Large-scale sexological surveys have not been conducted in Australia. As a consequence, much information offered here is based on small surveys and anecdotal evidence. Research undertaken by Coates over a period of seven years and confined to Western Australia (Coates 1987) indicates that, among a population of 678 young adults, 87 percent of females and 93 percent of males reported having engaged in self-pleasuring at least once in the preceding six months. More recent research undertaken by Ferroni

(1993), who reviewed 658 women, classified into three groups—namely, women with gynecological problems, women who had had a hysterectomy, and healthy women, respectively—found that 70 percent of her respondents reported autoerotic behavior.

Current mores about autoerotic behavior reflect the Judeo-Christian influence coupled with a more relaxed Australian attitude toward most aspects of sexual behavior. Self-pleasuring as a topic of conversation has, to a certain extent, lost its taboo status. Likewise, the use of pornographic material as a stimulus, either alone or with a partner, is a subject of discussion for some young people.

5. Interpersonal Heterosexual Behaviors

A. Children

There is little information available about types of sexual behavior and whether patterns of sexual experimentation have changed. However, anecdotal reporting indicates that Australian children are no different from children in other countries and engage in sexual rehearsal play. This is conventionally curbed by witnessing adults, although enlightened parents will take the opportunity to educate their children about private and public, acceptable and unacceptable, behavior. Many parents will tell their children that it is acceptable to engage in self-pleasuring as long as they confine it to the privacy of the bedroom. It is not customary for children to witness adult sexual interactions nor for children to be initiated in to sexual activity by an adult. There are no pubertal initiation ceremonies in the nonindigenous population.

B. Adolescents

Results of a survey of 2,000 respondents aged 16 to 25 years suggest that adolescents are probably more sexually experienced than their parents were at the same age (McCabe and Collins 1990). Intercourse is occurring at an earlier age than ten years ago and in greater numbers. The mean age of first intercourse is about 16 years, and by the age of 18, nearly 60 percent of young people report that they are sexually active. There is also a reported increase in the number of sexual partners at a given age.

Casual sex is still an important part of adolescent sexual activity, although most sexual experience in adolescents probably occurs in the context of a steady relationship. Explanations for the initiation of sexual intercourse include curiosity, peer pressure, and the need to be loved. The rates of sexual experience are greater in males than in females (Dunne et al 1993; Cubis 1992). Peer pressure from boys is strong and many young women report that their first experience of intercourse was not a positive one.

Sexual activity and socioeconomic status have not been shown to be related, but pregnancy and carrying to term are associated with lower socioeconomic status.

Pregnancy is no longer a reason to precipitate marriage, with less than 20 percent of detected adolescent pregnancies resulting in marriage prior to the birth of the baby.

Not surprisingly, data from the Family Planning Association and other sources indicate that adolescents are among the poorest users of contraceptives. Age, a reluctance to acknowledge to others that they are sexually active, and distrust of authorities are possible reasons for the low utilization of the services offered.

Recent research by Moore and Rosenthal (1991) indicate that young people continue to resist the use of condoms even in the context of safer sex practices and HIV/AIDS. Males are more likely to place the responsibility on their partners and females express a distaste for condoms. It has been suggested that heterosexuals do not believe that they are at risk, that AIDS has been seen as a disease of the sexually deviant or other stigmatized groups (e.g., drug users) and that HIV transmission has been identified with groups, not sexual practices (Kippax 1991).

C. Adults

Cohabitation, Marriage and Family: Structure and Patterns

Cohabitation is a common practice in Australia, to the extent that it is officially recognized for property distribution on dissolution. The term de facto has been in common usage for at least thirty years and is applied to couples who live together without undergoing a formal marriage ceremony. A high proportion of young people live together for a considerable period prior to marriage. Over 60 percent of adults believe that living together before marriage is acceptable and about 50 percent of all people under the age of 30 do live together prior to marriage. Thirty percent of these say that they do not believe in marriage. One third state that they would leave the relationship if they were not growing in it (Glazer 1993).

Since the 1970s, the age at first marriage has risen, with a resultant rise in the age of the primiparous mother. The average family size is around 2.4 children and there is a greater focus on women's having a career outside of the home.

Divorce and Remarriage

When Australians do marry, monogamy is the conventional custom. Divorce and remarriage have become increasingly accepted in the past twenty years, and it is estimated that one in four marriages will end in divorce, with the current rate being 11 per 1,000 marriages. Close to 60 percent of previously married men and 25 percent of previously married women, remarry (Castles 1992, 169, 172).

Nonmonogamous Relationships

Recently, in at least one capital city, a group in support of nonmonogamous relationships has been established. It is distinctly different from the "swinging" groups of the 1970s. The group advertises under the rubric "Beyond Monogamy" and advocates responsible and mutual polyfidelity.

Sexuality and the Physically Disabled

Since the United Nations International Year of the Disabled in 1979, Australia has been making a concerted effort to make provision for, as well as change the attitudes toward, people with disabilities. Recognition has been given to emotional relationships and sexual rights and the needs of both the intellectually and physically disabled. However, once again, the provision of education, counseling, and other services is variable. Predominantly dependent upon local expertise, interest, and influence, programs may or may not be offered. In Western Australia, a comprehensive education program has been developed for the intellectually disabled, whereas very little of a formal nature is provided for the physically disabled. In other states, there have been some exceptionally enlightened programs for adults with acquired disabilities.

Legislation, governing such things as antidiscrimination and equal opportunity, provide protection for the rights of the disabled. Community housing as opposed to institutional dwellings enhances possibilities for the disabled to exercise their sexual options.

Incidence of Anal and Oral Sex

There is no reliable data on the incidence of oral and anal sexual activities in Australia. Coates' Western Australia survey (1992) indicates that at least 73 percent of her sample had experience at least once with both fellatio and cunnilingus; 32 percent had experimented with anal sex. Both oral and anal sexual practices are included in information about safer sex practices with precautions to be taken to avoid HIV transmission. The general acceptance of such messages (with few notable, and predictable, objections) may indicate an assumption that these practices are within the norms of acceptable sexual relationships.

6. Homoerotic, Homosexual, and Bisexual Behaviors

A. Legal and Social Status of Gays and Lesbians

Homosexuality has been subjected to both legal and social sanctions. However, there has been a gradual reduction of hostility toward homosexuality and a concomitant change in legislation in the past twenty years. Under the equal rights legislation, same-sex couples are generally afforded similar rights to opposite-sex couples. This recognition has been extended to residency status in this country for the partner of a gay or lesbian person. Despite official acceptance and a generally sanguine attitude, there is still a prominent homophobic element within this society. Predominantly this is expressed against gay men through so-called poofter-bashing, where gangs of youths go to public gay venues for the express purpose of assaulting (presumed) gay men. Certain fundamentalist religions actively campaign for the reintroduction of legislation against homosexuality.

All states except Tasmania have repealed laws against same-sex activities between consenting adults in private. In Tasmania, all male-to-male sexual activity remains illegal. In Western Australia, the legislation may be unique in the English-speaking world, where the document is prefaced with a disclaimer to the effect that the parliament does not condone the behavior.

There is a strong and active network of gay men and lesbian women, with all the major cities and many rural areas having constituted organizations. A number of these organizations are at least thirty years old and have been at the vanguard of political activism and in the provision of counseling and education services. These organizations were also crucial to the early and positive response to HIV/AIDS policy development, education, counseling, and treatment. In addition there are support groups throughout the country for the parents and friends of gay people.

There are a number of domestic gay publications, the most notable quality magazines being *Outrage* and *The Advocate.* Typically, women are less well catered for, although there is a national networking newsletter called *Grapevine,* which provides a contact service. Most of the cities have dedicated bookshops, and all dealers of sexually explicit material stock magazines aimed at gay men.

The Sydney Gay and Lesbian Mardi Gras, held in March each year, is reported to be the largest in the world and attracts thousands, including many international visitors. The Mardi Gras parade is conducted through the streets of Sydney and is a popular event for families to attend on what is, normally, a warm summer evening. The Sydney City Council supports the Mardi Gras as an important income-generating event. A fundamentalist Christian group prays for rain to mitigate the success of the event.

B. Sexual Outlets and Relationship Patterns

Gay Men

The largest gay population is in the city of Sydney with Oxford Street being the best-known area for at least a particular subgroup to congregate. An area on this street known as "The Wall" is the place male sex workers congregate. Sydney, Melbourne, Brisbane, Perth, Adelaide, Canberra, and the Gold Coast all have a number of acknowledged gay and lesbian venues, including bars, restaurants, night clubs, and theaters. These venues are recorded in the publication *Gay Guide.* Smaller towns have similar venues, but tend to have a lower profile.

It is easy to stereotype the patterns of behavior for gay men, however, it would be more accurate to say that there is as much diversity in relationship and sexual patterns among the gay population as there is among the nongay population. The spectrum—from long-term monogamous relationships, serial monogamy, triads, groups, to frequent, anonymous sex, and sexual abstinence—would all be represented within the gay community.

One representative pattern of gay male behavior has most recently been documented by researchers from Macquarie University in New South Wales. The study revealed that urban gay men had high levels of knowledge about HIV transmission and had substantially changed their sexual behavior. Attachment to the gay community, defined as sexual, social, or cultural/political, was found to increase the likelihood of behavior change. Isolation and nonattachment decreased the chance of sustained behavior changes (Crawford et al., 1991).

In contrast, results of a study of men who use the beats in western Sydney, differ somewhat from the Macquarie study. Wherrett and Talbot (1991) found that 40 percent of men reported they practiced unprotected anal intercourse with casual partners, 10 percent with regular partners, and 95 percent of the sample reported having experience of anal/genital intercourse without condoms at some time in their lives. Forty-eight percent of men stated that they had had unprotected intercourse within the last six months. The authors suggest that the findings from these and other similar studies reveal that there are large numbers of men who have sex with men who are not attached to the gay community and are the least likely to adopt safer sex practices.

Lesbian Women

Lesbian women have had a much lower profile until relatively recently and would appear to be less well catered for in terms of venues. Some years ago, the women shared the male venues, often having a "women only" night. Today, at least in the larger cities, there are venues just for women.

Again the relationship patterns would cover the entire spectrum. A comparison between gay men and lesbian women in terms of fidelity and number of partners would probably show similarities with matched, so-called heterosexual groups.

Gay Parents

A number of both gay men and lesbian women have exercised their option to become parents. The methods used have ranged from selecting a sexual partner for the specific purpose of conceiving, to artificial insemination and IVF.

There have been examples of a parent's gaining custody of children on the grounds of the homosexual orientation of the other parent. However, homosexuality per se would not necessarily ensure loss of child custody.

Bisexuality

People who actively engage in sexual relationships with both men and women may be considered the invisible group. There is frequently a lack of recognition and acceptance by the gay and lesbian community, many of whom claim that those who identify themselves as "bisexual" in fact have not come to terms with their "homosexuality." Further, the concept of bisexuality is ignored by the general community.

Personal experience as a counselor and educator leads one to believe that there is a degree of covert bisexuality among males. One common mode of expression for married men in making regular visits to anonymous sex venues such as "T-Rooms" and Saunas. Prior to the recognition of HIV/AIDS, the author was aware of a number of bisexual groupings, mainly triadic relationships. Whether the number of self-identified bisexuals has declined, or simply gone underground because of prevailing attitudes, is unknown.

Data collected from 1986 to 1991 by a telephone counseling service for bisexual men and their female partners revealed that 59 percent of the male callers were married. Over that period, there was a consistent decline in the number of bisexual men who reported participation in unprotected male-to-male anal sex, paralleled by a small, steady increase in safer-sex knowledge levels. There were, however, a number of misconceptions about safer-sex behavior, with the role of oral sex in HIV transmission the least well understood. Younger men were more likely to participate in high-risk behaviors (Palmer 1991).

7. Gender Conflicted Persons

A. Transsexualism

Transsexualism is recognized as a medical condition in Australia and provision is made for sex reassignment. The program follows the model developed by John Money at Johns Hopkins University Hospital (Baltimore) in the United States. Because of the need to maintain surgical skills, there are only two designated venues for surgery to be conducted: one in South Australia, the other in New South Wales. The preparatory program, however, is offered in a number of cities.

The standard approach, after assessment and definitive diagnosis, is to provide a program of hormone therapy, social training, and counseling for a minimum period of two years prior to undergoing surgery. For some individuals, the program is too lengthy. Because of the close proximity of a number of Asian countries where relatively inexpensive surgery is offered, a number will opt out of the program and elect early surgery, not always with positive results.

All states and territories, except South Australia, have yet to make provision for changing the birth certificate and/or providing individuals with documentation that would allow recognition of their reassigned gender.

On the occasions where a transsexual has been confined to prison, there have been instances where the authorities have placed the person in a prison appropriate to her/his reassigned gender. There have also been instances where the contrary has occurred.

B. Transvestism

Self-reporting and anecdotal information indicates that a high proportion of people who cross-dress are professional men who are heterosexually oriented, in heterosexual relationships, and have children. It has also been estimated that one in ten men cross-dress.

Support groups for both transvestites and transsexuals exist in four of the states; however, there is no national body.

8. Significant Unconventional Sexual Behaviors

A. Coercive Sex

Child Sexual Abuse and Incest

The incidence of incest and child sexual abuse may be much greater than reported figures. In a survey of a thousand university students in the State of Victoria, Goldman and Goldman (1988) asked about childhood sexual experiences, and found that 28 percent of females and 9 percent of males reported some form of sexual abuse from adults; 76 percent of the perpetrators were known to the child. It is estimated that girls under the age of 18 face odds of between one in ten and one in four chances of sexual abuse within the family, generally by a father or stepfather (Allen 1990).

Child abuse and incest in the Aboriginal population has been noted as a major concern, anecdotal evidence suggesting that incidence may be substantial (Hunter 1992).

Legislation provides for an "age of consent," generally 16 years, and any "indecent dealings" is liable to a penalty of four years imprisonment with hard labor and "with or without a whipping."

There is legislation against "incest by an adult female," which states that any woman "who permits her father or son or other lineal ancestor or descendant, or her brother or half-brother, to have carnal knowledge of her . . . is guilty of a misdemeanor, and is liable to three years imprisonment with hard labor for three years" (Western Australia Criminal Code, 118).

Throughout the country, various crisis centers, refuges, support groups, and treatment centers provide facilities for both child and adult victims. Like most community organizations, funding is limited, volunteer support is a major factor, and there are never enough resources.

It is important to note that all facilities mentioned in this chapter pertain to the major population centers; rural Australia itself is very poorly served in all areas of sexuality.

Sexual Harassment and Coercion

It is estimated that sexual harassment in the workplace occurs for young women about 50 percent of the time in a first paid job, and is a significant risk for women throughout their working lives. Some years ago, the Federal Labour Government introduced legislation and promoted education in the area. Throughout Australia, government instrumentalities, nongovernment organizations, and many private companies now have provision for reviewing complaints. As understanding of what constitutes harassment improves and the mechanisms for lodging a complaint tested, the number of cases reported has increased. A number of men have lodged successful claims, although the majority of complainants are women.

Sexual Assault and Rape

Allen (1992) states that the so-called developed countries have comparable patterns of sexually abusive behaviors, and that although rates may vary between countries and regions, certain probabilities remain. It is estimated that occasional or habitual violence perpetrated by men against women occurs in at least a quarter (some research suggests a third) of all sexual relationships. It is estimated by workers in the area that one in five women will be a victim of sexual assault by the age of 18 years.

Most cities and large towns have counseling and other services for the victims of sexual assault. Many cases go unreported, however, a number of victims will seek the services of agencies such as a Sexual Assault Referral Center and may or may not be referred on to the police. Not all victims who report directly to the police are referred to an independent agency. Thus it is difficult to quantify the number of cases. As an example, however, the Sexual Assault Referral Center in Perth, Western Australia, servicing a total population of a little over a million, has approximately eight hundred new cases reported each year.

The incidence of reported male rape seems to be increasing. Generally men are most at risk when placed in all-male environments, such as prison.

B. Sex Workers (Prostitution)

The act of prostitution has never been illegal in Australia. But during the last decade of the nineteenth century and the first decade of the twentieth century, a range of legislative measures were enacted that made most prostitution-related activities illegal.

In the state of Victoria and the Australian Capital Territory, prostitution-related activities have been decriminalized and legislation enacted to provide for the lawful conduct of business. In all other states and territories, "living off the earnings or keeping premises for the purposes of prostitution" are illegal. In most states a policy of "control and containment" is operated through the local police (generally the vice squad). Through this policy, the number of brothels are limited, independent operators are closed down, and the workers in the brothels are required to undergo monthly medical checks. All workers must have a current health statement saying they are disease-free. Any worker who has an infective disease is not permitted to work. There is a very high level of condom usage with most workers charging substantially more if a client insists on sex without a condom. Many workers, however, have a technique for rolling on a condom, using their mouths and without the client's being aware.

Workers have their own magazine and newsletter that is aimed at being both informative and entertaining. There are also community organizations that provide support and information for people in the sex industry.

C. Pornography and Erotica

Since the 1970s, the dominant trend has been toward liberalization, facilitating the availability of sexually explicit material. Since 1971, principles applying to the classification and censorship of films, videos, and printed material have been generally agreed on by federal and state governments, thus abandoning the attempt to prohibit pornography. These principles relate to age, public offensiveness, consumer protection, and sexual violence against nonconsenting persons. Material classified as "restricted" may only be sold in designated areas of news agents and specialist shops, or be sealed if on open display. Films with a "restricted" category may not admit minors under the age of 18 years. One state does not permit "Restricted" films to be shown on a Sunday—a rather anachronistic situation.

Much of the material is imported, although Australia also has an active production industry. It is claimed that the Australian Capital Territory has the most liberal attitude and hence is the source of the majority of locally produced material. This claim has not be substantiated.

Recently, in at least one state, consideration has been given to the need for, or indeed the feasibility of, monitoring pornographic material obtained through computer sources.

9. Contraception, Abortion, and Population Planning

A. Contraception

According to Siedlecky and Wyndham (1990), there have been six successive waves of contraceptive innovation in Australia; the main methods used in the early part of the century were condoms, douching, withdrawal, and abortion. Later, quinine pessaries and other spermicides were the most-used methods. By the late 1940s, the diaphragm, first introduced in the 1920s, became popular, and the intrauterine device during the 1950s and early 1960s. The introduction of the oral contraceptive in 1961 dramatically increased the number of women using contraceptives.

Oral contraception is still the most frequently used method for Australian women under the age of 30. Older women tend to return to more traditional methods (especially the diaphragm, following adverse reports about IUDs and the pill). However, couples are increasingly choosing sterilization with more than 50,000 men and women undergoing sterilization per annum (Siedlecky and Wyndham 1990).

Depo-Provera has not been approved by the Australian Drug Evaluation Committee (ADEC) and is therefore is still officially on trial, although it has been used for twenty years for the treatment of cancers of the breast, uterus lining, and kidney. As the drug is commercially available, the ADEC has indicated that if a physicians have strong reasons for prescribing its use as a contraceptive, then they may do so. Its use in this manner has been controversial and is opposed by feminist groups. The short- and long-term side effects are not known and indiscriminate prescription without adequate information, documentation, and follow-up for clients—particularly its disproportionate use among disadvantaged women (institutionalized, blacks, migrants, and intellectually disabled)—has given rise to controversy.

Currently, a variety of contraceptives is readily available to most Australians. The most accessible are condoms, which are sold in supermarkets as well as pharmacies and "sex shops." Oral contraceptives have been available, on prescription, in Australia since the early 1960s, and an upward trend in the age of marriage has been attributed to its widespread use (Siedlecky and Wyndham 1990). The Family Planning Association provides accessible contraceptive advice and prescriptions. School-based education programs generally offer contraceptive information as part of the curriculum.

B. Teenage Pregnancy and Abortion

With regard to adolescent contraceptive behavior, Condon (1992) notes that approximately 25 percent of 15- to 19-year-olds become pregnant. Forty percent of these choose to terminate the pregnancy, which indicates that the pregnancy was unplanned and that contraceptive measures were either not used or failed.

C. Abortion

It is estimated that, despite restrictive laws, approximately 60,000 abortions are performed annually in Australia (Siedlecky and Wyndham 1990). Regulation of abortion is a matter of state legislation. During the 1960s, abortion-law reform groups were established in all states. This was often associated with the establishment of Family Planning Clinics and pro-choice, women's health services. The struggle to liberalize the laws has been ongoing and not very successful. In 1969, South Australia was the first state to make abortion legal. The Northern Territory adopted similar legislation.

In other states, wider interpretation of the laws has made abortion easier to obtain and lawful under certain circumstances. The reason is that the Australian judiciary has supported principles established by common-law decisions—for example, the Bourne case in England in 1938, in which the judge stated that abortion was lawful if performed in good faith and for the purpose of preserving the life of the mother, which is interpreted to mean not only her physical existence, but also her physical and mental health. However, in some states there have been no test cases and no precedent set, and the situation is far from satisfactory for all concerned.

Surveys of public opinion indicate that most people think that abortion should be legally available for a range of indications (Graycar and Morgan 1990; Anderson 1986). The Royal Commission on Human Relationships (1977) provided the most comprehensive account of all aspects of sexual and family behavior in Australia in the 1970s, and recommended abortion-law reform. The antiabortion lobby, represented mainly by the Right to Life Group, became organized in the early 1970s to defend the status quo against the push for legislative change from abortion-law reform groups. During the 1980s, attacks began with renewed vigor following activities in the United States and the introduction of more restrictive legislation. Activities have continued with picketing of abortion clinics and attempts at legislative change—for example, a campaign to withdraw rebates for termination procedures from the national health insurance.

In summary, it may be said that Australian women have sought abortion as a solution to unplanned pregnancy for at least the past one hundred years, in spite of the legal restrictions and prevailing moral attitudes. Restrictive abortion legislation does not save more babies but rather loses more mothers. The decline in morbidity and mortality arising from abortion has been a result of better techniques, use of blood transfusion and antibiotics, but also from changes in attitudes that have brought abortion into the open and allowed women to obtain earlier operations. There is still reluctance to allow women to decide for themselves, and abortion is likely to remain a contentious issue (Siedlecky and Wyndham 1990, 101).

D. Population Planning Programs

The documented history of population planning in Australia began with white settlement. It commenced with attempts to control Aboriginal populations through murder, the removal of children from their parents, and deliberate attempts to "breed out." At the same time, campaigns for increasing the white population through active immigration programs and aggressively promoting the role of wife and mother were adopted. Political, legal, medical, and religious institutions conspired to reduce women's options and to prevent access to contraception. Despite this, Family Planning Organizations have an honorable and effective history throughout Australia.

10. Sexually Transmitted Diseases

Australian figures on the rate of sexually transmissible diseases are similar to the rates in other developed countries. The age groups most affected are those between 15 and 30. The most common infections are chlamydia, gonorrhea, genital herpes, HIV, genital warts, syphilis, and hepatitis B. Penicillin-resistant gonococcal infection is on the increase.

Health and education services are generally good in the major cities and towns, however, many rural areas are dependent on local general practitioners. Practitioners, especially in the designated STD (Sexually Transmitted Diseases) clinics, are cognizant of the need to establish patient rapport and trust. Counseling is provided in government clinics as well as education.

Control of infection is mediated through preventative measures, the provision of expert services, and through expeditious contact tracing. Most STDs are reportable and a national register is maintained for epidemiological purposes. The data is published through the federal health agency in the *Community Disease Intelligence.*

The rate of infection among the indigenous population is higher than in the nonindigenous population for a number of reasons, including reduced access to education, poor living conditions, and generally lower standards of health care.

11. HIV/AIDS

Australia was one of the first countries to recognize the serious public health risk posed by HIV/AIDS and instituted health promotion strategies very early. In addition, resources were allocated to both private and public organizations to cater for those who were already infected and to target those who were considered to be most at risk. Despite pockets of resistance and some cases of extreme bigotry, the overall strategy has proved to be relatively successful. The predicted rates of infection for the end of the 1980s suggested a doubling of newly diagnosed cases, when in fact there has been a slight decline.

As of December 1992 the cumulative number of diagnoses of HIV infection in Australia was 16,788, with 82 percent being classified as acquired through homosexual/bisexual contact, 4.9 percent through intravenous drug use, and 2.8 percent through homosexual/bisexual contact and intravenous drug use. Six percent of infections were acquired through heterosexual sex and 3.4 percent were infected through blood transfusion. The cumulative total of women diagnosed was 408 and the number of children was 92. The current rate of new diagnosis is approximately 96 per 100,000 (*Australian HIV Surveillance Report*, April 1993).

Although HIV infection is recognized as a serious risk, knowledge and education does not always translate into changed behavior and attitudes. High-risk groups that need particular attention are those homeless young people who are associated with prostitution and drug use.

12. Sexual Dysfunction, Counseling, and Therapy

The incidence of sexual dysfunction in the community is unknown. There are, however a number of dysfunction services, both private and public. Community-based resources include organizations such as Rape Crisis Centers, Incest Survivor's Association, Women's Health Centers, Migrant Health Centers, Gay and Lesbian Counseling Services, various AIDS organizations, Marriage Guidance, and the Family Planning Associations. These all provide both crisis assistance and counseling services to varying degrees. All of these organizations are restricted by lack of satisfactory funding, since they are dependent upon government grants and fund-raising activities.

It is difficult to quantify the number of practitioners who specialize in sexual counseling and therapy. There are two major organizations that attempt to bring these practitioners together: the Australian Society of Sex Educators, Researchers, and Therapists and the Western Australian Sexology Society. In population terms, the state of Western Australia is much smaller than the Eastern states; however, it appears to be the trailblazer in sexology and has a well-coordinated network of practitioners and resources.

13. Advanced Education and Sexual Research

A. Advanced Education

There is only one university-accredited postgraduate program in sexology in Australia; this is offered through the Division of Health Sciences at Curtin University of Technology in Western Australia. The program was established in 1979 by this author. Students may enroll at postgraduate diploma level and advance to a master of science degree by research and to a doctor of philosophy by research. At the postgraduate diploma level, students may choose between majoring in counselling, education, or sexological research. The duration of the diploma program is two semesters; to obtain a master's degree requires a minimum of an additional two semesters; and for the doctorate, a minimum of a further four semesters.

Throughout the Australian university system, various professional programs, such as social work, medicine, nursing, and psychology, provide some elements of sexology in their courses. However, other than the options offered through Curtin University, there is no systematic and comprehensive program for students in the health and helping professions, nor in education.

In 1992, the Australian College of Veneriologists in collaboration with the Australian Society of Sex Educators, Researchers, and Therapists offered a program in sexual health counseling. These two organizations provide participants with a diploma on completion.

The Family Planning Association of Australia offers regular training programs for medical practitioners and nurses. In addition, ad hoc programs are offered for professionals and nonprofessionals. The Family Planning programs are nationally accredited and various professional organizations recognize these for continuing education credits. Address: Family Planning Australia, Inc. Lua Building, Suite 3, First Floor, 39. Geils C, P.O. Box 9026, Deakin, ACT 2600 Australia (Phone: 61-6/282-5298. Fax: 61-6/285-1244). The address for Family Planning Victoria is: 266-272 Church Street, Richmond 3121 Australia (Phone: 61-3/429-1868).

The address for the Australian Association of Sex Educators, Counselors, and Therapists is: P.O. Box 346, Lane Cove NSW, 2066 Australia (Phone: 61-2/427-1292).

B. Research

Most of the research dollars and interest have tended to be in the areas of fertility (control and enhancement) and in the area of HIV/AIDS. In vitro fertilization programs have had a prominent profile and work is undertaken in several states.

Of the research that has been undertaken to examine behaviors or attitudes, few have been based on random samples. Most studies have been limited to small, targeted, and often self-selected samples, and frequently relatively unsophisticated survey instruments have been used.

Several areas of current research suggest new political agendas. For example, funded surveys that have used whole population samples have looked at practices and attitudes surrounding HIV/AIDS, STDs, fertility, and reproductive technology.

The address for the Australian Society of Sex Educators, Researchers, and Therapists is: 21 Carr Street. Coogee, New South Wales 2034 Australia.

The address for the Western Australian Sexology Society is: c/FPA 70 Roe Street. Northbridge, Western Australia 6000 Australia.

The Journal of Sex and Marriage and the Family, published by the Family Life Movement of Australia, recently changed its name to the *Australian Journal of Marriage and Family*.

Four other Australian journals publish articles of interest to sexologists: *Australian Forum*, published bimonthly by Gordon and Gotch; *Healthright*, published quarterly by Family Planning Australia, New South Wales; *Australian and New Zealand Journal of Family Therapy*, published quarterly by the

Family Therapy Association, South Australia; and *Venerology*, published quarterly by the National Venerology Council of Australia.

Summary

The nonindigenous people of Australia reflect the cultural attitudes and behaviors of their predominately European origins. There are variations because of the cultural mix; however, the dominant religions, legislation, and education is essentially Western and public sexual morality reflects the values of these institutions.

ABORIGINAL AUSTRALIA

Aboriginal traditions are complex and varied. There are elements of the culture that are the exclusive province of certain individuals or groups and are not permitted to be revealed to others. Sensitivity on sexual matters has precluded any extensive anthropological study. The only detailed work is that of Ronald and Catherine Berndt, who spent more than thirty years observing, participating, and documenting Aboriginal cultures in the northern regions of Australia.

It is impossible for a non-Aboriginal person to present cultural traditions accurately and it would be impertinent to try. Through the assistance of Dr. Robert Tonkinson, Professor of Anthropology at the University of Western Australia, I present below some examples of traditional Aboriginal practices. There is no attempt to be inclusive nor comprehensive and the material should not be viewed as generalizable, nor necessarily current.

The concept of the Dreaming is of fundamental importance to Aboriginal culture and embraces the creative past—where ancestral beings instituted the society—the present, and the future. The Aboriginal worldview integrates human, spiritual, and natural elements as parts of the whole and is expressed through rituals (Tonkinson 1991).

While the basic social unit is the family, there is a complex system of classificatory kinship that dictates marriage rules. Kinship status imposes responsibilities and behaviors toward other kin. A basic feature of the kinship system is that the siblings of the same sex are classed as equivalent, so that, for example, the sisters of a child's mother would all be classed as "mother." The children of one's parents' siblings would therefore be classed as "brothers" and "sisters." Through this system, kinship may be extended to include people who do not have a blood relationship.

The moiety system of social classification provides correct intermarrying categories, although it does not determine marriage partners. Within moieties there are groupings which, for want of a better word have been classified as "clans" although a more accurate translation of the words used by the people themselves might be "crowd" or "lot." A clan is usually identified by an association with a natural species, for example, the barramundi clans (named after a species of fish), or Eaglehawk. Each clan has a dialect and each person is a member of one, linked dialect-clan pair, which is that of her or his father. This categorization has significance in all aspects of social activity and includes specific mythic and ritual knowledge and beliefs. The clan indicates territorial possession as well as belief system. Membership of the dialect-clan group defines a person's social position as well as their belief system (Berndt 1976).

A traditional, Aboriginal view of sexuality is that it is a natural urge, to be satisfied. It has symbolism beyond the individual, being linked to fertility in all its manifestations. Representations of sex, through songs, dances, and paintings, relate to the human activity and to seasonal change, to the growth and decay of plants, and to the regeneration of nature. Reproduction of humans and of the natural world is vitally important and obedience to ancestrally ordained laws is the responsibility of adult humans. The correct performance of rituals guarantees continuity of life-giving power and fertility from the spiritual realm (Tonkinson 1991).

1. Gender Relationships

In traditional Aboriginal societies, there was a pervasive egalitarian ethos that placed every adult as the equal of others of the same sex. The operation of the kinship system exerted an overall balance in male-female relationships (Tonkinson 1991). Earlier ethnographers have tended to present Aboriginal culture as a traditional male-dominant, female-subordinate, hunting and gathering society (Warner 1937; Parsons 1964). It has been argued, however, that this view is a narrow one generated through the androcentricity, and possibly the ethnocentricity, of the authors (Merlan 1988). Other authors have emphasized the complementary nature of gender roles, without conflict (Berndt 1980). The complexity of the Aboriginal worldview and the concept of the Dreaming may have contributed to the differing perspectives of the ethnographers. The Dreaming, which contains the lore of creation and the permanence of the interrelationship of all things, is maintained through the different contributions to it made by women and men. Women's narrative of the Dreaming deals with the rhythms of family life, while men's narrative deals with the rhythms of the life of the whole group. Thus there are male and female domains that are connected and complementary.

Gender difference is a significant aspect of Aboriginal symbolism and consequently there are gender-specific rituals. Many rituals relate to productive activities and utilize parallel symbols, for example the *woomera* (throwing stick used by males when hunting) and the digging stick (used by females when gathering insects). Certainly, men and women share a sense that both "men's business" and "women's business" are indispensable (Merlan 1988).

Specific areas are designated for men's rituals and women's rituals and women and men are excluded from each other's sites. Physical punishment would be incurred if there was intrusion into the domain of the opposite gender; however, the depth of meaning associated with the rituals ensures that the power of suggestion preserves sanctity. Because both men and women have ritual domains, there is a strong sense of propriety, and self-esteem is derived from this (Merlan 1988). While much ritual activity involves both sexes, mature men control both the ritual proceedings and the scheduling of activities.

2. Sexual Ceremonies and Rituals

A. Puberty Rituals

Initiation ceremonies assisted the transition from childhood to adulthood with highly elaborated rituals for boys. Modeled on death (of the boy) and birth (of the man) they dramatized separation from women, in particular from the mother. Rules of kinship dictated the allocation of roles and responsibilities in initiation as in all social behavior. Guidance, reassurance, and support were guaranteed, as was chastisement if rules were broken.

For females, puberty rites were simple. The transition to adulthood was based on sexual maturation and included sexual activity. However, menarche, marriage, and childbirth have not been ritualized or publicly celebrated in Aboriginal societies.

B. Defloration

Ritualistic defloration was practiced in some parts of Australia but no longer occurs. Ceremonies varied; however, one example dating back to the 1940s has been described by Berndt, and related to people from the northeastern region of Arnhem Land. Girls who were to undergo the ritual were called "sacred" and deemed to have a particularly attractive quality. The men made boomerangs with flattened ends, to be used as the instrument of defloration prior to ritualistic coitus. Men, girls, and boomerangs were smeared with red ocher, symbolizing blood. A special windbreak or screen was prepared for the girls, the entrance of which was called the sacred vagina. The screen was intended to prevent men from seeing "women's business."

Prior to her defloration, a girl may have lived in seclusion for a period of time with certain older women, observing food taboos. The older women taught the girls songs, dances, and sacred myths. At the end of the seclusion period, there was a ritual bathing at dawn.

In some areas, a girl may have lived in her intended husband's camp for a period of time. After the seclusion period, she would be formally handed over to her husband and his kin, and the marriage consummated.

In other areas, a girl may have been unaware that her marriage was impending and be seized by her intended husband and his "brothers" while she was out collecting food with the older women. Her husband's "brothers" had sexual rights to the girl until she had settled down in his camp (Berndt and Berndt 1988).

Earlier anthropological reports (Roth 1897, cited in Berndt 1988) described rituals that have involved the forced enlargement of the vagina by groups of men using their fingers, with possum twine wound round them or with a stick shaped like a penis. Several men would have intercourse with the girl and later would ritually drink the semen. Mitigating this was the second part of the ritual which allowed dancing women to hit men against whom they had a grudge with fighting poles without fear of retaliation.

C. Circumcision

Circumcision was a common, though not universal, practice. In many areas, Aboriginal men believed that the uncircumcised penis would cause damage to a woman, which was one reason why sexual activity of an uncircumcised boy was viewed negatively. Rituals associated with circumcision were secret and sacred and were considered "men's business." Full details have not been disclosed to outsiders and what is offered here are those aspects that are permitted.

Women danced close to the circumcision ground but were not permitted to watch. During totemic rituals, the boy who was about to be circumcised was present, but often could not see what was going on. It was at that time that he was told the meaning of the songs. Just before dawn, he would be led to a group of older men who used their bodies to form a "table" upon which the young boy was placed. After the circumcision, the boy returned to his seclusion camp and the rest of the group moved to another campsite, as happened after a death. In some areas, the foreskin was eaten by older men, in others the boy wore it in a small bag around his neck, in others it might have been buried.

There were a number of postcircumcision rites that included the young man's being taken on a journey around his totemic country.

At a later stage, subincision may have taken place. Again the initiate was taken into seclusion and, later, the procedure conducted using the human "table." The partially erect penis was held up and the incision made on the underside. Subincision of the penis was regarded as the complementary right to defloration. Stone blades were prepared while thinking of coitus, and it was believed that semen flowed more rapidly after subincision (Berndt and Berndt 1988). Subincision had religious validation, proved in many areas through reference to the penile groove of the emu or the bifid penis of the kangaroo. Subincision was not for contraceptive purposes, as was commonly believed by nonindigenous people. In fact in many areas, semen was not credited with having a role in procreation. In all areas of Australia, spiritual forces were believed to be central to procreation. Physiological maternity as well as paternity was denied, with the belief that a plant, animal, or mineral form, known as the conception totem, was assumed by the spirit-child who then entered its human mother (Tonkinson 1991).

D. Courtship and Marriage

Rules of kinship restricted sexual freedom and set the parameters for selection of spouses; however, premarital and extramarital sex was appropriate. It is expected that everyone marry. Marriage rules may give the impression that there was no room for the concept of "romantic love" in Aboriginal traditions. However, an insight into the nature of male-female sexual relationships may be obtained through some of the traditional myths, often expressed in song cycles. These include reference to affection, as well as physical satisfaction and mutual responsibility. The songs make explicit reference to circumcision rituals, to menstruation, semen, and to defloration.

One ritualistic means of courtship is reported through the Golbourn Island song cycles (Berndt 1976). In the songs, young girls engage in making figures out of string, the activity causing their breasts to undulate: this and the figures they make are designed to attract men. Undulation of the buttocks was also used, along with facial gestures, that indicate a girl was willing to meet a boy in a designated area. These activities usually occurred around the time of menarche. Menstrual blood had an erotic appeal for men and some sacred myths allude to that theme. Menstrual blood was also seen as sacred, and by extension women were sacred during their menstrual period.

In song and dance, intercourse and erotic play is celebrated as joyful and beautiful. Intercourse has significance as it maintains populations, both human and nonhuman, and therefore produces food. It is through intercourse that the seasons come and go, and it is only through the changing of the seasons that plants can grow.

Infant betrothal was an important aspect of Aboriginal cultures and was often associated with men's ritual activities, especially circumcision. In the Western desert region, for example, the main circumciser had to promise one of his daughters to the novice in compensation for having ritually "killed" him.

Girls were often given to their husbands while still prepubertal, but coitus did not usually commence until her breasts had grown. In this context, girls may have had their first sexual experience by the age of 9 and boys by the age of 12.

Standards of beauty or attractiveness varied; however, obvious physical disabilities were seen to be a disadvantage and, similar to Western culture, youth is most highly valued.

E. Love Magic

The use of songs, dances, and other rituals were used to attract a prospective lover or to rekindle passion in an existing relationship. Members of either sex employed love magic, which was thought to cause the person who was the object of it to become filled with desire. On occasions, a large-scale ritual dance of an erotic nature was used as a general enhancement of sexuality. Both sexes were involved, although the pairs of dancers who simulated intercourse were of the same sex. The intention, however, was aimed at arousing heterosexual desires (Tonkinson 1991).

3. Contraception and Abortion

Traditionally the Australian Aborigine, like other hunting and gathering societies, had low levels of fertility. Ethnographers have found little evidence of plant contraceptives or abortifacients. There is no evidence of infanticide's ever being used.

Current fertility rates among the indigenous population is lower than in the nonindigenous population. This in part may be due to the generally lower levels of health care and standards of hygiene and the higher levels of STD infections, all due to a serious neglect on the part of successive governments.

4. Homosexuality, Bisexuality, and Gender Dissonance

The Berndts (1988) have commented that the traditional way of life placed so much emphasis on heterosexual relationships that there has been little evidence (to ethnographers) of other modes of sexual expression. They do, however, mention that "homosexual experimentation and masturbation" are reported among boys and young men when temporarily segregated from the women. Berndt goes on to say that examples of female homosexuality is even more rare and that "the close physical contacts which Aborigines indulge in are deceptive in this respect" (Berndt and Berndt 1988, 195).

Contemporary urban life has demonstrated that homosexuality is known among the Aboriginal community, with gay and lesbian Aboriginals participating in the local gay culture.

There is no evidence in the literature of gender dissonance in traditional Aboriginal cultures.

5. Incest

The kin relationship, rather than a biological one, dictates the incest taboo (Tonkinson 1991). In traditional societies, the incest taboo extends to all the members of one's own moiety, with certain exceptions during sacred rituals. For example, during the defloration ceremony, a man inserts the defloration boomerang into a woman whose formal relationship to him is roughly the equivalent of his wife's mother; he then has coitus with her as a sacred ritual considered important from the point of view of fertility.

As mentioned previously, there is current concern that the incidence of child sexual abuse is increasing among the Aboriginal population. This may well be as a consequence of dislocation from traditional structures.

6. Education

Apart from the services available to all, there are a number of services specifically for Aboriginal populations. These include infant and maternal health and welfare services, fertility counseling, and STD and HIV/AIDS education programs. Nevertheless, there is a greater need for services to be extended, relevant, and accessible.

Summary

Some aspects of Australian Aboriginal cultures have been presented within the context of traditional societies. The majority of Aborigines living in Australia today have had their cultural heritage eroded by the dominant migrant culture and the urbanization of certain regions. Current attitudes and sexual behaviors are influenced by Western religions and Western law. The attitude of earlier generations of migrants has left Australian Aborigines with a shorter lifespan, lower fertility rates, and higher rates of infant mortality and sexually transmitted diseases, than nonAboriginal Australians. Various governments and other agencies are attempting to ameliorate this situation; however there is still a long way to go to achieve equity and to dismantle prejudice.

References and Suggested Readings

Allen, J. A. 1990. *Sex and Secrets: Crimes Involving Australian Women Since 1880.* Melbourne: Oxford University Press.

Australian Public Service Staffing Statistics Report, 1993.

Baxter, J. Summer 1992. "Power Attitudes and Time: The Domestic Division of Labour. *Journal Comparative Family Studies,* 23(2):165-82.

Berndt, R. M. 1976 *Three Faces of Love: Traditional Aboriginal Song-Poetry.* Melbourne: Thomas Nelson Ltd.

Berndt, C.H. 1980 "Aboriginal Women and the Notion of the 'Marginal Man.'" In R. M. and C. H. Berndt, eds. *Aborigines of the West: Their Past and Present.* Perth: University Western Australia Press.

Berndt, R. M., and C. H. Berndt. 1988. *The World of the First Australians.* Canberra: Aboriginal Studies Press.

Berndt, R. M., and R. Tonkinson, eds. 1988. *Social Anthropology and Aboriginal Studies: A Contemporary Overview.* Canberra: Aboriginal Studies Press.

Castles, I. 1992. *Year Book Australia 1992.* Canberra: Australian Bureau of Statistics.

Chisholm, J. S., and V. K. Burbank. 1991 "Monogamy and Polygyny in Southeast Arnhem Land." *Ethology & Sociobiology,* 12(4):291-313.

Clark, M. 1950. *Selected Documents in Australian History 1788-1850.* Sydney: Angus & Robertson.

Coates, R. 1992. *Parent's Prerogative Versus School Based Sexuality Education.* Occasional Paper 8. Perth: Edpak.

Coates, R. 1987. *Reports from the ATASKA Study. Occasional Paper 3.* Perth: Edpak.

Condon, J. T. 1992. "Adolescent Pregnancy: Abortion, Relinquishment for Adoption and Parenting." In R. Kosky, H. S. Eshkevari and G. Kneebone, eds. *Breaking Out: New Challenges in Adolescent Mental Health.* Canberra: National Health and Medical Research Council, 36-50.

Connell, R. W., et al. 1988. *Social Aspects of the Prevention of AIDS: Study A - Report No. 1: Method and Sample.* Sydney: Macquarie University.

Crawford, J., et al. 1991. *Social Aspects of the Prevention of AIDS Project.* New South Wales: Macquarie University.

Cubis, J. 1992. "Contemporary Trends in Adolescent Sexual Behaviour in Australia." In R. Kosky, H. S. Eshkevari, and G. Kneebone, eds. *Breaking Out: New Challenges in Adolescent Mental Health.* Canberra: National Health and Medical Research Council.

Dixson, M. 1976. *The Real Matilda: Woman and Identity in Australia 1788 to 1975.* Sydney: Penguin Books.

Dowsett, G. 1991. "Social Research on AIDS: Examples from Macquarie University, Sydney." *Venereology,* 4(1):38-42.

Dunne, M. et al. 1992-1993. *HIV Risk & Sexual Behaviour Survey in Australian Secondary Schools.* Canberra: Australian Government Publishing Service.

Edgar, D., and H. Glazer. April 1992. "A Man's Place? Reconstructing Family Realities." *Family Matters,* 31:36-39.

Ferroni, P. A. 1993. *The Effects of Hysterectomy and Gynaecological Conditions on Women's Sexuality and Self-Esteem.* Unpublished Doctoral Thesis ANU Canberra.

Glazer, H. 1993. *Lifematters.* Sydney: ABC Radio.

Goldman, J. D. G. 1992. "Children's Sexual Cognition and Its Implications for Children's Court Testimony in Child Sexual Abuse Cases." *Australian Journal Marriage & Family,* 13(2):78-96.

Goldman, R., and D. G. Goldman. 1988. "The Prevalence and Nature of Child Sexual Abuse in Australia." *Australian Journal Sex, Marriage & Family,* 9:49-106.

Grbich, C. 1992. "Societal Response to Familial Change in Australia: Marginalisation." *Journal Comparative Family Studies,* 23(1):79-94.

Hill, J. 1991. *Contraception and Fertility Regulation: The Law and Sexuality in Western Australia.* Perth: Family Planning Association of Western Australia.

Hunter, E. 1992. "Aboriginal Adolescents in Remote Australia." In R. Kosky, H. S. Eshkevari, G. Kneebone, eds. *Breaking Out: New Challenges in Adolescent Mental Health.* Canberra: National Health & Medical Research Council.

Keene, I. 1988. "Twenty-five Years of Aboriginal Kinship Studies." In R. M. Berndt and R. Tonkinson, eds. *Social Anthropology and Aboriginal Studies: A Contemporary Overview.* Canberra: Aboriginal Studies Press.

Loach, L. 1992. "Bad Girls: Women Who Use Pornography." In L. Segal and M. McIntosh, eds. *Sex Exposed: Sexuality and the Pornography Debate.* London: Virago.

McCabe, M. P., and J. K. Collins. 1990. *Dating, Relating and Sex*. Sydney: Horwitz Grahame.

Mercer, J. 1977. *The Other Half: Women in Australian Society*. Sydney: Penguin Books.

Merlan, F. 1988. "Gender in Aboriginal Social Life: A Review." In R. M. Berndt and R. Tonkinson, eds. *Social Anthropology and Aboriginal Studies: A Contemporary Overview*. Canberra: Aboriginal Studies Press.

Moore, S. M., and D. A. Rosenthal. 1991. "Condoms and Coitus: Adolescents' Attitudes to AIDS and Safe Sex Behaviour." *Journal Adolescence*, 14(3):211-227.

National Health and Medical Research Council. 1990. *Handbook on Sexually Transmitted Diseases*. Canberra: Australian Government Publishing Services.

Palmer, W. A. 1991. *Men Who Have Sex with Men in Australia: A Report of the Gammaline Telephone Counselling Service*. Melbourne: Health Department Victoria.

Parsons, T. 1964. *Social Structure and Personality*. New York: Free Press of Glencoe.

Pinto, S., A. Scandia, & P. Wilson. 1990. *Prostitution Laws in Australia*. Canberra: Australian Institute Criminology.

Rollins, B. 1989. *Sexual Attitudes and Behaviours: A Review of the Literature*. Melbourne: Australian Institute of Family Studies.

Siedlecky, S., and D. Wyndham. 1990. *Populate and Perish: Australian Women's Fight for Birth Control*. Sydney: Allen and Unwin.

Simon Rosser, B. R. 1992. *Gay Catholics Down Under: The Journeys in Sexuality and Spirituality of Gay Men in Australia and New Zealand*. Westport, CT: Praeger.

Sullivan, B. 1990. "The Business of Sex: Australian Government and the Sex Industry." *Australian and New Zealand Journal of Sociology*, 27(1):3-18.

Tonkinson, R. 1991. *The Mardu Aborigines: Living the Dream in Australia's Desert (2/e)*. New York: Holt, Rinehart & Winston.

Warner, W. L. 1937. *A Black Civilization*. New York: Harper.

Western, J. S. 1992. "Human Sexuality in Australia: The Quest for Information." In: *Rethinking Sex: Social Theory and Sexuality Research*. Victoria: Melbourne University Press.

Wherrett, L., and W. Talbot. 1991. *HIV/AIDS Prevention, Homosexuality and the Law*. Canberra: Department of Community Services and Health.

Bahrain
(*Al-Bahrayn*)

Julanne McCarthy, M.A., M.S.N.*

Contents

Demographics and a Historical Perspective

The State of Bahrain is an archipelago of some thirty-three islands, totalling 268 square miles, located in the middle of the southern shore of the Arabian Gulf, almost halfway between Shatt Al-Arab in the north and Muscat to the south. The islands lie approximately twenty miles from the eastern province of Saudi Arabia and two to eighteen miles from Qatar. Bahrain's neighbors are Saudi Arabia on the west and Quatar on the east. Bahrain has been joined by a causeway to Saudi Arabia since late 1986. This causeway has had a profound effect, and greatly influenced certain aspects of Bahrain

*The information in this chapter was gathered by the author and 28 Bahraini and expatriate professional colleagues. The organization and presentation of this material was done by Julanne McCarthy.

society. Bahrain Island, the largest in the group, is the location of the current capital city Manama. It is approximately thirty miles long and ten miles wide and is linked by causeways to the islands of Muharraq on the northeast and Sitra on the east coast. Outside the capital, the landscape is covered by fertile gardens and palm trees in the northern third, and there is the desert with the oil and gas reserves in the remainder. Most of the population lives in the northern portion, while the central desert area contains the remains of the hundred thousand or more *tumuli* (ancient burial mounds), and a few towns and villages. The southern third of Bahrain Island is mainly a noninhabited restricted area. Most of the islands are now joined by causeways to the main island, except the Hawar Island group which lies offshore.

Bahrain has long been a port of call—for more than 6,000 years—and cuneiform tablets describe in ancient times the fresh water springs, the dates, and the market place in Bahrain which attracted Gulf trading ships to the offshore harbor. These ancient travelers were shuttling between Mesopotamia, Bahrain, and the Indus Valley. Archeological finds have identified Bahrain as "Dilmun, the land of the living" mentioned in the Sumerian epic, *Gilgamesh.* Other archeologists have suggested that Bahrain was the Garden of Eden. Traditionally, people were farmers, fishermen, and merchants. There were no Bedouins or semi-Bedouins living in Bahrain (Taki, 1974). Since the late nineteenth century, the form of government has been a traditional monarchy with succession passed from father to son (unlike other Gulf and Middle East countries where succession is brother to brother). Between 1861 and 1971, Bahrain was a British protectorate. There were three social classes in Bahrain until 1932—royalty, merchants, and farmers (Khuri, 1980). The discovery of oil in 1932 led to many changes in traditional customs and initiated the beginning of a middle class in the society.

Bahrain saw a resurgence in its trading and commercial sector, and particularly growth in banking, during the 1970s because of the Lebanese civil war. Many institutions, with their expatriate work force, moved to Bahrain, attracted by its tolerable social environment. There are now expatriates from over sixty countries living in Bahrain and working in various government agencies, private businesses, service institutions, and family homes. There are also tourists from the Gulf and around the world visiting Bahrain. These current commercial activities, and the past contact with traders and people from different cultures, for centuries has given Bahrain a unique cultural pattern and a cosmopolitan air. The latter has not been seen in other Gulf cities, like Dubai, until recently. The people of Bahrain and their respect for, and tolerance of, different cultural values makes Bahrain unique in many ways from its neighbors.

The State of Bahrain has a land area of 268 square miles (695.26 square kilometers) and the 1991 census showed a population of 508,037 individuals including 323,305 (63.6 percent) Bahrainis and 184,742 (36.4 percent) expatriates. The mid-1996 population estimate is 586,000. Bahrain's population density of 765/square kilometer is one of the highest in the world. The Bahrain birthrate of 2.91 percent for 1981-1991 is still among the highest in the world, however lower than the previous 3.4 percent (Ahmed, A.A. 1995:2).

The 1991 demographic profile shows 50.9 percent of the Bahraini population are under 20 years of age, while the proportion over 60 years of age is 5.5 percent. Adult literacy is estimated at 84.1 percent (Baby, 1996a). Urban dwellers comprise 82 percent of the population. The structure of the expatriate population differs significantly from the local population as 52.9 percent of this segment are between 20 and 49 years of age, which is understandable as most expatriates are brought in to work. These individuals comprise a significant proportion of the work force, approximately 33 percent, and it should be noted they are living in Bahrain during their most sexually active years. The largest group of expatriates are from South Asia, with approximately 120,000 from India, Pakistan, Bangladesh, and Sri Lanka. Another large group are the Filipinos comprising more than 16,000 workers. The *1996 World Almanac* gives the ethnic distribution as Bahraini 63 percent, Asian 13 percent, other Arab 10 percent, and Iranian 8 percent. The main languages used in Bahrain are the official language Arabic, Farsi, and Urdu, (*The World Almanac*, 1996). English is widely understood and commonly used commercially. The 1993 per capita income was reported as $12,000 (*The World Almanac*, 1996), while based on GDP the 1996 per capita income is listed as $15,500 (Baby, 1996b:2).

Life expectancy at birth in 1995 is 71 for males and 76 for females. The birthrate is 24 per 1,000 population; the death rate 3 per 1,000, giving a natural annual increase of 2.1 percent. Infant mortality is 18 per 1,000 live births. Medical services are free.

The predominant religion in Bahrain is Islam, which is also the state religion. This has implications on all aspects of daily life and sexuality as there is no separation of church and state, religion and daily life. Religious affiliation is the most important single attribute determining an individual's social status in Bahrain society (Al-Sharyan, 1987:345). Religion continues as an all-encompassing pervasive guide which directs and divides up the hours of each day. Bahrainis are members of either the Sunni and Shi'ite sects of Islam, 30 percent and 70 percent respectively. The ruling family belongs to the Sunni sect. Many expatriates living in Bahrain are non-Moslem and are free to practice their respective religions openly and at their own places of worship such as churches (Anglican, Roman Catholic), chapels (Interdominational, Dutch Reformed-USA), and other places of public worship (e.g., Hindu temple). Other groups meet in homes or apartments (Mormons, a few local Jewish families) for prayer. Expatriate groups retain their own cultural values and language and generally socialize among themselves. There are many ethnic, cultural, and social clubs which advertise their activities which anyone can attend. The interaction of all these expatriates among their own groups and with Bahrainis will be developed further in this report with regard to aspects of human sexuality.

1. Basic Sexological Premises

There is a dearth of documented data regarding the nature of human sexuality in Bahrain. The data presented here are based on the few documented studies which are available. A thorough search was conducted of all the national bibliographies which have been compiled, government records, and the local print media, including newspapers, and local and regional journals in English. No one until recently conducted research in the realm of human sexuality in Bahrain; however, studies have been carried out on related areas by anthropologists, economists, doctors, nurses, psychologists, and social workers. All this data was pulled together, and with structured interview data, was used to write this basic document regarding the status of knowledge on, or related to, human sexuality in Bahrain according to the outline provided by the *Encyclopedia*'s general editor. It is hoped that researchers will be stimulated to study this topic in Bahrain and to present supplementary data from Arabic sources.

There may be a logical explanation why there is a dearth of literature regarding human sexuality, as the local culture, predominantly based on Islam, holds as a core value the suppression of external manifestations of sexuality in public, i.e., one should not present oneself in a sexually provocative manner. Believers are extolled not to draw attention to the body form, therefore the men's *thobe* (long, loose shirt-like garment) and the women's *jellabiya* (long, loose dress) are the preferred clothing style for many, at home and at work (unless there are uniform or safety restrictions). However, expatriates of all nationalities comment on the sheerness of some of the men's' summer white *thobes* and how a person's underwear is sometimes visible, which appears in contradiction to the stated norm. Personal preference in dress is allowed so expatriates and Bahrainis are seen wearing a variety of clothing styles. Suppression of sexuality is also seen in the practice of women covering their hair partially (*Muhtashima*) or fully (*Muhajiba*), and even their face partially (*Burga*) or fully (*Mutanaqiba*). The practice of veiling in public has increased during the last five years and can be seen among young as well as elderly women. Use of make-up, nail polish, and perfumes intending to draw attention are discouraged in public. Modesty in dress extends into the home. If a woman has chosen to veil, then even in the home she must veil in the presence of unrelated male relatives, but not in the presence of women, children, or her immediate male relatives. Covering of the body is also observed among siblings where even sisters, according to the Koran, are not to be uncovered among themselves. Among married couples, dress expectations vary and can cause some dissension. Some men state that in their own home they would like to wear shorts when it is hot but their wives do not approve. The Koran's injunction is that for the man, the middle area from the waist to the knees not be naked. It is acceptable for men engaged in athletics to wear shorts, and for fisherman or men in certain other occupations. There is an ingrained belief in some communities however that older males can lose their dignity and respect if they run or jog "half naked" in the streets or public parks (Fakhro, 1991:48).

Unrelated males and females are not to touch. The strict conservative definition is that touching is a sin. Great effort is made by everyone not to touch accidentally. As a local sign of respect and to purify oneself, people may spit to the side first before potential contact. This is a local custom and not dictated in Islam. Then in case of a accidental contact, e.g., while handing over change, the person is considered clean. Bahraini informants explained this is a traditional practice, and Catholic nuns reported being the recipients. Most expatriates have never seen or heard of this practice.

Other traditional social controls practiced include animadversion against eye contact between men and women, especially strangers. Lack of eye contact by a man to a woman is a traditional sign of respect. Likewise, a woman who is unveiled is strongly advised not to smile at strangers, (men outside her own family), and men and women should keep their eyes down when walking in public. Today these practices may or may not be followed in the workplace by people who see each other frequently, and also depending on the work situation (e.g., serving the public). However in public places, many people follow these injunctions. More recently, Westernized good manners such as courtesy, politeness, and cordial relations with customers and coworkers have been promoted in the private schools and service industry sector. Bahraini business leaders, through the public media and through in-house newsletters, are promoting good manners as being good for business. Total quality management concepts are being incorporated into the local businesses and society; however some resistance is met due to traditional values, e.g., women should not smile at an unrelated man.

The general aversion of speaking about sexual matters, or even the urogenital system, extends to doctor-patient relationships. Patients are reluctant to discuss their genitalia, and doctors are reluctant to ask about the genitalia and even omit these from a physical exam. This has resulted in junior doctors missing the correct diagnosis, and consultants later correcting the situation. As a result, there is suspected underreporting for various diagnosis, e.g., priapism in children with sickle cell disease (Al-Dabbous, 1991). This same reluctance has influenced studies regarding menopause in women which concentrate on osteoporosis and rarely mention psychosexual symptoms (Sadat-Ali, et al., 1993).

A. The Character of Gender Roles

Gender roles in Bahrain show a variety of manifestations and reflect the person's education level, socioeconomic level, religious sect, urban or village background, and the degree of contact with local expatriates, as well as travel, study, or work abroad. In Islam, women have the freedom to be a traditional mother or to work (Kahtanie, 1992:6). Women have had opportunities to expand their roles from their traditional roles in Bahrain during the last thirty years. Great strides have been made by many women in the fields of education, medicine, nursing, other health-related professions, finance, clerical work, computers, light manufacturing, banking, and veterinary science, for example. These women in successful jobs are having an effect on the characteristics of gender roles in Bahrain. A comparison between the past and today reveals the significant changes which have occurred, and some of the driving forces which have helped women to achieve higher economic status in Bahrain.

The traditional lifestyle of a Bahraini Shi'a village woman in 1960 was described by Hansen (1967). The Bahraini village lifestyle was similar to that described in Oman in 1974-1976 (Wikan, 1982), however, with a few differences, i.e., the wives of Bahraini fisherman and farmers worked outside the home. The fisherman's wife helped to clean and sell fish, while the latter helped their husbands in the fields and in marketing (Rumaihi, 1976:153). In contrast, women living in the towns and cities were exposed to very different circumstances as they were restricted to running their household and to child rearing. As a result, they developed very different lifestyles and gender roles. Among the wealthy, the epitome of status was to have nothing to do all day and to have all work done by servants (Waly, 1992).

During the latter part of the 1890s, an agent of change in the status of women was the arrival of the American missionaries sponsored by the Dutch Reformed Church of New Brunswick, New Jersey. The group established, in stages, informal classes in Arabic for boys and girls, then separate classes, and later formal classes, all held in Arabic. Families of various ethnic and religious groups in Manama sent their children to classes for free, and later a fee. There were complaints from conservative men regarding education for women; however, some girls had been taught in Koran schools (*al mutawa*) prior to this time. The American Mission School, now Al Rajah School, had its first university graduate, a licensed teacher, as school mistress for girls in 1919 (Anthony, 1984:231). The first secular boys school, Al-Hadaya Al-Khalifiya, was opened in 1919. The first secular girls school, Al-Khadija Al-Kubra, was established in 1928, and again there were complaints from conservative males (Belgrave, 1956:94). The Government, in spite of such protests, allowed female education to continue. The Government schools have always been separate but equal for the sexes, and reportedly they follow the same curriculum and use the same textbooks. The complete history of women's secular education has been reported by Duwaigher (1 964).

The early expatriate female teachers, Americans, Egyptians, and Lebanese, became role models for women in terms of possible educational achievements and different clothing fashions. As girls' schools became more prevalent, women were needed as teachers, and in the 1950s, the first Bahraini women traveled to Cairo and Beirut to study. Opportunities in the field of education working as teachers and principals were the first professional roles for women. The Government did not promote women studying abroad, but neither did it prohibit them.

A hospital-based Nursing School was established in 1959, and in 1961, two male nurses were sent to London for further study. In 1976, the College of Health Science was opened and there were opportunities for women and men in nursing, and later, in other health-related fields. Women continued to travel abroad for their medical studies to Jordan, Beirut, and Egypt, and they now hold positions as Heads of Departments, Deans, and Professors. There were never any Bahrain Government restrictions prohibiting women from traveling abroad for study, even when alone. In other Gulf countries, there are now restrictions on women traveling abroad alone. Of course, family restrictions and concerns determined, then and now, if a woman could travel abroad alone or accompanied. Women who are professionals now, when interviewed, said they knew of Bahraini women who had college degrees (their teachers or relatives), and some who had traveled abroad (doctors, teachers, or relatives), and they were their role models. When they were young, these women hoped that if they had good grades in school, then they also would have these opportunities. Of course, men always had these opportunities and were sponsored by their families or the Government.

Another important force for change was the discovery of oil in Bahrain and the operation of the Bahrain Petroleum Company (BAPCO) refinery under the auspices of Standard Oil of California and Texaco (Caltex). An influx of expatriate workers from the UK, New Zealand, USA, and elsewhere moved to Bahrain and lived in the oil town of Awali. Many Bahraini men obtained training and jobs at the refinery. Some Bahraini women worked in the homes of these expatriates, while men obtained jobs as drivers. Women for the first time now had their own money and became more active in the economic system (Taki, 1974). There had always been merchants in the cities in Manama and Muharraq, but now more of the economy was based on cash wages, and the refinery as a major employer contributed to the development of a new middle class (Khuri, 1980). By 1995, 18.4 percent of Bahraini women and 55.2 percent of expatriate women were working.

Today many females are attending school, which is still noncompulsory. In the past, there was a gender gap; however, now, a higher percentage of girls than boys attend (Baby, 1996b). Some girls still receive schooling only at home due to strict family values. Government standardized exam results show that females receive a disproportionate share of the high and excellent grades over their male counterparts. This trend has been seen for the last forty years (Belgrave, 1960:96). These educational trends have implications for women in terms of admission and access to scholarships to Bahrain University, where in the summer semester of 1996, 52 percent of the new students were women (Ahmed, 1996). Women have long been the majority at the university. Women with high grades are also meeting the criteria for admission to the Arabian Gulf Medical College and the College of Health Science. According to local bank managers who give applicants' exams, women score higher than men, and many clerical and teller jobs have been given to women, some of whom have worked up to the position of bank branch managers and executive officers (Moore, 1996). These women who have done well and obtained good jobs now have assumed some different roles in society, i.e., they may be supporting their elderly parents partially or fully; they may be making more money than their husbands who may have their *Tawyehi* (high school diploma) or less. Also, they may be more desirable to some men who want or need a partner who can help support the family and make possible extras, such as travel and private schooling for their children.

Anyone watching the Bahrain Government television channels sees what appears to be a male-dominated culture; and in the political sphere, this view reflects reality as there are no women in the Government at the level of Undersecretary or above. There are, however, eleven Director (head of Directorate) positions now held by women (Noor, 1996). Since the recent 1996 government changes, women holding government positions are less frequently seen on television as keynote speakers. This is the public "persona" of the culture. There is a wide divergence among intellectuals regarding how much power and opportunity are available to Bahraini women in reality.

One school of thought suggests that throughout a history of 6,000 years, women have held more power, authority, and responsibility in Bahrain than in other Gulf countries. Ebtihage Al-A'Ali (1991) states that since Dilmun times, men and women in Bahrain have held complementary positions, not competing positions. There was a Dilmun god of the sea, and a goddess of the land. When pearling was a major source of income, men went off in their boats for months at a time while their wives held their families together on shore (Noor, 1996). Some wives even worked outside the home to supplement their husband's income. The author states that there is nothing in the Koran prohibiting women from working, only local traditions that have developed. Ms. Al-A'Ali suggests that when Western companies became active in Bahrain after 1930, the reason they did not employ women was because of their cultural values and notions of men being dominating versus complementary. She posits that these formal organizations in Bahrain are based on imported models and thought. She concluded her report stating that one of the unique attributes of Bahraini society is that its island traditions do not restrict the employment of women in top management positions. Her thesis is supported by recent newspaper articles highlighting women who have achieved top positions in private banks and government sector businesses, such as petroleum engineering, and even as Directors in the Government (Moore, 1996; Noor, 1996).

A completely contrasting view regarding gender roles in Bahrain is presented by Farouk Amin (1982). He notes Bahrain was the first Gulf state to have education for women (1928), and female social organizations, e.g. Bahrain Young Ladies Association (1965). However, Faroul Amin also cites values hurting working women. Employers are reluctant to hire women due to their high fertility rates (the average family size in 1983 was 7.9). Many husbands are not in favor of their wives working, so women quit after marriage. Women are responsible for child care. Twenty percent of rural women are not allowed to study in school. Women have the right to refuse a mate suggested by their family, but not the right to choose. The opening of Bahrain University meant it was no longer necessary to send women abroad for study. The Government is not actively helping women through its policy on sex segregation in the schools, and by its policy of providing women study opportunities mainly in socially acceptable jobs, such as teaching, nursing, and secretarial work. In the 1980s, neither government job bonuses nor housing benefits were given to women. In conclusion, Amin (1982) notes that a value on masculinity, based on religious and traditional values, precludes a large number of women from continuing their study, working outside the home, and even choosing their own spouse.

A second pessimistic view of gender roles is presented by Al-Sharyan who states that the division of labor in Bahrain is not just an economic division, but also reflects lifestyle, prestige, and social honor. Also he states that the labor market is made up predominantly of culturally disadvantaged categories, i.e., nondominant women and immigrants (1987:353). Exploitation and sexual inequality have neither been reduced nor eliminated. Women did not demand more rights or could not, so, in order to establish wider access to resources, they tended to act so as to reinforce traditional social norms and values (1987:344). Women concentrated in particular specialities and are thus confined to a fairly narrow range of jobs within the occupational structure. As a result, there is a rigid differentiation in the labor market along sexual lines based on the patriarchal characteristics of the society which are now consolidated (1987:350). This is reflected in women being the leaders of organizations for the blind, deaf, handicapped, and nursing.

Gender roles in Bahrain probably fall in between the two extremes presented by the above studies. A Bahraini economist listed the five social ills which he felt most confined women to an inferior status in Arab society, i.e., the chastity requirement, early marriage, the dowry, polygamy, and divorce (Taki, 1974:11). Changes are slowly being seen in two of these practices, e.g., early marriage and the dowry. Another practice which prohibited women's development is veiling, which excludes women from many fields of activity (Boserup, 19:127). Some women have made it to top positions in spite of these "social ills," and 18.4 percent of Bahraini women are working and 55.2 percent of non-Bahraini women are working. No studies have been done on working women regarding marital status and number of children; what sacrifices were made by them; and if they are married, whether there is any correlation with their husbands' education level. Is there a "glass ceiling" in the Government, withholding jobs from women above the level of Director? What role does a girl's self-confidence play in pursuit of education, type of spouse, work opportunity after marriage, and family planning? What are the long-term implications of higher school grades of women, and their academic achievements at the college level in terms of their choices of marital partners, marital relations, the stability of their marriage, and the effect of their education on the educational success of their children? Who is the breadwinner and who is the boss? Further studies in these areas would be very informative for government planners and policy makers.

B. Sociolegal Status of Males and Females, Children and Adults

The sociological status of males and females as children, adolescents, and adults are clearly defined in the Koran and interpreted by the Bahrain legal system, which is based on a combination of Sharia law and British jurisprudence which are expressed through codes (Ziskind, 1990:41). All births are recorded and rights are granted according to the nationality of the father. Everyone in the country has access to free medical care after their birth, including expatriates. Bahraini women can sign their own operation permits in hospitals or use their thumb prints; however due to local tradition, the husband, or even other relatives, tend to sign permits. This practice is perpetuated by medical staff who ignore or who are unfamiliar with patients' rights. This practice has also been witnessed in Saudi Arabia (Abu-Aisha, 1985). Hospitals in Bahrain do not have statements regarding patients' rights and responsibilities.

All local children can have a place in the Government schools. Education is free for all Bahrainis and a place in the Government schools is provided for all who register. Girls have access to all areas, including religious studies and technical education. Expatriate parents send their children to various private schools, which are based on various preferences: ethnic (French School, Indian, Pakistani, Japanese, or Filipino), religious (St. Christopher's School–Anglican and Sacred Heart–Roman Catholic), or socioeconomic (Bahrain School, Al Hekma). Bahrainis who pass the entrance exam are entitled to attend Bahrain University and scholarships are available. The majority of students to date have been women, and more are of the Shi'ite sect.

Previously, during the 1960s, the Government made efforts to promote full employment for qualified male adults in companies such as BAPCO, the Defense Force, and other government ministries, and companies. However, now this is not economically feasible, so there is much competition for government and nongovernment jobs. Also the World Bank and other financial organizations are stressing the need for less government control and more free-market economic activity in the country. As a result, unemployment is becoming a national concern. How this will affect women's work opportunities is not known. All workers are protected by various work laws and due process rules for firing workers are enforced.

Men and women can own property inherited from their parents based on the rules of Islam for the distribution of property; however this differs according to Sunni or Shi'ite affiliation. Women keep their family name after marriage and all their property remains in their names, without becoming joint property or being held in their husband's name (Badawi, 1980:23). Women in Bahrain own many small businesses, shops, boutiques, and compounds of rental villas. All marriages and divorces are registered in the Court to ensure people are legally protected. Family disputes over property can be brought to the Courts for adjudication.

Bahrain had a "Special Treaty Relationship" with the United Kingdom until 1971. Now the political system of the country is a traditional monarchy under an Amir. All officials are appointed and there has been no suffrage for anyone since 1975 when the parliament was dissolved (Curtis, 1977). Formerly, there were elections for municipal councils and women and men both had the right to vote. The one Constituent Assembly election held in 1972 allowed only men to vote and there have been no subsequent elections.

Individuals, who violate the laws of the State or strictures regarding certain behaviors, are brought before the various Courts, and fined or confined. Even expatriates appear before the Bahrain Courts, which are held in Arabic, for traffic violations, medical negligence lawsuits, drug trafficking, theft, and visa violations. Other minor violations, including being seen eating during the daylight hours of Ramadan, may result in fines for expatriates and tourists. During Ramadan, the media informs residents and visitors of all restrictions.

There are certain individuals whose legal rights are not clearly defined due to their unclear birth status. These are the foundlings (*laqeet*) who have been abandoned, and whose family and nationality is unknown. They are basically homeless and have no papers. Between the early 1920s and the 1950s, the American Mission Hospital had an affiliated orphanage and school for these children. Later, during the 1950s and 1960s, the Government hospital was their legal residence until a job was found for them. Since the 1970s, they have been cared for in the Children's Home in Gudhaibia, which provides for these children with the help of volunteers.

Life is not easy for these individuals. The foundlings are taken care of and have access to free health care and education; however they have no documents and this prohibits them from obtaining any passport, owning property, procuring government employment, and other social benefits. The female foundlings are easily placed in permanent foster homes of Moslem Bahrainis, as under Islam they are not considered adoptable in the full Western sense. The females fare better and generally marry, and can inherit special gifts if any are willed to them. The males are not placeable in foster homes as they are not related to the women in the family, so rules of seclusion and veiling restrict placement. The males spend their lives in government institutions. They cannot be raised by non-Moslem Bahrainis.

C. General Concepts and Constructs of Sexuality and Love

Sexual suppression, except in a heterosexual marriage, is the expected norm in Bahraini culture. Within a legal marriage, the sexual relationship of the couple is between the husband and wife, and based on their religious beliefs and personal preferences.

Cleanliness is associated with sexuality. A person should be clean and attractive before and after engaging in sexual activity. Cleanliness may include removal of part or all body hair for women, and some or all hair for men also. Activities before sex include at least partial bathing, if not full bathing; use of attractive incense or perfumes; make-up for women depending on the couple's choice; and attractive lingerie, depending on personal choice and economic status. Some women attend exercise classes to tone up their bodies, however this is not the norm, and obesity among men and women is a problem in the Gulf (Bin Hamad, et al., 1991). Some couples may disrobe while others remain covered or partially covered during sexual activities. There have been no studies on practices related to sexuality in the home or bedroom. After sexual intercourse, all Moslems are expected to wash, and for the woman to wash completely, including her hair. If a woman arrives at a party with wet hair, then jokes may be made about her possibly preceding sexual activities.

Women who smoke are considered to be sexy by young men according to informants. Traditionally some Bahraini women smoked the hubbly-bubbly (*Al-gadow*) at home, at the village springs, and at parties when offered (Hansen, 1967:89). Bahraini women do not smoke cigarettes openly at work (unlike some expatriates), and are only occassionally seen smoking in their cars or at restaurants. Recently, security guards have noted that a few teenage girls and younger women have been noted to have cigarettes in their purses. The prevalence of smoking among working women in Bahrain is estimated to be 20 percent based on the one study published (Al-Khateeb, 1986). Women have a meeting house in Adliya where they can go to socialize and smoke. Middle Eastern women in countries other than the Gulf area, such as Jordan, Egypt, and Turkey smoke openly, however this is not a local custom. There have been no studies published in Bahrain regarding why women smoke; however a study in Saudi Arabia (AlFaris et al., 1995) stated that relief of stress was the most commonly admitted reason for smoking (48.9 percent), followed by no reason (28.5 percent), and imitation (12.2 percent).

Children are important in an Arab family. The traditional wedding wish says "from the woman children, from the man money." All men desire a boy to retain their name, and a woman will continue getting pregnant until she has a son to please her husband, and herself. After the birth of the first child, the father and mother relinquish their name to that child, until there is a male child. The man is called "father of" Abu . . . and the "mother of" Um . . . (Curtis, 1977:55). This practice reinforces the importance of children in the society and is not meant to denigrate or detract from a woman or man's status. If a couple has difficulty conceiving, there are two in-vitro fertilization (IVF) units in the country.

The Western concept of love is used by few members of Bahraini society to describe their feelings for their spouse. Parents will clearly state they love their children and their parents and have a duty towards them. An individual's relationship, in certain cases, may be closer with their parents, siblings, and children than with their spouse; this depends on the type of marriage they entered into.

The nature of family relationships has been reported in a thesis by Kahtanie (1992) who asked married Bahraini couples about their coping strategies when facing life strains in marital and parental roles. Twenty-five married couples attending a Health Center participated. The researcher noted that marriages in Bahrain are based on mutual understanding, but conflicts and frustration can occur when confronting stress. Participants described the parental role as one of the most important roles in Bahrain (Kahtanie, 1992:1). The participants however were not eager to share their coping mechanisms. Eighty percent said they would rely on God. Traditionally a couple's support system included parents, grandparents, and/or a neighbor; however now only 84 percent said they would ask these people for assistance. The remainder said they would handle the problems themselves. Twenty percent said the doctor was of no help. The chief causes of marital stress included nonacceptance by spouse, non-reciprocity and lack of give and take in the relationship, and role frustration (Kahtanie, 1992:23). Forty percent of the men said their wife was not a good sexual partner. Most of the couples adjusted to their lives by doing things to avoid differences, solving differences between them by yelling, shouting, and keeping out of the other's way. Their coping responses included not telling anyone of their problems because Bahrain is small and information can spread. Other coping mechanisms included controlled reflection versus emotional disharmony; comparison to other marriages; passive forbearance versus self-assertion, and selective ignoring. Sixty percent of the participants said they keep most of their feelings to themselves (Kahtanie, 1992:46).

The implications of this forbearance, ignoring, and internalization are mentioned by Kahtanie in conjunction with Chaleby's 1987 study on how unhappy marriages are reflected in various psychosomatic disorders seen, especially among women in Saudi Arabia. These women reported that incompatibility in intimacy and socializing, not meeting their husband before marriage, and polygamy lead to stress, which was expressed as complaints of backache, headache, pain syndromes, or other symptoms suggesting underlying anxiety (Chaleby, 1987).

An interesting trend detected by Kahtanie was that the higher the education of the woman, the less she was able to cope with problems in the marriage (1992:36). Avoidance coping mechanisms elicited by Kahtanie are reflected in other aspects of family life or work, e.g., people say "its not like we were prevented, we just did not ask or raise this issue." Personal adjustment and avoidance of confrontation is a core value in Bahraini society. This value is seen in other island cultures around the world (Hall, 1996) and has implications for how change is introduced or not introduced into a society.

2. *Religious and Ethnic Factors Affecting Sexuality*

A. Religious Values (*Din*)

The official religion of Bahrain is Islam, which is upheld through the country's laws, culture, heritage, and traditions. The majority of residents in Bahrain are followers of Islam. During the Friday noontime service in the mosque, the imams teach their congregation the religious point of view regarding all aspects of their life. At the time of the night prayer, special lecture activities are scheduled. There are special religious booklets, e.g.: *Al-moamalat Al-islamiyah* (about banking, charity, selling, and buying), *Al-Ebadat* (praying, social conduct, *Haj*, and fasting) available to guide people in their lives according to the Prophet's teachings. Non-Moslem expatriates are expected to respect the religion and customs of the country. There are three major illicit acts in Islam: fornication, alcohol consumption, and eating pork. According to Islam, sexual matters are private matters and sexual behaviors are appropriate only between married heterosexuals.

Islamic law requires people to be modest in their dress and the body must be covered in public. For a man, this includes the part from his hips to his knees, while for a woman this comprises all her body from the top of the head to the ankles excluding the face, hands, and feet. Expatriate women are not required to be covered completely in Bahrain, unlike Saudi Arabia; however they are expected to dress modestly in public.

While the practice of veiling exists in Bahrain, the percentage of women wearing a veil has varied through the years, depending on rural or urban habitation and social class. Veiling practices posed a difficulty to the early American mission doctors who were all men, and it was not until the 1930s that there was a female doctor, and then only for two weeks a year. In spite of this, one quarter of the operations at that time were on women, and in increasing numbers, Bahraini women gradually attended the mission hospital and were seen by male doctors (The American Mission Hospital, 1933-34:7). In the early days, a hole was made in the veil and the specific area of the mouth, face, or body was exposed. Today, some women or their husbands still request that the woman be seen only by a female doctor; however this is not always possible. Now more and more families choose to pay and attend the clinic of the "best" doctor in their speciality regardless of gender.

The superego, according to psychoanalytic theory, is the portion of the personality associated with ethics, self-criticism and the moral standard of the community. Two psychiatrists in Saudi Arabia describe Arab culture, particularly in the [Arab] peninsula, as characterized by a deeply rooted set of moral codes, social values, customs, and rituals of behavior. The collective attitude toward such conventions is rather strict and inflexible (Al-Khani and Arafa, 1990).

The traditional extended family (*atilab*), which has an authoritarian and hierarchical structure, has the main role in transmitting values and securing conformity, and is the basic and most influential social system. Al-Khani and Arafa state that this practice leads to the development of a superego developmental system that is characterized by the cultivation of shame (*Ayeb*) rather than guilt, and the enhancement of conformity and fear of other's criticism rather than individualism and self-criticism. A consequence in Saudi Arabia is seen in the number of patients, markedly males, who comprise 97.2 percent of clients who see a psychiatrist for the treatment of social phobias. These statistics reflect a cultural attitude that discourages females from seeking psychiatric care.

The study of superego development in Saudi Arabia and the concept of shame (*Ayeb*) needs to be considered as a possible explanation for some of the differences seen among Bahrainis in the practice of their stated religious beliefs. Followers of any religion vary from true and fervent believers who practice all aspects of their faith to those who follow certain aspects and disregard others. Situational ethics is a term used in the West to describe why the degree of compliance to religious rules is not always 100 percent, and how people justify their daily practice based on the situations encountered and what is/was the higher right. This term is not commonly used in relation to Islam; however, this report will show that men and women and/or their families decide what religious practices relating to human sexuality they will follow in their personal lives all the time, or some of the time, or which rules they will ignore completely depending on the social situation. Traditional cultural values, such as shame (*Ayeb*), at times, may supersede the higher religious ideals. Also according to Al-Sharyan, Eastern loyalty remains fixed and strong toward familial and tribal values whatever the influence of modernization (1987:342).

Bahrainis respond to differences in people's adherence to religious values in a mature way, i.e., people know when they should pray—Shi'ite three times a day and Sunni five times a day. The call to prayer from numerous minarets announces prayer time. People are not forced out of stores and restaurants during the "exact" prayer time. Although the Government television channels announce prayer times, programs are not discontinued for fifteen to twenty minutes as in Saudi Arabia. The attitude in Bahrain is that mature people and true believers know what they should do without coercion.

Islam condones sexual activity in marital heterosexual relationships (Fakhro, 1991). Homosexuality is forbidden (*haraam*). There is no enforced Bahrain state law prohibiting this practice which does exist. Anal sex is *haraam* ("the sky shakes when doing it"); however it is practiced between men and women, and men and men. Although prostitution is discouraged in the Koran, it is legal in Bahrain. There were early attempts to regulate it by Court decree (1937). Child abuse, including sexual abuse and incest cases, are seen by health care workers in Bahrain. Divorce is looked upon with strong disfavor by the Prophet; however divorce rates are increasing to the detriment of children and the elderly. Islam is vehemently against drinking alcohol, and prohibits the use for pleasure of any drug that can harm the intellect or the body, including tobacco (Fakhro, 1991). However, all the above practices are prevalent in Bahrain society to the detriment of health promotion programs in the society. As mentioned, while religious teachings expound ideal values, humans cannot always reach the ideal. This report will present some of the ideals and rules regarding aspects of human sexuality, and the current gaps seen between the ideal and reality.

B. Ethnic Values

There are more than sixty nationalities represented among expatriates living in Bahrain and they comprise about one third of the total population. Most of these individuals do not have the option of ever becoming a Bahraini citizen, unless they marry a Bahraini, perform in a special job category, or meet other stringent qualifications, such as religion or five-year residency status. As a result, most expatriates make no effort to become assimilated into the local culture. Some learn Arabic out of necessity due to their job; however, most join social organizations and clubs where they can meet their own compatriots. All these expatriate groups have brought their various religious, moral, and social values with them, and these are reflected in the variety of dress styles seen (sari, sleeveless blouses, tight pants, no bras, miniskirts, and jogging shorts) which are seen on the local streets, and in shops. Likewise attitudes towards alcohol use, pornography, prostitution, and unmarried and extramarital relationships vary from group to group and individual to individual. Concepts regarding degrees of nudity vary greatly and differences among expatriates are reflected where they take their children swimming. There is one private beach attended only by expatriates wearing bikinis and bikini briefs (women and men). Also at this beach, women are seen topless at times when they are changing their clothes. Because of the nudity, some Westerners do not take their children to this beach and limit their outings only to clubs or their residential compound pools.

Bahrainis are very tolerant of the expatriates and their different lifestyles. No restrictive dress codes have been passed; no religious police (*Muttawa*) censure people verbally or physically. People are arrested only for blatant, public violations of the Ramadan fast during daylight hours. Bahrainis must be credited for their highly hospitable culture and tolerance of people from different cultures and religions. Occasionally, situations arise because of the dichotomy of values, particularly regarding dress codes, which are a very obvious difference. Personal or public conflicts sometimes result which require resolution. Bahraini children are taught from a very young age that modesty and covering of the body is proper. Occasionally, a child may experience confusion when their first teacher is wearing a sari and the abdomen and arms are exposed, as well as her hair. Children report feeling uncomfortable at school during their first days because of the "embarrassment" which they feel seeing the teacher's abdomen. Parents explain about differences in national dress and these issues are resolved. More-public conflicts occur, but rarely, such as that seen in 1994 when mainly male and female expatriate runners in a competition jogged though some conservative villages wearing tank tops and jogging shorts. The local media later reported some stones were thrown at the runners. Such events subsequently have been routed through mainly desert areas away from the villages.

Ethnic attitudes towards other aspects of sexuality such as prostitution vary widely. In some cultures, such as Thailand, women know and accept that their husbands frequent prostitutes, while the Filipinos are mainly Catholic and such activity is considered a mortal sin. In spite of this prohibition, the Filipinos in Bahrain are attracted to the money available through prostitution and have the reputation of being one of the ethnic groups active in this practice.

3. Sexual Knowledge and Education of the Population

A. Government Policies and Programs for Sex Education

There is a national curriculum which is taught in the boys and girls schools using the same textbook. The course content offered to Intermediate School students is not labeled as sex education. An introduction to human anatomy and physiology is taught to students around the ages of 10 to 12, depending on a student's school entry age. This basic course is purely an anatomy and physiology approach to sexuality, and male and female informants said they learned about eggs, sperm, menstruation, etc. Family planning is now also covered in this course. There is no discussion of personal relationships or human sexuality, as this is considered *haraam*. There is little discussion of sexually transmitted diseases (STDs) as the emphasis is on normal anatomy and physiology. Some informants report that they did understand what their teacher said, so that when they started menarche, they already understood what was happening to their bodies; however, one woman reported that when she started menstruating, she was afraid she had hurt herself and cried, then told her mother. Another informant mentioned that the intermediate-level course was not enough. "She did not know how babies got out of the body, maybe through the rectum?" In her case, she did not understand about the birth process until she took another course in college. At the Tawyehi level (grades ten to twelve), further anatomy and physiology courses are taught only to those in the science stream or curriculum. Students in the arts or commercial streams have no further courses. There have been no studies reported on the effectiveness of these general intermediate-level courses, or senior school science courses, or the extent of knowledge or accuracy of knowledge among students or Tawyehi graduates.

Graduates from the College of Health Science reported that there were classes where students had to present topics and discuss material relating to the genitourinary system. The females said they were very embarrassed in the coed class, and were sweating; however the subject was taught as scheduled. Everyone felt more comfortable with the other subjects in the curriculum.

An expatriate physician in 1987 wrote the only article regarding the sexual responsibilities of physicians seen to date in the national medical journals (Gravesen, 1987). Other physicians have written on related topics such as reproductive fertility (Rajab, 1984), and urogenital problems of the elderly (E. Amin, 1984). In general, the term human sexuality is simply not used.

There have been no studies published in Bahrain regarding knowledge of women about the climacteric (menopause), and the physical changes they can expect, nor its effect on their libido. Two hospitals have started menopausal clinics to meet the needs of older women, and there have been a number of articles in the general press about the advances made in hormone replacement therapy. There are also no data available regarding women's knowledge regarding mammogram screening, pelvic screening for cancer, osteoporosis, or other preventive measures which are needed and available. Only recently have physicians in Gulf countries reported psychosocial symptoms related to menopause, in Kuwait (Al-Quttan and Omu, 1996) and in Saudi Arabia (Sadat-Ali, 1993). Reportedly, there is a reluctance among physicians to study osteoporosis in this age group, which showed a high incidence of the disease in the pilot study (Sadat-Ali, 1993), or other related topics. The general opinion expressed by female informants is that a lot of older women "suffer at home when going through the change."

Regarding human sexuality courses for the general public, there are lectures offered at the Primary Health Centers regarding pregnancy care and delivery; however there are no lectures addressing issues associated with "human sexuality." The Bahrain Family Planning association (B.F.P.A.)

also offers lectures; videos and booklets about family planning are available from their library.

B. Informal Sex Education

Informants mentioned a variety of informal sources for their early sex education, as most said parental instruction was rare and consisted of "don't touch it" or "don't let anyone touch." Regarding parental instruction, the range of responses included those who said, "I could never talk to my mother/father about that," "She/he did not encourage us to ask," "Mother didn't tell," and "We didn't ask mother," to those whose parents were supportive and "explained when asked," to parents who approached them first and "gave them books to read," and/or "explained everything to them." Some girls were told riding bikes and horses could be harmful, so they should be careful. All informants, men and women, said they discussed sex-related topics with their friends; some did or did not discuss such sex-related matters with their older or younger siblings. All informants likewise said that the media had an influence on their knowledge, including movies (Indian, Arabic, Western), music (Arabic, Western), and books and magazines. Some mentioned how their friends or coworkers, at the time of their engagement, gave them graphic information on "what to do" and "how to do it."

Human sexuality teaching to hospital patients can only be confirmed for cardiac patients attending the Shaikh Mohammed Bin Khalifa Bin Salman Al Khalifa Cardiac Center as their patient-teaching booklet (in Arabic and English) covers all aspects of sexual behavior after heart attacks and surgery. Urologists and obstetric/gynecology staff discuss human sexuality topics with their patients; however they have no teaching booklets for them.

4. Autoerotic Behaviors and Patterns

A. Children and Adolescents

Infibulation, clitoridectomies, and other forms of female genital mutilation have never been performed on Bahraini females. The practice is not seen in the entire Gulf region and Hicks clearly mentions this distinction (1993). It was practiced in the Saudi Arabian peninsula, in Yemen (Muhsen and Crofts, 1991). Some expatriate Moslem children and women born elsewhere, e.g., in the Sudan or Egypt who have been circumcised, are seen in Bahrain's medical facilities. It was only in July 1996 that Egypt banned circumcision of girls in all state medical facilities ("Girl Circumcision Ban," 1996); however barbers and doctors are still performing the procedure and girls are hemorrhaging to death in Egypt.

Informants report that Bahraini children around the ages of 2.5 and 3 begin to touch themselves in the genital region like children around the world. As soon as relatives see this activity beginning, the child is taught this is not socially acceptable, and every time the behavior is seen, the child is admonished verbally not to do it (physical punishment is not used). Bahraini children do not walk around naked and always have clothes on.

All the female informants report that their mothers from a very early age taught them how to sit with their legs together, to sit carefully and to ensure they are covered properly, and how not to sit (not to squat, and "not to let anything show"). Some report that they were taught how to wash their genitals in a proper way, and now they are teaching or taught it to their female children, e.g., with a closed finger and thumb position, and not with their fingers reaching and feeling. The prevalence of this particular washing method is not known. When girls reach the age of 10 to 12, their general play activities become restricted, and all reported their mothers told them their bodies would be changing and that they needed to behave in a careful manner. The concept of virginity and being careful with sharp objects was instilled in them. The incidence or types of autoerotic behaviors in this age group have not been studied.

B. Adults

Adult autoerotic behaviors have not been studied in Bahrain. A study was conducted in a conservative region of Saudi Arabia regarding women and breast self exams (BSE). Half of the women attending a clinic had information about BSE; however 12.1 percent said they did not think they should touch their breast, and 9.0 percent said it was embarrassing for them to do BSE (Akter et al., 1995). No studies have reported on whether men conduct regular self-exams for testicular cancer or have annual prostate exams. Annual prostate screening is not promoted, and rectal exams are done only upon patient request in many cases. These exams may be deleted due to the sexual overtones and the staff feeling uncomfortable conducting them. Further research on preventive health screening and cultural prohibitions would be informative.

Pornography is prohibited by law; however its definition is not clear. Magazines are seen in the country (e.g., *Playboy*) which are illegal, while *The Sun*, the United Kingdom newspaper typically featuring a topless woman on page three, is not. Men bring these magazines into the country and some keep them at their mothers' houses when their wives do not approve of them.

There are X-rated movies or blue movies available in Bahrain, as well as what may be called provocative movies which include a few seconds of partial nudity, belly dancing, or heavy petting. There have been cases reported of couples making X-rated movies or blue movies for themselves, and later these somehow got into others' hands which caused great embarrassment to those involved. Other blue movies have been smuggled in from distribution centers in Saudi Arabia or abroad. Expatriates have been arrested at the Saudi Causeway transporting such tapes in their cars.

Another video source of stimulation to men are the wedding party videos from Bahrain, Saudi Arabia, or Qatar which are copied and distributed unknown to the sister, relative, or sister's friend who held the original. Informants report that some of their brothers have seen and even sold copies of these videos, which include Gulf women with their hair uncovered, dressed in miniskirts, with tight clothes, or low-cut necklines. The adolescent boys and young men watch these movies when available.

Sexual devices are not sold in the country; however they are brought in by people who travel abroad. Informants said that some people keep them for their own use, while others are sold. Sexual devices are not defined as illegal by law. One incident was reported of a Saudi Arabian woman returning to Saudi Arabia who had bought a sexual device elsewhere. Saudi Arabian Customs could not take it from her because such items are not mentioned in customs laws, and the woman retained her device.

Aphrodisiacs from various sources are used, but their prevalence has not been studied. Some compounds from local or imported herbs are thought to have beneficial powers for improving male potency, female fertility, or for curing venereal diseases. Such herbs are available from traditional herbalists (*Al Ashab*) in the various *suqs*, or from traditional midwives. References on this topic are limited in content (Bushiri and Davis, 1996; Abdul and Saheb, 1990, and Abu-Zaid, 1966). The latter source in Arabic describes the herbs used in the Gulf and methods of treatment which were brought in from India, Syria, Sudan, and Egypt. Some individuals also request hormone shots from their physicians. Testosterone therapy should be avoided as much as possible; if used, then monitoring of the prostate is needed (E. Amin, 1984:30).

Alcoholic beverages are freely available in Bahrain through retail liquor outlets, hotel bars, and restaurants unlike other Gulf countries. Liquor is served openly to Bahrainis, expatriates, and tourists. Liquor has not always been so available. Traditionally, Arak, the local liquor made from dates, was confiscated by the police (British and local). Then foreigners were allowed to purchase liquor if they held a special permit. At this time, a black market in imported spirits flourished (Belgrave, 1960), and Arak was made by hidden stills. Then retail liquor outlets were licensed and sales flourished. Islam's prohibition of alcohol is based on its intoxicating effect on the brain (*khumr*). Modern scholars in the Tufseer advise people "don't put your hand in a dangerous thing." Hotel bars, restaurants, and clubs frequented by locals and tourists are also frequented by prostitutes.

Some individuals experiencing difficulties of any psychological or organic nature, including sexual, traditionally would go to the *mutta wa* (religious man or woman) and ask for assistance. The *mutta wa* would say words from the Koran to cure the person (Al-Maki, 1996:16). These psychosomatic cures were reportedly effective in some cases.

Fracture of the penis is a urological emergency situation which requires immediate identification and surgery in order to prevent morbidity to the patient. Prior to 1988, there were fewer than 100 cases reported in medical literature (Sandozi et al., 1988). Urologists in the Gulf during the last ten years have reported dozens of such cases. Fracture of the penis may occur during coitus, or by a direct blow, by abnormal bending of an erect penis, or through other sexual aberrations. Men report hearing a crack, then feel a sharp pain with subsequent loss of erection, deformity, discoloration, and swelling, but no micturation (painful urination) difficulties. If surgical treatment is not provided quickly, the condition results in serious morbidity, including deformation of the erect penis, weak erections, and reduced sexual performance. The surgical procedure is described by Taha et al., 1988.

Various reports have been published in the Gulf regarding penile fracture, including eight cases in Kuwait involving seven expatriates living without their wives. Their injury was self-inflicted in four patients and due to accidental trauma in three cases. In one case, a Sudanese male was trying to negotiate a hymen and vagina which had strictures due to the ritual practice of female circumcision and clitoridectomy (Sandozi et al., 1988). Numerous other cases have been reported in Abu Dhabi (Al-Saleh et al., 1985) and Qatar (El-Sherif et al., 1991), with nine cases in four years in the United Arab Emirates (Hamarnah, 1993), Bahrain (E. Amin, 1994), and Iran (Asgari et al., 1996). As mentioned, the incidence of this urological injury is generally low, but review of the literature shows the incidence of this injury is higher in the Arabian Gulf region (Hamarnah et al., 1993). Some authors suggest the various etiological factors include relatively large numbers of single male expatriates, and married men living away from their spouses, in a Moslem country which contributes to the genesis of this injury. Sandozi et al., suggest that excessive libido and sexual urges which cannot be relieved may play a part in the causation of penile fracture (1988). Expatriate workers in Saudi Arabia do not usually socialize with Saudi women and night life activities are rare due to segregation of the sexes, (Abbas and Satwekar, 1989). In Bahrain there are many opportunities to socialize including discos (Belgrave, 1968).

Priapism is a painful, persistent, penile erection without sexual excitement and is due to engorgement of the corpora cavernosa. Priapism can be self-induced with various drugs and occasionally cases are seen at medical facilities. Priapism is also a known complication secondary to sickle cell disease (SSD). Reports from the U.S.A. show that 50 percent of boys/men with SSD can be affected, i.e., report having one occurrence or more of priapism. Studies in the Gulf show that priapism is a common complication of SSD, e.g., in Saudi Arabia with 18.4 percent of SSD patients reporting at least one experience (Al-Dabbous and Al-Jama, 1993). In Bahrain the incidence of priapism prevalence is low at 2.0 percent (Rasromani et al., 1990:114), and the incidence of SSD is 2.0 percent, while the sickle cell trait is 11.2 percent.

Informants were asked about an incongruous aspect of culture seen in Bahrain. For example, American wrestling programs are seen on local television and in other Gulf countries. These programs are very popular and individual wrestlers are known by names. The wrestlers generally have extravagant make ups, hairstyles, and outfits. Some of these outfits are only tight bathing suits and this is shown on local TV. Informants state that wrestlers themselves are not seen as provocative as wrestling is a traditional sport from the days of the Ottomans, and it is seen as exercise, or family entertainment. However, it was noted that if a girl had tapes of wrestling matches and watched wrestling in an "entranced" manner, then that was another issue. Surprisingly, body-building competitions are held annually in Bahrain, and participants are Bahraini men.

While public autoerotic behaviors are infrequently seen in Bahrain, they are occasionally reported. An elderly Western expatriate visitor attending church was horrified as an expatriate male sitting next to her masturbated during the service. She reported she was afraid, but could not get up because the church was so crowded. Female Asian expatriates report situations where taxi drivers have begun masturbating while they were in the taxi. The reputation of this Asian group is rather low morally, which may be why they are exposed to more encounters of this nature. Expatriate women all note that in Bahrain theses incidents are very rare, unlike the frequency of similar incidents they were exposed to in Saudi Arabia, i.e., you could not look men in their eyes or below their chests.

5. Interpersonal Heterosexual Behaviors

A. Children

Sexual Exploration, Sex Rehearsal Play, and Rites of Passage

Children seen touching other children in any suggestive manner are firmly instructed that this behavior is not appropriate. All sexual exploration and sexual rehearsal play, if noted by the parents or relatives, is strongly extolled as forbidden.

All Bahraini boys are circumcised according to the requirement in the Koran. The procedure is usually performed in the first forty days after birth in a hospital or Health Center Day Case Unit. Traditionally, up until about ten to fifteen years ago, boys of 6 of 7 years of age were circumcised by a doctor or a traditional barber. This latter practice has been stopped in Bahrain, although it continues in Saudi Arabia and is thought to be a source of hepatitis C infections in that country (Arya, 1996:229). Traditionally, after the circumcision, money and sweets were distributed to other children in the family and to the boy's friends and neighborhood children (Curtis, 1977:55). This practice has now almost died out.

There are no ceremonies marking adolescence or adulthood. Children, upon reaching age 7, begin to attend the mosque regularly in order to learn more about their religion, and this is their rite of passage to full membership in the community.

B. Adolescents

There are no female puberty rituals in Bahrain. Women mention that when they reached the age of menarche, they informed their mothers, and the girls in return were told, "they were now a woman," "they needed to behave like a woman," "to be careful of covering," that "they could no longer play outside with children," and "to be especially protective of their virginity." Their mothers usually told other female relatives or friends that their daughter was now a woman, but there was no party or ceremony. Women reported gossiping to their sisters and how they were happy that they were normal.

A few studies have been done regarding the experience of menstrual cycle symptoms among Bahraini women (Al-Gaseer, 1990), Saudi women (Atallah, et al., 1990), and Kuwaiti women (Ibrahim et al., 1979). The age of onset of menarche in the region varies from 10 to 17 years of age with an average of 13 years. Women in the younger age groups, 17 to 24 years, report more menstrual symptoms, while educated women report more menstrual and premenstrual symptoms than single women (Al-Gaseer, 1990; Ibrahim et al., 1979). Some women report they called their period "my auntie"; other euphemisms include "Hajiya came," and "I gave birth."

Many Arab women reportedly do not use tampons because of the sexual connotation of placing something in the vagina; also they fear tampons will make their vagina wide. A third belief is that "washing out is cleaner" than keeping it inside. Some Westernized married women report using tampons, but they said unmarried girls and teenagers would never use them.

The traditional notion that a menstruating women is unclean (*Najis*) still pervades the belief system, although Al-Malki states this notion was rejected by the Prophet (1996:19,27). Menstruating women are not to fast on the affected days during Ramadan or on other religious days, but must make up these days later. A woman should not be divorced by her husband when she is menstruating; likewise sexual relations are prohibited during menstruation (Al-Faruqi, 1 988:72).

Once a women's menstrual cycle has started, there is only one occasion when it needs to be strictly regulated and that is when a women plans to go on *Umrah* or the *Haj*. A woman cannot go to Mecca and perform the prayers in the Kaabah or other rituals if she is menstruating. Girls or women with regular periods or irregular periods are given primolat N tablets for 21 days for suppression of the period, or sometimes birth control pills to regulate them, so they can plan on when to make *Umrah* or *Haj*, and they are ensured of being "clean."

The relationships between adolescent unmarried males and females, aside from family relationships, are strictly controlled by families. The majority of boys and girls attend segregated government schools until their graduation from Tawjehi (high school). There have been coeducational expatriate schools for decades in Bahrain, such as St. Christopher's, Sacred Heart, the Bahrain School (American), and the Indian School, which a percentage of Bahrainis have attended. During the last ten years, expensive coeducational private schools have opened specially catering to Arabic-speaking Bahraini and expatriate Arab students, e.g., Al Bayan, Ibn Khaldoon, and Al Hekma. In all the coeducational schools, boys and girls study together, take school trips with their parents' permission, and sometimes socialize. Dating in the Western sense is not the norm. This is the only opportunity for some students to meet members of the opposite sex. Students in mixed groups may also socialize in the shopping malls and hamburger and pizza places. Male teenagers are freer to spend time out of the house with friends, expatriate students, and workers.

C. Adults

Premarital Relations, Courtship, and Dating

Bahraini parents strictly control, or at least monitor, their daughter's meetings with men, and discourage anything more then necessary, talking relationships. As mentioned earlier, dating in the Western sense is not the norm. There are instances known where Bahraini women dated expatriate men, including those in the American military during the time of the Gulf Crisis and Gulf War (1990-1991), and these women actively sought out these relationships. These situations are very rare as most families are very strict. One informant reported recently seeing two Persian Bahraini women trying to pick up two American military men in Manama. The two men quickly declined and kept walking, as these relationships are strongly discouraged by the U.S. Military due to security and other reasons.

Sexual Behavior and Relationships of Single Adults

Single men have premarital sexual relationships, while single Bahraini women ideally do not. Single adults are expected to be chaste in their relations, and the girls are expected to be virgins at the time of marriage. A man may have an expatriate girlfriend or girlfriends, or a boyfriend in Bahrain or abroad. The prevalence of these patterns have not been studied among men, nor their prevalence in relationship to venereal disease in Bahrain.

Some Bahraini single women do have affairs. Reportedly, this behavior is very rare, and the meetings are conducted in hotels or elsewhere in Bahrain, and preferably where there are "no eyes," or when they are both abroad. A single women who is not a virgin will face difficulty finding a husband if she is known to have lost her virginity, "not by a normal condition," meaning not through marriage. An affair places her in an abnormal or doubtful situation. The women who are known not to be chaste will find it difficult to ever get married (Taki, 1974:1 1). A few rare marriages do occur, informants reported, but this is not common, as the man's family will be against the marriage if they have any knowledge that the girl is not a virgin. There have been no reports about Bahraini women traveling abroad for hymen repair surgery.

When expatriate women are seen with a man, it is generally assumed that they are "friends," or lovers until it is clarified that they are married. This attitude extends to Western or Asian women, all of whom are generally considered to have loose morals until their actions prove otherwise. The Government does not get involved in the affairs of expatriates unless a man files a claim of adultery against his wife. In these cases, the residence permits of the woman and her lover are usually revoked and they are deported. This is done quietly, unlike the 1990s' case in the United Arab Emirates which received worldwide press coverage.

Conservative Bahraini men and families, if they know someone is having an affair, will enforce certain rules of social behavior in order to protect their wives or families from this person's influence. They will not allow their wives to invite into their house a married or unmarried woman who is living with a man or who has a male "friend," even if the woman is the wife's coworker, compatriot, or friend. These same women are not allowed to sit in the wife's car seat, i.e., the front right passenger seat so they have to sit in the back seat. In most cases, the husband or extended family (*Allah*) even ask the woman not to see such a friend at all socially, because being together could affect the wife's name and they should not be friends. In some cases, an association is allowed to continue with conditions, and in some cases, it is continued in defiance of family wishes when the undesirable person is brought into the house.

Social sanction extends to men who bring their lovers or socially unacceptable partners to a party. One such situation occurred at an Embassy party, when an elderly man arrived with his much younger, diamond bedecked, Filipina guest. Suddenly there was a collective inhaling of breath and staring by the Bahraini dignitaries, and the frosty censure could be felt in the air immediately. The man was greeted as per custom, while the woman was totally ignored and spent her time among the women at the party.

Marriage and Family

Bahrain has the reputation among all the Gulf countries of being a place, "where people can marry who they want." All informants, males and females, agree this is true to a large extent. Women clearly state that the "woman has the right to say no" to any man who is recommended by her family. Farouq Amin amends this and states women have the right to refuse, but not the right to choose (1986). Men stated that, based on their subjective knowledge, perhaps 50 percent of marriages in Bahrain are arranged. In reality, this figure is 75 percent (Kahtanie, 1992:41). This incidence is much lower than in Oman or the United Arab Emirates. In the latter country, a law was passed in 1996 stating the man should see the woman before their marriage. Regardless of the stereotype in the Gulf that Bahrainis can marry who they want, there are still six different types of marriages seen in Bahrain, according to Kahtanie (1992). They include arranged marriage, cousin marriage, couples who have not met before, couples who met, forced marriages, and educated-later marriages. Both women and men reported that some men are now showing a preference for, and are choosing, educated working women, even those years older, who can be a partner and who can help in providing financial extras for the family (Taki, 1974; Kahtanie, 1992:39).

Marriage selection and choice of mates ideally follows the Islamic pattern, i.e., religion is the first selection factor, while the second factor is the monetary status or potential monetary state of the male and beauty in the female. According to the Koran, individuals cannot marry those who suckled at the same breast and are a milk brother, *Akh Bil Radha'a.* For all types of marriage, the permission of the father or brother is required, and in addition, for soldiers, military approval is needed. For members of the royal family, Amiri Court approval is required.

Marriage brokers (*al khatba*) are still used to arrange meetings in spite of telephones and automobiles, and even though 39 percent of marriages are consanguineous marriages (Al-Naser, 1993; Al-Arrayed, S., 1995). Many marriages are still arranged between families. The Islamic associations also play a role in helping individuals find a partner. Men and women can complete a questionnaire at their local association, providing information on education, age, background, and preferences. Association staff match applicants, and they and their families can arrange to meet.

Arranged marriages can succeed or fail. Men stated that the couple may "fall in love" or find they are compatible. A lot of these mainly younger couples also divorce during the first or second year; couples in these arranged marriages stay married, especially after they have a family. In some cases, one of the spouses (either man or woman) falls in love with the other, but this feeling may never be returned, e.g., the wife may say, "our marriage was arranged and he is a good father," and the man, meanwhile, has much stronger feelings for his wife or vice versa.

The reasons given for women agreeing so easily with their parents regarding arranged marriages include the following: girls are afraid to say no to their parents for any reason because of the way they were raised; the girl may not know any other man or does not have any feeling of attachment to anyone in particular; it is better to be married than unmarried (Taki, 1974); or a girl does not want to wait too long and to be told "the train has left." For all these reasons, a girl may acquiesce to her parents' wishes. A man, likewise, may easily follow his family's choice of wife for his first marriage, but if widowed, or if he marries a second time, the woman will be of his choosing.

Consanguineous marriages now comprise 39 percent of marriages, down from 45.5 percent in previous generations (Al-Arrayed, 1995). This trend for preferential first cousin marriage has serious health implications, including effects on sexual development for the children produced by these couples. The coefficient for inbreeding in Bahrain is 0.0145 (Al-Naser, 1993). The child mortality rate is Bahrain is three times that of Japan, even though Bahrain is ranked as an otherwise low-mortality population. The Bahrain Child Health Survey of 1989 showed that one quarter of births occurred between first cousins. The mortality rate for these offspring during their first month and first twenty-three months is two times higher than children of unrelated parents. The study showed that women who marry relatives, especially their first cousin, tend to marry younger, are illiterate, their parents were illiterate, and they live in rural areas. Other practices contributing to higher mortality include polygynous marriage, remarriage after divorce, short intervals between births, employment of women only in the home, breast feeding for an average of 10.6 months, malnutrition, and lower socioeconomic status. The author of the study suggested that the government needs to discourage first cousin marriage, to raise the marriage age to 18, to teach the illiterate about birth spacing which is part of Islamic teaching, and to allow polygamy only if the man can afford it (Al-Naser, 1993). Sheikha Al-Arrayed disagrees with the contraindications for consanguineous marriage and cites its traditional history and social benefits, even though 42.8 percent of her sample reported familial genetic diseases (1995).

Some Bahraini men marry expatriate women who are Moslems or non-Moslems. They meet while studying at European, American, or Asian universities, while working in hospitals, or while traveling. The man's family may accept or reject the woman, depending on her religion, country of origin, or other factors. Bahrainis may marry other Gulf Cooperation Council (GCC) nationals with family approval, and occasionally Indian or Pakistani Moslems, but rarely Westerners who have converted to Islam. In these cross-cultural marriages, it is the woman's choice what passport she wishes to maintain. Holders of non-Bahraini passports cannot own property in Bahrain.

Once the agreement of the two individuals has been given to marry, regardless of the type of marriage, then the families decide upon the monetary arrangements for the dowry (*mahr*), which is a gift symbolizing love and affection (Badawi, 1980:17). According to Islamic law, there is a marriage contract (*Al-Rayd*) for all Moslem marriages. This contract specifies the money the man and/or his family will pay at the time of the official engagement in the mosque, any "seconds" if all the money is not available at once, and the "last" money to be paid at the end of the marriage upon divorce or death. The first and second money can be paid to the woman, or to her father for holding. Any "second" money, in case of the early death of the man, is paid before the money in the estate is apportioned to other heirs; or any other money he may have borrowed or was holding for his wife is paid first, as the money was hers, *fit ajulain,* in life or death. The contract once signed is a legal document and is blessed in the mosque and then registered with the Courts.

The amount of the dowry paid in 1994 at the time of the engagement varied from BD400 to more than BD2000 according to the *Statistical Abstract 1994.* Distribution of dowries paid by non-Bahrianis are shown and also tracked in terms of amount and geographical distribution in the country (*Statistical Abstract 1994*: Table 3.53).

The current generation may use the woman's dowry to buy furnishings for the home, rather than having it held by the father or put into her separate bank account. This arrangement depends upon the couple and their relationship. The man's family may also be required to pay for an expensive hotel wedding reception. This depends on the families involved and the contract arrangements. Women report that they were told by their mothers from the time they were young, "never give your money to your husband." If their money is loaned to the husband, it is generally done legally with a contract.

The financial straits of some young men and their families make it difficult for these men to marry. During the last few years, several benevolent social organizations, including the various Islamic Associations, have arranged group weddings once a year, so some or all of the costs of the dowry and weddings are alleviated. These costs can be prohibitive for the young men and prevent them from marrying ("Mass Wedding," 1996). A description of a traditional Sunni wedding ceremony is given by Al-Khalfan (1993), and a Shi'ite ceremony is described by Hansen (1967).

After the engagement, which is equivalent legally to a Western marriage, the woman may move into the man's father's house. Ideally women do not become pregnant during this engagement time and should wait until after the public wedding ceremony. The engagement is usually less than one year, and longer engagements are discouraged. If the woman does become pregnant, the family then decides if a family or public wedding will take place.

During the "engagement" period, some couples decide unilaterally or mutually that they are not compatible and they will divorce. According to the *Statistical Abstract 1994,* 28 percent of the Bahraini divorces were before there was any sexual union, 16.5 percent for non-Bahraini divorces (*Statistical Abstract 1994*: Table 3.74). In the 1994 report, 19 percent of the marriages lasted longer than one year (*Statistical Abstract 1994*: Table 3.77). Once the Court grants a divorce, a delay of three months is required (*Al' Idda*) to ensure the women is not pregnant, then the divorce is finalized. Islam discourages divorce and teaches reconciliation is better.

A man can say the word *talaq* three times in his home to divorce his wife, then the couple has two options. They can see a religious man, a sheik, for his opinion, or attend a court. In both situations, the conditions surrounding the statement will be assessed, i.e., was *talaq* said in a calm manner or was the man under stress? Was the woman in a state of purity (*tuhr*)? If under stress, then the courts will consider *talaq* as said once. If said in a calm manner, then the legal divorce proceeding will go forward with review of the provisions in the marriage contract. The specific laws pertaining to divorce and inheritance are governed by Sharia law. The Shi'ite follow the *Ja'afari*, and the Sunni the *Maliki* rite.

Women can obtain a divorce for certain prescribed reasons: the man disappears or is absent; the man is impotent; if the marriage causes the wife mental or physical illness, e.g., man is a homosexual, wife battering, or adultery; non-support by the man; or if a special condition clause was included in the contract as a condition for marriage (Ramzani, 1985). In July 1996, a landmark divorce case was publicized in Bahrain's newspapers. A women was able to divorce her husband who had AIDS, as she said she was at risk for contracting it through sexual contact.

Marriage and divorce rates are tracked by the Central Statistics Organization. The general divorce rate is 1.7/100 population, and the general marriage rate is 7.5 (*Statistical Abstract 1994*: Table 3.45). The trend is one divorce for approximately every 4 to 4.5 marriages. Eighty percent of the marriages and 85 percent of the divorces were among Bahraini couples (*Statistical Abstract 1994*: Table 3.44). Bahrainis in 1994 also married Asians, other Arabs, other Gulf Arabs, Europeans, and Americans. The divorces followed the same general distribution (*Statistical Abstract 1994*: Table 3.44). Among Bahraini couples, 91 percent were married for the first time, while among expatriate couples, only 56 percent of the men were married for the first time. The age range of women marrying showed 1.6 percent were 19 years or younger, however this age range accounted for 8.9 percent of the divorces in 1994 (*Statistical Abstract 1994*: Table 3.43). Trends show young divorced men and women frequently remarry (*Statistical Abstract 1994*: Table 3.56).

If a woman was proven barren before the divorce, or if she wishes to keep her children and not have to give them to her mother or her ex-husband, then the woman may choose not to remarry, in which case, she will continue to live in her parent's house. Her family will continue to protect her and, now that she is divorced, she needs more protection from men who may assume she is "more easy" in her ways.

Ideally, a man informs his wife if he wishes to take another wife. However this is not always practiced. The woman may be told afterwards. She may discover the other marriage or marriages in a sudden way, e.g., during the Government census when the Government census taker is trying to determine which wife he is talking to; some find the other wife and husband in a new house she paid for, or in some cases, the wife may never know. There are Bahraini men who have families in Egypt, India, Philippines, or elsewhere, of which their Bahraini families are unaware. In some cases, the family only finds out when the man dies and the various wives make inheritance claims on the estate.

A man's marriage of another wife is generally not a valid claim for divorce, as a man may legally have up to four wives at one time. Most women do not want to share their husband and their family usually supports them (Taki, 1974). The possibility of polygamy makes wives anxious, especially if they are barren or fail to produce male children. Women voice their feelings of insecurity in a serious or joking manner, as they do not know if their husband already has another wife or if he plans to do so. He can also say to them, "if you do not do this, I will look for another." There is a greater risk for older women, as there is always the threat that the husband could take a younger wife. The latter is one concern which reportedly makes women keep menopause a secret, as they do not want their spouses to know of it out of fear that he may take a younger wife.

Women make great efforts to keep their husbands satisfied and traditionally this included placing packs of rock salt in their vagina after delivery (A. Mohammed, 1978; Rajab, 1978). The purpose of the salt crystals was to reduce the size of the vagina after delivery to normal or less than normal size so the man will feel more pleasure (Dickson, 1915; Hansen, 1967:108). The use of rock salt and its effects has been documented since the early twentieth century by the doctors at the American Mission Hospital in their annual reports, and in Kuwait and Saudi Arabia (Dickson, 1915) and Oman (Doorenbos, 1976). The main result was rock salt atresia of the cervix, so that in subsequent deliveries the cervix was so tough, it had to be cut to allow delivery. Another effect of the salt packs was unexplained elevation of the patients' temperature after delivery and suspected sepsis. Records show in 1938 that the first MRCOG consultant attended delivery of eighty-four patients and seventy-nine had rock salt atresia. The Ministry of Health took a proactive approach to this problem and registered, trained, and supervised all the traditional midwives. By the late 1970s this practice "was nearly died out" (Rajab, 1979:7). However cases are still seen, even as recently as 1996 in the Maternity Hospitals. In the latter case, an elevated temperature was noted and upon examination it was found the woman had inserted a vaginal pack of rock salt. Herbal passaries known as *mamool* were also used to tighten the vagina, drain lochia, and promote involution of the uterus (Al-Darazi, 1984:37-38). Some women used a combination of salt crystals, herbal pessaries, and antiseptic solutions. Vaginal douches of datol, a strong disinfectant, are still commonly used after childbirth. Regarding resumption of sexual relations after delivery, the wife usually stays with her mother for the first forty day after delivery and may have also stayed with her mother for one month prior to delivery (Curtis, 1977:47),

Serial monogamy is seen in Bahrain, and some women are divorced and remarried three or more times during their lifetime, and men marry more often. As women become older, their chances for remarriage lessen. There are no reports outlining the common causes of divorce, although in the one study conducted on coping mechanisms of Bahraini couples, marital sexual satisfaction was an issue raised by 25 percent of the husbands (Kahtanie, 1992). The Islamic rules of inheritance work against remarrying or polygamy, and the sons generally oppose remarriage which might engender other children, thereby affecting other inheritors (Taki, 1974).

Extramarital Relationships

There is a type of marriage referred to in the Koran as *al Mut'a*, or temporary marriage. At the time of the Prophet, this practice was allowed for the soldiers who spent many years away from their homes. If the woman the soldier kept became pregnant, then she was to become a full legal wife. The Prophet himself later stopped this practice, and Umar bin Khatab, shortly after the Prophet's time again instructed men to stop these type of alliances, as women should be taken as legal wives only.

This practice of temporary marriage has continued only among the Shi'ite. One example is described as seen in Sar Village by Hansen (1967:127). In this particular marriage, the girl did not leave her village to live with her husband in A A'li. Currently, the term *Al Mut'a* has taken on a new meaning. Men who are having an affair may use this term to describe their current relationship, however, there is no legal basis for this type of relationship today (Al-Faruq, 1988:6).

The extent to which Bahraini and expatriates are involved in extramarital affairs is not known. Anecdotal stories are passed around when an incident occurs, e.g., a Bahraini store owner was called to testify to the police about the good behavior of his Bahraini worker. The worker had severely beaten an Indian neighbor who was found to have been sleeping with the man's wife. Incidentally, this woman was "covered" whenever she appeared in public.

The Changing Nature of Bahrainian Marriage and Household

Three major changes have occurred in Bahrain which are driving forces for change in Bahraini families and family relationships. Household structures have changed from mainly extended families (*Allah*) of twenty to thirty members living under one roof, to variable forms including traditional extended households with several generations of family members to nuclear family households (no Arabic word to describe this) located in one of the new cities, e.g., Isa Town, Hamad Town, or a flat. Another major change in all types of households since the 1970s has been the introduction of Asian maids. These maids clean the house, cook, and depending on the family, assume a little or a lot of influence in child rearing practices. However, these maids are economically, and in terms of power, "the lowest of the low" (Al-Sharyan, 1987:350). Their presence has helped the wife to go out and work outside the home, as child rearing is done with the help of the maid. Formerly, the presence of a grandmother would have been the only means allowing a woman to work outside. A third change was the introduction of private automobiles in the 1950s. The automobiles allowed family members to take tours together, and men took their families to beaches and oases. More activities could be planned together as a family (Taki, 1974). These three factors have contributed to the breakdown of the extended family and increased prevalence of conjugal families.

Some women reportedly are very frustrated in their marriages. They are working at a job, running the house, may be making more than their husbands, and are not shown any interest or appreciation by their husbands. Some state that the husband's attitude is "I take your money and you do what I tell you." The men may be out every night visiting traditional coffee houses smoking *shisha,* playing chess or dominoes. They may be out drinking in hotel bars or restaurants. The men receive many invitations for lunch and the tendency is for them to take every opportunity to be out of the house. The men spend little time with the children and some have the attitude, "have them and wait until they grow up." Women get frustrated if their husbands are lazy. Traditionally, men and women lived separate lives in Bahrain and their social networks were segregated (Taki, 1974). The frustrations expressed by some women reflect the continuing trend of separate lives maintained by some husbands while their wives are expecting more from a marriage. Information on these divergent lifestyles and expectations would be helpful to increase public awareness, and to teach couples how to resolve these different expectations from a marriage in order to control the number of divorces.

Children and the elderly are suffering the consequences of divorce. The woman returns to her family with the children depending on their age, or the children go to the father and most likely a stepmother for their upbringing. If the woman remarries, her parents or the husband definitely have custody of the children. After marital breakups, society suffers a greater burden in terms of juvenile delinquency due to unsupervised children (Al-Falaij, 1991), an increase of malnutrition and infant mortality (Al-Naser, 1993), and abandonments of the elderly in Government hospitals.

Sexuality and the Physically Disabled and Older Persons

The physically disabled can marry in Bahrain and whether they do depends on their family and the extent of their problems. There are institutes for the blind (Noor Institute for the Blind), deaf (AlFarisi Rehabilitation Center for the Deaf), and handicapped (National Bank of Bahrain Rehabilitation Home for Handicapped Children) in Bahrain where they receive special training. Bahrain has long been the recognized leader in the Gulf for the training of the handicapped, and for providing them with education and employment opportunities.

If the man is affected with a handicap, the family may find him a bride locally, or more likely abroad, in India. The chance of a handicapped woman marrying depends on the effort made by the family on her behalf, and the presence of a maid to help her. Male informants stated that a handicapped woman would have difficulty marrying because of her limitations in organizing the house. People with mobility handicaps due to polio, birth injuries, or later trauma injuries do marry, but this depends on the injury. Again, if there is difficulty finding a spouse, families will find a wife for their son in India, while the daughter may remain at home her entire life.

Those who are mentally retarded generally do not marry, but there is no law prohibiting marriage. A case was cited where a family employed the son in the business and found him a wife. Male informants queried why anyone would want to marry a retarded woman, as she could not organize the home?

The elderly in Bahrain comprised 5.5 percent of the population according to the 1991 census. The elderly are defined as older than 60 years of age. The elderly remarry, but it is more likely the men will remarry. Marriage statistics for 1994 show that the oldest age for marriages was 40 to 44 for women and 50 plus for men. However, it should be noted that age is a relative matter. All births were not recorded in the past, so many 40- to 80-years-old do not know their exact age. Also, people adjust their birth dates, i.e., men have reported that they added years at the beginning of their working life so they could get Government employment at an earlier age. Others drop years, especially when in their 40s, by changing all their legal documents after saying a mistake was made earlier. Also when people are asked their age, many just underestimate it, e.g., one man said he was 45 when asked by a hospital surveyor. The surveyor reported she looked at him and thought to herself 60 to 65 minimum. The man saw her pausing and said, "50 to 55, whatever you like." The official Government retirement age is 55 for women and 60 for men. There has been no study on the relationship of changing of birth data in the official records and work benefits and entitlements. The life expectancy at birth in 1995 in Bahrain is 74.2 years for women and 69.9 years for men (76 and 71 respectively according to the *1996 World Almanac*), both figures being higher than the average for other Arab states, 64.1 and 61.5 years respectively (Baby, 1996b).

Regardless of the recorded age, the physical condition of the middle-aged or elderly affects their sexual ability. Among the elderly in Bahrain, long-term complications of diabetes, hypertension, and cardiovascular diseases can result in male impotence. Since the 1980s, penile prostheses have been available to treat men who are known to have organic causes of their impotence (Amin, E., 1984). This procedure is available in public hospitals and with greater confidentiality in private hospitals.

Incidence of Anal Sex, Fellatio, and Cunnilingus

There are no enforced legal restrictions in Bahrain regarding the practice of oral sex or anal sex. Informants reported that according to Islam, oral sex is allowed. The rationale is mutually satisfying sexual positions including oral sex are considered normal. Some women say they are reluctant to participate in oral sex, although Bahraini and Western women participate to keep their husbands satisfied.

Anal sex is considered abnormal activity and associated more with homosexual activity of which it is considered a possible precursor, so it is forbidden (*haraam*). Reportedly, if a man even asks his wife to perform anal sex, she has the right to file for divorce. Anal sex is practiced, however, and while the woman may not agree, the husband in some cases is threatening by saying "if you don't, I will go elsewhere." Also women do not file for divorce. Occasionally women discuss this activity with friends or doctors because of the discomfort they experience and the need for creams or suppositories to soothe small rectal tears. Some women find out about their brother's anal sex activities indirectly when they complain about discomfort and an inability to sit down. One informant reported that a friend's brother, who was engaging in anal sex for money, told his sister that he had no money and the man paid him BD50.

6. *Homerotic, Homosexual, and Bisexual Behavior*

A. Children and adolescents

There have been no studies or even articles published in English regarding these topics. In a few rare publicized cases involving a rape and/or a murder, it was revealed, for example, that an adolescent male was involved in a long-term homosexual relationship with an older expatriate male, or that a young boy was a victim of a homosexual rape by one man or a gang of boys. There are no statistics available on these topics since 1956.

B. Adults

Objective data are not available regarding adult behaviors relating to homoerotic, homosexual, or ambisexual behaviors. Very few male homosexuals openly admit their homosexuality and most get married to keep up appearances. Since homosexuality is *haraam* and abhorred according to Islam, most relationships are discrete in order to protect the family name or a spouse. Male informants report that there are now some Bahraini gay men who openly reveal that they are gay, and who state they have no intention of marrying, but this may be fewer than 5 percent of the gay men in the population. Anecdotal stories are related by informants; however, no one could contribute any information on specific behaviors, such as roles or courtship patterns. Islam prohibits homosexual or lesbian relationships, so most couples do not openly admit their relationships, and there is no way to legalize these relationships in Bahrain.

There is a homosexual community comprised of expatriates who are more open about their sexual orientation, e.g., Filipinos and Thais, who are unlike the Bahrainis who are very careful to hide their sexual proclivities. There was an incident in the early 1990s when twenty to thirty Filipino homosexuals were deported by the Government. Despite this, the Filipino gay community now flourishes as before.

Patterns in sexual outlets for homosexual men have not been studied. Filipinos report male drivers (Arabs or Asians) put their hands on the knee of the passenger, and the Filipino has to indicate his preference. Filipino men and others working in barber shops approach their customers by offering to massage them. Such approaches are reported by many men including Bahrainis and expatriates. Men report having to shop around for a barbershop where they feel comfortable and "don't have any problems." Women report friends and families warn other families where they should take their sons to have their hair cut and where not to leave their sons alone. Some parties in the desert reportedly are another venue which men use to meet potential contacts.

Women, as they are kept under more careful watch of their parents, meet other women in school, at friends' houses, weddings, or parties. Women are free to meet at any time, as they are always encouraged to socialize with other women. Only one informant personally knew a lesbian who had told him that she and her friends meet at school or the university, and that lesbians usually marry and have children while continuing their female relationships. This woman said there were a large number of Bahraini lesbians in the community.

The prevalence of lesbian relationships in Bahrain is not known. Male and female informants all mentioned they knew about Bahraini lesbians. Female relationships are considered "safe" by parents, so the women meet easily and often. Like the gay men, lesbians are frequently married and have children. Expatriate lesbians are more open about their sexual proclivities and these women dress in a style that is immediately identifiable by their countrymen, e.g., Filipina "T-birds," or Scandinavian lesbians among others. The incidence of female-to-female STD or HIV infections has not been reported.

Ambisexual (bisexual) adults usually marry in Bahrain and each spouse may have a lover on the side (lesbian, gay, or heterosexual). Only anecdotal stories are available regarding this topic, and there are no data on the prevalence of hidden bisexuality in Bahrain.

A question is frequently raised by expatriates regarding homosexual activity in the country. Are the men truly homosexuals, bisexuals, or heterosexuals? What role does opportunity for sexual release play in their behavior? A story was related about an incident in a hotel. Several Saudis gave money to the male Asian hotel clerk and told the clerk to find them some women. The clerk took the money. The men called down to the desk several times to find out where the women were. During the last call when the clerk said no women were available, the men said, "You come up then."

7. Gender Conflicted Persons

A. Transvestites, Transgenderists, and Transsexuals

Male transvestites or *benaty* (males dressing as females) are seen occasionally in public, e.g., attending a public festival, while in the hospital, or shopping. Informants report that this is "much more common in Kuwait." People are tolerant, mainly ignore them, and do not talk about them. A few comment on the behaviors seen, e.g., "high voice," "make-up," or "using a fan," but do not relate to the nature of the person. Bahrain men dressed as women have been reported as providing the entertainment at exclusive parties where expatriates are rarely invited. One female British author reported attending such a party as her introduction to the country a few years ago. It is not known what proportion of these male transvestites are homosexuals, bisexuals, or heterosexuals.

In some situations, men have been known to dress as women for other reasons, mainly in order to breach security, e.g., to get into a dormitory to visit a friend, to get into a female prison to visit someone, and to hide from the police. The latter practice has caused some problems, and now female security guards are being used in Government agencies, as only a woman can touch or search a woman. One Filipino passed as a female maid for a couple of years before being caught by his employer.

Cross-dressing by males is not considered an act of juvenile delinquency in other parts of the world; however in Bahrain, Saudi Arabia, and the rest of the Gulf region, which has strict religious based norms, cross-dressing is seen as a clear instance of alienation from traditional values (Al-Falaij, 1991). One study showed 4 percent of Saudi male juvenile delinquents were cross-dressing (Al-Ghamdi, 1986). While there are no published data for Bahrain on cross-dressing, 12.4 percent of male juvenile delinquents and 16 percent of female delinquents in one study in Bahrain were accused of moral delinquency (Buzaboon, 1986:151).

Women in the Gulf have a long practice of wearing the sirwal chemise—long full pants with long loose overshirts seen among all Pakistanis (males and females) and some Indians. This fashionable 'Punjabi-style' outfit is worn by men and women alike in Bahrain by many nationalities and is also fashionable in the West. The only differences between men's and women's styles are the type of material, style of buttons, and decoration. Loose pant suits are another preferred style of dress for women to preserve modesty. Women are frequently seen wearing loose pants in the whole Gulf region. There is no association between a woman wearing slacks and being lesbian among Gulf countries. There are lesbian Filipinas known as "T-birds" who dress like a man and who flatten their breasts. They purposely are trying to look like a man. There have been Scandinavians who have pointed out lesbians from their own country. They report, "See how they wear a shirt and pants like that. Only lesbians dress like this at home, so we can identity them easily."

The incidence of transgenderists has not been studied at all. None of the informants reported knowing any Bahraini who said, "I am this gender but trapped in this body." Westerners and Filipinos report knowing of people making such comments in their home countries.

Voluntary sex-change operations for completely gendered adults to the opposite sex are not done in Bahrain and they are illegal. This view is supported by the Koran and the Prophet's teachings (Al Herbish et al., 1996). If there is confusion regarding the sex organs of a child at birth, then investigations will be conducted to determine sex assignment of the person. Sex-change protocols followed for newborns are similar to those published in Saudi Arabia (Taha and Magbol, 1995). If the sex organs are predominantly those of a male, the male sex will be assigned; likewise if those of a female, the female sex is assigned. Unfortunately some problems are not apparent until the time of puberty (Abdul Jabbar, 1980; Farsi, et al., 1990). A study in Saudi Arabia on intersex disorders detected in puberty or later reported that all genetic males, known as females, accepted sex reassignment as males. Females incorrectly known as males did not readily accept sex reassignment, as culturally the male sex is preferred (Taha and Magbol, 1995; Al-Herbish et al., 1996). The nature and incidence of some cases in Bahrain have been reported by S. Al-Arrayed (1996).

The man's chances for remarriage are limited mainly by his financial resources and his ability to pay the marriage contract divorce settlement, and if he can afford the dowry for a new wife. Poor men unable to provide well for their families have been known to marry four wives, as there are currently no regulations regarding minimal income; however this is now being recommended (Ahdeya Ahmed, 1996). In other Gulf countries, men are being encouraged to take a second wife in order to reduce the numbers of unmarried local women. The U.A.E. Government extends soft loans to finance taking a second wife, and men already having foreign wives are now eligible.

B. Specially Gendered Persons

The *kaneeth* (xanith) is a specially gendered person reported historically in the Gulf (Wikan, 1982) and still seen today. The prevalence of these male transvestites/homosexuals is not known. None of our informants have personally known such individuals, however many reported they have heard others talk about this topic. Some informants described people they have known and/or their families. One Bahraini informant reported that "the person they knew like this was Omani and he lived in our neighborhood and he was the best cook." Another reported, "There is a man who is married, and he has children, but he is also like this." Others said, "This was more common in the past." Following up on this comment, a long-time expatriate resident mentioned "that soon after independence and after the British left, all the Omani men were sent back home in dhows from

Manama. People went to the sea front to see the dhows cast off. These men had worked as maids, (there were no female maids then), as singers in bands at women's parties, and were eunuchs." These Omani men sound like the description of the third gender *kaneeth* described by Wikan in Oman in the 1970s (Wikan, 1982).

When asked about the term *kaneeth*, Bahrani informants did not agree that the *kaneeth* is a third gender. The term in Arabic means a male or female homosexual. Bahrainis said some marry and have children, so are bisexuals according to the English definition. *Kaneeths* in Bahrain would not necessarily show feminine manners, or dress in a more feminine style, unlike those reported in Oman, but would wear a *thobe* or Western-style men's clothing.

8. Significant Unconventional Sexual Behavior

A. Coercive Behaviors and Neglect

Child Physical Abuse and Neglect

The incidence of child abuse has not been studied or reported in the medical literature in Bahrain. Articles published in Bahrain have alerted physicians to note and report suspected cases (Al-Ansari, 1992; Molloy et al., 1993). Two hospital informants noted knowing of only two cases of child abuse in the past eleven years in Bahrain, and in one case the mother was mentally disturbed, while in the second case the child was handicapped. Similar abuse of handicapped children is also mentioned in Saudi Arabia (Al-Eissa, et al., 1991). Two articles on childhood trauma in the Gulf (Bahrain and Saudi Arabia) did not mention if any of the cases were due to child abuse (E. Amin, 1979; Al-Otham and Sadat Ali, 1994). Nonaccidental burning of children is another type of abuse which may exist in Bahrain and which requires a team approach to detection and treatment (Saeed, 1992). Child abuse does exist in Kuwait, and is reported in increasing frequency (Al-Rashied, 1988), and in Saudi Arabia (Al-Essa, et al., 1991; and Qureshi,1992). A case of Munchausen Syndrome by proxy has been reported in Saudi Arabia (Al-Mugeiren et al., 1990) and doctors in Bahrain have been alerted to note such cases (Molloy, et al., 1993).

School teachers have also been educated regarding child abuse and are to report suspected cases of child abuse to the social worker. One study was conducted regarding teacher awareness of symptoms (Ali, 1996). Since schooling is not compulsory, or may be conducted at home with home study, teachers cannot know of the full extent of this problem. According to the Koran, children are to be treasured, and strict discipline and physical means of discipline are not commonly used. From ages 1 to 7, parents are exhorted to love and care for their children, and from 7 years onward to be as a friend to guide their child.

The extent of abuse to which children are subjected from the many maids employed in the country likewise is not known. However, Al-Rashied in 1988 noted in Kuwait that child abuse has been noted more often after increased reliance on baby sitters. Individuals report knowing of suspected abuse cases in Bahrain, and when they were confirmed, the maids were deported. In one example, a Filipina brought to work for a family was found using physical means to control the children and scaring them so much their personalities changed, which is how the parents first became aware of the problem. Another South Asian maid absconded, and was later caught working as a prostitute. The parents then wondered if she had been entertaining men in the home, as the children had reported previously that the maid used to lock them in their rooms when the parents were away.

Many of the cases of child abuse are not physical abuse or battered child syndrome, but neglect, or cases of failure to thrive. Bahraini doctors have been alerted to note these cases (Al-Ansari and Al-Ansari 1983). One expatriate, for example, reported thefts from her vegetable garden. The culprit was eventually caught and it was a young boy who was hungry. Investigation of the case showed there were four wives and forty children in the family and an unemployed head of the family. The expatriate dropped all charges. Social workers have reported finding neglected handicapped children who were being kept in boxes in the home so these children had severe contractures. In these cases, the mothers had many other children to care for. Side effects of medical procedures are sometimes not noted by parents among their large number of children until the damage is irreversible. Young children are sometimes left in cars overnight and they die in the extreme heat as their absence in the house was not noted. A study on the impact of family size on morbidity showed crowding, poor sanitation practices, low education, and poor personal hygiene resulted in more family visits to health centers (Nasib et al., 1 983).

The Bahrain Government has an effective means of helping abused children once identified. All reported cases of abuse and neglect are investigated and social workers and community health care nurses follow up each case, even daily, if it is felt this is needed. Even though all government health care services are free to all residents, utilization of psychiatric services for children by parents is low. In 1981 and 1982, the last published data, only .016 percent of children were referred for psychiatric help, while it is estimated 5 to 20 percent of children could benefit from the services. Boys outnumbered girls in conduct disorders, while girls had more reactive and neurotic disorders (AlAnsari and Al-Ansari, 1980). The possible underlying causes of childhood psychiatric problems were not discussed in the article.

Charity from the Government, the Red Crescent, or other family members may not be meeting all the physical needs of some families. Other agencies and social organizations provide needy families family aid

(Jameyat Al-Islah, Jameyat Al-Islamiya, Jamiyat Al-Tarbiat Al-Islamiya, Sunduq Al-Infaq Al-Khairi, and Al-Eslah Society's Welfare Committee). Only official begging is sanctioned in the country, i.e. women mainly are licensed and have a permit to visit shop owners to solicit charity and usually only during the month of Ramadan. However beggars (men and women) can be seen in many parts of the capital city on a regular basis.

Child Sexual Abuse

The worldwide current awareness of family sexual abuse started in the 1980s (Patten, 1991). The incidence of child sexual abuse in Bahrain has not been documented in any published reference. Hospitals keep their own statistics which are not officially reported. In contrast to rarely seen cases of battered child syndrome, several cases of sexual abuse are seen every week by hospital medical personnel, nurses, and social workers according to informants. The number of children seen by private doctors and in private hospitals is also not reported. A team of doctors and a psychologist are now addressing this issue, and perhaps data on prevalence and trends will be available in the future. The lasting impact on the children involved and their families, and the relationship of sexual abuse to dysfunctional families to broken homes due to other social factors, such as high unemployment, have not been studied or reported.

Sexual abuse is detected in various ways, including the wife catching the father and daughter. In some cases, bleeding in the genital or rectal area may be the first sign seen by parents or reported by the child; a skin rash or symptom of a sexually transmitted disease (STD) may be the first sign. Babies of six to eight months, toddlers, preadolescent, and adolescent children are the victims. In some cases the abuse is from a male relative (father, uncle, or brother), or outsider, or gang of boys who may be sexually abusing the male or female child in question. Cases are reported of maids playing with and sexually abusing male or female children. None of the reported cases are as extreme as the male mutilation seen in Saudi Arabia by a mentally disturbed mother (Hegazi, 1990). Incest and sexual abuse cases reportedly occur among Bahraini and non-Bahrainis, including South Asians expatriates. Health care personnel state Pakistanis are more frequently involved, however there are no clear data on trends.

The extent and frequency of police involvement in sexual abuse cases varies. If an outsider or group of boys is involved, and a male child was abused, then the police may be called. If a female child was abused and a male relative was involved, e.g. the father, then the police are not called. In these latter cases, the female child may more often be taken to a private doctor, or to no doctor. In the last ten years, there have been two publicized cases of young girls raped by expatriate men. One was a 5-year-old child playing outside her house. Neighbors and family members caught the expatriate Asian man and severely beat him. The second case involved an Asian school guard who raped a young preadolescent female student.

Pedophilia

Pedophilia has not been studied, however pedophilia regarding young boys is talked about and is not a new practice. During the late 1980s, there was a man reportedly raping young boys in the Muharraq area. The case was discussed opening by worried parents, but the outcome of this situation was not publicized. Bahraini pedophiles paying boys for sex both in Bahrain and abroad are known, and such cases are discussed openly by older members of the local community. Groups of older boys are sometimes involved in rapes of young boys, however this data are not reported. Pedophilia in Saudi Arabia, in contrast, is considered a major crime, and those caught are sometimes beheaded, depending on the extenuating circumstances such as alcohol use and kidnapping.

Rape: Acquaintance, Date, Marital, and Stranger Rape

The prevalence of rape is not reported. Isolated cases are known to occur, and a few have been reported in the print media, usually no more than one case in a year. Those reported in the media generally involved expatriates and sometimes Bahrainis. One case of homosexual rape of a young village boy by an older village boy resulted in the child's murder. Stranger rape does occur, e.g. one Asian woman (a maid), took a taxi ride late at night and was raped by the driver. She also contracted a severe case of genital herpes from this incident. The frequency of rape in Bahrain, in comparison to cities of 500,000 to 600,000 people, would provide valuable comparative data. Many Bahraini families possibly do not reports rapes due to the shame involved, and Asian women are reluctant to report also, so accurate figures are difficult to obtain, but underreporting of rape is the situation in all countries around the world. Marital rape has not been studied.

B. Sexual harassment

Sexual harassment has not been studied in Bahrain in the work place, nor in social situations. According to the Sura Al Noor, unrelated men and women ideally should talk about essential things only. Women government workers have been known to call and harass a male coworker over the telephone while at work, but this is very rare. Likewise the occasional male coworker has been known to harass a female coworker at work or in social situations. These incidents are reported as very rare, however the real prevalence is not known, as Asian females in particular are reluctant to report any problems or to cause trouble for fear of loosing their jobs. Bahraini females are also reluctant to report such cases due to the lack of witnesses and the shame of making the problem publicly known. There was one publicized case of telephone harassment, which continued after a Bahraini woman married. The harassment resulted in a murder plot, after which the man's body was discovered in the desert. The husband was jailed for life and the woman for a shorter term.

Women report that off-color jokes may be told in their presence when they are a member of a group. The men will "look out of the corner of their eye" to see if they were overheard. The women say they have been schooled not to respond in any way, or to indicate that they heard what was said.

Touching between men and women in public, such as holding hands, is seen occasionally, however at work it is limited to an occasional handshake. An unrelated man should not touch a woman according to Islam. Some women refuse to shake hands even in professional situations, or some wear gloves, or a glove on the right hand. This practice can be seen on the television during graduations and other public ceremonies when an official shakes everyone's hand.

Body language has been studied among the Arabs for many years and social distance is reportedly closer than seen in some Western countries. Men talking to men, and women talking to women may be standing within six to ten inches of each other. In Bahrain, however, this social distance appears to be extended between members of the same sex to twelve to eighteen inches so expatriates do not have the same "close" feelings as when talking to some Mediterranean nationalities. Among males and females, this talking distance is usually further apart at two to three feet. Very rare exceptions to this rule occur when someone is agitated and they may poke with a finger at an expatriate person's arm while making a point and usually without realizing what they are doing. Occasionally, a powerful man may put their hand on a woman's back, but this is rare and the expatriates say they feel uncomfortable. Among the various expatriate groups in Bahrain, this social distance varies depending on the age (hand holding seen among male or female teenagers) or the nationality. Hugging when meeting a person is more common among the Filipinos, while casual kissing is seen among all groups, including Bahrainis, at the airport upon departure or arrival. Hand holding among men is a common sight among grown men. Bahrainis, South Asians, and Filipinos are seen holding hands on the streets. The practice is also seen among some women, but it is less common.

Kissing between men is a common practice and is seen in the media, in public, and at work. Kissing on the cheek, forehead, and shoulder is a sign of respect, and among friends a sign of welcome. Kissing between women is also seen frequently in public and at work as a sign of respect, and of greeting, especially if the women have not seen each other recently or some one is returning from a trip.

C. Prostitution

Prostitution has existed in Bahrain for many years and the *British Agency Annual Reports* include data on this topic. There was an increase in prostitution reported between 1926 and 1937 in the British reports. A number of foreigners earning good pay came to Bahrain from Persia, Iraq, and India without their families, and this caused an increase in prostitution which is a matter of supply and demand.

The history of prostitution in Bahrain since World War I has been discussed in various sources. Designated brothel areas were established (Rumaihi, 1976:193). There was formerly a section of west Manama, between Naim and the Police Fort, known as "Gubla" and an area in Muharraq known as "Al Grandol." There were brothels in these areas with female prostitutes, and the male prostitutes were almost as numerous as women. A February 8, 1937, court decree ordered that prostitutes should live and work only in these two designated places. Prostitutes living or working elsewhere would be deported. The court ruling also ordered the deportation of those "highly professional" prostitutes. The female prostitutes were predominantly from Persia, Iraq, and Oman, with Persians commanding the highest prices, then Iraqis and Omanis respectively. The female prostitutes were all known as "Daughters of the Wind" according to Belgrave (1960); Bahraini informants report they were known as "Daughters of Love."

The male prostitutes were chiefly Omani boys (Belgrave, 1960). All the Omani men did not live in this area, as some also lived with families who could afford their services. Later, there were Bahraini women who were the children of former slaves also working in these areas, while Belgrave notes the presence of foreign women "who had become Bahrain subjects by the simple expedient of marrying Bahrainis" (1960). Among these various groups of women, some were divorced, more commonly they were poor, and a few married women did it for the money or even pleasure. The brothels themselves were attended by men of all socioeconomic classes and ethnic groups.

Bahrainis now in their early forties or older all reported a range of knowledge regarding this topic and the location of the districts. Some knew of such a former "Red Light" district, but they were not sure where it was exactly. Some said they used to visit it with their parents while on business trips, for example, to collect rent. Others reported they visited the area because it was where "all the action was." One informant said he collected bottles and cans for recycling and used the money to visit the ladies. Another informant reported she was very young, but she remembered seeing a man with a young boy. When she asked her mother why the man had the young boy, her mother answered "he is married to him."

The term *Grandal* is still used in another context by elderly people to describe or comment on an individual whose behavior is "loose" according to preferred standards. Such a woman is called a *Grandal*, or it is said she is acting like a *Grandal*. Older people listening understand the connotations of the term. The areas designated for prostitutes started to decline in the early 1970s, and prostitution activities became more dispersed throughout the country with the opening of hotels. Still, women reportedly can still be seen standing in doorways in the old Gubla area in Manama.

Various reasons are given for the decline of this area in town and the recent changes seen in prostitution patterns. First, in the early 1970s, there were major political and economic changes seen in Oman. The current Sultan deposed his father and began investing millions of riyals in major infrastructure improvements in the country. There was an improvement in job opportunities, so many Omanis returned home. Second, the local, economic development of the 1970s due to the boom in oil prices resulted in the building of many new apartment blocks so there were flats (apartments) available in many parts of the city. Also the British military wanted flats and villas in which to live, so there was a building boom, and then Bahrainis moved into these dwellings also (Taki, 1974). People could have more privacy away from their families. Third, the economic boom of the 1970s also meant people had more disposable income and could afford extras like paying for a small flat or small villa. Fourth, the economic boom of the 1970s resulted in an increase of expatriate laborers between 20 and 50 years of age, including those from the Philippines and Sri Lanka. These two groups, all informants state, are highly involved in prostitution in Bahrain. Some Filipinas are paid a monthly salary or gifts of sometimes up to BD400 (US$1,000) or more by their male friend. Because of the low opinion of Filipinas in general, women with families and even elderly women over 60 report being approached directly or indirectly for prostitution (money is brushed on their arm or flashed so they can see it). Finally, after Bahrain gained full independence from the United Kingdom in 1971, U.K. residents were granted special visa privileges, i.e., no visa was required for the first three months of entry. Many U.K. residents came to Bahrain and the United Arab Emirates in the Gulf looking for jobs and employment opportunities. Some of the British women found jobs, others sponsors, and others travel between Bahrain and the United Arab Emirates and are seen frequenting the hotels working as prostitutes. This visa law was changed in 1996, and a visa is now required for U.K. residents due to reciprocal changes instituted by the European Union.

After the opening of the Saudi Causeway in late 1986, local women experienced many problems while they were walking on the streets, in shopping malls, or attending parties in hotels. The Causeway also led to an increase in the number of incidents reported by women who said they or their friends were approached by Saudis. Western women with their children reported being approached in shopping malls by Saudi men and being offered money for their services. Bahraini women, because of the problems, began avoiding hotels even for wedding parties on Wednesdays, Thursdays, and Fridays to prevent such situations from occurring. Women working in public areas in Government buildings are given hotel phone numbers by Saudis, and many have requested job changes to less public areas as a consequence. These situations were predicted by Wilsher in 1982, and reflect an expansion of the prostitution activities described by Faroughy (1951:20) who stated that "prostitution forbidden in Saudi Arabia has greatly increased under the complacent eyes of the authorities and Bahrein has become a kind of 'pleasure island.'"

Solicitation for prostitution is quite open. Expatriate men report being approached by women in hotels and shopping malls. One first-time consultant visitor from the U.S.A. in 1989 was invited to look at a photo album of women by a taxi driver, taking him from the airport to his business appointment. The visitor reported being absolutely amazed to see this in a strict religious country. A Filipino man attending a hotel disco with a group of friends approached a Western woman and asked for a dance and was told "you cannot afford me."

The nationality of female prostitutes has changed through the 1980s and 1990s. During the 1980s, Filipinas could be seen going off with men they picked up, even while in family pizza restaurants. Sri Lankans were available on certain streets in various areas of Manama. Also there continues to be a main street in Adliya commonly referred to as the "meat market" where Filipinas walk about at night. New nationalities of prostitutes have been seen during the 1990s. Since the breakdown of Communism, Russians began traveling freely to the Gulf. Many came to Bahrain and the United Arab Emirates for shopping, and there was a billion dollars in Russian trade for the United Arab Emirates during 1995 alone. Some of the women also came to sell small items, while others came as prostitutes. Russian women were available in some of the expensive hotel restaurants frequented by Saudis, outside two- and three-star hotels and other restaurants frequented by other tourists. Many of them advertised their services for BD20 ($53) dollars by holding up two fingers. One informant asked to see the C.P.R. (Central Population Registry) residence cards of Russian women outside an expensive restaurant. They had current C.P.R. cards and their profession was listed as "business." By the summer of 1996, Bosnian female prostitutes were reportedly working out of one of the mid-size hotels. These women usually asked for the equivalent of BD25-50 or a gift such as a watch if money was not available. Adolescent Ethiopian prostitutes have been seen on the Exhibition Road area with pagers.

Prostitution is not illegal in Bahrain, and it must be mentioned that solicitation for prostitution is not as blatant in Bahrain as that seen in Abu Dhabi where women constantly walk up to men standing alone on the street, or while waiting for transport.

D. Pornography and Erotica

All pornographic materials are strictly prohibited by law and are confiscated by customs officials if detected. Most, if not all, expatriates coming to Bahrain are told that three items are strictly prohibited, i.e., pornography, items on the Israeli boycott list or made in Israel, and cultured pearls. The latter two classes of items are seen, however. Cultured pearls are not to be sold in Bahrain, but are worn, and the boycott list has changed since the Gulf War.

Pornography is available in Bahrain, e.g., magazines, as they are not picked up by security upon arrival as easily as metal items (by the metal detector), or drugs (by drug sniffing dogs) or computer diskettes containing pornography. All videos are viewed by customs agents at the airport upon arrival; others are retained and can be picked up later in Manama at the censorship office. Blue videos are still smuggled in, as well as items on the Israeli boycott list; these reportedly are "not that difficult to find." Arrests of individuals holding blue movies or computer diskettes containing pornography, and those caught selling them are sometimes publicized in the newspapers as a deterrent. Relatives and roommates may turn in the sellers or users to the police. Names of the culprits may be publicized in the press or withheld.

E. Sex-Related Murders, Suicide, Self-Mutilation, and Sex with Animals

Murders in Bahrain have been very rare for the first nine decades of the twentieth century. The British advisor reported in the *Bahrain Government Annual Reports Volume II 1937-1941* that "usually about one or two murders are dealt with by police during the year." This general trend continued until the 1990s.

The early reports also mentioned that "occasional murders may take place which are not detected, especially women and newly born children." These women were put to death by their relations because "they had dishonored the family. Killing a woman for this reason was considered by many Arabs to be justified" (Belgrave, 1960:100). Belgrave notes that he knew of cases where an unmarried girl was "put away" because she was pregnant, but he knew of no cases of a wife being killed because she was unfaithful. One case was related in the late 1980s of an expatriate Arab man and his brothers who managed to forcibly take the man's wife to their home country. They informed the wife's Western doctor they were going to have the woman and the child killed for bringing shame on the family. No action could be taken as there was no crime in Bahrain. This practice has been stopped in Bahrain for decades.

Currently, it is reported that the majority of pregnant, unmarried Bahraini women are sent abroad for abortions or practice self-induced abortion to avoid bringing shame on themselves and their family. Others may check into a maternity hospital, sometimes under a false name, and leave the child behind in the hospital.

Prostitutes in the former brothel areas were sometimes murdered by jealous lovers according to Belgrave (1960:103). More recently, during the last ten years, there were two sex-related murders involving Filipinas. The media reported one was murdered at work reportedly by a Pakistani lover, while the other body was found in a dumpster near a hotel.

Sex-related murders between individuals who are or were lovers have been reported, but they are very rare. During the last ten years, there were several publicized heterosexual cases in the media, e.g., a Filipino couple (the man murdered the woman, and then killed himself), and a South Asian woman was killed by her lover. There have been a couple of homosexual-related murders, for example, one village man killed his lover and buried him in the yard. And in another case, a younger Bahraini male (late teens) killed his elderly British lover.

Suicide due to shame about sexual matters is rare, but does occur. An Indian woman whose child was found to be HIV-positive confessed that she was involved with a Pakistani male. After an investigation, it was determined he had slept with a Filipina, who had been involved with a Saudi. The Indian woman committed suicide soon after the investigation, and her family (husband and son) were deported as they were HIV-positive.

Successful suicides versus parasuicides appear to be more common among Asians in Bahrain, particularly Indian males and females. Firearms, except for antiques, cannot be legally held by the general public in Bahrain, so serious suicide attempts are made by means of hanging, electrocution, drinking of kerosene or self-immolation, slitting of wrists to cause arterial bleeding, and drug overdose. Investigations published in the press show that the men are usually depressed over their financial situation or illegal residency status, while the women are having work difficulties (termination or warning letters), or family difficulties in India or locally. Some Indian women are trapped in abusive marriages to Bahrainis and have no place to seek assistance. Other precipitating factors may include sexual abuse by the husband's male relatives and other family situations.

One research study on suicide has been published to date (Metery et al., 1986). In 1981, the police suicide register showed 150 people attempted suicide mainly by ingesting drugs for a rate of 0.04 percent. Religious values (suicide is a mortal sin in Islam) and social stigma possibly contributed to the low rate (Metery et al., 1986). This study showed more women, generally unmarried in their twenties, attempted suicide, and 60 percent had attended their local health centers within the previous six months complaining of somatic symptoms such as headache and body aches. This study did not indicate the number of Bahrainis or non-Bahrainis listed in the suicide register. A growing pattern of self-induced drug overdoses is reported among Saudi women (Malik, et al., 1996), Kuwaiti (Emura et al., 1988), and Qatari women (El-Islam, 1974). The precipitating event(s) leading to suicide need to be studied.

Parasuicide survivors (impulsive attempts) are brought to health care facilities. A six-month audit of Medical Department admissions between late 1995 and early 1996 in one general hospital showed 1.08 percent of the admissions were parasuicide attempts, with a ratio of 4.5 females to males, the same ratio of Bahrainis to non-Bahrainis, and the same ratio of impulsive situations versus psychiatric histories. Causes of impulsive attempts included exam failures, problems at work, fight with a family member, recent divorce, recent parental death in the family, and marital arrangements.

One case of self-mutilation by a Thai male who became depressed, reportedly when his girlfriend left, was reported in the press. Urological surgeons in the large government hospital performed successful surgery in this case. Attempts of this nature are extremely rare (one case in ten years).

Another deliberate self-harm (DSH) practice known as "jumping syndrome" appears to be common in the Gulf States, and is seen increasing in prevalence in Qatar (El-Islam, 1974), Saudi Arabia (Mahgoub, 1990), and Kuwait (Suleiman, et al., 1986). Predominantly Asians, and mainly females with an average age of 29 years, are jumping off buildings in an attempt to kill themselves. Studies show that many have died, while others have had extensive fractures and required long-term hospitalization for an average of fifty-six days, which places a cost burden on the Gulf States free health services. The proportion of unsuccessful attempts resulting in minor injuries is not known. The females jumping in most cases had no history of previous psychological illness. Sexual and physical abuse are the most important factors which push females to deliberate self-harm (DSH). Some of the jumping syndrome survivors alleged that this was the reason, however sexual abuse was not proven (Sadat-Ali, et al., 1995:189). Reportedly this is the method of choice for suicide in Kuwait due to the non-availability of drugs (Suleiman, et al., 1986). Cases of jumping syndrome have not been reported in the media in Bahrain, however medical personnel have been alerted to this trend.

There have been no studies conducted regarding Bahrainis having sex with animals, and there are no local anecdotal stories discussed regarding this topic. An archaeology text by Bushiri (1992) discusses seals found in Bahrain and Kuwait from the Dilmun period which show intercourse between a man and a bull, which the man performed from behind the bull while holding the rear of the bull.

9. Contraception, Abortion, and Population Planning

A. Contraceptives

Attitudes regarding contraception vary from couples who accept all children as the will of God and who make no effort to prevent pregnancy, to those who plan, space, and limit their families. In the former situation, many women report it is the husband who feels more strongly about this issue and who refuses to use contraception. In some cases, the women want more children and the husband refuses, e.g., the woman may be the second or third wife and the husband has many children, including sons, from a previous marriage(s), so he may then have a vasectomy after only two children from the last wife. The wife may then feel cheated and express regrets. Other families quote the Koran's injunction to be able to provide for their children well, so they use various forms of birth control (condoms,

IUDs, or pills) to space their children. Spacing varies from one to three or even fifteen years. Women say, "My husband told me I can get pregnant again after three years," and men have said, "On my salary, I can only afford to have this number, so we needed to space our children." Among the college-educated, some boldly say "Two is enough." One Government publication reported that 50 percent of Bahraini families are using some form of contraception and another report states that 54 percent of married women are using contraception (Ahmed, A.A., 1995:15). The local birth rate of 2.91 percent is still one of the highest in the world. There are other factors motivating high pregnancy rates, including certain segments of society who are having children simply to outnumber other segments of society for potential political gains.

A group of Bahraini intellectuals from several specialties organized the Bahraini Family Planning Association (B.F.P.A.) in 1975. Bahrain has the only F.P.A. in the Gulf and is one of fifteen in the Arab region with their regional headquarters in Tunis. There are 165 country associations in the world with their main office in London. There are approximately 200 active members in Bahrain promoting the association's work. A survey was conducted by the association in 1983 to test the attitude and knowledge of the population regarding contraception. This initial survey showed promising results, and the association has been active ever since. The association has facilitated other research by providing data, contacts, or support to researchers, and several theses have been completed (Al-Darazi, 1984,1986; Al-Gaseer, 1990). The B.F.P.A. contributed U.S. $10,000 towards the costs of the 1996 National Family Health Survey of 5,000 randomly selected Bahrain families, including 26,000 individuals. The survey was sponsored by the Gulf Cooperation Council Ministers of Health and the U.N.D.P. The questionnaire included items relating to reproduction and sexual health. The report with analysis is expected in 1997.

The funding for the B.F.P.A. organization comes in part from funds redistributed by the B.F.P.A. Central Committee to countries around the world. The local president is on the B.F.P.A. Board, the Central Committee, and the Budget Committee. Other funds come from donations by local individuals, various institutions, and the Government, i.e., Ministry of Labor and Social Affairs. Contraceptive aids are given by the B.F.P.A. to the Ministry of Health for distribution to families in the Primary Health Clinics, Salmaniya Medical Center, or the Maternity Hospitals. The B.F.P.A. also accepts gifts of clothes and other items, which are distributed to needy families. Annual reports are prepared at the local, regional, and federation levels describing activities of the association.

The activities of the B.F.P.A. are geared toward increasing public awareness of the types of contraceptives available for family planning. There is no local opposition; however, an occasional non-Bahraini will raise opposition to their work. The association provides lectures to representatives of local groups who then go back and talk with members of their respective group. The B.F.P.A. has videos, cassette tapes, and pamphlets, as well as a library at their association headquarters in Gafool. The current five-year plan has four main goals which the group is trying to reach, i.e., youth awareness, promotion of counseling and family planning, empowerment, and development of volunteerism and fund raising.

Family planning nurses working in Maternal-Child Health indicate that there has been a trend toward increasing use of tubal ligations and vasectomies for birth control, even among village residents. B.F.P.A. and the staff nurses state that people are better educated about their options for birth control, have the desire to space children, and many want to limit children out of economic necessity, e.g., due to the recession and no jobs. Nurses praise the support of the Bahrain Family Planning Association and their assistance in providing free contraceptives, and at times clothing or goods to needy families.

Free contraceptive aids are available from the Government at all the Primary Health Centers and at the Government hospitals for all Bahrain's residents. Free tubal ligations and vasectomies are likewise available and are being used increasingly by older couples as a means of birth control. Health education courses regarding contraception are presented at the Government Primary Health Care Centers and videotapes are also available. The *1993 Annual Report for Primary Health Care in Bahrain* notes that "due to religious beliefs and traditional attitudes," a total of 4,573 visits were made during 1992 for family planning services. Out of these visits, 2,917 women initiated a contraception method, and 263 received IUDs. A total of 8,660 women received family planning counseling sessions, which was 7.8 percent of females in the child-bearing age (Fouzi Amin, 1993). A study conducted in one Health Center in the United Arab Emirates included 908 women between 15 to 44, and 50 percent of them were using some means of contraception (Blankensee et al., 1995).

Many doctors discuss birth control options including sterilization with grand multigravida (more than eight to ten children) and high-risk patients (those with repeated Cesarean sections and other complications) at the time of delivery. Doctors document when the patient refuses to have a procedure, or has signed a sterilization permit. After delivery, the doctors indicate if the patient has requested some form of birth control and what choice was made. The doctors' personal beliefs play a factor in whether birth control options such as a tubal ligation are even mentioned. Some couples, after making their own choice, may be told by a doctor that their choice to have a tubal ligation is *haraam* (forbidden). More assertive and more educated couples will find another doctor, while others may be ashamed or afraid to discuss this matter with another doctor. There are no institutional ethical standards to guide physicians regarding this matter, or to suggest that they refer couples to another doctor who is willing to discuss such matters. If a woman is declared unfit, e.g., mentally retarded or unfit to be a mother, the family can request she be sterilized.

Condoms are sold openly in grocery stores and pharmacies. There are many private clinics in Bahrain, and three private hospitals, where birth control information and supplies are available for a fee.

Data on birth control practices of the various expatriate populations are not reported. Misconceptions regarding pregnancy abound, and some Indian girls are prohibited by teachers and parents from swimming in coed pools for fear they will get pregnant. The knowledge of Syrian, Jordanian, Palestinian, and Beluchi women has not been studied, and they are the expatriates having the largest families.

B. Teenage Pregnancies (Unmarried)

Although unmarried pregnancies occur, their incidence and prevalence among Bahrainis and non-Bahrainis, and teenagers specifically, are not known. A Bahraini girl/woman and her family will try to cover up such a scandalous incident. Male informants all knew of women "in trouble," while female informants rarely knew of anyone.

Teenage pregnancies are not a major problem as seen in the West, because a girl's behavior is strictly monitored by her parents. A girl, from the time she is ten to twelve, is kept close at home when not in school. Even if she attends the University, her parents know where she is and her daily schedule. Most girls are married after completion of *Tawyehi* or college, and some later even in their thirties; however until she is married, a girl is expected to live at home. A Kuwaiti researcher supports this perception that "illegitimate pregnancy is a problem of small dimension in Moslem societies" (Hathout, 1979). No objective data are available on this topic.

The children of unmarried women, in the early part of the twentieth century, were at times murdered with the girl by family members (Belgrave 1960:101-102). Other infants were abandoned on municipal rubbish dumps, *Samadah*, at the corners of streets, or placed outside the hospital (Belgrave, 1960:103). Some of these foundlings were looked after in the American Mission Orphanage. Others were cared for in the Government hospital, and very often foundlings were taken in by women who had no family. Another view was noted by Charles Belgrave who wrote that "for the children there was very little stigma in illegitimacy" (1960:103). He said he knew several young men "who were proud of belonging to important families, though on the wrong side of the blanket."

Currently four to six abandoned children a year are referred to the Children's Home. The number of expatriate women and maids becoming pregnant is not known, as many return to their homes to deliver. Rare cases are reported in the media, e.g., an expatriate maid delivered a child which died and the body was buried in the garden, and later a child in the family uncovered the body while playing. In this case, the expatriate woman was deported. Other newspaper reports note court cases where, for example, a young boy found a dead baby wrapped in a cloth outside the home, and he told his mother who alerted the Police Station.

C. Abortion

Abortions are provided in Bahrain only under strict religious regulations, i.e., a person cannot decide to have an abortion because of lack of birth control or an unwanted birth or rape. Abortions for these reasons are illegal. One study was conducted in Kuwait on "unwantedness," so it is a phenomenon seen in the Gulf. In Kuwait, the women tried to induce abortion with medicines, violent exercise, or mechanical interference (Hathout, 1979). Objective data on this topic is not available for Bahrain.

A medically indicated abortion allowable by Sharia Law can be obtained in a government hospital, usually before three months, if the fetus has been found to be deformed, or with a congenital defect detected through ultrasound, amniocentesis, or other tests. Early abortions can also be performed if the pregnancy poses a threat to the life of the mother, and early deliveries are done if the woman has life-threatening conditions such as PET or placenta previa. The justification for these abortions is to save the woman's life and to preserve the family, as she has other children to care for, and "she is the root of the family while the fetus is the branch which is sacrificed to save the root" (Hathout, 1979). In the case of the fetus with a defect, the rationale for abortion reportedly is to prevent suffering.

The attitude to abortion, especially in the case of an unmarried pregnancy, varies from liberal, "Why didn't she have an abortion when she was outside the country?" to very conservative, "She had an abortion outside and this needs to be reported to the religious police." Some informants report that the majority of unmarried Bahraini women have abortions outside the country due to the shame (*ayeb*) of an illegitimate birth. Illegal abortions do occur in Bahrain. Informants reported, "She drank some liquid and had an abortion." Others report, "She was told to take seven to eight birth control pills for three days, but it did not work." Nurses report this latter method is seen and is effective. Some individuals try other self-induced methods which are more dangerous, including dilatation of the cervix, and insertion of items into the uterus. A Filipina abortionist was caught operating in Bahrain in 1995 after a Saudi client became septic due to the abortion and during interrogation revealed the abortionist to the police. All the considerable money the abortionist had in her bank account was confiscated by the Bahrain Government and she was deported.

D. Population Policy

The population growth of Bahrain is 2.9 percent, which is one of the highest in the world. The effect of this high population growth, and its effect on the country's growth and development, has been discussed in many reports and in the media. There is currently no government policy to educate people regarding the need to reduce population growth. All informants stated that there is no policy that women should be encouraged to use some means of birth control or to have a tubal ligation after so many children, e.g., four.

The Government has instituted a fee of BD100 (U.S.A. $265.00) for all expatriates who deliver in government facilities and who are non-entitled workers, or the spouses of non-entitled workers. This may be an indirect means of discouraging expatriate births, or a way of controlling their spacing. For many expatriates to pay BD100 a year out of a monthly salary of BD60-80 is a great burden. Likewise, the Government requires male workers to be making a minimal salary of BD250 before they can bring their families to Bahrain. Another means of controlling the number of expatriates and their burden on the health service is to deny residence visas for elderly relatives (over 65). Generally, work visas for government jobs are not given to expatriates over 60 to 65 years for men and 55 years for women.

Premarital counseling is encouraged by the Government and is provided free in the Primary Health Centers and government hospitals. In 1992, 545 couples received premarital counseling and among them, eighty-nine abnormal findings were detected (Fouzi Amin, 1993:27). Premarital counseling is being encouraged, but is not yet required among Bahrainis because of the high incidence of first cousin marriage (39 percent) and the high frequency of genes for blood disorders in the population, including sickle cell disease, G6PD deficiency, a variety of major and minor thalassemias (Nadkarni et al., 1991), as well as other congenital anomalies (Sheikha Al-Arrayed, 1996).

Other Arab countries, such as Egypt, have population control slogans such as "look around." Other Islamic countries, such as Pakistan and Iran, have developed programs to educate people to limit their families to two or three children. Bahrain has no public policy to date. Approximately 0.1 percent of the recent Ministry of Health budget has been spent on family planning, while 0.2 percent has been spent on control of illegal drugs, and 0.3 percent on medical exams of newly hired expatriate workers (*1991 Ministry of Health Report*).

10. Sexually Transmitted Diseases (STDs)

A. Incidence, Patterns and Trends of STDs

Venereal diseases were reported by the first American missionaries who arrived in Bahrain in the late 1890s and early 1900s (Rajab, 1979). The missionary doctors were able to test for gonorrhea in the early 1900s and found it was a common disease. Venereal disease in 1914 ranked next to malaria (Patterson, 1914). A high proportion of the population was suffering from the ophthalmic form of gonorrhea which was rampant according to the *Government of Bahrain Administrative Report* for 1926-1937, and the

Bahrain Government Annual Reports 1926-1960. Venereal infections ranked high, along with smallpox, malaria, dysentery, and trachoma.

Tracking of a second STD was started after a definite diagnosis for syphilis was possible by 1933-34 at the American Mission Hospital's Laboratory (1933-34:9). During the 1940s, there were over a thousand cases treated annually, and by 1948, venereal infections had spread even more, and 200 patients were treated as inpatients and 1,200 as outpatients. At that time, the Government took certain stern measures against foreign women of loose character (Al-Khalifa, 1982). Venereal infections started coming down after the introduction of new medicines, and Bahrain was the pioneer for the whole region in developing an infrastructure to improve health care. In 1952, the Public Health Department (P.H.D.) was separated out as a distinct entity, and its statistics show that after 1965, venereal infection trends are greatly reduced from the 1940s (Al-Khalifa 1982:219). The P.H.D. laboratory is the preferred lab for testing blood samples of infectious diseases and all positive samples are sent to them for confirmation and follow-up of personal contacts.

The incidence of STDs has been studied mainly in relation to their effect on urinary tract infections and antibiotic drug resistance (Yousef et al., 1991), infertility, and impotence, rather than the epidemiology of their occurrence and relationship to various types of sexual activity.

The overall frequency of male urethritis and STDs in Bahrain is low, 108/100,000 (541/500,000) versus 1,600/100,000 in the USA, however the isolates of *Nisseria gonorrhea* found are often highly resistant or show diminished sensitivity to penicillin (Yousef et al., 1991:94). The number of gonorrhea cases peaked in 1980 to over 600 cases/year. The 1994 figures were the same as 1990 (379 to 380 cases/year). Gonococcal infections in 1994 ranked third after influenza and chicken pox. In contrast to Bahrain's statistics, the first case of *Nisseria gonorrhea* in a pregnant Saudi woman was only reported in 1988 (Abdul Khaliq and Smith, 1988).

Syphilis cases reported to the P.H.D. in Bahrain have been increasing since 1990 from 37 to 104 cases in 1994 (*Statistical Abstracts 1994*). These rates (0.019 percent) are low in comparison to other parts of the Middle East and may reflect reporting inconsistencies or treatment outside Bahrain. A seven-year study conducted in Saudi Arabia on 90 percent of hospital births (Saudis and non-Saudis) showed an increase from 0.2 percent to 1.5 percent overall incidence of syphilis in 1986 (Abbas and Satwekar, 1989). This rate is high in comparison to European statistics, but lower than other Middle East and African data. Endemic syphilis is prevalent in the Middle East, and all cases of syphilis are treated as infectious until proven otherwise. Up to 20 percent of adult Bedouins in Saudi Arabia have been exposed to endemic syphilis *bejel* (Abbas and Satwekar, 1989). Secondary syphilis symptoms may be the first noted and treated. In Saudi Arabia, this has been reported by Basri and Smith (1991). In one case, the husband was being treated in a VD clinic but did not tell either of his wives, and one wife was never brought for treatment. In another case, a Somali bisexual had many sexual contracts, and in the third case the patient denied any extramarital contacts. A problem in Saudi Arabia which is difficult to overcome, is tracking of contacts. The first case of congenital syphilis was reported in Kuwait in 1987 (Hariri and Helin, 1987).

The seroprevalence of chlamydial infections was shown to be 44 percent of 100 pregnant women randomly screened in Bahrain. This suggests a high prevalence of chlamydial disease in the population, although some of the antibody-positive cases may be due to old ocular infections (Rajab et al., 1995). The USA average is 3 to 5 percent, and 15 to 20 percent in an STD clinic. In Saudi Arabia, the rates ranged from 10 percent of women seen in a gynecology clinic to 30.6 percent of men attending an STD clinic. Chlamydia overall accounted for 11 percent of all gynecological infections seen in one Saudi Arabian hospital (Qadri et al., 1993). Another study in a Saudi Arabian STD clinic showed 46 percent of males and 36 percent of female were affected, while 2 percent of men and none of the women attending a Primary Health Care clinic were affected (Qadri et al. 1993). Genital forms in Saudi Arabia were estimated at 38.4 percent and ocular forms at 61.6 percent. Chlamydial infections can be a cause of blindness, and is a familiar disease, especially where there is overcrowding, large numbers of children, lack of water, and poor hygiene. The prevalence of people with and without overt genital disease is higher in Saudi Arabia than in developed countries, but similar to rates seen in Bahrain. The role of chlamydia in female infertility due to blocked tubes was reported by Babag and Al-Mesbar (1993), who state that chlamydia is high in the Saudi Arabian population, but significantly higher in infertile women.

Hepatitis B is now classified as a sexually transmitted disease. The percentage of the Bahrain population affected is 2 percent (Mahnon and Fernandez, 1972). This incidence is higher in Saudi Arabia (14 percent) and 9 percent in Oman (Al-Dhahry et al., 1994). Saudi Arabia and Oman have high endemicity of hepatitis B, while Bahrain has more hepatitis C (4.7 percent) versus Saudi Arabia (0.2. to 5.0 percent) (Bakir, 1992). Currently, hepatitis C is not classified as an STD. A study on the risk of transmission of hepatitis B infection among family members in Bahrain showed a transmission rate of 26 percent (Parida and Effendi, 1994).

Human papiloma virus (HPV) is a sexually transmitted agent which has been shown to have a strong relationship with neoplasms of the female genitalia. One study showed the rate of infection among 25- to 35-year-old women in Bahrain to be 63 percent (Sunderaj, 1990).

B. Treatment for STDs

Treatment for STDs is provided free to all Bahrainis; however, due to the nature of the disease and its social implications, people generally attend private clinics, see consultants in the private hospitals, or even attend clinics outside Bahrain for treatment. There is a specialized private venereal disease clinic in the Gudaibiya area.

Prevention of spread of STDs through tracking of sexual contacts is a problem in the Middle East (Basri and Smith, 1991). Affliction with VD is seen as a sign of low morality, so patients vehemently deny any extramarital affairs. The men may not tell even their wives they are being treated. The men may have had casual sex (as seen in Saudi studies) while overseas, so their contacts are unknown and are lost. The Bahrain Public Health Department tries to determine all contacts. Other forms of prevention include vaccinating all newborns in Bahrain for hepatitis B according to WHO guidelines to prevent a burden later in the health care system. Other prevention efforts include public education lectures, programs in the media, and other methods. These programs do not include the incidence of these diseases in Bahrain nor their prevalence in the various ethnic groups, but mainly stress the need to make a general concerted effort to prevent them by good moral behavior.

One direct method for prevention of STDs has been tried in Bahrain, as in other Arab countries. During the late 1980s, the Jordanian Government started handing all single male travelers a card warning about the dangers of AIDS. Likewise in Kuwait, information pamphlets are distributed at the airport warning travelers about the dangers of sexual diseases outside the country. As many Arab men take single or male-only group vacations to the Far East and Europe, such prevention problems were instituted by several Arab countries. Traveling Bahrainis state that at the Bahraini Airport, pamphlets on STDs are likewise distributed, but men report this is not on a consistent or daily basis as in other countries. Another direct way of prevention, by prohibiting sex vacations, was in effect for awhile. Visas were required to travel to certain countries, e.g., Thailand. These restrictions have since been lifted.

There are Bahraini men who regularly travel to Thailand, Philippines, Hong Kong, or elsewhere for sex vacations. Some are unmarried, others married. Informants have reported that one single man was asked, "Aren't you afraid of contracting some disease?" he responded by saying, "God's will." He could not be convinced of the unsafe nature of his activities. Another married man makes two trips a year. When he was asked about safe sex, he shrugged his shoulders. Another man, a well educated and highly paid professional, would make Asian trips and repeatedly return with ophthalmic infections and expected his doctor to cure him again. The incidence of these trips is not known, nor how many use "safe sex" during these encounters. There are Bahraini women having affairs in Bahrain, usually in hotels or flats, as well as abroad. The number who have contracted STDs due to an affair have not been studied or reported. The annual number of venereal cases published by the Government does not distinguish among Bahraini and non-Bahrainis, nor do they make any distinction among those who contracted the STD from their husband or wife, through a local affair, or an affair abroad. There are no statistics regarding how many are divorced or unmarried and living on their own versus individuals living in parental homes. All this information is needed to detect trends and to plan effective prevention programs.

11. HIV/AIDS

A. Incidence, Patterns, and Trends

Doctors in Bahrain were first alerted in 1985 to the new disease called AIDS (*flocks al mana'ah al mukta sabah*), and lectures were given in 1989 and 1990. The first public reports on the occurrence of HIV in the population appeared in 1990. At that time, 95 percent of the HIV carriers reportedly were drug users, and 5 percent had received organs or blood outside the country (Fulafel, 1990). The latter group going to India have a risk of 1:12 of HIV seroconversion following transplantation in Bombay, based on figures from other Gulf countries (Al-Dhahry 1994:314).

HIV testing is done in government facilities. No consent is obtained from individuals before testing. Now all conscripts into the Bahrain military and civilian employees of the military are tested for HIV, HBV, HCV, sickle cell disease, G6PD deficiency, and other relevant factors depending on family history and country of origin. Staff are tested upon employment and during retroactive screening regimens. Patients attending the Shaikh Khalifa Bin Mohammed Al Khalifa Cardiac Center for any invasive procedure are all routinely checked for blood-borne viral diseases. Expatriates positive for HIV will not be treated at the Cardiac Center unless they have an emergency condition, and like all positive expatriates, will be sent to their home country immediately under Public Health Laws. Other hospital and clinic patients, excluding dialysis patients, are not routinely tested, and are checked based on the nature of their current signs and symptoms. If an HIV-positive result is returned, generally elective surgical procedures are canceled.

Expatriate workers recruited for all government health care facilities are tested, as well as maids, cooks, and beauticians who are processed through recruitment agencies and hired to work in Bahrain. Bahrain does not require an "AIDS-free certificate" for all expatriates, including wives and children, taking up residence before their arrival in the country, unlike Kuwait and Saudi Arabia, which require all expatriates taking up residence in the country to be HIV-free. The United Arab Emirates Health Department screens everyone in the country for HIV on a periodic basis as their expatriate work force comprises 70 percent of the population. Over 1,600 HIV-positive cases have been detected to date in the U.A.E., with the majority of cases detected among Asian expatriates who were deported.

HIV Incidence Among Newborns, Children, and Adults

HIV-positive status is seen among newborns in Bahrain. The incidence is not known, as women and babies are not being screened as done in 37 states in the USA, and elsewhere. The suspected rate of infection at the time of birth, or later from breast feeding is not known, nor the number of newborns who later revert to HIV-negative status.

Children of various ages have been detected positive for HIV and have died from AIDS. The first AIDS death in Bahrain in the 1980s was a child infected through a blood transfusion given abroad. The known routes of HIV transmission have been vertical, mother to child, and from blood transfusions received abroad. Infections from sexual abuse have not been revealed to date if such data are known. The rate of horizontal transmission among family members is also not known. A few adolescent HIV and AIDS cases have been seen in health care facilities.

The incidence of HIV infections among adults has been reported by the Government. More men than women have tested HIV-positive. The proportion of Bahrainis versus expatriates is not clearly indicated in the Government data. In 1991, according to Ministry of Health figures, 0.09 percent out of 7,374 blood donors were positive and 0.01 percent of 8,173 reporting for their preemployment physical exam. The trends show an increasing number of reported cases each year for men and women. All expatriates who test positive for HIV are deported according to the Government's Public Health rules (as are those with hepatitis B and C, tuberculosis, and leprosy). The potential drain of these expatriate individuals on health care funds, and the possibility of cross infection to others, are the rationale of the Government enforcement of deportation rules.

There are three main patterns of HIV infection seen among men. Intravenous drug users comprise the largest number. During the late 1980s, government media releases indicated IV drug use was the primary known source of HIV infection among men (Fulafel, 1990). Heterosexual, bisexual, or homosexual activities, including multiple sex partners in Bahrain or abroad, e.g., India, Thailand, Philippines, and Western countries, are the second source. Blood transfusions abroad, in countries where blood is not routinely tested, e.g., India, Philippines, remains a third route of infection.

There is a long history of hard drug use among men in Bahrain. Iranian opium was marketed between Iran, London, and Hong Kong by the British trading ships of the East India Company during the late nineteenth century and into the early twentieth century. Some opium was shipped to Bahrain via dhows. Opium was sold in herb shops in Manama called *Abdareen* shops. These sales continued during the 1920s and 1930s. There was widespread use among those of Persian descent, Beluchis, and Indians. People usually smoked opium, but as their tolerance developed, they began taking it orally. One man used to see his relative putting three to four pieces of opium in his mouth and drinking it with tea. Unlike the other groups, the Arabs only used opium for medicinal purposes to treat headache or stomach ache, and it was given in small quantities diluted in milk to put a child to sleep.

The use of opium later declined in the early 1940s when it was outlawed and became a controlled substance. Then new types of drugs, including IV drugs became prevalent. A study from 1980 to 1984 showed an annual increase in cases of drug involvement and narcotics dependence (Mattar, 1985). In 1991, the Bahrain courts heard 197 drug-related cases involving 433 drug users or traffickers of several nationalities.

Currently, drug use is strictly controlled and there are frequent arrests at the airport, mainly of expatriates who try to bring in heroin, opium, and hashish (marijuana). Other drug caches of heroin have been found at sea hanging on buoys. Occasionally, someone is caught, usually an expatriate trying to bring in drugs via the Saudi Causeway. In spite of controls at all ports of entry, supplies of drugs are readily available on the Island. School principals have openly told students what places to avoid, as they are known for drug sales. People report having relatives who are IV users of hard drugs. Money is given to them by family members to purchase drugs. Others may rob to support this habit. The Government newspapers every week contain information about court hearings for drug use, drugs confiscated at the airport, drug sales, or drug-related deaths—all among men. The incidence of these drug hauls is reported by the Ministry of the Interior. The incidence and prevalence of IV drug use among the population is not reported, but it is a major factor in HIV transmission in the country. Narcotics Anonymous has a local chapter, and reformed addicts attend, speak at local seminars, and give public lectures upon request. They talk about the twelve-step rehabilitation program and how it helped them, once they admitted they were addicted to drugs.

The extent of bisexual activities and the danger of HIV transmission due to these unsafe sex contacts has implications on the future health of the women to whom these men are married and their offspring. The frequency of interaction among homosexual and bisexual men is not known, however anecdotal stories show that Bahraini men have been known to have Western expatriate lovers in Saudi Arabia, and elsewhere, unknown to their Bahraini wives. Also, naive young women sometimes discuss their personal relations with coworkers, including their husbands' practices during intercourse, e.g., "needing a cucumber in his rectum."

The patterns of HIV infection among women in Bahrain differ from men. Their numbers are very low. The early cases in the 1980s were seen among women who contracted the virus during operations abroad, or from blood transfusions, e.g., from India. Their positive status many times was discovered when the patient attended a hospital for another procedure. More recently, women are being infected during heterosexual activities with their husbands or a lover; fortunately, these cases are rare to date. Transmission of HIV infection from a wife to her husband has occurred, but these cases are also rare.

Among health care workers, there have been no documented cases of HIV contracted through blood contact or sharp injuries. However, several cases and deaths due to hepatitis B and hepatitis C infections from patients are known in the community. The practice of deporting the HIV-positive expatriates, and deaths of some Bahrain patients from AIDS, has kept the known number of HIV cases in Bahrain below 200 for the last ten years. The published cases of AIDS are listed as 20 (Wahdan, 1995)

If there are data kept on the incidence of HIV among homosexuals, lesbians, and bisexual persons, they are not published, nor are they in the public domain.

B. Availability of Treatment, Prevention, and Government Policy

The Government of Bahrain provides free health care for all Bahrainis who are HIV carriers. Government workers must provide care for these individuals, and doctors are aware of all current treatments available abroad. All experimental medications are not available in the country; prophylactic antibiotics to prevent *Pneumocystis carrini* are available.

Regarding expatriates, the Government policy regarding HIV/AIDS includes the following:

1. Recruiting agencies need to test workers in certain service areas in their home countries, including maids, beauticians, cooks, and health care workers. In Saudi Arabia and Kuwait, all seeking residence, not just workers, are tested prior to arrival.
2. The above categories of workers are retested after arrival.
3. All expatriates found positive for HIV, HBV, or HCV are deported.
4. All expatriates who are later tested and found positive are deported.
5. There is no scheduled testing for all the inhabitants of the country. (Countrywide testing has been conducted in the UAE and Kuwait).
6. Local drug users who test positive are incarcerated if their behavior shows they are a risk to others, or upon the request of concerned family members.

Research regarding the topic of HIV is scanty. The Government conducted one study in the late 1980s regarding the population's knowledge about AIDS. The majority reported it was "an expatriate problem." Another study was conducted among military conscripts, and it showed the men knew about the disease, but some were unclear about transmission routes and prevention measures (Parida, 1992). A study conducted by medical students showed that only 5.9 percent of Bahrainis understood the modes of transmission for AIDS, and 32.2 percent believed it could be cured (Chand, n.d.). Obviously, more public health education is needed regarding the topic. A 1995 study on nurses' knowledge about AIDS has not been reported to date. In 1995, the Government announced appointments to a National AIDS Committee.

The United Nations resident coordinator and UN Development Program (UNDP) resident representative, Dr. Faysal Abdul Gadir, has been outspoken regarding shying away from the AIDS threat:

> Once again there is the problem of people not acknowledging that in fact it is a problem. . . . Forget for a minute the sociocultural view that it is impossible to contract it due to religious and social regulations. The reality is people are contracting the disease and we can't close our eyes and say it is the problem of industrial and non-Moslem countries. We cannot say it is irrelevant to us. It will mean a drain on the budget as the State will have to take care of each patient until he dies. (Gadir, 1996)

Lectures are provided occasionally to the public on HIV and AIDS in the Government Health Centers and videos are also shown. The Ministry of Health has distributed booklets in Arabic about AIDS. Indirectly, the Government provides knowledge about AIDS though the choice of movies shown on government controlled television channels (Arabic and English). The WHO sponsored an AIDS-awareness day in 1995. Discoveries of the latest AIDS advances are sometimes published in the local government-controlled newspapers (Arabic and English). During the 1996 Ninth International AIDS Conference, daily updated information was printed in the local English-language newspaper.

Public education about the dangers of AIDS is not provided on a continuing basis. There are no active government media programs, such as the public service advertisements seen on the television in the UK, USA, or other countries. There are no large posters shown on hoardings (signboards), or at bus stops or public malls as seen in India, Hong Kong, and Botswana. There are no notices about safe sex, or clean needles on the doors of pubic toilet stalls, or at the airport like you see in Australia or Hong Kong. The overall health education budget for the Ministry of Health in 1991 was 0.1 percent of the total budget or U.S. $120,000.00 (BD 56,229,000) for education regarding all areas.

12. Sexual Dysfunction

A. Definition of Sexual Dysfunction

The definition of sexual dysfunction can be based on the patient's perception and/or on underlying organic and psychological causes. There have been no reports published in the Bahrain medical journals on this topic, although various lectures on related topics have been presented.

B. Availability of Diagnosis and Treatment

The patients' perception of sexual dysfunction needs to be assessed accurately by urologists and other health care professionals. In some cases, the individual who is normal may be comparing himself to what others say they are capable of performing, e.g., intercourse once a week versus three times a day (E. Amin, 1994). Many patients are reluctant to describe sexuality and sexual aspects of their marriage, as seen in the study among primary health care patients conducted by Kahtanie (1992). Once a psychological basis for sexual dysfunction is diagnosed, the patients are referred to the psychiatrist if they agree. Many patients in Bahrain and the Gulf do not seek psychiatric help until their difficulties become more prominent and continuous and interfere with their marital or social life (Al-Khani and Arafa, 1990). Acceptance of psychiatric referrals has increased dramatically during the last ten years, although education level and perception of any shame associated with psychiatry still inhibit individuals getting the help they may need. Bahrain provides free psychiatric service for anyone in the country, and the Psychiatric Hospital and outpatient clinics are well staffed with highly trained Arabic- and English-speaking Bahraini and expatriate male and female doctors.

Individuals with addictions whose behavior is erratic, including their sexual activities, can receive free psychiatric treatment and can attend addiction clinics or drug detoxification programs. There are also long standing, self-help groups, such as Alcoholics Anonymous (held at American Mission Hospital), and a new local chapter of Narcotics Anonymous (founded in 1996). There are known cases where addicted individuals having HIV continued to be irresponsible in their sexual behavior, and their families asked to have them placed in jail to control them in the interest of the public welfare and prevention of cross infection.

Organic causes of sexual dysfunction are varied and their incidence is rising. The incidence of congenital anomalies in Bahrain is 20 percent. This figure is based on the 80 percent of deliveries which are conducted in the Ministry of Health facilities (excluding the military and private hospitals, and home births). Anomalies of the genitourinary system rank second at 2.5/1,000 after musculoskeletal at 2.8/1,000 (Al-Arrayed, 1987). This rate is lower than 21.6/1,000 in Al-Ain and 12.9/1,000 in Abu Dhabi, and 6.6-8.5 /1,000 in Saudi Arabia (Topley and Dowda, 1995). The author notes that all malformations, based on international studies, may not be noted at birth (only 43 percent), or during the first six months (82 percent). Other problems are noted later, especially those of a sexual nature, which may be detected only during adolescence, or later after marriage.

Organic causes of sexual problems seen in Bahrain and the Gulf area include undescended testis, hypospadias (Al-Arrayed, 1987), webbed penis (Husa and Al-Samarrai, 1990), intersex disorders requiring gender reassignment such as Turner's Syndrome, Kleinfelter's Syndrome, and XX genotype females/phenotype males, and XY women (Al-Arrayed, 1996). Expert surgical help is available, as well as penile prosthesis implants. Endocrinologists can provide adjuvant hormonal therapy, as needed. Clinical psychologists or psychiatrists can provide counseling for individuals and/or their families on gender identification and possible social outcomes. In order to prevent the continual rise in occurrence of organic causes of sexual dysfunction among the young, doctors are recommending genetic counseling for individuals before marriage and after birth of an affected child. A genetic counseling group clinic has been established; however participation is voluntary. Screening on 515 couples in a Health Center showed that among them, 89 had abnormal findings detected (Fouzi Amin, 1993). A similar recommendation for genetic counseling was made in Kuwait (Telbi, 1988).

13. Research and Advanced Education

There are no institutes or programs for sexological research in the State of Bahrain. Nor are there any post-college or graduate-level programs for the advanced study of human sexuality, or any sexological journals or periodicals. Occasionally, a related article will be published in the two national medical journals:

Bahrain Medical Bulletin. Editorial Officer. Box 32159, State of Bahrain. Tel: 0973-265 258; Fax: 0973-277 036

Journal of the Bahrain Medical Society. Editorial Office. Box 26136. Manama, State of Bahrain. Tel: 0973-742 666 (5-10 pm local time); Fax: 0973-715 559

There are also no national or regional sexological organizations among the six Gulf Cooperation Council member states (Bahrain, Saudi Arabia, Kuwait, Qatar, United Arab Emirates, and Oman). There is a Bahrain Sociologists Society, which has published a series of monographs in Arabic. Bibliographies available on Bahrain include:

Ailan, Redhy Mustafa. 1996. *Bibliography for Women in the State of Bahrain.* (In Arabic). Bahrain: Information Center for Women and Children.

Badu, Balghis, and Mary Awad. 1995. *Arab Women Bibliography: A Study Conducted in Eight Arab Countries.* Center for Arab Women Training and Research, Tunisia. (Includes French and English titles for Bahrain, Egypt, Jordan, Kuwait, Lebanon, Morocco, Palestine, Yemen; database to be updated annually.)

Davis, Gordon A. 1993. *Catalog of the Bahrain Historical and Archaeological Society Library.* (English titles). Bahrain: Historical and Archaeological Society, P.O. Box 5087, Juffair, Bahrain.

Manzer, Bruce. 1996. *BMED: An Index to Gulf Medical Journal Holdings in the Al Farsi Library (1979-1995).* Bahrain: Ministry of Health, Al-Farsi Library, College of Health Science, P.O. Box 12, Sulmaniya, Bahrain.

Sarhan, Mansoor Mohammed. 1995. *National Bibliography Vol. 1.* Fakhrawi Book Shop Printing & Publishing, Translation, Bahrain: P.O. Box 1643, Manama, Bahrain.

Statistical Abstracts 1994. 1995. State of Bahrain, Central Statistics Organization, Directorate of Statistics.

Information is available in English and Arabic on related topics in the following libraries:

Bahrain Family Planning Association Headquarters, Al-Qufool, Bahrain Tel: 0973-232233, 256622 Fax: 0973-276408

Al-Farsi Library, College of Health Sciences, P.O. Box 12, Ministry of Health, Al Sulmaniya, Bahrain. Tel: 0973 255555 ext. 5202 Fax: 0973 252569 Telex: 8511 HEALTH BN

References and Suggested Readings

Abbas, Samer M. A., and Sucheeta R. Satwekar. 1989. "Positive Treponematosis in Saudi Antenatals and Their Perinatal Outcome Over a 7-Year Period." *Saudi Medical Journal*, 10(4):301-304.

Abdul, Fawzi. 1995. "Penile Prosthesis: A Revolution in Treatment of Erectile Dysfunction." *The Journal of the Kuwait Medical Association*, 27(4):303-307.

Abdul, Hakeem H., and Hameed Saheb. 1990. *The Complete Book of Home Remedies.* New Delhi: Orient Paperbacks.

Abdul Jabbark F.A, M.A. Al-Meshari, M.A. Hafeez, and M.O. Malik. 1980. "Male Intersex XX: A Case Report." *Saudi Medical Journal*, 1(2):149151.

Adbul Khaliq, Suad A., and Eric L. Smith. 1988. "Gonoccaemia in Pregnancy: First Report of a Case in Saudi Arabia." *Saudi Medical Journal*, 9(1):86:88.

Abu Aisha, Hassan. 1985. "Women in Saudi Arabia: Do They Not Have the Right to Give Their Own Consent for Medical Procedures?" *Saudi Medical Journal*, 6(2):74-77.

Abu-Zaid, Abdul Aziz Umar. 1996. "Trade and Folk Medicine in Old Jeddah" (in Arabic). *Al- Ma'thurat Al Sha'biyyah: A Specialized Quarterly Review of Folklore*, (Qatar), 42 (April):82-96.

Ahmed, Ahdeya. 1996. "Strict Conditions Guide Polygamy." *Gulf Daily News* (English Edition), Bahrain, April 2, 1996:2.

Ahmed, Ahmed Abdulla. 1995. *An Overview of Health Services in Bahrain.* Bahrain: Ministry of Health Report.

Ahmed, Ahmed. 1996. "Jobs to Receive Priority." *Gulf Daily News* (English Edition), Bahrain, August 12, 1996:2.

"AIDS: 1985." *Bahrain Medical Bulletin*, 7(2):64.

Akhter, S.S., T. Filani, M. Gadella, and A. Al-Amir. 1995. "Beliefs and Attitudes about Breast Self Exam in Al-Qassim Region of Saudi Arabia: A Study of Women Attending Primary Health Care Clinics." *Saudi Medical Journal*, 16(6):493-497.

Al-A'Ali, Ebtihaj. 1991. *The Phenomenon of Women in Management: An Alternative Perspective and Implication in the Case of Bahrain.* Doctoral dissertation, University of Lancaster, United Kingdom.

Al-Ansari, Ahmed, and Batool Shubar. 1982. "The Child and Adolescent Psychiatric Population of Bahrain: Comparative Data." *Bahrain Medical Bulletin*, 4(3):83-87.

Al-Ansari, Ahmed, and Huda Al-Ansari. 1983. "Failure to Thrive." *Bahrain Medical Bulletin*, 5(1):23-26.

Al-Ansari, Ahmed Malalla. 1992. "Treatment Issues in Child Abuse and Neglect." *Journal of the Bahrain Medical Society*, 4(3):89.

Al-Arrayed, Ahmed S., and S. Chandra. 1996. "Prevalence of Antibodies to Hepatitis C Virus." *Journal of the Bahrain Medical Society*, 8(1):13-16.

Al-Arrayed, Sheikha. 1987. "Congenital Anomalies in Bahrain." *Bahrain Medical Bulletin*, 9(2):70-73.

Al-Arrayed, Sheikha Salim. 1995. "The Frequency of Consanguineous Marriages in the State of Bahrain." *Bahrain Medical Bulletin*, 17(3):63-67.

Al-Arrayed, Sheikha Salim. 1996. "Chromosomal Abnormalities in 500 Referred Cases in Bahrain." *Bahrain Medical Bulletin*, 18(1):2-4.

Al-Dabbous, Ibrahim A. 1991. "Priapism in Two Children with Sickle Cell Disease at Qateef Central Hospital." *Bahrain Medical Bulletin*, 13(3):1 04-106.

Al-Dabbous, I.A., and A.H. Al-Juma. 1993. "Priapism in Sickle Cell Disease in Qateef Central Hospital." *Saudi Medical Journal*, 14(5):440-442.

Al-Darazi, Fariba Abdulwahab. 1984. *Assessment of Bahraini Women's Health and Illness Cognitions and Practices.* Master of Arts thesis, University of Illinois, Chicago.

Al-Darazi, Fariba Abdulwahab. 1986. *Health and Illness Cognition Among Bahraini Women.* Doctoral dissertation, University of Illinois, Chicago.

Al-Dhahry, Said, Prabhakar Aghanashiniker, Harmoud Al-Marhuby, Meds Buhl, Abdullah Daar, and Mohammed Al-Husani. 1994. "Hepatitis B, Delta and Human Immunodeficiency Virus Infections Among Omani Patients with Renal Diseases: A Seroprevalence Study." *Annals of Saudi Medicine*, 14(4):312-315.

Al-Eissa, Y. A., et al. 1991. "The Battered Child Syndrome: Does It Exist in Saudi Arabia?" *Saudi Medical Journal*, 12(2):129-133.

Al-Falaij, Abduirahman Ali. 1991. *Family Conditions. Ego Development and Sociomoral Development in Juvenile Delinquency: A Study of Bahrain Adolescents.* Doctoral dissertation, University of Pittsburgh.

Al-Falaij, Abduirahman Ali. 1993. "Family Conditions, Ego Developmdnt and Sociomoral Development in Juvenile Delinquency: A Study of Bahrain Adolescents." *Journal of Bahrain Medical Society*, 5(3: 168).

Al-Faris, Eiad, Mona Al-Rajhi, and Mohammed Al-Nour. 1995. "Smoking Among Females Attending a Health Center in Riyadh, Saudi Arabia." *Annals of Saudi Medicine*, 15(5):525-527.

Al-Faruqi, Lamya. 1988. Women. *Muslim Society and Islam.* Plainfield, Indiana: American Trust Publications.

Al-Gaseer, Naeema. 1990. *The Experience of Menstrual Symptoms of Bahraini Women.* Doctoral dissertation, University of Illinois, Chicago.

Al-Ghamdi, H. 1986. "The Dynamic Forces in the Personalities of Juvenile Delinquency in the Saudi Arabian Environment." *Transcultural Psychological Research Review*, 23:248-250.

Al-Hariri, S., and 1. Helin. 1987. "Congenital Syphilis." *The Journal of the Kuwait Medical Association*, 21(4):335-338.

Al-Herbish, Abdulla S., Naser A. M. Al-Jurayyan, Abdulla M. Abo Bakr Mohammed, Ahmed Abdulla, Muneera Al-Husain, Abdulla A. Al-Rabeah, Pravinchandra J. Patel, Akram Jawad, and Asul I. Al-Samarrai. 1996. "Sex Reassignment: A Challenging Problemcurrent Medical and Islamic Guidelines." *Annals of Saudi Medicine*, 16(1):12-15.

Al-Jishi, A. 1982. *Bahrain Ministry of Interior Working Paper on Juvenile Delinquency.* Bahrain: Ministry of Interior Press.

Al-Khalifa, Abdulla bin Khalid. 1982. "The Inception and Development of Health Services in Bahrain." *Al-Watheeka (Journal of the Historical Documents Centre, State of Bahrain)*, 8 (Jan.):241-229.

Al-Khani, Mohammed, and Magdy M. Arafa. 1990. "Social Phobia in Saudi Patients." *Annals of Saudi Medicine*, 10(6):615-619.

Al-Khateeb. 1986. "Trends of Tobacco Smoking Among Physicians, Journalists and Teachers in Bahrain," *Bahrain Medical Bulletin*, 8(1):19-23.

Al-Malki, Noor. 1996. "The Superstitions of the Qatari people." *Al-Ma'thurat Al-Sha'biyyah: A Specialized Quarterly Review of Folklore* (Qatar), 42, (April):82-96.

Al-Naser, Yassa Essa. 1993. *Inequalities in Child Survival in Bahrain: The Role of Marriage Patterns in a Low Mortality Population.* Ph.D. dissertation, University of London.

Al-Mugeiren, Mohammed and Robert S. Genelin. 1990. "A Suspected Case of Munchausen's Syndrome by Proxy in a Saudi Child." *Annals of Saudi Medicines.* 10(6):662-665.

Al-Othman, Abdulla, and Mir Sadat-Ali. 1994. "Pattern of Pediatric Trauma Seen in a Teaching Hospital." *Bahrain Medical Bulletin,* 16(3):87-89.

Al-Quttan, Najeeba, and Alexander A. E. Omu. 1996. "The Pattern of Menopause in Kuwait and the Need for Hormone Replacement Therapy." *The Journal of the Kuwait Medical Association,* 28(2):152-157.

Al-Rashied, Abdullah A. 1988. "Introduction to the 'Battered Baby Syndrome'." *The Journal of the Kuwait Medical Association,* 22(3):193-194.

Al-Saleh, B. M. S., E. R. Ansari, I. H. Al-Ali, J. Y. Tell, and A. Saheb. 1985. "Fracture of the Penis Seen in Abu Dhabi." *Journal of Urology,* 134:274-275.

Al-Sharyan, Ahmed Ali. 1987. *The Cultural Division of Labour in Less Developed Countries: The Case of Bahrain.* Ph.D. dissertation, University of Exeter, UK.

Ali, Nadia. 1996. *Child Abuse.* M.A. Thesis: University of Texas, Austin.

Amin, Essa. 1979. "Statistics for Child Trauma." *Bahrain Medical Bulletin,* 5(2):19.

Amin, Essa. 1984. "Urological Problems of the Elderly." *Bahrain Medical Bulletin,* 6(1):29-30.

Amin, Essa. 1994. "Male Impotence." Monday Morning Doctors' Lecture Series. Bahrain Defence Force Hospital, April 11, 1994.

Amin, Farouq. 1982. *A Study of Bahrain's Family.* Bahrain: Government Press.

Amin, Fouzi. 1993. *Annual Report Primary Health Care.* Bahrain Ministry of Health, Primary Health Care.

Anthony, T.Ak 1984. *Documentation of the Modern History of Bahrain from American Sources 1900-1938: Historical Records of the American Mission,* New Brunswick, New Jersey. Al-Watheeka (Journal of the Historical Documents Centre, State of Bahrain), 4 (Jan.):243-229.

Arya, S.C. 1996. "Risk Factors in Acquiring Hepatitis C Infection in Saudi Arabia." *Annals of Saudi Medicine,* 16(2):229.

Asgari, M.A., et al. 1996. "Penile Fracture." *Journal of Urology,* 155:148-149.

Atallah, Nabih L., Nadia J. Sharkawi, and John J. Campbell. 1990. "Age at Menarche of School Girls in the Asir Region of Saudi Arabia with a Note on Adult Heights and Weights." *Saudi Medical Journal,* 11 (1):59-63.

Babag, Zainab A., and Adbulaziz Al-Mesbar. 1993. "The Role of Chlamydia Tranchomatis Infection in Infertility." *Annals of Saudi Medicine,* 13(5):423-428).

Baby, Soman. 1996a. "UN Praises Bahrain's Health Care." *Gulf Daily News* (English Edition), Bahrain, August 18, 1996:1.

Baby, Soman. 1996b. "Quality of Life in Bahrain Ranking Among the Best." *Gulf Daily News* (English Edition), Bahrain, August 18, 1996:2.

Badawi, Jamal A. 1980. *The Status of Women in Islam.* Plainfield, Indiana: MSA of US and Canada.

Bakir, T.M.F. 1992. "Age-Specific Prevalence of Antibody to Hepatitis C Virus (HCV) Among the Saudi Population." *Saudi Medical Journal,* 13(4):321 -324.

Basri, N.A., and E.L. Smith. 1991. "Three Cases of Secondary Syphilis Presenting in Different Departments." *Saudi Medical Journal,* 12(6):461 -463.

Belgrave, Charles H. 1960. *Personal Column.* London: Hutchinson and Co., Ltd.

Belgrave, Charles H. 1968. "Bahrain from Dhow to Discoteque." *Mid East,* 8 (May-June):32-37.

Belgrave, James H. 1975. *Welcome to Bahrain.* London: The Augustan Press.

Bin Hamad, Tahya, Emmanuel B. Larbi, and Jamila Absool. 1991. "Obesity in a Primary Health Centre: A Retrospective Study." *Annals of Saudi Medicine,* 11 (2):163-166.

Blanckensee, Diane J., Agnes M. Montague, Janine M. O'Keefe, Monica Steinback, and Jamil H. Ahsood. 1995. "Contraceptive Usage in UAE National Women." *Emirates Medical Journal*, 13:197-202.

Boserup, Ester. 1970. *Woman's Role in Economic Development.* London: George Allen and Unvin.

Bushiri, Ali Akbar. 1985-1986. "Dilmun Culture," *Dilmun (Journal of the Bahrain Historical and Archeological Society)*, 13:7-16.

Bushiri, Ali Akbar, and Gordon A. Davis. 1996. "Local Herbs Reputed to Have Aphrodisiac Powers." Unpublished manuscript.

Bushiri, Ali Akbar. 1992. *Dilmun Culture.* Bahrain: Ministry of Information, National Council for Culture, Arts and Literature.

Buzaboon, Bana Y. 1986. *A Study of Psychological and eNvironmental Factors Associated with Delinquency.* Doctoral dissertation, University of Wales.

Chaleby, K. 1982. "Traditional Arabian Marriage and Mental Health in a Group of Outpatients in Saudi Arabia." *Acta Psychiatry Scandinavia*, 77:139-142.

Chaleby, K. 1987. "Social Phobia in Saudi." *Social Psychiatry*, 22:167- 170.

Chand, Indira. n.d. "New AIDS Awareness Campaign Urged." *Gulf Daily News* (English Edition), Bahrain.

Curtis, Jerry L. 1977. *Bahrain: Language Customs and People.* Singapore: Tun Wah Press.

Dickson, H.R.P. 1915. *The Arab of the Desert: A Glimpse into Badawin Life in Kuwait and Sau'di Arabia.* London: n.p.

Doorenbos, H. 1976. "Postpartum Salt Packing and Other Medical Practices: Oman, South Arabia," In *Medical Anthropology*, Francis X. Grollig and H.R. Halley, eds. pp. 109-111. Paris: Mouton Publishers.

Duwaigher, Safia Muhammed. 1964. *Development of Women's Education in Bahrain.* Master's thesis, American University, Beirut.

El-lslam, M.F. 1974. "Hospital Referred Parasuicide in Qatar." *Egyptian Journal of Mental Health*, 15:101-112.

El-lslam, M.F. 1982. "Arabic Cultural Psychiatry." *Transcultural Psychiatry Research Review*, 19:5-21.

El-lslam, M.F. 1984. "Cultural Change and Intergenerational Relationships in Arab Families." *International Journal of Family Psychiatry*, 4:55-63.

El-Rufaie, Omer E., Abdul A. Al-Quorain, Faten A. Azzoni, and Suzan S. Al-Khalifa. 1991. "Emotional Aspects of Functional Abdominal Pain." *Saudi Medical Journal*, 11(6):450-452.

El-Sherif, A.E., W. Dauleh, N. Allowneh, and P.V. Jayan. 1991. "Management of Fracture of the Penis in Qatar." *British Journal of Urology*, 68:622-625.

Emura, M.K., N. Abdulla, A. Saudah, A.R. Al-Asfoor, and M.E. El-lslam. 1988. "Attempted Suicide by Drug Overdose in Kuwait." *Saudi Medical Journal*, 9:182-187.

Fakhro, Ali M. 1991. "Health Promotion Policies." *Bahrain Medical Bulletin*, 13(2):47-48.

Falafel, R.A. 1990. "AIDS: A Moral Issue or Public Hazard." *Journal of the Bahrain Medical Society*, 2(2):53-55.

Faroughy, Abbas. 1951. *The Bahrein Islands (750-1951): A Contribution to the Study of Power Politics in the Persian Gulf.* New York: Verry, Fisher and Company, Inc.

Farsi, Hasan M. Ali, Hisham A. Mosli, Mohammed M. Rawas, Tawriq N. Rehamy, and Sami A. Hemdi. 1990. "Persistent Mullerian Duct Syndrome in an Adult: A Case Report." *Annuals of Saudi Medicine*, 10(3):330-332.

Felimban, F. M. 1993. "The Smoking Practices and Attitudes Towards Smoking of Female University Students in Riyadh." *Saudi Medical Journal*, 14(3):220-224.

Gadir, Faysal Abdul. 1996. "Gulf Cannot Afford to Ignore AIDS Threat." *Gulf Daily News* (English Edition), Bahrain, July 19, 1996:1

"Girl Circumcision Ban." 1996. *Gulf Daily News* (English Edition), Bahrain. July 19, 1996:5
Goode, William J. 1962. *World Revolution and Family Patterns.* Glencoe, Illinois: The Free Press, Collier MacMillan, Ltd.
Gravesen, Roy. G. 1987. "Sexual Responsibilities of Physicians." *Bahrain Medical Bulletin,* 9(2):82-86.
Hall, Edward T. 1959. *The Silent Language.* New York: Doubleday & Co.
Hall, Edward T. 1966. *The Hidden Dimension* New York: Doubleday and Co.
Hamarnah, Samer Abdulla, Zubair Hadi Safiki, and Abdul Jabbar Mahdi Saleh. 1993. "Fracture of the Penis." *Emirates Medical Journal,* 11: 25-27.
Hansen, Henny. 1967. *Investigations in a Shi'a Village in Bahrain.* Copenhagen: National Museum of Denmark- Publications of the Ethnographical Series, Vol. 12.
Harrison, Paul. 1904. "Our Medical Work." *Quarterly Letters of the Arabian Mission,* (New Brunswick, New Jersey), 88 (January-March). Also in Anthony, T.A. 1984. *Documentation of the Modern History of Bahrain from American Sources 1900-1938: Historical Records of the American Mission,* New Brunswick, New Jersey. *Al Watheeka* (Journal of the Historical Documents Centre, State of Bahrain), 4 (Jan.):243-229.
Hathout, Hassan. 1979. "Unwantedness as an Indication for Abortion." *The Journal of the Kuwait Medical Association,* 13 (June):89-92.
"Health Check Law for Expats Clear. 1996." *Gulf Daily News* (English edition), Bahrain, 14 June 1996:4.
Hegazi, M., Hussain Fadaak, Alaa Saharty, and Ahmed Wafiq. 1990. "One Stage Penile and Urethral Reconstruction–A New Extension of Inferiorly Based Rectus Abdominus Myocutaneous Flap." *Annals of Saudi Medicine,* 10(5):564-566.
Hicks, E. K. 1993. *Infibulation: Female Mutilation in Islamic Northeastern Africa.* New Brunswick and London: Transaction Publishers.
Husain, Mohd. T., and Asal Y. Al-Samarrai. 1990. "Webbed Penis in Arab Children." *Annals of Saudi Medicine,* 10(5):531-534.
Ibrahim, M.E., H.M. Hathout, M.A.A. Moussa, and M.A. Razaq. 1979. "Gynecological and Obstetric Survey of the Ministry of Public Health Nurses in Kuwait." *The Journal of the Kuwait Medical Association,* 13(1):27-37.
Ismail, Mazin A. 1990. "The Role of the Primary Health Center in the Early Management of Infertility and Impotence." *Journal of the Bahrain Medical Society,* 2(2):134-136.
Johnson, Paul. 1958. *Journey into Chaos.* London: MacGibbon and Kees.
Kahtanie, Khadija. 1992. *A Study of Coping Strategies Experienced by Bahraini Married Couples When Faced with Life Strains in Marital and Parental Roles.* Master of Arts thesis, The University of Texas Medical Branch, Galveston.
Khalfan, Mohammed Ali. 1973. "How They Lived 2–The Dying Customs of Bahrain, Series 1–The Marriage Ceremony." *Dilmun (The Journal of the Bahrain Archaeological and Historical Society),* 5:14
Khuri, F.l. 1980. *Tribe and State in Bahrain.* New York: The University of Chicago Press.
Kutub, Muhammed. 1982. *Islam: The Misunderstood Religion,* Malaysia: Polygraphic Press Sdn. Bhd.
Mahgoub, O.M., , et al. 1990. "Deliberate Self-Harm in the Migrant Populations in the Eastern Province of Saudi Arabia," *Saudi Medical Journal,* 11:473-477.
Mahgoub, Osman M., Hassan B. Adbel-Hafeiz, Abdulaziz Al-Quorain, Hassan Al-ldrissu, Ghassab Al-Ghassab, and Ismail Absood. 1991. "Life Events Stress in Saudi Peptic Ulcer Patients of the Eastern Province." *Annals of Saudi Medicine,* 11(6):669-673.
Mahmon, E. Fernandez. 1992. "Experience of Hepatitis B in Bahrain." *Journal of the Bahrain Medical Society,* 4(1):64-66.
Malik, M., A. Belal, T.E. Mekter and H. Al-Kinary. 1996. "Drug Overdose in the Asir Region of Saudi Arabia," *Annuals of Saudi Medicine,* 16(1):33-36.

"Mass wedding job." 1996. *Gulf Daily News* (English edition), Bahrain, July 11, 1996.
Mattar, Ali. M. 1985. "Drug Abuse." *Bahrain Medical Bulletin,* 7(2):5355.
McDermott, Anthony. 1973. "Women in Saudi Arabia." *The Guardian* (London), May 2, 1973.
Metery, George E., Ali M. Matar, and Randah R. Hamadeh. 1986. "Early Recognition and Prevention of Attempted Suicide in Primary Health Care." *Bahrain Medical Bulletin,* 9(1):12-16.
Mohammed, Amina Abdulla. 1978. *Traditional Health Practices of the Post-Partum Bahraini Women.* Master of Arts thesis, University of Illinois, Chicago.
Mohammed, Farooq Amin. 1986. *Women and Social Change in Bahrain.* Master of Arts thesis, University of Essex, United Kingdom.
Molloy, June, Dunia Al-Hashimi, and Fadheela T. Al-Mahroos. 1993. "Children in Jeopardy: Munchausen Syndrome by Proxy." *Journal of the Bahrain Medical Society,* 5(3):154-159.
Moore, Richard. 1996. "Sky Is the Limit for a Career in Banking." *Gulf Daily News* (English edition), Bahrain, August 5, 1996:2.
Moore, Richard. 1996. "Keeping ALBA a Step Ahead," *Gulf Daily News* (English edition), Bahrain, August 8, 1996:3.
Muhsen, Zana, and Andrew Crofts. 1991. *Sold.* London: Warner Books, A Division of Little, Brown and Company, UK.
Nadkarni, Kishore V., Sheikha S. Al-Arrayed, and Jayant P. Bapat. 1991. "Incidence of Genetic Disorders of Haemoglobins in the Hospital Population of Bahrain." *Bahrain Medical Bulletin,* 13(1):1924.
Nasib, Tawfiq A., Randah R. Hamadah, and Haroutune K. Armenian. 1983. "The Impact of Family Size on Morbidity at a Primary Health Care centre in Bahrain." *Bahrain Medical Bulletin,* 5(2):65-72.
Noor, Eman. 1996. "Bahraini Women Forging Ahead." *Gulf Daily News* (English edition), Bahrain, August 8, 1996:5.
Parida, S.K. 41992. "Knowledge, Attitude and Behavior of Army Personnel Towards HIV Infection." Ninth International Conference on AIDS, Berlin.
Parida, S.K., and Khalid Effendi. 1994. "Viral Infection Among Family Members of Carriers of HbsAg in Bahrain." *Journal of the Bahrain Medical Society,* 6(2):61-63.
Patterson, Lucy M. 1904. "Two Weeks at the Hospital." *Quarterly Letters of the Arabian Mission.* (New Brunswick, New Jersey), 50 (April-June). Also in Anthony, T.A. 1984. *Documentation of the Modern History of Bahrain from American Sources 1900-1938: Historical Records of the American Mission,* New Brunswick, New Jersey. *Al-Watheeka (Journal of the Historical Documents Centre, State of Bahrain),* 4 (Jan.):243-229.
Patton, Michael Quinn. ed. 1991. *Family Sexual Abuse: Frontline Research and Evaluation.* California, Newbury Park: Sage Publications Inc.
Qadri, S.M.H., J. Akhter and K. Ignacio. 1993. "Incidence of Chlamydia Infections in a Large Metropolitan Hospital in Saudi Arabia." *Saudi Medical Journal,* 14(2):152-155.
Qureshi, Naseem A. 1992. "The Battered Child Syndrome: Does It Exist in Saudi Arabia?" (letter to editor) *Saudi Medical Journal,* 13(4):369-370.
Rajab, Khalil E. 1979. "Milestones in the Medical History of Bahrain with Special Reference to Maternity and Child Welfare." *Bahrain Medical Bulletin,* 1(1):6-9.
Rajab, Khalil E. 1984. "Getting Around Infertility." *Bahrain Medical Bulletin,* 9(2):58-60.
Rajab, K.E., A.A. Yousef, and S. Rustan. 1995. "Prevalence of Chlamydial Infection Among Pregnant Women in Bahrain." *Journal of the Bahrain Medical Society,* 7(1):17-19.
Ramzani, N. 1985. "Arab Women in the Gulf." *The Middle East Journal,* 39:258-276.
Rasromani, Khalil, Akbar M. Mohammed, Salwa Al Mahroos, and I. Mannan Khan. 1990. "Priapism in Sickle Cell Disease." *Bahrain Medical Bulletin,* 12(3):113-115.

Rumaihi, M.G.4 1976. *Bahrain: Social and Political Changes Since the First World War.* London and New York: Bowker (in association with the Centre for Middle Eastern and Islamic Studies of the University of Durham, North Carolina, USA).

Sadat-Ali, Mir, Abdulla Y. El-Hassan, Ezzidin M. Ibrahim, Hussain Al-Frehi, and Fahd Al-Muhanna. 1993. "Osteoporosis in Saudi Women: A Postmenopausal Pilot Screening." *Annals of Saudi Medicine,* 13(3):272-274.

Sadat-Ali, Mir, Ibraham Al-Habdan, and Sunil Marwah. 1995. "The Dilemma of Jumping Syndrome." *Journal of the Bahrain Medical Society,* 7(3):187-190.

Saeed, Tariq. 1992. "Non-Accidental Burning in Children." *Journal of the Bahrain Medical Society,* 4(3):90.

Sandozi, S., N.Z. Al-Awadhi, and S. Ghazali. 1988. "Fracture of the Penis: Experience of 8 Cases." *The Journal of the Kuwait Medical Association,* 22(3):274-276.

Sarhan, Mansoor Mohammed. 1995. *Bahrain National Bibliography Vol. I* (English version). Bahrain: Fakhrawi Book Shop Printing & Publishing.

Statistical Abstract 1994. State of Bahrain, Central Statistics Organization, Directorate of Statistics.

Suleiman, M.A., A.A. Nashef, M.A.A. Moussa, and M.H. El-Islam. 1980. "Psychological Profile of the Parasuicide Patients in Kuwait." *International Journal of Psychiatry,* 32:16-22.

Sunderaj, Shirley. 1989. "Human Papiloma Virus and Cervical Neoplasia in Bahrain." *Journal of the Bahrain Medical Society,* 1(1):8-11

Taha, S., A. Sharayah, B.A. Kamal et al. 1988. "Fracture of the Penis: Surgical Management." *Internal Surgery,* 73:63-64.

Taha, S.A. and G.M. Magbol. 1995. "The Pattern of Intersex Disorders and Gender Reassignment in the Eastern Province of Saudi Arabia." *Saudi Medical Journal,* 16(1):17-22.

Taki, Ali Hassan. 1974. *The Changing Status of the Bahraini Woman.* Bahrain: Oriental Press

Telbi, Ahmed S. 1988. "Neonatal Screening: The Need for Introducing a New Service in Kuwait." *The Journal of the Kuwait Medical Association,* 22(3):195-196.

The American Mission Hospitals Bahrain. *Persian Gulf: Report for 1933-34.* New Brunswick, New Jersey: Dutch Reformed Church Archives.

Topley, J., and A. Dewda. 1995. "Pattern of Congenital Anomalies Among UAE Nationals." *Saudi Medical Journal,* 16(5):425-428.

Wahdan, Mohamed H. 1995. "AIDS–The Past, Present and Future in the Eastern Mediterranean Region." *Eastern Mediterranean Health Journal,* 1(1):17-26.

Waly, Tarik. 1992. *Private Skies: The Courtyard Pattern in the Architecture of the House Bahrain.* Bahrain: Al Handasah Center Publication.

Wikan, Unni. 1982. *Behind the Veil in Arabia: Women in Oman.* Chicago: The University of Chicago Press.

Wilsher, Peter. 1982. "Leading the Saudi into Temptation." *Sunday Times* (London), November 21, 1982:18.

World Almanac and Book of Facts 1993. New York: World Almanac, A Scripps Howard Company, p.732.

Yousef, A. A., Mark R. Wallace, and Bendayna, K.M. 1991. "Male Urethritis in Bahrain: The Increasing Incidence of Resistant Gonorrhea." *Bahrain Medical Bulletin,* 13(3):94-96.

Yousef, A.A., M.R. Wallace, B.H. Baig, and K.E. Rajab. 1991. "Prenatal Serologic Screening in Bahrain." *Scandinavian Journal of Infectious Diseases,* 23:781-783.

Yousef, Aziz. 1994. "Prenatal Screening of Syphilis Toxoplasmosis and Hepatitis B in Patients Infected with HIV in Bahrain." *Transactions of the Royal Society of Tropical Medicine and Hygiene,* 88:60.

Ziskind, David. 1990. *Labor Laws in the Middle East.* Los Angeles, CA: Litlaw Foundation.

Brazil
(*República Federativa do Brasil*)

Sérgio Luiz Gonçalves de Freitas, M.D., with
Elí Fernandes de Oliveira and Lourenço Stélio Rega, M.Th.*

Contents

Demographics and a Historical Perspective

A. Demographics

Brazil occupies the eastern half of South America; with 3.28 million square miles, it is larger than mainland United States. Its neighbors include French Guiana, Surinam, Guyana, and Venezuela on the north, Columbia, Peru, Bolivia, Paraguay, and Argentina on the west, Uruguay in the south, and the Atlantic Ocean on the east. In the north, a heavily wooded Amazon basin and tropical rain forest covers half the country. All 15,814 miles of

* Additional comments in [. . . (RJN/SA)] are by Raymond J. Noonan and Sandra Almeida, or [. . . (Editor)] by Robert T. Francoeur.

the Amazon River are navigable. The northeast is semiarid scrubland, heavily settled and poor. With more resources and a favorable climate, the south central region has almost half the county's population, produces three-quarters of the farm goods and four-fifths of the industrial output. Most of the major cities are on the 4,600 miles of tropical and subtropical coastlines.

Seventy-seven percent of the 160 million Brazilians live in cities. Life expectancy at birth in 1991 was 62 for males and 68 for females, or 57 and 67 respectively according to the *1996 World Almanac.* The 1991 birth rate was 26 per 1,000 (1995 rate: 21 per 1,000) and the death rate in 1991 was seven per 1,000 and in 1995 nine per 1,000, giving an annual natural increase of 1.9 percent and 1.2 percent respectively. The age distribution is 35.2 percent for those under age 14; 15 to 59, 57.7 percent; and 60+, 7.1 percent. The 1991 literacy rate was 81 percent.

Brazil has one hospital bed per 270 persons, one physician per 848 persons, and an infant mortality rate of 57 per 1,000 live births in 1995. Socioeconomically, 80 percent of Brazil's population are classified as low income. Brazil's per capita gross domestic product in 1993 was $5,000.

B. A Brief Historical Perspective

The first European to reach the land that is now Brazil is generally believed to have been the Portuguese navigator Pedro Álvares Cabral in 1500. At that time, the country was sparsely settled by various indigenous tribes, whose decimated descendants survive today mostly in the Amazon basin. In the following centuries, Portuguese colonists gradually pushed inland, bringing along with them a large number of African slaves. Slavery was not abolished until 1888.

In 1808, the King of Portugal moved the seat of his government to Brazil when threatened by Napoleon's army and Brazil became a kingdom under Dom João VI. When Dom João returned to Portugal, his son Pedro proclaimed the independence of Brazil in 1822 and he was acclaimed emperor. In 1889, when the second emperor, Dom Pedro II, was deposed, the United States of Brazil was proclaimed as a republic. The country was renamed the Federative Republic of Brazil in 1967.

A military junta controlled the government between 1930 and 1945. A democratic government prevailed from 1945 to 1964 when the institution of new economic policies aggravated inflation and triggered a military revolt. The next five presidents were military leaders. Strict censorship was imposed and political opposition suppressed amid charges of torture and other human rights violations. In the 1974 elections, when the official opposition party made significant gains, some relaxation in the censorship occurred.

Brazil's agricultural production soared between 1930 and the 1970s. In the same years, vast mineral resources and a huge labor force enabled Brazil to make major industrial advances. However, soaring inflation and an unbalanced, two-tiered society with a very wealthy few and a majority of people barely managing to survive, led to a severe economic recession. Brazil's foreign debt, one of the largest in the world, required restructuring in 1982. Announcement of a comprehensive environmental plan to develop the Amazon basin brought an international outcry from environmentalists deeply concerned about the growing destruction of the Amazon ecosystem which is so vital to the world environment.

1. Basic Sexological Premises

A. Character of Gender Roles

Brazil being a typically Latin and machismo society, males enjoy a superior, almost demigod status. This is reinforced by the economic dependence of women. Only about 18 percent of the women are employed outside the home; the majority devote their time to caring for their house and children. Nevertheless, women do possess some privileges that protect them in the workplace. For example, they may retire five years earlier than men and maternal leave is available during illness of a child. A special pregnancy leave permits them to be away from work for 120 days after childbirth. However, all these apparent privileges significantly reduce the chances and competitiveness for women seeking to enter the work force.

[*Note*: In addition to the value of *machismo* mentioned above, Brazilian sexual attitudes and behaviors are strongly influenced by three other values—*marianismo, ediquetta,* and *pronatalism*—which are commonly shared with some minor variations across the Latino world of South and Central America. To avoid duplication in several chapters, these four basic values are described in detail in Section 1A, Basic Sexological Premises, in the chapter on Puerto Rico. The reader is referred to this material in Volume 2 of this *Encyclopedia.* (Editor)]

[The structure of sexual life in Brazil has traditionally been conceived in terms of a model focused on the relationship between sexual practices and gender roles—on the distinction between masculine activity (*atividade*) and feminine (*passividade*) as central to the order of the sexual universe. *Comer* (to eat) describes the act of penetration during sexual intercourse while *dar* (to give) describes those who passively offer themselves to be penetrated and possessed by their active partners. In some respects, these role distinctions are more fundamental than is sexual anatomy. For details on the implications of these premises, see Sections 5 and 6 below. (Editor)]

In 1986, the Delegacia da Mulher, The Women's Advocacy group, was formed to protect women against sexual and physical violence. All the employees of this agency are women, because women feel more secure filing complaints when they are speaking to other women. Only 3 percent of the members of Parliament are women. Feminist organizations are small, not very popular, and have little influence in society.

[Nevertheless, results of a national survey (representing 35 percent of the economically active women in the country) by *Veja/Feedback* described the average Brazilian woman over 25 as follows:

> She's married, has two children, entered the work market in the 1980s and wants to earn more. Contrary to her mother and grandmother, she recognizes that eternal marriage does not exist. All-providing husbands do not exist. She prepares herself almost by intuition to keep going alone in life.
>
> In everyday family life, she does everything for the children but gives less to the husband—a husband who still identifies the woman as the support of the home and the happiness. The two become estranged. For this woman busy with her own life, criminal violence and the preservation of health are preoccupations more important than sexual pleasure or the fear of getting older. For that woman who does not work outside of the house, the model of the ideal woman is exactly of one who sweats her body and the double shift [inside and outside the home]. (*Veja*, 1994, p. 11)

Over 20 percent of Brazilian families are supported exclusively by women (*Veja*, 1994, p. 11).

[This same 1994 survey (p. 15) reported the following primary concerns of women: violence against women, 98 percent; sexual abuse, 96 percent; daycare for children, 94 percent; equal salaries, 79 percent; free choice of contraceptives, 73 percent; more political participation, 73 percent; division of duties at home, 70 percent; and legalization of abortion, 56 percent. (RJN/SA)]

B. Sociolegal Status of Males and Females

From the legal viewpoint, Brazilian males and females have equal legal rights as children, adolescents, and adults. Adults, those over 18 years of age, both men and women, have the right and obligation to vote. Voting is mandatory. Each voter receives a receipt documenting his/her fulfillment of this obligation. Wages of a worker who does not have this receipt will be attached by the state in the month following the elections. Adolescents between 16 and 18 years of age have the right to choose to vote or not to vote.

[The traditional role of Brazilian women as housewife, derived from the nineteenth-century European ideal, was that of the "unproductive queen of the house," who was responsible for the respectability and harmony of the household and envied by the working woman. When one achieved the status of housewife, she gained dignity and a higher social status. However, growing numbers of Brazilian women have finally come to recognize their own power and the possibility of being an agent of change. In the last 20 years, the number of economically active women in Brazil grew by 70 percent to 23 million—39 percent of Brazil's population of women—a figure almost equal to the populations of Holland and Denmark combined (*Veja* 1994). (RJN/SA)]

A law restricting abortion has produced some discussion about women's rights that developed into a sort of political campaign.

Recently The List of the Rights of Children has been promoted with considerable publicity. The intention is to provide minors with greater protection against the violence they are victims of in the large cities. [Poverty and the inability of Brazil's majority poor to limit the number of offspring they have drives many youth to abandon their families and make their own lives on the street. Typical of Brazil's urban scene is the city of Salvador. In 1993, Salvador's 2.5 million inhabitants included a floating population of some 16,000 youths, working, playing, begging, stealing, and sleeping on the street. This was up 33 percent from an estimated 12,000 in 1990. About 100 Salvadorian street children are murdered each year by right-wing extremists. Social recognition of this problem and efforts to remedy it are vital to Brazil's future. (Editor)]

C. General Concepts of Sexuality and Love

The development of the communication media, especially television, has greatly influenced the concept of love and sexual behavior of the population. Every day, viewers of soap operas may witness episodes in which the sexual behavior of the protagonists is very permissive. This has definitely transformed Brazilian sexual relations in two ways. Such programs decrease sexual taboos and endorse sexual permissiveness especially in the areas of the sexually uncommon and "deviant" sexual behaviors.

Overall the sexual attitudes of Brazilians depend on gender, age, region of residence, and religious influences. The rural population and the migrant rural workers living in large cities suffer profound influences from Catholicism's religious teachings and ceremonies. This group is also characterized by a low level of education and culture. In this group, premarital and extramarital sexual contact is condemned. The Catholic Church approves only the natural means of family planning and condemns abortion. Ignoring Church doctrine, many in this group favor the contraceptive hormonal pill and surgical sterilization; the incidence of condom use is much lower. The Evangelical churches accept the use of the contraceptive pill as well as other methods, but are also vehemently opposed to abortion. Claims that the IUD is an abortifacient rather than a contraceptive method have caused its usage to be proscribed by Evangelicals. However, some government programs support use of the IUD in women of low income with numerous children.

Among Brazilians with a higher level of education, especially in the large cities, various forms of petting are acceptable as well as premarital sex and extramarital sex, the latter being less frequent than the former. A variety of contraceptives are accepted as normal, with a preference for the contraceptive pill, surgical sterilization, condom, and abortion, in that order. Brazil is the world champion of Caesarean births, 35 percent of all births. The majority of Caesarean section deliveries are accompanied by sterilization of the woman through tubal ligation.

In comparing attitudes toward sexuality and love among Brazilians of different socioeconomic levels and different regions of the country, it seems to us that two different societies exist. One culture maintains the traditional attitudes of the Third World; the other culture has been influenced by the modernization trends commonly seen around the world and has gradually adopted more permissive attitudes.

[Popular women's magazines have the purpose of transmitting the cultural norms, such as monogamy, similar to those in the U.S. and other countries. The August 1994 Portuguese edition of *Cosmopolitan*, called *Nova*, for example, highlights such issues for women as "A guide to self-confidence," "Attracting the right man," and "Monogamy: Is it possible to keep the fires hot?" (RJN/SA)]

2. Religious and Ethnic Factors Affecting Sexuality

A. Source and Character of Religious Values

The predominant religion in Brazil is Roman Catholicism, primarily because the Roman Catholic Church has determined that newborns must be baptized and officially registered as Roman Catholic at birth. In 1992, it was estimated that of the country's 148 million people, 70 percent are Catholics, 20 percent are Protestants (Baptists, Presbyterians, Pentecostals, Evangelicals, etc.), and 10 percent are Spiritualists (Mystics, Umbandists, Voodooists, etc.). The predominance of Christian religions has set the stage for the war against abortion, which is officially condemned as a crime. However, in most cities abortion occurs underground. For similar reasons, sexual education in the public schools is generally nonexistent.

B. Source and Character of Ethnic Values

Brazil has four distinct races of people: Caucasians, 54 percent; Mestizo (mixed race), 34 percent; Negroes, 10 percent; and Asians, 2 percent. There are also about 200,000 indigenous Indians. Portuguese, Africans, and mulattos make up the vast majority of the population, with Italian, German, Japanese, Indian, Jewish, and Arab minorities.

Brazil was colonized in 1500 by the Portuguese, making it the only Portuguese-speaking country in all of Latin America. Youth is highly valued in this nation where 51 percent of the population is under the age of 27. This is obvious in many aspects of Brazilian life. For instance, kissing and petting by couples in the streets, theaters, and public places are generally tolerated in liberal Brazilian society, despite conservative religious influences.

[In this respect, Brazilians tend to allow expressions of sexuality and eroticism that are quite unacceptable in other areas of the Latino world, especially in public. This disparity can be traced to a unique blend of Roman Catholic and native Indian values with a strong African influence. Like other Latinos, Brazilians have taboos and restrictions on public sexual behavior. However, Brazilians draw an important distinction between public and private behaviors that preserves traditional Indian and African values. "Within four walls, beneath the sheets, and behind the mask of *carnaval*, everything can happen!" "Everything," or *tudo*, refers to the world of erotic experiences and pleasure. The phrase *fazendo tudo*, "doing everything," means Brazilian men and women have an obligation to experience and enjoy every form of sexual pleasure and excitement, or more precisely those practices that the public world most strictly prohibits. This, however, must all be done in private, behind the mask, between four walls, or under the sheets.

[The concept of *tudo* is the key element in the domain Brazilians call *sacanagem* (DaMatta 1983). *Sacanagem* is an extremely complex cultural category, with no suitable English translation, except perhaps "the world of erotic experience" or the "erotic universe." Within this erotic world, erotic pleasure is an end in itself and the classifications of active/passive, the sex of the partner, and the acts engaged in are secondary. A Brazilian most clearly embodies the erotic ideal of *sacanagem* by doing everything, particularly those practices that the public world most condemns and prohibits. The transgression of public norms called for by *sacanagem* brings the playfulness of *carnaval* into everyday life (Parker 1987; Moitoza 1982; Francoeur 1991, 43-47). (Editor)]

[The African influence on Brazilian life and sexuality takes many forms. For instance, at all levels of Brazilian society, it is customary to offer a guest *cafézinho*, a small cup of espresso made by pouring water over powdered coffee through a cloth strainer. One way this custom is practiced illustrates the influence of how black magic brought to Brazil by slaves from Africa is still strong in some parts of the country. This custom can give the *casadoiras*, young women looking to get married, an opportunity to enhance their prospects of getting married. The young women believe that if they pour the coffee through their own panties and give the drink to their unsuspecting boyfriends, the men will be attached to them forever and will not be able to escape marriage. In *The Scent of Eros: Mysteries of Odor in Human Sexuality* (New York: Continuum Press, 1995, 83-84), Kohl and Francoeur have suggested a possible scientific basis of this folk custom which occurs in some African cultures, among African Americans in the southern United States, as well as in Brazil. The soiled undergarment used as a filter may contain pheromones which have been found in primate and human vaginal secretions. Released into the coffee, these may serve as a natural sex attractant or aphrodisiac. However logical it is in terms of what we know about vaginal pheromones, this suggestion is speculation and untested by experimental research. (RJN/SA)]

Racial prejudices exist, but they are concealed and racial conflict and skirmishes/clashes are rare, except when economic interests lead to attacks on indigenous peoples in the Amazon basin. Couples with clearly different ethnic origins are very commonly seen in any public gathering. There exists a great mingling of the races that gives Brazil a preeminently Mestizo population, especially in the north and northeast. In the south, those of European Caucasian descent, i.e., German, Italian, Spanish, and Portuguese, predominate.

[The expression *pé na cozinha* ("foot in the kitchen") illustrates the intermixing of the white and non-white races common in Brazil. The phrase goes back to the Brazilian colonial era when the slaves brought from Africa worked in the kitchens and the white masters would have sexual relations with them. Some of the offspring resulting from these illicit liaisons had very light traces of the African influence in their appearance and were considered to be white with their "foot in the kitchen," meaning they had some African features. *Pé na cozinha* is still used today to describe a person who has a vestige of African characteristics. (RJN/SA)]

3. Sexual Knowledge and Education

A/B. Government Policies, Sex Education Programs, and Informal Sources

It is necessary to emphasize that sexual education has been somewhat taboo in Brazil. In the past seven years, however, some sexual education programs have surfaced in the private schools. In São Paulo (1987), an experimental study of sexual education in five public schools revealed that sex education helped improve students scores in all their subjects as well as improved the relationships between parents, students, and teachers.

Truthfully, in Brazil, there is no government program for the sexual education of its youth. Recently, in the principal cities of the country, a Program of Adolescent Support surfaced that informs, orients, and teaches adolescents about their sexuality through educational interviews and seminars.

One study revealed that 72 percent of the men and 45 percent of the women received their first information about sex from friends and schoolmates. It also showed that in the large cities youth learned about sex mainly from movies and magazines. It seems that Brazilian families generally prefer that their offspring obtain their sexual information through the school system and published material such as adult and pornographic magazines. This frees the parents, who feel insecure speaking about sex, from ever mentioning such a "delicate subject" in the family circle and to their children.

One consequence of this lack of sexual education was uncovered in an unusual study of 150 women treated for anorgasmia. They were very poor and worked hard in the fields. They lived in rural areas without radio or television before they married, and had no time to watch television even when it was available. None of these women ever received any sexual education from family members or school. Over a third of them did not know that the sexual act was a normal part of marriage although they knew that prostitutes and other bad men and women engaged in *sacanagem* ("the world of erotic experience"). For these women, sexual intercourse was not a moral behavior but immoral and indecent. When they found out what sex was and that it was a part of marriage, they thought that their husbands were crazy and felt as if they had been raped. For these women, the lack of sexual knowledge was the major cause of anorgasmia. In addition, 20 percent of the wives abandoned the therapy because their marriages were destroyed by violence. For 80 of the women in this study, other factors were responsible for the anorgasmia. These poor rural women are not typical of the real universe of most Brazilian women (de Freitas 1990).

These women had access to sexual therapy only because AB-SEX, headed by the main author, introduced this therapy as a free part of Public Health in 1986 in São Paulo. At present, many of these patients are living in a big city and have been married more than ten years.

[On the television program, "Fantástico," in late 1994 on TV Globo, a national Brazilian network, reporters interviewed two researchers, Emídio Brasileiro and Marislei Espíndola from the city of Goiânia, who had conducted a sex survey over the preceding five years. The researchers, whose book, *Sexo: Problemas e Soluções*, was to be published by the end of the year, reported that children wanted to know what sex was for; adolescents wanted to know what sex was like; young adults at about 20 years old wanted to know how to avoid the consequences of sex; adults from about 30 wanted to know how to educate their children about sex; those over 40 think they know everything about sex; and those around 60 think it's too late. A few of the questions that these researchers said they were most often asked included: 1. Can a pregnant woman have sex? 2. When is a young person ready for his first sexual intercourse? 3. Sexually, is it easier to be a man or a woman? 4. If I have sex before or during a sports competition, will I decrease my physical performance? (RJN/SA)]

4. Autoerotic Behaviors and Patterns

A 1983 questionnaire survey indicated that boys and girls in an urban group of 3- to 5-year-olds played together in such a way as to touch or see each others' sexual organs, especially when no adults were present. When this type of behavior was observed in a school setting by some teachers in Colégio Batista Brasileiro in São Paulo, the main author was invited to provide some orientation for the teachers. As we know, this type of behavior in infancy is practically universal and independent of social class or ethnic origins.

As mentioned earlier, it is uncommon for parents to speak about sex to their children at home. When childhood sexual curiosities are not satisfied by the parents, the child naturally seeks answers on their own from other sources. Usually such persons or sources they turn to are not prepared or adequate to guide them efficaciously. In terms of self-pleasuring, the child is likely to encounter one of two attitudes or value judgments. One opinion, and probably the less frequently encountered, is that self-pleasuring is a normal component in the psychosexual development of children. The other opinion views masturbation as a negative road to human development.

Regardless of the value message encountered and the lack of external support, 92 percent of adolescent boys and 45 percent of girls engage in self-pleasuring. However, the fear of being found out by parents or other kin is a common accompaniment. In our research, 66 percent of the boys and 36 percent of the girls began self-pleasuring between 10 and 15 years of age.

While the Evangelical Protestants express a great preoccupation with, and a negative view of, self-pleasuring, Roman Catholic doctrine also condemns this behavior as disordered and seriously sinful, but seldom if ever mentions it. There are no significant statistics about childhood and adolescent autoeroticism.

5. Interpersonal Heterosexual Behaviors

A. Children

In a retrospective research project about child and adolescent sexual behavior, 57 percent of all adults played sex games as children (de Freitas 1991). The children in general do not receive any sort of sexual guidance or information from their parents, yet their sexual behavior seems generally adequate and appropriate for their developmental ages as psychologists understand this.

Going through the phases of sexual self-discovery and autoeroticism characteristic of infancy, the children imitate their parents and are influenced by peers and the mass media, movies, and television.

Recent research has uncovered that 60 percent of those interviewed admitted to having played doctor and other games that included the mutual touching of their bodies and the sexual parts when they were children. The majority engaged in this kind of play with children of both sexes. However, there was a tendency for girls to play more with girls, while boys also played mostly with children of the opposite sex.

We must call attention to the fact that only 60 percent of the subjects interviewed revealed having practiced this type of play in childhood, when it is well known that the frequency of this activity is much higher all over the world. From this we understand that many respondents omitted the truth from their information about their infancy. To speak of childhood sexuality is an intolerable outrage for many Brazilians. Even today in our culture, childhood sexuality is a taboo theme that cannot be mentioned with total tranquillity because of the intense anxiety it awakens in adults. Most adults want to forget the sexual experiences of their childhood because they were punished for demonstrating an interest in those activities. This perhaps explains the fact that many people, especially women over 45 years of age, did not answer the questions about sexual play in childhood.

While our observations and data are limited, two general forms of childhood sexual behavior have been observed. Children, 2 to 4 years old, generally limit themselves to speaking words of sex, showing their penises or buttocks, or even lifting the little girls' skirts and making drawings of nude girls or urinating boys. Children, 5 to 7 years old, seek closer contact with the opposite sex. Meanwhile, attitudes of punishment by the older family members for erotic play reinforce fear and redirect behavior towards self-pleasuring in private.

[In contrast with Euro-American sexual values that frown on sexual rehearsal play among children and adolescents, Brazilian culture expects young boys and girls to experiment with sexual pleasure and prepare for marriage within certain limits and in private.

[In the game *troca-troca*—literally "exchange-exchange"—pubescent and adolescent boys take turns, each inserting his penis in the other's anus. In addition, the early sexual interactions of adolescent boys and girls draw on a wide range of nonvaginal sexual practices, in particular on anal intercourse, in order to avoid both unwanted pregnancy and rupture of the hymen, still an important sign of a young woman's sexual purity (Parker 1987). (Editor)]

Clitorectomy does not exist in Brazil. Male circumcision exists only in the Jewish community. However, postectomy to shorten the prepuce is performed for uncircumcized boys with a long prepuce.

B. Adolescents

Puberty Rituals

Some social celebrations are observed when girls celebrate their fifteenth birthday. In some rural cities, this involves a "Big Party" with the fathers presenting their daughters to society and the girls dancing their first waltz. In upper-class urban families, these girls are then allowed to court and have a boyfriend. [See discussion of *quinceañera* in Section 2, "Latino Perspectives," of the USA chapter in Volume 3 of this *Encyclopedia.* (Editor)]

Premarital Sexual Activities and Relationships

The period of puberty involves biological, psychological, and sociological transformations. In Brazilian girls, menarche occurs between the ages of

10 and 13, having already had the partial growth of the breasts and the hips. Research shows that 62 percent of Brazilian mothers try to teach their daughters about their first menstruation before it occurs. Meanwhile, 38 percent of the young women confess not having any knowledge of the phenomenon before it happened.

Research indicates that the first menstruation in girls causes a strong emotional reaction that prompts the girls to inform their mothers. It is rare that girls hide their menarche from their mothers, although 15 percent of the subjects interviewed reported that as their response. The reaction of the boys to the signs of sexual maturation and their first nocturnal emission depends on the level of information they have received from their older friends. Unlike girls' reaction to menarche, boys almost always hide their first nocturnal emission from their parents, preferring to tell their older friends. The sexual maturation of puberty brings interest in the opposite sex, but the majority only start dating about age 15.

Sexual intercourse is generally initiated between the ages of 12 and 17 for men and 17 to 20 for women, again confirming a more permissive standard for men than for women. About the age of 16, dating becomes more intimate with non-coital sexual contact more evident. By age 16, 17 percent of the men and 8 percent of the women have had sexual intercourse. Only 40 percent of the women and 52 percent of the men revealed that their first sexual experience was positive and pleasant.

Research on adolescents in Botucatu, a rural area of the São Paulo district, and in the capital of São Paulo district revealed sharp differences in the sexual behavior of adolescents. In the rural cohort of 290 adolescents we found that 65 youngsters or 22.4 percent had already had heterosexual contact between ages 13 and 19 years. Nineteen of these adolescents had experienced coitus while 46 had only played sex games without having penile-vaginal intercourse. Of this group, 60 percent had a pleasant sexual experience and 40 percent felt guilt, mental anguish and remorse. By comparison, in a parallel group of 290 youths in the city of São Paulo, a similar number and percentage of adolescents had already had heterosexual contact. However, the breakdown was reversed, with 41 youths or 13.8 percent having experienced coitus, and 24 engaging in non-coital sex play, or outercourse. In the urban cohort, sexual contact was pleasurable for 69.3 percent. This demonstrates that the urban Brazilians are more liberal and more venturesome in their sexual behavior. About one quarter of all women are pregnant when they get married.

C. Adults

Premarital Courtship, Dating, and Relationships

In research conducted by AB-SEX (1991), 81 percent of adult men reported having had premarital relations, while 53 percent of women reported the same behavior. Again this was more commonly reported in the large cities.

The preoccupation of women with virginity is more evident in the rural zones in the interior of the country, and less so in the state capitals. Among college students in the larger cities, who are politically active and quite influential, there is often a shame attached to being a virgin.

Recent data indicates that single adults suffer from pressure to be married, but about 7 percent of Brazilian women between the ages of 35 and 45 years of age have children without being married, only 2 percent of whom marry after the birth of their first child. Single men between the ages of 37 and 46 prefer to remain single, even if their partners have children. There are many couples in the lower economic class who start a family and have many children without being married.

Marriage and the Family

The majority of marriages occur between the ages of 20 and 25, about 65 percent of all marriages. As in the developed nations, the small family model has become the standard. An accentuated fall in fertility has been noticed, since we have gone from the average of 6.3 children per woman in the 1960s to a current average of 2.8 children. This has come as a result of a series of transformations to which we generally refer as the process of modernization of Brazilian society.

In Brazil, monogamy is the fundamental pattern; bigamy and polygamy are illegal. Research in 1991, reported by IPPM (Institute of Market Research of São Paulo), found that in São Paulo, 54 percent of the people are opposed to female adultery while an equal number are against male adultery. Extramarital sex is acceptable under "certain circumstances" to 25 percent of the men and 23 percent of the women. People in smaller cities and economically lower are more rigorous in their opposition to extramarital sexual relations.

The average frequency of marital intercourse ranges between twice a week and three times per month. However, more and more of those interviewed say that they might feel happier if they had sex more often; they often added that they would feel less anxiety (*E acrescentam que seriam menos nervosos*).

[Based on the University of Chicago's report on sexuality in America which had recently been released, TV Globo, a national network, in the last quarter of 1994 conducted a mini-survey of the frequency with which Brazilians have sexual relations. On the television program "Fantástico," they reported that 17.6 percent of Brazilians have sexual relations once a week, 35.9 percent have none, and 46.5 percent do so two or more times per week. They also interviewed two researchers, Emídio Brasileiro and Marislei Espíndola, who had conducted a sex survey over the preceding five years. These researchers reported finding that men appeared to be more liberal about sex but actually were more conservative, in comparison to women who were apparently more conservative but actually were more liberal. (RJN/SA)]

In 1978, divorce was legally recognized after twenty-five years of Parliamentary discussion. The most frequent cause of divorce is extramarital sex, 33 percent, followed by excessive use of alcohol, physical violence, personality incompatibility, and irreconcilable differences. Usually it takes from two to four months to obtain a divorce. Divorced persons are not allowed to remarry for at least three years. Bigamy is considered a felony and a guilty verdict is accompanied by a jail term to be determined by a judge. The majority of divorces occurs between three to seven years after marriage. Frequently the divorcing couple has no children, 41 percent, or only one child. Divorce after twenty to thirty years of marriage is rare, and seems to be connected with andropause (the Brazilian term for male menopause) or menopause.

In one out of every five divorces, the mother retains custody of the child, while the male must pay alimony usually equal to 30 percent of his salary. In cases where the male refuses or stops paying alimony to the ex-wife, he is immediately arrested by order of the courts.

Sexuality and Older Persons

[Lucia Helena de Freitas, a Brazilian psychologist and gerontologist, studied the sexuality of a group of retired commercial workers who participated in the cultural activities of a social club. She found that 73.8 percent of them still had sexual relations, with 35.7 percent doing so two or three times a week, 21.4 percent once a week, and 16.7 percent less often. Almost all the interviewees (90.5 percent) felt the necessity of having sexual relations; 95.2 percent believed that sexual desire does not end with age, with 40 percent saying that it increased with age and 59 percent thinking the opposite. However, 33.3 percent believed that pleasure during the sexual act increased with age, as opposed to 66.7 percent who said the pleasure decreased. Regarding orgasm, 28.6 percent said they were able to reach it quickly against 40.5 percent who said they needed more time. Only 13.5 percent of women said they experienced a change in their sexual life as a result of menopause; some said they reached orgasm more quickly once they stopped menstruating. In the case of men, 4.8 percent acknowledged problems of impotency. Freitas concluded that with the advance of age, typically the frequency of sex decreases but the quality does not. (*Manchete* 1992, 40). (RJN/SA)]

Incidence of Anal and Oral Sex

IPPM's (Institute of Market Research of São Paulo) survey revealed that at least 23.5 percent of São Paulo residents (Paulistanos), 12.6 percent of Rio de Janeiro residents (Cariocas), and 18.8 percent of those in other Brazilian cities reject oral sex because they consider it abnormal. Also, 53 percent of the Paulistanos, 38.6 percent of the Cariocas and 45.7 percent of those in other cities consider anal sex abnormal; 10 percent refused to answer.

The belief that oral and anal sex are abnormal sexual practices has its origin in many sources. One of these is the moral order, based in the Catholic tradition. This tradition believes sex in itself to be a mortal sin if it does not involve vaginal intercourse for the purpose of procreation within matrimony and condemns all other erotic practices. Thus all sexual activities without a procreative end are considered taboos and sexual perversions that should be avoided.

In spite of this prohibition, many people go against the conventional sexual standards, since the primary message of Brazilian folk culture—*fazendo tudo*—prompts a freedom of sexual expression in private where anything can happen and everything is possible, encouraging everyone to broaden one's repertoire of sexual practices even when they violate public sexual norms in private.

The IPPM survey, for example, showed that at least occasionally 52.9 percent of Cariocas, 37.8 percent of Paulistanos, and 42.1 percent of other Brazilians have practiced anal intercourse. Statistical analysis revealed that men 30 to 45 years of age were three times more likely to solicit anal sex than women. These results confirm that among married couples, as elsewhere, it is generally the male that initiates new sexual practices, while the female frequently is limited to accepting passively her partner's solicitation. This presents a "delicate situation" for the female who is pressured to accept anal or oral sex because there are no legal restrictions in Brazil.

The emphasis on *fazendo tudo, tesão* (excitement), and *prazer* (enjoyment) promotes "rather elaborate and varied forms of sexual foreplay, a strong emphasis on oral sex, and especially a focus on anal sex (Parker 1987, 164). Interviews of 5,000 men and women throughout Brazil revealed that over 50 percent of those surveyed in Rio de Janeiro and over 40 percent of those in the rest of Brazil reported practicing anal sex at least occasionally (Santa Inêz 1983, 41).

Carnaval

In Brazilian sexual culture, the annual celebration and unrestrained exuberance of Carnaval is typical of

> an erotic universe focused on the transgression of public norms through a playfulness reminiscent of . . . one's adolescent sexual experience and the excitations they produced play[ing] themselves out again repeatedly throughout adult life. They undercut the effects of sexual prohibitions and make polymorphous pleasures such as oral and anal intercourse, an important part even of married, heterosexual relationships. Such acts [whether engaged in with same or other gendered persons, with a nonspouse or stranger], along with the *tesão* or excitement which is thought to underlie them and the *prazer* or enjoy-

ment which is understood to be their aim, are essential to the Brazilian sexual culture, with its context of 'no shame,' 'within four walls,' 'beneath the sheets,' or 'behind the mask.' (Parker 1987, 165)

6. Homoerotic, Homosexual, and Ambisexual Behaviors

[The categories of homosexuality (*homossexualidade*), heterosexuality (*heterossexualidade*), bisexuality (*bissexualidade*), and a distinct homosexual identity (*identidade homossexual*) were introduced into Brazilian culture in the mid-twentieth century by social hygienists, medical doctors, and psychoanalysts.

[Despite their current prevalence in the media, these concepts of sexual classification remain in large measure part of an elite discourse. As mentioned in Sections 1B and 2A, Brazilian sexual culture is centered on the distinction between masculine activity (eating (*comer*), conquering and vanquishing (*vencer*), owning and possessing (*possuir*), and feminine passivity (giving, being penetrated, dominated, subjugated, and submissive). In keeping with the overriding importance of every male considering himself macho, the Brazilian male considers himself heterosexual, man, *homem* as long as his dominant mode of sexual expression involves active phallic penetration, regardless of the gender of the partner being possessed and penetrated.

[If the category of "men," or *homens*, seems clear, its counterpart is less so. Those who *dão* (give or submit) include biological women or *mulheres*, and others, the biologically male *viado* (deer), *bica* (worm, intestinal parasite), and the feminine form of *bicho* (best translated as queer or faggot). Though endowed with male anatomy, the *viado* or *bicha* is linked with the fundamentally passive social role of *mulher*, not *homem*. Within these categories, a male can have sexual relations with *mulheres*, *viado*, and *bicha* and maintain his masculine (heterosexual) identity provided he exercises phallic dominance. In any discussion of sexual behaviors, gender orientation, and AIDS education, it is essential to keep in mind this Brazilian folk model.

[The interplay between traditional and modern medical models of sexual behavior is evident within the open, shifting, and flexible subculture of *entendidos* and *entendidas* (those who know) in Brazil's larger cities. Organized around same-sex practices and desires, this subculture is found in certain bars, beaches, saunas, discos, and the like. *Entendidos* (studs) are sometimes contrasted with *homens*, and the traditional *bicha* as the passive partner of the active *bofe*. Both the *entendidos* and *bofe* are considered masculine *homens* despite their participation in same-sex activity.

[The same dichotomy structures the increasingly open presence of the once almost invisible "lesbian" subculture where *sapatão* (big shoe, dyke, or butch) contrasts with *sapatilhão* (slipper or femme dyke) (Parker 1987). (Editor)]

In Brazil, homosexuals communicate among themselves with their own subculture language, including the signal of an earring in the left ear for gay men and a left ankle bracelet for lesbians. This combination of in-group verbal and nonverbal communication allows homosexual persons to function in a generally hostile environment.

The recent IPPM (Institute of Market Research of São Paulo) survey made it clear that homosexuality is one of the areas of human sexuality most marked by prejudice. Over half, 51.5 percent, of Paulistanos, 57.1 percent of Cariocas, and 56.3 percent of those in other cities oppose homosexuality. On the other hand, a small number of those interviewed, only 13.5 percent, 8.7 percent, and 9.4 percent respectively in these same areas, consider homosexuality normal conduct. We do not have data concerning the number of homosexuals in the country, but it is probable that it is similar to that of other Latin American countries.

The social status of homosexuals is favorable only among those who have achieved fame in the arts, music, theater, movies, television, and haute couture. A homosexual orientation and lifestyle seem to facilitate self-promotion and professional success in these fields. In other areas of professional life, homosexuality is not a positive factor. In recent research in São Paulo, it was found that homosexuals, especially those with an exaggerated behavior, were usually rejected for employment following interviews with the company psychologists, although these same psychologists deny being prejudiced against homosexuals. In some areas, such as sales, there are minimal chances for an overt homosexual to find employment. Discrimination is also strong against overt lesbians. But, since they are generally more discreet and less overt in their behavior, they are not as easily identified. They only call attention to themselves when they are on a date with a younger (fem) lover, or when they cause a scene triggered by jealousy when the (fem) lover speaks to men.

Legal problems arise only when homosexuals become physically violent or when they wish to marry legally. Brazil's laws do not permit homosexuals or lesbians to marry.

Homosexual prostitution, especially when transvestites are involved, is the object of frequent police raids. However, this repression does not appear to have much effect on this, considering the open activity at night on the streets in the large cities.

Religious restrictions on these sexual practices are stronger among the Catholics, 68 percent of whom condemn homosexual behavior, even though there are cases involving homosexual priests who continue to practice their duties. The Catholic Church officially teaches that homosexual activities are contrary to the procreative purpose of sex.

The Protestants do not persecute homosexuals but instead seek to help them recuperate through faith in God. There are many cases where homosexuals, who were passive (bottoms) and prostituted themselves, have been regenerated or cured, becoming heterosexual to the extent of marrying and having children. They even lost their effeminate behaviors. (*Os protestantes não perseguem os homossexuais, mas procuram ajudá–los na recuperação, em que homossexuais passivos e que ate se prostituíam na noite, tornaram–se heterossexuais, casando–se, tendo filhos e perdendo os trejeitos efeminados.*)

7. Gender Conflicted Persons

There are no legal restrictions on transvestites in Brazil. However, in Brazil, transvestism is a marginal phenomenon (*um fenômeno marginal,* implying "practiced by a criminal element of society"). Transvestites are often men who work during the day and at night apply makeup, dress as women, and work the street or nightclubs to prostitute themselves with men or bisexual couples. Legally they are considered prostitutes and treated as such by the police.

In Brazil, sex-change surgery for transsexuals is considered to be mutilation surgery and legislation prohibits surgical treatment of a transsexual. Participation in such medical treatment is considered a felony for both the patient and surgeon.

Some transsexuals have gone to Europe to be operated on and change their sexual identity. However, these are isolated cases because the majority of the transsexuals are content to dress as women at night and prostitute themselves.

Surgical techniques are well developed in Brazil so that many cases of congenital ambiguous or anomalous genitals are regularly corrected with surgery. These operations try to preserve the sexual (gender) identity adequate to the patient.

8. Significant Unconventional Sexual Behaviors

A. Coercive Sex

Sexual violence is a crime for which there are provisions in The Brazilian Penal Code. The law protects citizens against sexual assaults in four categories: *estupro* or rape; *tentativa violenta ao pudor,* a violent attempt against *pudor* (meaning chastity, decency, modesty, virtue, purity, and more), or sexual molestation involving violence; *posse sexual através de fraude,* or sexual possession through fraud; and *atentado ao pudor mediante fraude sem violência,* or an attempted violation of *pudor* involving fraud.

The first two categories of sexual assaults involve violence and if grave physical harm results, the crime is viewed as aggravated and the convicted offender subject to a heavier sentence. In some cases, even if the victim consented to or invited the sexual partner, the law considers violence to have been part of the sexual act. These are usually cases where the victim is under 14 years of age, mentally incompetent, or unable to offer physical resistance.

Sexual Abuse, Incest, and Pedophilia

Sexual relations involving an adult or older adolescent with a child is legally termed sexual victimization (*Victimização Sexual*). When sexual victimization involves a relative of the victim, it is classified as incest.

Since 1982, there have been more reports of this type of behavior because of the feminist movement and the fact that females are the most common victims. The frequency of such acts is very difficult to establish because only the gravest and most brutal cases become known to the authorities. Research conducted in São Paulo by Azevedo between December 1982 and December 1984 showed that only a small percentage, about one in twenty-five cases of incest and pedophilia are reported to the authorities.

Research in greater São Paulo found that 87 percent of the cases of pregnancy in girls up to the 14 years of age resulted from incest perpetrated by the father, uncle, or stepfather of the victim. About 6 percent of the victims surveyed by Azevedo were males. In 70 percent of the cases of incest, the biological father was the perpetrator. The majority of such aggressors were 30 to 39 years old and blue collar workers.

Rape and Sexual Harassment

Rape is punishable by a minimum sentence of three years solitary confinement (*reclusão*) in prison. The sexual violence documented in police and court records is deceptive because most cases of sexual violence are not reported to crime detection units and because the requirements of the law to gain a conviction of either sexual violence or seduction are excessive. A man can only be found guilty of a crime of seduction if the women is under the age of 18, and even then a guilty verdict is rare. Only a male who seduces an under-age, minor virgin and continues having coitus with her is at risk of being convicted of seduction. If convicted, he may be sentenced to two to four years in prison. If the woman seduced is under the age of 14, then the crime becomes one of rape and the minimum sentence is three years in jail. If the woman seduced is over 18 years of age, there is no crime unless there is a serious threat, violence, or suspected violence.

Domestic Violence

[Being beaten by a husband is no longer just crying at home, suffering in silence, and ashamed to say anything. It is now judged as a crime and taken seriously by society. With the opening of the doors on August 6, 1985, of the 150 women's precincts (Delegacias da Mulher), police stations directed by women who specialize in domestic violence against women, Brazilian women made a great gain. These police stations became the arm of the judiciary most trusted and least feared to be used by the people. For many years, the beating of women was not seen by policemen as a crime, but rather a minor domestic affair that did not involve them. This picture has now changed significantly. Initially, 80 percent of the cases involved women who had been beaten two or three times by their husband; today, the majority file a report at the first strike. An average of three hundred women are seen each day (*U.S. News & World Report* 1994, 40-41; *Veja* 1994, 20).

[In 1991, Brazil's highest appeals court threw out the "honor defense" in adultery cases that allowed men who were accused of murdering their wives and/or their wives' lovers to escape punishment by arguing that they were defending their honor (*U.S. News & World Report* 1994, 41). (RJN/SA)]

B. Prostitution

Prostitution, whether heterosexual or homosexual, is not a criminal offense in Brazil unless it involves public solicitation or *pudor em público* (a public violation of *pudor,* meaning chastity, decency, modesty, virtue, purity, and more). In 1970, liberation of the press which strongly influenced sexual liberty, accentuated reduction in female prostitution in the larger cities. Meanwhile, the increase in libertinism (*o aumento da libertinagem,* meaning debauchery, hedonism, immorality, and more) has facilitated the appearance of male prostitution in public places, for both heterosexual and homosexual contacts. The presence of houses of prostitution (*casas noturnas*) has decreased, being replaced by massage parlors, telephone callgirls, and street soliciting. A large number of motels have appeared throughout the larger cities, often catering only to couples seeking private encounters or to prostitutes and their clients.

Statistics on the total number of prostitutes in Brazil do not exist, but the police estimate their number at about one million for the whole country.

There is a Prostitutes Association or union (Associação de Prostitutas) founded in 1986, with its main purpose to obtain recognition of prostitution as a legal profession. So far, this effort has produced no results.

C. Pornography and Erotica

The military regime that dominated Brazil from 1964 to 1985 repressed the publication of erotica and sexually explicit films. Since 1985, there has been a great surge in the number of pornography shops and erotic films, videos, and publications. Presently both hard- and soft-core pornography is easily accessible in Brazil. Both television and cinema theaters exhibit erotic films. Scenes showing sex with children or animals are strictly avoided, as is any depiction of sadomasochism, although sexual cruelty and violence may sometimes be shown.

[In 1995, a growing concern about the spread of AIDS, confusion over sexual values among the young, and the competition among television's prime-time soap operas to stage the steamiest love scenes provoked a social backlash against Brazil's fabled comfort with sensuality. In July 1995, the weekly news magazine *Veja* identified 95 nude shots, 74 sex acts, and 90 scenes with smutty dialogue in a week's worth of programming on the five major networks. Complaints from individuals, local governments, and church groups have prompted the federal government to investigate the prevalence of sex on prime-time television and recommend steps to control this (Schrieberg 1995). (Editor)]

D. Paraphilias

Some specialists deal with paraphilic clients, but there are no statistics on the incidence or types of paraphilias encountered in clinical practice, or among the general population.

Bestiality or zoophilia is a widely distributed sexual practice both geographically and historically. Its frequency is greater among adolescents in the rural areas, generally constituting a temporary sexual outlet or experimentation rather than a long-term behavior. Our surveys found that 12 percent of Paulistanos and Cariocas and 17 percent of other, nonurban respondents reported erotic contact with animals in their childhood or adolescence. This behavior is much rarer among Brazilian women.

9. Contraception, Abortion, and Population Planning

A. Contraception

Forty years ago in the rural areas of Brazil, families not infrequently had between ten and twenty children. In recent years that number has decreased, especially in the large cities. The average number of children in a family has gone from 6.3 in 1960 to 2.8 in 1993.

Some progress has been made by the federal government in contraception and sexual education. Since 1986, the government has directed its efforts to educate young women in the use of contraceptives in order to reduce the number of teenage unmarried pregnancies. The programs are run by nurses and social workers who also teach the use of the contraceptive pill and condom use for STD prevention. These programs operate mostly in the large cities, such as São Paulo, Rio de Janeiro, Brasília, Belo Horizonte, and Recife.

Some branches of the federal government, such as SUS (Sistema Único de Saúde) offer free distribution of contraceptive pills as an IUD replacement for women who do not want to become pregnant. Research undertaken by the IPPM (Institute of Market Research of São Paulo) showed that 73 percent of those interviewed favor family planning in Brazil. In Rio de

Janeiro, the number reached 83 percent of the women and 78.9 percent of the men. Only 8.5 percent of those interviewed in Rio de Janeiro and 6.8 percent of those in other cities declared themselves totally and radically opposed to birth control.

[Although 75 percent of Brazil's 154 million people are Roman Catholic, the world's largest Roman Catholic population, every relevant statistic shows that most people ignore the Church's teachings on contraception and abortion. In a June 1994 survey of 2,076 Brazilian adults, 88 percent of the respondents said they did not follow the Church's teachings; for women 25 to 44, this figure was 90 percent. On a national scale, Brazil has experienced one the the most radical reductions in family size recorded in modern history. With 40 percent of adult Brazilian women working outside the home, the fertility rate in the developed south is below the replacement level of 2.1 children per woman; in the impoverished northeast, it is 4.0 but this is well below the 5.8 recorded in the region in 1980 (Brooke 1994).

[About two-thirds of the married women practice some form of contraception; 43 percent use oral contraceptives and 42 percent have been sterilized. The government, pressed by the Catholic bishops, has maintained laws against abortion and sterilization and blocked legislative efforts to provide free contraceptives through Brazil's national health service. Virtually all clinics that dispense contraceptives and information are maintained by private groups. Although opinion polls show that Brazilian women want universal access to modern contraceptives, they have little power to press this in the political establishment. Brazil has no women as state governors or Supreme Court justices; women hold only 4.7 percent of the seats in the 580-member Congress; and no women in the Brazilian Bar Association are directors, although 52 percent of the Association's members are women (Brooke 1994). (Editor)]

[The Brazilian woman is having fewer children than in the past. The average number of children for Brazilian women has been steadily decreasing over the last four decades. The 1991 Census reported an average of 2.7 children as compared to 6.28 children in 1960, 5.76 children in 1970, and 4.35 children in 1980 (*Anuário Estatístico Brasileiro 1992*, cited in *Veja*, 1994, 75). The decrease may be attributed to several factors, including the use of contraceptives, sterilization, and abortion, as opposed to the worldwide economic and social reasons for the decline.

[In contrast with the 1994 report by Brooke cited above, the Instituto Brasileiro de Geografia e Estatística—Anticoncepção, 1988, cited in *Veja* (1994, 75) reported that the majority of women, twenty-three million women or 62 percent, do not use a contraceptive method. As a result 1.4 million unwanted pregnancies result in abortion (Alan Guttmacher Institute, cited in *Veja*, 75). Of the methods of contraception that are most used, the oral contraceptive pill is used by 43 percent of the women, sterilization is used by 42 percent, 7 percent use the calendar method, 2 percent use condoms, 1 percent use the IUD, and 5 percent use other methods (Instituto Brasileiro de Geografia e Estatística—Anticoncepção, 1988, cited in *Veja,* 75). The pill, sterilization, and the IUD account for 86 percent of the contraceptive use in Brazil, as compared to their combined use of 38 percent in other "developed" countries (Instituto Brasileiro de Geografia e Estatística—Anticoncepção, 1988, World Health Organization—Reproductive Health, 1990, cited in *Veja,* 75).

[Among the live births, 32 percent are done by Caesarean section, the highest rate in the world, as compared to 29 percent in Puerto Rico, 24 percent in the United States, 10 percent in England, and 7 percent in Japan (World Health Organization, 1991, cited in *Veja* 1994, 75). One reason for the high incidence of Caesarean deliveries in Brazil can be traced to the high number of women who choose to have a tubal ligation done at the same time to limit future births. United Nations statistics show that maternal mortality is also high, with 150 deaths per 100,000 births, as compared to 3 deaths, 12 deaths, and 1,000 deaths per 100,000 births for Japan, the United States, and Guinea, respectively. In the rural areas, 35.6 percent of the births are done at home versus 7 percent in the urban areas.

[Of those people who use condoms, women at every age level buy fewer condoms than men. A Brazilian company reports that, on average, 12 percent of the condoms bought are bought by women and 88 percent are bought by men. The breakdown by age level is as follows: among those 15 to 19, 5 percent are bought by women and 95 percent by men; from ages 20 to 24, 18 percent by women and 82 percent by men; from ages 25 to 29, 19 percent by women and 81 percent by men; from ages 30 to 39, 23 percent by women and 77 percent by men; and from ages 40 or older, 28 percent by women and 72 percent by men (Dispomed Comercial Ltda., cited in *Veja,* 75). (RJN/SA)].

B. Teenage Unmarried Pregnancies

There are no reliable statistics on the number of unwed teenage pregnancies in Brazil.

In recent research among adolescents, we found that 16 percent of the subjects approved of the IUD as a contraceptive method while 48 percent disapproved. Meanwhile, the lack of information about sexuality and contraception has caused many single adolescent females to become pregnant. In São Paulo, 54 percent of the adolescent males interviewed considered women's preoccupation with pregnancy a female problem for which the female is solely responsible. Even with the risk of AIDS infection, 35 percent of the adolescents refused to use condoms because they believe it takes away from their pleasure. All these factors contribute to an increasing number of unwed teenage pregnancies. SUS has an unwanted pregnancy education and prevention program for female adolescents in several regions of São Paulo, and similar programs exist in other capital cities. Practically nothing is available in the rural areas.

Many young women faced with an unwanted pregnancy resort to clandestine abortion clinics to hide the pregnancy from family. When the unwanted pregnancy does not end in a clandestine abortion, it is more frequent for the unwed adolescent mother to remain single than to marry the father. In the majority of cases, 51.8 percent, the young fathers shirk their responsibility as a parent.

C. Abortion

With the increase in sexual activity, the number of abortions in Brazil is slowly growing. Article 128 of the Penal Code of 1940 allows only two reasons for legal abortion: when the pregnancy is the result of rape or when there is no other way to save the woman's life.

Abortion statistics are not reliable or consistent. In 1989, the World Health Organization reported nearly 5 million abortions a year in Brazil, about 10 percent of the number of abortions performed worldwide. A research study in São Paulo, 1993, revealed 4.5 million induced abortions per year in Brazil. The incidence is highest among women ages 15 to 19, with 136 abortions per every 1,000 women in this age bracket. Nationally, there are 8.3 illegal abortions for every 100 pregnancies. Brazil records about 400,000 hospitalizations for medical complications of abortions annually; in the United States only 10,000 women experience complications requiring hospitalization.

In 1989, a National Research of Health and Nutrition study conducted by the Institute of Geography and Statistics (IBGE), found the index of abortions greater among women of the southeast, 16.4 percent, than among women of the northeast, 14.4 percent. These two regions accounted for 75 percent of all the pregnant women in Brazil. These statistics are informative when one recalls that the southeast region has a higher standard of living than the northeast. In the poorer northeast, there were 45 pregnant women per 1,000 women; in the more economically developed southeast, the rate was 33 per 1,000 women. This is in keeping with the hypothesis that a higher standard of economic development and better standard of living leads to a lower number of pregnancies. A second factor in the incidence of clandestine abortions is the number of previous pregnancies a woman has had. Of 13,862,844 women who were pregnant in the past five years, 14.9 percent terminated a pregnancy at least once. Among women who had had four previous pregnancies, 47.1 percent terminated the fifth pregnancy. Among women who had had five previous pregnancies, 77.1 percent terminated a subsequent pregnancy.

Several reasons are commonly cited to justify the legalization of abortion in Brazil: (1) a woman's right to control her own body, (2) socioeconomic factors such as the lack of support and sustenance for children resulting from unwanted pregnancies, (3) "if so many people are doing it, why not legalize it?" (4) fetal malformations, (5) therapeutic abortions are already legal to save a mother's life, and (6) abortion is already allowed in cases of rape. Other factors supporting the legalization of abortion include the increase in sexual promiscuity, which increases the number of illegal abortions, and the chaos in the official system of public health, which reduces the distribution of contraceptives that could reduce the incidence of illegal abortions.

Presently, a task force of the Federal Council of Medicine is proposing the legalization of abortion for cases where the fetus will be born with serious or irreversible physical or mental problems. If this proposal is approved by The National Congress, then abortions will become legal in private or public hospitals, up to the twenty-fourth week of gestation, with the consent of the pregnant woman and the affidavit of two doctors. However, abortion continues to be a crime in Brazil today.

D. Population Control Efforts

There are numerous efforts to promote a reduction in the population growth in Brazil. It is worrisome to find that São Paulo has 16.4 million inhabitants, being the second largest city in the world, second only to Tokyo, Japan, with 20 million inhabitants. Government campaigns carried on television and in newspapers inform people on the need to prevent an excessive growth of the population that does not have the necessary infrastructures, especially work and food supplies, to support it. Haphazard, uncontrolled population growth has led to the appearance of abandoned children, beggars, and would-be criminals (*marginais desocupados*) with nothing to do, all of whom are a heavy burden to a society without sufficient support structure.

The small family model has been in place in the large Brazilian cities since 1960, when the average of 6.3 children per family started to drop to the current 2.8 children per family. In rural areas, which comprises the largest area of the country, the average number of children in a family is still high at 5.7. However, we can assume that an accentuated drop in fertility in Brazil has resulted from the family planning campaigns. Reports tell us that 65 percent of the Brazilian couples of reproductive age use some type of contraceptive, with female surgical sterilization predominating. For example, in the United Kingdom female sterilization accounts for 8 percent of all contraception, in Belgium 5 percent, and in Italy 1 percent. In Brazil, female surgical sterilization accounts for 27 percent of the contraceptive usage. Hormonal therapies account for 25 percent, IUDs 1.3 percent, and vasectomies 0.7 percent. Other less-effective methods account for 11 percent of all contraception used.

10. Sexually Transmitted Diseases

A. Incidence, Patterns, and Trends

The incidence of gonorrhea, which had diminished considerably until 1960, increased greatly with the sexual liberty that developed in the 1970s. Syphilis also increased during that period of greater sexual promiscuity. With the advent of AIDS, the condom that had been used solely by prostitutes to avoid disease or pregnancy became the principal method of protection against the transmission of the HIV virus, and in the process benefited the campaigns against other STDs in our country.

In Brazil, STDs have increased significantly in the younger population, fifteen to twenty years old. Based on statistics from several States, we estimate that 15 percent of the youth has already contracted a venereal disease. This amounts to about 2.2 million youths.

The Ministry of Health wants to encourage the war against the incidence of STDs through educational campaigns. They believe that any serious effort to control STDs must begin in the schools. According to Dr. Belda, venereal diseases are symptomatic of what he called a "social sickness," because their basic causes are connected to the behavior of individuals and communities. Among the factors cited as responsible for the changes in sexual conduct are the increase in promiscuity, variation in sexual customs, the migration of populations, and greater ease in transportation. We also admit that the increasing use of contraceptives also serves to increase promiscuity. Along with increased promiscuity, there is increased risk of contracting venereal diseases such as syphilis, gonorrhea, venereal lymphogranuloma, chancroids, inguinal granuloma, genital herpes, condyloma acuminatum, and HIV.

The most frequent STDs are syphilis and gonorrhea. The other STDs are not very common and escape the Health Ministry's statistical control. Syphilis is found in men in its primary phase, mostly because of its obvious clinical signs. However, it goes unnoticed in women, being confused with other vulvar inflammations. When it is diagnosed in women, it is most often in the secondary phase as a part of prenuptial exams. That is why the campaigns must especially reach groups such as prostitutes, homosexuals, and unwed youth.

Despite the lack of credible data, there is much evidence to indicate a new surge in gonorrhea in Brazil. In Rio de Janeiro, the incidence of gonorrhea grew by 120 percent between 1968 and 1972 while the population grew only 6 percent.

11. HIV/AIDS

A. Incidence and Transmission

At the end of 1992, The Ministry of Health reported a total of 31,466 cases of AIDS in Brazil. An estimated 450,000 Brazilians are infected with the

HIV virus but present no clinical signs characteristic of the disease. São Paulo has the largest number of cases, 18,755 patients, followed by Rio de Janeiro with 4,933 cases and Rio Grande do Sul with 1,468 cases. Out of a total of 31,466 AIDS patients, 13,874 have already died, according to a report from the AIDS Division.

The known cases of AIDS in newborns are few and rare. Recent reports indicate only 634 perinatal cases. Of all the occurrences, 3.6 percent or 1,143 were found in people under 15 years of age. Among adolescents, ages 15 to 20, the incidence of AIDS associated with IV drug use has risen from 3 percent in 1980 to 24 percent in 1993. While there has been a reduction in the number of infections transmitted by sexual contact, authorities are increasingly concerned about this rising transmission of the virus among IV drug users. According to the latest report (1993), 19,060 of the 31,466 total AIDS cases were victims of heterosexual, bisexual, or homosexual transmission. Another 8,508 have contracted the disease through contact with infected blood. In adults, the ratio is seven infected males for every one female infected with the virus.

In a research project in Rio de Janeiro involving 1,350 men and women between 15 and 59 years of age, the authors found that 100 percent of homosexual and bisexual respondents were informed about AIDS. However, only 38.8 percent of the men and 18.3 percent of the women had changed their sexual practices to avoid AIDS. The government campaigns stress the importance of using the condom as a means to avoid AIDS. Many homosexuals and bisexuals do not use condoms because it "inhibits sexual pleasure." They say the use of the condom is not well accepted because a man may be offended if a woman insists he use one or a woman may become suspicious if a man uses one. Weighing the risks of losing a partner who already loves you against the risk of contracting AIDS, many people choose to take the risk of contracting the disease.

In the Brazilian cultural tradition, the notion of homosexuality is more related to a passive (receptive) versus an active (penetrative) role. "The medical/scientific model has often been reinterpreted in traditional folk concepts, with their emphasis not on sexual object choice, as in the categories *homossexualidade* or *heterossexualidade*, but rather on *atividade* and *passividade*. In popular thought, the category of *homossexuais* or 'homosexuals' has generally been reserved for 'passive' partners, while the classification of 'active' partners in same-sex interactions has remained rather unclear and ambiguous (Parker 1987, 162). This causes some men to classify themselves as heterosexual, when in reality they are homosexual or bisexual. The result is that many AIDS prevention programs adopted from the United States to reach males engaging in anal intercourse do not reach their target audience. The disease is spreading among homosexuals and heterosexuals alike as a consequence of poor sexual knowledge and a lack of care. There has not been any research among lesbians, but it seems to us that there has not been an increase in disease among these women except among those who use IV drugs (Paiva 1995).

B. Availability of Treatment and Prevention Programs

Prevention programs for AIDS, using the slogans "Use a Condom" or "Practice Safe Sex" copy the North American models and do not take into account the particularities of sexuality in Brazil (Parker 1987). The practice of anal sex, as noted in Section 5C, is much more common between men and women in Brazil than in the United States where it is a more frequent behavior among homosexuals.

There is a great mobilization of the community in a program of AIDS prevention through the development of several societies, the organization of lectures (*palestras*), the showing of films, professional health courses, the distribution of pamphlets, and information on radio and television programs. Meanwhile, religious groups protest and critique the campaigns because they seem to support solely the use of the condom and the disposable syringe. They believe it would be more educational and formative to discourage homosexuality, promiscuous sex, and drug use.

There has been no lack of the drug AZT. Even though it is a very expensive drug and not very efficacious in the treatment of AIDS, it has been distributed freely to patients with HIV who report to the Health Centers. Presently, Brazil is fourth worldwide in the number of AIDS cases, according to the World Health Organization. The United States has the most cases, followed by Uganda and Tanzania. France is fifth and Zaire is sixth (1992 data). Several years ago, Parker noted that:

> it is clear that a careful examination of the cultural context in Brazil inevitably leads to the conclusion that the health problem posed by AIDS and facing Brazilian society is potentially far more widespread and serious that has thus far been acknowledged . . . . Brazil is facing an epidemic disease that is potentially as devastating as the other serious public health problems that already exist there, and a combination of prejudice, short-sighted planning, and economic instability has left Brazilian society almost entirely unprepared to confront it. (Parker 1987, 169)

Presently, much attention has been given to the protection of those who work in the Health Industry and have contact with the high risk groups in the general population, especially adolescents. The voluntary testing for HIV has been encouraged, and there is a campaign to protect those who test positive against discrimination.

12. Sexual Dysfunction, Counseling, and Therapies

A/B. Concepts of Sexual Dysfunction and Treatment

Sexology has been a medical specialty in Brazil since September 30, 1980. But, the majority of the physicians and the public are not aware of this.

Brazilian culture exalts the virile man and erectile dysfunction is considered a great shame. This leads men to depression and the common practice of not admitting they are impotent and blaming the woman when forced to admit it. Various sexual therapy clinics have emerged in the large cities, some of them without any modern scientific basis. There are a few legitimate groups that deal mostly with male sexual dysfunctions; a breakdown of such clinical treatment includes lack of erection 52 percent, ejaculatory problems 26 percent, and reduced libido 22 percent.

The use of vascular surgery is very common for male erectile dysfunction, followed by the insertion of a prosthesis to improve erection, for problems of an organic origin. Psychotherapy and hormone therapy are used in psychogenic problems.

Since 1986, the Department of Sexology of the ARE—Várzea do Carmo in São Paulo has been exclusively dedicated to the treatment of female sexual dysfunctions. Their case distribution is: inhibited sexual desire/arousal 37 percent, anorgasmia 61 percent, and vaginismus 2 percent. In a study of 150 clients at this clinic, Sergio L. Freitas found that 80 percent of the treated women were cured of their symptoms while 20 percent dropped out of therapy for several reasons. Half of the women treated did so without their husband's knowledge. The husband's machismo jealousy and pride will not permit them to seek help openly. It was necessary to combine psychoanalytical and gynecological methods, and the techniques of Helen Singer Kaplan's *New Sex Therapy*, with a reconditioning and remedial sexual education. The main causes of sexual disturbances were related to sexual disinformation, negative early sexual experiences, and a poor-quality sex life. The average age was 32 years old. Treatment lasted from three to ten weeks. We found that 27 percent of the women were married without knowing that the sexual act was normal conduct in matrimony. Sixty percent were virgins when they married; 87.7 percent found their first sexual relation to be somewhere between bad and awful; 13.3 percent found it to be acceptable; while none rated their early sexual experiences as either good or great.

The training of professionals for diagnosis and treatment takes place at the institutes mentioned in Section 13A. Certificates are awarded at a postgraduate level, following both theoretical and practical training through the observation of cases in active therapy.

Recent economic conditions have taken their toll on Brazilian sexuality. In a tropical land soaked with sensuality, economic anxieties are tarnishing a point of Brazilian national pride: bedroom performance. Harried by an annual inflation of 2,500 percent, two-thirds of the adults surveyed in 1994 complained that the economic crisis was dampening their libido. Brazil's sex crisis is manifest at the dilapidated motels that line the roads into Rio de Janeiro. These establishments, featuring ceiling mirrors and suggestive names like "Lipstick," "Pussycat," and "L'Amour," offer hourly rates. Opened in the economic go-go years of the 1970s, many of these 225 motels in Rio are now deteriorating for lack of maintenance. Once discreet, they now fight to survive by advertising on television and offering promotions like discount lottery tickets or free lunches. Even so, Rio's motel industry trade association estimates that motels are renting their rooms at discounts averaging 40 percent. Respondents in a Brasmarket poll listed the following reasons in descending importance for the flagging sex drive: insecurity, lack of money for a date, street crime that keeps people at home, and lack of money for a motel.

13. Sexual Research and Advanced Education

A. Institutes and Programs for Sexological Research

Sexology was recognized as a medical specialty in Brazil in 1980. Some postgraduate courses are offered at the Institute Saedes Sapietiae and at the Institute Havelock Ellis. These courses have been run by the Department of Sexology—ARE—Várzea do Carmo since 1986, by Dr. Sérgio Freitas. They offer practical training in sexology to professionals in the areas of psychology, nursing, social work, and medicine. The text *Becoming a Sexual Person* (Robert T. Francoeur, 2nd ed., New York: Macmillan, 1991) has been utilized as the basis for graduate courses in sexology, along with research in the area of sexuality and behavior of the Brazilian woman, since 1992. Interest for this clinical specialty has had a recent impulse because of the XI World Congress of Sexology, held in June 1993 in Rio de Janeiro.

Among the organizations carrying on research, promoting courses, and running conventions on human sexuality in Brazil are the following:

Brazilian Association of Sexology (AB-SEX) (Associação Brasileira de Sexologia). Dr. Sérgio Luiz G. de Freitas, M.D., President. Address: Rua Tamandaré, 693 - Conj. 77, 01525-001 São Paulo, SP, Brazil.

Brazilian Sexual Impotency Research Society. Sociedade Brasileira de Pesquisa sobre Impotência Sexual. Roberto Tullii, M.D., Director. Address: Alameda Gabriel Monteiro da Silva, 1719, 01441-000 São Paulo, SP, Brazil.

Brazilian Sexual Education Association. Associação Brasileira de Educação Sexual. Address: Alameda Itú, 859, Apto 61, 01421-000 São Paulo, SP, Brazil.

Brazilian Society of Sexology. Isaac Charam, M.D., President. Address: Praça Serzedelo Correia, 15, Apto 703, 22040-000 Rio de Janeiro, RJ, Brazil.

Brazilian Society of Human Sexuality. Sociedade Brasileira de Sexualidade Humana. Address: Av. N.S. Copacabana, 1072, s. 703, 22020-001 Rio de Janeiro, RJ, Brazil.

Sexology Nucleus of Rio de Janeiro. Núcleo de Sexologia do Rio de Janeiro (NUDES). Address: Av Copacabana, 1018, Grupo 1109, 22060-000 Rio de Janeiro, RJ, Brazil.

National Sexology Commission of The Brazilian Federation of the Societies of Gynecology and Obstetrics. Comissão Nacional de Sexologia da Federação Brasileira das Sociedades de Ginecologia e Obstetrícia (FEBRASGO). Address: Edf. Venancio 2000, Bloco 50, Sala 137, 70302-000 Brasília, DF, Brazil.

Paranaense Commission of Sexology. Comissal Paranaense de Sexologia. Address: Rua General Carneiro, 181 - 4º andar. Maternidade do Hosp. de Clínicas, 80060-000 Curitiba, PR, Brazil.

Department of Sexology - ARE - Várzea do Carmo. Departamento de Sexologia - ARE - Várzea de Carmo. Address: Rua Leopoldo Miguez, 257, 01518-000 São Paulo, SP, Brazil.

B. Sexological Publications and Journals

The only sexological journal published in Brazil is *Jornal da AB-SEX*, published since 1986 by the Brazilian Association of Sexology (AB-SEX) (Associação Brasileira de Sexologia). Address: Rua Tamandaré, 693, Conj. 77, 01525-001 São Paulo, SP, Brazil.

Some newspapers, magazines, and other popular periodicals publish columns dealing with sexual interests that provide an insight into Brazilian sexual cultures and behaviors. These include *Notícias Populares* (SP), *Claúdia*, *Nova*, and *Carícia* (Editora Abril).

14. Sexual Behaviors of Aboriginal Indians

A. Puberty Rituals and Premarital Activities

The behavior of several indigenous tribes of Brazil is similar, except for some variations particular to each native culture. The indigenous groups, such as the Kapalo, Xavantes, Tupinambas, and the Alpinages, have developed similar rituals for children and adolescents.

A girl is promised as a future bride while she is still very young, usually about 5 years of age. The future groom is a male adolescent, about 16 years old, who will marry her when she enters puberty and has her first menstruation. After her first menstruation, the girl is taken to the women's house (*Oca*). There she will remain for an entire year without being permitted to see sunlight or trim her hair. After a year's time, she is removed from the house and prepared for the nuptial party. She will be married to that same young man, who is now about 26 years of age.

Among the Kapalo, rituals of preparation for the male adolescent begin when he completes his sixteenth birthday. He must pass tests of courage, physical endurance, and resistance to pain. The boy must run through the forest for several kilometers while carrying a tree trunk. He must climb a tree and insert his arm into a bee or wasp hive, descending only after he has been stung several times. He must not hurry his descent nor run from the tree. He must also not scream or cry in pain. The boy must also demonstrate his skill in hunting and fishing with arrows (nets and hooks are not permitted for fishing). After passing all these tests, he is considered to be an adult. He will no longer live in the boys' house and must now reside in the unmarried men's house (*Oca*). He will then begin to take part in the adult fights and competitions.

At this point he begins his sexual initiation. He may have sexual relations with any widow, older single women, and his older brother's wife. Sexual intercourse occurs mostly between people of different generations: the older generation teaches the younger generation.

Virginity is of secondary value. Girls usually lose their virginity before their wedding. The explanation is simple. The young women and men are not knowledgeable of the ways of the world. They marry old people of the opposite sex so they can learn from them.

B. Sexual Behaviors of Single Adults

Because girls are married about age 5, there is a lack of young single women. Young men thus must be content with much older women. Although most are postmenopausal and sterile, there is the advantage of having a wife who knows how to cook, tend the fire, and keep the house. Thus, single young men will take any old woman for a bride, even if they do not find her attractive. As soon as it becomes possible, she will be traded for a younger wife. Men can only have sexual relations with fertile women after they have executed at least one enemy in a ritual killing.

Sometimes, the parents of the groom offer him an enemy to execute. However, if he wishes to marry a young woman, he must capture and kill an enemy himself. Because of this ritual, a single young man very seldom marries a fertile young woman before he is at least thirty years old. Men may only take part in war expeditions between the ages of 26 and 40 years of age. A man that has never imprisoned any slaves is labeled a "bad apple," or weak, timid, and cowardly (*Mebek*). He will never marry.

C. Cohabitation, Marriage, and Monogamy

There is cohabitation without marriage but once married a woman's fidelity is demanded. Older men may reserve for themselves a high number of women, especially if they have gained power or prestige as warriors, medicine men, or Great Chiefs (*Caciques*). Old men are privileged, they can even reserve prepubescent (premenarche) girls for themselves. When a *Cacique* receives a young girl from her parents, he will wait for the first menstruation before having sexual intercourse with her. It is taboo to have sexual relations before menarche. There are frequent cases where there is reciprocal affection between a couple, and they remain united until the death of one of the consorts.

Dissolution of a marriage occurs with ease and frequency. Any incident as simple as a domestic disturbance or indisposition can lead to separation.

The major cause of breach is the wife's adultery. In these cases, the mildest punishment is for the wife to be returned to her parents. A man may also repudiate, or even kill an adulterous woman, according to the tribe's natural laws. However, a man's adultery is received with approval by the community, which is amused by it. When a pregnant woman, widowed, divorced, or with a traveling husband, has sexual relations with another man, there is the difficulty in determining the father of the child. Such children, known as *Maraca*, "fruit of two seeds," are buried alive immediately following their birth.

This procedure also occurs any time twins are born. They believe twin children are generated by antagonistic spirits and must therefore be sacrificed.

After a birth there are some sexual prohibitions. The husband must abstain from sexual relations from the beginning of the pregnancy until the child can walk by itself, or is at least a year old. This is the reason why men may have several wives (polygyny). In this manner, a man only has sexual relations with the same wife two years after the beginning of pregnancy.

References and Suggested Readings

"Abortos Ilegais Chegam a 6 Milhões por Ano." November 9, 1990. *O Estrado de São Paulo*, p. 12.

Azevedo, Maria A. 1985. *Mulheres Espancadas: Violência Denunciada.* São Paulo: Editora Soma.

"Brasil Realiza 10% dos Abortos no *Mundo*." January 1, 1989. *Folha de São Paulo.*

Brooke, James. September 2, 1994. "With Church Preaching in Vain, Brazilians Embrace Birth Control." *The New York Times*, A1 and A3.

"Cirurgias Clandestinas Chegam a 5 Milhões." July 2, 1987. *Folha de São Paulo.* Caderno C, p. 7.

Da Matta, Roberto. 1983. "Para Uma Teoria de Sacanagem: Uma Reflexão Sobre a Obra de Carlos Zefiro." In Joaquim Marinho, ed. *A Arte Sacana de Carlos Zefiro.* Rio de Janeiro: Editora Marco Zero, pp. 22-39.

Da Mata, Roberto. 1978. *Carnavais Malandros e Heróis: Para Uma Sociologia do Dilema Brasileiro.* Rio de Janeiro: Zahar Editores.

Fernandes, Florestan. 1989. *Organização Social dos Tupinambas.* São Paulo: Editora Hucitec.

Freitas, Sérgio L. G. 1989. *Sexologia ao Alcance de Todos.* São Paulo: Editora Comunidade (out of print).

Freitas, Sérgio L. G. 1993. *Relatório Freitas—Comportamento Sexual da Mulher Brasileira.* São Paulo: Editora Soma.

IPPM. 1983. *Hábitos e Atitudes Sexuais dos Brasileiros.* Cultrix e Lab. Syntex do Brasil.

Loyola, M. A., ed. 1994. *AIDS e Sexualidade: O Ponto de Vista das Ciências Humanas* ["AIDS and Sexuality: The Point of View of the Social Sciences"]. Rio de Janeiro, RJ, Brasil: Relume Dumará/Universidade do Estado do Rio de Janeiro.

Manchete. 1992 (October 10). "Sexo Depois dos 60" ["Sex After 60"], p. 40.

Maybury-Lewis, David. 1983. *Sociedade Xavante.* São Paulo.

Muraro, R. M. 1983. *Sexualidade da Mulher Brasileira: Corpo e Classe Social no Brasil* ["Sexuality of the Brazilian Woman: Body and Social Class in Brazil"]. Petrópolis, RJ, Brasil: Vozes.

"O Brasil Tem 10% dos Abortos Feitos no Mundo." November 9, 1990. *Folha de São Paulo,* Caderno C, p. 4.

Paiva, Vera. 1995. "Sexuality, AIDS and Gender Norms Among Brazilian Teenagers." In: Han ten Brummelhuis and Gilbert Herdt, ed. *Culture and Sexual Risk: Anthropological Perspectives on AIDS.* Amsterdam: Gordon and Breach Science Publishers.

Parker, R. G. 1991. *Corpos, Prazeres e Paixões: A Cultura Sexual no Brasil Contemporâneo* ["Bodies, Pleasures and Passions: Sexual Culture in Contemporary Brazil"]. Trans. M.T.M. Cavallari. São Paulo, SP, Brasil: Editora Best Seller. English translation published as *Pleasures and Passions: Sexual Cultures in Contemporary Brazil.* Boston: Beacon Press.

Parker, R. G. 1987. "Acquired Immunodeficiency Syndrome in Urban Brazil." *Medical Anthropology Quarterly.* n.s., 1(2):155-75.

Parker, R. G. 1985. "Masculinity, Feminity, and Homosexuality: On the Anthropological Interpretation of Sexual Meanings in Brazil." *Journal of Homosexuality,* 11(3/4):155-63.

Parker, R. G. 1984. "The Body and Self: Aspects of Male Sexual Ideology in Brazil." Paper presented at the 83rd Annual Meeting of the American Anthropological Association. Denver, Colorado.

Parker, R., C. Bastos, J. Galvão and J. S. Pedrosa, eds. 1994. *A AIDS no Brasil* ["AIDS in Brazil"]. Rio de Janeiro, RJ, Brasil: Relume Dumará/Associação Brasileira Interdisciplinar de AIDS/Instituto de Medicina Social, Universidade do Estado do Rio de Janeiro.

Rega, Lourenço S. 1989. *Aspectos Éticos do Abortamento.* A monograph.

Saffioti, H. I. B., and M. Muñoz-Vargas, eds. 1994. *Mulher Brasileira É Assim* ["The Brazilian Woman Is Like This"]. Rio de Janeiro, RJ, Brasil: Editora Rosa Dos Tempos Ltda.

Santa Inêz, Antonio Leal de. 1983. *Hábitos e Atitudes Sexuals dos Brasilieros.* São Paulo: Editora Cultrix.

Schrierberg, David. October 9, 1995. "Samba Warnings: Porn and Promiscuity Provoke a Backlash." *Newsweek,* p. 52.

Suplicy, Marta. 1994. "Sexuality Education in Brazil." *SIECUS Report,* 22(2), 1-6.

Suplicy, Marta. 1985. *De Mariazinha a Maria.* Petrópolis: Editora Vozes.

Suplicy, Marta. 1983. *Conversa Sobre Sexo.* Petrópolis: Editora Vozes.

U.S. News & World Report. 1994 (April). "Battered by the Myth of Machismo: Violence Against Women Is Endemic in Brazil," p. 41.

Veja Especial: Mulher: A Grande Mudança no Brasil ["*Veja* Special: Woman: The Big Change in Brazil"], August/September 1994.

Canada

Michael Barrett, Ph.D, Alan King, Ed.D., Joseph Lévy, Ph.D.,
Eleanor Maticka-Tyndale, Ph.D., and Alexander McKay, Ph.D.

Contents

Preamble

Given Canada's ethnocultural, linguistic, religious, and urban/rural diversity (see Section A below), and its sociological and gender diversity (Section B), we have wondered whether it is possible to present an overview of the sexuality of Canadians. The risk in attempting to do so is that one will "homogenize" the rich diversity by taking the "average" opinion or the median frequency of specific behaviors as a reflection of what Canadians are like sexually. On the other hand, a focus on different subgroups within the population may beg the question of whether Canada has a national identity pertaining to sexual customs, beliefs, and practices. At the national ("macro") level, there are quantitative data about some aspects of behavior—although there have been no large-scale studies of adult sexual behavior in Canada—but it is often difficult to interpret such information in ways that would further our understanding about the particularities of "Canadian" sexuality. On the other hand, studies on selected populations in specific settings, the "micro" approach, are often designed to describe or explain the behavior of that group, but they are seldom done in ways that would permit comparisons across Canada or over time. While sexological research in Canada has grown significantly over the last twenty years, it is still a new field and these limitations on our national database are neither surprising nor insurmountable. Our compromise, therefore, has been to incorporate elements of both the macro and micro approaches, to provide quantitative information where possible, and to make cautious inferences where empirical evidence is lacking.

Demographics and a Historical Perspective

A. Demographics

Although geographically Canada is the largest country in the Western Hemisphere with 3.85 million square miles including the Yukon and Northwest Territories, only about 10 percent of its land mass is suitable for permanent large-scale settlement and only slightly more than that for permanent agriculture. The 1997 population of more than 30 million inhabitants is distributed unevenly among the ten provinces and two territories with Ontario, Quebec, British Columbia, and Alberta accounting for 84 percent of the total (Table 1). Most people live in cities (about 80 percent), primarily in the southern regions of the country, with the three largest metropolitan centers around Toronto (Ontario), Montreal (Quebec), and Vancouver (British Columbia) accounting for over one quarter of these urban dwellers. A 5,300 km shared border with the United States, a recently signed free-trade agreement, and extensive consumption of U.S. media, expose Canadians to strong economic and cultural influences from a country with over nine times its population. However, the history, composition (e.g., religious and ethnocultural mix, socioeconomic diversity), and structure (e.g., legal, medical) of the two neighbors differ in ways that have an important influence on sexuality in the two countries.

Canada's ten provinces, plus the Yukon and Northwest Territories, are linked through a central federal government but the various levels of federal, provincial, regional, and municipal government have differing levels of responsibility for health, education, social welfare, legislation, and other areas that impact upon sexuality and sexual health.

The proportion of the population over 65 (12 percent in 1995) is projected to increase to about 16 percent within the next twenty years given continued high levels of immigration (approximately 200,000 per year) and continued low fertility rates (1.67 in 1995). In contrast, the proportion

Table 1

Population Distribution in Canada (1996)

Province/Territory	Population (in Thousands)	Percentage of Total
CANADA (April 1, 1996)	29,857.4	
Newfoundland	571.2	1.9
Prince Edward Island	137.3	0.5
Nova Scotia	941.2	3.2
New Brunswick	761.9	2.6
Quebec	7,366.9	24.7
Ontario	11,209.5	37.5
Manitoba	1,141.7	3.8
Saskatchewan	1,021.1	3.7
Alberta	2,774.5	9.3
British Columbia	3,835.7	12.8
Yukon	31.1	0.1
Northwest Territories	66.2	0.2

Source: *Quarterly Demographic Statistics*, Statistics Canada, Catalogue No. 91-002, Vol. 10, No. 1, July 1996.

under 15 (21 percent in 1995) is projected to decline further to about 16 percent over the same period (Beaujot 1991). The large segment of the population now in the middle years, i.e., the "baby boom" generation born between the late 1940s and the early 1960s, has exerted considerable influence on social and cultural patterns in Canada from the "sexual revolution" of the late 1960s to the economic expansion of the 1980s. This generation currently holds many of the positions in government, business, health care, and the media, and might therefore be expected to influence public policy in relation to sexuality (i.e., in areas such as education, law, health care, etc.).

The changing age structure of the population, coupled with high life expectancy (75 years for men; 81 years for women in 1995), and a declining rate of natural population increase (0.6 percent in 1995), are all characteristic of the demographic transition seen in other industrialized northern countries (see basic demographic data for Canada in Table 2). The birth rate in 1995 was 13 per thousand persons, the death rate 7 per thousand, and the infant mortality rate 7 per thousand live births. Although the total fertility rate has been below replacement level for twenty-five years (about 1.7 children per woman in 1995), a natural population increase of 0.6 percent per year, coupled with a comparable rate of net immigration (0.6 percent), gave Canada a growth rate of 1.2 percent in 1995, one of the highest among the world's industrialized countries. Net immigration contributed a little over 50 percent of Canada's population

Table 2

Basic Demographic Data for Canada (1995)

Total population:	29,955,000 (July 1, 1996 est.)
Total population:	29,606,100 (July 1, 1995 est.)
Total population:	29,251,300 (July 1, 1994 est.)
Births:	380,300
Deaths:	210,600
Natural increase:	169,700
Birth rate:	13.0/1,000 population
Death rate:	7.2/1,000 population
Rate of natural increase:	5.8/1,000 population (0.58%)
Immigration:	220,100 (est.)
Net immigration:	185,100
Net immigration rate:	6.3/1,000 population (0.63%)
Total population increase:	354,800
Annual population growth rate:	1.2%
% population growth from natural increase:	47.8%
% population growth from net immigration:	52.2%
Population doubling time:	58 years
Total fertility rate (est.):	1.66 births per woman aged 15-49
Life expectancy at birth:	male 75 years; female 81 years

Data from: *Annual Demographic Statistics*, 1995. Statistics Canada, Catalogue No. 91-213-XPB, 1996. See also Dumas and Belanger (1995).

increase in 1995 and current trends suggest that immigration will continue to have a significant impact on Canada's demographic future. In 1995, Canada had one hospital bed per 149 persons and one physician per 484 persons. Literacy was 96 percent in 1994. The 1995 per capita domestic product was $22,200.

By law the federal government is required to state in advance of any year the intended total number of immigrants, refugees, etc., that will be admitted to Canada in that year. The five-year period from 1989-94 specified about 250,000 immigrants per year (emigration is approximately 40,000 per year). The level for 1997 has been set between 195,000 and 220,000. Immigration patterns over the past ten years and in the future will continue to alter the already varied ethnocultural composition of the Canadian population, particularly in the larger urban centers to which a high proportion of immigrants have been drawn. Canada's changing ethnocultural composition, discussed in Section C below and also in Section 9D, is of interest. The continuing trend to ethnocultural diversity suggests that a wide range of attitudes, traditions, and practices surrounding marriage, sexuality, sex role expectations, and sexual taboos will be present as a source of both variety and potential conflict in Canadian society.

B. A Brief Historical Perspective*

At the time that European explorers first arrived, the area now called Canada was already occupied by indigenous peoples who came to be called North American Indians (now First Nations) and Inuit. People with aboriginal ancestry currently represent about 3.7 percent of Canada's population.

The French explorer, Jacques Cartier, who reached the Gulf of St. Lawrence in 1534, is generally regarded as the founder of Canada, although John Cabot, an English seaman had sighted Newfoundland thirty-seven years earlier, and Vikings are believed to have reached the same area centuries before either Cartier or Cabot. The French pioneered settlement by establishing Quebec City in 1606, Montreal in 1642, and declaring Canada a colony in 1663. The British acquired Acadia (Nova Scotia) in 1717 and captured Quebec in 1759. By 1763, Britain had gained control of the rest of New France. The Quebec Act of 1774 gave the French in Upper Canada the right to their own language, religion, and civil law. The English presence in Canada increased during the American Revolution when many American colonists loyal to the crown moved north to Canada. Fur traders and explorers pioneered paths to the west, with Sir Alexander Mackenzie reaching the Pacific in 1793.

Upper and Lower Canada, later known as Quebec and Ontario, and the Maritime Provinces developed their own local legislative assemblies in the 1700s, and reformers called for a more responsible government. The War of 1812 between Britain and the United States delayed the move toward a more democratic government, but by 1837 political agitation had led to rebellions in both Upper and Lower Canada. Lord Durham's report recommended union of the two parts into one colony, to be called Canada. This union continued until 1867 when the Dominion of Canada was established with Ontario, Quebec, Nova Scotia, and New Brunswick. A federal system of government was developed, modeled on the British parliament and cabinet structure under the Crown. In 1982, Canada ended its last formal legislative link with Britain by assuming control over its constitution. In 1987, the so-called Meech Lake Agreement would have assured constitutional protection for Quebec's efforts to protect its French language and culture. Its failure in 1990 sparked a separatist revival which remains a major issue for the country. In 1992, the Northwest Territories approved creation of a self-governing homeland for the 17,500 Inuit living in the Territories, to be known as Nunavut, "Our Land."

C. Ethnocultural Composition: Ethnic Origins and Recent Immigration

The face of Canada, as is true for the United States and Australia, has been shaped by immigrants. European settlers from the United Kingdom (U.K.)

*R. T. Francoeur, the *Encyclopedia*'s editor, provided this brief historical perspective.

and France are considered the two founding nations of Canada (and the current ethnic composition of the population still reflects that background). However, many First Nations groups were already inhabiting the region when these settlers arrived, including Cree, Dakota, Dene, Gitksan, Gwich'in, Huron, Innu, Inuit, Mohawk, Micmac, Naskapi, Ojibway, Saulteaux, and Salish. In the 1991 census, over one million people (3.7 percent of the population) identified either single or mixed aboriginal ancestry.

Canada's 1991 census provides the most accurate and current profile of the the ethnic origins of people living in Canada. A review of that data by Renaud and Badets (1993) and selected observations from a major study on families in Canada (Vanier Institute of the Family 1994) are used below to summarize the increasingly diverse ethnocultural composition of Canadian society.

Ethnic origin is taken to mean the cultural or ethnic group to which one's distant relatives belonged. In the 1991 census, respondents were asked to indicate whether their ancestry was a single ethnic group (e.g., French) or multiple (two or more groups, e.g., British and French). Rounded percentages for the largest groupings were: British, i.e., all United Kingdom countries (28 percent), French, i.e., French, Acadian (east coast French) or Quebecois (23 percent), British and French (4 percent), British, French, and other (14 percent), other European (15 percent), Asian (6 percent), Aboriginal, i.e., First Nations people (4 percent), and other (6 percent). Overall, 31 percent of Canada's population in 1991 reported ethnic origins other than British or French.

A report by Badets and Chui (1994) documents the changing pattern of immigration to Canada that has produced such ethnocultural diversity. While early immigrants to Canada came predominantly from the United Kingdom and Europe, that trend has shifted, particularly during the 1980s and into the 1990s. Between 1981 and 1991, 48 percent of immigrants to Canada were born in Asian countries, 25 percent in Europe and the United Kingdom, 10 percent in Central and South America, 6 percent each in the Caribbean and Africa, and 4 percent in the United States. In 1991, about 16 percent of Canada's population was born outside the country, which is not much different from the 15 percent figure reported thirty years earlier. Of these, 54 percent were from Europe and the United Kingdom and 25 percent from Asian countries. Most of the 4.3 million people in Canada in 1991 who were born outside the country either have become or will become Canadian citizens.

Of the 217,000 immigrants to Canada in 1994, about 94 percent settled in four provinces (Ontario, British Columbia, Quebec, and Alberta), predominantly in one of the three largest metropolitan areas (Toronto, Montreal, and Vancouver). It is not surprising, therefore, that 38 percent of Toronto's population in 1991 was not born in Canada. This rich ethnocultural diversity in some areas of the country provides a variety of sociosexual customs and gender role expectations that must be considered in education, health care, and public policy related to sexuality. These issues include: developing effective ways to prevent HIV infection among communities of First Nations people and other ethnocultural groups; differing attitudes and beliefs toward sexuality between first-generation immigrant parents and their children or between recent immigrants and the "predominant" culture; cross-cultural differences in gender role expectations, deference to authority, emphasis on reproduction and child rearing as the rationale for marriage; arranged marriages; attitudes and policies toward women who experienced genital mutilation in their country of origin (see Omer-Hashi and Entwistle 1995); the desire of some groups to use sex selection to provide a child of the preferred sex, usually male; and varied traditions concerning public discussion about sexuality, sex education, and discussion between the sexes about sexual problems and dysfunctions.

D. Linguistic Diversity

As expected from the ethnic origins of the population, 61 percent of Canadians reported English as their only first language (i.e., the one they learned at home in childhood and still understand), 24 percent French, and 13 percent one of the "nonofficial" languages (1991 census). Most French-speaking Canadians live in Quebec (81 percent of Quebec's population identified French as their first language), but there are groups of Acadians in New Brunswick and French-speaking communities in other parts of Canada. Immigrants (those not born in Canada) accounted for about two thirds of those whose first language was neither English nor French and for about three quarters of those who spoke a language other than English or French at home.

1. Basic Sexological Premises

A. Character of Gender Roles

At present over half of Canadian women who are raising children also do additional paid work outside the home. Although single (never married) women and men are equally likely to be employed (59 to 60 percent for both sexes in 1981 and 1991), the proportion of married women employed increased from 47 percent in 1981 to 56 percent in 1991. This represents a major change in the employment experience of women and is a reflection of changed economic circumstances, more single parent families, and the altered gender role expectations and opportunities for women over the last twenty years. However, 71 percent of women in 1991 were employed in one of five occupational groups (teaching, nursing/health care, clerical, sales, and service) compared to about 30 percent of men in these sectors (Ghalam 1993). This clearly demonstrates that though men and women are approaching equality in labor force participation, the labor force remains sex segregated with men and women concentrated in different areas.

In her book, *Gender Relations in Canada,* Marlene Mackie (1991) identified the evolution of feminism and of the feminist movement in Canada as a major influence on gender role expectations, on women's social and economic status, on their perceptions of themselves as agents for change, and hence on the social and interpersonal aspects of relationships within and between the sexes. The most recent wave of that movement, beginning in the late 1960s, has gradually altered the legislative landscape regarding equal employment, pay equity, access to legal abortion and contraception, sexual harassment, maternity leave, day care, and a range of other issues that affect women's social and economic well-being. Mackie (1991) suggests that the "official" beginning of the feminist movement in Canada occurred in the period that preceded the federal government's decision, in 1967, to establish the Royal Commission on the Status of Women. The commission's mandate was to assess the prevailing situation regarding the position of women in Canada and then to "recommend what steps might be taken by the Federal Government to ensure for women equal opportunities in all aspects of Canadian society" (Mackie 1991, 255). Three years later, after hearings across Canada, the commission issued its report which contained 167 recommendations (Mackie 1991).

Mackie suggests that three dimensions of feminism—liberal, socialist, and radical—have each had an impact on different spheres of life in Canada. Liberal feminism mobilized action to establish the Royal Commission and guided the emergence and agenda of large national organizations such as the National Action Committee on the Status of Women, the Canadian Advisory Council on the Status of Women, and the provincial liaison groups. These groups have acted to achieve equity in the workplace, fair property rights when marriages end in divorce, and a host of other changes that reformed the existing social system. Socialist feminists challenged the oppression of women within the economic system and within the family and approached some of the same agenda items as liberal feminism but from a different perspective. Their focus on both class and gender issues aligned this branch of feminism with the concerns of lesbians, immigrant women, and women of color (Adamson et al. 1988, as cited in Mackie 1991). Radical feminists and socialist feminists, says Mackie, share the premise "that the dominant male culture promulgates a picture of reality that buttresses patriarchy and denigrates women." (Mackie 1991, 260). Citing Adamson et al. (1988), Mackie views radical feminism as instrumental in the establishment of rape crisis centers, in campaigns against pornography, and in founding shelters for battered women. The lesbian/gay liberation movement has taken place almost concurrently with the women's movement and embodies and is informed by many of the same concepts of gender equality, personal freedom, and human rights.

From an institutional and legislative perspective, it would appear that liberal feminism has influenced contemporary government policy and corporate practice. These changes have been the source of some conflict. For example, the Toronto-based group R.E.A.L. Women of Canada (Realistic, Equal, Active, for Life), founded in 1983, now has chapters in all provinces and is the most prominent of the organizations opposing at least some of the legislative and social trends encouraged by the feminist movement. This group opposes policies that it believes either undermine the family or promote homosexuality as an acceptable alternative to heterosexual marriage. It advocates programs that would allow women to choose to stay at home with their children (e.g., through tax credits that would permit this option in lieu of universal day care). The organization is on the right politically and in terms of social policy and gender relations, and it espouses a more traditional and restrictive sexual philosophy than that of most Canadians. The growth of the political and religious right in Canada, although it has occurred to a lesser extent than in the U.S., suggests strong dissatisfaction, in this group, with some aspects of the trend to more egalitarian gender relations. Men's rights groups in Canada, e.g., In Search of Justice, also believe that some of the legislative changes influenced by the feminist movement have unfairly disadvantaged men. Most of their efforts have centered on issues of child custody and support following divorce.

The nascent men's movement in Canada—not to be confused with men's rights groups—has at least two "branches." One emphasizes the consequences for men of traditional, socially imposed male roles and seeks new ways to be male. The other, represented by groups such as Men Against Sexism, considers patriarchy and men's violence to be the major threats to women and seeks to change the structures and forms of social organization that perpetuate domination of one group by another at the interpersonal, social, or international level (see Kaufman 1987). The latter group has an annual white ribbon campaign to highlight men's opposition to violence against women.

B. Sociolegal Status of Males and Females

In the formation and enforcement of laws and policies, Canada is a federation of provinces and territories. Some areas of jurisdiction—e.g., the criminal code that governs sexual assault, divorce, and censorship—are federal and require the passage and modification of laws by the Canadian parliament. The enforcement of most laws, through policing and the courts, however, as well as jurisdiction over matters of education, civil conduct (e.g., allowable conduct in various locations, property offenses, alcohol, and tobacco laws), family law (e.g., division of property in divorce, parental rights, and responsibilities), and delivery of health care, are within provincial or local jurisdiction. Consequently, it is difficult to draw conclusions that apply across the country. In some locations, most notably Quebec and British Columbia, federal and local laws have been applied in a manner that supports greater equality between men and women and protection of various segments of society from discrimination. In others, e.g., Alberta and Saskatchewan, there has been a more limited interpretation and application of related federal legislation and passage of fewer provincial laws providing protection of groups and guarantees of equal treatment.

Equality before the law regardless of gender and sexual orientation is a relatively modern development in Canada. Legislation and court rulings that established such equality, though generally considered to have begun in the late 1800s with the "Person's" case in which women were included in all legal documents under the status of "person" (prior to this only men were included), are primarily a phenomenon of the past thirty years. Several landmark changes which will be referred to throughout this chapter include:

1969—Sweeping legislative changes, referred to as "getting the government out of the bedrooms of the nation," were initiated by parliament. These struck down a variety of laws restricting sexual activities, including the dissemination of information on birth control, and enshrined in law the principle that any activities between two consenting adults, conducted in private, were beyond the jurisdiction of law.

1970s—Universal provision of medical care without direct payment was instituted in each province. With this change, medical diagnostic and treatment procedures associated with sexuality, such as treatment for gender dysphoria, difficulties in sexual functioning, birth control, abortion, and infertility, became available to all Canadians without direct cost.

1968-1985—A series of changes in the laws governing divorce. Prior to this period, divorce required a parliamentary decree and could be granted only for reasons of adultery. The criteria for granting divorce were broadened and their application transferred to the courts. This change saw an immediate and sharp increase in the number of divorces granted across the country. It is noteworthy that property settlements and child custody matters are within provincial jurisdiction and so vary across the country.

1980s—A series of changes in Quebec family law took Quebec from the position of having the most conservative to having the most progressive set of provincial statutes. Under the new laws, women were guaranteed an economic and legal status independent of that of their husbands. This was symbolized in women's retaining their name in marriage and included equal sharing of family property, decision making, and of roles and rights as parents. Prior to this, for example, wives were under their husbands' control in determination of residence, property was owned wholly by men unless special contracts were arranged prior to marriage, decisions about children (e.g., with respect to medical care, education, and residence) were exclusively under the control of fathers (at least in law), and the line of inheritance was primarily from father to son with considerably less to wives and daughters.

1982—The Canadian Charter of Rights and Freedoms was declared law. This has been the basis for court challenges of other legislation, policies, and actions that have restricted or dictated rights and access, primarily of women, people with various disabilities, and homosexuals to areas and services in Canadian society (e.g., jobs, housing, insurance, particular medical services, spousal benefits, and parental rights).

1985—"Rape" was removed from the Criminal Code and replaced by several categories of assault that involve sexual contact, and laws addressing sexual contact with children were revised. Of note is the fact that the new law removed the onus of proof of lack of consent from women, and allowed women to file charges of sexual assault against their husbands. More recent changes and court rulings have further modified legal proceedings in this area. These are discussed in Section 8A.

1988—A Supreme Court of Canada decision overturned the laws restricting women's access to abortion. This continues to be a contentious issue among Canadians, but eight years after this ruling, abortion still remains outside the jurisdiction of the Criminal Code.

1996—The federal parliament amended the Canadian Human Rights Act to include sexual orientation as a "category" protected legislatively against discrimination. The Act already made it illegal to discriminate on the basis of race, religion, age, sex, marital status, or disability.

While many other legislative changes and court rulings have influenced the sociolegal status of various groups of Canadians, these are generally considered among the landmarks that have established the contemporary position of men and women, adults and children, and people of different sexual orientations.

Today, men and women are equal before the law in Canada and the Canadian Charter of Rights and Freedoms enshrines this principle. Both the public and private sector have adopted policies to increase the proportion of women in those work settings in which they have been traditionally underrepresented, and employment equity legislation has been implemented in the public sector in some provinces to rationalize pay scales according to job requirements. Men continue, however, to predominate in positions of power and leadership (e.g., government and major corporations).

Equal treatment of lesbian and gay individuals in law and in areas of employment, housing, etc., is increasing, to a sizable degree because of court challenges and threatened challenges (which have used the Charter of Rights and Freedoms) to eliminate discriminatory practices. Equal treatment does not exist, however, with respect to parental rights, spousal relationships, employee benefits, and other such issues, although court decisions continue to set precedents in the absence of legislated change (see Section 6). It is increasingly common for large corporations to extend such benefits even though they are not yet required in law to do so.

Current legislation regarding nonconsensual sexual behavior does not discriminate on the basis of sex (e.g., sexual assault law applies to both sexes). Children under the age of 14 cannot consent to sexual activity with an adult (i.e., anyone 18 or over) and an adult engaging in such activity with a child could be charged with "sexual interference," or "sexual assault" (since consent, even if given, is not legally recognized) (MacDonald 1994). An "invitation to sexual touching" would also be illegal if the invitee was under 14. In the foregoing offense categories, a person of 12 or 13 would be deemed able to give consent if the other person was not more than two years older and was not in a position of authority over the complainant.

The acts associated with sexual interference and invitation to sexual touching are also proscribed when done toward a person 14 to 17 by someone in a position of trust, authority, or dependency. The legislated age of consent for anal intercourse is 18, in contrast to 14 for other sexual activities, but this was effectively reduced to 14 by court decisions in 1995. There is also a statute on "corrupting children" (i.e., anyone under 18) by exposing them to adultery, sexual immorality, habitual drunkenness, etc., but this provision is rarely prosecuted (MacDonald 1994).

Although Canadian law defines adults as those 18 or over, there are provincial variations affecting such things as tobacco, alcohol use, and age of consent to medical treatment. For example, it is illegal to sell tobacco products to someone under 18 in Canada, but that age was raised to 19 in Ontario. The ages at which it is legal to sell alcohol to someone vary across the provinces, ranging between 18 and 21 years. Consent to treatment provisions also vary by province. For example, for several years Quebec has set 14 as the general age of consent, including birth control, abortion, and STD treatment. Ontario's Consent to Treatment Act, passed in 1994, was designed primarily to regulate treatment, particularly of those incapacitated or vulnerable in some way, when existing law is unclear. It also applies to treatment of children. For example, physicians, nurses, and clinic staff working outside hospital settings may treat children of 12 or even 11 without parental notification based on the practitioner's judgment of the child's capacity to give informed consent. Contentious areas in this regard might include prescribing birth control pills, pregnancy counseling, or diagnosis, counseling, and treatment for STDs. Notification of parents when the child does not wish them to be informed is left to the prudent judgment of the practitioner, and confidentiality of records would be handled in a similar manner. However, if the treatment is given in a hospital setting, parental consent to treatment would be needed for children under 16. Some other provinces set age of consent to treatment closer to the age of 16. These issues reflect the current attempts to balance children's rights and parents' rights when the two appear to be in conflict. A similar balancing in relation to acceptance of children's testimony in court is also taking place in Canada (see Section 8A on sexual abuse).

Canada is in a stage of change with respect to matters of law and policy regarding the status of men, women, children, the variously abled and disabled, and individuals of differing sexual orientations. If the trends of recent years continue, the change will be in the direction of provision of greater guarantees of equal treatment, increased access to a variety of sexual health services, protection of individual rights, and protection against discrimination. However, there are segments of Canadian society that challenge these changes and have mounted various campaigns to limit their scope. The future picture with respect to legal matters cannot be predicted.

C. General Concepts and Constructs of Sexuality

There have been no systematic, large-scale national studies on the sexual attitudes or conduct of Canadian adults. In November 1993, a major Canadian polling agency (Decima Research) conducted a national telephone survey of 1,610 Canadian residents randomly selected from the ten provinces (*Maclean's*/CTV Poll, 1994) in which a variety of questions involving sexual attitudes were included. [Note: Neither the Northwest Territories nor the Yukon were included due to their sparse population; sample sizes in the less-populated provinces were increased to reduce province-by-province errors.] The following sampling of the survey findings provides some background for subsequent speculation on Canadians' perspectives on sexuality and public policy. Given the small sample size and the methodological limitations of such a study, the results are at best indicative.

Most survey respondents felt that in the last ten to twenty years, Canadian attitudes on sexual matters had become far more permissive (43 percent) or more permissive (30 percent), with a higher percentage of those over 55 years old viewing the change as far more permissive (e.g., 59 percent of 55- to 64-year-olds vs. 32 percent of 25- to 34-year-olds). One reflection of the change in permissiveness is Canadian attitudes toward premarital sex (i.e., premarital intercourse). In a 1990 national survey of adults, Bibby and Posterski (1992) found that 80 percent agreed or strongly agreed that premarital sex was acceptable. This compares to 68 percent in agreement in 1975. Approval ranged from 92 percent among 18- to 34-year-olds (vs. 90 percent in 1975) to 59 percent of those 55 and over (vs. 42 percent in 1975). Slightly more people disagreed than agreed that a person should have more than one sexual partner before marriage (50 percent disagree, 39 percent agree, and 11 percent have no opinion). In a 1995 study with a similarly representative sample of Canadian adults, Bibby (1995) found continued high levels of acceptance of sex outside of marriage (this includes "premarital" and "intermarital" activity) among the young (89% of 18- to 34-year-olds approved) and an ongoing increase in acceptance among older Canadians (62% of those over 55 approved vs. 42% in 1975). Bibby

(1995) attributed the latter shift to aging of the baby boom generation that came of age in the 1960s, and suggested that by 2010 about 85% of Canadians would approve with 15% remaining opposed.

With respect to having an extramarital affair, 80 percent of respondents to the *Maclean's*/CTV poll said it was never OK, 10 percent not usually OK, and 6 percent sometimes or always OK. This response did not differ according to gender, but respondents from Quebec and French-speaking respondents in general were less likely to say "never OK" (about 65 to 67 percent vs. 79 to 91 percent in the other provinces). Respondents were somewhat less likely to condemn extramarital affairs under all circumstances (e.g., "it is totally unacceptable for a married person to have an affair"). In this case, 70 percent agreed or strongly agreed whereas 22 percent disagreed and 7 percent strongly disagreed. Men were slightly more likely to be accepting than women. There was no difference based on age, but respondents from Quebec were much less likely to agree strongly that it was always unacceptable (19 percent) and more likely to disagree or strongly disagree (45 percent). Bibby (1995) also found low levels of approval in that 85% in 1995 said that extramarital sex was always or almost always wrong (compared to 78% in 1975). Although, responses differed by age (78% for 35- to 54-year-olds vs. 90% for those 18 to 34 and 55 and over), Bibby noted that overall, Canadian's attitudes toward extramarital sex have become less approving over the last 20 years. This does not seem to be a simple reflection of aging of the population since young people are among the most disapproving.

When asked if they considered masturbation to be a healthy part of one's sex life, 8 percent strongly agreed, 57 percent agreed, 30 percent disagreed and 5 percent strongly disagreed. There were no sex differences in agreement, older respondents were less likely to agree (although 52 percent of those 65 and older agreed), and Quebec again had the highest agreement with 78 percent overall considering masturbation to be a healthy part of one's sex life.

When asked if they would feel uncomfortable talking with their children about sex, few indicated that they would be uncomfortable (about 17 percent). This indirect declaration of comfort was evident for both sexes and for the age groups most likely to be involved in rearing young children or teens. It is unlikely that this perceived comfort always translates into actual discussion, particularly in the area of sexual decision-making. For example, Bibby and Posterski (1992) found that while a sizable percentage of teens identified parents as the first source they would consult when making decisions about what is "right and wrong" (45 percent), or about school (45 percent) or a major problem (31 percent), fewer chose parents first for decisions about "sex" (8 percent) or relationships (7 percent); friends were most likely to be chosen in both of the latter categories (55 percent and 75 percent respectively).

Legislation prohibiting discrimination on the basis of sexual orientation is now common in most provinces and this trend, although actively opposed by some individuals and groups, reflects a shift in Canadian attitudes

(Section 6 discusses gay/lesbian issues in more detail). Two of the *Maclean's*/CTV survey questions assessed attitudes toward homosexuality. When asked if "it would be fine if one of my kids turned out to be gay", 11 percent of respondents strongly agreed, 45 percent agreed, 29 percent disagreed, and 14 percent strongly disagreed. Women were more accepting than men in this regard (64 percent of men agreed vs. 49 percent of women), younger were more accepting than older respondents, and those in Quebec were more likely to agree (85 percent) than in the rest of Canada (46 percent). On the statement "It would bother me if openly gay and lesbian people were teaching in the schools," the responses generally paralleled those above (56 percent would not be bothered, 44 percent agreed that they would be bothered; women were slightly more accepting than men). Bibby (1995) also found evidence of increasingly accepting attitudes toward homosexuality (32% said it was not at all wrong and 16 % sometimes wrong in 1995), up from 38% acceptance in 1990 and 28% in 1975. This still leaves half the population considering homosexuality always or almost always wrong. Interestingly, Bibby (1995) also found that between 1990 and 1995, during a period of active debate about inclusion of gay rights in the Human Rights Code (which occurred in 1996), approval of the idea that gays and lesbian should have the same rights as other Canadians dropped from 80% in 1990 to 67% in 1995. Bibby saw it as somewhat paradoxical that "just when Canadians are exhibiting both an increasing acceptance of homosexuality and greater social comfort with lesbians and gays, they now are also exhibiting increasing discomfort with the idea of extending them equal rights" (Bibby 1995, 74). One might argue that this is a temporary shift based on a tendency of some Canadians to be displeased with both sides in periods of acrimonious and politicized debate.

Television, the print media, and film provide Canadians with regular reminders of social policy issues related to sexuality (pornography, prostitution, sexual abuse, etc.). While these themes will be examined in later sections, survey respondents' attitudes on selected examples give an indication of the prevailing dynamic on such matters. For example, 52 percent agreed that prostitution should be legalized with a slightly higher proportion of males than females and of Quebecois versus non-Quebecois agreeing. Interestingly, agreement was lowest among 18- to 24-year-olds (33 percent agreed but 57 percent disagreed including 26 percent who strongly disagreed). In contrast, 60 to 64 percent of 35- to 54-year-olds agreed. Concerning the acceptability of people watching sexually explicit movies, 60 percent of males versus 34 percent of females said it was sometimes or always OK and 25 percent of males versus 48 percent of females said it was never OK. The statement "pornography is always degrading to women" yielded agreement from 69 percent of respondents (58 percent of men and 80 percent of women). Since respondents gave higher levels of agreement to the idea that "erotic magazines and movies can help make your sex life more interesting" (50 percent of males and 38 percent of females agreed) it would appear that Canadians make some distinction between the term "erotica" (which they associate with pleasure) and pornography (which they associate with harm). As we show in Section 8, it is the latter distinction that forms the basis for current obscenity law in Canada.

Taken collectively, the foregoing observations support the conclusion that more Canadians in the 1990s than in prior years accept, or are at least tolerant of, a wider diversity of forms of sexual conduct, expression, and communication. This is particularly the case in areas outside the domain of marriage, as seen in the continued lack of acceptance of extramarital sex by the vast majority of Canadians and by increased acceptance of an unmarried couple living together (in 1995, 78% of Canadians approved, Bibby 1995). However, as Bibby and Posterski (1992) observed, these changes are more a result of population change than of individual change.

> The sexual revolution changed the way Canadians viewed sex outside of marriage. But, having succeeded in transforming attitudes and behavior about sex, the revolution has long been over. What we have witnessed in the past decade or so is the transmission of the new sexual values from first-generation revolutionists to their offspring. The reason the national figures of acceptance have risen over the past twenty years is not because young people are becoming more permissive than their parents. Rather, the protests of grandparents troubled by the changes have—with their passing—been relegated to history. (Bibby and Posterski 1992, 40)

Of note is the consistently greater acceptance and tolerance of diverse forms of sexual expression on the part of French-speaking (primarily resident in the province of Quebec) as compared to other Canadians. This theme, repeated in other sections of our review, is considered by sociologists to be related to a general decline in the influence of the Roman Catholic Church in Quebec coupled with the rapid move of women into the labor force in this province; again, this is reflective not so much of a change in individual attitude, but of population and demographic changes over the years.

2. Religious and Ethnic Factors Affecting Sexuality

A. Religion and Religious Observance

The 1990 Statistics Canada *General Social Survey* reported the religious affiliation of Canadians 15 and over as: 45 percent Roman Catholic, 30 percent Protestant (United Church of Canada, Anglican, and other), 12 percent no religious affiliation (this percentage is almost double what it was ten years earlier), and 9 percent other religious denominations. These figures reflect the British and French origins of the country and the historical predominance of British and European immigration. Other non-Christian religious affiliations beginning with the First Nations peoples and extending to subsequent immigration by different groups include: Judaism, Buddhism, Islam, Hindu, and Sikh. The Christian "fundamentalist" religious presence that has challenged sex education and secular sexual laws and attitudes in some parts of the U.S. is less prevalent in Canada, although "conservative" religious groups are among the only ones that have increased in numbers in recent years.

Attendance at religious services is declining. In 1990, 24 percent attended at least once a week, 12 percent once a month, and 27 percent once a year. Those 65 and over were more likely to be weekly attenders in 1990 (42 percent) than those of younger ages (15 to 24 years): 15 percent; 25 to 44 years: 18 percent; 45 to 64 years: 32 percent). Church attendance has declined since 1985 in all age groups. Nevertheless, a telephone survey of 4,510 adults conducted in 1993 by the Angus Reid Group (a major polling agency) for *Maclean's* (a national news magazine with wide distribution) (April 12, 1993) reported that 78 percent affiliate themselves with a Christian denomination, 74 percent disagree with the statement "I am not a Christian," and about 65 percent stated belief in traditional Christian theological doctrines.

The trend to secular beliefs that conflict with Church doctrine is seen in the fact that, among self-described Roman Catholics polled, 91 percent approve of artificial birth control, 82 percent condone premarital sex, 84 percent would allow priests to marry, 55 percent view homosexual behavior as morally acceptable, and only 20 percent support the Church's stance that abortion should be opposed in all circumstances except when the life of the women is at risk. At the other end of the spectrum, when a church moves away from traditional patterns, as the United Church of Canada did by accepting the ordination of non-celibate, homosexual clergy, a sizable minority felt the church was becoming too liberal in its teachings. Those on the conservative end of the belief spectrum within their denominations are the most active opponents of abortion and proponents of "abstinence-only" sex education in the schools.

Among the almost 4,000 15- to 19-year-old high school students surveyed by Bibby and Posterski (1992), though 79 percent identified themselves with a particular organized religious denomination, only 19 percent of 15-year-olds and 13 percent of 19-year-olds attended weekly religious services, 15 percent said they received a high level of enjoyment from their involvement in an organized religion, and 24 percent viewed themselves as committed. Despite the apparently low and declining interest in organized religion (10 percent considered religious involvement "very important"), 24 percent rated "spirituality" and 46 percent "the quest for truth" as very important. Bibby and Posterski (1992) found that teens are highly receptive to spiritual and values-related issues. Supernatural beliefs also appeared to be more common than one might expect based on religious involvement. For example, the percentages agreeing with various supernatural beliefs were: God exists (81 percent), Divinity of Jesus (80 percent), some people have psychic powers (69 percent), life after death (64 percent), astrology (52 percent), extrasensory perception (52 percent), contact with the spirit world (44 percent), and I will be reincarnated (32 percent). These percentages are similar in most respects to those for adults asked the same questions in a 1990 survey (see Bibby and Posterski 1992).

These data suggest that while most Canadians are moving away from active involvement in religious institutions, they retain a core of religious beliefs and an interest in spiritual ideas and philosophies. Given this trend, it would be expected that the specific teachings of and stands taken by religious institutions on issues of sexuality might have less influence on Canadians today than they did in the past. This is illustrated most explicitly in the attitudes of French Canadians compared to the teachings of the Roman Catholic Church. For some newer Canadians, however, results of some research suggest that affiliation with religious institutions and involvement in their activities may remain important, with churches, temples, and mosques providing a center for activities of ethnic communities (Maticka-Tyndale et al. 1996). Though to date there are no large-scale studies of the influence of religion and religious involvement in different immigrant groups, results from research by sociologists across North America suggest that the teachings of religious institutions will have more influence on individuals and communities where involvement in those institutions is higher.

B. Ethnocultural Diversity and Sexuality

Canada's ethnocultural diversity has a variety of implications for sexuality and sexual health. Behavior is strongly influenced by social and cultural factors and recent immigrants to Canada, in particular, may face complex challenges in understanding and adapting to a new culture. However, it is difficult in a brief review to encompass the ways that cultural traditions in other spheres of social life both reflect and create expectations regarding sexual behavior for Canada's varied ethnocultural groups. In most cases, national statistical data on specific aspects of sexual behavior do not exist, and it is rare to find qualitative studies focused on the broad aspects of sexual activities and beliefs within different ethnocultural communities. Concerns about AIDS and sexual abuse have generated some research within selected communities, including a network of studies in several ethnocultural communities. The largest of these, the federally funded *Ethnocultural Communities Facing AIDS* study, was conducted in collaboration with representatives from six communities—Chinese, South Asian, Horn of Africa, English-speaking Caribbean, North African Muslim, and Latin American—in the three cities that receive the largest proportion of immigrants to Canada (Montreal, Toronto, and Vancouver). This project used a combination of ethnographic and survey techniques and had two goals: (1) the development of a knowledge base about cultural and psychosocial factors influencing sexual behaviors that place people at risk for HIV infection; and (2) formation of recommendations for prevention programming in these communities. Overviews of results and recommendations from the qualitative phase of research were published in the six-booklet report, *Many Voices:HIV/AIDS in the Context of Culture* (see Health Canada, 1994a-f for community reports; see also Adrien et al. 1996; Maticka-Tyndale et al. 1996; Godin et al. 1996; Singer et al. 1996).

3. Sexual Knowledge and Education

A. Government Policies and Programs

Because Canadian political structures and social life are based on a relatively nonintrusive conception of democratic society, formal sources of sex education have, for the most part, refrained from overtly imposing specific "doctrinal" sexual values on Canadians. For example, institutions such as the public schools have generally not sought to inculcate particular views on the acceptability of premarital sex. Instead, the school is more likely to offer information and guidance intended to help students make informed decisions about their sexual behavior; counseling and health facilities generally operate from the premise of providing information and care (e.g., to decrease sexually transmitted disease and unwanted pregnancy) regardless of position or status. This is not to say that sex education in the schools is free of ideology or that some Canadians would not wish stronger influence for their particular ideological position. Nevertheless, it appears that school-based sexuality education generally aspires to a non-doctrinal stance based on democratic principles (see McKay 1997).

Since education in Canada falls under provincial rather than federal jurisdiction, the Ministry of Education (or Department of Education) for each of the ten provinces and two territories usually has its own guidelines and/or curricula for sexuality education and its own procedures for implementing them. However, there are various programs through which the national government collaborates with the provinces and/or operates independently in this area, particularly within the context of health promotion and protection. The federal government provides funding for a variety of provincial organizations and researchers concerned with education and treatment pertaining to sexual health (AIDS, STDs, sexual abuse prevention, women's reproductive health, etc.). Two main branches of Health Canada, the Health Programs and Services Branch, and the Health Protection Branch, have mandates that include issues related to sexual and reproductive health. For example, a joint venture between these branches led to production of the *Canadian Guidelines for Sexual Health Education* (Minister of Supply and Services 1994). The *Guidelines* were developed by a national working group coordinated by the Sex Information and Education Council of Canada (SIECCAN), a non-profit educational organization, under a contract agreement with the Division of STD Prevention and Control (part of the Bureau of HIV/AIDS and STD within the Laboratory Center for Disease Control of the Health Protection Branch). The *Guidelines* present a unifying framework, a philosophy, and a set of principles to unite and guide those providing, planning, or updating sexual health education programs and/or services for people of all ages across Canada. The *Guidelines* can be used as a frame of reference for assessing both the overall network and the individual components of existing sexual health education programs and related services at the national, provincial, or local level. However, the document cautions against a single "authoritative" definition of sexual health as a static phenomenon that can be readily identified, and hence prescribed, by experts. Sexual health education is seen as "a broadly based, community-supported enterprise in which the individual's personal, family, religious, and social values are engaged in understanding and making decisions about sexual behavior and implementing those decisions" (Minister of Supply and Services 1994, 4).

Another joint venture that involved the federal government and the provincial ministries of health and education supported development and evaluation of "Skills for Healthy Relationships," a program about sexuality, AIDS, and other STDs for early high school students. Developed by the Social Program Evaluation Group at Queen's University, Kingston, Ontario, the program is now available to any school/school board or Ministry of Education that wishes to assume the cost of duplicating the materials (available from the National AIDS Clearinghouse of the Canadian Public Health Association). An in-service training session for teachers is an important component of the program, as was the large-scale program evaluation done independently by researchers not involved with development or implementation of the program (Warren and King 1994). Other federal and provincial/territorial government programs related to HIV/AIDS prevention and treatment (Section 11) and to other aspects of sexual health will be discussed as the relevant topics arise throughout the chapter.

Sexuality Education in Elementary and Secondary Schools

All provinces and territories have school programs that include sexuality education although the content, and extent of implementation, varies considerably between provinces and within different parts of the same province. While school-based sexuality education programs are a provincial responsibility, the federal government has a variety of programs through which it can assist sexuality education in schools or sexual health education for all ages in the community. As noted above, a variety of government departments may support researchers and community organizations in diverse sexuality education programs and services. Local public health units within specific municipalities of each province are also actively involved in public education about contraception, AIDS and other STDs, sexual abuse, and other aspects of sexual health, and they may do so in school settings as well.

There have been only a few national surveys of the availability of sexuality education in Canadian schools (for reviews, see Barrett 1990; 1994) and no detailed national studies of the classroom content of sexuality education that would indicate the extent to which provincial guidelines and curricula are translated into classroom programming. There is, however, enough information from individual provinces to indicate significant advances in sexuality education over the past ten years fueled to a large extent by emerging concerns about HIV/AIDS, other STDs, and sexual abuse, and also by ongoing concerns about teen pregnancy.

Survey findings throughout the 1980s and 1990s have consistently shown broad public support for some form of sexuality education in the schools (Lawlor and Purcell 1989; Ornstein 1989; McKay 1996) and this is particularly so for HIV/AIDS education (Verby and Herold 1992) which now appears in many curricula in grades five and/or six (ages 9 to 11). Although it is often difficult for such studies to include detailed assessment of respondents' opinions about specific content, or their views on the more subtle aspects of philosophy and attitudes that they might wish to see inculcated, Canadians appear to be strongly supportive of the school's involvement in sexuality education. Nevertheless, a minority perceives contemporary sex education to be skewed toward liberal, secular attitudes, particularly in the areas of abortion, homosexuality, teen sexuality, and access to contraceptive information and services, and actively promulgates a more restrictive agenda in all of these areas. Although historically this view has been expressed as an opposition to sexuality education in the schools, at present it is more likely to focus on either the specific value positions that schools should adopt, the appropriateness of particular topics (e.g., homosexuality, contraception, and abortion), or the ways in which student behavior should be influenced (e.g., abstinence-only programs).

There are few settings other than schools through which almost all young people can be reached with a planned educational program that addresses the broad range of topics subsumed under the heading of sexuality education. Sexuality education in schools is almost invariably integrated into a broader program of Health Education, Personal and Social Relationships, Family Life Education, Religious and Moral Education, etc., but this varies between provinces (or even within provinces) and there is therefore no standard national curriculum for sexuality education. However, most school curricula are based on a statement of principles and a guiding philosophy that emphasizes self-knowledge, acceptance of individual development, social obligations, personal values, the avoidance of problems (e.g., sexual coercion, teen pregnancy, STDs, etc.), and to a lesser and varied extent, the development of satisfying sexual relationships. Material is presented in a hierarchy based on age appropriateness with a number of previously excluded or delayed topics now appearing at earlier ages (e.g., AIDS and avoidance of sexual exploitation).

Sex education in schools is evolving in Canada, from first-generation programs that focused primarily on knowledge about reproduction and birth control (on the assumption that students would translate this information into self-protecting behavior), to second-generation programs that included factual information plus skills in communication and relationships (on the assumption that these generic skills would translate as above) (Kirby 1992; Kirby et al. 1994; McKay 1993), to the newly emerging third-generation programs that are rooted in conceptual models of behavior change that include knowledge acquisition, development of attitudes and behavioral intentions in support of sexual health, motivational supports, and development of situation-specific skills. The Skills for Healthy Relationships program for grade nine students (aged 13-14) described above is an example of this approach (Warren and King 1994). This gradual transition in Canadian sexuality education (most programs are second-generation type) reflects an increasing desire of educators and public health professionals to design interventions that affect sexual health behavior and outcomes. One of the complaints about traditional sex education has been that it does not work, i.e., teen pregnancies and STDs remain high. The problem is that early sex education programs simply anticipated such outcomes although they were neither designed for nor taught in ways that would achieve these specific behavioral objectives. Students did become more knowledgeable and more insightful about their own and other people's feelings and behavior—both desirable outcomes—but this type of knowledge-based sex education is not generally expected to have a major impact on behavior (for a review, see Fisher and Fisher 1992). With the growing concern about AIDS and other STDs, schools are being asked to influence behavior (postponing sexual involvement, encouraging abstinence, increasing condom use and safer sex practices, etc.) and not just to increase knowledge.

While Canada has experienced localized opposition to sex education in the schools, that opposition today, as noted above, is seldom to the school's involvement in sexuality education per se, but to the presumed "liberal" values of such programs. Public discourse on this issue has affected curriculum development to varying degrees across Canada and it is against the competing pressures of heightened expectation, anticipated "traditional" opposition, and limited resources, that school-based sexuality education continues to develop. A detailed overview of recommended or required sexuality education content in Canadian elementary and secondary schools is beyond the scope of this chapter (for a recent review, see Barrett 1994).

Outcomes of School-Based Sexuality Education

The final report on the Skills for Healthy Relationships program (Warren and King 1994) is the largest study ever undertaken in Canada on the long-range outcome of a school-based sexuality education program. As noted above, the program was developed by the Social Program Evaluation Group at Queen's University, Kingston, Ontario, with the collaboration and support from provincial and territorial ministries of education and health, the Council of Ministers of Education, Canada, the National Health and Research Development Program, and the AIDS Education and Prevention Unit through the National AIDS Contribution Program of Health Canada. The Skills for Healthy Relationships program provides grade nine students (age 13-14) with a carefully structured and theoretically based educational intervention on AIDS, other STDs and sexuality. It features cooperative learning (small groups), parent/guardian involvement (six interactive activities), active learning (role playing, behavioral rehearsal), peer leaders (in small groups, modeling skills), video instruction, and journaling and development of a personal action plan (assertiveness goal). The skills component is a major feature of the program, and outcome measures, assessed by questionnaires just after students had taken the program and one and two years later, included indicators of change related to these skills (assertiveness, communication with parents, regular condom use if sexually active, etc.). The comparison groups in each of the four provinces in which the program was tested were students who took their school's regular grade nine AIDS/STD program.

Two years later, students who took the program said they had been changed by the program in a number of ways: more comfort talking about personal rights with a partner (72 percent), talking about condoms (67 percent), ability to refuse or negotiate something I don't want to do (58 percent in both cases), more assertive (53 percent), and always use condoms with my partner (61 percent) (Warren and King 1994). Compared to the nonparticipant group, participants at the two-year follow-up:

- were more likely to have gained compassion toward people with AIDS;
- had more positive attitudes toward homosexuality;
- showed greater knowledge of HIV/AIDS;
- were more likely to express the intent to communicate with partners about condom use;
- were no more likely to have the intent to use condoms (this was initially high in both groups);
- were no more likely to report "always" using a condom (about 41 percent of both groups said they always did so; about half reported using a condom the last time they had intercourse); and
- females were more likely to declare that they would respond assertively if they were pressured unwillingly to have sex.

As would be expected, in the period from grade nine to eleven, the proportion of students who had experienced intercourse increased for both sexes in both groups. However, the percentage of both sexes who said they had ever had intercourse was slightly lower in the participant group two years after the program (51 percent comparison vs. 42 percent participant for males; 49 percent comparison vs. 46 percent participant for females). The students from both groups who were most likely to have unprotected intercourse were those who took risks in areas such as alcohol consumption, use of cannabis, and skipping classes. They were also more likely to be doing poorly in school (Warren and King 1994). These latter observations highlight the important behavioral influence of social and relationship factors that may well be difficult to change through school-based interventions alone.

In Canada, Orton and Rosenblatt's (1986; 1991; 1993) pioneering research on a multisectoral approach to pregnancy prevention in Ontario showed that rates of adolescent pregnancy declined more rapidly in the late 1970s and early 1980s in those localities that provided young people with both school-based sexuality education and access to clinical services. Orton (1994) points out that the usual practice of reporting only province-wide data for teen pregnancy has tended to obscure the "inequality gap" between individual localities with respect to the decline in teen pregnancies. We have therefore been less likely to note the successes in localities that combined prevention programs in both the educational and public health sectors, and also less able, and willing, to recognize and target resources toward those settings that needed special assistance because they were less advantaged for providing such programs (e.g., rural and northern localities). Orton (1994) argues that: "Policies and programs of sexual health have the potential to reduce social inequalities by reducing rates of adolescent pregnancy and STDs, and also by reducing the wide variation in rates between jurisdictions and groups within Canada" (p. 223).

Based on an analysis of policies and programs in education, public health, and social services in Ontario, Orton (1994) argues that "intersectoral collaboration can contribute to greater and more equitable access to sexual health education and services" but that such collaboration requires "strong policy directives at all three ministries" (p. 222). Her findings in Ontario argue for "the effectiveness of centralized policy direction (public health), and the ineffectiveness of a decentralized approach (education and social services) to achieve equitable access to effective programs" (Orton 1994, 223). The planning document, *Toward Sexual and Reproductive Health in Saskatchewan*, from a province attempting to strengthen sexual health education, shows how a centralized initiative from the Ministry of Health invited multisectoral collaboration in program and policy development (Saskatchewan Health 1993) along the lines that Orton (1994) recommends.

There are a number of issues facing the continued growth and improvement of sexuality education in Canadian schools. For example, the duration, content, and quality of such education varies considerably between schools and within and between provinces, but it is uncertain whether governments will continue to give sexuality education the required priority and resources. Canadian schools face increasing financial and staffing constraints and there is a growing demand to focus more on basic areas like language skills, science, computer technology, etc., which may lead, by default or design, to either lower priority for sexuality education or to a more limited, problem-centered focus on selected topics. Given the various sexual ideologies, religious traditions, and ethnocultural backgrounds within the Canadian population, it has been difficult to find a broad public consensus on how to deal with controversial issues in schools (teen sexuality, homosexuality, etc.). The past climate of cautiousness and conflict on such issues still continues to impede implementation of high-quality sexuality education programs in many areas. The goal identified in the *Canadian Guidelines for Sexual Health Education*, i.e., universal access to a broadly based, comprehensive, and integrated approach to sexual health education, suggests high national expectations and intentions, but uncertain resources and competing priorities are part of the reality facing attempts to fully implement such a program.

Sexuality Education and Related Services Through Public Health Units and Other Such Agencies

Provincial and Territorial Public Health Units play a major role in sexual health education and related services in Canada, and they are often in the forefront of community sexual health education campaigns. For example, the Program Requirements and Standards section of Ontario's *Mandatory Health Programs and Services Guidelines* (Ontario Ministry of Health 1989) lists four pages of expectations and program standards for sexual health and STDs. Boards of health and public health nurses are the front line staff involved in addressing these issues with clients of all ages and socioeconomic status. The demands on this growing bureaucracy have increased in recent years in response to changing patterns of sexual behavior among youth, increasing ethnocultural diversity and immigrant populations in cities, population aging, AIDS, concerns about sexual abuse prevention for all ages, and other such issues. In the face of growing demand and limited resources, provision of service is varied across Ontario (this is probably true for all provinces) and, for the same reasons, the additional mandate to do community needs assessments and outcome evaluations of sexual health programs is also difficult to sustain.

Various nongovernmental agencies are also involved in sexuality education and related services. The Sex Information and Education Council of Canada (SIECCAN), founded in 1964, maintains a resource library and information service, publishes the *Canadian Journal of Human Sexuality* and the *SIECCAN Newsletter*, provides consultation services and professional education workshops, and facilitates development of new resources such as the *Being Sexual* series (Ludwig and Hingsburger 1993), *After You Tell* (Ludwig 1995), and the previously described *National Guidelines for Sexual Health*

Education. The Planned Parenthood Federation of Canada (PPFC) has a long history of advocacy, education, and resource distribution on contraception and sexuality. PPFC administers the Sex Education and Research Clearinghouse (SEARCH), a national center for distribution and development of sexuality education resource materials. Local Planned Parenthood offices now provide sexual health education and services and some, such as The House, in Toronto, administer adolescent health centers that are equipped to address a broader range of health issues than contraception and pregnancy counseling. The Canadian AIDS Society and local AIDS committees and organizations do educational outreach that includes some aspects of sexuality education, as do other groups with particular concerns about sexuality such as the Disabled Women's Network and the British Columbia Coalition on AIDS and Disability. The Canadian Public Health Association, the Canadian Association of School Health, the Canadian Infectious Diseases Society, the Society of Obstetricians and Gynecologists of Canada, and a number of other nongovernmental organizations contribute at the national level to public sexuality education.

B. Informal Sources of Sexual Knowledge

Despite the growing role of schools and public health authorities in public education about such topics as contraception, STDs, and HIV/AIDS prevention, informal sources (peers, family, and the media) are probably the primary influence on sexual attitudes and knowledge. Adolescents have been the focus of most research in this area.

For example, when asked to list their main sources of AIDS information, grade eleven students (*N* = 9,617) surveyed in the *Canada Youth and AIDS Study* ranked television first, followed respectively by print materials, school, family, friends, and doctors/nurses (King et al. 1988). The first three rankings were the same for grade seven (*N* = 9,925) and grade nine (*N* = 9,860) students. Although these informal sources were identified as the main source of AIDS information for Canadian youth, a majority of the young people surveyed said they would have preferred a more formal source of information, such as doctors or nurses.

Ornstein's (1989) study of AIDS-related knowledge, behavior, and attitudes of Canadian adults (*N* = 1,259) found that, similar to the students in King et al.'s study, television (39 percent) and newspapers (23 percent) led the list of respondents' self-identified "main sources of information about AIDS." Magazines were identified by 9 percent and health authorities (e.g., physicians, nurses, hospitals, and clinics) by only 2.5 percent. In the survey phase of the *Ethnocultural Communities Facing AIDS* study, conducted in English-speaking Caribbean, Latin American, and South Asian communities (only men from the South Asian communities participated in the survey), the rank ordering of where respondents preferred to get information about HIV/AIDS was identical in all three communities and to both of the two earlier studies (Maticka-Tyndale et al. 1995). Ornstein's (1989) conclusion that "in the main, Canadians rely on the mass media rather than more specialized publications to learn about AIDS" (p. 52), clearly applies regardless of age and probably also regardless of ethnocultural background.

While various forms of media, particularly television, have been Canadians' main source of information about AIDS, the picture changes somewhat when sources of information on sexuality in general are examined. Again, informal sources of information predominate. However, with sexuality in general, as opposed to AIDS, peers and family become the most commonly cited sources of information. The World Wide Web and other computer-assisted information systems are having a growing impact on students' access to sexuality-related content, but the potential of this medium as a formal resource for sexuality education (see Humphreys et al. 1996) has yet to be exploited.

When King et al. (1988) asked a national sample of students about their main sources of information about sex, grade seven (aged 11-12) and grade nine (aged 13-14) students ranked family first out of six possible sources of sex information. Though friends were ranked fifth by grade seven students, they rose to third for grade nine students, and first for grade eleven students. The latter group ranked family a close second. Friends remained first for college/university students with family dropping to third place, replaced by print materials in second. Interestingly, school dropouts ranked previous schooling first, friends second, and family third as their main sources of sex information. In a comparable study of Newfoundland students done in 1991, Cregheur et al. (1992) found that grade eleven students (aged 16-17) ranked friends first as their main source of information about sex, followed by school, television, family, and print materials. Interestingly, compared to the King et al. (1988) national sample, grade eleven students in the Cregheur et al. study (1992) were less likely to cite friends, family, television, and print materials as their main sources of information about sex and more likely to cite school.

The role of peers and parents as important informal sources of information and support is evident from the results of three studies. King et al.'s (1988) study of Canadian teens found that overall, teens agreed that they talked with their close friends about sex (increasing from 56 percent in grade seven to 75 percent in grade eleven), that people of the opposite sex like them (51 percent in grade seven, 73 percent in grade eleven), and that they discuss their problems with their friends (62 to 71 percent). Among grade nine students questioned in a 1992 evaluation of the "Skills for Healthy Relationships" program (see Warren and King 1994), 59 percent of females and 38 percent of males agreed that "I can talk to my mother about sexual matters" (26 percent of females and 41 percent of males agreed that they could talk to their fathers about sexual matters). Finally, Herold's (1984) study of young women visiting a birth control clinic found that two thirds of the women had received birth control information from girlfriends, about half from schools or reading materials, 25 percent from their mothers, and 2 percent from their fathers. The importance of peers is highlighted in Herold's (1984) conclusion that

> peers provide teenage girls with information, legitimization and support. Girlfriends are the most important source of information about birth control, and teenage girls who are socially isolated in the sense of having few friends often delay getting birth control because they lack peer support. (p. 105)

The impact of informal sources of learning on sexual values is a much discussed issue in Canada. In a study of values and sex education in Montreal-area, English-language high schools, Lawlor and Purcell (1988) surveyed 667 grade nine and grade eleven students about a variety of topics related to sex education. Asked where they learned their moral values related to sexuality, the students again ranked peers at the top. Friends away from school were ranked first, followed respectively by classmates, home, television and movies, books and magazines, in school from teachers, in school from religious teaching, and rock/pop music and lyrics. It is noteworthy that these students ranked rock/pop music and lyrics last out of a possible eight sources of sexual values, since there has been increasing speculation in the Canadian media that popular music and rock videos may have a negative impact on the sexual attitudes of young people. For the eight sources for learning sexual values, the most pronounced gender difference was for the item "in the home" which was ranked third by grade nine girls and second for grade eleven girls, but fifth by both grade nine and grade eleven boys.

While public policy and sex education literature generally acknowledge the important role that parents play in the sexual development of children, there has been surprisingly little research on the direct communication of sexual knowledge from parents to their children. In a study of 200 Canadian university women (Herold and Way 1983), subjects reported which sexual topics they had discussed with their parents. Eighty percent had talked about attitudes towards premarital sex with their mothers, 55 percent with their fathers; 70 percent had discussed contraception with their mothers, 29 percent with their fathers; 15 percent had discussed oral sex or masturbation with their mothers, 2 percent with their fathers; and 9 percent had talked about sexual techniques with their mothers, less than 1 percent with their fathers.

Several general observations can be made based on these studies. First, family, peers, and media form a triad of influence and education with respect to issues related to the sexuality of young Canadians. In general, there is a developmental shift that occurs in the relative place of family, peers, and media sources during adolescence. Between about grade nine (13 to 15 years of age) and grade eleven (16 to 17 years of age) peer influence rises to top rank and that of family decreases in importance, in some cases even outranked by the more impersonal media (e.g., print materials). In addition, at least for university women, mothers in particular have been a potential source of information and influence in matters of sexuality. The foregoing results support Bibby and Posterski's (1992) observation that the apparent changes in attitudes and conduct are not individual changes but a "coming of age" of a new generation of Canadians—the children of the "sexual revolution" generation—who are forming their own reference groups of information and influence.

4. Autoerotic Behaviors and Patterns

> In the insufficiently heated bedroom on the northwest corner of the house in Park Place, I was taken by surprise by the first intimations of a pleasure that I did not at first know how to elicit from or return to the body that gave rise to it, which was my own. It had no images connected with it, and no object but pure physical sensation. It was as if I had found a way of singing that did not come from my throat.
>
> —A man's recollection from his boyhood in
> *So Long, See You Tomorrow,* William Maxwell (1980)

In the early 1900s, the first sex education classes in Ontario schools taught young boys about the dangers of masturbation. Students were told that seminal fluid contained a vital force that nourished the brain and muscles, and that wasting it through any sexual excess, but particularly through masturbation, was physically and mentally depleting to the individual. Furthermore, students were also told that a man could pass this depleted condition on to his offspring. These dual beliefs in vitalist physiology and in the inheritance of acquired characteristics provided the "secular" rationale for prohibitions that were already part of the religious teachings of the time. Canada's long-abandoned eugenic sterilization law of 1902 had its origins in the period when such teaching became popular (for review, see Bliss 1970). Sex education at that time was generally silent on female masturbation—often ignoring its very possibility—but when it was mentioned, the dire consequences for reproductive health and mental stability were strongly emphasized. Mothers were told to be watchful lest their children fall into the habit that, they were warned, was notoriously difficult to break.

Over ninety years later, masturbation has gone from being a sin to a normal part of sexual development in children and a healthy aspect of sexual expression in adults. This general impression would have to be documented from qualitative sources, since we have been unable to locate any published national data on masturbation frequency in any age group. Survey results cited in Section 2C indicate that a majority of Canadians adults view it as a healthy expression, although a sizable minority either disagreed (30 percent) or strongly disagreed (5 percent) with this view. Sex education literature almost invariably refers to masturbation as normal, and recommendations for parents usually pertain to the importance of privacy and of not instilling guilt. Sexuality education for children and young adults with developmental disabilities places particular emphasis on teaching in this area since public masturbation, even when it arises through lack of social skills, can lead to embarrassment, restriction of social opportunities by caregivers, or exploitation by others. The Sex Information and Education Council of Canada (SIECCAN) publishes and distributes a seventeen-booklet sexuality education series for people with developmental disabilities—*Being Sexual: An Illustrated Series on Sexuality and Relationships*—that includes clearly illustrated, detailed, sex-positive information about female masturbation (Ludwig and Hingsburger 1993) and male masturbation (Hingsburger and Ludwig 1993). The series is designed for people who have problems with language, learning, or communication, and all books are translated into Blissymbols, making the series the only resource of its kind in the world. Blissymbolics, a symbolic language developed by C.K. Bliss and described in *Semantography*, published in 1949, was intended to be a means of communication across all language groups. It is now used by people with disabilities, and others, to facilitate expressive speech. The Canadian organization responsible for this work is Blissymbolics Communication International.

A recent paper on childhood masturbation written by Canadian authors relies on U.S. statistics for occurrence and incidence data to suggest that 90 to 94 percent of males and 50 to 60 percent of females have masturbated during their lifetime, that the highest incidence is among 16- to 20-year-olds (86 percent masturbate; the frequency is higher in males than females), and that masturbation declines with age in men but increases toward middle age in women (Leung and Robson 1993). While some religious groups consider masturbation to be sinful or an unacceptable indulgence, the common reaction in Canada appears to range from benign acceptance (and little discussion) to enthusiastic approval, reflective of the general shift toward a larger proportion of the population's acceptance and endorsement of various forms of sexual expression.

5. Interpersonal Heterosexual Behaviors

A. Children

There have been no national studies on the sexual behavior or sex-role rehearsal play of Canadian children. While it seems likely that sexual curiosity and exploratory play would follow patterns similar to those described by U.S. researchers (see Martinson 1994), we do not know of any studies that would provide empirical support for this conjecture in Canada.

B. Adolescents

It is important to place the sexual behavior of Canadian adolescents as a group within the context of prevailing social, political, and economic conditions and of other individual variables such as their personal characteristics and relationships, their attitudes toward sexuality, and their increasing exposure to sexual images and information through television, films, and magazines. Although it is misleading to generalize about such a diverse group, the findings of two national studies with large samples described earlier offer important insights into the sexual attitudes and behavior of Canadian adolescents. The *Canada Youth and AIDS Study* (Social Program Evaluation Group, Queen's University, King et al. 1988) is the only large-scale national study of both the attitudes and sexual behavior of Canadian adolescents and young adults. The sample included approximately 19,500 grade nine and eleven students, 14 to 17 years of age. "Project Teen Canada" 1992, which replicated a national survey of 15- to 19-year-olds conducted in 1984, had a sample of 3,600 15- to 19-year-olds and investigated attitudes and beliefs (not behavior) about a range of topics including sexuality (Bibby and Posterski 1992). These sources are used below as a starting point to examine the sexual attitudes and behavior of Canadian adolescents.

Sexuality and Self-Esteem

Self-concept refers to the way individuals describe their abilities, personalities, and relationships; whereas, self-esteem refers to the value placed on these personal characteristics (King et al. 1988). Research has repeatedly demonstrated strong associations between self-concept, self-esteem, and sexual conduct, particularly for adolescents. These are therefore important concepts to consider in this section on adolescent sexual conduct. In King et al.'s national study, while Canadian teens generally agreed that they had confidence in themselves (88 to 90 percent of grade seven, nine, and eleven males, 81 to 87 percent females) (King et al. 1988), ambivalence is reflected in a variety of areas, particularly for young women. Between 51 percent and 53 percent of grade seven, nine, and eleven females reported that they would "change how I look if I could" (vs. 37 to 38 percent for males); 37 percent of grade seven females and 51 percent and 54 percent of grade nine and eleven females agreed with the statement "I need to lose weight" (vs. 21 to 24 percent for males); and 32 to 41 percent of females agreed that "I often feel depressed" (vs. 27 to 30 percent for males). At the same time, 84 to 89 percent said "I have a lot of friends," 81 to 84 percent said "I am a happy person," and 71 to 74 percent said "the future looks good to me."

Similar findings on self-esteem of Canadian 11- to 15-year-olds are reported in *The Health of Canada's Youth* (King and Coles 1992), part of an international collaborative study designed to collect comparative health-related information on young people in Austria, Belgium, Canada, Finland, Hungary, Norway, Poland, Scotland, Spain, Sweden, and Wales. In the section on social adjustment, King and Coles (1992) observe that "compared with young people from European countries, young Canadians are experiencing more strain in their relationships with their parents and even with each other" (p. 96). Yet Canadian students were more likely than those in most other participating countries to find it easy to talk to friends of either sex about things that really bother them. This concurrence of positive self-regard on the one hand, and anxiety or dissatisfaction with specific areas of their lives on the other, has also been noted in other studies of slightly older Canadian youth as well.

For example, Bibby and Posterski (1992) also noted the generally high self-esteem of teens (e.g., 82 percent of females and 90 percent of males agreed that the statement "I can do most things well" described them either very well or fairly well). However, these adolescents had concerns about a number of areas including achievement in school (this was an issue for both sexes) and personal safety (a major concern for females). About three times as many females as males (56 percent vs. 20 percent) agreed that there was an area "within a mile (or kilometer) of your home where you would be afraid to walk at night." About 95 percent of both young women and men plan to have careers but there appears to be a continuing gender gap in areas that may impact on sexual and gender relationships. For example, females were more likely than males to rate certain values as "very important" (concern for others, 75 percent vs. 48 percent; forgiveness, 71 percent vs. 45 percent, and honesty, 82 percent vs. 56 percent) (Bibby and Posterski 1992).

Though these studies support the general contention that Canadian adolescents have a relatively positive self-concept and high self-esteem, they also demonstrate clear and important gender differences. Young women express specific concerns about appearance and safety, and focus greater attention on values that relate to relationships than those of individual achievement or success. Considerably fewer young men, on the other hand, show concern for appearance or focus attention on relationship values and, by and large, they seem unconcerned about personal safety. These characteristics are of particular importance when considering their potential influence on relationships between young men and women and the ability of each to realize the expectations they have set for their futures.

Attitudes Toward Sexuality and Relationships

Attitudes toward sexual intercourse before marriage (i.e., "premarital sex") have been widely used as an indicator of sexual permissiveness. In King et al.'s study (1988), among grade eleven students (age 15 to 17), 13 percent said unmarried people should not have sex and 76 percent said it is all right for people to have sex before marriage if they are in love (74 percent female, 78 percent male) (agreement combines "strongly agree" and "agree" categories on a five-point Likert scale) (King et al. 1988). In their slightly older sample in 1992, Bibby and Posterski found that: 86 percent of females and 88 percent of males agreed with sex before marriage for people in love (the value was 93 percent for both sexes in Quebec); 51 percent of females and 77 percent of males agreed with sex before marriage when the people involved liked each other (81 percent and 91 percent respectively in Quebec); 40 percent of females and 73 percent of males agreed that sexual relations were OK within a few dates (60 percent and 82 percent respectively in Quebec); and 5 percent of females and 20 percent of males agreed with sexual relations on a first date if people like each other (9 percent and 23 percent respectively in Quebec). A study of attitudes toward use of power in sexual relations among college students in Quebec (Samson et al. 1996) found that the majority of students refused to see the expression of sexuality as a locus of power but viewed it more in the context of shared affection and pleasure. The tendency toward increasing permissiveness with greater levels of affection is a long-standing North American tradition among young people and adults. The greater levels of approval among Quebec students may be characteristic of the more sex-accepting attitude of Quebec society in general and particularly of the francophone segment of the population. In contrast to their attitudes toward premarital sex, only 9 percent of young people in Bibby and Posterski's (1992) total teen sample approved of extramarital sex (12 percent vs. 9 percent for francophone and anglophone Quebec teens) with this figure falling to less than 5 percent for Catholic teens who attended church two to three times per month.

Bibby and Posterski (1992) found that 87 percent of teens outside of Quebec approved of unmarried people living together (95 percent among francophone Quebecois and over 80 percent among Catholic students in Quebec). Among teens outside of Quebec, 65 percent approved of people having children without being married (88 percent among francophone Quebecois).

In the areas of homosexuality and gay rights, teens were more likely to support social justice and rights for the gay population (68 percent approval overall outside of Quebec, 83 percent in Quebec) than to approve of homosexual relations (33 percent approval outside of Quebec, 55 percent among francophone Quebecois). King et al. (1988) found a sizable percentage of grade seven, nine, and eleven students agreeing that "homosexuality is wrong" (45 percent, 42 percent, 38 percent respectively) and a surprisingly small percentage agreeing that they would feel comfortable talking with a homosexual person (18 percent, 22 percent and 29 percent respectively). With increasing discussion of gay rights and homosexuality in the media, these numbers would probably be different in 1997 although there remains a dichotomy between many young people's acceptance of gay rights and their acceptance of homosexuality. Since students with the lowest tolerance for people with AIDS also had the most negative attitudes toward homosexuality, and vice versa (King et al. 1988), the widespread mandating of HIV/AIDS education in Canadian schools in recent years may well lead to greater compassion for people with AIDS and less stigmatizing of gay people because of their presumed association with AIDS. Indeed a 1992 study (Warren and King 1994) of over 2,000 grade nine students from four provinces who received an educational program about sexuality and AIDS ("Skills for Healthy Relationships") found that 23 percent considered homosexuality to be wrong (vs. 42 percent in the 1988 national sample) and 60 percent felt that "homosexuals should be allowed to be teachers" (vs. 39 percent in the 1988 study).

This background information on sexual attitudes and self-esteem provides a context for discussing the specific sexual behaviors of Canadian adolescents.

Sexual Behavior of Adolescents

The 1970s and 1980s saw gradual changes in sexual behavior of Canadian young people consistent with the "sexual revolution" in attitudes that began in the 1960s. University students were the common research sample for many of the past studies on sexual behavior of youth, since parents and school boards were generally disinclined to give approval for questions on the specifics of sexual behavior in surveys of younger teens. Although similarly restricted on some topics (e.g., questions about oral sex and anal sex were asked only of college/university students, school dropouts, and "street youth"), the *Canada Youth and AIDS Study* provided evidence that "young people are more sexually active than adults may realize." For example, 31 percent of grade nine males (14 to 15 years old) and 21 percent of females reported at least one instance of sexual intercourse. For grade eleven students (16 to 17 years old), the figures were 49 percent and 46 percent respectively (see Table 3 for more recent data from similar groups). For comparison, among first-year college/university students (19 to 20 years old), 77 percent of males and 73 percent of females had ever had intercourse. Hence, a sizable majority of Canadian teens have had at least one experience of vaginal intercourse by the time they are 19 and the majority of Canadians initiate sexual intercourse between 15 and 19 years of age.

Over half of younger teens have engaged in some form of sex play. For example, about 74 percent of grade eleven students (75 percent of the males; 73 percent of the females) and over half of grade nine students (61 percent of the males; 53 percent of the females) have experienced "petting below the waist" (King et al. 1988). Among the reasons offered for their first experience of sexual intercourse, 19-year-olds in the 1988 sample reported love (48 percent of the females; 24 percent of the males), physical attraction (8 percent of the females; 25 percent of the males), curiosity (16 percent of the females; 12 percent of the males), passion (8 percent of the females; 11 percent of the males), and drug and/or alcohol use (6 percent for both sexes). King, Coles, and King (1990) found that about 2 percent of both male and female 19-year-olds identified themselves as either homosexual or bisexual, but the details of their self-identification and behavior were not obtained.

In a late 1980s study of Quebec grade eleven high school students (*N* = 1,231, average age, 17 years) Otis et al. (1990) found that French- and English-speaking boys did not differ in the proportion who had experienced intercourse (62.4 percent vs. 54.1 percent), in number of partners among those with such experience (3.4 vs. 4.1), or in likelihood of condom use (46.9 percent vs. 48.8 percent). English-speaking male high school students were less likely than their francophone counterparts to report that a partner was using the birth control pill to prevent conception (33.7 percent vs. 48.8 percent). Among francophone versus anglophone high school girls however, differences were apparent in terms of intercourse experience (61.5 percent vs. 30.1 percent), number of lifetime partners (2.8 vs. 1.8), use of the birth control pill (56 percent vs. 22 percent) and use of condoms (30.9 percent vs. 83.7 percent). These differences may reflect more long-standing relationships or sexual experience among francophone girls (age at first intercourse was 14.9 vs. 15.7) or a greater emphasis among francophone students on contraception and less so on STD prevention (see also Otis et al. 1994). In a recent review of research on the sexual behavior of different populations of high school students in Quebec, Otis (1996) noted that 12 to 23 percent of first-year and 47 to 69 percent of fifth-year high school students had ever had intercourse. Among those who had ever had intercourse, 1 to 8 percent reported same-sex sexual activity, 7 to 37 percent anal sex, and 1 percent involvement in prostitution. A sizeable minority of this group had six or more partners (12 to 22 percent for 15-year-olds; 27 to 47 percent for 18-year-olds, depending on the study).

Although peer pressure in its broadest definition undoubtedly affects teens in many ways, only a minority state that they feel pressure from their friends to be sexually active. Among grade nine students, 16 percent of males and 8 percent of females agreed that they felt such pressure (21 percent and 6 percent respectively for grade eleven students) (King et al. 1988). However, a sizable proportion of younger teens may have some uncertainty on this matter since 55 percent of grade nine students surveyed by Bibby and Posterski (1992) responded "don't know" to the statement "I am not influenced by my peers" (41 percent agreed that they were not so influenced, 14 percent agreed, implying that they were). Even if peer group pressure does not usually influence the decision to be sexually active, peer group norms probably influence this and other important aspects of sexual behavior (e.g., decision to use condoms, safer sex practices, attitudes toward gender equity, etc.). Sexual health educators encourage the development of such peer norms as a positive reinforcement for "healthy" sexual behavior.

A recent evaluation study of the "Skills for Healthy Relationships" sexuality curriculum (Warren and King 1994), provides the most up-to-date national information available on the prevalence of vaginal, oral, and anal sex among grade nine and eleven students in Canada (3,750 grade nine and 3,000 grade eleven students from eight school boards in four provinces) (Table 3). Overall these findings indicate a large increase in experience of both vaginal and oral sex between grades nine and eleven and considerable similarity between the sexes in both grades (particularly in grade eleven) in terms of their reported experience of both behaviors. As we will note later in relation to sexual behavior of university students, similarity of acts between the sexes does not necessarily mean similarity of motivation, interpretation, or expectation with respect to these activities.

Table 3

Occurrence of Vaginal, Oral, and Anal Sexual Activity in a Large Sample of Canadian Teens (1992)[1]

	Percentage Responding in Each Category			
	Grade 9 (*N* ~ 3,750)		Grade 11 (*N* ~ 3,000)	
	Female	Male	Female	Male
Vaginal sex				
Never	80	73	53	51
1 or 2 times	7	11	8	13
3 or more	13	16	39	36
Oral sex				
Never	79	73	53	52
1 or 2 times	8	11	11	13
3 or more	13	16	36	35
Anal sex				
Never	96	94	92	90
1 or 2 times	3	3	5	3
3 or more	1	3	3	7

[1] Respondents were students in the experimental and comparison groups of the Skills for Healthy Relationships program evaluation (8 school boards in 4 provinces) (Warren and King, 1994). Grade 9 students are generally 13-15 years old; grade 11, 16-17 years old.

C. Adults

Premarital Relations, Courtship, and Dating

This material is addressed in Sections 5B above and in the section below.

Sexual Behavior and Relationships of Single Adults

Most of the research on premarital or non-marital sexual activity of single Canadian adults has been done on university students. The *Canada Youth and AIDS Study* reported that about 77 percent of men and 73 percent of women in college/university had experienced intercourse, 68 percent of males and 64 percent of females had engaged in oral sex, and 14 percent of males and 16 percent of females had at least one experience of anal sex. Among those who had had intercourse, 23 percent of the females and 15 percent of the males said they had only ever had one partner (two partners, 9 percent for males, 15 percent for females; three to five partners, 28 percent for males, 35 percent for females; six to ten partners, 22 percent for males, 17 percent for females; and eleven or more partners, 27 percent for males, 11 percent for females) (King et al. 1988). About 7 to 8 percent of both sexes reported having had a sexually transmitted disease (King et al. 1988). These findings are for first-year university students and probably underestimate the average experience of students in all years.

In the most recent review of sexual behavior of college students in Quebec (1 to 2 years younger on average than university students), Samson et al. (1996) reported that 76 percent had ever had intercourse. Within this group, 9 to 14 percent reported experience of anal sex, 8 percent same-sex contacts, and 27 to 42 percent had 4 or more partners. For university students (Otis 1996), 86 to 90 percent had sexual intercourse, 18 percent had anal sexual contact, and 35 percent had 5 or more partners. In a study of anglophone and francophone university students (*N*= 1,450 men and women from four universities in Montreal), Lévy et al. (1993) found that 88 percent of French-speaking versus 81.5 percent of English-speaking men had had intercourse at least once; the values for females were 88 percent versus 74.5 percent. While the sexes did not differ within language groups, French-speaking women were significantly more likely to have had intercourse than English-speaking women. This was also true for oral sex experience (86 percent vs. 79.2 percent in French-speaking vs. English-speaking men; 85.4 percent vs. 73.1 percent in French-speaking vs. English-speaking women).

This trend toward convergence of the overt sexual behavior of male and female university students in Canada (and elsewhere) has been noted since the early to mid-1970s (Barrett 1980). In terms of the occurrence of different sexual activities in a sample of 585 francophone university students in Quebec, one might suggest that this behavioral convergence is complete (Frigault et al. 1994; Table 4). However, it would be incorrect to assume that similarity between the sexes in terms of sexual acts implies that similar "causal paths" influenced those activities (Maticka-Tyndale 1991). For example, Table 4 shows male/female differences in the perception of which sex has the greatest influence on the decision to engage in sexual activity. While neither sex assigned that role "mostly" to their partner (about 3 percent for both males and females), males were much more likely to perceive themselves as the influencer whereas females perceived the decision to be equally shared or only slightly more influenced by the male. Females were also more likely to report that they had experienced sexual harassment or mistreatment and more likely to think often or very often about AIDS in the context of their sexual relationship. Despite the conver-

Table 4

Sex Roles and Aspects of Sexual Experience Among Francophone University Students (1994)

Activity or Experience (in the past year unless otherwise indicated)	Percentage Giving the Response	
	Female (N = 316)	Male (N = 269)
Ever had sexual intercourse	90.8	81.4
Ever had oral-genital sex	88.8	80.3
Ever had anal sex	18.7	18.7
Have you had a steady partner in the last year?	76.4	66.8
Who has the greatest influence on the decision to engage in sexual relations?		
Mostly you	8.4	28.1
You a little more so than partner	9.9	22.7
Equal	53.8	39.4
Partner a little more than you	24.8	6.4
Mostly partner	3.1	3.4
Have you had sexual relations with someone when you definitely didn't want to?		
Never or rarely	93.9	92.7
Have you ever given in to a partner's pressure for sexual relations?		
Never or rarely	78.3	72.4
Experiences of sexual harassment		
Unwanted physical advances (touching, kissing)	31.7	21.7
Physical violence of a sexual nature	6.7	1.1
Do you think about AIDS in the context of your sexual relationships?		
Never	41.4	42.3
Rarely, seldom	33.0	43.8
Often, very often	25.6	13.9

Data from Frigault et al. (1994). Respondents average age 21 years, 95% never married, 90% raised Catholic, all university-level students in Montreal, 1.5% said they were homosexual, 0.9% bisexual.

gence of behavior, we suspect that sex differences in the social and interpersonal contexts for sexual activity are important considerations, and that these differences may be even more common among university students in other parts of Canada.

Maticka-Tyndale's (1991) study of factors that predicted Quebec college (i.e., CEGEP) students' (N = 866) perception of their susceptibility to

HIV/AIDS also showed clear evidence of sex differences despite considerable similarity between the sexes in overt behavior. (Note: Quebec is the only province with a two-year intermediate "college" program [CEGEP] between the end of grade eleven [age 16] and the beginning of university. CEGEP students are generally 17 to 21 years old and therefore younger than university students.) Maticka-Tyndale's conclusion about this group of students was as follows:

> Though the actions may be converging, the causal factors associated with male and female sexuality are decidedly different. If there is concern for understanding male and female sexuality, or with devising programs which will encourage changes in sexuality to reduce risk, it is these causal factors which must be addressed, not merely the final acts. (Maticka-Tyndale 1991, 60-61)

Since there have been few Canadian studies on ethnocultural differences in sexual behavior, Maticka-Tyndale and Lévy's (1992) comparison of sexual experiences among Quebec CEGEP students is of interest. Their results demonstrate differences between students from different ethnic backgrounds, but since the sample size is small (total *N* = 317, group sizes 10 to 196), the results should be viewed with caution. In their comparison of francophone Canadian, English Canadian, Greek, Haitian, Italian, and Jewish (both English- and French-speaking) students, French Canadians (*N* = 196) indicated the broadest range of heterosexual experiences (88 to 98 percent reported kissing, body kissing, body caressing, and genital caressing), 80 percent had oral sex, and 75 percent had experienced intercourse. At the same age, Greek (22 percent), Italian (33 percent), and anglophone Jewish students (38 percent) were the least likely of all groups to have engaged in intercourse, and Greek students were less likely to have participated in oral sex (27 percent) than were the other nonfrancophone Canadian groups (48 to 65 percent), and less likely to report body kissing (44 percent), genital caressing (29 percent), and the other noncoital behaviors.

Respondents who had experienced sexual intercourse were also compared on their use of various contraceptive methods. The question asked about methods they had ever used and, therefore, more than one response was possible. Among all students, the most common methods were the pill (43 to 81 percent across all groups), condom (45 percent to 88 percent), and withdrawal (45 to 67 percent). Some students may have sequentially tried several methods. For example, withdrawal, which is often employed in early experiences, was used at some time by about one half or more of all six groups (Greek students were not included in this analysis because of the small number with intercourse experience). Haitian and French Canadian students were significantly less likely to report this method (45 percent and 49 percent) than were English Canadians. Haitians were more likely to report "none" (37 percent), compared to 6 percent for French and English Canadian and francophone Jewish students and 11 and 12 percent for Italian and anglophone Jewish students. Haitian students were also less likely to report condom use (45 percent vs. 72 to 88 percent for the other groups). Interestingly, the differences noted above in some aspects of behavior were not generally observed in relation to personal assessment of AIDS risk among these Quebec students. The Haitian population in Montreal warrants special mention with respect to AIDS risk because their higher incidence of AIDS at the beginning of the AIDS "epidemic" in Canada led to the early, and incorrect, assumption that Haitians had a special susceptibility within the group.

Overall, these results suggest that most Canadian young adults will experience some tension between their own attitudes, expectations, desires, and behaviors as well as between these and the expectations set by their family and cultural milieu. The reported behaviors of young men and women suggest a move away from what was typically referred to as a "double standard" (i.e., the application of differential norms, expectations, and penalties to the sexual actions of men and women). However, if one considers both the observed differences in some aspects of self-concept, self-esteem, and relationship values and the findings from research on the situational, personal, and interpersonal factors influencing male/female sexual conduct, it is clear that certain gender differences still prevail. With respect to comparisons between ethnocultural groups, research demonstrates both differences and similarities within and between Canada's ethnic groups. These observations reinforce our introductory contention that generalizing one pattern to all Canadians is not just difficult, but probably impossible.

The ethnocultural differences in actual behavior reported in the Quebec study (Maticka-Tyndale and Lévy 1992) reflect a common phenomenon in Canada's larger cities. First- and second-generation students from different cultural backgrounds do not all adopt the behavioral pattern of the dominant culture. Agencies providing sexuality education, counseling, and related services have had to become more conscious of the impact that Canada's linguistic and ethnocultural diversity can have on gender role behavior, attitudes toward different types of sexual activity, dating customs, and a range of other issues that can directly or indirectly affect sexual health.

The current sexual behavior of French Canadian young adults in Quebec reflects, and in many respects exceeds, the pattern of liberalization seen elsewhere in North America and in other parts of Canada. For example, a review of studies of young adults and adults in Quebec found that among 20- to 24-year-olds, 89 to 93 percent had intercourse, with a high proportion (over 50 percent) reporting four or more partners. Among adolescents and young adults who were involved with youth centers that address problems of social adaptation, 70 to 93 percent had intercourse, of whom 48 to 60 percent had more than six partners, and 5 to 15 percent had been involved in prostitution (Otis 1996). English Canadian youth and young people from other ethnocultural backgrounds are more similar than different in many aspects of their behavior, although young adults, overall, are not as homogeneous a group as their portrayal in the media might suggest.

Marriage and Family: Structure and Patterns

Profiling Canadian Families, a 1994 report by the Vanier Institute of the Family, used data from the 1991 Canadian census to provide a current profile of Canadian marriage patterns and family structure. The Institute's broad and unconventional definition of family contrasts with the structural definition applied in statistical analyses. They state:

> Family is defined as any combination of two or more persons who are bound together over time by ties of mutual consent, birth and/or adoption and who, together, assume responsibilities for variant combinations of some of the following: physical maintenance and care of group members; addition of new members through procreation and adoption; socialization of children; social control of members; production, consumption and distribution of goods and services; and affective nurturance-love. (The Vanier Institute 1994, 10)

While this definition acknowledges the continuing trend toward varied family constellations within Canadian society, it does not easily conform to that used for the purpose of statistical data gathering. Statistics Canada defines family in structural terms as

> a now-married couple (with or without never-married sons and/or daughters of either or both spouses), a couple living common-law (again with or without never-married sons and/or daughters of either or both partners), or a lone parent of any marital status, with at least one never-married son or daughter living in the same dwelling. (Dumas and Peron 1992)

The latter definition applies to the marriage, family, and divorce information that follows.

About 84 percent of Canadians lived in families in 1991. Because Canadian law does not recognize the "spousal" relationship of gay and lesbian couples, this number probably underestimates the percentage who perceive themselves as part of a family. Among those in families, 46 percent are married with children, 29 percent are married without children, 13 percent are lone-parent families (about one fifth of these are male lone-parent families), 6 percent are common-law without children, and 4 percent are common-law with children.

Several trends have been documented in the structure and form of Canadian marriages and families that have a direct impact on sexuality. These include age of first marriage, divorce rates and subsequent remarriage, number and timing of children, and spousal and parent roles.

Age at first marriage in 1991 was about 28 for men and 26 for women and represented an increase of three years since the early 1970s. This trend toward later first marriage is relatively recent and reverses the earlier trend toward younger age at first marriage observed throughout the first half of this century. It has accompanied the changes in attitudes and practices with respect to premarital sexual activity, the increase in formation of common-law unions, lengthening of time of education, and entry of women into the labor force in increasing numbers.

As already discussed, initiation of sexual activity occurs well before marriage for the majority of Canadians (ten years or more on average). Though there are no reliable studies of sexual activity in the early part of the century, it is generally accepted that premarital sex, to the degree it is practiced today, is a phenomenon of the latter part of this century in Canada. In addition, marriage is no longer the first step for establishing a couple union. Among those born in the early 1960s, about 70 percent of women who married before the age of 25 had previously lived common-law (78 percent for men); the figure for women married before the age of 20 was 96 percent (99 percent for men). The proportion of all couples living in common-law relationships doubled in Canada from 6 percent to 10 percent between 1981 and 1991.

In the *Ethnocultural Communities Facing AIDS* study, differences in proportion of respondents currently living common-law were documented for three participating groups. Nine percent of women and 17 percent of men in the English-speaking Caribbean communities, 8 percent of women and 5 percent of men in the Latin American communities, and 2 percent of men in the South Asian communities were in common-law relationships (Maticka-Tyndale et al. 1996). Of all the provinces, Quebec has the highest percentage of common-law couples (19 percent of all couples were living in a common-law relationship in 1991). This represents more than a doubling in ten years (from 8 percent in 1981) and indicates a general trend among the young in Canada, and particularly in Quebec, to begin their cohabiting relationships prior to marriage and for some to continue to do so in lieu of marriage. Common-law couples are most prevalent in the Yukon (23 percent) and Northwest Territories (27 percent).

A second factor influencing marriage and family structure has been the large-scale entry of women into the labor force. In 1990, for example, 70 percent of couples with children under 19 had both partners employed compared to 30 percent in 1970 (Vanier Institute 1994). This has provided women with greater independence and is considered an important influence on the delay in age at first marriage, age of first childbirth, single-parent (mother only) families, and divorce rate. It has also produced tensions within families as many individuals and couples find it difficult to meet their own and others' expectations with respect to spousal, parental, broader familial, and occupational responsibilities.

Canadians are having fewer children and delaying the birth of the first child to a later age. Average age at first birth was 23.3 years in 1971, 24.8 years in 1981, and 26.4 years in 1991 (Vanier Institute 1994). In addition, there is an increase in the number of single-parent families both as a result of divorce and of single women (and a small number of single men) raising children without partners. About 13 percent of families in Canada are "lone parent" families with 83 percent of these involving female parents (Vanier Institute 1994). Some of the foregoing factors are addressed more comprehensively in Section 9D. Here we note only that these factors have an important influence on family structure, sexuality, and couple relationships.

Before 1968, divorce was permitted only if one of the partners had committed adultery. The divorce rate throughout the 1950s and early 1960s was around 200 divorces per 100,000 married women per year. The 1968 Divorce Act expanded the grounds for divorce to include: acts such as adultery or physical or mental cruelty; permanent marriage breakdown (e.g., desertion, imprisonment, or living apart for at least three years). The divorce rate rose steadily through the 1970s to around 1,100 per 100,000 married women in 1981. A revised Divorce Act in 1985 made marriage breakdown the sole grounds for divorce; conditions included separation for one year or more (accounting for 93 percent of all divorces in 1986), adultery, physical cruelty, and mental cruelty (see Dumas and Peron 1992).

The number of years of marriage prior to divorce is decreasing and the incidence of divorce per marriage is increasing. Possibly 40 percent of couples married in the early 1990s will experience divorce. The rising divorce rate has increased the pool of people available for remarriage and as a consequence about one third of all marriages in 1990 were remarriages for at least one partner. Despite the changing patterns described above, the average Canadian married in the 1960s will probably spend about thirty-five to forty years of their life married to someone.

Of course, these data and trends can only be examined for those counted as "families" in various government and research documents. What must be remembered is that some Canadians also form what the Vanier Institute's definition would clearly identify as a "family," but their experiences are not represented in these data. These include gay and lesbian couples who form long-term commitments, share responsibilities and care for each other, and who may also raise children. They include the sometimes more communally shared commitments to fulfilling the responsibilities of family life found in some native communities. In the absence of research and documentation, we can only recognize that these alternative relationship and family forms exist, but cannot draw any conclusions about their prevalence or life course.

Together the changes described above portray Canadian marital and family relationships as units with flexible boundaries. Later marriages, common-law unions, divorce, and remarriage speak of the flexibility of boundaries with an increasing number of individuals moving in and out of marriage or marriage-like relationships. Canadians remain committed to marriage, however, with most spending more than half of their adult lives in marriage or marriage-like relationships.

Children are more likely to experience the influence of several parent-like individuals in their lives and to be aware of and familiar with a variety of relationship types as an increasing number of parents move through several partnerships. Courts, however, remain relatively conservative in their custody and visitation rulings in cases of divorce, at times restricting custody and access to children on the part of a parent who is openly involved with a sexual partner who is not her spouse. This appears to reflect a dominant view of the preferred family form for child rearing as consisting of a heterosexual, married couple. This is evident, in particular, with respect to a parent who is gay or lesbian, with courts most commonly granting custody, whenever possible, to a nongay or lesbian parent and often restricting or placing limits on visitation on the part of the gay or lesbian parent.

Sexual Behavior of Adults

In the absence of a Kinsey-type national survey of sexual behavior, Canadians have historically relied on U.S. statistics to draw inferences about the situation in Canada. Such inferences are less common today as social scientists increasingly document ways in which Canadians differ from their American neighbors in family patterns, laws, attitudes, and health. However, the only available Canadian data typically pertain to selected groups (teens, university students, gay men, etc.) rather than to the adult population as a whole, and come from studies done for a specific purpose (e.g., to assess risk behaviors related to HIV infection, to determine the occurrence and incidence of coercion in sexual relationships, etc.). This makes it difficult to obtain a global sense of the sexual behavior of adult Canadians.

The 1990 *Health Promotion Survey* from Statistics Canada asked a few questions about adult sexual behavior (e.g., number of partners, opinions about various methods of preventing STDs; age at first intercourse, etc.). Among the approximately 6,000 respondents to the question on the age at first intercourse (excluding those who refused to answer or had not had intercourse, approximately 3.3 percent in each case), the results were: under 15, 4.7 percent; 15 to 16, 16.3 percent; 17 to 19, 38.2 percent; 20 to 24, 32.9 percent; 25 to 29, 6.0 percent; over 29, 2.0 percent. These results were for the entire sample of adults of all ages.

Three more recent surveys conducted by Health Canada provide some information on selected aspects of adult sexual behavior in Canada. These are the National Population Health Survey (NPHS), conducted in December 1994 and January 1995, and the Canada Health Monitors (CHM) surveys (1994 and 1995). Given the range of issues addressed in such surveys, the focus of sexuality-related questions that are included is often on selected behaviors associated with health risks, rather than on the broader psychosocial aspects of sexuality and relationships. For example, the CHM (1994) survey found that among 15- to 19-year-olds who had experienced intercourse in that year, 44 percent of males and 33 percent of females had more than one sexual partners. Comparable figures for 20- to 24-year-olds were 41 percent for males and 19 percent for females; for 25- to 29-year-olds, 20 percent for males and 8 percent for females; and for those 30 and over, 14 percent for males and 4 percent for females. These findings approximate those from the NPHS 1995 study which had a total sample size of approxmately 7,200 (in comparison to CHM 1994 which had about 2,200). CHM 1994 also found that among 15- to 19-year-old males, 41 percent said they used a condom always or most of the time with a regular partner whereas 85 percent did so with a non-regular partner. This type of survey information is of some interest for STD or HIV/AIDS prevention but it does not provide the kind of insight into the social context and intra/interpersonal dynamics of behavior that would be afforded by a national study focused broadly on sexuality and sexual health (e.g., comparable to the recent study in the United States by Laumann et al. 1994).

The previously cited Decima Research poll (*Maclean's*/CTV Poll, 1994) and a comparable national telephone survey in 1995 (*Maclean's*/CTV Poll, 1995) provide information on selected aspects of adult sexual activity in Canada (Table 5). While the decline in frequency of sexual activity with age (i.e., from the mid-50s onward) is expected, it is difficult to analyze this finding in more depth because the results are uncorrected for marital status and access to partners, and also because it is unclear how respondents interpreted the term "have sex." Similarly, the fact that about one in ten said they had had an affair while married is of interest, but we do not know how men and women of different ages understood the term "affair" or how they might have responded to the question, "Have you ever had sex with someone other than your partner while married?" The fact that we have such limited national data on adult sexual behavior is an impediment to informed public discourse, policy development, and provision of sexual health education and related services.

Studies of adult sexual behavior and attitudes in Quebec reveal a significant shift away from the traditional sexual script that linked sex, marriage, and reproduction, to one that places greater emphasis on communication and pleasure. There are few Canadian studies that address the frequency of different sexual behaviors of married and cohabiting adults let alone the more complex variables of pleasure, desire, and sexual satisfaction. The work of Samson et al. (1991, 1993) is therefore of particular interest in this respect. Their research addressed these questions in a study of married

Table 5

Selected Data on Sexual Activity of Canadian Adults

	Percentage Responding in Each Category						
	Two or More Partners in Past Year[1]		Ever Had an Affair While Married[2]	Frequency of "Having Sex" per Month			
	Male	Female		None	1-5	6-10	11+
Male (total)	—	—	13.9	—	—	—	—
Female (total)	—	—	7.3	—	—	—	—
18-24	32	18	7.3	15	38	17	30
25-34	30	5	7.5	6	25	34	35
35-44	4	4	10.1	9	30	33	28
45-54	18	1	17.4	16	41	31	13
55-64	5	0	13.2	23	52	17	8
65+	5	2	6.5	54	42	2	2

[1] *Maclean's*/CTV Poll (1994). *N* = 1,610 respondents across Canada contacted by telephone.

[2] *Maclean's*/CTV Poll (1995). *N* = 1,200 respondents across Canada. Those never married (10% women, 19% men) and not responding to this question (8% women, 3% men) are not included in the average.

and cohabiting, heterosexual, French-speaking Montreal adult residents (*N* = 212, mean age 36.9) surveyed in the late 1980s. Based on the respondents' estimates of their annual number of intercourse experiences, they found weekly intercourse frequency rates varied with age as follows: 3.1 times per week (18- to 24-year-olds), 2 times/week (25 to 34), 1.8 times/week (35 to 44), 1.6 times/week (45 to 54), 0.8 times/week (55 to 64), and 0.9 times/week (65 or older). Overall, male and female subjects (respondents were not each others' partners) did not differ significantly in reported average frequency. Duration of relationship influenced intercourse frequency, with those in "new dyads" (less than two years) averaging four times per week, in "young dyads" (two to ten years) averaging 2.3 times per week, and those in "older dyads" (over ten years) averaging 1.4 times per week. This difference held even when age was factored out (Samson et al. 1991).

Composite sexual satisfaction scores were calculated from questions on frequency, desire, pleasure, and overall assessment of the respondent's sexual life. These scores did not correlate with either age or duration of relationship, but those with the higher satisfaction scores reported significantly more frequent intercourse. Respondents also rated their general satisfaction with their regular partner. Overall, 50 percent of the respondents said they were "fully satisfied" with their regular sexual partner. This was the upper response on a scale that proceeded from "fully satisfied" to "not at all satisfied" and suggests a high level of satisfaction in this sample. The fact that general satisfaction did not correlate with age or duration of relationship but did correlate with intercourse frequency suggests some link between intercourse frequency and relationship satisfaction, although response bias may confound the findings (e.g., satisfied subjects may overestimate intercourse frequency).

Respondents were also asked about occurrences of active oral-genital sex in the preceding year, where "active" is defined as "stimulated with the mouth the genitals of their regular sexual partner" (Samson et al. 1993). Overall, 80 percent had engaged in active oral-genital sex (no difference between the sexes), but the percentages were higher for younger groups (e.g., 90 percent for those 18 to 34, 81 percent for those 35 to 54 and 38 percent for those over 55). Those with higher than average education (13 years or more) were more likely to engage in the behavior than those with less (88 percent vs. 74 percent). The average weekly frequency rates according to age grouping were: 1.6 times per week (18 to 34), 0.8 times per week (35 to 54) and 0.4 times per week (55 plus). There was no sex difference in average reported frequency, but, as with intercourse, oral-genital sex was more frequent in new and young dyads versus older dyads. Frequency was also greater in couples with no children and in those who had one child compared to those with two or more children. These differences remained when age and length of relationship were factored out. As with intercourse frequency, oral-genital sex frequency also correlated with both sexual satisfaction and general partner satisfaction, perhaps because these behaviors are correlated with each other and are an increasingly common part of the sexual script of many adults (Samson et al. 1993). The authors also noted that for those who engaged in oral-genital sex, neither "religiosity" nor church attendance affected annual frequency (although "religious" people were less likely to include oral sex in their sexual repertoire).

During the 1960s, a number of factors began to influence sexual values in Canada, including the introduction of the contraceptive pill, the increasing media coverage of sexuality, and the opening up of public discourse about sexuality that began in the 1960s and continued into the 1970s and 1980s. The concurrent impacts of the feminist movement, the gay rights movement, changes in legislation, and the increased freedom in the media to portray and "commercialize" sexuality, produced conflict with, and gradual change of, many traditional attitudes and behaviors. These changes have occurred across Canada, but francophone Quebec appears to have changed more, and more rapidly in some respects (see Lévy and Sansfaçon 1994). The development of sexology as an academic discipline in Quebec in the early 1970s may have had a modest or—as Gemme (1990) suggests—a major influence on these changes. What can be said with certainty is that since Canada's only university department of sexology was founded at the University of Quebec at Montreal in 1969, sexologists in Quebec have had an opportunity to document these changes in a segment of the population, francophone Quebecois, in a way that has not occurred to the same extent for Canada as a whole. As is true elsewhere in Canada, the research emphasis in the 1980s and 1990s has been on youth, primarily university students, preuniversity CEGEP students, and, more recently, younger high school students.

The most recent data on sexual behavior of Canadian adults comes from a 1995 mailed survey of 1,713 respondents (return rate about 60%) who were proportionally representative of the overall population in terms of community size, gender, marital status, education, ethnic origins, and age. The latter included 35% aged 18 to 34, 38% aged 35 to 54, and 27% aged 55 or over (Bibby 1995). Responses to the question "How often do you engage in sex?" yielded the following national percentages: daily (3%); several times a week (25%); once a week (25%); two-to-three times a month (14%); once a month (9%); hardly ever (13%); never (11%). Bibby noted some provincial variations (e.g., 35% of Quebec respondents said several times a week or more vs. 24% in Ontario) but gave no explanation for the differences.

Not surprisingly, people under 40 reported higher frequencies. Once a week or more was reported by 58 to 78 percent of men and women aged 18 to 49 (never was 2 to 7 percent). Although this rate was lower for 60- to 69-year-olds (men 30 percent with 5 percent never; women 25 percent with 41 percent never) and for those over 70 (22 percent for men with 25 percent never; 7 percent for women with 58 percent never), Bibby points out that about 1 in 5 men and 1 in 15 women over 70 reported this upper end of his scale of frequency of sexual activity. Bibby also found little difference in the weekly frequency of sexual activity of various religious groups although married Roman Catholics (64 percent) were slightly more likely to report weekly or greater sexual activity than the conservative or mainline Protestant denominations (50 to 55 percent). Those with no religious affiliation reported 77 percent, a finding that Bibby explains as related to the younger age of this group rather than to religious affiliation. Other data on adult sexual behavior are discussed below in the context of condom use and safer sex practices (Sections 10 and 11).

Ethnocultural Variations in Sexual Behaviors of Single Heterosexually Experienced Adults

Because the focus of the survey phase of the *Ethnocultural Communities Facing AIDS* study was on heterosexual transmission of HIV/AIDS, only certain questions were asked about sexual activity. In this study, 377 men and women from the English-speaking Caribbean communities in Toronto, 364 men from the South Asian communities in Vancouver (the survey team was advised that it was inappropriate to survey South Asian women about sexual matters), and 352 men and women from the Latin American communities in Montreal were surveyed. Participants were located through community organizations and in locations where members of each community were known to congregate. To insure a broad representation from each community, the samples were stratified by age (respondents ranged from 16 to 50 years), time since immigration to Canada, and also by gender in the Latin American and English-speaking Caribbean communities. Great care was taken in developing appropriate wording of the survey items and in translation of those items to the dominant ethnic language in the Latin American (Spanish) and South Asian (Punjabi) surveys. Table 6 summarizes responses of single adults to questions on current sexual partnerships and sexual activity during the past year. (Note: Given the limitations of such a study, including wide age range and small sample size in particular subgroups, the results should be interpreted with caution. However, these are the only data of their kind available for specific ethnic communities,

Table 6

Sexual Behavior of Single[1] Heterosexually Experienced Respondents in the *Ethnocultural Communities Facing AIDS* Study: English-Speaking Caribbean, South Asian, and Latin American Communities

	Percentage Responding in Each Category				
	English-Speaking Caribbean		South Asian	Latin American	
	Women (N = 190)	Men (N = 187)	Men (N = 364)	Women (N = 176)	Men (N = 176)
Total number single respondents (N)	119	106	123	91	95
Number sexual partners in past year					
None	6	9	5	8	17
1	46	34	17	74	38
2-5	39	46	49	11	35
6 or more	9	10	29	8	11
Number with any sexual partners in past year	N = 103	N = 91	N = 117	N = 84	N = 82
New sexual partner in past year	54	70	75	28	51
In a long-term relationship	69	65	41	65	59
Number in long-term relationship	N = 71	N = 62	N = 47	N = 50	N = 45
Monogamous	79	60	65	94	84
Partner monogamous	36	54	52	68	93

N values in brackets = total respondents in survey sample.

Data adapted from Adrien et al. (1996).

[1] Includes never married and previously married (separated, divorced, widowed).

and given Canada's changing pattern of immigration and increasing ethnocultural diversity [see Section 1], they merit attention in this chapter.)

Different patterns of relationship formation are evident in each of the communities as well as for men and women (Table 6). Overall, men reported a larger number of sexual partners and a higher proportion entered sexual relationships with new partners in the previous year. However, the variations between men and women across the different groups were as great as those between men and women in any one group. These results, and others from this study support the observation that has already been made that diverse patterns of sexuality are represented in Canada's population.

Sexuality and Disability

While Canadians are aware of the social rights of people with disabilities, the issues surrounding sexuality and disability do not appear to have impacted greatly on public consciousness. The concern about sexual abuse of people with disabilities may be an exception to this generalization. However, health care professionals and people with disabilities have raised the profile of sexual health issues (privacy, autonomy, rights to information, services, etc.) in the last twenty years and there is a growing literature on the sexual implications of various disabling conditions and chronic illnesses.

The first major conference on sexuality and physical disability in Canada took place in Toronto in 1974. Cosponsored by the Canadian Rehabilitation Council for the Disabled and the Sex Information and Education Council of Canada (SIECCAN) and intended as a local event, it drew 150 participants from across Canada, an indication of the limited attention the topic had received prior to that time. Subsequent changes in attitudes and awareness have led to increased education on sexuality and disability among rehabilitation and health care professionals, either in their original training or through in-service workshops and seminars. For example, SIECCAN representatives have conducted over a hundred of the latter events in the last twenty years, and other organizations, such as the former Alberta Institute for Human Sexuality in the 1970s and 1980s, have also raised professional consciousness in this field.

In British Columbia, the Sexual Medicine Unit at the University Hospital, Shaughnessy Site, pioneered the development of assessment and treatment strategies for sex-related consequences of physical disabilities and chronic illness, including training of sexual health care clinicians in this specialty area (Miller et al. 1989), and research on sexuality and spinal cord injury (Szasz 1989), sperm retrieval for fertility enhancement (Rines 1992), sexual implications of multiple sclerosis in both sexes, and a variety of other such areas. Across Canada, a number of associations for people with disabilities or chronic illnesses now provide resource materials on the sex-related aspects of specific conditions, and some, such as the Multiple Sclerosis Society of Canada, have been particularly active in public education and professional training about sexuality and multiple sclerosis (Barrett, 1991). Recent issues of the *Canadian Journal of Human Sexuality on Sexuality and Disability* (1992) and *Sexuality and Cancer Treatment* (1994) also reached a national audience of professionals.

The Disabled Women's Network has produced a number of publications addressing sexuality and disability issues including a guide for health care professionals (DAWN 1993a) and a resource book on health care for women with disabilities (DAWN 1993b). Although there are no national professional or consumer groups that focus specifically on sexuality and physical disability, a variety of advocacy groups address this issue—e.g., the British Columbia Coalition for the Disabled has an AIDS and Disability program and the Coalition of Provincial Organizations of the Handicapped has also written on sexual rights of disabled persons (COPOH 1988). In 1992, Linda Crabtree began publishing *It's Okay*, which grew into a 32-page, consumer-written quarterly on sexuality, sex, self-esteem, and disability distributed across Canada and internationally (Crabtree 1994). Currently edited and published by Susan Wheeler (1996), *It's Okay* is the first and only publication of its kind in Canada that provides a forum for personalized discussion of sexual health and relationship issues for people with a variety of disabling conditions.

Sexual issues that affect people with developmental disabilities (sex education, privacy, contraception, marriage, sterilization, etc.) have been an ongoing focus of attention and policy development since the early 1970s. At the provincial level, most schools, Associations for Community Living, and residences for developmentally disabled children and adults have acknowledged the right to sexuality education and counseling, and have developed curricula and other services to meet those needs. In Ontario, a network of groups concerned with sexuality education, counseling, and related services has formed an umbrella organization, the Ontario Sexuality and Developmental Disability Network (OSDDN), to facilitate communication, professional development, resource sharing, and advocacy within the field. There is still too little training in sexuality for professionals who work with developmentally disabled clients, although in-service workshops in this area are increasingly common. These have resulted, to a great degree, in response to recognition of the frequency of occurrences of sexual abuse of people with disabilities (Roeher Institute 1992; Sobsey 1994; Sobsey et al. 1994). The Federal government's Family Violence Prevention Division has funded national and local programs to prevent abuse of people with disabilities, and the National Clearinghouse on Family Violence assembles and distributes resource materials on this topic including those on sexual abuse. The National Health Research and Development Program (NHRDP) of Health Canada has also funded national research on sexual abuse of people with disabilities (e.g., Mansell and Wells 1991).

Sexuality education for disabled teens and adults increasingly recognizes the positive as well as the problem-prevention aspects of sexuality and

Canadian resources reflect this trend (Ludwig 1991; Maksym 1990). The previously mentioned seventeen-booklet series, *Being Sexual: An Illustrated Series on Sexuality and Relationships*, published by SIECCAN in 1993, is the only resource of its kind in the world to include Blissymbol translation of key messages along with the English text. It is designed specifically for use with people who have problems with language learning and communication and includes a user's guide and explanation of all Blissymbols used in the text of each book (SIECCAN 1993).

It is generally accepted that people with developmental disabilities have the right to contraception and to other services available to any individual in society, although this theoretical right implies that support will be available to access such services and this is not always the case. The Canadian Supreme Court in the "Eve" decision effectively prohibits sterilization of people with developmental disabilities unless they are able to give informed consent. Although it is now more common for people with developmental disabilities to marry, the right to marry is confounded by at least three different types of legislation (Endicott 1992). In some settings, e.g., Ontario and the Northwest Territories, it is against the law for any person to issue a marriage license to or to perform a service of marriage for someone who the person might reasonably know is mentally handicapped. This statute has been changed in Ontario to omit reference to mental handicap and to place the restriction on people who "lack the capacity to marry," but as Endicott (1992) points out, this provision may discourage marriage even if it does not violate the Canadian Charter of Rights and Freedoms. In other provinces, e.g., Alberta, Manitoba, and Quebec, a person who has been declared incapable in other areas, such as handling finances, is considered incapable of marrying unless he/she provides certification from a doctor or other "official" source that he/she understands the responsibilities involved in marriage. British Columbia and Prince Edward Island prohibit marriage for people with developmental disabilities, whereas Saskatchewan, New Brunswick, Nova Scotia, Newfoundland, and Yukon have no law blocking marriage (i.e., people should have the "capacity" to marry, but there are no statutes to enforce the rule about capacity) (Endicott 1992).

Incidence of Anal and Oral Sex

Since the 1969 change to the Criminal Code, sexual activity in private between consenting adults has generally not been a criminal concern in Canada. Previously taboo behaviors such as oral and anal sex have become increasingly common in the heterosexual population, but even with the recent research interest generated by concerns about HIV/AIDS, there have been few population studies on the incidence of these behaviors. A late 1980s study in Montreal, Quebec, reported that 75 percent had engaged in oral sex and 15 percent in anal sex in a sample of heterosexual university students (mean age 22 years); 64 percent of both sexes reported engaging in unprotected (without condom use) oral sex and about 6 to 7 percent in unprotected anal sex (Samson et al. 1990). Section 5C provides other limited data on these behaviors in adults.

In the *Ethnocultural Communities Facing AIDS* study (see Table 6 and prior references), participants who had initiated new sexual partnerships in the past year were asked about anal intercourse in these relationships. In the English-speaking Caribbean communities, 20 percent of women and 21 percent of men reported anal intercourse, as did 17 percent of women and 41 percent of men in the Latin American communities, and 41 percent of men in the South Asian communities (Maticka-Tyndale et al. 1996). Qualitative, in-depth interview methodologies have demonstrated different meanings attached to anal intercourse. For some, for example, this is an alternative to vaginal intercourse when it is necessary to maintain virginity. Both incidence and meaning would have to be taken into consideration in creating a profile of sexuality; however, there is no research available that fully explores these issues.

Although sexual activity in private between consenting adults is not generally a concern of the Criminal Code, anal intercourse is listed as an offence punishable on summary conviction. It is not "illegal" when engaged in, "in private, by a husband and wife, or by any two persons, each of whom is eighteen years of age or more, both of whom consent to the act." In law, a person under 18 cannot consent to anal intercourse; age of consent for most other sexual activities is generally 14, although a number of restrictions apply to 14- to 17-year-olds, some of which will be discussed elsewhere (for review, see MacDonald 1994). An act is considered not to have been done in private if a third person participates or is present (e.g., group sex or if someone is watching or able to observe because of the setting). This provision of the Criminal Code has been used to prosecute gay men, but it sends an indirect signal to heterosexuals about the taboo nature of anal sex, at least in the "official" sense that any law implies disapproval. This taboo may well be an impediment to safer sex practices or to disclosure of STD infections acquired in this way.

6. Homosexual and Bisexual Behavior

A. General Observations

There has been little historical analysis of same-gender sexual activity in Canada, and the record that exists in court documents, press reports, and other archival material is sometimes confounded by the various coded ways in which same-sex activity and relationships were described. In his history of the regulation of gay and lesbian sexuality in Canada, Kinsman (1987) notes that native societies had a variety of names and meanings for same-sex relations, that English and French colonists in the nineteenth century used labels such as "crime against nature," "secret sin," "sex perversion," "sexual immorality," "social evil," "sodomy," and "buggery" (the latter was proscribed in Canadian law until 1969), and that "homosexuality" and "lesbianism" appeared only with the emergence of the medical and social sciences in the early 1900s and "gay" only recently. He offers evidence of cross-dressing by white women in nineteenth-century Canada (this activity provided access to economic and social privilege and perhaps to erotic relationships with women) and of the emergence of male homosexual networks in the 1880s, which created a public consciousness and identity for this disapproved, and now publicly labeled category of men called homosexuals. He recounts the recent emergence of gay and lesbian networks in the 1950s and 1960s and the legislative and political changes that led, in 1969, to the decriminalizing of homosexual acts between consenting adults over the age of 21. The subsequent legislative changes of the 1980s and 1990s reflect the emerging legal protection of the rights of gays and lesbians concurrent with a gradual shift in public acceptance of gay relationships.

Until 1996, neither the Canadian Charter of Rights and Freedoms (1982) nor the Canadian Human Rights Act explicitly prohibited discrimination on the basis of sexual orientation, although both had been interpreted in that light. In 1996, the federal parliament made this position "official" with a change to the Human Rights Act prohibiting discrimination on the basis of sexual orientation. Federal practice has already been altered in the military after a 1992 decision in which a woman, released from the Canadian military because of her lesbian relationship, successfully challenged the ruling. The decision noted "that the military's policy prohibiting homosexuals is not valid, because it violates the constitutional guarantee of equality and freedom of association" (Bell 1991). The human rights codes in all but three provinces (Alberta, Newfoundland, and Prince Edward Island) and one territory (Northwest Territories) prohibit discrimination in housing, employment, and access to services. However a wide range of rights now extended to married and common-law heterosexual couples are not available to gay couples, and legislative change in these areas has therefore been one of the focuses of gay rights activity in Canada. The presence of publicly gay members in the federal parliament and of an increasing number of provincial and municipal gay politicians is a reflection of changing public attitudes in this area. Nevertheless, Kinsman's (1987) identification of homosexuality as one of the "battlefields of sex" in Canada is probably still correct—the others are prostitution, abortion, women's reproductive rights, sexuality of youth, pornography, and sexual violence against women and children.

Metropolitan Community Church and other churches in Canada covenant gay relationships in a public ceremony, but this is not legally recognized as a marriage. While no law expressly prohibits marriage, a 1974 court decision on this matter ruled that the definition of marriage meant an opposite-sex couple. Since common-law couples in Canada now receive most of the employee benefits that accrue to married couples, many municipalities and some corporations are extending these benefits to gay couples (i.e., domestic partnerships based on the same conditions of relationship that apply for common-law couples). Since the gay and lesbian population in Canada includes people with a variety of relationship and lifestyle choices, there is not universal agreement in the gay community about whether couples in general should have privileges that others do not, or whether gay couples want to be governed by statutes designed primarily for heterosexual couples with children. Nevertheless, altering existing legislation and policies that discriminate against gay couples has been used as one way of achieving social equity.

A 1994 Ontario provincial government bill that would have extended spousal benefits to same-sex couples was defeated, not on the basis of the economic and social benefits, but because it included a redefinition of family and extension of adoption rights, both of which are contentious issues in some segments of the population. The government's removal of these portions of the bill just prior to the vote did not alter the outcome. As with other areas of contention about sexuality and public policy, this issue will probably be decided in the Courts rather than the legislature.

B. Gay and Lesbian Adolescents

While men have generally self-identified as gay at an earlier age than women, it appears that young people of both sexes are now self-identifying as gay, lesbian, or bisexual at an earlier age. This may be explained by the increasing acceptance of gay people, the visible presence of a supportive gay community, and greater awareness of sexuality. However, many gay youth have strongly negative experiences in high school, either because of overt discrimination if they are open about their orientation or because fears of mistreatment keep them from disclosing. Gay bashing still occurs, and this fear, coupled with uncertainty and self-recrimination about their sexual feelings and the difficulty of finding people to confide in, can make this an intensely negative period in the lives of gay youth. Because they are often stigmatized and isolated, it is likely that gay youths have a higher risk of suicide than do teens on average. Counseling and support services for gay youths are now available in some cities, and a number of programs, such as the Sexual Orientation and Youth Project of Central Toronto Youth Services, have helped to sensitize and train teachers and health professionals about these issues. Overall, gay youths in Canada still face major challenges in their personal development, particularly if they live in smaller cities and rural areas. A telephone hotline for gay, lesbian, and bisexual youths established in Ontario in 1994 was overwhelmed with calls for advice and information, requiring the provincial government to offer additional funding to meet the demand.

The process of self-identification and coming out has been discussed extensively in Canada, but there is little quantitative research done to document these experiences for gay and lesbian youth. In interviews with sixty gay and lesbian youth (average age 19), Schneider (1991) identified the factors frequently named as contributing to their labeling themselves gay or lesbian—most chose more than one factor. Emergence of same-sex attraction and feelings was mentioned most often by both sexes, but males were more likely to identify this as "general same sex attraction" (7 percent of females vs. 73 percent of males) whereas females associated their sexual feeling with falling in love with someone of the same sex (83 percent of females vs. 10 percent of males). Same-sex sexual experience was identified by 33 percent of females and 37 percent of males as a validation of their ability to experience pleasure with the same sex and of the sense that "it seemed right for them." Males were more likely than females to identify "casual and anonymous sex over an extended period of time" as a factor in their self-identification as gay (0 percent of females vs. 40 percent of males). Although a number of young men who listed this option said they often felt guilty about such encounters and vowed to stop them, they also noted that the experiences contributed to their recognition that their attraction was toward men.

Lack of interest in the opposite sex (10 percent of females vs. 33 percent of males) was a relevant factor in that most had dated heterosexually and were aware of their disinterest, but it was less influential as a salient clue in self-identification because many assumed early on that they would eventually be attracted to opposite-sex partners. More than half identified "contact with lesbians/gays" (67 percent of females vs. 50 percent of males) as an important influence suggesting that positive role models reinforce self-acceptance. This seems likely since such contact was also the most common contributor to their feeling positive about their lesbian/gay identity (93 percent of females vs. 80 percent of males). First long-term relationship contributed to self-identification for 73 percent of females and 37 percent of males (Schneider 1991).

These findings are consistent with the self-identification and coming-out processes encountered in other countries with restrictive religious and social traditions surrounding homosexuality. The effect of these negative social attitudes and experiences is reflected in the high levels of thoughts of suicide or suicide attempts, periods of extreme anxiety and depression, social withdrawal, and loneliness—all of which occur in teens but were often associated by this group with their struggles surrounding sexual orientation and acceptance by others (Schneider 1991).

Canadian schools have been slow to introduce adequate discussion of gay and lesbian sexuality into school curricula, and those that attempt to do so often encounter strong opposition from organized groups from the religious right—the larger mainstream denominations may be less restrictive and some even supportive. The only high school curriculum resource guide in Canada on homosexuality and homophobia was developed by the Toronto Board of Education in the late 1980s amidst extensive public debate. The Board approved the curriculum guide in 1992. The Toronto Board of Education's Student Support Services program also administers a Human Sexuality program in which an educator/counselor visits local high schools to talk directly about homophobia and to let gay/lesbian/bisexual students know, without singling them out, that the board has a counseling and support group designed to address their needs. At the time of writing, this was the only program of its kind in Canada and one of two such programs in North America.

C. Service Agencies

There is an extensive network of lesbian/gay/bisexual organizations, service agencies, and interest groups in most large Canadian cities, and national organizations such as EGALE (Equality for Gays and Lesbians Everywhere), and provincial ones, such as the Coalition for Lesbian and Gay Rights in Ontario, provide a centralized focus on particular issues.

Most of the large Protestant church denominations in Canada accept ordination of gay and lesbian clergy. Unitarian-Universalist churches were the first to ordain gay and lesbian clergy who are in sexual relationships and to have an official policy of welcoming gay and lesbian members and affirming their relationships. Of the large Protestant denominations in Canada, only the United Church of Canada, after prolonged and divisive debate, has extended acceptance into the clergy to those who are in sexual relationships. All others require, at least in terms of "official" policy, that gay and lesbian clergy be celibate. This applies also in the Roman Catholic Church in which celibacy is required of priests (only men are permitted to be priests) regardless of sexual orientation. Most large denominations also have identified groups for gay and lesbian members (Dignity—Roman Catholic and Integrity—United Church) and some, such as the United Church of Canada, are seeking ways to find congregations prepared to accept qualified openly lesbian/gay ministers.

Canada has many gay/lesbian organizations at the provincial and local levels. Some address social justice and legislative and policy issues, others emphasize community service and education. The various AIDS Committees across Canada have drawn heavily on the gay community for expertise in all areas of their mandate and also for volunteer work and peer support. In addition, local groups such as PFLAG (Parents and Friends of Lesbians and Gays) in Ontario also provide information and mutual support for families of gay/lesbian youth or adults.

D. Behavioral Patterns

There have been few large-scale studies of gay male sexual behavior in Canada and none of lesbian sexual behavior. *Men's Survey 90* surveyed the sexual practices of 1,295 men (mean age 34, 73.7 percent with partial or complete college education) recruited from twelve bars and three bathhouses in Toronto in 1990 (Myers et al. 1991). This is the largest number of gay and bisexual men ever surveyed in Canada but the results may not apply to smaller cities or rural areas elsewhere in the country. The study was designed to investigate AIDS knowledge, attitudes, and behavior. The AIDS-related findings will be reported in Section 11B.

About 48 percent said they had had sex only with men in their lifetime, 35.3 percent had previously had sex with women but had only done so with men in the past year, and 13 percent were bisexual. The reported number of partners in the past year ranged from none (6 percent), one (16.8 percent), two to nine (37.8 percent), ten to fourteen (12.4 percent), fifteen to twenty-four (9 percent), to twenty-five plus (18.1 percent). Among those who reported a current relationship with a man (35.8 percent), 33.9 percent said it was monogamous, 55.7 percent that it was not or presumed not to be monogamous, and 10 percent were uncertain. 5.4 percent had a regular female sex partner.

When asked about sexual activity in the past three months, 11 percent said none, 28.4 percent said no anal sexual activity, 39.9 percent said protected (i.e., with condom) anal sex, and 20.7 percent unprotected (no condom used) anal sex. In the latter group, the measure was based on even one act of unprotected anal sex and the percentage was higher for a monogamous partnership (31.4 percent) versus 14.1 percent for unpartnered men. Other sexual practices reported in the previous three months included mutual masturbation (81.7 percent), insertive oral-genital sex (76.2 percent), deep tongue kissing (75.9 percent), receptive oral-genital sex without seminal contact (74.1 percent), receptive and insertive oral-anal sex (33.9 percent and 27.9 percent), and receptive oral-genital sex with ejaculation (27 percent). Unprotected anal sex in the last three months was more common in men under 35, in those with high school or less versus college education (26.7 percent to 30.7 percent vs. 17.5 percent to 18.6 percent), and in men who were previously heterosexual or previously bisexual in their behavior.

Lévy et al. (1994a) have also studied sexual behavior and safer sex practices in a sample of gay men in Montreal, Quebec; see Section 11, Table 17.

7. Gender Conflicted Persons

Although Canadians have become less rigid in their gender role expectations for both sexes in recent decades, their reaction to cross-dressing and cross-gender behavior is often a mixture of discomfort and fascination. The popular media have given considerable coverage to issues of transsexualism, transvestism, sex reassignment surgery, and cross-dressing, and Canadians are generally aware of these matters. Sex reassignment surgery has been available in Canada since the Gender Identity Clinic was established at Toronto's internationally recognized Clarke Institute of Psychiatry in the early 1970s.

Canada has four centers that do sex reassignment surgery as part of the treatment for gender identity disorders: the Gender Identity Clinic at the Clarke Institute of Psychiatry in Toronto, Ontario (Blanchard and Steiner 1990); the Gender Dysphoria Clinic at the Vancouver General Hospital in British Columbia (Watson 1991); the Human Sexuality Unit at the Montreal General Hospital in Quebec (Wilchesky and Assalian 1991); and the joint program of the Department of Sexology, University of Quebec at Montreal and Le Comité sur le Transsexualité of Centre Hospitalier de l'Hôtel Dieu, also in Montreal. All programs employ more or less similar formats and criteria for treatment, although the Vancouver program is reportedly somewhat less restrictive in the circumstances under which it approves hormone treatment and surgery. The Vancouver program uses a variety of factors to develop a "management plan." These include "intensity of cross-gender identification, degree of obsession with cross-dressing, extent of investment in versus abhorrence of sex and reproductive organs, desire for cross-gender hormone administration, need versus fantasy of sex reassignment, and nature of eroticism." "Sexual orientation is considered an independent factor not directly relevant in the evaluation of gender disorders" (Watson 1991, 4). The plan may include a combination of hormonal treatment, psychotherapy (individual, family, and group), speech therapy, and vocational rehabilitation. The decision about referral for surgery is based on "the extent of cross-gender identification and proven ability to adapt in the chosen gender role" (Watson 1991, 8), the latter evidenced by a minimum of one year living in the new role.

The program at the Clarke Institute of Psychiatry requires a one-year "real-life test" prior to hormonal treatment and a minimum of two years living in the cross-gender role before approval is given for surgery. Specific requirements that must be met before recommendation for surgery is approved include: employment or student status in the new role (this requirement is a potential source of conflict with current or future employers); change of all documents (bank account, driver's license, health insurance, etc.) providing proof of cross-living (employer letter, statement of earnings, etc.); proof of divorce in the case of those who are legally married (a protection for the surgeon) and other such requirements (Clemmensen 1990). The rationale for these restrictions, which can generate anxiety and animosity among patients, is that postoperative regret and poor outcome are more likely if these criteria are not followed. The Montreal General Hospital group has similar criteria and a varied program that includes a strong emphasis on group support (Wilchesky and Assalian 1991). The Department of Sexology/Hôtel Dieu program was established in the early 1970s and follows assessment criteria similar to those described above for the Clarke Institute. It is different from the others in that the

Department of Sexology does the assessments, therapy, and recommendation for surgery for the hospital clinic and is also an active center for research on gender identity. Group counseling is provided, but when the department itself offers such groups, it is because the activity includes a research component, not because it is a standing service.

The legal status of postsurgical male-to-female and female-to-male transsexuals is uncertain in Canada. Although the health plans in about one half of provinces will cover surgery and it is legal to change one's birth certificate postoperatively, the law appears to define one's sex based on chromosomal composition. In a 1992 legal decision in Ontario, the judge annulled the marriage of a woman and a female-to-male transsexual on the grounds that the law does not permit marriage between two people of the same sex. This means that a postoperative male-to-female transsexual can legally marry another female (and this has occurred in Canada) and that postoperative transsexuals who marry (the issuing of a marriage license is based on appearance and not genetics) and later seek divorce, may have their marriage declared invalid.

At the social level, transsexuals face significant problems with education, employment, and social acceptance. Support groups are present in some large cities and previously active organizations, such as FACT (the Federation of American and Canadian Transsexuals), Gender Serve, and Metamorphosis Research Foundation, all in Ontario, have shown the importance of such support and education services for people with gender conflicts.

8. Significant Unconventional Sexual Behaviors

A. Coercive Sex

Sexual Abuse of Children

In Canada, child abuse refers to physical, sexual, and emotional abuse or neglect. All provinces and territories, except the Yukon, require any person who knows of or suspects such abuse to report it to child welfare authorities. The Yukon identifies teachers and childcare workers as the groups with a legal duty to report. It is difficult to estimate the prevalence of child abuse because of the secrecy and privacy involved and because jurisdictions vary in what and how they report (e.g., some record both allegations and investigations while others report only the latter [Johnson 1996a]).

Sexual contact between children and adults is strongly proscribed in Canada, and the phenomenon of child sexual abuse is now increasingly recognized as a long-standing problem that has been insufficiently addressed at all levels of society. Major reports of such abuse in the past ten years have focused public and professional attention on child abuse in general and sexual abuse in particular. For example, the criminal conviction of Catholic brothers for physical and sexual abuse of male residents at a Roman Catholic orphanage in Newfoundland, the growing reports of sexual abuse of children in some Aboriginal and First Nations communities in which poverty, alcoholism, and drug use are widespread, and the response to disclosure of similar abuses of large numbers of children in a small Ontario community have been among the most publicized of many such accounts. These incidents reinforced the concerns expressed in the *1984 Badgley Commission Report, Sexual Offenses Against Children and Youth,* which indicated that by age 16, approximately 5 to 9 percent of males and 15 to 20 percent of females had experienced some form of unwanted sexual touching, and that 1 to 3 percent of females under 16 had experienced forced intercourse (Lindsay and Embree 1992).

Changes in the Canadian Criminal Code in 1987 expanded the old provision that prohibited sexual intercourse with a person under 14 to include the following category of sexual interference:

> Every person who, for a sexual purpose, touches, directly or indirectly, with a part of the body or with an object, any part of the body of a person under the age of fourteen is guilty of an indictable offense and liable to imprisonment for a term not exceeding ten years or is guilty of an offense punishable on summary conviction. (MacDonald 1994, 16)

Since children under 14 are not assumed to be able to give consent, "it is not a defense that the complainant consented to the activity that forms the subject matter of the charge" (MacDonald 1994, 16). MacDonald (1994) notes that the prohibition on sexual activity with a person under 14 does not apply if, "the child is at least twelve years old, is consenting, and the other person involved is less than two years older than the child and is not in a position of trust, authority or support toward the child" (MacDonald 1994, 17). In addition, there is a statute on "invitation to sexual touching," which makes it an offense

> to invite, counsel, or incite a person under fourteen to touch him/herself or any other person, directly or indirectly, if the invitation is made for a sexual purpose. For example, it is a criminal offense to suggest that a young boy masturbate for the voyeuristic pleasure of the person making the suggestion. (MacDonald 1994, 16)

Sexual contact between an adult and a child would also fall under the sexual assault section of the Code (a child cannot give legal consent to the contact), thus adding to the variety of provisions in Canadian law that address sexual contact between adults and children.

In 1994, the Institute for the Prevention of Child Abuse published an incidence study of reported child abuse and neglect based on a sample of

2,447 child maltreatment investigations from the cases of fifty-four children's aid societies in Ontario in 1993 (Trocme et al. 1994). This is the first such province-wide study, and since the investigation used measures of abuse and neglect similar to those employed in the U.S., some cautious comparison may be possible. (Note that cases opened more than once in any year are counted as separate investigations; the duplication rate is thought to be about 25 percent). In Ontario, it is mandatory for children's aid societies to investigate all reports of abuse. These are then deemed "substantiated" (there is sufficient evidence for the investigator to conclude that abuse occurred), "suspected" (can neither substantiate nor rule out abuse), or "unfounded" (there is sufficient evidence that maltreatment did not occur). In the case of sexual abuse investigations reported in the Trocme et al. study, the behaviors involved were touching/fondling genitals (30 percent substantiated in 1993), exposure (33 percent substantiated) and intercourse (40 percent substantiated). Showing pornography to a child is also included as abuse. When more than one type of abuse took place for any child, the most intrusive was the one recorded.

The annual incidence of sexual abuse refers to the number of children under 14 mistreated in a particular year. Among all categories of sexual abuse of children in Ontario in 1993, the substantiated incidence rate was 1.6/1,000 (29 percent of cases) versus 1.5/1,000 suspected and 2.4/1,000 unfounded, for a total report rate of 5.4/1,000 children under 14 in 1993. Sixty percent of substantiated cases involved touching/fondling of genitals (0.95/1,000 substantiated rate) and 25 percent involved intercourse (0.4/1,000 substantiated rate). Using a comparison of the incidence rates (substantiated plus suspected) in the Ontario study and prevalence data from the national report of the Committee on Sexual Offenses Against Children and Youth (1984), Trocme et al. (1994) estimate that between 25 percent and 50 percent of sexually abused children (depending on the method of calculation) are identified by the child welfare system.

Police investigations took place in 75 percent of substantiated nonparental sexual abuse cases (criminal charges were laid in 31 percent of substantiated cases), whereas police investigation occurred in 63 percent of substantiated parental sexual abuse cases (criminal charges were laid in 46 percent of these substantiated cases). This pattern reflects the increasing police involvement in Canada in cases of sexual abuse reported to children's aid authorities. Among all cases of substantiated sexual abuse, the perpetrator was the child's father or stepfather in 16 percent and 14 percent of cases respectively, another male in 62 percent, a mother in 1 percent.

Although the overall incidence of substantiated child maltreatment in the Ontario study is about one half that in the U.S.A. in 1990 (21/1,000 vs. 43/1,000), this difference is almost entirely due to the higher rate of child neglect in the U.S.A. (4.64/1,000 vs. 2.0/1,000). The substantiated sexual abuse rates were very similar in both countries (1.57/1,000 vs. 1.65/1,000 in the U.S.).

Has the growing public concern about sexual abuse of children led to the fabrication of such allegations in divorce or child custody proceedings? In Canada, the Divorce Act governs both custody and access and requires that the courts consider the best interests of the child as the standard in such cases. Zarb's (1994) detailed analysis of the legal situation in Canada indicates that legal decisions in this area are rare because such matters are usually settled without a trial. When a trial does occur, transcripts are often kept confidential. She notes that when allegations are unfounded, the court generally awards unsupervised access, and sometimes full custody, and that unproven accusations lead to supervised or unsupervised access depending on the judge's perception of the best interests of the child. In weighing the rights of an accused parent (almost invariably the father) against the possible risk to the child, Zarb indicates that Canadian courts should and do err on the side of caution.

Zarb (1994) points out that there is a greater occurrence of allegations of sexual abuse on interim applications for custody, but she argues that this does not necessarily mean that false allegations are generally and cynically used as a "bargaining chip" in such cases. Among the possible reasons for unfounded allegations, she cites (1) the excessive influence of media reports that lead to overinterpretation of innocuous behavior as abuse, (2) the emotional fragility of newly separated parents, (3) the belief among some adults that children do not know enough about sex to be able to make up events and therefore that there is no reason to doubt their reports, (4) the lack of trust in separated couples, and (5) the fear that failure to report suspicions may lead to accusation of negligence. When accusations are founded, Zarb notes that case law offers "no clear consensus in Canada with respect to how much contact a child victim of incest should have with his or her abusive parent after disclosure" (Zarb 1994, 108). She sees a consensus for continued access in such cases (in Canadian law access means, at a minimum, the right to make inquiries and to get information about the child's schooling, health, etc.) only when the child wants it, when the abusive parent has affirmed that the child's accusation was correct, and when the other parent can protect the child from the offending parent if necessary. In the absence of judicial consensus on many of the contentious issues surrounding child abuse investigations and their sequelae, Zarb (1994) sees the need for much more research on the prevalence of sexual contact between adult relatives and children and on the related issue of "the child's best interests" when such allegations are made and/or substantiated.

When child sexual abuse cases go to court, there have been a number of recent changes in Canadian law and procedure that make the experience less onerous for the child witness while respecting the right of an accused to a fair trial. Young's (1992) review of evidentiary issues in cases of child sexual abuse in Canada cites measures that include: use of screens so that the child witness need not see the accused while testifying, use of closed-circuit television, use of videotaped statements, and increasing acceptance of children as reliable witnesses under appropriate circumstances. All have been challenged as contrary to the rights of the accused, but Young (1992) sees the legislative trend leaning toward a balance that recognizes the past disenfranchisement of children in the courts for reasons that some now consider invalid. A booklet published by the Sex Information and Education Council of Canada (*After You Tell*, Ludwig, 1995) uses clear language, illustrations, and Blissymbol translation to explain the sequence of events, including legal procedures, that follows disclosure of sexual abuse.

Sexual Harassment

Sexual harassment is illegal in Canada under the Canadian Human Rights Act and also under all provincial and territorial acts respecting human rights. Aggarwal's (1992) detailed review notes that the first such documented case in Canada occurred in Ontario in 1980 when the Ontario Board of Inquiry determined that "sexual harassment amounts to sex discrimination prohibited under the Ontario Human Rights Code." This decision has become the basis for judgments by human rights tribunals in other provinces and at the national level.

In 1983, the Canadian Human Rights Commission adopted a definition of sexual harassment as including:

> (1) verbal abuse or threats; (2) unwelcome jokes, remarks, innuendoes, or taunting; (3) displaying of pornographic or other offensive or derogatory pictures; (4) practical jokes which cause awkwardness or embarrassment; (5) unwelcome invitations or requests, whether indirect or explicit, or intimidation; (6) leering or other gestures; (7) unnecessary physical contact such as touching, patting, pinching or punching; (8) physical assault. (Aggarwal 1992)

There are now many different definitions of sexual harassment being applied in labor relations codes, university policies, and guidelines covering a range of agencies and work settings. Most definitions, such as that adopted at one Canadian university, indicate that sexually harassing behavior "is sexual in nature and is unwanted by the person to whom it is directed." In order for a behavior to constitute sexual harassment, it "must affect the recipient's employment, instruction, or participation in university activity or interfere with the recipient's environment, performance, or evaluation" (cited in Aggarwal 1992).

Although the application of these codes has been a source of debate in some settings, there appears to be general agreement that sexual harassment is a problem and that some form of control and/or redress is needed. A 1991 poll cited by Aggarwal (1992) indicated that 37 percent of women and 10 percent of men had experienced such harassment; other studies of selected groups have indicated larger percentages, mostly of women, frequently involving incidents in the workplace, and often unreported.

Most provincial human rights codes specifically identify sexual harassment in the workplace as a violation. Ontario's 1990 Code, for example, specifies that every person should be free from:

1. a sexual solicitation or advance made by a person in a position to confer, grant, or deny a benefit or advancement to the person where the person making the solicitation or advance knows or ought reasonably to know that it is unwelcome.
2. a reprisal or threat of reprisal for the rejection of a sexual solicitation or advance where the reprisal is made or threatened by a person in a position to confer, grant, or deny a benefit or advancement to the person. (Aggarwal 1992)

This definition implicitly notes that sexual harassment is a misuse of power and constitutes a "poisoning of the work environment" and is not simply misunderstood courtship behavior. Nevertheless, misunderstandings in this area abound and most procedures appear to incorporate the intentions of fairness to each party, confidentiality (although not anonymity of the complainant with respect to the respondent), adjudication, and the potential for remedy without formal disciplinary proceedings. It would be unwise to assume universal agreement and comfort with harassment codes, particularly on university campuses where such policies have been cited as a threat to academic freedom and to open discourse on discomforting topics. Defenders claim that such policies, and the administrative machinery needed to adjudicate them, are not simply a way of reinforcing "political correctness" but a means of addressing a problem that disadvantages not only women but other groups such as gay/lesbian/bisexual students or employees.

Many policy and procedural guides on sexual harassment now include harassment on the basis of sexual orientation. This is consistent with the inclusion of sexual orientation as a protected category in most provincial human rights codes. The Criminal Code also has sections on "stalking," the persistent following or watching of someone. It is also illegal to watch or beset a person's residence or place of work. The popular media have reported on entertainment celebrities being "stalked," usually women stalked by men, and have thereby raised awareness of this phenomenon in the general population.

Sexual Abuse and Sexual Assault (Rape)

Readers interested in an overview of legal and legislative aspects of sexual assault can find an excellent review of Canadian trends in the 1980s and early 1990s in *Confronting Sexual Assault: A Decade of Legal and Social Change*

(Roberts and Mohr 1994). In addition, the Canadian Panel on Violence Against Women received 800 submissions and heard thousands of personal stories from individuals in 139 communities across Canada. The Panel's final report, *Changing the Landscape: Ending Violence, Achieving Equality* (Minister of Supply and Services 1993), while providing a broad sampling of personal stories and recommendations concerning women's experience of violence in Canada, is less reliable as a source of statistical data on the incidence or occurrence of such experiences. The large volume of publication and government activity in the area of sexual abuse and assault during the 1980s and into the 1990s is a reflection of the consciousness raising that has occurred in the past ten to fifteen years. The report of the 1984 Committee on Sexual Offenses Against Children and Youth and the more recent revelations of sexual abuse of children in care (see Gripton and Valentich 1990) are but two examples of this burgeoning awareness.

Although forced sexual intercourse is a serious offense, the word "rape" is no longer used in the Criminal Code of Canada. The offenses of rape and indecent assault were replaced in the code in 1983 by the categories of sexual assault (level I), sexual assault with a weapon (level II—victim threatened with a weapon or caused bodily harm), and aggravated sexual assault (level III—victim is maimed, disfigured, or has her or his life endangered during the assault).

The new laws have produced several important changes in how sexual assault is viewed and treated in the courts. First, it is now possible to charge one's spouse with sexual assault, something that could not be done under the former "rape" laws. Second, the law is nongender or sexual orientation specific. Thus, assault of men by women, and assault by someone of the same gender are all offenses under this law (though, to date, charges have rarely been brought in the latter). Finally, it is less common for interrogations of victims about past sexual behaviors or the specific sexual acts that occurred to be permitted in court proceedings. The specific circumstances under which such interrogations may occur are now prescribed in a bill that outlines how questions of consent and mistaken belief of consent should be handled in court proceedings.

Possible maximum prison sentences for levels I to III sexual assaults are ten years, fourteen years, and life respectively, although sentences are usually less, and many occurrences that would probably meet the legal definition of sexual assault, particularly level I, go unreported or do not go to trial.

The first level of these offenses, sexual assault, is not defined in the code. Sexual assault incorporates the legal definition of assault (use of force or threat of force on a person against her/his will) coupled with the idea that the assault was of a sexual nature or violated the sexual integrity of the victim. The prevalence of sexual assault, or of offenses that would have legally constituted sexual assault had they been reported, is difficult to assess, but some authors suggest that only one in ten of such occurrences is reported. Recorded sexual assault statistics for Canada in 1995 list 28,216 incidents (10 percent of all violent incident reports) with 97 percent level I and 3 percent level II or level III. The national report rate of 124/100,000 population in 1992 was 10 percent higher than in 1991, consistent with a trend of about a 12 percent per year increase since the new assault law was introduced in 1983. This probably reflects an increase in reporting although the incidence may also have increased. Rates varied from 64/100,000 in Quebec to about twice that in Ontario, and 895/100,000 in the Northwest Territories (Statistics Canada, 1992; Roberts, 1994). Nonsexual assault rates show similar variability. The rate of level I sexual assault in Canada in 1995 (approximately 100 per 100,000) was 11.9% lower than in 1994, the second year in a row of decline after the prolonged period of increase from 1983. This rate was still 35.5% higher than in 1985 (Johnson 1996a; Hendrick 1996). At present, it is difficult to assess the relative contribution of the varied factors (law reform, better reporting, and increased incidence of offences) that led to the 1983-1993 increase and the recent 1994-95 decline in level I sexual assault incidents (Johnson 1996b). In contrast to level I sexual assaults, the less common level II and level III assaults have declined since 1985; both dropped about 35% between 1991 and 1995 (Hendrick 1996).

In 14 percent of level I incident reports in 1992, the police did not pursue the case beyond preliminary investigation. The "unfounded" rate (i.e., police have determined that a crime was not committed) for level I to III cases has been fairly consistent at 10 to 15 percent since 1983. To say that a report was "unfounded" does not necessarily imply that an intentionally false allegation was made. When there is sufficient evidence to lay a charge, the case is "cleared by charge." This happened 49 percent of the time for level I reports in 1992, 57 percent for level II, and 64 percent for level III, indicating that charges occur more often in cases in which the definition of the offense is clear and therefore more likely to lead to conviction. Clearance rates for all charges have increased since 1983 (43 percent in 1983-85 vs. 50 percent in 1990-92). In 1991-92, incarcerations occurred for 60 percent of level I convictions and 90 percent for levels II and III. An analysis of reports to selected police departments in Canada in 1992 found that 84 percent of assault victims were female, 98 percent of those charged were male, most of those charged were over 25 years of age (67 percent) and most assaulted were under age 18 (63 percent). About 20 percent of assailants were reported as strangers, 32 percent as casual acquaintances, and 28 percent as parents or other family members. The reported assaults usually took place in a private dwelling (63 percent), 61 percent involved threat of physical force, 1 percent involved firearms, and 18 percent other weapons.

To what extent do official reports reflect actual experience? Statistics Canada's *Violence Against Women Survey* (1993) surveyed 13,300 Canadian women 18 and over to assess their experience of physical and sexual violence. The study was reported to be the first national survey of its kind anywhere in the world (*The Daily*, Statistics Canada, 1993). The specific findings on "sexual assault" are based on recent and lifetime experience of "unwanted sexual touching" ("Has a stranger or man other than a spouse or boyfriend ever touched you against your will in any sexual way, such as unwanted touching, grabbing, kissing, or fondling?") and of "sexual attacks" ("Has a stranger, date or boyfriend, spouse or other man ever forced you or attempted to force you into any sexual activity by threatening you, holding you down, or hurting you in some way?"). Using these definitions, 39 percent reported experiencing one of these since age 16 (24 percent sexual attack, 25 percent unwanted sexual touching, and 10 percent both). Overall, 58 percent had more than one lifetime experience of sexual touching and 42 percent of sexual attack; 5 percent reported at least one experience of either in the previous twelve months (Roberts 1994). While the experience had negative emotional impact in 85 percent of cases, only 6 percent said they had reported these incidents to police (11 percent in the case of sexual attacks, 4 percent for sexual touching) and of those reported to police, 63 percent of the complainants were under the age of 18. Reasons for not reporting included: the incident was too minor (44 percent overall; 28 percent for sexual attack vs. 53 percent for unwanted sexual touching), the expectation that police would not be able to do anything (12 percent), protection of privacy (12 percent), or it was dealt with in other ways (12 percent) (Roberts 1994).

When participants in the *Ethnocultural Communities Facing AIDS* study were asked whether they had ever been coerced or forced to have sex with someone against their will. Thirty-seven percent of women and 19 percent of men from the English-speaking Caribbean communities, 5 percent of men from the South Asian communities, and 8 percent of women and 1 percent of men in the Latin American communities reported they had. Of particular interest is the fact that in the English-speaking Caribbean communities, percentages reporting coercion or force were higher for those who had been in Canada longer (34 percent of those in Canada longer than fifteen years, men and women combined, vs. 20 percent of those in Canada less than fifteen years). This was so even when age and marital status were held constant, suggesting that coercion is a more common experience here than in the Caribbean (Maticka-Tyndale et al. 1995).

In the *Violence Against Women Survey*, the lifetime reports of unwanted sexual touching and sexual attacks (collectively referred to as "sexual assault" according to the expanded legal definition) were usually linked to dates or boyfriends or someone known to them and less often to strangers (19 percent). Based on reports of one or more such experiences in the previous twelve months (5 percent of the sample), Roberts (1994) estimates that 18 percent of women aged 18 to 24 years had experienced some form of sexual assault. Figures for the other age groups were: 8 percent (25 to 34), 5 percent (35 to 45) and 2 percent (45 to 54) (results exclude data involving marital partners). In addition, report rates among women with post-secondary education were double those for respondents with high school education or less (Roberts 1994).

Treatment for Victims and Offenders

Treatment for children and adults who have been sexually abused is in great demand and despite the growth in such services in recent years, the need outstrips both financial resources and the availability of adequately trained professionals. Canada has over seventy community-based, sexual assault services staffed primarily by volunteers. These kinds of services (telephone crisis lines, accompaniment of victims in hospital, police interviews, court, counseling and support groups, etc.) are responding not only to current reports of assault but to past abuse that is only now being dealt with as a result of publicity surrounding this issue.

Marshall (1992) recommends three areas of societal response to sexual offenses: preventing or at least reducing the incidence; assistance to victims; dealing with offenders through incarceration and specialized cognitive-behavioral treatment programs. He notes that treatment programs for sex offenders have been employed with some success in Canadian penitentiaries, hospitals, and community-based outpatient clinics. Since most offenders will eventually be released, such treatment is considered a vital part of social policy. Marshall (1992) cites recidivism rates of 10 percent in a five-year follow-up study of treated offenders who had a comprehensive program that addressed five target areas: cognitive factors, sexual issues, social functioning, life management, and relapse prevention; for untreated offenders the recidivism rate was 35 percent. Antiandrogen treatment is used with some offenders during treatment and subsequent to release.

"Gating" (i.e., immediate rearrest upon release) of offenders who have completed their sentences, but are still considered dangerous, has been used in Canada as has the placing of conditions on released offenders (e.g., restricting men who have committed offenses against children from going near schools, etc.). The former has been declared in violation of charter rights and a current test case in Ontario will determine whether the latter does so as well. Both issues reflect the extensive concern that prevails in Canada around the risk of sexual assault and abuse. Growing public awareness of the long-term consequences for many victims of sexual abuse has undoubtedly contributed to the perception of dangerousness that colors public discourse about sexuality.

Sexual Coercion and Assault—College and University Students

DeKeseredy and Kelly (1993) conducted a national study of sexual mistreatment and assault on university campuses using a sample of 1,307 men and 1,835 women from classes in over forty universities and community colleges across Canada. Respondents were young (median age 20 for females, 21 for males), unmarried (about 80 percent for both sexes; those married were asked to respond based on their dating relationships), and primarily in their first or second year of study (66 percent). The results presented here are for women's reports of their experiences of abusive behavior in dating relationships and men's reports of their own abusive behavior. (For commentary on the study and the circumstances of its public release, see Gartner 1993, Fox 1993, and Kelly 1994.)

The study determined incidence rates (past year) and prevalence rates (since starting university or college) for a variety of experiences that were described in detail in the research questionnaires and that corresponded, in some cases, to legal definitions of sexual harassment or level I or II sexual assault. For example, "Have you ever given in to sex play (fondling, kissing or petting but not intercourse) when you didn't want to because you were overwhelmed by a man's continual arguments and pressure?" yielded an 18.2 percent incidence response (7.8 percent of men said they had been the source of such an outcome for a female partner in the past year) and 31.8 percent prevalence (14.9 percent of men said they had exerted such pressure on a partner since beginning university/college; see Table 7.

DeKeseredy and Kelly (1993) suggest that their reported incidence and prevalence figures for sexual abuse in dating relationships may be underestimated, that the problem is as serious in Canada as has been reported for the U.S.A., that the attempt of some males to "mirror the dynamics of patriarchal marriages" in their dating situations may contribute to mistreatment of their partners, and that men and women bring different interpretations of consent to such relationships. Kathleen Cairns (1993) at the University Calgary has identified the different self-perceptions and scripts that many men and women in university bring to these interactions (sexual entitlement on the part of males and sexual accommodation on the part of females) and suggested that attention to such scripts could provide a basis for understanding and eventually reducing the incidence of coercive behavior. She proposes that sex education for young women should focus on assertiveness and refusal skills, on "development of a sense of self as sexual subject, and on the related understanding of the nature of female sexual desire" (Cairns 1993, 211). Young men should learn how to develop a broader awareness of sensuality, feeling, and of girls and women as persons; both sexes need to recognize that it is social-derived sexual scripts and power differences, not immutable biology, that leads to sexual coercion.

Research by Sandra Byers and her students at the University of New Brunswick also adopts a sexological rather than purely legalistic and legislative approach to understanding and changing sexually coercive behavior (see Byers 1991; O'Sullivan et al. 1994; O'Sullivan and Byers 1993). For example, Byers and Lewis (1988) found that desired level of sexual activity was the same for men and women in 90 percent of dating for college age couples, that women were no more likely than men to refuse a partner's

Table 7

Incidence and Prevalence Rates for Different Aspects of Sexual Abuse Reported by a National Sample of Canadian University/College Students

Situation	Incidence[1] (%)		Prevalence[1] (%)	
	Women ($N = 1{,}835$)	Men[2] ($N = 1{,}307$)	Women ($N = 1{,}835$)	Men[2] ($N = 1{,}307$)
Have you given in to sex play (fondling, kissing or petting, but not intercourse) when you didn't want to because you were overwhelmed by a man's continual arguments and pressure?	18.2	7.8	31.8	14.9
Have you had sex play (fondling, kissing or petting, but not intercourse) when you didn't want to because a man threatened or used some degree of physical force (twisting your arm, holding you down, etc.) to make you?	3.3	1.1	9.4	2.2
Has a man attempted sexual intercourse (getting on top of you, attempting to insert his penis) when you didn't want to because a man used some degree of physical force (twisting your arm, holding you down, etc.) but intercourse did not occur?	3.9	0.6	8.5	1.6
Have you given in to sexual intercourse when you didn't want to because you were overwhelmed by a man's continual arguments and pressure?	11.9	4.8	20.2	8.3
Have you ever had intercourse when you didn't want to because a man threatened or used some degree of physical force (twisting your arm, holding you down, etc.) to make you?	2.0	1.7	6.6	1.5
Have you had intercourse when you didn't want to because you were drunk or high?	7.6	2.2	14.6	4.7

[1] Incidence (in the past year), prevalence (since beginning university/college).

[2] Male responses indicate percentage who said they had been the source of such experiences for a woman.

Data from DeKeseredy and Kelly (1993). Median age for females 20 years, for males 21 years.

sexual initiation (although men initiated more often), that when disagreements occurred in desired level of sexual activity men did not, in the vast majority of cases, try to persuade, coerce, or force their partners, and that most stopped the unwanted activity when asked. While these and other findings suggest that Canadian college students are at various stages in the transition to more egalitarian gender and sexual relationships, the level of mistreatment experienced and perceived by college and university women remains a significant issue on many campuses.

Sexual Assault and Coercion of People with Disabilities

There is a high prevalence of sexual assault and abuse in the lives of people with physical or developmental disabilities and this area has generated a variety of educational, research, and prevention programs (The Roeher Institute 1992; Sobsey 1994; Sobsey et al. 1994). The Disabled Women's Network has been particularly active in raising awareness of this issue at both the local and national level through pamphlets for consumers and an educational guide for health care professionals. The federal government's Family Violence Prevention Division funds a variety of programs that deal with violence in general and sexual abuse in particular against people with disabilities.

Physician-Patient Sexual Contact

Patient-physician sexual involvement is an important area of professional misconduct that has received increased attention in Canada in recent years. Subsequent to the report in Ontario of the Task Force on Sexual Abuse of Patients (TFSAP 1991), an act was passed (Regulated Health Professions Amendment Act, 1993, SO1993,c37) which identified "strict guidelines for reporting such activity and disciplining physicians" (Lamont and Woodward 1994). A task force of the College of Physicians and Surgeons of Ontario (CPSO) mandated to respond to the report that the CPSO had commissioned identified three categories of impropriety that would receive different penalties. They were:

1. Sexual impropriety: any behavior such as gestures and expressions that are sexually demeaning to a patient or that demonstrate a lack of respect for the patient's privacy.
2. Sexual transgression: any inappropriate touching of a patient, short of sexual violation, that is of a sexual nature.
3. Sexual violation: sex between a physician and a patient, regardless of who initiated it, including but not limited to sexual intercourse, genital-genital contact, oral-genital contact, oral-anal contact and genital-anal contact. (CPSO 1992, as cited in Lamont and Woodward 1994, 1434)

The Committee on Physician Sexual Misconduct established by the College of Physicians and Surgeons of British Columbia (1992) proposed ninety-seven different recommendations for responding to the issues surrounding patient-physician sexual contact. The College also funded a mailed survey of all practicing physicians in British Columbia (4,513 responses, 72.3 percent response rate, 78.9 percent males) which found that 20.7 percent of the responding physicians, and 62.3 percent of psychiatrists, had seen a patient who reported having had sexual contact with another physician (Maurice et al. 1994a). Female physicians were more likely than male physicians (31.2 percent vs. 17.8 percent) to indicate that they had heard such a revelation from a patient. Among the physicians who were asked questions about their personal behavior, 3.5 percent of the 1,414 who responded (69.5 percent response rate) said they had had at least one sexual experience with someone who was a current patient at the time of the sexual contact (3.8 percent of male vs. 2.3 percent of female respondents). This figure was 7.4 percent for those who said they had had sexual contact with a former patient (8.1 percent of male vs. 4.3 percent of female respondents).

Maurice et al. (1994b) have also surveyed members of the public in British Columbia to assess their opinions and experience concerning patient-physician sexual contact. Questionnaires mailed to 6,000 women and 2,000 men yielded 2,456 responses (2,079 women, 376 men). When asked whether a physician had ever touched their private body parts for what seemed to be sexual reasons, 4.7 percent of the women and 1.3 percent of the men said yes. In addition, 6 percent of women and 2.5 percent of men said a doctor had made sexual remarks that upset them and 0.3 percent reported sexual activity with a former physician (0.7 percent with a doctor who was their current physician at the time of the contact).

Ontario and British Columbia have now passed legislation that requires physicians to report to their provincial medical college (i.e., registration body) any suspicions or knowledge they may have of physicians engaging in sexual contact with patients.

A large sample of Canadian obstetricians and gynecologists (i.e., 782 members of the Society of Obstetricians and Gynecologists of Canada, response rate 78 percent) has also been surveyed on this issue via mailed questionnaire (Lamont and Woodward 1994). Based on the CPSO definitions of impropriety, transgression, and violation: 37 percent of female respondents and 19 percent of males said they were aware of actions by a colleague that fitted one of the categories; fewer (10 percent overall) knew another obstetrician-gynecologist who had done so; 3 percent of males and 1 percent of females reported such involvement themselves; and 4 percent and 2 percent respectively said they had been accused of such involvement; 97 percent said such contact was never therapeutic and 58 percent saw it as an abuse of power. Respondents varied in the type of penalty they felt should be applied for different levels of offense, with a hierarchy based on level and with females generally favoring stronger penalties (e.g., 39 percent of females vs. 21 percent of males favored permanent loss of license for a sexual violation, 11 percent vs. 3 percent for a transgression). Respondents differed on the amount of time they felt should elapse before it was permissible to begin a relationship with a former patient that might lead to sexual activity (never acceptable, 14 percent; 6 months to over one year, 53 percent; OK after public termination of the professional relationship, 11 percent). The Canadian Medical Association has recently published a Policy Summary on these matters both to guide physicians and the public and to generate discussion and ongoing review of the policies (CMA Policy Summary 1994).

Sexual Homicide

Although sexual homicide is rare, the horror of such events and the publicity surrounding them is a source of considerable anxiety and concern in Canada. As a consequence, amendments have been proposed to the Criminal Code, the Prison Reformatories Act, and the Corrections and Conditional Release Act that would permit continued incarceration of dangerous offenders even after their court-imposed sentences for previous crimes have been completed. Using homicide statistics from 1974-86 in Canada, Roberts and Grossman (1993) found that about 4 percent of recorded homicides were sexual homicides (i.e., murders that occur as part of the commission of a sexual offense). Over this period, the number of such homicides did not increase nor did the proportion of homicides classified as sexual homicides. The victims were primarily female (85 percent) and the perpetrators were almost exclusively male (99 percent). Compared to the period 1961-70 when 20 percent of the victims were under age 21, the more recent period had 49 percent under the age of 21. About 30 percent of such crimes involved a stranger and 33 percent an acquaintance. Close family members were infrequently victims in contrast to other homicides (about 12 percent of all murders were of spouses) and alcohol and drugs were involved in 25 percent of sexual homicides, slightly less than for homicides in general. The wide publicity given to sexual homicides has focused attention on all aspects of sexual assault and violence. Research and public policy initiatives address the complex problems of preventing sexual assault of all kinds, of treating victims and their families, of treating offenders, most of whom will eventually be released from prison, and of predicting dangerousness of adults after the fact and of youth before they offend.

B. Prostitution

While prostitution among consenting adults has never been illegal in Canada per se, the practice has long been considered immoral, and the Criminal Code has been used to prosecute prostitutes and more recently their customers. In 1983, the Special Committee for the Study of Pornography and Prostitution (the Fraser Committee), established by the Justice Minister in 1983, was mandated to examine all aspects of prostitution in Canada and to make recommendations for changes in what was perceived, at the time, to be an unenforceable law on solicitation. In their 1985 report, the Fraser Committee made more than a hundred recommendations, including one that prostitution-related activities by both prostitutes and customers be removed from the Criminal Code and another that small-scale, nonresidential commercial prostitution establishments should be allowed to operate. The federal government, however, did not act upon these two recommendations. The Committee's fifteen recommendations dealing with adult prostitution included the proposal that because it was the nuisance aspect of public solicitation by adult prostitutes that most concerned the public—teen prostitution will be addressed below—an addition to the nuisance provisions of the criminal code pertaining to solicitation would help to alleviate this problem (Gemme 1993).

In a recent review of legal, criminological, and sexological perspectives on prostitution in Canada, Gemme (1993) examined the implications of legal changes made subsequent to the Commission's report. He notes that although prostitution is not strictly illegal,

> almost all activities which permit one to practice prostitution are illegal (solicitation; to deliver service to many in the same place; to operate or to find oneself in a bawdy house; to transport toward this place; to initiate someone into prostitution or to live from the prostitution of others. (Gemme 1993, 227)

The increased visibility of street prostitution in Canadian cities throughout the 1980s may account for both the public perception that it is a "serious problem" (about 25 percent of Gallup poll respondents said so in 1984, 1988, and 1992) (Wolff and Geissel 1992) and for the 1985 change in the law which prohibited not only solicitation, as in the past, but also communication for the purpose of prostitution. In attempting to eliminate the nuisance effect of prostitution on nonparticipating members of the public, the law also defined automobiles as a "public place" in which such communication might occur. These changes were intended to decrease street prostitution, to make it easier to get prosecutions, and to prosecute both clients and prostitutes (Gemme 1993).

One effect of the 1985 change in the law was an increase in the recorded number of prostitution offenses from 1,225 in 1985 to 10,134 in 1992. Of the latter, about 90 percent were for communicating (reflecting a significant increase in client prosecutions) with the remainder split between procuring and bawdy house convictions (Wolff and Geissel 1992). Jurisdictions may vary in the extent to which they prosecute and, although they cannot legislate in areas already covered by the Criminal Code, some have applied municipal regulations in order to facilitate prosecution (e.g., Montreal prostitutes convicted in one area were prohibited from being found in that area for one year). In assessing the law's application in Montreal, a city that accounted for 16 percent of Canada's reported prostitution offenses in 1992, Gemme (1993) and Gemme and Payment (1992) made the following observations:

1. Police efforts to implement the law in areas where prostitution was prevalent reduced the number of prostitutes in those areas, but shifted them to other areas, including residential ones, without reducing total numbers.
2. Arrests were easier and more frequent, since the courts had agreed that charges could be laid even though an undercover officer was "posing" either as a prostitute or client. The vast majority of communication arrests of potential clients involved a police officer posing as a prostitute.
3. Although 20 to 25 percent of prostitutes were male, only 11 percent of prostitution arrests were of males and no clients of male prostitutes were arrested (since police officers were less inclined to "pose" in that situation).
4. Although the pursuit of equity in application of the law has led to more clients being charged, the overall approach to prostitution in Canada continues to marginalize sex trade workers and often exposes them to mistreatment and abuse, experiences that preceded the entry of many into prostitution (e.g., 44 percent of Gemme's (1993) interviewees reported sexual abuse and 33 percent rape prior to entry into prostitution).

Adolescent prostitution is a significant concern in the large cities where adult prostitution is also more common (e.g., Toronto, Montreal, Vancouver, Calgary, and Edmonton accounted for about 80 percent of all recorded communicating offenses in 1992) (Wolff and Geissel 1994). Given the sizable number of runaway and subsequently homeless youths who gravitate to the urban core, service agencies are called upon to address the reasons for their running away from home (which may include physical or sexual abuse) and the subsequent consequences should they become involved in prostitution. While it is a criminal offense in Canada "to obtain or attempt to obtain the sexual services of a person under age eighteen, for consideration (i.e., any kind of payment or reward)" (MacDonald 1994, 19), Wolff and Geissel (1994) suggest that adolescent prostitution is a survival strategy arising from prior stressors and that supportive environments may be more important than legislative measures in addressing this problem.

C. Pornography and Erotica

Canadians have a long history of debate over what legal sanctions the government could or should impose on sexually explicit books, magazines, films, etc. As these materials became more readily available in the 1970s, it became popular to attempt to distinguish between obscenity and pornography on the one hand and erotica on the other. The growth of video sales, cable television, satellite technology, computer networks, and other communication technologies has made access to a wide range of sexual materials, particularly film and video, both more common and more likely to be used and approved at some level by women and men. For example, a 1992 Gallup Poll reported that 55 percent of Canadians 18 and over felt that adults should be able to buy or rent videos with explicit depictions of sexual intercourse; 37 percent said no and 7 percent had no opinion. Approval was highest in Quebec (69 percent), in accord with the more permissive and accepting attitudes of Quebecois in the area of sexuality, and lowest in Atlantic Canada (49 percent). Approval was higher among men (64 percent) than women (46 percent) and among young versus older respondents (66 percent of those over 65 disapproved vs. 30 percent for those 18 to 29).

The current Obscenity Law—pornography is only mentioned in a new section on "child pornography"—applies to the making of a book, film, magazine, object, sex aid, recording, painting, etc. that "corrupts public morals." "For the purposes of this Act," the law states, "any publication a dominant characteristic of which is the undue exploitation of sex, or of sex and any one of the following subjects, namely crime, horror, cruelty, and violence, shall be deemed obscene" (p. 22). MacDonald (1994) points out that obscenity is that which exceeds contemporary standards of community tolerance. The court's perception of this standard has shifted over time so that "nowadays hard-core pornography involving consensual adult sex is not considered legally obscene. However, scenes of sexual violence, degradation, and humiliation are still generally prohibited. Depictions of ejaculation upon another person, for example, are sometimes held to be degrading and therefore obscene" (MacDonald 1994, 22).

Despite a 1985 government committee report (Fraser Commission 1985) that could find no evidence for a causal link between pornography and crimes against women, Canadian public opinion and legislative sentiment has leaned toward legal control, particularly when sexuality and violence are involved. A 1992 Supreme Court decision in the Butler case adopted the notion that it was social harm, not necessarily the explicitness of the sexual content, that should be proscribed. Justice Sopinka's judgment argued that "we cannot afford to ignore the threat to equality resulting from exposure to audiences of certain types of violent and degrading material. Materials portraying women as a class as objects for sexual exploitation and abuse have a negative impact on the individual's sense of self-worth and acceptance." The decision, which now guides the way obscenity cases are charged, interpreted, and prosecuted in Canada, is based on the judge's definition of harm, i.e., that the material "predisposes persons to act in an antisocial manner as, for example, the physical or mental mistreatment of women by men, or what is debatable, the reverse." Avoidance of the presumed harm associated with pornography is, according to the judgment, "sufficiently pressing and substantial to warrant some restriction of the full exercise of the right of freedom of expression."

The guidance offered by the Butler decision does not alter the Criminal Code, which still includes the defense of serving the public good, i.e., "No person shall be convicted of an offense under this section if the public good was served by the acts that are alleged to constitute the offense and if the acts alleged did not extend beyond what served the public good." The notion of doing good while doing harm is difficult, but apparently not impossible, to reconcile.

In practice, it is the local police who lay charges and customs officials who detain books and magazines destined for entry into Canada. Rather than have the matter decided after the fact, some provinces such as Ontario have boards that view, in advance, all videos and films approved for distribution or showing. Nevertheless, it is still possible for local police to charge distributors of material approved by the board and for subsequent prosecution under federal law. Despite official statements to the contrary, it appears that Canada Customs has been particularly restrictive on publications destined for the gay/lesbian/bisexual audience. Both Glad Day Books in Toronto, a pioneer in marketing gay/lesbian literature, and Little Sister's Book and Art Emporium in Vancouver, have initiated law suits over books blocked by Customs. The latter is being supported by the British Columbia Civil Liberties Association in a current (1994-95) challenge to the provisions of the Customs Act that have allowed customs to ban and detain books. The detentions usually apply to visual or verbal descriptions of sex with violent overtones (sadism and masochism, bondage, etc.) but other materials are also stopped if the title implies restricted content. Ironically, even a book by American feminist Andrea Dworkin, an opponent of pornography but not a proponent of Canada's new "harm-based" law as a way of dealing with it (Toobin 1994), has been stopped at Customs. Shortly before the Little Sister's case began, Canada Customs removed depictions of anal penetration from its guidelines for detaining or banning books, a restriction that probably contradicts provincial human rights code provisions that prohibit discrimination based on sexual orientation.

Human rights legislation in Canada may also be invoked in attempts to limit access to sexually explicit materials. For example, in early 1993 the Ontario Human Rights Commission established a board of inquiry to address complaints that local stores selling *Penthouse* and *Playboy* created a "poisoned environment" for women. Although the board of inquiry was halted in late 1993, the issues surrounding legislative regulation of sexual depictions is likely to continue.

Canada's new "child pornography law," introduced in 1993, makes it an offense punishable by a maximum of ten years imprisonment to make, print, publish, or possess for the purpose of publication, any material classified as "child pornography." Possession is also prohibited and punishable by up to five years. In both cases, someone charged could be found not guilty "if the written material alleged to constitute child pornography has artistic merit or an educational, scientific, or medical purpose." Child pornography is defined as "a photographic, film, video, or other visual representation, whether or not it was made by electronic or mechanical means" that has one or more of the following features: (1) it "shows a person who is or is depicted as being under the age of eighteen years and is engaged in or is depicted as engaging in explicit sexual activity"; (2) "the dominant characteristic of which is the depiction, for a sexual purpose, of a sexual organ or the anal region of a person under the age of eighteen years"; or (3) "any written material or visual representation that advocates or counsels sexual activity with a person under the age of eighteen years that would be an offense under this Act" (MacDonald 1994, 23).

This law was tested in a court hearing in Toronto in 1995. Five paintings and thirty-five pencil drawings by Toronto artist Eli Langer were seized by police from a gallery exhibition because they were claimed to violate the existing child pornography law. Although charges were eventually dropped against the artist, the hearing was held to test whether the local court had the authority to destroy or confiscate the paintings and drawings or whether they should be returned to the artist. Some of the drawings, which are not based on real children and did not employ models, are nevertheless explicit depictions of sexual activity of children with each other, by themselves, and with adults, which is included in clause 1 of the law. Testimony that addressed the concept of harm, an issue pertinent to current obscenity law, argued that pedophiles would be stimulated by such works to the point of committing offenses. Defense witnesses challenged such a direct causal link arguing that the hastily drafted law was too broad and a threat to artistic freedom—the drawings are a product of the artist's imagination—which threatens other artists as well as educators and researchers. The drawings were eventually returned to the artist.

Court proceedings on obscenity cases have been a common occurrence in Canada, and the courts, rather than legislators, appear to be the ultimate arbiters who weigh research evidence and public opinion in such matters. The recent development of phone sex lines, computer sex services, and other such means for accessing sexually explicit content are also testing the Canadian penchant for legislation in such areas. Although it is subject to some legal restriction, sexually explicit material is widely available in Canada.

9. Contraception, Abortion, and Population Planning

A. Contraception: Attitudes, Availability and Usage

Although contraceptive pills, condoms, and other forms of contraception were available in Canada prior to 1969, it was only in that year that the law was changed to legalize the advertising, dissemination, and distribution of such methods for the purpose of contraception. The establishment of the

Family Planning Division within the federal ministry of health in 1972 was consistent with the government's policy that adult Canadians should be able to determine voluntarily the number and spacing of their children. An important aspect of the division's work was to support development of community public health programs to reduce teen pregnancy. When the division was discontinued in 1976, due in part to opposition from quarters opposed to its mandate, the loss impaired development of services in smaller communities that needed both the resources and initiative provided by this kind of federal program (Orton and Rosenblatt 1993).

Contraceptive information and services are now generally available through public health units, Planned Parenthood centers, private physicians, pharmacies, and a variety of clinics and health centers. While knowledge about contraceptive methods is generally good, application of that knowledge, in terms of both motivation and finding a method suitable for each individual, is still a significant issue, particularly for teens and young adults.

While availability of contraceptive education and services for adults and teens has increased in the last ten to fifteen years, a 1990 *Report on Adolescent Reproductive Health* (Health and Welfare Canada 1990) noted that teens, particularly in rural areas, still lacked adequate access to contraception and related sexual health services. To the extent that this deficiency reflects teen discomfort with the settings in which such services are located, some high schools have established Sexuality Health centers (Campbell 1991) and some jurisdictions have introduced condom machines in the high schools (A. Barrett 1992). Neither of the above is a common occurrence in Canadian schools. Such programs generally arise only after an assessment of community needs and consultation with parents. When they do occur, they probably reflect an already high level of community acceptance. Overall, the school-based sexuality education programs described in Section 3A and community agencies, such as public health units, Planned Parenthoods, etc., are the most likely "official" sources through which students can get accurate information about contraception.

Contraceptive Practices

For a variety of reasons, including religious conviction, some Canadians choose to use natural family planning methods (symptothermal method, etc.) and a number of organizations (e.g., SERENA) and agencies (clinics in Catholic hospitals) offer education and support for users of this method. Overall, however, Canadians are most likely to use pill, condoms, and IUD early in their sexual lives with sterilization (tubal ligation and vasectomy) being a popular method in later years.

Although young adults who are regularly involved with a sexual partner are most likely to use birth control pills for contraception, public health officials have encouraged the additional use of condoms as added protection against STDs. Free condom distribution by public health units has been used as a means to promote "dual protection" among pill users (Ullman and Lathrop 1996). In a survey of 249 male and 237 female urban, heterosexually active (in the past year) university students, Myers and Clement (1994) found that 52.2 percent of males and 39.7 percent of females reported condom use during vaginal intercourse. All respondents indicated at least one instance during the past year in which they had not used a condom during intercourse. Table 8 gives some of their choices from a list of fifteen possible reasons for not using a condom the last time they had unprotected intercourse.

Table 8

Reasons Identified by Heterosexual University Students for Not Using a Condom the Last Time They Had Unprotected Sexual Intercourse[1]

Reason for Not Using a Condom During Last Act of Unprotected Sexual Intercourse[2]	Percentage Citing the Reason	
	Female	Male
Was with regular sex partner	55.7	49.1
Thought we were safe	44.3	47.4
Did not have a condom[3]	24.6	45.6
Did not want to use one	27.0	35.3
No sex with anyone else	25.8	24.3
Sex was so exciting[4]	17.4	30.6
Partner didn't want to use one[5]	13.8	27.8
Using drugs or alcohol[3]	4.2	13.3
Had just met partner[5]	4.2	12.1
Was embarrassed to buy	3.6	5.2

[1] Results from Myers and Clement (1994, p. 52). Sample includes 249 male and 237 female heterosexually active university students (average age ~ 22 years). 83.6% of respondents had used condoms at some point in their lives, 69.4% in the last year.

[2] Percentages add up to more than 100 since some respondents picked more than one of the fifteen possible reasons on a list of options.

[3] sig. diff., $p < 0.001$

[4] sig. diff., $p < 0.005$

[5] sig. diff., $p < 0.05$

In their replies to attitudinal questions about sex and condom use (strongly agree 1 to strongly disagree 5), females more strongly disagreed than males with the statements "safer sex is boring" (mean scores of 4.1 for females vs. 3.7 for males), "condoms are a turnoff" (3.4 for females vs. 3.1 for males), "it's safe for long-term lovers to have whatever sex they want with each other" (2.6 for females vs. 2.4 for males), "it's hard to have safer sex with alcohol or drugs" (3.2 for females vs. 2.6 for males), and "it's hard to have safer sex with an attractive person" (4.0 for females vs. 3.4 for males). Although both sexes agreed that "sexual enjoyment is an important part of life," females gave slightly more agreement (1.9 for females vs. 1.7 for males) (Myers and Clement 1994). Overall, female university students showed more positive attitudes toward condom use and a stronger belief in their ability to use condoms than did male university students. This, in turn, translated into more conscientious practices reported by women than men. Two important subtexts in negotiations about condom use are a behavioral norm of serial monogamy among Canadian university students (i.e., there is never more than one partner, but partnerships do not last for more than a few months) and the traditional cultural norm that leads women to trust and defer to their partners, and men to expect this.

In a 1991 study of young adults (aged 15 to 29) in Quebec, 14.7 percent of sexually active respondents said they had never used a condom (9 percent for ages 15 to 19, 15.2 percent for ages 20 to 24, 16.8 percent for ages 25 to 29 years old). Another 41.3 percent said they had stopped using them (28.5 percent for ages 15 to 19, 40.2 percent for ages 20 to 24, 48 percent for ages 25 to 29), and 44 percent said they still used them (62.5 percent for ages 15 to 19, 44.6 percent for ages 20 to 24, 35.2 percent for ages 25 to 29). Among those in the total sample who were respectively either currently using or had previously used condoms, the reasons for ever having used condoms (multiple choices possible) were: contraception (77 percent, 83 percent), danger of STD (65 percent, 45 percent), new partner (29 percent, 27 percent), many partners (11 percent, 8 percent), and had or have an STD (2 percent, 4 percent) (Santé Quebec 1991). The findings suggest that many young people in Quebec may use condoms for contraception early in their sexual interactions and then shift to other methods of contraception and away from condoms as they get older and perhaps more established in a relationship.

Among college students (CEGEP) in Quebec, 18 percent said they had not used a contraceptive method the first time they had intercourse, 14 percent used a condom and the pill, 11 percent the pill only, and 55.3 percent a condom only. When asked about the contraceptive method used the last time they had sexual intercourse, 4.2 percent said none, 18 percent said the condom and pill, 49.2 percent the pill only, 26 percent the condom only, and 1.7 percent used other methods (Samson et al. 1996). In a study of contraceptive use by 745 sexually active anglophone and francophone university students in Montreal and Ontario, Lévy et al. (1994b) found that in the previous six months (1992-93) 72.4 percent overall reported using the pill, either alone (35.4 percent) or in combination with a condom (19.1 percent) or with other methods (17.9 percent), whereas condom use with the pill or other methods was less common (41.7 percent). The sizable percentage using some method of contraception (97.7 percent) and the lower percentage incorporating condom use (41.7 percent) is consistent with the suggestion that pregnancy prevention still predominates over STD/HIV prevention in the decision-making of a sizable percentage of university students. Although most students had only one partner in the previous six months (85.2 percent), having had more than one partner was the variable that correlated most strongly with condom use. Condom use was less common among those with higher coital frequency.

Tonkin's (1992) study of 15,549 students in grades seven to twelve in public and independent schools in British Columbia provided data on a variety of social and health-related issues affecting young people. With specific reference to sexual activity and contraceptive use, he found that 33 percent of males and 28 percent of females in the sample had ever had intercourse. For those in grade twelve (ages 17 to 18), the figures were 55 percent for males and 52 percent for females. Among the British Columbia high school students who were currently "sexually active," 64 percent of males and 53 percent of females said they used a condom in their last experience of sexual intercourse. Overall, 49 percent of sexually active students said they used condoms, 25 percent birth control pills, 8 percent withdrawal, 2 percent other methods, and 13 percent no method; 3 percent said "not sure."

A convenience sample of 660 15- to 18-year-old females in Toronto (Insight Canada Research 1992) found that among the 41.8 percent who said they were sexually active, the contraceptive methods used were condoms (29 percent), condoms and the pill (24 percent), the pill (22 percent), condoms and foam (4 percent), other (3 percent), or no birth control (26 percent).

The 1995 Canadian Contraception Study (Boroditsky et al. 1996) used a self-administered questionnaire to assess the contraceptive attitudes and practices of a random sample of 1,428 women aged 15 to 44 (57.5 percent married, 42.5 percent unmarried) drawn from 20,000 households that had previously agreed to be subjects in market research studies. Based on all respondents in the sample, the percentages currently using various methods of birth control were as follows: the pill (30 percent); condom (25 percent); male sterilization (14 percent); female sterilization (12 percent); IUD (11 percent); no method (15 percent); none because pregnant or trying to get pregnant (7 percent); withdrawal (5 percent); hysterectomy/menopause (3 percent); cream/jelly/foam (3 percent); rhythm (3 percent); IUD (1 percent); and diaphragm (1 percent). Not surprisingly, sterilization (male or female) was used by 38 percent of all married women versus 7 percent of not currently married women of all ages. Since the study did not determine the proportion of young unmarried women who were sexually active, or lesbian, it is not known what proportion of the 15 percent of nonusers had no need of contraception. However, among teens who have ever used the pill, 35 percent said they started using it before their first intercourse, 22 percent as soon as they became sexually active, and 33 percent within one year.

In the *Ethnocultural Communities Facing AIDS* study, respondents in long-term relationships were asked about their current contraceptive practices. Eighteen percent of women and 28 percent of men from the English-speaking Caribbean communities reported no contraceptive use, compared to 12 percent of South Asian men, and 20 percent of women and 24 percent of men from the Latin American communities. Condoms were the most common contraceptive reported in all communities (62 percent of women and 54 percent of English-speaking Caribbean men, 47 percent of South Asian men, 37 percent of women and 44 percent of Latin American men), followed by oral contraceptives (49 percent of English-speaking Caribbean women and 33 percent of men, 26 percent of South Asian men, 30 percent of Latin American women and 22 percent of men) (Maticka-Tyndale et al. 1996).

Based on his research with university students, William Fisher (1989), from the University of Western Ontario, has described a "Contraceptive Script" that Canadians typically follow. This script outlines a common progression of contraceptive methods that are used as individuals first become sexually active and form committed relationships. When young Canadians first become sexually active they typically use either no contraception or one or a combination of condoms and withdrawal. The use of oral contraception is usually begun after a woman has been sexually active for a period of time, or when she considers her sexual partnership to have become "long-term" or "committed." When relationships are terminated, it is not uncommon for contraceptive practices to return to an earlier form (e.g., to cease using oral contraception and rely on withdrawal or condoms in new partnerships), though as women move through a larger number of partnerships, they more typically continue using oral contraceptives. Though there has been no single large- scale national study to test Fisher's script, the studies cited here, and others, consistently provide support for the conclusion that the Contraceptive Script is commonly followed.

B. Teen Pregnancy

Canadian statistics on teen pregnancy do not distinguish between married and unmarried teens, nor is it possible to determine the extent to which marriage may have been precipitated by unintended pregnancy (although this tendency is much less likely than twenty years ago). Given that teen marriage rates are low and that most teen pregnancies are assumed to be unplanned and unwanted, Canadians generally approach teen pregnancy as a problem (although this may not be so in some northern Aboriginal or First Nations communities where teen sexuality and pregnancy are less stigmatized).

A major review of teen pregnancies in Canada from 1975 to 1989 (Wadhera and Strachan 1991) provides background to the current situation. The pregnancy rate is established by combining data on registered live births, therapeutic abortions in hospital (and only since 1990 in free-standing clinics), plus registered stillbirths, hospitalized cases of spontaneous abortion, etc. From 1975 to 1989, the teen pregnancy rate (births per 1,000 women aged 15 to 19) dropped from 53.6 in 1975 to 41/1,000 in 1987 and then increased to 42/1,000 in 1988 and 44.1/1,000 in 1989. This trend was similar for younger teens (15 to 17) and older teens (18 and 19) although rates were lower in the former (27/1,000 in 1989 vs. 67/1,000 for 18- to 19-year-olds).

At the end of the 1980s, Canada's teen pregnancy rate (44.1/1000 for 15- to 19-year-olds in 1989) was similar to those of France (43/1000) and England and Wales (45/1000), higher than those for Sweden (35/1000) and the Netherlands (14/1000), and lower by more than one half that of the United States (Wadhera and Millar 1996a). The variability in teen pregnancy rates in the different provinces and territories of Canada in 1988 (Table 9) was probably due more to social and demographic factors than to differences in the proportion of teens who had ever had intercourse (also shown in Table 9). In 1990 to 1993, pregnancy rates for 15- to 19-year-olds remained higher than in the mid-1980s, ranging from 47.3 to 48.1/1000 (Wadhera and Millar 1996b). Given the greater likelihood of contraceptive

Table 9

Teen Pregnancy Rates and Teen Sexual Intercourse Experience for Canada, the Provinces and Territories in 1988[1]

Province/Territory	Rate/1,000 Teens Aged 15-19	Percent Ever Had Sexual Intercourse[2]	
		Grade 9 (13-14)	Grade 11 (15-16)
CANADA (1988)	41	26.0	46.0
Yukon	85	40.2	56.2
Northwest Territories	145	41.7	59.5
British Columbia	45	23.6	41.4
Ontario	39	22.3	43.1
Alberta	55	30.4	47.7
Saskatchewan	58	22.2	52.1
Manitoba	60	22.0	43.2
New Brunswick	36	30.6	50.5
Nova Scotia	44	32.5	56.1
Prince Edward Island	36	24.3	47.5
Newfoundland	35	37.0	54.7
Quebec	29	28.3	45.9

[1] Source: Wadhera and Strachan (1991).

[2] *Canada Youth and AIDS Study Technical Report* (King, M., Coles and King, A., 1990. Based on data for 1988).

use by sexually active teens described elsewhere in this chapter, this increase is somewhat surprising, although a number of other sociodemographic and behavioral factors might explain it (e.g., earlier cohabitation, a larger proportion of sexually active teens, and greater "risk taking" behavior in other domains of life, changes in the age structure of sexual partnerships, and increased opportunities for successful parenting by older teens).

Given the tendency of teenaged females to have somewhat older male partners, a sizable percentage of the males involved in the pregnancies of 18- to 19-year-olds may not have been "teens" themselves. An analysis of U.S. teen pregnancies and births (which occur at a significantly higher rate than in Canada) reported that 70 percent of the male partners were over twenty (Males 1992). A comparable national analysis has not been done in Canada, but an update on adolescent birth statistics for the City of Toronto in 1993 (Phillips 1994) revealed a similar pattern to that in the U.S. Of the 364 births to 15- to 19-year-olds in Toronto in 1993, 54 percent ($N = 196$) had a record of the father's age. Of these fathers, 25 percent were 15 to 19, 45 percent were 20 to 24, and 30 percent were over 25. Among the 18- to 19-year-old females (65 percent of the births in the sample), the father's age was 15 to 19 for 18 percent, 20 to 24 for 51 percent, and over 25 for 31 percent. Among the 15- to 17-year-old females who gave birth, fathers' ages were 15 to 19 (44 percent), 20 to 24 (30 percent), and over 25 (26 percent). The available data covering STD cases for 1992 also support the conclusion that a sizable percentage of STD cases in female adolescents were acquired from males over the age of 19. Although these results cannot be generalized to the entire population, they are an indication that the majority of teen pregnancies may not involve male teen partners. It is not known what proportion of the pregnancies were either planned or desired.

In 1989, 58 percent of pregnant 18- to 19-year-olds gave birth (66 percent in 1975), 36 percent had induced abortions (25 percent in 1975 when abortion was less accessible), and 6 percent had other recorded pregnancy terminations (9 percent in 1975). In 1989, the absolute number of births to 15- to 17-year-olds was 46 percent less than in 1975, and to 18- to 19-year-olds, 40 percent less. Given the personal consequences of teen pregnancy for parent and child, prevention of unwanted pregnancy remains an important sexual and reproductive health issue in Canada (Wadhera and Strachan 1991).

C. Abortion

In 1988, the Supreme Court of Canada effectively decriminalized abortion in Canada by declaring the existing law (revised in 1969) unconstitutional. Prior to this, abortion was illegal unless done by a doctor in an approved hospital, following certification by the hospital's therapeutic abortion committee that the woman's life or health would be endangered if the pregnancy continued. The Supreme Court decision was based on a woman's right to "life, liberty and the security of the person" under Canada's Charter of Rights and Freedoms. That decision has not eliminated the continuing struggle by some antiabortion groups to discourage abortion and block legal access to it. Campaign Life Coalition, Alliance for Life, Canadian Physicians for Life, and Human Life International are among the best known of the groups supporting this view. The groups most identified with retaining and improving women's right and access to abortion and educating about these issues are, respectively, the Canadian Abortion Rights Action League (CARAL) and Childbirth By Choice. A major impetus to change in the Canadian law has been the repeated charging, conviction, and subsequent acquittal of Dr. Henry Morgentaler for providing illegal abortions, i.e., illegal because, although medically safe and performed in a clinical setting, it was not done in an accredited hospital.

Dr. Morgentaler has now established clinics in a number of Canadian cities; all have been extensively picketed and some have been directly attacked—the original Toronto clinic was destroyed by arson in 1983. Many providers of abortion in clinics and hospitals continue to experience varying levels of picketing and/or harassment by protesters. In several provinces (e.g., Alberta and Ontario), the harassment of patients, staff, nurses, and/or the physicians who perform abortions has led to injunctions to prevent protesters from demonstrating directly in front of some clinics or physicians' residences.

The impact of public attitudes and disagreements about abortion, and the continuing acrimony surrounding this issue, extends widely into debates about sexuality education in schools, availability of clinical services, public health policies, and religious beliefs. A 1989 national survey found that 27 percent of Canadians thought abortion should be legal under any circumstance, 59 percent legal under certain circumstances, 12 percent illegal under all circumstances and 3 percent had no opinion. This pattern of response has been consistent since 1975 (Muldoon 1991). In 1989, at the time that the federal government was considering a bill to recriminalize abortion (i.e., effectively a return to the 1969 version of the law), a national opinion poll commissioned by CARAL found that 62 percent disagreed with this plan, 28 percent agreed and 9 percent had no opinion or did not reply. One year later, after the bill had been passed by the House of Commons and sent to the Senate for approval, a similar poll had responses of 66 percent, 25 percent and 9 percent respectively. The Senate defeated the "recriminalization" bill in January 1991. This meant that no federal law was in place and that abortion would be dealt with, as in other medical matters, by provincial and medical regulations. That is the current situation.

At present, all provinces except Prince Edward Island provide varying degrees of access to abortion in hospitals and all but PEI (which pays under special circumstances) will pay some or all of the cost under health plan coverage. There are now a total of sixteen free-standing clinics (i.e., separate from hospitals) in Canada that provide abortion (none in Saskatchewan, PEI, or the territories) with the host province paying full costs in two provinces, partial costs in four, and no costs in the remaining four. Access to abortion still varies considerably across Canada, and there is significant financial hardship involved for women in many settings, particularly in remote Northern areas and in PEI, Newfoundland, and Saskatchewan (the three most rural provinces). Abortion continues to be a focus and flash point for differing beliefs and ideologies about sexuality and social policy.

When asked to identify the circumstances of pregnancy under which they would consider legal abortion acceptable, Canadians surveyed in 1990 gave higher approval under conditions such as harm to the woman's health (82 percent), pregnancy from rape or incest (73 percent), or the strong chance of serious defect in the baby (69 percent), than under specific social conditions such as low family income (38 percent) (Muldoon 1991). These distinctions have prevailed in such surveys for over twenty years and suggest that Canadians, although generally approving of legal access to safe abortion, also have opinions about the criteria they would like to see used when such decisions are made.

A recently released summary of data on therapeutic abortion in Canada (Health Division, Statistics Canada 1996) indicates that 106,255 abortions were performed in Canada in 1994, 32.3 percent of them in free-standing clinics (see Tables 10, 11 and 12). This represents 27.6 abortions per 100 live births and 14.7 abortions per 1,000 women aged 15 to 44. (For comparison, the 1992 abortion rate per 100 live births was 37.9 in the United States versus 25.6 in Canada [Health Reports 1996].) The incidence of unreported abortions is unknown but probably quite low. It has been suggested that the increase in the absolute number of abortions in the late 1980s and early 1990s has been due to a prolonged economic recession. Women under 20 accounted for about 20 percent of abortions, and over half of the women who sought abortions already had one or more children.

One problem for Canadian women seeking access to hospital abortions has been the waiting time involved. This is an issue not only because of increased risk and anxiety, but because of the restrictions placed on late

Table 10

Abortion Data for Canada (1994)

Year	Total Abortions[1]	Abortions per 100 Live Births	Percent Abortions Reported from:		
			Hospitals	Clinics	United States
1994	106,255	27.6	67.4	32.3	0.3
1993	104,403	26.9	69.5	30.2	0.4
1992	102,085	25.6	69.1	30.5	0.5

[1] Abortion rate (1994): 14.7 abortions/1,000 women aged 15-44.

Source: Health Division, Statistics Canada (1996).

Table 11

Age-Specific Abortion Rates and Percentages for Canada (1994)

Age Group	Age Specific Abortion Rate/1,000 in Age Group[1]	Percent Distribution of Known Hospital Abortions According to Age Group
15-19	15.2	19.9
20-24	31.4	30.1
25-29	20.2	21.5
30-44	8.0	27.9

[1] Abortion rate (1994): 14.7 abortions/1,000 women aged 15-44.

Source: Health Division, Statistics Canada (1996).

Table 12

Marital Status and Prior Abortion History of Women Receiving Abortions in Canada (1994)

Percent Abortions in 1994 According to Marital Status[1]		Percent Abortions in 1994 According to Prior Abortion History[1]	
Single	63.7%	No prior abortions	65.5%
Married	21.1%	One	21.3%
Separated	3.3%	Two	5.8%
Common Law	4.3%	More than two	2.1%
Divorced	2.6%	Unknown	5.3%
Unknown	5.0%		

[1] Based on known cases in hospitals only.

Source: Health Division, Statistics Canada (1996).

abortions in some settings. Data collected on 59,694 therapeutic abortions conducted in hospital settings in 1992 showed that almost 90 percent were within the first twelve weeks of pregnancy. Time since conception for all cases was: less than nine weeks (35.5 percent); nine to twelve weeks (53.5 percent); thirteen to sixteen weeks (6.7 percent); seventeen to twenty weeks (1.7 percent); over twenty weeks (0.3 percent); and unknown (2.2 percent). The so-called abortion pill, RU 486, which disrupts gestation early in pregnancy, has not yet been approved for testing or release in Canada.

D. Population Planning

To the extent that a population policy attempts to influence the size, rate of growth, distribution, age structure, or composition of a population, Canada does not have such a policy. Federal government policy ensures the right of people to regulate the number and spacing of their children but does not directly advocate increasing population size through more births, although the fertility rate has been below replacement for twenty years. A de facto policy favoring continued growth is suggested by the setting of higher immigration levels (approximately 250,000 per year) for the 1989-94 period than in previous years. However, the government reduced total projected immigration levels for 1995 to 190,000-215,000 (actual arrivals in 1993 were 230,000) and altered procedures so that new immigrants (as opposed to refugees whose numbers increased in 1995) would not place as great a strain on social service funding. These changes are intended to meet economic objectives rather than demographic ones. Levels set for 1997 project 195,000-220,000, which would probably give a population increase from net migration of about 180,000.

One province, Quebec, offers a financial incentive to women who give birth in any year, presumably as a means of maintaining the francophone population (and perhaps total population as well, since Quebec's fertility rate is the lowest in Canada). Quebec also has some influence on immigration to that province (i.e., to maintain Quebec's share of total population at 25 percent), an agreement arising from Quebec's relationship with the rest of Canada, and an option that some other provinces also wish to exercise. In fact, the actual proportion of immigrants to Canada who settle first in Quebec has been dropping annually from 22.4 percent in 1991 to 12.5 percent in 1994 (Dumas and Belanger 1996). Overall, Canada has no stated national policy concerning distribution of the population. Immigrants settle predominantly in only a few provinces where jobs and other family members are located (e.g., over half of all immigrants come to Ontario, 25 percent of these to the Metropolitan Toronto area), but this is the result of circumstance and economics and not as a guided policy decision regarding population distribution.

Population trends in Canada, including slower growth and changing age distribution, will affect a number of areas that impinge directly or indirectly on sexuality and on the allocation of resources for programs and services related to sexual health. From an economic standpoint, an aging and more slowly growing population requires policy decisions about: maintaining economic viability; training and retraining to sustain a competitive labor force; regional disparity based on population age and size; and maintaining health care and pension plans (Chui 1996).

10. Sexually Transmitted Diseases

A. Incidence, Patterns, and Trends

The final report of the Royal Commission on New Reproductive Technologies argues that a countrywide strategy is needed to prevent STDs and that this "must become a priority if we are to reduce the prevalence of infertility among Canadian couples in the future" (Royal Commission on New Reproductive Technologies 1993). Research done for the commission showed that many people lacked adequate access to quality reproductive health services that could either reduce their risk of acquiring STDs or provide rapid diagnosis and treatment. This was noted particularly for isolated and rural areas, and for many adolescents, single adult women, people with disabilities, and cultural and linguistic minorities.

About one third to one half of women who acquire an STD (usually chlamydia or gonorrhea) will develop pelvic inflammatory disease (PID), representing about 80 percent of all cases of PID. It is difficult to estimate accurately the rates of PID, but Health Canada data cited in the report gave age-specific rates of between 243/100,000 and 306/100,000 for women in the four age groups 15 to 19, 20 to 24, 25 to 29, and 30 to 34. STDs appear to play only a small role in male infertility in Canada, but the incidence data presented in Table 13 suggest that STDs are a concern for both sexes.

Table 13

Number and Percentage of Selected Reportable Sexually Transmitted Disease Cases by Age and Sex in Canada (1995)

	Number of Reported Cases (Percentage of All Cases)			
Categories (Age/Years)	**Gonoccocal Infection**	**Early Symptomatic Syphilis**	**Chlamydia**	**Hepatitis B**
Rate	18.6/100,000	0.4/100,000	122.9/100,000	10.5/100,000
Total	5,500	111	36,375	2,815
Male	3,032 (57.2)	64 (57.7)	8,739 (24.0)	1,805 (64.1)
Female	2,268 (42.8)	39 (42.3)	27,622 (76.0)	984 (35.0)
Under 15	100 (1.8)	0 (0.0)	573 (1.6)	77 (2.8)
15-19	1,267 (23.0)	9 (8.1)	12,091 (33.2)	176 (6.3)
20-24	1,459 (26.5)	18 (16.2)	13,523 (37.2)	360 (12.8)
25-29	1,009 (18.3)	20 (18.0)	5,361 (14.7)	482 (17.1)
30-39	1,167 (21.2)	33 (29.7)	3,638 (10.0)	860 (30.6)
40-59	409 (7.4)	23 (20.7)	826 (2.3)	684 (24.3)
60+	37 (0.7)	8 (7.2)	62 (0.2)	135 (4.8)

Note: Numerical totals may not match since age and/or sex unspecified in a small proportion of cases.

Data source: Division of STD Prevention and Control, Bureau of HIV/AIDS and STD, Laboratory Centre for Disease Control, Health Canada, October 1996.

The *Canadian Communicable Disease Report* (supplement) (*Canadian STD Guidelines*), updated in 1995, provides Canadian guidelines for prevention, diagnosis, management, and treatment of sexually transmitted diseases (*CCDR* supplement 1995). Such guidelines first appeared at the national level in 1988/89 in response to a recommendation of the now disbanded Expert Interdisciplinary Advisory Committee on Sexually Transmitted Diseases in Children and Youth. Despite the decreasing incidence of some sexually transmitted diseases, STDs remain the most common reportable infections in Canada (Gully and Peeling 1994). Reporting rates for gonorrhea have declined in both sexes since 1980 to a 1995 rate of 18.6/100,000. The most recent summary of national STD statistics (Table 13) reports 5,500 cases of gonococcal infection (57.2 percent in males) in 1995 distributed according to age as shown in Table 13. The overall population rates by province varied in 1992 from 2 to 13/100,000 in Newfoundland, PEI, Quebec, and New Brunswick, to 22 to 46/100,000 in Nova Scotia, Ontario, Alberta, and Yukon, to 72 and 115/100,000 in Saskatchewan and Manitoba respectively, and 488/100,000 in the Northwest Territories. The overall rate in 1995 (18.6/100,000) continues a significant decline from 233/100,000 in 1981 to 109/100,000 in 1987 to 34/100,000 in 1992.

Rates of early symptomatic syphilis declined in Canada from 5.7/100,000 in 1984 to 0.9 in 1989, then increased to 1.4 in 1991 and declined again by 1995 to 0.4/100,000. The rates for all age groups except 15- to 19-year-old females declined between 1991 and 1992. Since then the rates are lower for both sexes in this age group (see 1995 data, Table 13), although the rate in 1995 is considerably higher for females. Early symptomatic syphilis in young females is a concern because of the reduced likelihood of detecting a primary chancre on the cervix or in the vagina (as opposed to on the penis) and hence the possibility of delay in initiating treatment (*Canada Communicable Disease Report* 1994). A similar increase in the U.S. was linked to the association of crack, cocaine, and prostitution, and that may also be true in Canada. Early symptomatic syphilis rates vary across Canada, although the Yukon rate of 10.7/100,000 in 1992 was almost five times that in the next highest province.

Latent syphilis has declined over the last decade (under 4/100,000 in 1992) although rates have increased in women 20 to 24 and 30 to 39. Congenital syphilis cases reported each year have also declined from twenty new cases in 1985 to three in 1991 and five in 1992.

Given that the Royal Commission on New Reproductive Technologies identified STDs as the primary preventable cause of infertility among Canadians, the continuing high incidence of chlamydial infection, particularly among young women, is a major concern. The national rates of 182/100,000 in 1991, 169/100,000 in 1992 and 123/100,000 in 1995 conceal sizable sex and age differences in reported number of cases (Table 13) and in rates (24/100,000 for males vs. 76/100,000 for females in 1995). Provincial rates also varied considerably from lows in Newfoundland and Ontario to highs in the Yukon and Northwest Territories. Both diagnosis and treatment for chlamydia are widely available in Canada, but there are significant problems with control of this disease because many people show no symptoms, the duration of infectiousness is long, and many people do not complete their course of medication if symptoms clear up quickly (Gully and Peeling 1994). These issues are particularly significant for teenage females who have the highest rates in Canada for chlamydia (Table 14).

Table 14

Rates for Selected Sexually Transmitted Diseases Among Canadian Teens (15-19 Years of Age) (1992-1995)

		Males		Females	
		Cases	Rate/100,000[1]	Cases	Rate/100,000
Chlamydia	1992	2,047	207.2	13,235	1,403.0
	1993	2,077	208.6	12,744	1,342.1
	1994	1,914	190.4	11,567	1,208.4
	1995	1,662	163.8	10,427	1,080.4
Gonococcal infections	1992	781	79.0	1,644	174.3
	1993	596	59.9	1,185	124.8
	1994	433	43.1	947	98.9
	1995	411	40.5	856	88.7
Early symptomatic syphilis	1992	5	0.5	27	2.9
	1993	2	0.2	5	0.5
	1994	2	0.2	8	0.8
	1995	1	0.1	8	0.8

[1] Age specific rates.

Data source: Division of STD Prevention and Control, Bureau of HIV/AIDS and STD, Laboratory Centre for Disease Control, Health Canada, October 1996.

Among the nonreportable STDs, herpes simplex 2, and human papilloma virus (HPV) infections are the most worrisome in Canada. Although it is difficult to obtain accurate national data, the evidence suggests that HPV is becoming more common, particularly in the younger age groups. Herpes simplex 2 seroprevalence has probably also increased in Canada in the last ten years as in the U.S. There were approximately 55,000 recorded patient visits for genital herpes in Canada in 1993, a number that includes multiple visits and probably underestimates the prevalence of infection.

There have been no studies specifically addressing perception of risk for STDs and actions taken by individuals to prevent STDs, though studies on prevention of sexual transmission of HIV/AIDS, and some on contraceptive use also address STD prevention through condom use. In the Santé Quebec study (1991), about 50 percent of women and 60 percent of men in all age categories perceived themselves to be at risk of contracting an STD. When asked what factors they thought would increase the likelihood of their using condoms (responses were "agree," "more or less agree," "disagree"), the statement "partner requested it" was the only one that received more "agree" than "disagree" responses (66 percent agree, 23 percent disagree). Other suggested options that might have influenced condom use were: if condoms were less expensive (32 percent agree, 54 percent disagree), condoms were more accessible (38 percent vs. 53 percent), thinner condoms (26 percent vs. 58 percent), better knowledge about how to use them (24 percent vs. 69 percent), and more use of condoms by those around me (36 percent vs. 55 percent).

11. HIV/AIDS

The tragedy of HIV/AIDS has focused public attention on a wide range of sexual, ethical, and public policy issues touching all segments of society. Its devastating impact on gay men, on people with hemophilia, and increasingly on other segments in society, has forced Canadians to address not only the pragmatic aspects of prevention and treatment, but also the core questions of homophobia, discrimination (not only toward gay men and lesbians, but also toward people who are ill or disabled), our attitudes toward different sexual practices, our comfort with explicit discussions of sexual behavior, and a broad range of issues unresolved during the "sexual revolution" of the 1960s and the "gay rights revolution" of the 1970s.

A. Incidence, Patterns, and Trends

As of October, 1996, Health Canada had received reports of 14,185 cases of AIDS (92.8 percent in adult men, 6.1 percent in adult women and 1 percent in children under 15 [Table 15]), (Health Laboratory Center for Disease Control [LCDC]). However, the LCDC has estimated that only about 85 percent of cases will eventually be reported (i.e., for a variety of reasons, underreporting is about 15 percent). Because there are also delays in reporting in any year and because the annual figures are corrected for such delays and for underreporting, Canada probably had considerably more cases of AIDS in adults to the end of 1996 than shown in Table 15.

By 1994, Canada had a total of 380 cases of AIDS reported per 1 million population. Compared to the thirty-one European countries, this rate was higher than all but Spain (699), Switzerland (617), France (578), and Italy (426). The comparable rate in the United States was 1,542 per million population (Frank 1996). Based on known cases of people with AIDS reported in Canada in 1994 (n = 1,156), 92.4 percent were male and 7.6 percent female, distributed according to age as follows: up to 14 years (1.0 percent); 15 to 19 (0.1 percent); 20 to 24 (1.8 percent); 25 to 29 (11.9

Table 15

Reported Cases of AIDS in Canada as of September 30, 1996[1]

Age Group	Sex	Total Reported Cases	Percent of Total	Reported Deaths
Adults	Male	13,169	92.8	9,578
	Female	866	6.1	565
	Subtotal	14,035	98.9	10,143
Pediatric[2]	Male	80	0.6	52
	Female	70	0.5	47
	Subtotal	150	1.1	99
	Total	14,185	100.0	10,242[3]

[1] Source: Bureau of HIV/AIDS and STD, Laboratory Centre for Disease Control, Health Canada, *Quarterly Surveillance Update: AIDS in Canada,* October 1996. Total cases reported since 1979.

[2] Children under 15 years of age.

[3] Delays for both AIDS reporting and death reporting make it inadvisable to subtract the latter from the former to calculate the number of Canadians living with AIDS.

percent); 30 to 39 (46.7 percent); 40 to 59 (35.3 percent), 60 and over (3.3 percent) (*Canada Communicable Disease Report* 1996).

It is estimated that over 80 percent of the deaths to date have been gay men. While men who have sex with men accounted for 79 percent of all new cases of AIDS in 1987, that percentage had dropped to 69 percent in 1994 (*CCDR* 1996). In contrast, injection drug use, which was the risk factor associated with 1 percent of new cases in 1987, accounted for 6 percent of cases reported in 1994. Based on the experience of AIDS in adults to 1994, the risk factors identified with transmission were: homosexual/bisexual activity (77 percent), injection drug use (3 percent), both of the above (4 percent), heterosexual activity (9 percent), receiving HIV infected blood or clotting factor (4 percent), and no identified risk factor (4 percent) (LCDC 1994).

It is unknown how many people in Canada are currently infected with HIV. One estimate from the *Canadian Communicable Disease Report* (1992) put the number at 30,000 to 40,000. In the 1996 *CCDR*, the estimate was 45,000. Estimates cited by Remis and Sutherland (1993) state that the prevalence of HIV infection among homosexually active men is 10 to 15 percent. The same report cites seroprevalence estimates in intravenous drug users ranging from 1 to 2 percent in the city of Toronto to 15 to 20 percent in the city of Montreal. Seroprevalence estimates from seven separate studies on adult women indicate seroprevalence rates per 1,000 adult women of 0.1 in Alberta, Saskatchewan, Manitoba, Prince Edward Island, Yukon, and Northwest Territories, 0.2 to 0.3 in British Columbia,

Ontario, New Brunswick, and Nova Scotia, 0.6 in Quebec, and 1.2 in Newfoundland. Four provinces, Ontario, British Columbia, Alberta, and Quebec, account for 95 percent of all cases in Canada.

Shifts in the epidemiology of the disease and the potential for further change make it difficult to predict the incidence and distribution of HIV infection among specific populations. For example, the proportion of all cases of AIDS in adults resulting from male-to-male sexual transmission decreased from 81.5 percent in 1988 to 73.5 percent in 1992 and 1993. The proportion of adults with AIDS who are injection drug users has been increasing from 4.6 percent in 1988 to 10.2 percent in 1993 (LCDC 1994). The number of people who acquired AIDS from blood products (hemophiliacs and others) peaked in 1988 and blood testing initiated in 1985 has almost eliminated this risk factor. (A national commission is currently investigating the Canadian blood supply [Krever Commission] and has identified populations who received blood products during or prior to 1985, but had not been notified or tested.) Reported cases of AIDS in women increased in each of the three-year periods between 1982 and 1990, and the cumulative incidence of AIDS in women in Quebec is almost four times the national average (probably because of the higher number of immigrants from countries where AIDS is more common) (Remis and Sutherland 1993).

B. Prevention, Treatment, Government Programs and Policies

The development of strategies and policies to prevent the spread of HIV infection has required basic research on Canadians' knowledge about AIDS, their attitudes toward people with AIDS, their perception of the government's role in prevention and treatment, and on aspects of their behavior that might place them at risk of infection. As of the mid-1980s, there had been no large-scale national surveys available as a basis for addressing such questions. In late 1988, the Institute for Social Research at York University conducted a national telephone interview survey of a representative sample of 1,259 Canadian adults to obtain data relevant to these issues (Ornstein 1989). By the time of the survey, there had been considerable public discussion about AIDS in the media and most respondents were knowledgeable about transmission, the distinction between AIDS and HIV infection, and the effectiveness of different methods of prevention. Nevertheless, 26 percent believed that blood donors were at risk of infection and another 5 percent did not know. In addition, a sizable minority (9 to 12 percent) believed that HIV could be spread by food preparation, that it could be cured if treated early, and that people who were infectious would show symptoms of the disease. Another 12 to 18 percent did not know the answers to these questions.

Among the groups or agencies that respondents perceived as having a major responsibility for AIDS education (as opposed to "some" or "should not be involved"), parents were identified most often (82 percent), followed by doctors and STD clinics (about 75 percent), federal and provincial governments, public health agencies, and community AIDS organizations (58 to 70 percent). While 45.6 percent said churches should have some responsibility, 35.2 percent said they should not be involved. It is perhaps a reflection of Canadians' deference to medical and parental authority that doctors and parents were rated so highly, since neither group has been a major source of HIV/AIDS information for most people. Indeed, television and newspapers were the most frequent sources of AIDS information identified by respondents (39 percent and 23 percent respectively).

Ornstein (1989) summarized his findings on Canadian attitudes toward some of the sociopolitical aspects of AIDS as follows:

1. Sixty-nine percent of Canadians would permit their child to continue to attend a school class taught by a teacher who was infected with HIV, and another 8 percent would do so with qualifications.
2. Eighty percent of Canadians believe that HIV infected persons should be legally protected from discrimination by landlords and employers. [Note: Discrimination in employment based on HIV status is generally prohibited in Canada and people with AIDS cannot be summarily dismissed because of that status.]
3. By more than a two-to-one majority, Canadians support anonymous testing for HIV. [Note: Although AIDS is a reportable disease, anonymous testing for HIV infection is available in some clinics. In addition, samples may be submitted anonymously by a physician who knows the identity of the donor.]
4. There is very strong support for allowing physicians to demand a test for HIV from patients they suspect to be infected and for compelling HIV-infected individuals to disclose the names of their sexual contacts.
5. About 60 percent of Canadians oppose providing needles to injection drug users. [Note: Needle exchange programs are now operating successfully in a number of Canadian cities.]
6. A nearly two-to-one majority indicates support for allowing high school students to obtain condoms in their schools (Ornstein 1989, 101).

Public knowledge and attitudes have continued to evolve since Orenstein's survey as have programs at the governmental, corporate, and community level. In 1990, the first phase of Health Canada's National AIDS Strategy was introduced. The goals were to stop transmission of HIV, to seek effective vaccines, drugs, and therapies, and to ensure for the care of people with HIV/AIDS and their caregivers, families, and friends. Funding for phase two of the National AIDS Strategy was approved in June 1993 for a five-year period that will end in June 1998. One component of the strategy is the HIV/AIDS Prevention and Community Action Programs (PCAP). As described by Frank (1996), the program's mandate includes: research into prevention and behavior; policy development; collaborative projects involving interaction between different levels of government; and support for non-governmental agencies and service providers. Information on projects funded through the program, and on other national and provincial HIV/AIDS-related activities, is available from the National AIDS Clearinghouse of the Canadian Public Health Association (CPHA) (400-1565 Carling Ave., Ottawa K1Z 8R1).

The 11th International Conference on AIDS held in Vancouver, British Columbia, in July, 1996, focused Canadian attention on the scope and complexity of the global aspects of AIDS and on emerging and ongoing issues that need attention in Canada. For example, an October 1996 joint news release from the Canadian Public Health Association and the Canadian Centre on Substance Abuse highlighted the increasing prevalence of HIV infection among injection drug users (and secondarily among their partners and children). HIV prevalence has increased from 10 percent in 1990 to 20 percent in 1996 at the major needle-exchange program in Montreal, and a similar pattern has been noted among injection drug users in Vancouver. A task force funded by Health Canada is currently holding consultations on a "National Action Plan on HIV/AIDS." Priorities include needle exchanges, methadone access and treatment, and enforcement policies. Similar concerns were raised in a recently released report on *HIV/AIDS in Prisons: Final Report* (*Canadian HIV/AIDS Policy and Law Newsletter* 3(1):13-14, October 1996) which noted that HIV infection is ten times higher among prisoners than in the general population, and that numerous studies on prison populations between 1989 and 1994 had found seroprevalence rates of 1 to 7.7 percent. The report recommended provision of sterile injection equipment or methadone treatment as has been done in several European countries to reduce the spread of HIV infection in this population and to others when they are released.

Recent reports from the British Columbia Centre for Excellence in HIV/AIDS indicate that treatment programs using multiple anti-viral drug therapy, including protease inhibitors, has reduced the death rate among patients in British Columbia's AIDS drug-treatment program. The quarterly rate dropped from 70/1000 at the beginning of 1994 to 23/1000 by the end of 1996. The long-term efficacy of this type of treatment is unknown, but such advances in treatment and prevention show the importance and impact of government support in the field. Given the time frame for planning and research on HIV/AIDS prevention and treatment, it is of some concern that early in 1997, the federal government had not yet announced whether it would support a renewal for phase III of the National AIDS Strategy.

C. HIV/AIDS Issues in Various Ethnocultural Communities

In late 1989 and early 1990, Health Canada (then called Health and Welfare Canada) initiated national consultations to identify the specific needs of ethnocultural communities with respect to HIV/AIDS prevention. The

Ethnocultural Communities Facing AIDS project arose from those discussions. Epidemiological and demographic data gathered in the first phase were used to identify six participating communities (South Asian and Chinese in Vancouver, communities from the Horn of Africa and English-speaking Caribbean Communities, and Latin American and Arabic-speaking communities in Montreal). Community-identified representatives for each group formed the six Regional Research Groups, which met regularly with the researchers. Each community group included community leaders, health care professionals, people working in the AIDS field, and others. Six indepth reports were produced as a result of the qualitative research (focus groups in each community and interviews) (Health Canada 1994a-f; available from the National AIDS Clearinghouse). The reports illustrate "the ways in which individual life experiences in the country of origin, combined with the challenges of recent emigration, can affect sexual health." Selected observations from the reports give an indication of the type and complexity of issues involved for the different communities.

Many recent immigrants find Canada to be a country of relatively liberal sexual values compared to their country of origin. Because they often come to Canada with more conservative sexual norms and customs than found in "mainstream" Canadian culture, members of some ethnocultural groups require HIV/AIDS prevention education programs that are designed to be culturally appropriate for their particular group. In some of these ethnocultural communities, an explicit discussion of sexuality between parents and children or between men and women is taboo. For example, in a focus group, Punjabi women discussed how "some girls do have sexual experiences before marriage, but will never talk about them because doing so would 'wreck their reputation'" (Health Canada 1994e, 11). Or as a woman from the Horn of Africa commented, "Since our childhood, sex was presented to us negatively, and there is no way we can appreciate talking about it" (Health Canada 1994b, 16).

In addition, in some of these culturally distinct Canadian communities, there is a denial of the existence of gay, lesbian, and bisexual behavior among community members. As one focus group participant from the South Asian community suggested, "A man who has sex with men won't accept the fact that he is gay" (Health Canada 1994e, 12). Or, as told by a study participant from the Horn of Africa, "People do not want to acknowledge or believe that homosexual behavior, or gay men, lesbians, and bisexuals, exist in their community. This denial leads those men and women who want to have same sex relationships to hide their behavior 'in the closet'" (Health Canada 1994b, 14).

Negotiating condom use is particularly difficult in some of these communities. For example, in the Chinese communities, "Most people who participated in interviews and focus groups report that condoms are not being used to prevent AIDS and other STDs. Women feel they are powerless to instigate condom use with their husbands or male partners, because it raises issues of 'trust' and 'promiscuity'" (Health Canada 1994f, 13). In some ethnocultural communities, condoms are seen as preventing a male from fulfilling his role in procreation or in maintaining his family line or the racial group. A woman from the English-speaking Caribbean islands suggests that within her communities, "There's a general conception that the condom equals genocide. You commonly hear men saying, 'my seed has to flow'" (Health Canada 1994c, 12).

The findings of the qualitative phase of the *Ethnocultural Communities Facing AIDS* project illustrate that the values, norms, and customs related to the discussion of sexuality, sexual orientation, gender roles, and condom use, among other issues, are sometimes unique to particular ethnocultural communities. In the third, survey phase of this project, questions were asked about various sexual experiences, risk perception, condom use, and psychosocial determinants of condom use with new sexual partners. Table 16 summarizes a selection of results in each of these communities.

Table 16

Selected Responses to Questions Related to HIV/AIDS Risk and Perception of Risk in Communities Participating in the Ethnocultural Communities Facing AIDS Project

	Percentage Responding in Each Category				
	English-Speaking Caribbean		South Asian	Latin American	
	Women (*N* = 190)	Men (*N* = 187)	Men (*N* = 364)	Women (*N* = 176)	Men (*N* = 176)
AIDS is a problem in our community:					
Agree	50	48	30	90	86
Neither agree nor disagree	11	8	39	7	11
Disagree	38	44	32	2	3
Believe at risk for HIV infection:					
Yes	32	30	11	29	40
Maybe	38	41	29	30	25
No	30	29	60	40	35
Have been tested for HIV	38	37	21	30	32
Frequency of condom use with new partners:					
Never	12	6	13	12	14
Sometimes	62	66	38	59	56
Always	26	29	47	28	30

Data adapted from Maticka-Tyndale et al. 1996.

Perceptions of personal risk and of the degree to which AIDS poses a problem varied between communities. For example, respondents from the Latin American communities were most likely, and those from the South Asian communities were least likely, to consider AIDS a problem in their communities. South Asian men were least likely, by far, to consider themselves at risk for HIV infection, and also the least likely to have been tested for HIV. No more than four individuals from any of the communities reported that they had tested positive for HIV infection. Reports of condom use with new partners support the conclusion that a minority in each of the communities is using condoms consistently. There was no statistical association between frequency of condom use and perception of risk in any of the communities.

The survey also examined the major psychosocial determinants of planning to use condoms in future sexual relationships. Both the strength of these determinants and their specific content varied across the communities. These results, together with those from the qualitative phase underscore the need, in Canada, to develop HIV/AIDS intervention strategies suitable for the target audience's ethnocultural identity.

D. National, Provincial, and Local Resources for Prevention

The Canadian AIDS Society, a coalition of over ninety local AIDS Committees and other community-based organizations, is actively involved in advocacy, public education, treatment, care, and support for people with AIDS. Most community AIDS initiatives in Canada began in, and are sustained by the gay community, with support from all levels of government and the local community. The second revised edition of the Society's *Safer Sex Guidelines* (Canadian AIDS Society 1994) provides authoritative guidance for educators and counselors on assessing the risk of HIV transmission via different sexual behaviors and on reducing that risk.

Examples of other governmental, non-governmental, and community programs and services related to HIV/AIDS prevention are referred to in other parts of Section 11.

E. Safer Sex Practices of Selected Populations

Gay and Bisexual Men

In 1991-92, the first national survey in Canada to assess possible effects of different variables on HIV test-seeking and sexual behavior of men who have sex with men was conducted in thirty-five cities across Canada (Myers et al. 1993). The sample of 4,803 men (20.9 percent over the age of 22) was recruited from gay-identified settings in seven geographical regions, and questionnaires, administered in English or French, were used for data collection. The salient measure of sexual risk-taking reported in the study was at least one instance of unprotected anal intercourse in the previous three months. Overall, 22.9 percent reported at least one instance of unprotected anal intercourse, 64.7 percent said that they had had an HIV test, and 11.8 percent reported that they were HIV positive.

Comparisons based on city size (cities with a population under 500,000, 500,000 to 1 million, and over 1 million), indicated that those from smaller cities were considerably less likely to have been tested (55.2 percent vs. 63.2 and 69.2 percent) and somewhat more likely to have engaged in unprotected anal intercourse (26.3 percent vs. 23.5 percent and 20.9 percent).

Lévy et al. (1994a) reported higher levels of condom use during anal sex among francophone gay men who were in occasional versus stable partnerships, and lower levels of condom use in both groups during oral sex (Table 17). The findings are consistent with other reports of increased use of safer sex practices among multipartnered gay men.

Table 17

Condom Use and Sexual Behavior in Francophone Gay Men: A Comparison of Men in Stable Partnerships and Men with Occasional Partners

	Percentage of the Group Reporting the Behavior	
Sexual Activity in Past Six Months	**Stable Partnerships[1] (*N* = 276)**	**Occasional Partners[2] (*N* = 336)**
Fellatio (active)	92.6	92.8
Used condom[3]	3.8	9.4
Fellatio (received)	94.1	96.7
Used condom	3.9	6.4
Anal sex (active)	54.6	43.0
Used condom	61.3	90.7
Anal sex (received)	51.5	34.8
Used condom	59.9	92.9

[1] 66% said the relationship was exclusive.

[2] 29% said they had one partner in the last 6 months (Average for group = 10).

[3] Condom used means in all such activities in the previous 6 months.

Data from Levy et al. (1994a).

High School Students

The *Canada Youth and AIDS Study* reported on the knowledge, attitudes, and behavior with respect to AIDS of over 38,000 Canadian youth aged 11 to 21 (King et al. 1988). The study, which provided a fairly comprehensive picture of the sexual behavior of Canadian high school students, found that 31 percent of males and 21 percent of females had had intercourse by grade nine. By grade eleven, these percentages increased to 49 percent for males and 46 percent for females. AIDS was second to pregnancy as the outcome of sexual intercourse that high school students worried most about. Although this study did not measure condom use among high school students, 48 percent held negative attitudes toward condoms.

In a late 1980s study of grade eleven students ($N = 1,275$, average age 17 years) in Montreal, Quebec, Joanne Otis and her colleagues found that 53 percent of respondents who had had intercourse (about 60 percent of both sexes) said they used a condom the first time. Only 18.2 percent said they did so constantly thereafter; 67.2 percent reported using the pill for contraception (Otis et al. 1990). The best predictor of a student's stated intention to use a condom with a future new partner was whether or not the female was using oral contraception, i.e., the intention to use condoms was lowest if it was assumed that the female would be taking the pill, and greatest if she was not. Otis et al. (1990) proposed that Canadian educators should reinforce the acceptability and desirability of condom use with a new partner, even if the female partner is using oral contraception (see also Otis et al. 1994). In a recent review of studies on adolescent sexual behavior, Otis et al. (1996) made the following observations related to HIV prevention among high school students in Quebec in 1995: (1) 50 to 75 percent said they had used a condom at first intercourse, an increase between 1988 and 1995; (2) about 50 to 60 percent of all sexual contacts involved condom use and 13 to 48 percent used a condom in all their sexual relations; (3) 22 percent of 15-year-olds and 39 percent of 18-year-olds said they had taken an STD test and 14 percent of high school teens had taken an HIV test. In the population of adolescents surveyed at youth or leisure clubs and at youth centers (for young people with social or other problems), the number were higher in all categories. For example, at youth and leisure clubs 65 percent reported condom use at first intercourse, 38 percent used condoms in all their sexual relations, and 41 percent had taken an HIV test.

Studies in the provinces of Alberta and Nova Scotia have also reported on the frequency of condom use among high school students. In the Alberta study, 41 percent of "sexually active" high school students indicated that they either did not or infrequently used condoms, and 59 percent reported that they frequently or always used condoms during sexual intercourse (Varnhagen et al. 1991). In a more recent study of Nova Scotia high school students, 55 percent reported using condoms "more than just some of time"; 35 percent always used condoms (Langille et al. 1994). Although the reported frequency of condom use among Canadian high school students is less than adequate for HIV/AIDS prevention, this group appears to use condoms more frequently than either college/university students (e.g., King et al. 1988; Ramsum et al. 1993) or adults (e.g., Ontario Ministry of Health 1992).

College/University Students

Because they are mostly young, single, highly sexually active, and accessible to researchers, college/university students have been widely used in studies of knowledge, attitudes, and behaviors related to HIV/AIDS. The *Canada Youth and AIDS* study found that among college students, 77 percent of males and 73 percent of females had at least one experience of intercourse. Sixty-eight percent of the males and 64 percent of the females reported having oral sex; 14 percent of the males and 16 percent of the females reported having anal sex. Numbers of partners for males and females respectively was: one (23 percent, 36 percent); two (12 percent, 17 percent), three to five (29 percent, 26 percent), six to ten (17 percent, 14 percent), and eleven or more (19 percent, 7 percent). Forty-four percent of males and 30 percent of females identified AIDS as the outcome of sex that worried them most (pregnancy was much higher at about 60 percent and other STDs much lower at 4 percent). When those who had intercourse were asked about condom use, the responses for males and females respectively were: always (19 percent, 11 percent), most of the time (16 percent, 9 percent), sometimes (43 percent, 52 percent), and never (22 percent, 28 percent) (King et al. 1988).

A comparison of British Columbia university students surveyed in 1988 (in the same year as the *Canada Youth and AIDS* study) and again in 1992 indicated no change in the number who reported being sexually active within the last six months (62 percent), a slight decline in the proportion with multiple partners (i.e., 2 to 7 partners in the last 6 months) from 30 percent to 24 percent of those who were sexually active, and some increase in the proportion using condoms "always" (17 percent to 25 percent in 1992) or "most times" (6 percent to 15 percent). However, the number reporting never used condoms (51 percent vs. 40 percent in 1992) or sometimes used (26 percent vs. 20 percent in 1992) remained high (Ramsum et al. 1993). This study is consistent with the findings of other studies of university students that have found that although they are highly knowledgeable about HIV/AIDS, this group's perceived risk has not been sufficient to overcome some of the barriers to consistent condom use (e.g., immediate accessibility, inconvenience, peer group perceptions, religious beliefs, influence of alcohol, etc.) (Ramsum et al. 1993).

Another study of college students in Montreal found that perceived risk of HIV infection was correlated with having a friend who had had an HIV test and having more than one coital partner. For women, the level of trust in a relationship was also correlated with perceived risk of HIV ("I trust this person, I must be at low risk"). For men, their confidence in their ability to assess whether or not it was necessary to use condoms with a particular partner was also correlated with perceived risk of HIV infection (Maticka-Tyndale and Lévy 1993). Recent reviews on condom use among college students in Quebec (Otis et al. 1996; Samson et al. 1996) found:

47 to 67 percent used condoms at first intercourse, an increase from 1983-1995; condom use was less common with a regular partner (38 percent) than with occasional partners (66 percent; 34 percent had taken an STD test and 14 percent an HIV test). The comparable findings among university students (Otis et al. 1996) were: 42.5 percent said they used condoms at first intercourse, fewer used condoms with a regular partner (34 percent) than with an occasional partner (88 percent), and 14 percent had taken an HIV test. Current prevention efforts with this group are increasingly using theoretically based approaches to behavior change (Fisher and Fisher 1992) that stress information, motivation, and behavioral skills (IMB), and identification with people known to have AIDS (i.e., influencing personal perception of risk). Because empirical research increasingly indicates that educational interventions based on an IMB approach are successful in helping people perform sexual health problem-prevention behavior, the IMB approach is recommended by Health Canada's *Canadian Guidelines for Sexual Health Education* (Minister of Supply and Services Canada 1994).

Street Youth

Street youth represent a particularly high-risk group for HIV infection because of the greater likelihood of involvement in prostitution, IV drug use, unprotected homosexual or bisexual activity, and backgrounds of family disruption, abuse, and attendant low self-esteem. As part of the *Canada Youth and AIDS* study, 712 street youth aged 15 to 20 were interviewed about their sexual practices and HIV-risk behavior (Radford et al. 1990). Ninety-four percent of the sample was sexually active, 32 percent never used condoms, 32 percent used condoms sometimes or most times, and 26 percent always used condoms; 75 percent used drugs and 12 percent occasionally injected drugs (half using shared needles). Needle-exchange programs in several major cities have helped reduce the spread of HIV in street youth, but this selected population remains at high risk and is therefore the focus of significant outreach programs by a variety of youth-serving agencies. The First National Conference on HIV/AIDS and Youth held in Toronto in 1989 led to publication of a *National Inventory of AIDS Organizations for Youth,* listing over a hundred such organizations and agencies across Canada.

First Nations People

Few studies have investigated the incidence of HIV infection among First Nations People in Canada. One study of a high-risk population in the city of Vancouver found an infection rate of 6 percent among First Nations People (Rekart et al. 1991).

The *Ontario First Nations AIDS and Healthy Lifestyle Survey* (Myers et al. 1993) is the largest Canadian study to date on the HIV/AIDS-related knowledge, attitudes, and behavior of First Nations People. At the time the study was initiated in 1989-90, there was little AIDS education for this population, but there was significant concern about the risk of infection in such close communities with a tradition of early sexual activity and ongoing experience of "social, economic, psychological, spiritual, and political concerns" and of other factors contributing to "the inequities in health that First Nations People experience" (Myers et al. 1993). Consultation with four Provincial Territorial organizations (Association of Iroquois and Allied Indians, Grand Council Treaty Number Three, Nishnawbe-Aski Nation, and the Union of Ontario Indians) resulted in interviews with 658 individuals (about an equal number of males and females) from eleven First Nations communities across Ontario.

In this sample of First Nations People, overall knowledge of HIV/AIDS was relatively low. For example, although 97.6 percent knew that "A person can get AIDS from having sex without a condom with someone who has AIDS," 85.3 percent incorrectly believed that donating blood could result in HIV infection for the donor; 18.3 percent gave an incorrect answer and 49.1 percent were uncertain in response to the item "Using Vaseline with a condom makes it weak and easier to break." Of the respondents who had heard of AIDS, 6.8 percent reported having been tested for HIV (7.8 percent of this group had tested positive) and 71.9 percent felt they had no risk for HIV infection. An additional 18.9 percent felt they had only a small chance of getting AIDS. About 40 percent of the men and 18 percent of the women had two or more sexual partners in the past year. Approximately 16 percent of the respondents reported having participated in anal sex at least once in their lifetime. In the twelve months prior to the survey, 29.8 percent of the respondents reported no sexual activity, 44.8 percent inconsistently used HIV-infection prevention measures when having sex, 12.1 percent never used condoms for vaginal or anal intercourse, and 13.3 percent reported engaging in only mutual masturbation or always using condoms for vaginal and anal intercourse. A recent analysis of the data on condom use from the study identifies a range of sociodemographic and behavioral factors associated with use or non-use of condoms, and discusses the findings in the context of the limited research available on safer sex practices in First Nations populations (Burchall 1997).

The authors of the *Ontario First Nations AIDS and Healthy Lifestyle Survey* concluded from their findings that in order to be successful, HIV/AIDS prevention efforts aimed at First Nations People must be culturally appropriate. They write, "The approach must be holistic and rooted in the culture, traditions, and customs of aboriginal communities, and therefore must embrace the entire community including the youth, parents, elders, and community leaders" (Myers et al. 1993, 63). For a country of considerable multicultural diversity, this principle of cultural appropriateness is an important facet of HIV/AIDS prevention efforts aimed at Canadian audiences.

F. The Direct and Indirect Costs of AIDS

Efforts to figure the costs of AIDS commonly focus on calculating the direct medical costs of treating persons with HIV and AIDS, the costs of health care professionals' salaries, research, hospital care, medication, and psychological support for affected families and close relatives. The direct medical costs of treating one Canadian with HIV/AIDS from the time of infection to death is estimated at between $150,000 and $215,000.

Seldom, if ever, considered are the indirect costs of the disease in lost future earnings caused by AIDS-related deaths. In a pioneering 1995 study sponsored by the British Columbia Center for Excellence in HIV/AIDS, economist Robin Hanvelt and colleagues (1994) estimated that AIDS has already cost Canada $3.3 billion in lost future earnings for all the men aged 25 to 64 years old who died from AIDS between 1987 and 1992. The average estimated loss of future earnings per death was $651,200 in 1990 figures. The total loss in future earnings attributable to HIV/AIDS in Canada was exceeded only by those for ischemic heart disease, suicide, motor-vehicle accidents, and lung cancer. Hanvelt believes his calculations, based on a six-year study of 5,038 Canadian men who died of HIV/AIDS, are conservative. While the annual future loss of income remained relatively stable or declined for other causes of death, earnings lost through HIV- and AIDS-related deaths more than doubled from $309 million in 1987 to $817 million in 1992. Hanvelt estimates that in the indirect costs of AIDS-related deaths in Canada will exceed $1.5 billion in 1996.

Combining estimates of direct and indirect costs of HIV/AIDS provides a clearer and more realistic picture of the social costs in terms of lost creativity, skills, knowledge, and productivity resulting from the premature death of thousands of young people.

12. Sexual Dysfunction, Counseling, and Therapy

Dr. Stephen Neiger, the founder of the Sex Information and Education Council of Canada, was probably the first practitioner to introduce "modern" sex therapy to the Canadian scene in the early 1960s. Neiger's behavioral approach to the common sexual dysfunctions (primary or secondary anorgasmia, vaginismus, and painful intercourse in women, erectile dysfunction, and premature ejaculation in men) was a contrast and challenge to the traditional belief that treatment of such problems required psychotherapy to determine their root causes. Neiger viewed many such problems as a product of inadequate education, cultural taboos, and the anxiety and negative reinforcement generated by unrealistic performance expectations. The growing North American interest in sex therapy in the early 1970s, spurred by the release of Masters and Johnson's *Human Sexual Inadequacy*, and by the prospect of rapid, symptom-oriented treatment, led to increasing demand for such help and the implicit expectation that medical professionals would be adequately trained to provide it.

While such training has indeed become more available in Canada and more accessible to Canadian therapists because of developments in the U.S., the situation at present is quite limited. Canadians do have wide access to counseling about sex-related topics since professionals from a variety of backgrounds (physicians, social workers, psychologists, public health nurses, occupational therapists, school guidance counselors, and clergy) may be trained, to varying degrees, to assist with sexual concerns as part of their broader work requirements. They do this counseling in a variety of settings, including private practice, hospitals, community health centers, family service agencies, sexual assault centers, etc., and are bound by the ethical standards of their professions and individual agencies. Such individuals have generally not been trained as sex therapists and would probably refer clients with problems that required such therapy. There are still few people trained as sex therapists and few opportunities for such training in Canada. The Department of Sexology at the University of Quebec at Montreal and the Department of Family Studies at the University of Guelph in Ontario are the only institutions in Canada to offer postgraduate training and degrees in sex therapy (see addresses in Section 12B).

Since there are no official self-regulating colleges of sex therapy in the provinces or nationally, as there are for other medical specialties, the question of who is a sex therapist and how they are trained is a continuing issue in Canada. Alexander's (1990) review of sexual therapy in English-speaking Canada identifies this concern about standards for training and practice as a primary reason for the formation of the Board of Examiners in Sex Therapy and Counseling in Ontario (BESTCO) in 1975. The ten founding therapists, all members of the Ontario Association for Marriage and Family Therapy (OAMFT), established criteria for training and certification of therapists that they then applied to themselves and to subsequent members. They assumed that provincial or national certification of sex therapists was imminent and that the group would be prepared for that event. That step toward regulation of sex therapists has not taken place. BESTCO remains the only group in Canada that has a formal, nonstatutory certification procedure for certifying already-accredited marriage and family therapists who wish to have their specialization in sex therapy recognized by a body of their peers.

Some sex therapists in Canada are certified by the American Association of Sex Educators, Counselors, and Therapists (AASECT), by the U.S.-based Society for Sex Therapy and Research (SSTAR), by the American Board of Sexology, and/or by other comparable international organizations specifically identified with sex therapy; others are certified for work in their field, e.g., medicine, nursing, psychology, pastoral counseling, marriage and family therapy, etc., which may or may not require specific advanced training before unsupervised practice in sex therapy can be done. For example, physicians can do sex therapy but do not have a formal requirement for certification of that specialty, despite the scarcity of such training in most medical schools. On the other hand, there are many physicians in Canada who are specialists in sexual medicine, but whose specialty is still not recognized by the Royal College of Physicians and Surgeons of Canada.

Only physicians and psychiatrists are permitted to bill the provincial health plans for sex therapy services, but their numbers are insufficient to meet the demand. Private sex therapy can be expensive for the average person, although some insurance plans will cover part of the cost of therapy if done by psychologists, social workers, or other health professionals covered by specific plans. Because of Canada's size and the location of therapists in large urban centers, sex therapy is simply not available to most people in smaller communities.

Canada has also had a chronic shortage of trained therapists who can work with people with paraphilias, gender disorders, psychiatric disorders, or medical conditions with sexual implications. Professionals who treat children and adults who have been sexually abused or assaulted, and those working with sex offenders, also require more training in sexuality than is currently available.

Sex therapists are expected to have accredited training in marital, family, and relationship therapy and to then acquire advanced skills and experience in sex therapy. The options for the latter in Canada include:

1. attending the week-long, Intensive Sex Therapy Training Institute offered at the University of Guelph, Ontario, prior to the annual Guelph Sexuality Conference;
2. obtaining supervision time with a therapist credentialed as a supervisor by a recognized accrediting body (AASECT, BESTCO, etc.);
3. taking the clinical training program in the Department of Sexology in the University of Quebec at Montreal (in French); or
4. becoming a member of a sexual medicine unit that trains therapists (e.g., the Sexual Medicine Unit at the University of British Columbia has had a long-standing program to train nurses and social workers as sexual health care clinicians, an excellent grounding for subsequent certification in sex therapy).

Continuing issues influencing the development of sex therapy in Canada include:

1. Feminist redefinition of "dysfunction" and development of new models for thinking about sexual response in the context of women's experience, rather than as a biologically mandated sequence of physiological events;

2. recent technological and pharmacological developments in the treatment of erectile dysfunction (e.g., injections and vacuum constriction devices), sexual desire disorders, and paraphilias;
3. the relationship between sex therapists and self-help movements such as the twelve-step programs for sex and love addiction (e.g., Sex and Love Addicts Anonymous);
4. the debate about the role of therapists in facilitating recovered memories of childhood sexual abuse and the therapeutic, legal, and political implications of practice in this area; and
5. dealing equitably with ethnocultural differences pertaining to sexuality. For example, the Canadian Medical Association recently banned physicians from doing the procedure referred to as ritual circumcision (Brighouse 1992) or genital mutilation (Omer-Hashi and Entwistle 1995), which is common in some parts of Africa and requested by some immigrants to Canada.

13. Research and Advanced Education

A. Sexological Research and Postgraduate Programs

Most sexological research in Canada is done by individuals or groups linked either directly or indirectly with universities. This work almost invariably occurs within specific academic disciplines (e.g., history, sociology, psychology, women's studies, philosophy, medicine, epidemiology and public health, education, family studies, criminology, etc.) rather than in a university department of sexology. The Department of Sexology at the University of Quebec at Montreal is the only department of sexology in Canada. Founded in 1969, it offers Bachelor's and Master's programs in human sexuality taught in French by approximately twenty full-time academic staff representing many fields of specialization. The master's program, which began in 1980 and was officially recognized by the university in 1985, offers internships, projects, courses, and other practical training in counseling and sex education (Dupras 1987). Candidates for the master's program in counseling come primarily from related fields, such as medicine, psychology, criminology, and social work, while those in the education stream usually come from the Bachelor of Human Sexuality Program (Dupras 1987; Gemme 1990). The Department is the major center for research on human sexuality in Quebec and also publishes *Bibliosex*, a biannual bibliography of sexuality literature in Canada and internationally.

Some academic departments in other parts of Canada offer graduate programs in human sexuality (e.g., University of Guelph, Department of Family Studics), but it is more common for graduate research on sexuality topics to occur within master's and Ph.D. programs in specific academic disciplines. Since 1978, the Family Studies Department has sponsored an intensive week-long annual June conference and training institute on sexuality at the University of Guelph, Ontario. The Departments of Psychology at both the University of Western Ontario and the University of New Brunswick are two examples of strong graduate research training in sexuality within a particular field. The Department of Sociology and Anthropology at the University of Windsor has the largest complement of sociologists—four—in a single department who are actively conducting research in sexuality. The department offers three undergraduate courses and one graduate seminar in sexuality, and students are able to pursue an undergraduate honors or a master's degree specializing in Family and Sexuality.

A number of medical faculties also provide postgraduate training in sexology. For example, the Sexual Medicine Unit at the University of British Columbia offers a clinical and research setting through which residents in Obstetrics and Gynecology and in Psychiatry can obtain advanced training. A number of other hospitals have Sexual Medicine Units or similar specialized services (e.g., the Sexual Health Unit at Montreal General Hospital), but there have been no national reviews of postgraduate sexuality training for physicians or for any of the other health disciplines, either as it pertains to research training, the subject of this section, or sex therapy training, which was discussed in Section 12.

In her report to a 1994 gathering of Chinese and North American sex educators and researchers in China, Byers (1995) noted that training in sexological research within specific disciplines is highly variable across Canada. Such training often occurs only because a faculty member hired for expertise in another academic area is also interested in sexuality. This situation makes the necessary multidisciplinary requirements of sexological training more difficult to find, and trainees, particularly in smaller centers, may not have easy access to a network of like-minded colleagues. She notes that this fragmentation has made it hard for sex research to flourish as a field in English Canada, even though individual researchers and research groups have achieved considerable recognition (Byers 1995). For example, the Gender Identity Unit at Toronto's Clarke Institute of Psychiatry is internationally known for research on transsexuality, the Social Program Evaluation Group at Queen's University in Kingston, Ontario, has published major studies on adolescent sexual behavior, the Department of Psychology program at the University of New Brunswick is well known for research on the psychology of male-female sexual interactions in dating and longer-term relationships, the Sexual Medicine Unit at the University of British Columbia is known particularly for work on sexuality, disability, and chronic illness, researchers in the Sociology and Anthropology Department at the University of Windsor have developed international reputations for their qualitative and multimethod research on homosexuality and on sexual transmission of HIV, and the research done in the Department of Psychology at the University of Western Ontario has influenced Canadian policy and practice in the prevention of teen pregnancy, STDs, and HIV infection. Despite these achievements, the discipline-based focus of much sex research has made it difficult to achieve a public profile for the sexological research community in Canada.

The Canadian Sex Research Forum, founded in 1969, is Canada's only national organization dedicated to a multidisciplinary focus on sexological research. The *Proceedings* of the CSRF meetings have been published annually by the Sex Information and Education Council of Canada, first in the *SIECCAN Newsletter* (1982-1985), then in the *SIECCAN Journal* (1986-1991), and now in the *Canadian Journal of Human Sexuality* (1992-present). In Quebec, l'Association des Sexologiques de Québec promotes various aspects of sexual science, and the biannual journal *Revue Sexologique/Sexological Review* publishes national and international papers, the majority in French, many by Quebec researchers.

There appear to be many more people doing sexuality research in Canada than the approximately one hundred Canadians who are members of CSRF and/or the Society for the Scientific Study of Sexuality (SSSS). A systematic record of this large group would both identify, and perhaps unify, those individuals who, despite their primary identification with another academic discipline, also share a common interest in sexology. Such a record would also enhance training and supervision of sex researchers by facilitating cross-disciplinary communication. This issue is one of many that a workshop at the 1993 Canadian Sex Research Forum meeting identified as a major deficiency in the training of many sex researchers in Canada and internationally (Aronoff, McCormick and Byers 1994).

B. Canadian Sexological Organizations and Publications

Addresses of Organizations

L'Association des Sexologues de Québec, 695 St. Denis, Suite 300, Montreal, Quebec, Canada H2S 2S3

Sex Information and Education Council of Canada (SIECCAN), 850 Coxwell Avenue, East York, Ontario, Canada M4C 5RI

Canadian Sex Research Forum, c/o Pierre Assalian, M.D., Executive Director, 1650 Cedar Avenue, Room B6-233, Montreal, Quebec, Canada H3G 1A4

The Department of Sexology, University of Quebec at Montreal, 455 Boulevard Rene Levesque East, Montreal, Quebec, Canada H3C 3P8

Planned Parenthood Federation of Canada, 1 Nicolas St., Suite 430, Ottawa, Ontario, Canada K1N 7B7

Sexological Publications

Three Canadian publications provide a professional focus on sexological issues and research:

Canadian Journal of Human Sexuality (4 issues per year), Sex Information and Education Council of Canada (SIECCAN), 850 Coxwell Avenue, East York, Ontario, Canada M4C 5RI

Revue Sexologique/Sexological Review (2 issues per year), c/o Editions I.R.I.S., 4932 rue Adam, Montreal, Quebec, Canada H1V 1W3

Bibliosex (2 issues per year), c/o Professor Robert Gemme, University of Quebec at Montreal, Department of Sexology, Case Postale 8888, Canada H3C 3P8

Conclusions

Four themes run through this profile of sexuality in Canada. The first is of a country composed of a variety of ethnocultural groups including the oldest, Aboriginal inhabitants, the dominant English and French residents, and the newer arrivals from a variety of countries. Though there has been little "group specific" research, the available evidence suggests that different groups can have quite distinctive cultural attitudes and practices in the area of sexuality. Canada's French-Canadians, about whom there has been considerable research, consistently demonstrate attitudes that are more accepting and permissive than those of other Canadians; they initiate sexual activity somewhat earlier than others, and are more likely to form committed partnerships without the legal status of marriage. Quebec, the province where the majority of French-Canadians live and the location of Canada's only Department of Sexology, has demonstrated the greatest acceptance of individual choice in sexual matters, and has the most egalitarian family laws of any province in the nation. Considering the historical domination of the Roman Catholic Church in Quebec, these results demonstrate the reduction of influence of religious institutions in the lives of French-Canadians, a change that is now occurring for some other groups of Canadians as well. While French-Canadians set one end of a continuum of attitudes and practices, each ethnocultural group in Canada has its own distinctive pattern of attitudes and practices, each embedded in unique communities and community institutions.

The second theme is of a country in which formal services, research, and education in sexuality are scattered and varied. In some regions, these are comprehensive and sophisticated, in others they are sparse and few. Research, graduate and postgraduate training, and therapeutic and clinical work in sexuality are not organized or provided in a coherent manner and are highly dependent on the presence of interested individuals. Sexuality as an academic discipline, and sexual health services beyond those related to reproduction and sexually transmitted diseases, are not generally recognized or supported through national associations or university departments.

The third theme is of a country that is in the process of reconceptualizing gendered and sexual relationships in its laws, culture, and policies. This is seen in the recent changes in laws, and in court challenges in areas such as sexual assault, sexual harassment, pornography and obscenity, access to medical procedures as part of sexual and reproductive health, and guarantees of equal treatment and rights for all Canadians regardless of gender, ability, or sexual orientation. It is also seen in the changing portrayals of sexuality in culture.

Finally, Canada is a country in which liberal and conservative (or permissive and restrictive) perspectives on sexuality compete for influence in the marketplace of ideas and ideology. To date, changes in legislation and policy have been in the direction of supporting individual rights, freedom of choice and expression, and recognition of diversity. Not all Canadians support these changes, however. Whether this direction will continue as part of Canada's future will be influenced, in part, by developments in all four of these themes.

Acknowledgments

We are grateful for the diverse contributions that the following individuals made during the preparation of this chapter: Diana Powell, Mary Bissell, Jo-Anne Doherty, Christine Donald, Bill Fisher, Louis-Robert Frigault, Jeanne Guillaume, Katharine Kelly, Ross Laver, Wayne Millar, Alan Mirabelli, Joanne Otis, Robin Rowe, and Dot Whitehouse. Thanks also to Robert T. Francoeur for his encouragement and support as editor of this *Encyclopedia* and to the many authors and researchers whose work we have relied upon for this chapter.

References and Suggested Readings

Adamson, N., L. Brislan, and M. McPhail. 1988. *Feminist Organizing for Change: The Contemporary Women's Movement in Canada.* Toronto: Oxford University Press.

Adrien, A., G. Godin, P. Cappon, S. Manson-Singer, E. Maticka-Tyndale and D. Willms. 1996. Overview of the Canadian Study on the Determinants of Ethnoculturally Specific Behaviours Related to HIV/AIDS. *Canadian Journal of Public Health,* 87(Supp. 1):S4-S10.

Aggarwal, A. P. 1992. *Sexual Harassment: A Guide for Understanding and Prevention.* Toronto: Butterworths Canada Ltd.

Alexander, E. 1990. "Sexual Therapy in English-Speaking Canada." *SIECCAN Journal,* 5(1):37-43.

Aronoff, D., N. McCormick, and S. Byers. 1994. "Training Sex Researchers: Issues for Supervisors and Students." *Canadian Journal of Human Sexuality,* 3(1):45-51.

Badets, J., and T. W. L. Chui. 1994. "Canada's Changing Immigrant Population." *Statistics Canada, Focus on Canada Series,* Catalogue No. 96-311E.

Barrett, A. 1990. "Condom Machines in High Schools: Better Late Than Never." *SIECCAN Newsletter,* 25(1):1-5.

Barrett, F. M. 1980. "Sexual Experience, Birth Control Usage and Sex Education of Unmarried Canadian University Students: Changes Between 1968 and 1978." *Archives of Sexual Behavior*, 9:367-389.

Barrett, M. 1994. "Sexuality Education in Canadian Schools: An Overview in 1994." *Canadian Journal of Human Sexuality*, 3(3):199-207.

Barrett, M. 1990. "Selected Observations on Sex Education in Canada." *SIECCAN Journal*, 5(1):21-30.

Beaujot, R. 1991. *Population Change in Canada: The Challenges of Policy Adaptation.* Toronto: McClelland and Stewart.

Bell, L. 1991. *On Our Own Terms: A Practical Guide for Lesbian and Gay Relationships.* Toronto: Coalition for Lesbian and Gay Rights in Ontario.

Bibby, R. W. 1992. *The Bibby Report: Social Trends Canadian Style.* Toronto: Stoddart Publishing.

Bibby, R. W. and D. C. Posterski. 1992. *Teen Trends: A Nation in Motion.* Toronto: Stoddart Publishing.

Blanchard, R., and B. Steiner, eds. 1990. *Clinical Management of Gender Identity Disorders in Children and Adults.* Washington: American Psychiatric Press Inc.

Bliss, M. 1970. "Pure Books on Avoided Subjects: PreFreudian Sexual Ideas in Canada." Canadian Historical Association, Annual Meeting, Winnipeg, pp. 89-108.

Boroditsky, R., W. Fisher, and M. Sand. 1996. The 1995 Canadian Contraception Study. *Supplement of the Journal of the Society of Obstetricians and Gynaecologists of Canada,* 18(12):1-31.

Brighouse, R. 1992. "Ritual Female Circumcision and Its Effects on Female Sexual Function." *Canadian Journal of Human Sexuality*, 1(1):3-10.

Burchall, A.N. 1997. Condom Use Among First Nations People Living On-Reserve in Ontario. M.Sc. Thesis. Graduate Department of Community Health, University of Toronto, Canada.

Byers, S. 1991. "Gender Differences in the Traditional Sexual Script: Fact or Fiction." *SIECCAN Journal*, 6(4):16-18.

Byers, S. 1995. "Sexology in Canada: A Growing Field." Paper presented at the First Symposium on Sexology: East and West, in Beijing, China, October, 1993. *SIECCAN Newsletter* (in *Canadian Journal of Human Sexuality*, 4(1):79-83.

Cairns, K. 1993. "Sexual Entitlement and Sexual Accommodation: Implications for Female and Male Experience of Sexual Coercion." *Canadian Journal Human Sexuality*, 2(4):203-213.

Campbell, E. R. 1991. "Establishing Adolescent Sexuality Health Centres in High Schools: The Ottawa Carleton Experience." *SIECCAN Newsletter*, 26(2):4-7.

Canadian AIDS Society. 1994. *Safer Sex Guidelines: Healthy Sexuality and HIV, A Resource Guide for Educators and Counsellors.* Ottawa, Ontario: Canadian AIDS Society.

Canada Communicable Disease Report. 1994. "Syphilis Trends in Canada, 1991-1992." Ottawa: Health Canada, vols. 20-14.

Canada Communicable Disease Report Supplement 1996. Notifiable Diseases Annual Summary. Volume 2252, June.

Canada Communicable Disease Report Supplement. 1995. *Canadian Guidelines for the Prevention, Diagnosis, Management and Treatment of Sexually Transmitted Diseases in Neonates, Children, Adolescents and Adults.* Ottawa: Health Canada.

Canadian Institute of Child Health 1994. *The Health of Canada's Children.* Ottawa, Ontario: Canadian Institute of Child Health.

Chui, T. 1996. Canada's Population: Charting into the 21st Century. *Canadian Social Trends.* Autumn. Catalogue. No. 11-008-XPE.

Clemmenson, L. H. 1990. "The 'Real-Life Test' for Surgical Candidates." In *Clinical Management of Gender Identity Disorders in Children and Adults.* Blanchard, R. and B. W. Steiner, eds. Washington: American Psychiatric Press Inc.

CMA Policy Summary. 1994. "The Patient-Physician Relationship and the Sexual Abuse of Patients." *Canadian Medicine Association Journal,* 150(11):184A-C.

College of Physicians and Surgeons of British Columbia. 1994. *Crossing the Boundaries: The Report of the Committee on Physician Sexual Misconduct.* British Columbia: College of Physicians and Surgeons of British Columbia.

Committee on Sexual Offences Against Children and Youth 1984. *Sexual Offences Against Children (Vol. 1).* Ottawa: Canadian Government Publishing Centre.

COPOH. 1988. *Dispelling the Myths: Sexuality and Disabled Persons.* Winnipeg, Manitoba: Coalition of Provincial Organizations of the Handicapped.

CPSO 1992. *Report on the Task Force on the Sexual Abuse of Patients Recommendations Reviewed by Council.* Toronto, Ontario: College of Physicians and Surgeons of Ontario.

Crabtree, L. 1994. *It's Okay: Adults Write about Living and Loving with a Disability.* St. Catharines, Ontario: Phoenix Counsel Inc., One Springbank Drive, St. Catharines, Ontario L2S 2K1.

Cregheur, L. A., J. M. Casey and H. G. Banfield. 1992. *Sexuality, AIDS and Decision-Making: A Study of Newfoundland Youth.* St. John's, Newfoundland: Office of the Queen's Printer.

The Daily and The Daily, Statistics Canada. Alphabetized under "T."

DAWN 1993a. *Women with Disabilities: A Guide for Health Care Professionals.* Toronto: Disabled Women's Network.

DAWN 1994b. *Staying Healthy in the Nineties: Women with Disabilities Talk about Health Care.* Toronto: Disabled Women's Network.

DeKeseredy, W., and K. Kelly. 1993. The Incidence and Prevalence of Woman Abuse in Canadian University and College Dating Relationships. *Canadian Journal of Sociology,* 18(2):137-159.

Dumas, J., and A. Belanger. 1996. *Report on the Demographic Situation in Canada 1995.* Ottawa: Statistics Canada, Catalogue No. 91-209E.

Dumas, J. and Y. Caron. 1992. *Marriage and Conjugal Life in Canada.* Statistics Canada, Catalogue No. 91-534E.

Dupras, A. 1987. "The Graduate Program (Master's Degree) in Sexology at the University of Quebec at Montreal." *SIECCAN Journal,* 2(1):25-32.

Endicott, O. 1992. "Can the Law Tell Us Who Is Not 'the Marrying Kind'?" *Entourage,* 7(2):9.

Fisher, W. A. 1989. Understanding and Preventing Teenage Pregnancy and Sexually Transmissible Disease/AIDS. *SIECCAN Journal,* 4(2):3-25.

Fisher, J. and W. A. Fisher. 1992. "Understanding and Promoting AIDS Preventive Behaviour: A Conceptual Model and Educational Tool." *Canadian Journal of Human Sexuality,* 1:99-106.

Fox, B. J. 1993. "On Violent Men and Female Victims: A Comment on DeKeseredy and Kelly." *Canadian Journal of Sociology,* 18(3):321-24.

Frank, J. 1996. 15 Years of AIDS in Canada. *Canadian Social Trends.* Summer Catalogue No. 11-008-XPE.

Fraser Commission Report. 1985. *Pornography and Prostitution in Canada: Report of the Special Committee on Pornography and Prostitution in Canada,* vols. 1,2. Ottawa: Minister of Supply and Services Canada.

Frigault, L. R., J. Lévy, L. Labonté, and J. Otis. 1994. *La Santé, la Vie Sociale et la Sexualité des Étudiantes et Étudiants de l'Université de Montréal.* Montreal, Quebec: Department of Sexology, University of Quebec at Montreal.

Gartner, R. 1993. "Studying Woman Abuse: A Comment on DeKeseredy and Kelly." *Canadian Journal of Sociology*, 18(3):313-20.

Gemme, R. 1990. "Sexology in Quebec." *SIECCAN Journal*, 5(1):3-10.

Gemme, R. 1993. "Prostitution: A Legal, Criminological and Sociological Perspective." *Canadian Journal of Human Sexuality*, 2(4):227-37.

Gemme, R. and N. Payment. 1992. "Criminalization of Adult Street Prostitution in Montreal, Canada: Evaluation of the Law in 1987 and 1991." *Canadian Journal of Human Sexuality*, 1(4):217- 20.

Ghalam, N.Z. 1993. "Women in the Workplace." *Canadian Social Trends, Statistics Canada.* Spring, pp. 2-6.

Godin, G., E. Maticka-Tyndale, A. Adrien, S.M. Singer, D. Willms, P. Cappon, R. Bradet, T. Daus and G. LeMay. 1996. Understanding the Use of Condoms Among Canadian Ethnocultural Communities: Methods and Main Findings of the Survey. *Canadian Journal of Public Health*, (87 supp. 1):33-37.

Gripton, J., and M. Valentich. 1990. "A Church in Crisis: Child Sexual Abuse in the Catholic Church." *SIECCAN Journal*, 5(4):37-45.

Gully, P. R., and R. W. Peeling. 1994. "Control of Genital Chlamydial Infection." *Canadian Journal Infectious Disease*, 5(3):137-39.

Hanvelt, R. A., et al. "Indirect Costs of HIV/AIDS Mortality in Canada. *AIDS*, 8(10):F8-F11.

Health and Welfare Canada. 1990. *Report on Adolescent Reproductive Health.* Ottawa, Ontario: Health Services and Promotion, Minister of Supply and Services, H39-185/1990E.

Health Canada. 1994a. *Many Voices, HIV/AIDS in the Context of Culture: Report for the Latin American Community.* Ottawa: Health Canada.

Health Canada. 1994b. *Many Voices, HIV/AIDS in the Context of Culture: Report for the Communities from the Horn of Africa.* Ottawa: Health Canada.

Health Canada. 1994c. *Many Voices, HIV/AIDS in the Context of Culture: Report for the English-Speaking Caribbean Communities.* Ottawa: Health Canada.

Health Canada. 1994d. *Many Voices, HIV/AIDS in the Context of Culture: Report for the Arab-speaking Community.* Ottawa: Health Canada.

Health Canada. 1994e. *Many Voices, HIV/AIDS in the Context of Culture: Report for the South Asian Communities.* Ottawa: Health Canada.

Health Canada. 1994f. *Many Voices, HIV/AIDS in the Context of Culture: Report for the Chinese Communities.* Ottawa: Health Canada.

Health Division, Statistics Canada. 1996. *Therapeutic Abortions, 1994.* Statistics Canada, Catalogue No. 82-219-XPE.

Health Reports. 1996. *Health Reports*, 8(2):49-50.

Hendrick, D. 1996. Canadian Crime Statistics, 1995. *Juristat* 16(10). Canadian Centre for Justice Statistics. Statistics Canada, Catalogue No. 85-002-XPE.

Herold, E. 1984. *Sexual Behaviour of Canadian Young People.* Markham, Ontario: Fitzhenry and Whiteside.

Herold, E. and Way. 1983. "Oral-Genital Behaviour in a Sample of University Females." *Journal of Sex Research*, 19:327-38.

Hextall, N. 1989. An Evaluation of the Teen-Aid Program in Saskatchewan. *SIECCAN Newsletter*, 24(1):3-13.

Hingsburger, D., and Ludwig, S. 1993. *Male Masturbation.* Book 5 in *Being Sexual: An Illustrated Series on Sexuality and Relationships.* East York: Sex Information and Education Council of Canada.

Humphrey. T., L. Gibson and K. Maki. 1996. Sex Ed on the Web: Exploring Solutions to Traditional Instructional Challenges. *Canadian Journal of Human Sexuality*, 5(4).

Insight Canada Research. 1992. *The Adolescent Female and Birth Control.* Toronto, Ontario: Insight Canada Research.

Johnson, H. 1996A. Children and Youths as Victims of Violent Crimes. *Juristat* 15(15). Canadian Centre for Justice Statistics. Statistics Canada, Catalogue No. 85-002.

Johnson, H. 1996b. Violent Crime in Canada. *Juristat* 16(6). Canadian Centre for Justice Statistics. Statistics Canada, Catalogue No. 85-002-XPE.

Kaufman, M., ed. 1987. *Beyond Patriarchy: Essays by Men on Pleasure, Power and Change.* Toronto: Oxford University Press.

Kelly, K. 1994. "The Politics of Data." *Canadian Journal of Sociology*, 19(1):81-85.

King, A. J. C., R. P. Beazley, R. W. Warren, C. A. Hankins, A. S. Robertson, and J. L. Radford. 1988. *Canada Youth and AIDS Study.* Kingston, Ontario: Social Program Evaluation Group, Queen's University.

King, M. A., B. J. Coles, and A. J. C. King. 1990. *Canada Youth and AIDS Study Technical Report.* Kingston, Ontario: Queen's University, Social Program Evaluation Research Group.

King, M. A. and B. J. Coles. 1992. *The Health of Canada's Youth.* Ottawa, Ontario: Minister of Supply and Services Canada.

Kinsman, G. W. 1987. *The Regulation of Desire: Sexuality in Canada.* Montreal: Black Rose Books.

Kirby, D. 1992. "School-Based Programs to Reduce Risk-Taking Behaviors." *Journal of School Health*, 62:280-87.

Kirby, D. et al. 1994. "School-Based Programs to Reduce Sexual Risk Behaviours: A Review of Effectiveness." *Public Health Reports*, 109(3):339-60.

Laboratory Centre for Disease Control. 1994. *Quarterly Surveillance Update: AIDS in Canada. April 1994.* Ottawa, Ontario: Bureau of Communicable Disease Epidemiology, LCDC, Health Canada.

Lamont, J. and C. A. Woodward. 1994. "Patient-Physician Sexual Involvement: A Canadian Survey of Obstetricians-Gynecologists." *Canadian Medical Association Journal*, 150(9):1433-39.

Langille, D. B., R. Beazley, J. Shoveller. and G. Johnston. 1994. "Prevalence of High Risk Sexual Behaviour in Adolescents Attending School in a County in Nova Scotia." *Canadian Journal of Public Health*, 85(4):227-230.

Laumann, E. O., J. H. Gagnon, R. T. Michael, and G. K. M. Harding. 1994. *The Social Organization of Sexuality:Sexual Practices in the United States.* Chicago:The University of Chicago Press.

Lawlor, W., and L. Purcell. 1988. *A Study of Values and Sex Education in Montreal Area English Secondary Schools.* Montreal, Quebec: Department of Religion and Philosophy in Education, McGill University.

Lawlor, W., and L. Purcell. 1989. "Values and Opinions about Sex Education Among Montreal Area English Secondary School Students." *SIECCAN Journal*, 4(2):26-33.

Leung, A. K. C. and W. L. M. Robson. 1994. "Childhood Masturbation." *Clinical Pediatrics*, April, pp. 238-241.

Lévy, J.J., and D. Sansfaçon. 1994. "Les Orientations Sexuelles." In F. Dumont, S. Langlois, and Y. Martin, eds. *Traité des Problèmes Sociaux.* Montreal: Institut Québécois de Recherche sur la Culture, pp. 455-71.

Lévy, J.J., A. Dupras, M. Perrault, M. Dorais, and J.-M. Samson. 1994. *Déterminants des Comportements Sexuels des Hommes Homosexuels Francophones de Montréal.* Rapport de recherche, Département de Sexologie, Université du Québec à Montréal.

Lévy, J.J., L.-R. Frigault, A. Dupras, J.-M. Samson, and P. Cappon. 1994. *Déterminants des Stratégies Contraceptives Parmi des Étudiantes Universitaires du Québec et de l'Ontario.* Rapport de recherche, Département de Sexologie, Université du Québec à Montréal.

Lévy, J.J., A. Dupras, J.-M. Samson, P. Cappon, L.-R. Frigault, and A. Larose. 1993. *Facteurs de Risques Face au SIDA et Comportements Sexuels des Étudiants Universitaires de Montréal.* Rapport de recherche non publié. Département de Sexologie, Université du Québec à Montréal.

Lindsay, D., and J. Embree. 1992. "Sexually Transmitted Diseases: A Significant Complication of Childhood Sexual Abuse." *Canadian Journal of Infectious Disease,* 3(3):122-28.

Ludwig, S. 1991. *Sexuality: A Curriculum for Individuals Who Have Difficulty with Traditional Learning Methods.* Newmarket, Ontario: Municipality of York Public Health.

Ludwig, S., and D. Hingsburger. 1993. *Female Masturbation.* Book 6, in *Being Sexual: An Illustrated Series on Sexuality and Relationships.* East York: Sex Information and Education Council of Canada.

Ludwig, S. 1995. *After You Tell.* Toronto: Sex Information and Education Council of Canada. Available in English and French.

Mackie, M. 1991. *Gender Relations in Canada: Further Explorations.* Markham: Butterworths Canada Ltd.

Maclean's. 1993. "Special Report: The Religion Poll."

Maclean's. April 12.

Maclean's/CTV Poll. 1994. "Canada Under the Covers." *Maclean's,* January 3, 1994. 107(1). Additional data from Decima Research, Toronto, Canada, provided by *Maclean's.*

Maclean's/CTV Poll. 1995. *Maclean's.* January 2, 1995. Additional data from Decima Research, Toronto, Canada, provided by *Maclean's.*

Maksym, D. 1990. *Shared Feelings: A Parent Guide to Sexuality Education for Children, Adolescents and Adults Who Have a Mental Handicap.* Downsview, Ontario: The Roeher Institute.

Males, M. 1992. "Adult Liaison in the 'Epidemic' of 'Teenage' Birth, Pregnancy and Venereal Disease." *Journal of Sex Research,* 29:525-45.

Mansell, S., and D. Wells. 1991. *Sexual Abuse of Children with Disabilities and Sexual Assault of Adults with Disabilities: Prevention Strategies.* Ottawa: Health Canada, National Clearinghouse on Family Violence.

Martinson, F. M. 1994. *The Sexual Life of Children.* Westport, Connecticut: Bergin and Garvey.

Maticka-Tyndale, E. 1991. "Sexual Scripts and AIDS Prevention: Variations in Adherence to Safer Sex Guidelines by Heterosexual Adolescents." *Journal of Sex Research,* 28:45-66.

Maticka-Tyndale, E., and J. J. Lévy. 1992. *Sexualité, Contraception et SIDA chez les Jeunes Adultes: Variations Ethno-Culturelles.* Montréal: Editions du Méridien.

Maticka-Tyndale, E., G. Godin, G. LeMay, A. Adrien, S. Manson-Singer, D. Willms, P. Cappon, and R. Bradet. 1996. "Phase III of Ethnocultural Communities Facing AIDS: Overview of Findings." *Canadian Journal of Public Health,* 87(supp. 1): S38-S43.

Maurice, W. L., S. B. Sheps, and M. T. Schecter. 1994a. *Sexual Involvement with Patients: A Survey of All Clinically Active Physicians in a Canadian Province.* Unpublished report.

Maurice, W. L., S. B. Sheps, and M. T. Schecter. 1994b. "Physician Sexual Misconduct: Public Opinion and Experience." Presented at the Canadian Sex Research Forum meeting, Elora, Ontario, September 1994. Unpublished report.

Maxwell, W. 1980. *So Long, See You Tomorrow.* New York: Knopf.

McKay, A. 1993. "Research Supports Broadly-Based Sex Education." *Canadian Journal of Human Sexuality,* 2(2):89-98.

McKay, A. 1996. Rural Parents' Attitudes Toward School-Based Sexual Health Education. *Canadian Journal of Human Sexuality,* 5(1):15-23.

McKay. A. 1997. Sexual Ideology and Schooling: Toward a Democratic Philosophy of Sexuality Education. PhD Thesis. Graduate Department of Theory and Policy Studies in Education, University of Toronto, Canada.

Miller, S., G. Szasz, and L. Anderson. "Sexual Healthcare Clinician in Acute Spinal Cord Injury Unit." *Archives of Physical Medicine Rehabitation*, 62:315-20.

Minister of Supply and Services Canada. 1993. *Changing the Landscape: Ending Violence, Achieving Equality. Final Report, The Canadian Panel on Violence Against Women.* Ottawa: Minister of Supply and Services Canada, Catalogue No. SW45-1/1993E.

Minister of Supply and Services Canada. 1994. *Canadian Guidelines for Sexual Health Education.* Ottawa: Minister of Supply and Services, Catalogue No. H39-300/1994E.

Muldoon, M. 1991. *The Abortion Debate in the United States and Canada: A Sourcebook.* New York: Garland Publishing.

Myers, T. and C. Clement. 1994. "Condom Use and Attitudes Among Heterosexual College Students." *Canadian Journal of Public Health*, 85:51-55.

Myers, T., L. M. Calzavara, R. Cockerill, V. W. Marshall, and S. L. Bullock. 1993. *Ontario First Nations AIDS and Healthy Lifestyle Survey.* Ottawa: Canadian Public Health Association.

Myers, T., D. Lucker, K. Orr, and E. Jackson. 1991. *Men's Survey '90. AIDS: Knowledge, Attitudes and Behaviours. A Study of Gay and Bisexual Men in Toronto.* Toronto: AIDS Committee of Toronto.

Omer-Hashi, K. and M. Entwistle. 1995. Female Genital Mutilation: Cultural and Health Issues and Their Implications for Sexuality. *Canadian Journal of Human Sexuality*, 4(2):137-147.

Ontario Ministry of Health. 1992. *Ontario Health Survey 1990.* Toronto: Ontario Ministry of Health.

Ornstein, M. 1989. *AIDS in Canada: Knowledge, Behaviour and Attitudes of Adults.* Toronto: Institute for Social Research, York University.

Orton, M. 1994. "Sexual Health Education in Ontario: A Survey of Three Sectors." *Canadian Journal of Human Sexuality*, 3(3):209-25.

Orton, M. and E. Rosenblatt. 1986. *Adolescent Pregnancy in Ontario: Progress in Prevention (Report 2).* Hamilton, Ontario: McMaster University, School of Social Work, Ontario Adolescent Pregnancy Project.

Orton, M. and E. Rosenblatt, E. 1991. *Adolescent Pregnancy in Ontario 1976-1986: Extending Access to Prevention Reduces Abortions and Births to the Unmarried (Report 3).* Hamilton, Ontario: McMaster University, School of Social Work.

Orton, M.J. and E. Rosenblatt. 1993. *Sexual Health For Youth: Creating a Three Sector Network in Ontario.* Toronto: Ontario Study of Adolescent Pregnancy and Sexually Transmitted Diseases, Faculty of Social Work, University of Toronto.

O'Sullivan, L. F. and E. S. Byers. 1993. Eroding Stereotypes: College Women's Attempts to Influence Reluctant Male Partners. *Journal of Sex Research*, 30:270-282.

O'Sullivan, L. F., K. A. Lawrance, and E. S. Byers. 1994. Discrepancies in Desired Level of Sexual Intimacy in Long Term Relationships. *Canadian Journal of Human Sexuality*, 3(4)313-316.

Otis, J., G. Gaston, J. Lambert, and R. Pronovest. 1990. "Adolescents and Condom Use: The Difference Between Contraception and STD/AIDS Prevention." 6th International Conference on AIDS, San Francisco, 1990. Unpublished data in text is from this study.

Otis, J., D. Longpré, B. Gomez, and R. Thomas. 1994. "L'Infection par le VIH et les Adolescents: Profil Comportemental et Cognitif de Jeunes de Milieux Communautaires Différents." In: *Éduquier pour Preventir le SIDA.* N. Chevalier, J. Otis, and M.-P. Desaulniers, eds. Quebec: Publications MNH.

Otis, J. 1996. Santé Sexuelle et Prévention des MTS et de l'Infection au VIH: Bilan d'une Décienee de Recherche Auprès des Adolescent(es) et des Jeunes Adultes Québecois(es). Ministère de la Santé et des Services Sauciaux (Québec).

Phillips, J. 1994. *Adolescent Births and STDs and Age of Male Partner.* Toronto Department of Public Health, Community Health Information Section, unpublished internal update, June 30, 1994.

Radford, J. L., A. King, and W. K. Warren. 1990. *Street Youth and AIDS.* Kingston, Ontario: Social Program Evaluation Group.

Ramsum, D. L., S. A. Marion, and R. G. Mathias. 1993. "Changes in University Students' AIDS-Related Knowledge, Attitudes and Behaviours, 1988 and 1992." *Canadian Journal of Public Health,* 84(4):275-278.

Rekart, M. L., J. Barrett, C. Lawrence, and L. Manzon. 1991. "HIV and North American Aboriginal Peoples." VII International Conference on AIDS, Florence, Italy, June 16-21.

Remis, R. S. and W. D. Sutherland. 1993. "The Epidemiology of HIV and AIDS in Canada: Current and Future Needs." *Canadian Journal of Public Health,* 84(supp. 1):534-38.

Renard, V. and J. Badets. 1993. "Ethnic Diversity in the 1990s." *Canadian Social Trends,* Autumn, 17-22.

Rines, B. 1992. "Fertility Enhancement for Spinal Cord Injured Men and Their Partners." *Canadian Journal of Human Sexuality,* 1(4):201-6.

Roberts, J. V. 1994. "Criminal Justice Processing of Sexual Assault Cases." *Juristat Service Bulletin.* Canadian Centre for Justice Statistics, 14(7):1-19.

Roberts, J. V. and M. G. Grossman. 1993. "Sexual Homicide in Canada: A Descriptive Analysis." *Annals of Sex Research,* 6:5-25.

Roberts, J. V. and R. M. Mohr. 1994. *Confronting Sexual Assault: A Decade of Legal and Social Change.* Toronto: University of Toronto Press.

Roeher Institute. 1992. *No More Victims: Manuals to Guide the Police, Social Workers and Counsellors, Family Members and Friends, and the Legal Profession in Addressing the Sexual Abuse of People with a Mental Handicap,* 4 vols. North York, Ontario: The Roeher Institute.

Royal Commission on New Reproductive Technologies. 1993. *Proceed with Care: Final report of the Royal Commission on New Reproductive Technologies,* Vol 1. Ottawa: Minister of Government Services Canada.

Samson, J. M., J. J. Lévy, A. Dupras, and D. Tessier. 1990. "Les Comportements Sexuels des Montréalais Francophones." *Contraception, Fertilité, Sexualité,* 18:277-84.

Samson, J. M., J. J. Lévy, A. Dupras, and D. Tessier. 1991. "Coitus Frequency Among Married or Cohabiting Heterosexual Adults: A Survey in French Canada." *Australian Journal of Marriage and Family,* 12(2):103-109.

Samson, J.-M., J. J. Lévy, A. Dupras, and D. Tessier. 1993. "Active Oral-Genital Sex Among Married and Cohabiting Heterosexual Adults." *Sexological Review,* 1(1):143-156.

Samson, J.M., J. Otis, and J. J. Lévy. 1996. Risques Face au SIDA Relations de Pouvoir et Styles de Communication Sexuelles chez les Étudiantes des Cégeps Francophone du Québec. Rapport de recherche. Départemente de Sexologie. Université du Québec à Montréal.

Santé Québec. 1991. *Enquête Québécoise sur les Facteurs de Risques Associés au SIDA et Autres MTS; La Population des 15-29 Ans.* Québec: Ministère de la Santé et des Services Sociaux.

Saskatchewan Health. 1993. *Toward Sexual and Reproductive Health in Saskatchewan: Report on the Advisory Committee on Family Planning to the Minister of Health.* Regina, Saskatchewan: Saskatchewan Health.

Schneider, M. 1991. "Developing Services for Lesbian and Gay Adolescents." *Canadian Journal of Community Mental Health*, 10(1):133-150.

SIECCAN. 1992. "Sexuality and Disability." *Canadian Journal of Human Sexuality*, 1(4).

SIECCAN. 1993. *Being Sexual: An Illustrated Series on Sexuality and Relationships.* (17 booklets) East York, Ontario: Sex Information and Education Council of Canada.

SIECCAN. 1994. "Sexuality and Cancer Treatment." *Canadian Journal Human Sexuality*, 3(2).

Sobsey, D. 1994. *Violence and Abuse in the Lives of People with Disabilities.* Baltimore, MD: Paul H. Brookes Publishing Co.

Sobsey, D., D. Wells, R. Lucardie, and S. Mansell. 1994. *Violence and Disability: An Annotated Bibliography.* Baltimore, MD: Paul H. Brookes Publishing Co.

Statistics Canada's Violence Against Women Survey. 1993. *The Violence Against Women Survey.* Ottawa: Statistics Canada.

Statistics Canada. 1990. *General Social Survey.* Ottawa: Statistics Canada.

Statistics Canada 1992. *Canadian Crime Statistics: Sexual Assault.* Catalogue No. 85-205. Ottawa: Statistics Canada.

Szasz, G. 1989. "Sexuality in Persons with Severe Physical Disability: A Guide to the Physician." *Canadian Family Physician*, 35:345-351.

Szasz, G., and C. Carpenter. 1989. "Clinical Observations in Vibratory Stimulation of the Penis of Men with Spinal Cord Injuries." *Archives of Sexual Behaviour*, 18(6):461-473.

Task Force on Sexual Abuse of Patients. 1991. *Final Report of the Task Force on Sexual Abuse of Patients.* Toronto: College of Physicians and Surgeons of Ontario.

The Daily. 1993. *The Violence Against Women Survey.* Statistics Canada, November 18, 1993, Catalogue No. 11-001E.

Tonkin, R. 1992. *British Columbia—The Adolescent Survey.* Burnaby, British Columbia: The McCreary Centre Society.

Toobin, J. 1994. (October 3). "Annals of Law: X-Rated." *New Yorker.*

Toronto Board of Education. 1992. *Sexual Orientation: Focus on Homosexuality, Lesbianism and Homophobia. A Resource Guide for Teachers of Health Education in Secondary Schools.* Toronto: Toronto Board of Education.

Trocmé, N., D. McPhee, K. T. Kwok, and T. Hay. 1994. *Ontario Incidence Study of Reported Child Abuse and Neglect.* Toronto: Institute for the Prevention of Child Abuse.

Ullman, R. and L. Lathrop. 1996. Impact of Free Condom Distribution on the Use of Dual Protection Against Pregnancy and Sexually Transmitted Disease. *Canadian Journal of Human Sexuality*, 5(1):25-29.

Vanier Institute of the Family. 1994. *Profiling Canada's Families.* Ottawa: Vanier Institute of the Family.

Varnhagen, C. K., L. W. Svenson, A. M. Godin, L. Johnson, and T. Salmon. 1991. "Sexually Transmitted Diseases and Condoms: High School Students' Knowledge, Attitudes and Behaviours." *Canadian Journal of Public Health*, 82(2):129-31.

Verby, C., and E. Herold. 1992. "Parents and AIDS Education." *AIDS Education and Prevention*, 4:187-98.

Wadhera, S., and J. Strachan. 1991. "Teenage Pregnancies, Canada, 1925-1989." *Health Reports*, 3(4):327-47.

Wadhera, S. and Millar, W.G. 1996a. "Pregnancy Outcomes." *Health Reports*, 8(1):7-15.

Wadhera, S. and Millar, W.G. 1996b. *Reproductive Health: Pregnancies and Rates*, Canada, 1974-1993.

Warren, W. K., and A. J. C. King. 1994. *Development and Evaluation of an AIDS/STD/Sexuality Program for Grade 9 Students.* Kingston, Ontario: Social Program Evaluation Group, Queen's University.

Watson, D. B. 1991. "Overview of Vancouver General Hospital's Gender Dysphoria Clinic." *SIECCAN Journal,* 6(1):3-8.

Wheeler, S. 1996. *It's Okay.* 5(1). Sureen Publications, Box 23102, 124 Welland Ave., St. Catharines, Ontario, Canada L2R 7P6.

Wilchesky, M., and P. Assalian. 1991. "Assessment and Treatment of Transsexuals: The Montreal General Hospital Approach." *SIECCAN Journal,* 6(1):47-50.

Wolff, L. and D. Geissel. 1994. "Street Prostitution in Canada." *Canadian Social Trends, Summer, 1994.* Statistics Canada, Catalogue No. 11-008E.

Young, A. H. 1992. "Child Sexual Abuse and the Law of Evidence: Some Current Canadian Issues. *Canadian Journal of Family Law,* 11:11-40.

Zarb, L. H. 1994. "Allegations of Childhood Sexual Abuse in Custody and Access Disputes: What Care Is in the Best Interests of the Child? *Canadian Journal of Family Law,* 13:91-114.

China
(*Zhonghua Renmin Gonghe Guo*)

Fang-fu Ruan, M.D., Ph.D., and M. P. Lau, M.D.

Contents

Demographics and a Historical Perspective

A. Demographics

The People's Republic of China is the largest country in Eastern Asia, embracing 3.7 million square miles. China has the largest population of any country in the world, 1.2 billion (1995).The vast majority of Chinese,

Editor's Note: In this chapter, Dr. Fang-fu Ruan's report and analysis of sexual attitudes and behavior in China follows our standard thirteen-topic structure. In Section 14, Dr. M. P. Lau provides a summary and analysis of the Kinsey-like *Sexual Behavior in Modern China: A Report of the Nationwide "Sex Civilization" Survey on 20,000 Subjects in China* (1992). Readers should consult Section 14 for additional information on specific topics discussed by Fang-fu Ruan.

92 percent, are Hans (ethnic Chinese, or Han Chinese), but the other fifty-five ethnic groups encompass 91.2 million people (about 8 percent of China's population). Minority nationalities with populations of over one million are Mongolian, Hui, Tibetan, Uighur, Miao, Yi, Zhuang, Bouyei, Korean, Manchu, Dong, Yao, Bai, Tujia, Hani, Kazak, Dai (Thai), and Li.

Slightly larger than the contiguous 48 United States, China is bordered by Korea in the east, Mongolia in the north, Russia in the northeast, Kazakhstan, Kirghizstan, and Tajikstan in the northwest, Afghanistan and Pakistan in the west, India, Nepal, Sikkim, and Bhutan in the southwest, and Myanmar (formerly Burma), Laos, and Vietnam in the south, and the Pacific Ocean in the east. Across the seas to the east and southeast are Japan, the Philippines, Malaysia, Brunei, and Indonesia. Only one tenth of the land is cultivated, although the eastern half of China is one of the best-watered lands in the world, with three great rivers and vast farmlands.

Twenty-seven percent of the 1.2 billion population are urban. The population density is 326 per square mile. The 1995 life expectancy at birth was sixty-seven for males and sixty-nine for females. The 1991 birth rate was twenty-two per 1,000; for 1995 eighteen per 1,000. The death rate in 1991 and 1995 was seven per 1,000, for a 1.5 and 1.0 percent annual natural increase respectively. The 1992 literacy rate was 78 percent, with nine years of schooling required and 96 percent attendance in primary school. China has one hospital bed per 382 persons, one physician per 648 persons, and an infant mortality rate of fifty-two per 1,000 live births in 1995. The 1993 per capita gross domestic product was $2,200.

B. A Brief Historical Perspective

The remains of various humanlike creatures, who lived as early as several hundred thousand years ago, have been found in many parts of modern China. The oldest human remains found in China were those of "Peking man," who lived approximately 578,000 years ago. Neolithic agricultural settlements, dating from about 5000 B.C.E. have been found in the Huanghe basin. Imperial China lasted almost 4,000 years, from the Xia dynasty (c. 2200-1500 B.C.) to the Qing dynasty (A.D. 1644-1911). Bronze metallurgy reached a peak during the Shang Dynasty of Northern China (c. 1500 B.C.E. to c. 1000 B.C.E.), along with Chinese pictographic writing. Imperial China was marked by a succession of dynasties and interdynastic warring kingdoms. The range of Chinese political and cultural domination waxed and waned, expanding from the north to the south and west at various times, as science, technology, and culture flourished in great sophistication. Rule by non-Hans (foreigners), the Mongols during the Yuan Dynasty (1271-1368) and the Manchus in the Qing Dynasty (1644-1911), did not alter the underlying Chinese character of the culture.

Cultural and political stagnation in the nineteenth century left China vulnerable to internal rebellions that left tens of millions dead and Russian,

Japanese, British, and other foreign powers exercising control over some key parts of the country. Imperial rule ended in 1911 with the formation of the Republic of China in 1912. Between 1894 and 1945, China was involved in major conflicts with Japan. In 1895, China gave up Korea, Taiwan, and other territories. Japan seized the northeast provinces of Manchuria in 1931, and invaded China proper in 1937. Following World War II, China regained the territories it had previously lost to Japan. In 1949, the People's Republic of China was proclaimed by Chinese Communist leader Mao Zedong; the nationalist Republic of China (Kuomintang) retired to Taiwan.

The Great Leap Forward, 1958 to 1960, tried to force the pace of economic development through intensive labor on huge new rural communes and emphasis on ideological purity. The program was abandoned when it encountered serious resistance. In 1965, the Great Proletarian Cultural Revolution was launched in an effort to reestablish the revolutionary purity of the principles of Chairman Mao Zedong with massive purges and the forced relocation of millions of urban teenagers into the countryside. This effort gradually petered out as pragmatism regained its influence. Despite the violent repression of democratic demonstrations by over 100,000 students and workers in the 1989 Tiananmen Square outside Beijing's Great Hall of the People, China has followed a painfully slow, halting, but definite transition and adjustment to a partial free-market economy and more democratic policies.

1. Basic Sexological Premises

A. Character of Gender Roles

In order to understand and evaluate the recent situation of gender roles in China, it is necessary to begin with some understanding of the roots of female oppression in the traditional Chinese society and family. In its earliest history, China was a matriarchal society, until Confucius and Mencius defined the superior-inferior relationship between men and women as heaven-ordained more than two thousand years ago. In traditional Chinese society, women should observe the Three Obediences and the Four Virtues. Women were to be obedient to the father and elder brothers when young, to the husband when married, and to the sons when widowed. Thus the Chinese women were controlled and dominated by men from cradle to grave. The ideal of feminine behavior created a dependent being, at once inferior, passive, and obedient. Thus for more than 2,000 years, for the vast majority of Chinese women, belonging to a home was the only means to economic survival, but they had no right to select a husband, let alone the right to divorce or to remarry if widowed. They had no right to their physical bodies. Those who defied such institutionalized oppression were persecuted, ostracized, and sometimes driven to suicide. [This may not apply to the lower class and marginal people. (Lau)]

The functional importance of all women in traditional China lay in their reproductive role. In a patriarchal and authoritarian society, this reproductive function took the form of reproducing male descendents. Since descent was patrilineal, a woman's position within her natal family was temporary and of no great importance. The predominant patrilineal household model, in combination with early marriage, meant that a young girl often left home before she was of significant labor value to her natal family. Hence, education or development of publicly useful skills for a girl was not encouraged in any way. Marriage was arranged by the parents with the family interests of continuity by bearing male children and running an efficient household in mind. Her position and security within her husband's family remained ambiguous until she produced male heirs. [Then she might become manipulative and exploitive. (Lau)] In addition to the wife's reproductive duties, the strict sexual division of labor demanded that she undertake total responsibility for child care, cooking, cleaning, and other domestic tasks. Women were like slaves or merchandize.

A real liberation and revolution in the female's role has occurred in the People's Republic of China (PRC). The first law enacted by the PRC government was the Marriage Law of 1950. The law is not only about marriage and divorce, it also is a legal statement on monogamy, equal rights of both sexes, and on the protection of the lawful interests of women and children. [However, it took years for the law to become more than words on paper and move into real life. (Lau)]

B. Sociolegal Status of Males and Females

The Changing/Unchanging Status of Women

In 1954, the constitution of the People's Republic of China restated the 1950 principle of the equality of men and women and protection of women: "Article 96. Women in the People's Republic of China enjoy equal rights with men in all spheres of political, economic, cultural, social, and domestic life."

Under this principle, major changes happened in the social roles of women in the PRC, especially in the areas of work and employment, education, freedom in marriage and divorce, and family management. For example, 600,000 female workers and urban employees in China in 1949 accounted for 7.5 percent of the total workforce; in 1988 the female workforce had increased to 50,360,000 and 37.0 percent of the total. [Most women continue to be employed as cheap labor, but this is not a condition limited to China. (Lau)]

A neighborhood survey in Nanjing found that 70.6 percent of the women married between 1950 and 1965 had jobs. Of the women married between 1966 and 1976, those employed stood at 91.7 percent, and by 1982, 99.2 percent of married women were breadwinners.

A Shanghai neighborhood survey reported 25 percent of the wives declared themselves boss of the family, while 45 percent said they shared the decision making power in their families. Similar surveys in Beijing found that 11.6 percent of the husbands have the final say in household matters, while 15.8 percent of families have wives who dominate family decision making. The other 72.6 percent have the husband and wife sharing in decision making. A survey in Nanjing revealed that 40 percent of the husbands go shopping in the morning. Many husbands share kitchen work. Similar surveys of 323 families in Shanghai found 71.1 percent of husbands and wives sharing housework. (Dalin Liu's study of *Sexual Behavior in Modern China* (1992) contains statistical data about domestic conflicts and the assignment of household chores.)

Although the situation of women changed dramatically from what was before, in actuality, women still were not equal with men. For example, it is not unusual to find that some universities reject female graduate students, and some factories and government institutions refuse to hire women. The proportion of professional women is low. Of the higher-level jobs such as technicians, clerks, and officials, women fill only 5.5 percent. Of the country's 220 million illiterates, 70 percent are women. Women now make up only 37.4 percent of high school students and only 25.7 percent of the university-educated population. Moreover, actual discrimination against women still exists, and continues to develop now. Many women have been laid off by enterprises that consider them surplus or redundant. Only 4.5 percent of the laid-off women continued to receive welfare benefits, including bonuses and stipends offered by their employers. Many enterprises have refused to employ women, contending their absence from work to have a baby or look after children are burdensome.

Male-Preferred, Female Infanticide, and the Sex Ratio Problem

China was, and in many ways still is, a Confucianist country. Confucianism said that: "There are three things which are unfilial, and to have no posterity is the greatest of them." In Chinese society "having posterity" means "having a male child." Therefore, having no boy is regarded as the worst possible problem a family can have, psychologically, economically, and sociologically.

Even before the founding of the PRC, when there was no birth control at all, China already had female infanticide. For example, in 1948 in China, the nationwide average sex ratio (male to female) was 109.6 males for every 100 females; in Dalian it was 194.0:100.

According to a survey done by gynecology professor Gu Zusan, 80 percent of rural families want a boy, not a girl. Therefore, one of the side effects of the government's "one child" policy is the practice of female infanticide. For example, the sex ratio in a community in Wuhan (1982) among those under one year of age was 154 (154 males for every 100 females); in a village in Hubei Province (1982), the sex ratio was 503.

In the 1970s, China's newborn sex ratio was 106:100. It was probable that in Wuhan, Hubei, and other places as well, female infanticide was being practiced. Even the government Beijing newspaper *Zhongguo Fazibao* (China Law News) reported this problem (September 11, 1986): "According to the survey by Zungqing Women Association, there were 2,800 cases of female infanticide in Zungqing in 1984. It was a very serious and severe problem." The newborn sex ratio in China has risen year by year. In 1986, it was 110; in 1987, 111; and in 1990, 112. In September and October 1992, a nationwide survey of 380,000 newborns showed the sex ratio was as high as 118.5.

C. General Concepts of Sexuality and Love

In mainland China today, the only sexual behavior that is acknowledged to be legally and morally permissible is heterosexual intercourse within monogamous marriage. A wide variety of sexual behaviors are explicitly proscribed. Thus, prostitution, polygamy, premarital and extramarital sex (including cohabitation arrangements), homosexuality, and variant sexual behavior are all illegal. Because even normal sexual expression is viewed with contempt as a less important activity of life, not only are pornography and nudity banned, but any social activity with sexual implications—such as dancing—may be subject to restrictions. Even the marriage relationship is given little consideration. For example, according to official statistics, approximately 360,000 married persons live apart from their spouses, and this figure increases at a rate of 100,000 per year. Most of these separations occur because individual citizens are not free to move from one place to another, or to change their places of employment.

Public policy and law related to sexuality seriously and severely impacts individual and social lives. Contemporary China is a noteworthy example of a totalitarian government's attempt to control or repress the sexual aspects of the individual's life. It exemplifies, as well, how sexually repressive policies are not actually effective in inhibiting sexual desire in private lives, nor in curbing the struggle for human sexual rights and freedom.

The major move toward democracy in mainland China after Mao was the "Democracy Wall" movement during 1978 and 1979. During this brief period, the government allowed young people to express their desire for personal freedom and democracy by placing "big character" posters on a wall that came to be known as the "Democracy Wall." The Democracy Wall was also used for advocating sexual liberation. The author vividly recalls visiting the wall on February 20, 1979, and seeing two poems about sexual rights. One was titled "The Eulogy of Sexual Desire," the other "Open Sex." In posters like these, China's youth first made a courageous stand on the importance of sexual openness to their country's modernization.

During the nationwide demonstration by university students in the winter of 1986-87, there were also some posters advocating sexual freedom. While sexual liberation was not a major explicit goal of the 1989 democracy movement, its importance was understood, and its value implicit in one of the loveliest events that occurred then. During the hunger strike in Tiananmen Square, a wedding was held for one of the leaders of the demonstrators. The bride and groom, the maid of honor (the General Commander Chai Ling, now an internationally known heroine of the struggle for democracy), and the best man (Chai's husband, the Vice General Commander Feng Congde) were all fasting, as were the classmates attending the wedding. Yet all the celebrants were laughing joyously. The wedding was the ideal symbol of the connection between the longing for liberty, and the desire for love, romance, marriage, personal happiness, and fulfillment.

[In 1996, Suiming Pan, head of the Institute for Research in Sexuality and Gender at the Renmin University of China in Beijing, analysed 11 social surveys on sexuality in Chinese cities between 1986 and 1995 and reinterviewed 103 men and 73 women. The ten factors list below, which Pan (1996) identified as affecting sexological research and studies in China, also reveal some important insights into the general concepts of love and sexuality that prevail in the Chinese culture.

1. For most people, the Chinese sexual vocabulary is either cryptic or considered dirty and abusive.
2. The more familiar with each other people are, the more difficult it is to talk about sex.
3. There is often a sexual undertone between heterosexual interviewers and interviewees.
4. Many tragic or socially illegitimate sexual matters would rather be forgotten than discussed with the interviewees.
5. Female interviewers are often considered "bad women."
6. Pornography, sex workers, and non-marital sex are illegal in the minds of Chinese people.
7. Ordinary people do not understand why researchers study sexuality.
8. Most ordinary people are unable to evaluate and express their own sexual feelings, or even their behavior.
9. Most females feel like vomiting when questioned about sexual matters.
10. Ordinary people think that if you ask a question about a kind of sexual behavior or relationship, then it means that you really like it yourself.

The first nine of these ten points reflect ignorance, stigma, and inhibition, with only the last point expressing a common sense viewpoint frequently encountered in other countries. (Editor)]

2. *Religious and Ethnic Factors Affecting Sexuality*

A. Source and Character of Religious Values

China is a multireligion country, with a vast proportion of the population professing no religion. Some worship ancestors and/or Shens ("kindly spirits"). Many subscribe to more than one of the main religions: Buddhism, Taoism, Islam, Catholicism, several major Protestant religions, and Confucianism. Taoism, as a religion, is considered a genuine indigenous religion of China in the sense that Buddhism, Islam, Catholicism, and Protestantism were imported from foreign countries, while Confucianism is taken to be more secularly oriented in doctrine.

Confucianism is based on writings which are attributed to Confucius (551-479 B.C.), the first great educator, philosopher, and statesman of China, and his followers, including Mencius (372-289 B.C.), a political thinker who believed in democracy. Confucianism dominated Chinese sociopolitical life for most of Chinese history.

Confucius and Mencius themselves expressed rather a positive view of human sexuality. For example, The Master (Confucius) said, "I have not seen one who loves virtue as he loves sex" (*Confucian Analects Book IX*, chapter 17); "Food and drink and the sexual relation between men and women compose the major human desires" (*The Book of Rites*, one of the major Confucianism classics, chapter 9). In *The Works of Mencius*, one of the major Confucianism classics (book 6, part 1), we find: "Eating food and having sex are both of human nature."

It was not until much later that sexual conservatism became a feature of Neo-Confucian philosophy. The crucial change was initiated by several famous Neo-Confucianists, including Ch'eng I (1033-1107), and Chu Hsi (1130-1200). Ch'eng I summarized the Neo-Confucian viewpoint as "Discard human desires to retain the heavenly principles."

When asked whether it was justifiable for a widow to remarry when pressed by poverty and hunger, he replied, "It is a small matter to die as a result of starvation, but a serious evil to lose chastity toward one's dead husband by remarrying." Chu Hsi stressed the inferiority of women and the strict separation of the sexes, and forbade any manifestation of heterosexual love outside of wedlock. Chu Hsi laid the foundations of Neo-Confucianism as the sole state religion. It encouraged a puritanical and strictly authoritarian form of government, including the establishment of censorship and thought control. However, the government had difficulty enforcing these views on the lower class or *sciao-ren* (the non-exemplary class of people).

Taoism has both a philosophical and a religious tradition in China. Although philosophical Taoism flourished early in the fifth century B.C., Taoism as a religion did not develop until the first century A.D. Next to Confucianism, it ranks as the second major belief system in traditional Chinese thought. The philosophy of Taoism outlined in the Lao-tzu's *Tao Te Ching* offers a practical way of life. Both philosophical and religious Taoism included in their classics some positive ideas about sex. For example, from Lao tzu's *Tao Te Ching*: "All things have their backs to the female and stand facing male. When male and female combine, all things achieve harmony" (chapter 42, translated by S. Mitchell, Harper & Row, 1988). And from Taiping Jing (*The Canon of Peace and Tranquility*), an early classic of religious Taoism: "Through the way of copulation between husband and wife, the Yin and Yang all obtain what they need and Heaven and Earth become peace and tranquility;" "Based on one Yin and one Yang, Heaven allows both man and woman to exist and to be sexually attractive to each other, therefore life can be continued."

Yin-Yang is a major philosophical concept developed during the Zhou dynasty (1027-221 B.C.). The concepts of Yin and Yang may be found in the majority of important Chinese classics, including such a major classic of Confucianism as the *I-Ching*, and such a Taoist classic as the *Tao-te-ching*. Thus, the Yin-Yang philosophy is among the most important unifying concepts of Chinese culture. According to the Yin-Yang philosophy, all objects and events are the products of two elements, forces, or principles: Yin, which is negative, passive, weak, and destructive; and Yang, which is positive, active, strong, and constructive. It was very natural for the Yin-Yang doctrine to become the basis of Chinese sexual philosophy. The Chinese have used the words Yin and Yang to refer to sexual organs and sexual behavior for several thousand years. Thus *Yin Fu*, "the door of Yin" means vulva, *Yin Dao*, "the passageway of Yin" means vagina, and *Yang Ju*, "the organ of Yang" means penis. The combination of these words into the phrases *Huo Yin Yang* or *Yin Yang Huo He*—"the union or combination of Yin and Yang"—describes the act of sexual intercourse.

Buddhism was first introduced into China in the first century A.D. from India. Chinese Buddhism was of the Mahayana (Great Vehicle) school, so named to distinguish it from the earlier form of Buddhism known as Hinayana (Lesser Vehicle). Among Tibetan peoples, it is distinguished by its emphasis on the Buddhist Tantras. Most Buddhist schools denied sexual desire, and traditionally Buddhist monks have been celibate. But, it is not the case of the school of Mi-tsung (Mantrayana, or Tantrism). Sex was the major subject of Mi-tsung. Mi-tsung was very similar with some sects of Taoism, and stressed the sexual union.

Even Mi-tsung said that *Buddhatvam yosidyonisamas-ritam* ("Buddheity is in the female generative organs"). In China, " Tibetan Esoteric Sect" (Tibetan Mi-tsung) flourished in the Yuan Dynasty, especially from the time of Kubilai Khan (A.D. 1216-1294).

Islam reached China in the mid-seventh century through Arab and Persian merchants. Islam has a large following among ten of China's minorities: Hui, Uighur, Kazak, Tatar, Kirghiz, Tajik, Ozbek, Dongxiang, Salar, and Bonan. The number of believers is about 14 million, mostly in Xinjiang, Gansu, Ningxia, Yunnan, Qinghai, Inner Mongolia, Henan, Hubei, Shandong, Liaoning, Beijing, and Tianjin.

Catholicism was introduced into China as early as A.D. 635. By 1949, the number of Catholics in China had reached 2.7 million. Protestantism was introduced into China in 1807. After the Opium War, missionary activity increased and Christianity became a part of the Chinese culture. For example, T'ai-p'ing-T'ian-Kuo, a great peasant rebellion in the Ging Dynasty, from 1851 to 1864, was under the banner of God and Christianity. By 1949, China had 700,000 Christians. Generally speaking, Catholicism and Protestantism strengthened the sex-negative and repressive attitudes in China at an official level.

B. Source and Character of Ethnic Values

There are some differences in sexual lifestyles among the different ethnic groups in China. For example, among Tibetan ethnics, plural marriages including polygyny and polyandry exist beside monogamous marriages. In some Tibetan families, brothers may share one woman as a common wife. There is also great variety in the way one religious factor impacts on the sexual attitudes in different ethnic groups. For example, Islam takes on slightly different expressions among its many followers in ten of China's minority nationalities: Hui, Uygur, Kazak, Tatar, Kirgiz, Tajik, Dongxiang, Salar, and Bonan. [Similar accounts of the material in this section can be found in Ng and Lau (1990) and Bullough (1976). The *Yearbooks* of the *Encyclopedia Britannica* provide the latest updates on the religious and ethnic compositions of the population. (Lau)]

3. Sexual Knowledge and Education

A. Government Policies and Programs for Sex Education

In line with its general policy of suppressing any discussion of sexuality, the Chinese government neglected the development of sex education courses for the general curriculum. It was not until the early 1980s that model programs were developed, and even then, discussion was usually limited to the necessity of using contraception to limit population growth. In the 1950s, 1960s, and 1970s, not only was there a complete lack of systematic sex education, but only a few booklets on sexuality had been published. The most popular one, *Knowledge of Sex* (*Xing-di-zhi-shi*), was published in 1957. Most of these booklets are devoted to social topics, such as love and marriage, and medical topics, such as sexual dysfunctions. Only a few pages discuss aspects of sexual relationships such as arousal, sexual responses, and frequency of intercourse. Yet, for more than twenty years, *Knowledge of Sex* was virtually the only sex booklet available to a population of eight to nine hundred million people. (See also Sections 14B and 14C.)

In 1980, heartened by the end of the Cultural Revolution, a few authors and publishers began to produce new materials. The first effort was a new edition of *Knowledge of Sex* published by People's Medical Publishing House. The first printing of 2.5 million copies, released in June 1980, was sold out almost immediately, and some people resold their copies at nearly double the original price.

Between 1980 and 1984, more than ten new sex booklets were published. Two of them became bestsellers. The first, *Required Readings in Wedding Hygiene* was originally published in September 1980, and by November 1981 had already been reprinted eight times, for a total of more than 7.5 million copies. The second, *Questions and Answers about Wedding Hygiene*, was published in July 1984 with a printing of 4.2 million copies.

Finally, in the mid-1980s, four major types of pressure led national and local officials to acknowledge the need for sex education programs. First, the population growth continued to be a very serious problem. A birth control program had been instituted in January 1973, but it became unavoidably clear that to implement the program effectively, young people would have to be given sexual information essential to understanding and using contraception. Second, rates of teenage pregnancy, juvenile sex crime, and sexually transmitted diseases seemed to be increasing. It was stated that sex education offered the best hope for diminishing these problems. Third, medical professionals felt that the numbers of patients they were treating for sexual dysfunction demonstrated a need for improved education. And finally, as a result of the new "open-door" policy of receptiveness to Western cultural influence, and a simultaneous increase in personal freedoms, the Chinese people were expressing a desire to improve their lives, including their sexual lives.

The first high school sex education courses were introduced in 1981 in Shanghai. In early 1986, forty Shanghai middle schools, about 10 percent of the city's total, introduced an experimental sex education course for coed classes in the 12- to 13-year age group. In addition to helping students understand the physiological and psychological changes they were undergoing, the course was designed to teach hygiene and sexual morality. By June 1986, nearly a hundred Shanghai middle schools gave sex education courses. And, by February 1988, 6,000 middle schools all over China had instituted sex education courses. Thirteen of the twenty-eight provinces, including Shanghai, Jiangsu, Tianjin, and Helongjiang, had made sex education courses part of the standard middle school curriculum. In February 1988, the State Council announced that sex education courses would be established in middle schools nationwide.

From January to October 1985, a special series of columns entitled "Essays on Sex Education" by the author of this chapter was published in *Required Readings for Parents*, the leading national monthly magazine on child and adolescent education. The series consisted of ten rather long articles on various aspects of sexuality and sex education. It was the first systematic treatment of such topics to be published since the founding of the People's Republic of China in 1949. The "First National Workshop on Sex Education" was held in Shanghai on July 22 to August 7, 1985. This was the first such conference convened in mainland China since 1949. It was an interdisciplinary workshop, attended by more than eighty professionals from eighteen provinces, most them of in the fields of birth control, sociology, urology, and high school and college education. The author was the major instructor. Also in 1985, the author served as chief editor, and as a major contributor, for a large updated volume of the *Handbook of Sex Knowledge*, published by the Scientific and Technological Literature Publishing House in Beijing in October. Although it was intended to be the most up-to-date text of its kind, the book could not include any descriptions of sexual positions, or any nude illustrations (except anatomical drawings). Despite these self-imposed restrictions, the first printing was limited to 500,000 copies by the government. After the author left China for the United States at the end of 1985, he was asked to prepare a new version to include the knowledge of the prevention of AIDS. In 1988, the revised edition was jointly published by the Scientific and Technological Literature Publishing House and the People's Medical Publishing House, one of the two publishers officially permitted to publish books on sex. Yet in 1988, the government allowed the showing of a film that explicitly referred to the *Handbook*. The movie, entitled *Mandarin Duck Apartments* (to the Chinese, a pair of mandarin ducks symbolizes an affectionate couple), includes a scene in which an old woman counsels a young newlywed who feels that sex is dirty and shameful. The old woman shows her the *Handbook*, explaining that findings in sexual science show that women have as much right as men to enjoy sex.

After the Tiananmen Square massacre in 1989, the government fell into its old habit of including sexual restrictions in a wave of political repression. But, because of the huge pressure from population control, STDs, and the prevention of teenager pregnancy, the government cannot inhibit and stop sex education any more. The sex education classes, exhibitions, meetings, and publications are still continued and developing in China today. [Pei-Kum Yao has chronicled in detail the development of adolescent sex education since 1920, in Appendix III of Dalin Liu's *Sexual Behavior in Modern China*, 1992. (Lau)]

B. Informal Sources of Sexual Knowledge

Given the government's authoritarian control described in the section above, it is obvious that informal sources of sexual information, such as television talk shows, radio phone-in programs, and popular magazines commonly found in more democratic and open countries are very limited in China because they are illegal and severely punished. [Underground sources continued to flourish, and official control has been relaxing as more emphasis has been shifted from ideology to economy. (Lau)]

4. Autoerotic Behaviors and Patterns

Self-pleasuring is still condemned by most of the Chinese people, included even some sex educators and sex researchers. It was widely said that frequent self-pleasuring will cause neuroses, sexual dysfunctions, and even severe diseases. Although in 1985, the author pointed out in his popular article "On Masturbation" and in his *Handbook of Sex Knowledge* that self-pleasuring is normal sexual behavior, neither harmful nor sinful, it will take time for people to accept this updated viewpoint on self-pleasuring. According to *A Report of the Nationwide "Sex Civilization" Survey on 20,000 Subjects in China* (1992), only 39.0 percent of students of colleges and universities said that they engaged in self-pleasuring, male students (59.0 percent) much higher than female students (16.5 percent). But Dr. Lee's survey in 1989 in Shanghai showed that 93.1 percent of male students of colleges and universities said that they engaged in this behavior. In the *"Sex Civilization" Survey*, 15.9 percent of married couples said that they engaged in self-pleasuring. (See also Sections 14B, 14C, and 14D for data on masturbation among adolescents, college students, and married couples in the 1992 nationwide survey by Dalin Liu.)

5. Interpersonal Heterosexual Behaviors

A/B. Children/Adolescents

Because of the pervasive social pressures, reinforced by some medical messages and the lack of sexual education, sexual expression other than heterosexual marital sex, including sexual play and sex rehearsal play, both alone and with peers, are punished when discovered. Such behavior is seldom if ever reported or commented on in public. No puberty rites are observed to mark sexual maturation.

Premarital Sexual Activities and Relationships

A study in a major city in Quangdong province found that of 123 young women undergoing premarital examinations, 75 (61 percent) had already experienced intercourse. In 1991, a survey in which questionnaires were distributed to a random sample of 1,003 unmarried university students in Beijing, including equal numbers of men and women, of 559 respondents, 106 (19 percent) said they have engaged in sex. Lack of private space is a major problem for young lovers. Many young people have little choice but to meet in parks. And where, five years ago, couples were likely to sit demurely together on a bench, it is now acceptable to hug and kiss, ignoring people passing by only a few feet away. Some couples disappear into the bushes. In Dalin Liu's 1992 survey, 18 percent of the married couples admitted to having sex with a previous partner; 86.3 percent of those sampled approved of such encounters. (See also Sections 14B and 14C for data on premarital courtship and sexual attitudes and behavior among adolescent males and females and college students in the 1992 nationwide survey.)

C. Adults

Unmarried Adults

For several thousand years, the Chinese people have tried to adhere to the simple dictum: "Get married at a marriageable age." And for centuries it would have been true to say that no Chinese would want to remain single for his/her entire life. But in recent years, China's unmarried population has been growing at a steady rate. For example, in 1982, there were 11,267,000 unmarried Chinese people aged between 28 and 49 years old, or 4.36 percent of the total 28 to 49 age range, of these, 10,556,000 were male (93.67 percent) and 714,000 female (6.33 percent). (See also Sections 14C and 14D for data on premarital sexual attitudes and behaviors among college students and married couples in the 1992 nationwide survey.)

Recently, the Chinese people have started to replace the old-fashioned social concepts with ones that respect the rights of the unmarried; to remain single is now as much a personal right as the right to marry. An important factor in this shift was a greater respect for the rights of freedom, which should prove a blessing both to individuals and society.

[In every public park in China, a large billboard at every entrance warns against "offence against public decency," just as there are notices in dance halls prohibiting anyone from "dancing with faces or cheeks touching the partner's." In reality, such "indecencies" are practiced by most people, and law enforcers are becoming more and more tolerant.

[An analysis of detailed observations of courtship and petting behaviors engaged in by married, unmarried, and status-unknown couples in 13 public parks in six Chinese cities, Beijing, Guangzhou, Zheng-zhou, Hohe-haote, Chong-qing, and Xian, during the summers between 1985 and 1989 provides an insight into the heterosexual courtship behavior of young Chinese couples in that era. In the five years, from 1985 to 1989, petting behavior in the public parks increased, forcing the authorities to be more tolerant of behavior that previously was unacceptable. The decreasing social control by the authorities reflected more tolerance in the society's political direction. Attitudes toward public petting were the most diversified in Beijing. The most permissiveness was found mainly in the blue-collar parks in contrast to the parks used mostly by white-collar workers and "cadres." Finally, in a country with a strong tradition of double standards in sexual morals for females and males, it was surprising that in Beijing, only 31 to 40 percent of the females were fully passive and at least 18 to 27 percent intiated petting to a small degree when it came to less intimate petting behavior in more private settings in the parks. "It could never be imagined in the old days that so many females would allow themselves to be petted in public, even if they were absolutely passive" (Pan 1993: 184).

[In 1987, there was the movement against "bourgeoisc liberalization," and in 1989, a "counterrevolutionary rebellion" in Beijing. It is uncertain whether and how these efforts could or did affect the petting limits, but it seems that the grimmer a movement is, the more timid the petting couples are, and the less permissive the nearby people are to the pettings. It is also interesting to note that no amount of social control, be it by propaganda, moral condemnation, or daily administrative measures, is as effective as a large-scale political movement once every few years in reinstating the official petting limits (Pan 1993:192; Burton 1988). (Editor)]

Cohabitation

Beginning in the late 1970s, the increased tolerance of nonmarital cohabitation in the West began to influence China's younger generation. College students and young intellectuals in particular were attracted to this lifestyle. Some of the younger or more open-minded sociologists also asserted the necessity of overcoming the disadvantages of traditional marriage. Actually, the act of cohabitation might be an act of defiance and courage, or simply a consequence of overcrowding and the lack of living space. These young Chinese risked being arrested.

The definitions of unmarried cohabitation used in compiling official statistics make it difficult to estimate the popularity of this behavior in the sense it is understood in the West. The official figure of 2.69 million couples in unmarried cohabitation in 1989 seems low, considering that some areas report that as many as 50 percent of couples living together live in unmarried cohabitation. As for couples marrying under the legal age (22 for males; 20 for females), China's State Family Planning Commission reports that 6.1 million such marriages took place in 1987 alone. According to China's 1990 census, 5.8 percent of 15- to 21-year-old males and 15- to 19-year-old females were "married." That means that 8.5 million Chinese "married" under the legal age. Two and a half million babies—10 percent of all births—were born to underage couples in that year. The same news article reports an estimate by the Marriage Administration Division of the national Department of Civil Administration that 30 percent of China's "married" couples are living together without having received an official marriage certificate, and that the number is growing (see Section 9D).

Marriage and the Family

Although China has a long history of polygamy, in contemporary mainland China, only monogamy is legal and morally permissible. On May 1, 1950, the new Marriage Law was promulgated. It stated that " The New-Democratic marriage system, which is based on the free choice of partners, on monogamy, on equal rights of both sexes, and on the protection of the lawful interests of women and children, shall be put into effect," and that "Bigamy, concubinage, child betrothal, interference with the remarriage of widows, and the exaction of money or gifts in connection with marriage, shall be prohibited." The revised marriage law of 1980 followed the same principles as the 1950 law.

Marital Sex

A surprising 91 percent of the 8,000 married couples interviewed by Dalin Liu (1992) in cities and rural areas expressed satisfaction with their spouse. However, when Dalin looked deeper, he found that the average Chinese couple has intercourse four to seven times a month, with peasants invariably reporting 25 percent more sex than city couples. However, 34.1 percent of the rural couples and 17.2 percent of city couples admit to less than one minute of foreplay or none at all. Consequently, 44.7 percent of urban wives and 37 percent of rural wives experience pain during intercourse. Only 16.8 percent of rural couples kiss or embrace apart from lovemaking. (See also Section 14D for data on marital sex and satisfaction among married couples in the 1992 nationwide survey.)

Marital dissatisfaction is very common in China today. Some estimate that as many as 60 percent of the Chinese are unhappy with their marriages. A survey of 3,000 young people in Wuhan, the capital of Hubei Province, showed that only 20 percent of respondents were satisfied with their marriage. In a survey of 600 couples, all residents of big cities, 70 percent said they were unhappy with their sex lives. A random survey of married couples in Shanghai found that 45 percent were unhappy with their sexual relationships. A survey of 6,000 divorce cases in five large cities, including Beijing, Shanghai, Guangzhou (Canton), Wuhan, and Xi'an, by ten newspapers showed that 72 percent of divorces are caused by disharmony of sexual life.

Divorce

Although the divorce rate is not very high in China, it is increasing rapidly. In 1978, some 170,449 couples divorced; 1979, 192,894 couples; 1980, 180,378 couples; 186,891 couples in 1981; 210,930 couples in 1982, 420,000 couples in 1983, and 450,000 couples in 1984. In 1985 and 1986, the annual average was 500,000 couples. The divorce figure rose to 587,000 couples in 1987, and 630,000 couples in 1988. In 1989, nationwide official statistics show that 9,851,000 couple applied for marriage; 9,348,000 couples, about 95 percent, were approved and given a marriage certificate. In the same year, 1,307,000 couples applied for divorce; 752,000, about 58 percent, were approved and given divorce certificates. The marriage rate was 16.8 per 1,000 persons and the divorce rate 1.35 per 1,000 persons.

[With rapid economic growth creating new hopes and expectations, and Government interference in personal lives receding steadily, the divorce rate in Beijing more than doubled from 12 percent in 1990 to 24.4 percent in 1994, according to the *Beijing Youth Daily*. This statistic compares the number of marriages and divorces in a given year. While the national divorce rate in mid-1995 was 10.4, far behind that in the United States and European nations, officials admit that the divorce rate is rising all over China, and faster in the cities than in rural areas. Among the factors contributing to the new trend are the new social and economic freedom, the rising expectations that women bring to marriage, and a remarkable increase in extramarital affairs. More than 70 percent of divorces are currently initiated by women with the most common reason being an extramarital affair on the part of the husband.

[Increasingly, among urban Chinese and even among government officials who once actively opposed divroce, divorce is being viewed as a an acceptable alternative to an unhappy marriage. Many officials even recognize a positive side to divorce. When both parties agree, a divorce can be granted in three days; not long ago, the wait was years. Important as the government's attitudinal shift is, a larger factor is the growing expectations women bring to marriage today, and their growing demands in an era of expanding opportunity. In the past, women were happy to settle for a stable income, a home, and children. To these expectations, women are now adding romance, sex, and affection. While women increasingly enjoy more independence and choices in career, place to live, husband, lover, they are also more subject to unemployment. Meanwhile, the shift has also brought a resurgence of traditional male values, including the right to have an affair.

[Prior to the current surge in divorces, China experienced two other waves of rapidly rising divorce rates, the first occurred in the 1950s when returning victorious Communist soldiers abandoned their farms and rural wives to move to the city; the second came during and just after the Cultural Revolution, between 1966 and 1980 (Faison, 1995). (Editor)]

Extramarital Sexual Activities

Sex between consenting adults is technically not illegal in China, but the police have broad powers to suppress activities that they consider antisocial. Elderly women who staff local "neighborhood committees," the grassroots eyes and ears of the government, also try to stop activities of which they disapprove. But discreet affairs have a good chance of escaping detection and interference. Means of birth control were not always available to unmarried youths, but women knew they could get an abortion. Extramarital affairs seem to occur much more than generally believed, although they are conducted in such secrecy that little statistical information is available. Perhaps the best evidence of these affairs is divorce rates: about one third of the divorces in Beijing from 1984 to 1985 were caused by extramarital relationships. In the Third Symposium of Family Problems in 1991, an expert said that 40 percent of divorces are caused by extramarital sexual relationships. If these findings are at all typical, then the increasing divorce rate must reflect an increase in the number of extramarital relationships.

A survey in Beijing found that members of at least 10 percent of the sample of 600 couples had had extramarital sex. Perhaps most significant is a nationwide survey that 69 percent of the people surveyed did not think extramarital affairs are wrong. In Dalin Liu's 1992 survey, 69 percent condoned extramarital sexual relations.

Incidence of Oral and Anal Sex

Several factors influence both attitudes towards and experience with oral and anal sex. In a 1989 survey with 1,279 respondents in 27 cities, nearly seven out of ten Chinese reported they have had anal sex with heterosexual partners. Professor Pan found that only 6 percent of the 600 heterosexual couples he surveyed in big cities had had anal intercourse at least once.

In ancient erotic art and fiction, oral sex, including mutual "69" oral sex, is not unusual. Considering the lack of information about sexual behaviors that prevailed until recently and Dalin Liu's finding that 34 percent of rural couples and 17 percent of urban couples engaged in less than a minute of foreplay, it is not likely that oral sex is as common as it was in ancient China. No general survey data is available. Many modern Chinese think oral sex is too "dirty." In 1988, a survey of 140 homosexual males in Shanghai revealed that only nineteen persons, 13.6 percent, said they had had oral sex, and only four persons, 2.8 percent, had experienced anal sex. At a 1990 World Health Organization meeting on the spread of AIDS in China, Pan reported that 7.7 out of 10 Chinese have had anal sex with a heterosexual partner. Little data are available on anal sex among homosexuals because of the taboo character of that population and studies on same-sex behavior (Burton 1990). (Dalin Liu's *Sex Culture in Ancient China* provides extensive information about sexual deviance in China.)

6. *Homoerotic, Homosexual, and Ambisexual Behaviors*

Male homosexuality may have been a familiar feature of Chinese life in remote ancient times. The official Chinese historical records indicate that during the Spring-Autumn and Chin-Han Era (770 B.C. to A.D. 24), male same-sex behavior was not a crime or considered immoral behavior. On the contrary, it was sometimes the noble thing to do. For example, in Western Han (206 B.C. to A.D. 8), ten of the eleven emperors each had at least one homosexual lover or shared some same-sex behavior. During the Western and Eastern Jin and Southern and Northern Dynasties (A.D. 256 to 581), male homosexuality seemed also acceptable in the broader upper-class society.

Considering the many and varied records of homosexuality in ancient China, one would expect to find evidence of homosexuality in modern China. However, literature regarding contemporary homosexuality is scarce at best, although it is available in Taiwan and Hong Kong. Thus it was a genuine breakthrough when, through a rather unique and unexpected set of events, the situation of homosexuality in China was openly discussed for the first time in a positive context. In 1985, Ruan, the author of this chapter, using a pen name Jin-ma Hua, published an article in a widely circulated Chinese health magazine, *To Your Good Health.* The article pointed out that homosexuality has occurred in all nations, all social strata, and in all eras in human history, and that homosexuals deserve a reasonable social status. Many of the readers of *To Your Good Health,* most of them gay, wrote to the magazine's editor in response to the article.

By April 1986, a total of sixty letters had been received by the editor of *To Your Good Health,* and forwarded to Ruan. A striking aspect of the letters from gay men is their immense relief at having an opportunity to express their feelings. Many letters expressed their writers' pain and conflicting desires for confidentiality and a chance to overcome their isolation. Clearly the chief source of pain for China's gay men derives from the fear of societal punishment, including arrest, and possible sentence to labor reform camp or prison.

The mental pressure and anguish arising from the fear that their true identity might be discovered is often unbearable. The social pressure, pain, and inner conflict homosexuals suffer can be so intense that they come to consider or even attempt suicide. Of the fifty-six who responded to Hua's article, fifteen, or more than 25 percent, mentioned suicide attempts. Of all the hopes and dreams expressed in these moving letters, three types of aspirations were outstanding. The first concerned the human rights issue—the belief that society should accept homosexuals and their right to express their sexuality without social or legal condemnation. The second concerned the issue of freedom to interact with other homosexuals—the wish that society would provide them with means to make contacts and form relationships, just as it does for heterosexuals. The third concerned the issue of knowledge—the wish that objective and scientific studies would be conducted and publicized in order to improve societal understanding. In twenty letters, the hope that some agency would facilitate social contacts among homosexuals took the form of a request that "Dr. Hua" or his publishers do so. In Hua's article, two actual cases of gay life in Hubei and Shanghai had been described. All twenty letters requested the names and addresses of these two men in order to establish contact with them. Some men, though they did not use the word for "club," expressed the wish to create this type of organization. There were eighteen letters pointing out the need for development and/or publication of more information about homosexuality.

Regarding the legal situation of homosexuals in mainland China now, although there is no specific statement concerning the status of homosexuals in the current Criminal Law of the People Republic of China, Article 106 says, "All hooliganism should be subjected to arrest and sentence." In practice, homosexual activity has been included in "hooliganism." As noted above, even the small sample of letters Ruan received contained a report of a man who received a five-year jail term for homosexuality.

Silence, especially a silence based on repression and enforced ignorance, must not be mistaken for approval or tolerance. When public figures do speak out on homosexuality, it is usually to condemn it. For example, in the 1990s, a famous attorney even wrote that "homosexuality . . . disrupts social order, invades personal privacy and rights and leads to criminal behavior." A leading forensic psychiatrist said that "homosexuality is against social morality, interferes with social security, damages the physical and mental health of adolescents, and ought to be a crime."

Another common reaction to the suggestion that homosexuality exists in China is denial. Clear evidence of the official denial of homosexuality was provided by the internationally well-known sexologist, Dr. Richard Green, the series editor of "Perspectives in Sexuality: Behavior, Research, and Therapy." In his "Series Editor's Comment" for Ruan's book *Sex in China: Studies in Sexology in Chinese Culture,* he wrote:

> Less than a year before the 1989 massacre in Tiananmen square, I lectured on human sexuality at Peking Union Medical College. I described my research on the nonsexual behaviors of young boys that predicted later homosexuality. I asked the physicians in the audience whether comparable childhood behaviors were found among Chinese boys. I was told that there were no homosexuals in China. (Ruan, 1991)

But, this official attitude of denying homosexuality in China can no longer be justified. In late 1991, officials in Shanghai, the largest city in China, recognized that there are about 10,000 homosexuals in the city. Actually, the number of homosexuals may be over 200,000, according to the *World Weekly* (September 1, 1991). Changzheng Hospital in Tianjin, the third largest city in China, reported in a medical paper that in the past four years, out of 366 STD cases, at least 61 cases of syphilis resulted from male homosexual behavior; 80 percent of the cases involved anal sex, 10 percent oral sex, and other 10 percent anal plus oral sex. Most of the cases (80 percent) had participated in sexual activity in public toilets. More than 80 percent of their homosexual partners were strangers. Their ages ranged from 16 years to 60 years, with two thirds of the group falling between 20 and 30 years of age. Most of them were workers, some were cadres, teachers, and others.

Yet another reaction is to admit that perhaps homosexuality does exist in China, but to insist that when it occurs, it is the result of Western influence; it was referred to as "spiritual pollution," and "Western social diseases," originating in "Western ideology and thoughts."

Finally, there are those who, when faced with undeniable evidence of homosexuality, respond by seeking to eliminate it. Even many physicians still fail to recognize homosexuality as simply one possible sexual orientation. For example, in Harbin, one of the largest cities in northeastern

China, physicians now use the discredited approach of "treating" homosexuality with electric shock therapy to discourage erotic thoughts.

In ancient times, Chinese culture was characterized by a very tolerant attitude toward same-sex female behavior. Lesbians in China today are even more closeted than gay males. (See also Xiaomingxiong—alias Samshasha, 1984, and Lau and Ng, 1989).

When Ruan received letters from homosexuals all over China in 1985 and 1986, not one was from a woman. The only women who are willing to discuss their homosexuality are the few who have already been imprisoned for this behavior and have little to lose. An exception to the usual difficulty in locating lesbians is the experience of Chinese journalists He and Fang, who were actually more successful in contacting lesbians than gay males in their 1989 survey of homosexuality in China. They wrote six stories about lesbians compared to one about gay males.

He and Fang had to rely on interviews with women who were jailed for "sex crimes," or crimes of violence inspired by sexual jealousy. Because so many investigations of female homosexuality are based on interviews with prisoners, it has been all too easy for Chinese people to develop a stereotype of lesbians as immoral, frustrated people (Sheridan and Salaff 1984).

In early 1992, a new and more humane homosexual policy emerged. This started with two young lesbians in Wuwei County, Anhui Province, whose parents opposed their homosexual relationship very much. The angry parents finally reported the affair to the local police department. After several months of investigation, the police department of Wuwei County arrested these two female lovers and restrained them fifteen days on charges of "misconduct."

The Wuwei County police department then referred the case to higher institutions until the Public Security Department of Central Government in Beijing heard the case. The Public Security Department replied and instructed the county police that since under current laws there is no article that specifies punishment for such behavior and relationship, it could not treated as "misconduct." Therefore, the Wuwei Police Department released the two women and let them live together as "husband" and "wife." Usually the older woman takes the role of "husband," and wears male clothing, while the younger one takes the role of "wife" and prefers to stay in the home. It is a very good signal to show that at least some police officers, especially senior ones, have started to change their attitude toward homosexuality and other sexual variations. But, recently a reversal still occurred. In May 1993, the government closed down the first gay saloon, "Men's World," in Beijing, which appeared on November 22, 1992, and came out in public on February 14, 1993.

(See also Sections 14B, 14C, and 14D for data on views of homosexuality and the incidence of same-sex behavior among adolescents, college students, and married couples in the 1992 nationwide survey.)

7. Gender Conflicted Persons

Recognition of transsexualism in human society is a relatively recent phenomenon, especially in the closed society of mainland China. In January 1983, with the author's assistance, the first male-to-female transsexual surgery was performed in the Plastic Surgery Department of the Third Hospital of Beijing Medical University.

The greatest difficulty facing transsexuals in China is that of gaining the acceptance of their families and society. It is nearly impossible to obtain permission to perform transsexual surgery. A psychiatrist told the author that he had seen two transsexual patients who, after being repeatedly denied transsexual surgery, used knives to remove the penis by themselves. The problem is not a lack of appropriate surgical techniques and facilities. In fact, both general plastic surgery and such precise surgical techniques as reimplantation of severed fingers are very advanced in China. Dr. Xia, in the Plastic Surgery Department of the Third Hospital of Beijing Medical University, has successfully operated simultaneously on a male-to-female transsexual and a female-to-male transsexual with mutual exchange and transplantation of ovaries and testicles; this surgery took nineteen hours. If permission were given, transsexual surgery could be performed with little difficulty in most large hospitals. The problem is really perceptual and ideological. The absence of scientific research on the subject means that there is nothing to counteract the statements of the popular press, which describes transsexualism as not merely outlandish, but as evidence of the inroads of "decadent Western culture." This ideological tone effectively inhibits surgeons' willingness to perform transsexual surgery.

[In early Chinese history, hundreds of males were castrated every year to become eunuchs. Some of these were transsexuals. In other words, transsexuals in the past had a legal option transsexuals do not have in China today. (Lau)]

8. Significant Unconventional Sexual Behaviors

A. Coercive Sex

Rape and Pedophilia

Rape, pedophilia, and any behavior which "subjects women to indignities or carries out other gangster activities," are all clearly illegal, according to Articles 139 and 160 of the 1980 Criminal Law of the People's Republic of China. It is very interesting to note that although China has an official policy severely repressing sex and heavily punishing sex crime, nevertheless, such crimes in mainland China continue to increase from year to year. The Chinese government does not publicize the number of sex crimes, but some figures are available from academic articles. For example, in Shanghai, the largest city in China, the number of rapes increased from 100 percent (as the basis for comparison) in 1979 to 377 percent in 1983. Nationwide, the number of reported rapes rose from a base 100 percent in 1979 to 340 percent in 1983. (See also Section 14E for data on sex offenders in the 1992 nationwide survey.)

Teenage rapists in particular increased from a base of 100 percent in 1980, to 150 percent in 1981, 192 percent in 1982, and 311 percent in 1983. While there was a slight decrease in 1984, the absolute number still increased, and in 1985 by 42.5 percent over the previous year in Shanghai.

In China, every year a lot of people were shot by the government as the penalty of crime. Many of them were related to crimes of sex, love, and marriage. In Beijing, the capital of the People's Republic, for instance, out of fifty-two cases of the death penalty in 1984, crimes of sex, love, and marriage accounted for 67.4 percent of all death penalties.

The juvenile crime rate from 1979 to 1981 increased more than 25 percent. Statistics from three cities in 1980 to 1983 showed 13 percent of juvenile crimes involved sex crimes. Most of them were 13 to 15 years old. Forty percent of male delinquents charged by the Juvenile Delinquent Correction Institution were charged with "sexual crimes and mistakes," 95 percent of the female delinquents, some as young as 12 years, were charged with sexual violations, which may or may not have involved rape.

Incest and Sexual Harassment

Certainly, incest and sexual harassment exist in China. No general survey data is available. "Sexual harassment" as a new word in Chinese (*Xingsaorao*) translated from English is now used in China. Traditionally, it was included in the concept of *liumong xingwei* or *tiaoxi funu,* both terms indicating any behavior which sexually subjects women to indignities. *Liumong xingwei* and *tiaoxi funu* are clearly illegal, according to Articles 139 and 160 of the 1980 Criminal Law of the People's Republic of China.

B. Prostitution

China's first brothels were likely established in the Spring-and-Autumn period (770 B.C. to 476 B.C.) by the famous statesman and philosopher Guan Zhong (? to 645 B.C.), who used them as a means of increasing the state's income. It is clear that the institution of government-run prostitution reached its peak in the Tang (A.D. 618 to 905) and Sung (A.D. 960 to 1279) Dynasties. In ancient China, where most women had no opportunity to acquire an education, and formal contact between men and women was frowned upon, it was the role of the courtesan to entertain a man and be his friend. Every prominent official, writer, artist, or merchant customarily left his wife at home when he traveled; instead he was accompanied by women skilled in making men feel comfortable. Courtesans with literary, musical, or dancing ability were especially desirable companions, and many became famous historical figures. However, the prostitutes working in privately owned brothels mainly provided sexual services. (See also the profile of a female prostitute in Section 14E for data on prostitution in the 1992 nationwide survey.)

From the Sung to the Ming Dynasties, government-run and privately owned prostitution existed side by side in China. Early in the Ging Dynasty, from A.D. 1651 to 1673, the Manchu Emperors Shun-chih and Kang-hsi gradually abolished both local and imperial governmental involvement in operating prostitution. Thus, for most of the Ching Dynasty, prostitution in China was a private enterprise. For most of the Republican period in mainland China (1912 to 1949), some prostitutes were registered while others plied their trade illegally.

When the Chinese Communists took power, one of the first social changes they introduced was the abolition of prostitution. Only one month after the Communist army took control of Beijing (Peking) on February 3, 1949, the new municipal government announced a policy of limiting and controlling the brothels. Less that eight weeks after the founding of the People's Republic of China on October 1, 1949, more than 2,000 Beijing policemen raided and closed all 224 of the city's brothels, arresting 1,286 prostitutes and 424 owners, procurers, and pimps. Other cities soon followed suit. In Shanghai, China's most populous city, there were 5,333 arrests of prostitutes between 1950 and 1955.

In October 1957, in a new attempt to maintain order, the 81st Session of the Standing Committee of the First National People's Congress adopted a new law entitled Rules on the Control of and Punishment Concerning Public Security of the People's Republic of China. The legislation announced the policy on banning prostitution. In 1979, at its Second Session, the Fifth National People's Congress adopted the first criminal law in the PRC, The Criminal Law of the People's Republic of China, which took effect January 1, 1980. Under this Law, the punishment for coercing prostitution was more severe: "Article 140: Whoever forces a female to engage in prostitution shall be sentenced to a fixed term of imprisonment of 3 to 10 years."

The severe repression of prostitution did not prevent its accelerated revival in the late 1970s and throughout the 1980s and 1990s. The first official report of the recurrence and development of prostitution in mainland China appeared in March 1983. It reported that

> According to the incomplete statistics from the three largest cities, Beijing, Shanghai, Tianjin, and four provinces, Guangdong, Fujian, Zhejiang and Liaoning, from January, 1982 to November, 1982, more than 11,500 persons were discovered to be involved in prostitution. More than 1,200 persons were owners and pimps of underground

> brothels; more than 4,200 women were prostitutes; and 1,800 persons, including 223 visitors from foreign countries, Hong Kong and Macao, were customers of prostitutes. Fifteen hundred people were fined, 790 were detained, 691 were arrested, and 662 were sent to labor camps. More than 900 underground brothels were banned and closed.

The growth of prostitution in Guangzhou (Canton) alone was amazing. In 1979, only 49 pimps, prostitutes, and customers were caught. In 1985, this number had increased to approximately 2,000. In one month of 1987, 11,946 people were arrested for involvement in prostitution, and in both the preceding and following months the figures rose to more than 13,000.

Prostitutes and their customers appeared everywhere, in hotels, inns, hair salons, single-family homes, apartments, dormitories, underground brothels, and taxis, in every city and every province. Between January 1986 and July 1987, eighteen prison camps for prostitutes were opened, and by December the number of camps had more than tripled to sixty-two.

Statistics collected in 1986 in the city of Guangzhou (Canton), in Guangdong province, supply some information about the men who patronize prostitutes. In 1986, of the 1,580 customers who were caught, 41 percent were from the city, 34.5 percent from other parts of the province, 15.3 percent from other provinces, 6.1 percent from Hong Kong and Macao, and 3.7 percent from other countries. Fully two thirds of the customers were Communist party members and county officials.

There is no doubt that economic motives fuel the current rapid growth of prostitution in mainland China. The possibility of earning as much as 10,000 Yuan new income in only two or three months versus the average Chinese income of only about 100 Yuan per month is a powerful incentive.

Since the late 1980s, even harsher measures were taken in the effort to curtail prostitution, including arrests of foreign citizens. In June 1988, in the Shenzhen Economic Zone, which abuts Hong Kong, there was a mass arrest of 122 prostitutes and 100 customers. In the small town of Deqing, about a hundred miles west of Canton, a man accused of being a pimp was executed.

The opposition to prostitution also has an ideological basis. In the lexicon of China's Communist leadership, "prostitution" is a very bad word. Deng Xiaoping, the top leader in China, is particularly strong in his opposition to prostitution and advocates severe penalties because he believes it tarnishes his country's reputation. According to a formal report, more than 200,000 prostitutes and customers were caught in 1991 alone, and more than 30,000 prostitutes were sent to forced labor camps, 80 percent of them street walkers.

Some of those arrested in the antiprostitution movement received sentences as severe as the death penalty. In Wenzhou city, Zhenjiang province, a woman and a man were sentenced to death because they had owned several underground brothels, employing fourteen prostitutes. In Beijing a 55-year-old man was given a death sentence because in 1988 he had allowed prostitutes to use the offices in a hospital about twenty times.

C. Pornography and Erotica

In China, erotic painting and erotic fiction occurred over 1,000 years ago, in the Tang dynasty. The official prohibition of erotic art and literature started as early as about eight hundred years ago, in Yuan dynasty. After the founding of the People's Republic of China on October 1, 1949, a strict ban on erotic fiction and pornography of any kind was imposed nationwide. In the 1950s and 1960s, the policy of banning erotica was very effective. In the whole country, almost no erotic material was to be found. There were few difficulties implementing this policy until the mid-1970s.

Then, the legalization and wide availability of pornography in several Western countries during the late 1960s and early 1970s, coupled with China's growing openness to the outside world, increased the supply of such material available for underground circulation.

In recent years, the suppression of pornography has become a very serious political and legislative concern. The number of arrests and the severity of sentences on people involved in pornography have both increased in the attempt to suppress it entirely.

By the late 1970s, "X-rated" films and videotapes were being smuggled into China from Hong Kong and other countries. (In China, these are known as "yellow videos" and "yellow" refers to erotica). Yellow videos quickly became a fad. At first, the only people who could view these tapes were rather highly placed party members and their families, since only they had access to videotape players, which were very rare and expensive in China at that time. Before long, however, "yellow videos," including the well-known American pornographic movie *Deep Throat*, were available to more people, although still very secretly and only through small underground circles. Some people used the tapes to make money; tickets for video shows were very expensive, usually 5-10 Yuan per person (at the time most people's monthly salary was only about 40 to 50 Yuan).

Sometimes people who were watching these tapes engaged in sexual activity, even group sex. Because yellow videos were usually shown in small private rooms to very small audiences whose members knew each other well, a party atmosphere often prevailed. It was very easy for young people to initiate sexual activity when they were aroused by what they saw.

At about the same time, erotic photographs, reproductions of paintings, and books were also smuggled into mainland China. They, too, were sold at a great profit. One small card with a nude photo would cost as much as 5 to 10 Yuan.

There was a strong reaction at the highest levels of the Chinese Communist Party and the Government. The police were ordered to confiscate every type of pornographic material, from hand-copied books to "yellow" audiotapes and films. Severe penalties were ordered for all people involved in the showing or viewing of "yellow" videos, and, in April 1985, a new antipornography law was promulgated. The nationwide crackdown on pornography led to numerous arrests and confiscations in city after city. For example, by October 1987 in Nanchang, the capital of Jiangxi Province, forty-four dealers in pornography had been arrested and 80,000 erotic books and magazines confiscated. It was reported that an underground publishing house with 600 salesmen had been circulating erotic materials in twenty-three of China's twenty-eight provinces, making a profit of 1,000,000 Yuan (in that period about $300,000 U.S.) in two years.

A Shanghai Railway Station employee was sentenced to death because he and four other persons organized sex parties on nine different occasions; during these they showed pornographic videotapes and engaged in sexual activity with female viewers. The other organizers were sentenced to prison, some for life.

The climax of this wave of repression seemed to occur on January 21, 1988, when the twenty-fourth session of the Standing Committee of the Sixth National People's Congress adopted supplemental regulations imposing stiffer penalties on dealers in pornography. Under these regulations, if the total value of the pornographic materials is between 150,000 Yuan and 500,000 Yuan, the dealer shall be sentenced to life imprisonment.

In a nationwide strike against pornography, beginning a few weeks after the Tiananmen Square massacre, on July 11, 1989, 65,000 policemen and other bureaucrats were mobilized to investigate publishing houses, distributors, and booksellers. By August 21, more than 11,000,000 books and magazines had been confiscated, and about 2,000 publishing and distributing centers, and 100 private booksellers were forced out of business. But then Deng Xiaoping, China's top leader, went further by declaring that some publishers of erotica deserved the death penalty. It may be at least one of the most severe political punishments against "pornography" ever suggested by a national leader anywhere in the world. After this, in July 1990, the Supreme People's Court issued a new decree stating that the death sentence is the proper penalty for traffickers in prostitution and/or pornography.

9. Contraception, Abortion, and Population Planning

A. Contraception

All kinds of contraceptive measures, from condom to pill, are available and used in China's practice of family planning. In 1989, it is estimated that more than 70 percent of couples of child-bearing age are using contraceptives, over 8.8 million males have undergone sterilization injections or operations, including a new reversible sterility operation. For females, the most popular birth control method is the intrauterine devices (IUDs). Used by 60 million women in the country, the IUD accounts for 41 percent of the total contraceptive measures; female sterilization operations constitute 36 percent. Research on a variety of oral contraceptives in the country has also reached advanced levels and these are available to the public. Breakthroughs have recently been reported in the development of medicines for terminating early pregnancy. In 1992, a survey showed that 83.4 percent of married couples have adopted contraceptive practices, 40 percent of them are using IUDs, 39 percent female sterilization, 12 percent male sterilization, 5 percent oral pills, and 4 percent condoms. (See also Sections 14B, 14C, and 14D for data on contraception usage among adolescents, college students, and married couples in the 1992 nationwide survey.)

B. Unmarried Teenage Pregnancies

See Section 5C.

C. Abortion

In China, abortion as a secondary measure to terminate an unwanted pregnancy is not only a legal right, it is even a legal responsibility. If a woman already has a child, she will be asked to terminate her unplanned pregnancy by abortion in the first trimester and even as late as the second trimester. Generally speaking, in mainland China one third of pregnant women have undergone an abortion. From 1985 to 1987, 32,000,000 abortions were done, 80 percent of these pregnancies being the result of failed contraception. (See the discussion of "Fewer births—the one-child policy," in Section D below).

D. Population Control Efforts

China's population policy consists of two components: decreasing and limiting the quantity of population; and improving the quality of population. To reduce the numerical growth of the population, three main measures are practiced: late marriage, late childbearing, and fewer births—the "one-couple-one-child policy." The basic measure used to improve the quality of the population involves efforts to prevent birth defects. (See also Sections 14B, 14C, and 14D for data on attitudes toward government limitation of family size among adolescents, college students, and married couples in the 1992 nationwide survey.)

This dual population policy is proving to be effective: China had 200 million fewer babies born in 1988 than in 1970. The result has been a saving of 3 trillion yuan ($802 billion). China has successfully controlled its annual population growth rate to less than 1.5 percent, as compared with 2.4 percent in underdeveloped countries and 2.2 percent in Asia. During the 1960s, the average Chinese woman gave birth 5.68 times (the figure includes infant deaths, still births, and abortions). This dropped to 4.01 during the 1970s and to 2.47 in the 1980s. The average population growth rate dropped from 2.02 percent during the period from 1949 to 1973 to 1.38 percent from 1973 to 1988.

Late Marriage

Generally, until the recent past, the Chinese people were controlled on the local level by *danwei*—the unit or institution one belongs to. In order to marry, a couple must have a legal registration and a permit letter from his/her *danwei*. Usually one's *danwei* leader checks one's age—while the minimum legal marriageable age is 22 for males and 20 for females, "later marriage age" policy stipulates an age of 27 to 28 for males and 24 to 25 for females in order to help in the control of population.

A 1991 survey in Nanjing, the former capital of China and the capital of Jiangsu Province, showed that the average marriage age was 27.5 for males and 25.8 for females. In 1949, the average first marriage age for females was 18.57, in 1982 it increased to 22.8 years old.

Late Childbearing

Married women are urged not to have a baby before 25 to 28 years of age, but no later than 30 years of age, in order to achieve the twin goals of later childbearing and healthier birth.

Fewer Births, the "One-Child Policy"

From the late 1970s to the early 1980s, China's family planning policy evolved from "One couple two children," to "One couple better one child," and then to "One couple only one child." From advocating "One couple one child" the government moved to punishing parents who have more than one child. In 1988, the "one-child policy" became a little more flexible, to allow couples in rural areas with one daughter to have a second child with planned spacing.

[By the mid-1990s, the "one-child policy" had produced an obvious but unintended and serious sex imbalance that is already producing some major improvements in the very low position women have traditionally held in this male-dominated society. Initially, the traditional preference for sons coupled with the "one-child policy" has led to ultrasound scans during pregnancy followed by selective abortion for female fetuses. In January 1994, a new family law took effect that prohibited ultrasound screening to ascertain the sex of a fetus except when needed on medical grounds. Under the new law, physicians can lose their license if they provide sex-screening for a pregnant woman (Reuters, 1994). Even after birth, "millions of Chinese girls have not survived to adulthood because of poor nutrition, inadequate medical care, desertion, and even murder at the hands of their parents" (Shenon 1994).

[The 1990 census showed about 205 million Chinese over the age of 15 were single in a total population of 1.2 billion. Overall, three out of five single adults were male. However, government figures show that, while the vast majority marry before they turn 30, eight million Chinese in their 30s were still single in 1990, with men outnumbering women by nearly ten to one. Demographics suggest that by the turn of this century, tens of millions of Chinese men will be unwilling or willing lifelong bachelors.

[A government-sponsored computer-dating service, the Great Wall Information Company, founded in Beijing in 1989, and others often sponsored by provincial and city governments, are swamped by eager men searching for a mate. One of the most popular television shows nationwide is "We Meet Tonight," a cross between a talent show and the "Dating Game," hosted by Ms. Yang Guang since its first showing in 1990.

[With women in short supply, the men are learning to be realistic and not set their expectations too high. In reality, the women now set the standards, making their choice of a prospective husband based on the intelligence, education, and financial status of many candidates. Another benefit for the women, prompted by the concurrent move towards a free market economy in which scarcity equals value, is that women can no longer be treated as chattel.

[Custom has held that a man should marry a woman several years younger and with less education than he has. This left older unmarried women, especially those with more education, almost no hope of finding a husband. With the growing shortage of single women, increasing numbers of men are being forced to consider marrying an older woman. There is a saying being heard more commonly in the countryside that a man who marries a woman three or more years older has found a bar of gold and benefits from her maturity.

[On the negative side, Chinese sociologists and journalists have suggested that the drastic increase of unwilling bachelors in a society that values the family and sons above all else may well produce an increase in prostitution, rape, and male suicide. Bounty hunters have already found a lucrative market for abducting young city women and delivering them to rural farmers desperate for brides.

[To restore the balance of sexes, some observers suggest the government could be forced to offer incentives like free higher education and tax breaks to encourage couples to have girls. This could result in a huge change in the way women are treated throughout the society (Shenon 1994).

[India is facing a similar sex imbalance with similar factors, the value of male offspring and efforts to reduce population growth. With 900 million people, India has nearly 133 single men for every hundred single women. In the industrialized world, sex ratios are more balanced; in some cases,

Japan and the United States in particular, unmarried women outnumber single men, fifty-four to forty-six (Shenon 1994). (Editor)]

Healthier Birth, or "Preventing Birth Defects"

Every year in China, 13 infants per 1,000 are found to suffer from physical defects. The death rate is 26.7 per 1,000 and the deformity rate is 35.7 per 1,000. Most are the victims of inbreeding and such hereditary diseases as some mental illnesses, hemophilia, and chromosome defects. This is a big burden to society and the families that have a child with a serious birth defect.

Since 1988, Dr. Wu Ming, a famous expert in medical genetics has joined the author of this chapter in publications, speeches, and lectures advocating the prevention of birth defects. The basic information was written by the author of this chapter in his book *New Knowledge on Prevention of Birth Defects,* published in Beijing by People's Medical Publishing House in 1981. This was the first book of its kind since 1949 and the founding of the People's Republic of China.

In the early 1980s, the concept of healthier birth, or prevention of birth defects, had already become an important component of China's policy of population control. In 1986, the Ministry of Health and the Ministry of Civil Administration stipulated that a medical examination would be a national requirement for marriage approval.

Gansu province is one of the poorer provinces in China. Out of its population of 23,000,000, more than 260,000 are mentally retarded. This has become a very severe social burden for the province. In 1988, Gansu province adopted a law to force persons who have severe hereditary or congenital mental retardation (I.Q. 1) to be sterilized before marriage, or abort any fetuses conceived, in order to prevent severe birth defects. From January 1989 to June 1991, 6,271 mentally retarded persons were sterilized. Later, several other provinces, including Fujian, Guangdong (Canton), Henan, Liaoning, and Sichuan, adopted the same law. Premier Li Peng and Ms. Peng Peiyun, the minister in charge of the State Family Planning Commission, have spoken out in support of this local law. This indicates that sterilization of mentally retarded persons may become national law in the near future.

In January 1994, a new family law went into effect that banned sex-screening of fetuses (mentioned above) and forbade couples carrying serious genetic diseases to have children. Marriage was prohibited for persons diagnosed with diseases that "may totally or partially deprive the victim of the ability to live independently, that are highly possible to recur in generations to come, and that are medically considered inappropriate for reproduction." A list of the applicable diseases was published shortly after the law went into effect (Reuters 1994).

10. Sexually Transmitted Diseases

Since the 1980s, there had been a dissemination of sexually transmitted diseases to every province and all the major cities in China. Statistics show that in sixteen major cities, the average incidence of STDs was 21.02 per 100,000 in 1987. In some cities, the incidence was as high as 336 per 100,000, resembling that in some Western countries. In Helongjiang province alone, the incidence of STDs increased at the rate of 8.9 times/per year from 1982 to 1988. By the end of 1988, when this province had the fourth highest incidence in the country, 4,558 cases had been reported; and it was estimated that reported cases represented only 20 percent of the total incidence. Nationwide, the number of STD cases reported from 1980 through the end of 1988 was 140,648, with more than 56,000, over 39 percent of these, occurring in 1988 alone. In 1992, the figure of 45,996 new reported STDs cases was 4.86 percent higher than in 1991.

11. HIV/AIDS

China has one of the lowest incidences of AIDS in the world. The first case of AIDS discovered in China, in June 1985, was that of an American tourist. As of August 1989, only three cases of AIDS had been discovered. All three were infected abroad. Also, by July 27, 1989, only twenty-six cases of HIV infection had been diagnosed. In October 1989, the first AIDS case in a native Chinese citizen was identified. The patient had sought medical care using an assumed name and was found to be suffering from secondary syphilis. The hospital later tested his blood serum and found it was HIV-antibody positive. By the time the young man was identified, he had already left the country. According to the head of the National AIDS Center, this patient said he had had homosexual relationships with foreigners. By December 1, 1992, 969 cases of HIV positives and twelve cases of AIDS patients were reported; nine of the twelve AIDS patients had already passed away as of mid-1993. (Gil (1991) has provided a valuable early ethnographic and epidemiologic perspective on HIV/AIDS in the People's Republic based on field visits to Beijing, Chengdu, and Kunming, the latter in Yunnan province, site of China's most severe nidus of HIV infection.)

In December 1996, the Health Ministry announced an official count of 4,305 cases of HIV infection. Privately, experts admit the real number already exceeds 100,000 cases (Wehrfritz 1996).

The accelerating spread of HIV/AIDS in China has recently been linked with the cultural aversion to giving blood. This aversion fosters a seller's market that all but guarantees an impending disaster. Most donors are poor migrants struggling to make ends meet. Some make their living as sex workers as well as from selling blood, and some are drug addicts. In addition, government clinics commonly reuse the needles used to draw blood, and only a third of the nation's blood supply is screened for HIV contamination.

The sale of blood inevitably leads to people willing to exploit and profit from the shortage. The government has recently broken up rings of blood brokers, known as "bloodheads," who have kidnapped or drafted people as donors by paying corrupt officials heading work units. The bloodheads then sell the blood to local government blood stations where directors may be willing to overlook the source and its risk just to have an adequate blood supply. In late 1996, a draft law was circulating among senior health officials that would outlaw the buying and selling of blood for clinical use. While such a law could definitely reduce the risk of HIV infection in the normal course of transfusions and surgery, it would leave China with a drastic shortage of essential blood. Officials could fall back on coercion, mandating regular blood donations for members of the military, police, and state unions. The cost of bringing the public health clinics' blood donation practices up to minimal standards for this age of AIDS will be prohibitively expensive, although this has to be done to avert disaster. Another approach already initiated by the government is to reeducate the people. Pop star Jackie Cheung has been recruited by China's Red Cross to help break the cultural aversion to donating blood with popular songs with the humanitarian appeal to "Reach out, spread some love today." This approach has worked in Hong Kong, but the change in attitude there took forty years (Wehrfritz 1996).

12. Sexual Dysfunction, Counseling, and Therapies

Professor Dalin Liu's survey showed that 34 percent of rural couples and 17 percent of urban couples said they engaged in less than a minute of foreplay, sometimes none at all. Not surprisingly, 37 percent of rural wives described intercourse as painful. While urban couples may be more adventurous sexually, they are not necessarily more satisfied. Professor Suiming Pan's sample of 600 couples were all residents of big cities, and 70 percent of them said they were unhappy with their sex lives, and a random survey of married couples living in Shanghai found that 45 percent were unhappy with their sexual relationships. According to Professor Kang Jin, president of the Shanghai Committee of Rehabilitation of Male Dysfunctions, in 1989 at least 20 percent of China's adult male population was suffering from some type of sexual dysfunction. Now, clinics of sexual counseling, sex therapy, or Western and/or traditional Chinese sexual medicines have been established in most big cities (see Section 5C).

13. Sexual Research and Advanced Education

No sex research existed between 1949, when Mao and his Communist Party took control over mainland China, and 1979. There were some studies on reproductive system and reproductive endocrinology, but these were in the biological and medical fields, not behavioral studies. However, since 1979 and especially after 1985, sex research became an apparently growing, even prosperous, field. China's sex research was started and developed under the names of "sex education" and "sexual medicine," two fields that are accepted and permitted by the government and society. Before the beginning of the open-door policy in 1979, even sex education and sexual medicine were non-existent.

The year 1982 saw a breakthrough for sexology in China. In that year, Robert Kolodny, William Masters, and Virginia Johnson's *Textbook of Sexual Medicine* (1979) was translated into Chinese under the guidance of Professor Wu Jieping, with the actual translation being done by his graduate students. The Chinese edition entitled *Xingyixue (Sexual Medicine)* was published by Scientific and Technological Literature Publishing House, Beijing. It is the first contemporary and updated Western sex book published in China since the founding of the PRC in 1949.

The year 1985 marked another turning point for sexuality education and sexology in China. In that year, Ruan's article, "Outline of the Historical Development of Modern Sexual Medicine," was published by the *Encyclopedic Knowledge*, and his series, "Essays on Sex Education: Ten Lectures," were published in *Required Readings for Parents.* From July 22 to August 7, 1985, the First National Workshop on Sex Education was held in Shanghai, with Ruan as the major instructor. In October 1985, the *Handbook of Sex Knowledge*, the first large modern book on sexuality written by Chinese and in Chinese, was published in Beijing by Scientific and Technological Literature Publishing House, with Ruan as editor-in-chief. All of these events were strong signs indicating the establishment and development of sexology in China. More and more sexual social surveys, publications on sex, and development of academic sexological journals and societies have followed.

As early as 1984, a project on survey and analysis of sex, love, marriage, family conflict, and crimes was carried out by the Beijing Society for Studies on Marriage and Family. This project was headed by Ms. Wu Cangzhen, Associate Professor of Marriage Law at China Politics and Law University in Beijing.

The most famous and important sexual social survey is the Shanghai Sex Sociological Research Center's *National Sex Civilization Survey* headed by Dalin Liu, professor of Shanghai University. Using 40 paid assistants and volunteer interviewers, between February 1989 and April 1990, the center obtained responses to a 239 questions surveyed from 19,559 people in over half of China's twenty-seven provinces. The 1992 publication in China caused a sensation all over South-East Asia. Planned and executed from beginning to end without government order or interference, this survey was supported by private Chinese sponsorship. It has already greatly contributed to a more uninhibited dialogue about sexual issues within China and has strengthened the status and prestige of Chinese sexologists, and facilitated the organization of various regional and national associations and national and international conferences. An American translation of this monumental work will be published in 1997 by Continuum Publishing Company, New York. The most striking trend found in this study is the deterioration of the strong tie between sex and marriage. This survey was published in December 1992 in Shanghai by Joint Publishing, Sanlian Books Company, entitled *Zhongguo Dangdai Xingwenhua—Zhongguo Lianwanli "Xingwenming" Diaoza Baogao (Sexual Behavior in Modern China—A Report of the Nationwide "Sex Civilization" Survey on 20,000 Subjects in China).* It is a large volume, with 866 pages and 677,000 characters. (See Section 14, Addendum for details on this nationwide survey.)

Between 1985 and 1991, sex researcher Pan Suiming, Associate Professor of the Department of Sociology at the China Renmin University in Beijing, and his assistants conducted seven social surveys of sex. "Behavioral Analysis of Heterosexual Petting in Public—Observations on Chinese Civil Parks" reported on 23,532 cases between 1985 and 1989 in thirteen parks in six cities. "Dissemination of Three Kinds of Sexual Information and the Accepter's Response" involved 1,610 respondents in Shanghai, 1989; "Influence of Sex Knowledge and Attitude on Sexual Behavior—The Condition, Motive, and Orgasm" had 603 samples in Beijing, 1988-89, and "Relations Between Satisfaction of Sexual Life and the Marriage" was based on 977 samples in Beijing, 1989. Seven hundred sixty-six respondents participated in the "Chinese Readers' Answers to the Questionnaire in the Chinese Edition of The Kinsey Report since 1989," with the research still in progress. "Deep Sexual Behavior Survey—Relations of Sexual Mores, Ideas, Affection, and Behavior," with 1,279 samples in twenty-seven cities, 1989, indicated that nearly seven out of ten Chinese have had anal sex with heterosexual partners, and that men reached orgasm about 70 percent of the time in contrast to 40 percent for women. "A Sampling Survey on Students' Sexual Behavior in Every University and College in Beijing" examined 1,026 respondents in 1991.

Between 1985 and 1992, more than three hundred books on sexuality were published in mainland China, including the Chinese translations of classical works by Sigmund Freud, Havelock Ellis, Margaret Mead, Alfred C. Kinsey, and R. Van Gulik. The first professional academic journal of sexology, *Sexology of China,* was published in March 1992 by Beijing Medical University.

On May 23, 1988, the country's first college-level sexology course was introduced at China People's University in Beijing. This special two-week program, called "Training Workshop on Sex Science," consisted of workshops on twenty topics, conducted by seventeen professors and experts. The program was attended by 120 people from twenty-six of China's twenty-eight provinces. As of mid-1993, 26.7 percent of the universities and colleges in China have a course on human sexuality or sex education.

Since 1987, a series of six nationwide conferences on sexology have been held in China. For example, the Sixth Chinese Congress of Science of Sex, was held on May 3, 1992, in Nanjing, the capital of Jiangsu Province. About five hundred experts attended the congress, over four hundred academic papers in the fields of sex education, sociology of sex, psychology of sex, sexual medicine, and STDs were accepted by the congress. The First International Conference of Sexology was held on September 12 to 15, 1992, in Shanghai. Over twenty participants came from thirteen foreign countries, and over three hundred participants from all over China. About a hundred academic papers on sexual medicine, sex education, sociology of sex, and psychology of sex were accepted by the conference.

There are two important Chinese sexological periodicals:

Sexology (formerly *Sexology of China, Journal of Chinese Sexology*) (started in 1992). Journal Address: Beijing Medical University, 38 Xue Yuan Road, Beijing 100083, The People's Republic of China. Editor's Address: The Public Health Building (Fourth Floor), Beijing Medical University, No. 83 Hua Yuan Road, Beijing 100086, China

Apollo and Selene. A bilingual Chinese/English magazine of sexology published in Shanghai by the Asian Federation for Sexology started in the summer of 1993. Address: Asian Federation (Society) for Sexology., 2 Lane 31, Hua Ting Road, Shanghai, the People's Republic of China.

The main sexological organizations in China are:

Chinese Sex Education Research Society. Director: Dr. Jiahuo Hong. (Founded in Shanghai in 1985.). Address: The Shanghai College of Traditional Chinese Medicine, 530 Ling Ling Road, Shanghai, 200032, The People's Republic of China

Shanghai Sex Education Research Society, founded in Shanghai in 1986. Address: The Shanghai College of Traditional Chinese Medicine, 530 Ling Ling Road, Shanghai, 200032, The People's Republic of China.

Sexology of China Association (Founded in Beijing in 1995; preparatory committee founded in 1990). Director: Professor Guangchao Wang, M.D. Address: Beijing Medical University, 38 Xue Yuan Road, Beijing, 100083, The People's Republic of China.

Institute for Research in Sexuality and Gender. Address: Professor Suiming Pan, Director, Post Office Box 23, Renmin University of China, 39# Hai Dian Road, Beijing 100872, People's Republic of China; Fax: 01-256-6380.

Chinese Association of Sex Education. Address: Mercy Memorial Foundation, 11F, 171 Roosevelt Road, Section 3, Taipei, Taiwan. Republic of China. Phone: 886-2/369-6752; Fax: 886-2/365-7410.

China Family Planning Association. Address: 1 Bci Li, Shengguzhuang, He Ping Li, Beijing, People's Republic of China.

China Sexology Association. Address: Number 38, XueYuan Lu, Haidion, Beijing 100083, People's Republic of China. Phone: 86-1/209-1244; Fax: 86-1/209-1548.

Shanghai Family Planning Association. Address: 122 South Shan Xi ltoad, Shanghai 200040, People's Republic of China. Phone: 86-21/2794968; Fax: 86-21/2472262 Ext. 18.

Shanghai International Center for Population Communication China (SICPC). Address: 122 South Shan Xi Road, Shanghai 200040, People's Republic of China. Phone: 86-21/247-2262; Fax: 86-21/247-3049.

*14. The 1989-1990 Survey of Sexual Behavior in Modern China: A Report of the Nationwide "Sex Civilization" Survey on 20,000 Subjects in China**

M. P. LAU

A. The Survey

This is the report of a survey of sexual behavior in the People's Republic of China, conducted from 1989 to 1990. Unprecedented in scope and scale, the survey involved twenty-eight sites (cities, towns, and villages) in fifteen of the twenty-seven provinces or autonomous regions. A total of 21,500 questionnaires, with 239 items covering a wide range of variables were distributed, and 19,559 of the returned replies were found suitable for study. About five hundred investigators were involved, including about two hundred field workers, most of whom were female volunteers. There was a caucus of about forty core leaders, with coordinating headquarters at the Shanghai Sex Sociology Research Center. The main academic leaders were Dalin Liu, Liping Chou, and Peikuan Yao of Shanghai and Minlun Wu (M. L. Ng) of Hong Kong.

This study has been compared to the *Kinsey Reports* (1948, 1953) in the popular media (Burton, 1990). For the first time in history, we have extensive scientific data on the sexual behavior of the contemporary Chinese, who comprise 22 percent of the world population. Information is available on puberty, romantic love, mating, marriage, marital life, marital sex, premarital sex, extramarital sex, abortions, divorces, as well as data on

---

*Editor's Note: The following section is adapted from M. P. Lau's detailed analysis of the original 1989-1990 Chinese version of the nationwide Kinsey-like survey of *Sexual Behavior in China.* This survey was published in Chinese in 1992; an English translation is scheduled to be published by Continuum (New York) in 1997. Lau's review-essay was published in *Transcultural Psychiatric Research Review* (1995, volume 32, pp.137-156). The *Encyclopedia*'s editor, R. T. Francoeur greatly appreciates the permission of Dr. Lau and Laurence J. Kirmayer, M.D., editor of the *Transcultural Psychiatric Research Review,* to include Lau's critique in this chapter.

family planning, women's issues, prostitution, pornography, sexual transgressions, and sexual variances, both as to attitudes and behavior.

In this review-essay, I provide a synopsis of some of the major findings of the survey through eight profiles of male and female adolescents and college students, urban and rural married couples, a female prostitute, and a male sex offender. I will then present a brief critique of the study methodology and suggestions for future research.

B. Adolescent Sexuality

In this section, I present two composite profiles constructed from ninety-one tables of statistics compiled during the national survey of twenty-eight secondary (or middle) schools in ten Chinese cities or suburbs. Secondary schools were not common in the countryside and the rural population was difficult to survey. In all, 6,900 questionnaires were issued and 6,092 were collected and analyzed. Each questionnaire contained forty-two multiple-choice questions with some open response categories. While the sample surveyed is not representative of all secondary schools owing to resource constraints, attempts were made to achieve as much diversity as possible. Some significant influences on sexual attitudes and practices were demonstrated, such as exposure to modernization, degree of enlightenment, and gender differences.

In 1989, there were 47,717,000 secondary school students in China (4.29 percent of the national population of 1,111,910,000), of whom 58.4 percent were male. Fully 97.8 percent of children reaching school age were sent to primary schools, and 74.6 percent of primary school graduates proceeded to secondary schools. There are six grades in each secondary school: Junior Middle 1, 2, and 3, and Senior Middle 1, 2, and 3, and the age range is normally 12 to 18. In the sample studied, the mean age was 15.53 (SD = 1.78). The features described in the profiles represent the means, modes, medians, or usual ranges, or the proportions in the sample. There is a wealth of detail in the book for further reference.

Profile 1: An Adolescent Female

The typical female adolescent respondent is a 15.5-year-old student in an urban or suburban secondary school. She comes from a stable family of workers or cadres, and has one sibling. She reached puberty at age 13, with menarche in the summer, and development of secondary sexual characteristics. (This is a later age compared with secondary school students in Hong Kong or Japan, but earlier than that described in China twenty-five years ago). At age 14.5, she began to have sexual interests, and desired to associate with boys, mostly for socialization or mutual assistance, or because of a "crush" on a boy for his good looks, but she has been too shy or "busy" to take action. (For comparison, a Japanese peer would have begun to have such interests and desires at age 12 to 13). She acquired most of her sexual knowledge from books, magazines, and movies, and would feel excited by casual physical touches and by conversation on sexual topics.

Among the secondary school girls in the survey, 7.4 percent wished for some bodily contact with a male, and 12.1 percent reported having been aroused to desire sexual intercourse. (Again, these percentages are much lower than those of Japanese peers). More than a third of secondary school girls reported having male friends since age 14, without infatuation and often in group settings. By 15.5 years of age, 11.1 percent were dating boys and 6 percent were "in love." The legal age for a female to marry in China is 20, and most girls think marrying early is not good or "would affect study."

Only 4.7 percent of adolescent girls reported a history of masturbation, usually since age 13.5; about 50 percent said they continued the practice. (In Japan, 9 percent of secondary schoolgirls have masturbated, and most persist in the habit). While 44.3 percent of female adolescents stated masturbation is "bad," almost 40 percent said they did not understand the question.

Less than 2 percent of adolescent girls have engaged in each of kissing, hugging, or sexual touching and only 1 percent reported having sexual intercourse (slightly higher in southern China). These rates are far below those in Japanese schoolgirls (up to 25.5 percent and 8.7 percent, respectively).

In well-developed urban areas, adolescent sex education has been available in classrooms, but has focused on physiology and hygiene, with little information on coitus, pregnancy, childbirth, contraception, homosexuality, paraphilias, and sexually transmitted diseases. Secondary schoolgirls would like more guidance on issues of romantic love, sexual impulses, and socialization. They discuss sexual issues with their mothers, sisters, and female peers, but not with teachers or fathers.

Profile 2: An Adolescent Male

The typical male adolescent respondent is a 15.5-year-old secondary school boy who comes from a stable family of workers or cadres and has one sibling. He has had seminal emissions since age 14.5, and most have been spontaneous nocturnal emissions. He has started developing secondary sexual characteristics. (These maturational milestones are later than those of a similar youth in Japan, but earlier than those in China twenty-five years ago.) At age 14.5, he began to show sexual interests, and wished to associate with girls, mostly because of attraction to their appearance or "tender disposition," but he was too shy or "busy" to act upon his feelings. (A Japanese boy would have commenced to have such interests and desires at age 12 to 13). He obtained most of his sexual knowledge from books, magazines, and movies, and has seen pictures of female nudity and experienced some casual sexual touching.

About one third of adolescent males reported desire for bodily contact with females, and 42.9 percent said they had been aroused enough to crave sexual intercourse. (Again, these percentages are much lower than those of Japanese peers).

Although almost half of male adolescents said that they had had female platonic friends since age 14, often in group activities, only 12.7 percent were currently dating a girl, and 7.6 percent reported being "in love." The legal age for a male in China to marry is 22, and most boys agree that marrying early is not good or "would affect study."

Only 12.5 percent of male adolescents reported a history of masturbation, usually starting at age 13.5; half reported they had continued the practice. (In Japan, 30 percent of junior high school students have masturbated, and fully 81.2 percent of those in senior high school, with most students continuing the habit). More than half of adolescent males consider masturbation "bad," but 21.2 percent said they did not understand the question.

Less than 5 percent of secondary school males have engaged in each of kissing, hugging, or sexual touching, and 0.9 percent have had sexual intercourse (slightly more in Southern China). (These rates are remarkably low compared to those in Japan, where up to 23.1 percent of high school boys have experienced sexual kissing and 11.5 percent coitus).

Adolescent boys tend to discuss their needs and problems with male peers, rather than with teachers, parents, or siblings.

C. College Students

In 1989, there were about 82,000 post-secondary students in China. A study of this group is of immense importance as they are destined to become the future leaders of the country. Intellectually well endowed and highly educated, they are still young, malleable, open minded, and sensitive to new ideas and trends. In the process of maturation as scholars, they confront the various phenomena associated with modernization and accelerating change. They interact with a "campus culture,' which may be a cultural melting pot and a frontier of novel concepts and ideologies. Restricted by demands for sexual abstinence and expectations of monogamy, they try their best to cope with their libido and desire. Their perceptions, perspectives, beliefs, and behavior will have profound effects on the future of nation-building, participation in the world community, and global stability.

This section presents two composite profiles condensed from 136 tables of statistics collected during the survey of twenty-four post-secondary colleges (including universities, teachers' colleges, academies of traditional medicine, training centers for cadres and security personnel, and an oceanography institute) in nine metropolitan areas. The institutions were selected according to practicality and diversity. Questionnaires with sixty-three items were distributed in classrooms and the purpose of the investigation explained. Confidentiality was assured. In addition to the group administration, some individual interviews were conducted. A total of 3,360 valid replies were analyzed. The mean age was 20.28 years ($SD = 3.13$) with 56.8 percent male.

Profile 3: A Female University Student

The typical female college student in the survey is a 20-year-old student in the faculty of arts. Her father was college-educated and holds a professional, technical, or managerial job. She had menarche at age 13.5, followed by the development of secondary sexual characteristics. She was unprepared for menarche and sought advice from her mother or peers. She received little sex education and acquired most of her sexual knowledge from books, news media, novels, peers, her mother, and her sisters. She found her teachers and parents "ignorant, busy, uncaring, conservative, and rigid." She would feel excited by depictions of sexual matters, and has been exposed to nudity through pictures in the media.

She thinks romantic love should be allowed but "properly guided," that the main purpose of copulation is to have a family, and that the female can be an active partner during sexual intercourse. She believes that premarital sex may be acceptable if the partners are mutually in love and willing, but extramarital sex should be censured, even if consensual. She considers homosexuality to be a perversion or illness, and would offer comfort to a homosexual friend and advise him or her to seek psychiatric treatment. She feels that homosexuality is something to be ashamed of and pitied but not severely punished.

Fully 70 percent of college women were not content with their bodies, with concerns about being overweight, hirsute, or other features; 25 percent were not satisfied with their secondary sexual characteristics, for example, thinking that their breasts are undersized. While 15.6 percent did not like their own gender, 42.8 percent stated they would prefer to be a male if they had a choice.

Among the college women surveyed, 16.5 percent had a history of masturbation, starting from age 13 to 14 and 8.2 percent still masturbated at a frequency of about once a week. Most respondents thought masturbation is "harmless" and "normal."

While 63.4 percent of female college students in the sample desired a heterosexual relationship, only 6.3 percent of them had had a sexual partner. Sexual contacts (including kissing, embracing, genital touching, and coitus) were infrequent and covert and commonly began after age 17. Contraception involved the use of "safe periods," pills, or condoms.

While 5.8 percent reported an inclination towards exhibitionism and 2.8 percent were predisposed to transvestitism, interest in other paraphilias was uncommon. The majority (87.3 percent) of college women reported that on seeing a nude female in a public bathroom, they would probably feel indifferent, but 3.9 percent said they might "come to like it."

Homosexual contacts were infrequent: 8.4 percent reported having been kissed or caressed, 3.2 percent had experienced homosexual masturbation, and less than 3 percent reported genital-to-genital contacts; 0.7 percent reported they would engage in homosexual contact if the opportunity arose.

Profile 4: A Male University Student

The typical male college student in the survey is a 20-year-old student in the faculty of engineering, science, or medicine. His parents had post-secondary education, and his father is a professional, technical, or managerial worker. He had his first seminal emission at age 14.5, followed soon by the appearance of pubic and then facial hair. (Compared with his secondary school counterparts, his sexual development started at a slightly later age). He received little sex education and was quite unprepared when he had his first seminal emission. He did not ask anyone for an explanation.

He acquired most of his sexual knowledge from books on hygiene and health, news media, novels and pornographic art, and from his male peers. He found his parents and teachers insensitive and outdated in knowledge and attitude. He holds liberal views about romantic love and is permissive about reading sexual material. He thinks that masturbation is harmless and normal. He believes that sexual intercourse would enhance love and give physical pleasure, as well as serving the purpose of building a family. He endorses the idea of a female being an active partner during sexual intercourse.

He thinks premarital sex would be acceptable if the partners are both willing and mutually in love, especially if they are prepared to marry each other, and extramarital sex, if consensual, may be permitted under certain circumstances. He would be quite aroused by references to sexual matters, and has seen pictures of nudes in the media, but is unlikely to have seen women in the nude.

One fourth of college males were not satisfied with some of their secondary sexual characteristics, such as sparsity of pubic hair or perception of the penis as undersized. A larger proportion (70 percent) were not content with other aspects of their body, such as shortness of stature, presence of pimples or freckles, and sparsity or grayness of scalp or facial hair. Gender dysphoria was uncommon, and only 8.3 percent of male college students surveyed wished to be female.

Almost two thirds of college males (59 percent) had a history of masturbation, starting at age 14 to 16, and 39.5 percent continued to masturbate at the rate of about once a week. Sexual contacts, including kissing, embracing, genital touching, and coitus, were reported to be infrequent and mostly covert. These activities usually began after age 17 and the male tended to take an active role. Only 12.5 percent of college males reported that they had had sexual partner(s), usually only one. Contraception involved "safe periods," condoms, and coitus interruptus.

While most male college students considered homosexuality a perversion or illness, to be sympathized with and offered treatment, 11.9 percent conceived of homosexuality as normal behavior for a small group of people. Homosexual contacts were infrequent, with 7.0 percent reporting kissing or caressing, 8.6 percent homosexual masturbation, and less than 3 percent genital-to-genital or anal touching; 1.5 percent would consider seeking someone out to engage in homosexual activity.

Paraphilias were rare among male college students, with 5.6 percent feeling prone to exhibitionism, but hardly any reporting other paraphilic tendencies. On seeing a nude male in a public bathroom, most would feel indifferent, but 5.4 percent said they might come to "like it."

When asked how they would respond if they found out that their fiancee had lost her virginity to another male, 20 percent of male college students said that they would leave her, but 60 percent would find it tolerable.

D. Married Couples

This section presents composite portraits of an urban couple based on 6,210 married persons surveyed in fifteen cities (nine coastal and six inland urban centers), and a rural couple typical of 1,392 married residents surveyed in three villages. A mixture of random and non-random sampling methods was used, steering a fine line between what was practical (e.g., considering the difficulties of gathering data from illiterate or unsophisticated persons) and what would be theoretically desirable (e.g., relative representativeness). A total of 396 tables of actuarial data were compiled, covering a wide range of sexual, marital, and family variables. There was a preponderance of female interviewers and interviewees. Many volunteer field workers came from women's groups, such as labor unions, family planning units, and obstetrical teams, and they were able to build good rapport with women respondents, who often appeared eager to share their intimate knowledge of family life with those whom they could trust. Overall, 68. 1 percent of urban and 78.2 percent of rural interviewees were female.

Profile 5: An Urban Couple

The spouses in the typical urban married couple in the survey were about 36 to 37 years of age and of above-average education compared with the general national population. They reported their health status as average or above average. The husband was a professional, technical, office, or managerial worker, and had received slightly more education than his wife, being twice as likely to have attended a post-secondary institute. The wife was a professional, technical, factory, or office worker. They have been married for about eleven years. They married of their own will, after an introduction by a third person and a period of courtship.

They consider mutual "love" and "understanding" more important in marriage than material comfort, political views, or evaluation by society. They believe that the purpose of marital sex is primarily to satisfy emotional and physical needs, rather than to fulfill an obligation or a "tradition" or to achieve reproduction, and there should be no prudery about it. They have sexual intercourse four to five times per month on average. The couple would like to have children because the latter "would add interest to life" and it is an aspect of "social responsibility." They would like to have a boy and a girl.

Of urban couples surveyed, 60 percent considered their marriage satisfactory, with greater satisfaction reported by the male partner, those with more education, those in professional, technical, or managerial positions, and those in the earlier years of marriage. Of those surveyed, 55.5 percent indicated good or fair (25.3 percent) levels of sexual satisfaction. Husbands reported greater enjoyment of coitus and gave more importance to coital frequency, styles of intercourse, and climaxes. The duration of foreplay tended to be brief, most often less than ten minutes, and gave less pleasure to the woman. In case of sexual disharmony, 44 percent felt there should be open discussion, 13.4 percent would seek medical help, and 24 percent would just "leave it" alone. Most couples endorsed women taking initiative in sex, such an attitude being especially common among males, the better educated, and in the southern cities. As urban married women gain more freedom, independence, and self-esteem, they feel less compelled to have sex against their will, and would ask to be excused without feeling guilty.

Most couples experienced their first sexual intercourse on their wedding night, but prenuptial sex was admitted by 24.9 percent of urban husbands and 15.8 percent of urban wives. It should be noted that premarital coitus was most often (80 percent) consummated with a "future spouse," and such behavior was endorsed by a majority (90 percent) of the urban couples polled. Sex before matrimony with someone who is not a "future spouse" tended to occur among urban youths in southern China, soldiers stationed in cities, and the less educated. (The number of abortions of premarital pregnancies has been on the rise, reaching 16 percent of those age 20 and over and single in a city in Jiangsu, and 90 percent of first abortions in a city in Zhejiang, both cities in the vicinity of Shanghai.)

Higher frequency of intercourse was associated with younger age, the earlier years in marriage, highest or lowest levels of education, being a manual or service worker, more privacy of the bedroom, temperate climate, and greater sense of obligation to perform. Sexual intercourse occurs most often just before sleep among younger and middle-aged couples, and at "no fixed time" among the young and the elderly. In terms of sexual practices, 56.5 percent of couples change positions during sex, and 65.2 percent are nude sometimes or often during sex; nudity during sex is more frequent among the young, the better educated, and in the southern cities.

Questions about orgasms were not asked as the investigators had found it quite difficult to elicit such information, but enjoyment of "sexual pleasure" was found to depend on the techniques, experience, and relationship; sexual pleasure had a more gradual onset in women, both physiologically and psychologically. Most couples reported they experienced sexual pleasure frequently (especially males) or sometimes (especially females), with highest rates in southern China. In a sampling of 1,279 men and women in 41 cities, Suiming Pan found men reach orgasm 7.2 times out of every 10 attempots; this contrasts with 4.1 times for women. In Dalin Liu's survey, one third of the urban women and one fourth of the rural women claimed to experience a feeling of pleasure (*kuaigan*) "very often," while 58.2 and 76.8 percent, respectively, experienced it "sometimes."

A history of masturbation was obtained from 17.1 percent of respondents—much more often from husbands than from wives, and from couples in southern cities—but nearly all of the respondents claimed it happened only occasionally. While 41.7 percent regarded masturbation as a "bad habit" and 13.1 percent considered it normal, fully 30 percent gave no clear answer. Only 0.5 percent admitted homosexual experience, but considerable denial or ignorance was suspected.

Among urban husbands, 10.2 percent admitted to a history of extramarital sex. Extramarital sex was more common among service or manual workers, or businessmen, those less than 25 years of age or more than 56, and those espousing a liberal or hedonistic attitude towards life. Urban wives were unlikely to have risked extramarital sex, but it was more likely to occur in middle age. These rates are far below those published in the Kinsey reports (1948; 1953). Nevertheless, the impact of extramarital affairs may be considerable. During divorce proceedings in five cities in China in 1985, the occurrence of extramarital affairs was confessed in two thirds of the cases. In Shenzhen, a town bordering Hong Kong, 91.8 percent of divorce cases in 1987 involved a "third person." While 66.2 percent of married urban respondents said that they accept the national policy of having only one child per family, 28.5 percent think such a restriction unreasonable. If they had only a daughter, 35.5 percent would want to have one more child, but not if this would incur punishment from the government. Birth control measures used by urban couples included: diaphragms (42.8 percent), tubal ligation (9.4 percent), other mechanical means (18.3 percent), pills (5.9 percent), vasectomy (2.3 percent), other methods (e.g., "safe periods," coitus interruptus, unknown) (15.5 percent), and none (5.8 percent).

Sexual knowledge was generally quite limited and resource material not readily available, especially to women. About two thirds (62.4 percent) of urban couples had read one of the four popular basic manuals on sexual knowledge available at the time of the survey, such as the one written for the newly wed, which mostly consider anatomy and physiology. Additional sexual knowledge was obtained from books, movies, and radio (35.6 percent), through personal experience (22.7 percent), and from same-sex peers or those in counseling positions. Most couples (70.4 percent) are interested in reading or viewing media with sexual themes, but 48.9 percent have found opportunities lacking. Women would like to know more about child education and physical hygiene, while men are interested in sexual techniques and interpersonal skills. Although 61.8 percent of urban couples would explain the birth process to a child, 25.4 percent would evade the question, and the rest would express displeasure or indifference, or give a false answer.

Profile 6: A Rural Couple

The typical rural married couple surveyed were about 35 years old, of average education compared with the general national population, and reported their health status as average or above average. They were engaged in farming, herding, fishing, or forestry, and were unlikely to have received post-secondary education. They have been married for about 11 years; he at age 23 and she at 22. They married of their own will (wholly or partly), although match-making was prevalent until one or two generations ago, and still occurred in a few locales.

They consider "love" and "understanding" more important in their union than the opinions of society. They believe that the main aims of marital sex are to fulfill physical and emotional needs, to go along with tradition, and to accomplish reproduction, and that they need not be prudish about it. They have sexual intercourse five to six times per month on average. They would like to have children, mostly for the sake of old age security, but also to propagate their lineage.

Of rural couples surveyed, 65 percent regard their marriage as satisfactory. Greater satisfaction was reported by the female partner, those better educated, and those under 25 or over 45 years of age. In case of sexual disharmony, 44 percent would engage in open discussion, 23.2 percent would seek medical help, and 21 percent would just "leave it" alone.

Most married rural couples experienced sexual intercourse for the first time on the wedding night, but premarital sex was admitted by 7.3 percent of rural husbands and 17.3 percent of rural wives. Premarital coitus was usually performed with a future spouse, and such behavior was endorsed by the vast majority of rural couples surveyed. Sex before marriage with someone who was not a future spouse occurred more commonly among older males and females when the feudal system allowed sexual permissiveness in certain forms of social transactions, and also among those who are younger, more educated, and liberal minded.

Higher frequency of intercourse was associated with more demand by the husband and greater compliance by the wife, having been married for a longer duration, and temperate climate. Sexual coitus occurred most often just before sleep, but also often "at no fixed time," as rural couples tended to have a less structured schedule of daily life compared with their urban counterparts.

About half (45 percent) of rural couples reported changing position during sex, and 57.2 percent said they were nude sometimes or often during sex; sexual nudity was more common among the young, the less educated, and in southern climates. In Shanxi province, some farmers traditionally sleep naked.

A history of masturbation was obtained from 10.1 percent of rural husbands or wives, more often from those in the South; nearly all described it as episodic. Most (73.4 percent) considered masturbation a "bad habit," but 9.6 percent deemed it "natural." Only 2.3 percent admitted homosexual experiences, suggesting considerable ignorance about the term.

Among rural married couples, the level of sexual satisfaction reported was good (66.6 percent) or fair (27.6 percent), with wives more easily satisfied than husbands. The duration of foreplay tended to be brief, usually five minutes or less, but neither partner had high expectations of gratification from it. Most couples endorsed women taking initiative in sex (this attitude was more common among males, the better educated, and in south China), but they would still prefer the male partner to be more active.

Among rural husbands, 9.3 percent admitted to a history of extramarital sex; higher rates were found among service or manual workers or businessmen, those under 25 or over 56 years of age, and those who gave evidence of a "pleasure-seeking predisposition" on several attitude measures. Rural wives were unlikely to have experienced extramarital sex.

Most rural couples would like to have a boy and a girl, but 48.5 percent would accept having only one child. After having a daughter, 60.3 percent want an additional child, and 6 percent still want one at the risk of sustaining some official penalty. In a 1989 survey, 68.1 percent of rural women wanted to have two children, 25.7 percent wanted one child, and 3.1 percent did not want children. Slightly lower percentages were found among rural men. Contraceptive methods utilized include: diaphragm (50.8 percent), tubal ligation (21.8 percent), pills (7.5 percent), vasectomy (1.2 percent), others (12.3 percent), and none (6.4 percent). On the other hand, infertility due to sexual dysfunctions was common (e.g., more than 25 percent of about 40,000 family planning counseling cases seen in 1984 to 1989), but most were said to be somewhat amenable to medical or herbal therapy.

Sexual knowledge was generally quite deficient, and resources not easily available, although 77.1 percent of rural couples had read one of the four popular basic manuals on sexual knowledge available at the time of the survey. Otherwise, the pattern was similar to that of urban couples. While 47.8 percent of rural couples would explain the birth process to a child, 33.8 percent would evade the question, and the rest would ignore or upbraid the child, or give a false answer.

Comment

An overview of the accounts of urban and rural married couples given in this section shows the emergence of two patterns: (1) respondents who are traditional and conservative in ideology, cautious and guarded towards novel ideas, moralistic and suppressive of self-expression, and less imbued with modern education tend to reside inland and in rural territories, are service or manual workers, and are more commonly female; and (2) respondents who are modernistic and individualistic in orientation, liberal and open in attitude, rational and objective in deliberation, and have been exposed to more contemporary and/or Western ideology tend to reside in urban areas, near sea-coasts or in southern China, are professionals or technical workers, and are more often male.

Of course, there are many exceptions to these broad generalizations. Those who are not well educated may also be gullible and suggestible, and experience sexual permissiveness as a relic of feudal systems, such as variations of a master-slave relationship, indigenous forms of marital or quasi-marital arrangements or cohabitation, such as concubinage and other forms of polygamy (McGough, 1981). Other situational, subcultural, idiosyncratic, or deviant variations in sexual behavior are noted throughout the book. The investigators also present detailed analyses of factors affecting sexual satisfaction and sexual pleasure as well as data on marital cohesion, domestic conflicts, marital breakdown, and sex in old age.

We see in this section a spectrum of variations in sexual behavior corresponding to the different stages of adaptation and change, resistance and retrenchment in response to modern and Western ideologies. There has been a general liberalization of attitudes, which is not yet matched by comparable changes in practice. Keenly aware of the dangers of an abrupt eruption of sexual instinctual drive, and deeply ingrained in a tradition of moderation and communal responsibility, the writers of the book repeatedly urge caution, restraint, and "proper socialization." While stressing the importance of being knowledgeable and educated, and of individual entitlement and gratification, heavy emphasis is also placed on family harmony, social stability, and the inculcation of moral values by advice and counseling, didactic education, and "propaganda." An analysis of sexual mores and superego and their possible practical impacts can be found in the books by Ng (1990) and by Wen and colleagues (1990) and in the paper by Ng and Lau (1990).

E. Sex Offenders

In the 1980s, rates of crime in China rose in leaps and bounds, with alarming increases in sexual offenses in the young and relatively less increase in violent crimes. This section presents composites of a female prostitute and a male sex offender with modal characteristics abstracted from 137 tables of statistical information, gathered in a survey of inmates of prisons and reformatories, supervised by security and reform officials, with guarantees of strict confidentiality. These institutions were located in nine areas, with most of the respondents from Shanghai (49 percent), Chengdu (22.8 percent), and Soochow (11 percent). A total of 2,136 subjects took part,with 67.5 percent males; 385 were female prostitutes.

Unfortunately, the various kinds of sex offenses were lumped together (except for female prostitution), and the data analyzed as a whole. Subjects included categories of "criminals," people with "infractions of the law," and those accused of "misconducts (wrongdoings, misdemeanors)." The judicial system gives latitude to officials to grade antisocial behavior and to dispose of violators according to pragmatic and situational considerations. For details and the extent of variations, the reader must refer to the book under review and its bibliography.

Profile 7: A Female Prostitute

The typical incarcerated female prostitute in the survey was 20 years old and came from a rural family, financially "average" or "above average." She was discontented with her lot and inclined to seek more money, pleasure, or adventure. She left school early and may have retained some part-time manual work. She may have been betrothed or married, with an "average" or discordant relationship, but a sex life that has been mostly satisfactory. Although emphasizing feelings as an important element in human relationship, she was cynical about romantic love, and may have become bitter and vindictive after she had been cheated or abused. She was ambivalent towards traditional feminine roles, chastity, and sexual restraint, but still viewed them as ideals and wished that she could conform.

She first ran afoul of the law after age 15. She was often seen as a victim of circumstances as well as an offender, and evoked sympathy from public officials, who would subject her to criticism, warning, "education," and "administrative discipline," before instituting legal penal measures, such as labor reform, and "thought reform." While incarcerated, she would indulge in daydreaming or in artistic diversions to sublimate her libido.

The number of prostitutes, pimps, and their patrons known to the law has been increasing rapidly in China, especially in Shanghai and Guangzhou. Prostitutes make up most of the nation's female sex offenders. The survey data and clinical observation show that prostitutes tend to be young and immature, vain and "insatiable," given to pleasure-seeking rather than to toil and tedium, vulnerable to temptation, and deficient in self-restraint. Also noteworthy are the contributing social factors of inequality of gender status, lack of emotional nurturing and support for dependency needs in parental and marital homes, and the prevalence of opportunities for deviant outlets. The survey also uncovered the "low quality" or "poor civilization" of the parents and other family members, in the forms of less education, ignorance, narrow world views, weakness of bonding, and lack of moral guidelines. These social forces need to be considered in any plans for prevention. After release from jail, 20 to 30 percent of female sex offenders released in Shanghai relapse. Relapse rates depend on the intensity of rehabilitation.

Profile 8: A Male Sex Offender

The typical incarcerated male sex offender in the survey was about 28 years old and single. He had some secondary school education and was a manual worker or tradesman. He had his first seminal emission at age 16.5, still has nocturnal emissions once or twice a month, and masturbates about six times a month. He first witnessed sexual coitus at age 17, most likely at a peer's home or in a movie or videotape. He admits having "average" or "strong" sexual desire, and exposure to sexual scenes tends to arouse him and predispose him to errant sexual behavior.

He came from a home where his parents, especially his mother, had little education but an "average" or "comfortable" income, yet he still tended to feel deprived. He seldom talked to his parents and felt that family life was dull and meaningless. The family was generally permissive, but would express anger when a sexual offense or misconduct was committed. In a small percentage of cases, there was another family member with a history of criminal or sexually promiscuous behavior.

He emphasized the importance of sex and love, but relished instant pleasure. He would choose a partner based on appearance, feelings, and temperament, and would want a mate for sexual purpose even at an early age and outside the boundaries of wedlock. He likes movies, music, socializing, gossiping, womanizing, gambling, detective stories, and martial arts. He would be easily aroused by sexual material but may not act on it. Such material has become increasingly public and readily accessible. He probably has a few friends with a history of sexual offense or misconduct. He acquired his sexual knowledge mostly from his peers or the media, rather than from parents, siblings, or teachers, and has often found his questions unanswered.

Most offenders were convicted of their first sexual offense before age 29. The most common offenses were "hooliganism" (a vague umbrella term comprising various kinds of uncivil, indecorous, unmannerly, or licentious behavior), "promiscuity," rape, and sex with a minor. Other male sex offenses included bigamy, extramarital relations, abetting prostitution, male prostitution, incest, and enforced sex with the aged or the disabled. There has been a trend to commit crimes less by violent means, and more by deception and enticement. The survey data and clinical observation show that the male sex offenders are generally immature, chauvinistic, and emotionally needy. They are said to be of "low quality," and their families and social backgrounds are described the same way. Married male sex offenders reported fairly good marital and sexual relationships with their spouses, with frequent sexual intercourse (about ten times per month).

Upon conviction, most offenders expressed regret and cooperated with the sentence. While in prison, they try to suppress their sexual drives, but 6.3 percent admit to masturbation and 0.7 percent to homosexual activity. While some psychological or medical therapy may be provided for this sexual frustration, there has been no general policy to cope with the problem.

F. Comments on the Research Methods

Technically, the nature and scope of this survey made the task very difficult. Sexuality is a matter of privacy and confidentiality and a topic often misunderstood and stigmatized. The peasantry was difficult to reach, in terms of both logistics and communication. There was little financial support, especially after the Tiananmen events. However, there was a ground swell of moral support from both inside and outside China, and many "comrades" from the tightly organized, stratified bureaucratic infrastructure in the nation, especially from women's groups, contributed their time, energy, and ingenuity, frequently working "to the point of exhaustion." Professor Liu and the core leaders were able to marshal the support of diverse groups at various levels in governmental, academic, educational, legal, labor, industrial, literary, media, and publishing sectors. The results have been partially presented at conferences inside and outside China, but since the book was written in Chinese, a wider dissemination of the findings awaits translation into other languages. An English translation of this full report is planned for 1997 by Continuum (New York), the publisher of this *International Encyclopedia of Sexuality*.

The investigators were well aware of the limitations of the study. They experienced numerous stumbling blocks and frustrations, and encountered criticism and derision. It was not possible to obtain a completely representative sample, but a study of selected mainstream or significant groups in accessible locales is still very meaningful. Efforts were made to collect data from diverse parts of China, and a mixture of random and non-random sampling was used. The large sample sizes may allow statistical adjustments for some of the biases in further analysis.

The questionnaires were as comprehensive as circumstances permitted. In the interest of not being too intrusive, many questions were addressed only to attitudes and beliefs, as respondents would feel too hesitant to report actual behavior or practice in some areas.

Limitation of time and resources precluded the compilation of an index. Materials on some special topics are scattered throughout the book. For example, data on homosexuality have to be found laboriously from more than ten places, and information on premarital sex must be traced from some eight sources among the pages. Bibliographical notes are appended to each section, but even the names of European authors are written in Chinese.

G. Discussion and Conclusion

This ground-breaking study is of immense value from a heuristic and theoretical point of view. No study of human sexuality can be complete without including a major human culture of the world and its most populous country. This study should provoke further questions at biological, psychological, sociocultural, and historical levels, and stimulate the emergence of new hypotheses and concepts, both in Chinese and other cultures. The methodology developed can serve as a template for future testing and improvement.

The practical import of this study cannot be overemphasized. It should equip the nation with more knowledge to meet the challenges of sexuality both at the individual and at the societal levels. Wary of the perils of a sexual "revolution" with sudden release of pent-up drives, the authors repeatedly stress the importance of an interpersonal perspective and "sociological imperative." Despite the authors' claim to be non-authoritarian, many opinions and conclusions are judgmental and moralistic and delivered in a didactic, paternalistic tone not usually encountered in scientific writing.

As much as it is a towering accomplishment, this study should be placed in perspective by considering directions for future research. Professor Liu came up with a short list of tasks: further analysis of the data collected; more publicity and application of findings, and further study of special groups, such as homosexuals, ethnic minorities, the aged, the disabled, and servicemen. This inventory, however, is very limited and should be amplified to include the following: (1) improvement of the questionnaires and methodology; (2) extension of sampling, to include more under-represented groups, including the overseas Chinese, and to allow further cross-cultural comparisons; (3) replication of the study and follow-up in longitudinal studies; (4) detailed case studies of individuals, subcultures, communities, families, institutions, opinion leaders, practitioners, practices, policies, and polities in this field; (5) further interpretation in cultural and historical terms and contribution to theory building; and (6) study of the impact of sociocultural changes and biological breakthroughs.

Conclusion

TIMOTHY PERPER, PH.D.

Because the People's Republic of China is one of the most populous nations, decisions made by its people and by its government about sexuality directly affect its population growth and therefore have global importance. Since the establishment of the People's Republic in 1949, China has undergone immense and sometimes profoundly convulsive changes. A half-century ago, China was devastated by years of civil and external war, its people widely illiterate, and its poverty profound. No matter what one feels about the Mao dynasty—if that word is metaphorically permissible—the achievements of the Chinese people in the past fifty years have been awe-inspiring. China has become a major industrial power and its population is widely literate.

From the 1949 revolution onward, China's government has increasingly become deeply involved in the reproductive decision making of its citizens. Those who study sexuality and understand its implications for world population growth must surely hope that China's own scholars, and others who know its rich history, many languages, and varied cultures, will continue and expand their studies of sexuality in China. Because China is both a crucible and a harbinger of the future, these studies will be invaluable for documenting how decisions made by the Chinese people and government will inevitably affect the future of everyone on the earth.

Acknowledgment for Section 14: A Report of the Nationwide "Sex Civilization" Survey on 20,000 Subjects in China

The secretarial help of Christine H. K. Lau and of Lucie A. Wilk is hereby gratefully acknowledged.

References and Suggested Readings

Bullough, V. L. 1976. *Sexual Variance in Society and History.* Chicago: University of Chicago Press. Chapter 11: "Sexual Theory and Attitudes in Ancient China."

Burton, Sandra. 1990 (May 14). "China's Kinsey Report." *Time Magazine,* p. 95.

Burton, Sandra. 1988 (September 12). "The Sexual Revolution Hits China." *Time Magazine,* pp. 66-67.

Evans, Harriet. 1997. *Women and Sexuality in China: 1949 to the Present.* New York: Continuum.

Gil, V. E. 1991 (November). "An Ethnography of HIV/AIDS and Sexuality in the People's Republic of China." *Journal of Sex Research,* 28(4):521-37.

Kinsey, A. C., W. B. Pomeroy, and C. E. Martin. 1948. *Sexual Behavior in the Human Male.* Philadelphia: W. B. Saunders.

Kinsey, A. C., W. B. Pomeroy, C. E. Martin, and P. H. Gebhard. 1953. *Sexual Behavior in the Human Female.* Philadelphia: W.B. Saunders.

Kolodny, R., W. Masters, and V. Johnson. 1979. *Textbook of Sexual Medicine.* Boston: Little, Brown.

Lau, M. P. 1995. "Sex and Civilization in Modern China." (A review-essay on *Sexual Behavior in Modern China,* by Dalin Liu, M.L. Wu (Ng), and L Chou). *Transcultural Psychiatric Research Review,* 32:137-156.

Lau, M. P., and M. L. Ng. 1989. "Homosexuality in Chinese Culture." *Culture, Medicine, and Psychiatry,* 13:465-488.

Lieh-Mak, F., K. M. O'Hoy, and S. L. Luk. 1983. "Lesbianism in the Chinese of Hong Kong." *Archives of Sexual Behavior,* 12(1):21-30.

Liu, Dalin, M. L. Ng, L. P. Zhou, and E. J. Haeberle. 1992/1997. *Zhongguo Dangdai Xingwenhua: Zhongguo Lianwanli Xianwenming Diaozha Baogao. [Sexual Behavior in Modern China: Report on the Nationwide Survey of 20,000 Men and Women.]* (In Chinese) First Edition, 1992. Shanghai: Joint Publishing Co. English translation published by Continuum (New York), 1997.

Liu, Dalin L. 1993. *The Sex Culture of Ancient China* (In Chinese). Ningxia People Publishers and Xinhua Bookshops. ISBN 7-277-00935-1/I.204.

Liu, Dalin L., and M. L. Ng, eds. 1993 *Chinese Dictionary of Sexology.* Helungjian: People's Publication Co.

McGough, James P. 1981. "Deviant Marriage Patterns in Chinese Society." In A. Kleinman and T. Y. Lin (eds.). *Normal and Abnormal Behaviour in Chinese Culture* (pp. 171-201). Dordrecht, Holland: D. Reidel.

Ming, Wu. 1981. *New Knowledge on Prevention of Birth Defects.* Beijing: People's Medical Publishing House.

Needham, Joseph. 1983. *Science and Civilization in China, Volume 5, Part V: Spagyrical Discovery and Invention: Physiological Alchemy.* "Sexuality and the Role of Theories of Generation." Cambridge, UK: Cambridge University Press.

Ng, M. L. (ed.). 1990. *Theories of Sex.* Hong Kong: Commercial Press.

Ng, M. L., and L. S. Lam, (eds.). 1993. *Sexuality in Asia. Selected Papers from the Conference on Sexuality in Asia.* Hong Kong College of Psychiatrists.

Ng, M. L., and M. P. Lau. 1990. "Sexual Attitudes in the Chinese." *Archives of Sexual Behavior,* 19(4):373-388.

Pan, Sui-ming. 1996. "Factors Inhibiting Chinese People from Answering Questions on Sexuality." A presentation at the combined Eastern/Midcontinent meeting of the Society for the Scientific Study of Sexuality, Pittsburgh, PA, May 3-5, 1996.

Pan, Suiming. 1996. "A Sampling Survey on Students' Sexual Behavior in Every University and College in Beijing." *Street.* Number 10:35-38. Also in *China Journal of Research in Youth,* Number 11.

Pan, Suiming. 1995. "Sexuality and Relationship Satisfaction in Mainland China." *Journal of Sex Research,* 7(4):1-17.

Pan, Suiming. 1994. "A Sex Revolution in Current China." *Journal of Psychology and Human Sexuality (U.S.A.),* 6(2):1-14. Full text published in *Chinese, in Research in Youth,* Number 2, 1994.

Pan, Suiming. 1994. "Chinese Wives: Psychological and Behavioral Factors Underlying Their Orgasm Frequency." *China Psychology* (Published in Chinese), No. 8.

Pan, Suiming. 1994. "Deep Sexual Behavior Survey—Relations of Sexual Mores, Idea, Affection, and Behavior," (Full text published in Chinese) *Chinese Psychology Health,* Number 7, pp. 168-171.

Pan, Suiming. 1993/1994. "Deep Sex Survey: Relationship Among Sexual Ideas, Orgasm, and Behavior. A paper given at the Conference on Gender Issues in Chinese Society, Miami Beach, Floorida USA, August 1993. Published in part in Chinese, *Chinese Psychology Health.* 1994. Number 7.

Pan, Suiming. 1993 (September). "Marriage and Sexuality in Current Beijing City" *Beijing Marriage in the Late 1980s.* Beijing: Beijing Government.

Pan, Suiming. 1993. "Quantitative Behavioral Analysis of Public Heterosexual Petting in Chinese Civil Parks." In: Ng and Lam, (eds.). *Sexuality in Asia.* Hong Kong: Hong Kong College of Psychiatrists, pp. 173-184.

Pan, Suiming. 1993. "China: Acceptability and Effect of Three Kinds of Sexual Publication." *Archives of Sexual Behavior*, 22(1):59-71.

Pan, Suiming. 1991. "Influence of Sex Knowledge and Attitude on Sexual Behavior—The Condition, Motive, and Orgasm." Privately published in *Textbook of Socio-Sexology* for use by sociology students at Remin University of China, Beijing.

Pan, Suiming. 1990. "Relations Between Satisfaction of Sexual Life and the Marriage" In *Research in the New Development of Marriage in Beijing City*. Edited by The Beijing Society for Research in Marriage and Family. Beijing: The Office of Social Science Planning of Beijing City Government.

Pan, Suiming. "Chinese Readers' Answers to the Questionnaire in the Chinese Edition of the Kinsey Report since 1989," Unpublished.

Pan, Sui-ming, and P. Aggleton. 1995. "Male Homosexual Behavior and HIV-Related Risk in China" In *Bisexualities and AIDS: International Perspectives*. London: Taylor and Francis Group Ltd.

Reuters News Service. 1994 (November 15). "New Chinese Law Prohibits Sex-Screening of Fetuses." *The New York Times*.

Ruan, Fang-fu. 1985. "Outline of the Historical Development of Modern Sexual Medicine." *Encyclopedic Knowledge*. Beijing: China Encyclopedia Press.

Ruan, Fang-fu. 1985. *Essays on Sex Education: Ten Lectures. Required Readings for Parents*. Beijing: Beijing Press.

Ruan, Fang-fu. 1991. *Sex in China: Studies in Sexology in Chinese Culture*. New York: Plenum Press.

Ruan, Fang-fu [using pseudonym J. M. Huaj]. 1985. "Homosexuality: An Unsolved Puzzle." *Zhu Nin Jiankang* (To Your Good Health), 1985(3):14-15.

Ruan, Fang-fu, ed. 1985/1988. *Xing Zhishi Shouce* (Handbook of Sex Knowledge). Beijing: Scientific and Technological Literature Publishing House. Revised 1988 edition published jointly by the Scientific and Technological Literature Publishing House and the People's Medical Publishing House. This book consists of 18 chapters as follows: (1) Science of Sex; (2) Sex Organs; (3) Sex Hormones; (4) Sexual Development; (5) Psychology of Sex; (6) Sexual Response; (7) Sexual Behaviors; (8) Sexual Hygiene; (9) Sexual Dysfunctions; (10) Sexual Varieties; (11) Sex Crime; (12) Sex and Marriage; (13) Sex and Reproduction; (14) Sex in Illness; (15) Sex and Drugs; (16) Sex in the Aged; (I7) Sex Therapy; and (18) Sex Education.

Ruan, Fang-fu, and V. L. Bullough. 1988. "The First Case of Transsexual Surgery in Mainhand China." *Journal of Sex Research*, 25:546-547.

Ruan, Fang-fu, and V. L. Bullough. 1989a. "Sex in China." *Medical Aspects of Human Sexuality*, 23:59-62.

Ruan, Fang-fu, and V. L. Bullough. 1989b. "Sex Repression in Contemporary China." In: P. Kurtz, ed. *Building a World Community: Humanism in the 21st Century*, pp. 198-201. Buffalo, New York: Prometheus Books.

Ruan, Fang-fu, and K. R. Chong. 1987 (April 14). "Gay Life in China." *The Advocate*, 470:28-31.

Ruan, Fang-fu and Y. M. Tsai. 1987. "Male Homosexuality in the Traditional Chinese Literature." *Journal of Homosexuality*, 14:21-33.

Ruan, Fang-fu and Y. M. Tsai. 1988. "Male Homosexuality in Contemporary Mainland China." *Archives of Sexual Behavior*, 17:189-199.

Ruan, Fang-fu, V. L. Bullough, and Y. M. Tsai. 1989. "Male Transsexualism in Mainland China." *Archives of Sexual Behavior*, 18:517-522.

Sankar, Andrea. 1984. "Spinster Sisterhoods." In M. Sheridan and J. Salaff, eds. *Chinese Working Women*. Bloomington, Indiana: Indiana University Press.

Shapiro, J. 1987 (October 18). "Scenes from the Kalideidoscope: Chinese Lives." *The New York Times Book Review*, p. 7.

Shenon, P. 1994 (August 16). "A Chinese Bias Against Girls Creates Surplus Bachelors." *The New York Times*, A1, A8.

Sheridan, M., and J. Salaff, eds. 1984. *Chinese Working Women*. Bloomington, Indiana: Indiana University Press.

Van Gulik, R. H. 1961; 1974. *Sexual Life in Ancient China: A Preliminary Survey of Chinese Sex and Society from ca. 1500 B.C. till 1644 A.D.* Leiden: E. J. Brill.

Wehrfritz, G. 1996 (November 11). "China: Blood and Money: The Marketplace Has Helped Spread AIDS." *Newsweek*, p. 50.

Wen, S. H., J. D. Zeng, and M. L. Ng. 1990. *Sex and Moral Education*. Hong Kong: Joint Publishing.

Xiaomingxiong. 1984. *History of Homosexuality in China. (Zhongguo Tongxingai Shilu).* Hong Kong: Samshasha and Pink Triangle Press.

Zhang, Xinxin, and Sang Ye. 1986. *Chinese Lives: An Oral History of Contemporary China.* Edited by W. J. F. Jenner and Cheng Lingang. New York: Pantheon Books.

Zhang, Xinxin, and Sang Ye. 1986. *Chinese Profiles: An Oral History of Contemporary China.* Beijing, China: Chinese Literature; distributed by China Book Trading Corp.

The Czech Republic and Slovakia (*Ceská Republika* and *Slovenská Republika*)

Jaroslav Zverina, M.D.*

Contents

Demographics and a Historical Perspective

A. Demographics

On January 1, 1993, the seventy-four year old Czech and Slovak Federal Republic ended peacefully when the Czech and Slovak Republics were established as separate nations. The two republics are located in east central Europe. Together, the two republics are about the size of the state of New York, with 49,365 square miles.

The Czech Republic is bordered by Poland on the north, Germany on the north and west, Austria on the south, and Slovakia on the east and southeast. The 30,450 square miles of the Czech Republic are divided between hilly Moravia in the east and the plateau of Bohemia in the west

*Partial translation by Anton Ros, M.D., and Lynne Ros.

surrounded by mountains. The 1995 population of 10.4 million had an age distribution of 21 percent below age 15, 69 percent between ages 15 and 64, and 10 percent age 65 and older. Three quarters of the people live in the cities. Ethnically, 94 percent are Czechs, 3 percent Slovaks, 0.6 percent Polish, 0.5 percent German, and 0.3 percent Gypsy. This official number of Gypsies is probably incorrect because many Gypsies reported themselves as Czech or Slovak. A more realistic estimate would be about 100,000 or approximately one percent of the population in the Czech Republic, double that of the Polish and German minorities. In terms of religion, 39.8 percent are atheist, 39.2 percent Roman Catholic, and 4.6 percent Protestant. Czech life expectancy at birth in 1995 was 70 for males and 77 for females. The birth rate was 13 per 1,000 people and the death rate 11 per 1,000 population, for a natural annual increase of 0.3 percent. The Republic has one hospital bed per 98 persons, one physician per 323 persons, and an infant mortality rate of nine per 1,000 live births in 1995. Literacy in 1993 was 100 percent with ten years of compulsory education. The 1993 per capita gross domestic product was $7,200.

Slovakia is bordered by Poland on the north, Hungary on the south, Austria and the Czech Republic on the west, and the Ukraine on the east; the Carpathian mountains are in the north and the fertile Danube plain in the south. Slovakia has about half the population of the Czech Republic, with 5.4 million people. Its 18,933 square miles makes it about 62 percent the size of its former partner. Ethnically, 86 percent of the people are Slovak and 11 percent Hungarian. The official number of Gypsies in 1991 was 80,627 or 1.5 percent; the actual figure is probably double this, somewhere about 150,000 or 3 percent of the population. Sixty percent are Roman Catholic and 8 percent Protestant.

The 1995 birth rate was 15 per 1,000 population, the death rate nine per 1,000 poppulation, for a natural annual increase of 0.5 percent. The infant mortality rate was ten per 1,000 live births in 1995. Literacy in 1993 was 100 percent. The 1993 per capita gross domestic product was $5,800.

B. A Brief Historical Perspective

Slovakia was originally settled by Illyrian, Celtic, and Germanic tribes and became part of Great Moravia in the nineth century. It became part of Hungary in the eleventh century. After being overrun by Czech Hussites in the fifteenth century, it returned to Hungarian rule in 1526. The Slovaks dissassociated from Hungary after World War I and immediately joined the Czechs of Bohemia and Moravians to form the Republic of Czechoslovakia. This union ended December 31, 1992.

The Czech Kingdom has a long tradition as a self-standing European country dating from the ninth century, when Bohemia and Moravia were part of the Great Moravian Empire. This later became part of the Holy Roman Empire. Under the kings of Bohemia, in the fourteenth century,

Prague was the cultural center of Central Europe. Bohemia and Hungary became part of the Austro-Hungarian Empire until 1918.

In 1939, Hitler dissolved the state of Czechoslovakia, made protectorates of Bohemia and Moravia, and proclaimed Slovakia independent. Soviet troops entered Prague in 1945 and the communists seized power in the elections of 1948. Communist rule ended with Vaclav Havel's "velvet revolution" in November 1989. Because these two countries were one nation for eighty years, they are treated together in this chapter.

1. Basic Sexological Premises

A. Character of Gender Roles

The prevailing character of gender roles in the republics is traditionally European, with masculinity connected with social dominance. While the Communist dictatorship verbally proclaimed and endorsed full female emancipation during its forty-year rule, the socioeconomic status of women was low. The number of women employed was very high, but their role in family care and child rearing was commonly underestimated.

B. Sociolegal Status of Males and Females

In both civil and criminal law, both genders are fully equal. Basic schools, colleges, and universities are coeducation. Both men and women have the same political rights.

C. General Concepts of Sexuality and Love

According to Christian tradition, love is a basic ethical category in sexuality. Most couples base their relationship on romantic love. Under the forty-year Communist dictatorship, the erotic and sexual were kept out the mass media. With the growing impact of AIDS and the changing political atmosphere after the 1989 revolution, there came a shift to more open discussions about sexuality and sexual morality.

2. Religious and Ethnic Factors Affecting Sexuality

A. Source and Character of Religious Values

Christianity is the dominant religious influence in both Republics, with Roman Catholics in the majority in both countries. In the Slovak Republic, 60.3 percent are Catholic, 30 percent other, mainly Protestant, and 9.7 percent not church-affiliated. In the Czech Republic, 39.7 percent are not church-affiliated, 39.2 percent are Catholic, and 21.1 percent other, mainly

Protestant. Religiosity is a much stronger influence in Slovakia than it is in the Czech Republic.

B. Source and Character of Ethnic Values

Except for the Gypsy population, the other ethnic minorities, Hungarian, Polish, German, and Ukrainian, blend homogeneously with each other and with the 54 percent Czech and 31 percent Slovak majorities.

3. Sexual Knowledge and Education

A. Government Policies and Programs

Basic knowledge about sexual anatomy and physiology is provided as a part of the basic school curriculum. However, information about contraception, sexual hygiene, and safer sex practices are only rarely and inconsistently covered. Almost universally ignored are topics like homosexuality, paraphilias, and sexual assaults (exhibitionism, rape, incest, and sexually motivated murder).

B. Informal Sources of Sex Education

As a consequence of the lack of formal education, children and young people get the greater part of their information about sex from peer groups. The most important sources of sex information for the young are parents, books, television, and other mass media sources.

In 1990, an unusual and curious national political party was founded with a main goal of promoting sex education and spreading information about human sexuality. This Independent Erotic Initiative (NEI) publishes a party magazine, the *NEI-Report,* which has become one of the successful and popular magazines in the Czech Republic. *NEI-Report* includes tasteful and tasteless exotic articles: cartoons; articles by sexologists dealing with sexual problems and dysfunctions, contraceptives, sexual hygiene, STD, and AIDS; articles by celebrities; letters from readers about their exotic experiences; and explicit photos that give the magazine commercial value. The articles are written by journalists, physicians, educators, and other experts, as well as celebrities and ordinary readers.

Data from a 1994 representative sample of 1,719 men and women over age 15 years in the Czech Republic indicated that 45 percent of the men and 35 percent of the women learned about sex from their peers, 26 percent of both sexes from books, 12 percent of men and 21 percent of women from parents, 15 percent and 14 percent respectively from newspapers and magazines, and 12 percent and 9 percent from television, films, and radio (Zverina 1994).

4. Autoerotic Behaviors and Patterns

Self-pleasuring is seen as an important and natural part of normal sexual activity and motivation. Myths about the unnaturalness and harmfulness of autoeroticism are rarely mentioned, although letters from readers to sex publications indicate that, despite negative beliefs and fears, people do engage in autoeroticism. This applies to both children and adults. Only rarely do parents complain to physicians about the sexual practices of their children.

In a representative sample of 1,719 Czechs over age 15 years, 83 percent of the men and 50 percent of the women reported masturbating sometime in their lives, with the average age for first masturbation being 14 years for men and 17 years for women. Five percent of the men and 10 percent of the women said masturbation poses a health risk (Zverina 1994a).

5. Interpersonal Heterosexual Behaviors

A. Children

The sexual games of children are usually played in secret, and ignored if discovered by parents. They are not the objects of special sanctions in most families.

B. Adolescents

Puberty Rituals

There are no special or institutionalized rituals that recognize either puberty or the initiation of a nonmarital sexual relationship.

Premarital Sexual Activities and Relationships

First sexual intercourse usually occurs between ages 17 and 18. Criminal law sets the minimum age of consent to sexual intercourse at age 15 for both men and women. This law applies equally to both heterosexual and homosexual intercourse. Premarital sexual intercourse is very common, with 98 percent of women having had sexual intercourse before marriage. Premarital sex is accepted, and quietly tolerated, but not openly accepted or endorsed by parents for women under age 18. The average number of premarital sexual partners is one or two for women and two to four for men.

In a representative sample of Czech adults over age 15 years, the average age reported for first coitus was 18.1 years for men and 18 years for women. More than 40 percent of these first experiences occurred in a cottage or outdoors; without contraceptives for 57 percent of the men and 64 percent of the women; and with an "occasional partner" for 34 percent of the men and 12 percent of the women (Zverina 1994a).

In 1993, a representative survey of Prague youths, ages 15 to 29, was sponsored by the *MF DNES* newspaper and carried out by the author of this chapter with the collaboration of DEMA, the Institute for Social Investigations. Seventy-eight percent of the men and 83 percent of the women reported having had sexual intercourse, with the average age for first coitus 17.3 years for men and 17.4 for women. In this same survey, sexually active men reported an average of 8.1 coital partners while women reported an average of 6.6 partners. Nearly two thirds of the men and 73 percent of the women reported having a sexual partner in the previous year. Only one sexual partner was reported by 9 percent of the males and 18 percent of the women. One in five males and 12 percent of females reported having had more than ten sexual partners in their lives. The most common sexual expression was vaginal coitus: 96 percent of sexually active men and 99 percent of sexually active women. Fellatio was refused by 16 percent of the women surveyed, while anal heterosexual intercourse was reported by 22 percent of the men and 16 percent of the women (Zverina 1994b).

C. Adults

Premarital Courtship, Dating, and Relationships

Courtship and dating customs are similar to those in other Eastern European countries and are based on the romantic model. There are no major differences in the dating and courtship patterns of young Czechs or Slovaks living in the cities or rural areas. There are no special courtship customs such as *Fensternl*, or window courting, which occurs in rural Bavaria, or similar customs in the Scandinavian countries.

In both republics, the age of first marriage is relatively low, about 21 years, for most men, with their brides generally being about a year younger. Two socioeconomic factors have contributed to this relatively low age of first marriage. During the forty years of communist rule the government supported early marriage with a system of government benefits and loans. Under communism, and down to the present, it has been extremely difficult for a single man or woman to obtain a flat or apartment. In addition, marriage and having a first child is an important social signal of having grown up and achieved adult status.

Marriage and the Family

As in most parts of the world, heterosexual monogamy is the dominant pattern of sexual behavior in the Czech and Slovak Republics. As is occurring elsewhere in Europe and North America, serial or successive monogamy is becoming a common modification. The 1990 Czech marriage rate was 8.8 per 1,000 inhabitants; the divorce rate 40.81 per 100 marriages. The average age of first marriage was 23.7 for men and 21.3 for women (Zverina 1994a). In Slovakia, the marriage rate was 7.6 per 1,000 inhabitants; the divorce rate 35.2 per 100 marriages.

In the 1994 study of Czech adults over age 15 years, men reported an average of 12.2 sexual partners, women 5.1 partners, with 1.8 and 1.9 partners respectively for the previous year. The average coital frequency in heterosexual partnerships was 8.4 times monthly. Three-quarters of the men and 82 percent of women reported being "fully satisfied with their sexual life" (Zverina 1994a).

Sexual promiscuity is unusual, and most extramarital heterosexual activities are situational or have a pairbonding character. Several studies indicate an incidence of extramarital intercourse at between 25 percent and 35 percent of husbands and wives, with extramarital sex more frequent for men. Most of these extramarital activities are short-lived and infrequent. Reasons for extramarital sex have not been studied, although it is likely that sexual variety and the attraction of a new experience are common motivations. Eighteen percent of men and 31 percent of women held that extramarital sex is "ethically unacceptable behavior" (Zverina 1994a).

In recent decades, there has been an escalating problem of single parent families, mostly divorced mothers with children. More than 70 percent of marriages ending in divorce have a minimum of one minor child. Single mothers have a state-guaranteed minimum standard of living and the economic support from the father of their children. Czech and Slovak society is not hostile to unwed mothers or divorced women.

The birthrate in both republics is relatively low, and still decreasing. The birthrate in 1978 was 18.4 per 1000 inhabitants. In 1992, it had dropped to 12.2 per 1000. Most married couples plan to have one or two children. Planning for more than two children in a family is unusual. Surveys suggest that coital frequency for most married couples is one to three times per week.

Sexuality and the Physically Disabled and Aged

Sexual behavior and sexual problems of mentally and physically handicapped persons are only rarely mentioned in public. The same is true for medical sexologists and marriage counselors. Since the dissolution of communist control in the "velvet revolution" of 1989, there has been a growing activity of different nongovernment organizations seeking to promote the care and well-being of the physically handicapped.

As elsewhere, there are more single women than single men over age 60. Older women are less likely to find an acceptable partner than older single men. We know that interest in sex in the later years has a direct connection with the availability of an appropriate sexual partner. An additional problem in the republics is that the living standard in state facilities for older persons is not conducive to couples' maintaining intimate relationship. In most cases, the state facilities for the elderly are based on a collectivist model.

Incidence of Oral and Anal Sex

Oral sex is widely accepted and practiced by Czechs and Slovaks. Respondents in several surveys indicated that about 70 percent of men and women engage in oral sex as a part of their sexual intimacy. The frequency of anal intercourse, on the other hand, is low among heterosexuals, with only about 5 percent of heterosexual women reporting this experience. In most cases where reported, the activity was exceptional and infrequent.

Sexual practices in both republics are not the object of legal regulations. The sexual behavior of consenting adult partners is free from any restriction by criminal law.

6. Homoerotic, Homosexual, and Ambisexual Behaviors

A. Children and Adolescents

Same-gender sexual experiences may be a natural part of the sexual play and exploration of children. However, their prevalence does not appear to be high. Only about 10 percent of men and 5 percent of women in the heterosexual population report having had same-gender experiences in childhood and early adolescence. In the population of gay men and lesbians, such experiences are, of course, more common.

B. Adults

Attitudes towards homosexuality among the greater part of the population are hostile or ambivalent. Homophobia and hostility towards homosexual people are more common among people in the lower socioeconomic classes. The pandemic of AIDS has brought some changes, mostly in the attitudes towards gays. It seems there is a greater tolerance of stable gay partnerships and couples, and the existence of gay clubs and associations. However, 33 percent of men and 41 percent of women in the 1994 adult survey considered homosexuality a disease. Twenty-two percent of both Czech men and women fully accept homosexuality. Only 2 percent of the men and 1 percent of the women reported a homosexual experience; 1 percent of both male and female respondents self-identified as homosexual, with another 1 percent unsure (1994b). In the adult Czech survey (1994a), 3 percent of men and 4 percent of women reported a homosexual experience. In more than 60 percent of male homosexual coitus, condoms were not used.

In the new penal law code, which went into effect in the republics in 1990, no distinction is made between heterosexual and homosexual behaviors. The ages of majority and of legal consent to sexual intercourse, 18 and 15 years respectively, are the same for both heterosexuals and homosexuals. This new code revoked the criminalization of homosexuality that existed in the previous code. At present, there is a movement to reduce the intolerance and inequities homosexual persons experience socially. These involves paying more attention to the situation of homosexual men and women in the workplace, in schools (both students and teachers), and in the army.

Most gay and lesbian associations are engaged in a movement to legalize the unions or marriages of homosexual couples. Some kind of legalization of long-term homosexual partnerships is supported by important politicians. The attitudes of the Catholic Church on homosexuality is at present still fundamentally rigid and hostile. Some Protestant Christian churches, on the other hand, are traditionally more liberal and less rigid. Coming out appears to be more of a problem for gay men than for lesbians.

Bisexual behavior is more common among homosexual persons than among the heterosexual majority. About 60 percent of the homosexual men surveyed and more than 70 percent of the lesbians reported having had heterosexual intercourse at some time in their lives. Among heterosexual men and women surveyed, only 12 percent of the men and 5 percent of the women reported some same-gender sexual contacts. Most of the same-gender contacts reported did not involve coitus.

While homosexual men tend to be more sexually promiscuous than lesbians, the frequency of anonymous sexual contacts under poor aesthetic conditions is decreasing. One hope: that this is connected with the increasing sex and AIDS-prevention education programs. The prevailing pattern at present is stable, long-term gay and lesbian relationships.

Sexual practices among homosexuals in the republics is the same as in other parts of the Western world. Among homosexual men, active and passive (receptive), anal intercourse is common. Condoms and lubricant gels are used with growing frequency.

7. Gender Conflicted Persons

Fetishistic transvestism is a paraphilia with seemingly low incidence among males in the two republics. In some cases, transvestite males bring their problems to sexological counseling centers. Most of these problems are connected with the partner's/wife's hostility toward the client's cross-dressing and its impact on their sexual practices.

The prevalence of transsexualism also appears to be low, as in other European countries. Interestingly, the sex ratio of transsexuals in the republics' sexological centers is the opposite of what it is in western Europe.

In the records of the Institute of Sexology at the Charles University in Prague, for instance, there are three times as many female-to-male transsexuals as male-to-female transsexuals. In most western European gender clinics, twice as many male-to-female transsexuals are reported as female-to-male. Colleagues in Poland report a ratio similar to that in Prague. Different social conditions and gender viewpoints in east and west European countries may be a factor in this difference in ratios.

Treatment for transsexual persons follows the common step-by-step practice in respected gender clinics around the world. Initial counseling and screening is followed by months of psychotherapy and sociotherapy. In allowing the client to adapt better to a reversal in gender role, it is possible to change the patient's name to a gender neutral one; in Czech and Slovak, the given and family names usually indicate the person's gender. However, some names are gender neutral and the same for either a male or a female.

Following months of hormone treatment, the decision for anatomical sex-reversal surgery can be made. Sex-reassignment surgery, which involves plastic surgery and gonad removal with consequent infertility, is required for an official and complete sex-reversal procedure.

Sex-reassignment surgery is available for both female-to-male and male-to-female transsexuals as part of the health insurance system. From a medical point of view, transsexuals are seen as people with inappropriate development of secondary sexual characteristics. In the Czech republic, about eight patients a year request official sex-change surgery.

8. Significant Unconventional Sexual Behaviors

A. Coercive Sex

Sexual Abuse, Incest, and Rape

The statistics on criminal sexual delinquencies are low in both republics when compared with most west European countries. Twelve percent of women in the 1994 adult Czech survey reported an experience with rape, while 5 percent of the men admitted forcing sex on a woman. The victimization of women, according to our experience, is lower than in western Europe. For example, approximately 18 percent of women in our surveys stated that they had been the object of sexual abuse as a child. In our 1994 preliminary results, 5 percent of the men and 8 percent of the woman reported sexual abuse during childhood. About 20 percent of the women reported having experienced some sort of sexual aggression from men. Most of these assaults are not reported to the police or other authorities. Sexual victimization of males is less frequent, probably about 8 percent to 10 percent.

Sexological investigations of criminal sexual delinquents requested by the police and courts are generally grouped in three main categories:

(1) indecent exposure, (2) sexual molestation or abuse of children and minors, and (3) rape and other sexual assaults.

In recent years, greater attention has been paid to sexual abuse and incest. The common experience is that the most threatened individuals in terms of sexual abuse and incest are children in single-parent families. The most frequent perpetrator is a step-father or the boyfriend of the mother of the victimized child.

A woman who reports a rape is subjected to a very careful and long investigation by the police. Hearings and questioning of the woman can last up to five hours or more. Once a charge is made, the woman cannot withdraw it. Nor can she discuss the accusation with anyone other than the police. If she does, she can be prosecuted for false accusation. At the court hearing, the woman has to answer questions from the court, the defense attorney, and the accused male, in what can be a very traumatizing experience. Similar procedures are followed in cases of child abuse.

At present, there are no special centers for counseling and support of the victims of rape and sexual abuse, although establishment of such centers is being considered.

When apprehended, perpetrators of sexual assault are examined both from psychiatric and sexological perspectives. In cases of psychopathological or paraphiliac motivation, the court can commit the perpetrator to compulsory treatment in a hospital psychiatric department or in an outpatient clinic. Specialized sexological departments in most psychiatric hospitals are staffed with personnel trained in treatment of dangerous sexual delinquents.

Sexual Harassment

Men can be sued for comments and sexually explicit (dirty) language, but accusations and court cases involving accusations of men making sexual advances to women, using indecent language, or sexually harassing women are rare.

[A 1996 report by J. Perlez, suggests that Central European countries and corporations are being slowly influenced by Western concepts of sexual harassment. In a high-profile case in the Czech Republic, a manager at Komercni Banka, a major state bank, was dismissed after a secretary filed a sexual harassment complaint against him. In a 1995 case involving the same manager, the bank refused to act. (See additional comments in Section 8A of the chapter on Poland) (Perlez 1996). (Editor)]

B. Prostitution

Little is known about prostitution in the Czech and Slovak Republics. There are probably several thousand prostitutes working in Prague. Some work in massage parlors and exotic clubs, but most frequent hotels, bars, and restaurants. Since the collapse of the Communist regimes, there has been a migration of Czech and Slovak prostitutes to West Germany, and from Eastern European countries to the Czech and Slovak Republics.

Nine percent of men and no women reported paying for sex, while no men and only 3 percent of the women had engaged in sex in exchange for money (Zverina 1994a). Among young Czechs, ages 15 to 29, 14 percent of males reported intercourse with a female prostitute, with a 60-percent use of condoms in these contacts. Three percent of the young women reported having sex for money, with a 50-percent condom use (Zverina 1994b).

C. Pornography and Erotica

The republics have no indigenous pornographic publications, but *Playboy*-like hard-core magazines are imported from Scandinavia, Germany, and Austria. These magazines are not available in regular stores, and where they are available, they are labeled "Not for Minors." The situation is similar for sexually explicit videos.

In our 1994 preliminary results, 4 percent of the men and 8 percent of the women thought that pornography should be prohibited; 11 percent and 20 percent respectively thought pornography to be dangerous.

D. Paraphilias

Paraphiliacs, at present, have more opportunities for communication and contact than they had under the communist rule. Some sexual contact magazines and advertisement services now exist for these people. Most of the interest is in sadomasochism and fetishistic practices.

Some people with ego-dystonic paraphilias seek help at the counseling centers and sexological departments. More frequently sexologists are called on to treat paraphiliacs who have been arrested as perpetrators of some sexual crime. In such situations, consultation with a psychotherapist is required, and treatment can be paid for by the national health insurance.

9. Contraception, Abortion, and Population Planning

A. Contraception

The birthrate in the Czech republic is very low. In the Slovak republic, it is comparable with some more successful countries from this point of view in Europe. About 49 percent of all children are not planned, but only 1.4 percent of all newborns are placed for adoption.

Data on the use of contraceptives in the two republics demonstrates a major problem, in that almost half of all pregnancies are unwanted. Withdrawal, coitus interruptus, is by far the most common contraceptive method, being relied on by 40 percent of the Czech women at risk and 51 percent of the Slovak women at risk (1991 data). Barrier methods, particularly the condom, are used by 31 percent of Czech women and 24 percent of Slovak women. The hormonal contraceptive pill is used by 8 percent and 6 percent respectively; sterilization by 2 percent and 5 percent respectively. The low incidence of hormonal contraception and surgical sterilization is a national problem. This is compounded by the seemingly high frequency of condom use. This datum should be understood as an artifact of the surveys because the 31 percent and 24 percent of women reporting condom use does not mean regular and consistent use, but rather occasional and even one-time use. In reality, condom popularity is both republics is very low in comparison with western European countries.

In preliminary data from Zverina (1994b), 39 percent of young Czech males reported condom use with a stable partner and 40 percent with a casual partner. Women reported condom use in 36 percent of coitus with a stable partner and only 20 percent with a casual partner. Forty-one percent of men and 35 percent of women reported using a condom with occasional partners. Condom use in anal intercourse and fellatio was the exception. Among Czech adults, male and female contraceptive use is shown in Table 1.

Table 1

Male and Female Contraceptive Use Among Czech Adults

Method	Men (Percent)	Women (Percent)
Withdrawal	41	38
IUD	17	23
Condoms	19	22
Oral contraceptives	16	22
Natural/Rhythm		12

B. Teenage Unmarried Pregnancies

The number of pregnancies in women under age 15 is low. In 1989, for example, the Czechoslovakian figure was 110 pregnancies in this age group, 0.03 percent of all pregnancies in that year. Seventy percent of these pregnancies were terminated by abortion, mostly legal induced abortions; forty ended in childbirth.

In the same year, 42,145 women age 15 to 18 years were pregnant, 10.8 percent of all pregnancies that year. Close to two thirds of these pregnancies ended in childbirth. Slovak and Czech teenage women have very little access to contraception. Contraceptive pills can only be obtained from a gynecologist, and the attitude of many gynecologists toward hormonal contraception for young women is inappropriately negative. Contraception counseling centers for teenagers promote abstinence in place of other contraceptive methods. Some counseling centers for teenagers, however, work under the supervision of British family planning organizations and provide contraceptive without charge.

C. Abortion

Laws regulating induced abortion were liberalized in 1956. Between 1956 and 1986, women seeking an abortion had to present their request to special "abortion commissions." From 1987 on, pregnant women could obtain an abortion simply by requesting it. Induced abortion is legal until the twelfth week of gestation. Abortion for medical reasons or to protect the woman's health is legal up to the twenty-fourth week of gestation. Illegal abortions are rare. In the 1994 adult survey, 60 percent of women and 58 percent of the men were fully "pro-choice." Three percent of both men and women believed induced abortion should be prohibited by law.

In the last two years, the number of legally induced abortions has declined. More than 80 percent of all abortions in the two republics are performed in the first two months of gestation, as "mini-interruptions." RU-486 is not available. The number of legally induced abortions per 1,000 women in 1991 is shown in Table 2.

Table 2

Rate of Legally Induced Abortions (per 1,000 Women), Czech Republic and Slovakia, 1991

Age Group	Czech	Slovak
Under 19	24.6	14.9
20-24	76.1	58.9
25-29	81.2	67.0
30-34	63.6	52.6
35-39	42.8	35.6
40-44	15.1	12.1
45 plus	1.4	0.9

D. Population Control Efforts

In recent decades, the government has made some efforts to promote population growth. All of these efforts utilized economic incentives. Money was provided for the support of each additional child at above the standard of normal living. Families with three or four children received increased support and benefits. All of these efforts had only a temporary effect, and no substantial long-term success.

At present, the state population policy is relatively liberal. The goal is to enhance the social and reproductive responsibility of the people. The state supports some sexual education programs. Nongovernmental organizations also sponsor activities including education programs aimed at improving contraceptive use and lowering the number of legally induced abortions for nonhealth reasons. It is estimated that more than 70 percent of all pregnancies in the two republics are unwanted and unplanned. This is the greatest problem in population policy for both countries.

10. Sexually Transmitted Diseases

A. Incidence, Patterns, and Trends in STDs

At present, the incidence of STDs and AIDS is relatively low. In the young Czech survey, only 7 percent of males and 16.5 percent of females reported some experience with a sexually transmitted disease. This is due to forty years of communist policy, which, in a substantial way, restricted the free movement of people. After the frontiers were opened in 1989, the movement of people into and out of the country increased. This new mobility and migration is already increasing the number of STD cases in the larger cities and in regions near the western frontier.

In the 1980s, no more than four cases of syphilis were reported annually per 100,000 inhabitants. In 1991, the rate of new syphilis cases was 1.3 per 100,000, with more women than men affected.

In the 1980s, the annual incidence of gonorrhea had been under 100 cases per 100,000 inhabitants. In 1991, 71 percent of all cases were men between ages 15 and 24. In 1992, the incidence of gonorrhea increased significantly in some regions, on the north and west frontiers, and in Prague. This is one of the first signs of a new STD epidemic developing under new social conditions.

Our own clinical experience reveals a remarkable increase in the incidence of all other STDs, including genital warts, papilloma virus infections, genital herpes, nonspecific urethritis, pelvic inflammatory disease (PID), chlamydia, and cervical carcinoma.

B. Availability of Treatment and Prevention Efforts

The law requires that all new cases of classical venereal diseases be reported to the state Dermatovenereological Department. Infected persons are also required by law to give health professionals information about all sexual partners. Diagnosis and treatment for STDs is easily available in all the larger cities, at dermatovenereological departments, clinics, and gynecological and urological departments.

The main factor in the primary prevention of STDs is responsible sexual behavior. Sexual education should be started at a very young age and should include information of the health risks of sexual behavior. Some particular groups, "at-risk populations," need special attention to sexual education programs, for example the propagation of safer sex information among promiscuous heterosexuals, homosexuals, prostitutes, and highly mobile minorities (tourists and professional drivers). Sexologists in both countries are not completely satisfied with the present situation in sex education. The involvement of the mass media, radio, and television, is very small in this area.

11. HIV/AIDS

A. Incidence, Patterns, and Trends

Thus far, the incidence of HIV infection in the republics is low. At the end of 1992, there were 143 known cases of HIV infection in the Czech republic, 93 of them being homosexual or bisexual men, and 30 hemophiliacs or blood-transfusion recipients. Only one IV drug user has registered. Ten cases involved heterosexual transmission and 9 cases had unknown sources. Of the 143 known cases, 11 were women and 7 were children under age 15. Persons with suspected HIV infection or AIDS are protected under a special law guaranteeing their personal freedom to seek or refuse testing.

AIDS is still a very rare diagnosis. At the end of 1992, only 32 cases of AIDS were known in the Czech republic. Twenty-six of these were homosexual or bisexual men, 3 transfusion recipients, 2 heterosexual men, and 1 foreigner.

The low incidence of HIV infection in both republics is well demonstrated by the results of several preventive and anonymous screenings for HIV. In one study of 66,095 patients with an STD, only 23 persons were found to be HIV positive, In another anonymous testing of 2,554 persons, only nine persons were HIV positive.

For 96 percent of the Czech men and women, the main source of information about HIV/AIDS is the mass media. Knowledge about HIV/AIDS has resulted in safer sex practices for 22 percent of the men and 14 percent of the women (Zverina 1994a).

B. Treatment, Prevention, and Government Policy

There are centers for HIV/AIDS investigation and treatment in both capital cities, Prague and Bratislava. Anonymous testing for HIV is available in all larger cities free of charge. Government policy fully respects the international standards of the World Health Organization.

National centers for HIV/AIDS have been operating in both countries for several years. The respective Ministries of Health Care have been coordinating governmental activities with nongovernmental organizations and institutions. An AIDS-Help society, SAP [*Spolecnost AIDS Pomoc*], was founded in 1991. Sexual education is actively promoted by the sexological societies and by the Czech and Slovak Family Planning Associations (SPRSV [*Spolecnost pro Planovani Rodiny a Sexualni Vychovu*] in Czech and SPR [*Spolecnost Planovaneho Rodicovstva*] in Slovakia). Many hot lines and telephone counseling services are operating with varying professional standards.

Programs for training counselors and health professionals are just being organized. Work with "at-risk" populations does not have a long tradition, because such groups were not acknowledged by the communist government. An organization for prostitutes was started in 1992. Propagation of safer sex information among promiscuous homosexual men and promiscuous heterosexuals is possible with the collaboration of gay self-help groups like the Lambda Klub, and through erotic magazines and video-rental clubs.

The author's 1993 survey of 984 residents of Prague (*N* = 485 males; 499 females) between the ages of 15 and 29 contained thirty questions about past and present sexual behavior designed to elicit information of the risk of HIV infection. The most frequent sources of information about HIV/AIDS were books and magazines (more than 50 percent of males and females). Parents and school were the main information source for less that 10 percent of the respondents. More than 90 percent of the male and female respondents were appropriately informed about HIV transmission, although 20 percent believed that the virus could be spread by insects, kissing, or sneezing. Five percent of the males and 2 percent of the women believed that hormonal contraception protects against HIV infection. One in four males and females felt threatened by the risk of infection. One in four males and one in five females had changed their sexual behavior as a result of this fear, with a decrease in sexual partners and increase in condom use being the most common changes.

Twenty-nine percent of males and 16 percent of women stated they would break with a partner if they learned that he/she was HIV-positive. Twenty-three percent of the men and 17 percent of the women believed persons with HIV/AIDS should be kept in isolation. Eleven percent of males and 20 percent of the female respondents had been tested for HIV infection at least once.

Preliminary results of the survey of Prague youth indicates that approximately a third of the youth of Prague are at very low risk for the infection, because of their monogamous lifestyle, avoidance of risky sexual practices, regular use of condoms, or complete sexual abstinence. Approximately 5 percent of the men and women were at high risk because of a combination of sexual promiscuity, risky sexual practices, coitus with IV drug users, and failure to use condoms. Now that information about this risk group is on the record, it can become the subject of a government-sponsored prevention campaign.

12. Sexual Dysfunction, Counseling, and Therapies

The investigation and treatment of sexual dysfunction has a long tradition in Czechoslovakia. Since the founding of the Institute of Sexology at Charles University in Prague in 1921, sexual dysfunctions have been a primary interest. Czech and Slovak sexologists have adopted a psychosomatic approach to couple sexual problems and sexual dysfunctions. Strong emphasis is given to the quality of the therapeutic contact and to psychotherapeutic activities. Most of the clinical sexologists came into sexology from psychiatry.

Prague has a long tradition of investigating the vascular etiology of erectile dysfunctions. One of the pioneers of surgical treatment of vasculogenic impotence is Professor Vaclav Michal at the Institute of Clinical and Experimental Medicine in Prague.

About one in six Czech men and women reported experiencing some sexual dysfunction in their lives (Zverina 1994a). Counseling and psychotherapy for sexual problems are available at some psychological centers in the health system and in social institutions, particularly marriage counseling centers that operate in all the larger cities in both countries. Medical diagnosis and treatment of sexual dysfunctions in both men and women are free of charge at present for all ages and social groups. Some medications, of course, are provided with partial payment by the patients.

13. Sexual Research and Advanced Education

The main center for sex research has traditionally been the Institute of Sexology at Charles University in Prague, founded in 1921. Research in this Institute has centered on behavioral sexology and on some andrological problems. The founder of the Czech School of Medical Sexology, Professor Josef Hynie, spent some time at several of the world-renowned centers of early sexology, particularly the Magnus Hirschfeld Institute of Sexology in Berlin. Professor Jan Raboch has made important investigations in both andrology and behavioral sexology. In 1977, Raboch was president of the International Academy of Sex Research (IASR). Prague has twice been the site of an annual meeting of the IASR.

Czech psychiatry is well known for its sexological research. In the early 1950s, Kurt Freund began his studies using penile plethysmography to investigate male sexual orientations. Ales Kolarsky and Josef Madlafousek, at the Prague Center of Psychiatric Research, extended Freund's work in penile plethysmography with important publications. Research on social aspects of sexology are just beginning at a new center founded by the Faculty of Philosophy of Charles University.

In early 1993, the Czechoslovak Sexological Society separated into two different and independent societies in Prague and Bratislava. Milan Zaviacic and colleagues at the School of Medicine, Comenius University, Bratislava, have carried out pioneering anatomical and physiological research on female ejaculation (urethral expulsions) and the so-called Graffenberg spot.

Undergraduate programs in sexology are included in some Medical, Pedagogical, and Law Faculties. Postgraduate study is possible only in medicine, in the medical sexology program. Admission to this postgraduate specialization is limited to those who have successfully completed the program in psychiatry or gynecology. Rarely are admissions made from other medical specializations.

The main sexological institutions in the Czech and Slovak Republics are:

Sexuologigky Ustav. Address: 1. Lekarske Fakulty, Univerzity Karlovy, Karlovo Namesti 32, 120 00 Praha 2, Czech Republic

Sexological Society. Address: Karlovo Namesti 32, 120 00 Praha 2, Czech Republic

Spolecnost pro planovani rodiny a sexualni vychovu, SPRSV—National Family Planning Association. Address: Podoske Nabrezi 157. 140 00 Praha 4, Czech Republic

The Sexological Institute and The Slovak Sexological Society. Address: Polna, 811 08 Bratislava 1, Slovak Republic

The School of Medicine. Comenius University, Bratislava. Address: Sasinkova 4, 811 08. Bratislava 1, Slovak Republic

References and Suggested Readings

Perlez, Jane. 1996 (October 3). "Central Europe Learns about Sex Harassment." *The New York Times*, p. A3.

Zverina, Jaroslav. 1991. *Lekarska Sexuologie* (*Medical Sexology*). Prague: H&H.

Zverina, Jaroslav. 1994a. Sexual Behavior of Men and Women in the Czech Republic, 1994. Some preliminary data supplied by the author. (In press.)

Zverina, Jaroslav. 1994b. Some Preliminary Results on the Sexual Behavior of 984 Young People (15-29 Years; 485 Men and 499 Women) in Prague: A Representative Sample. Some preliminary data supplied by the author. (In press.)

Finland
(*Suomen Tasavalta*)

Osmo Kontula, D.Soc.Sci., Ph.D., and Elina Haavio-Mannila, Ph.D.

Contents

Demographics and a Historical Perspective

A. Demographics

Finland lies in northern Europe where Russia, Sweden, and Norway are its neighboring countries. Roughly five million inhabitants occupy this 130,119-square-mile country, with 64 percent in urban areas. The population is ethnically very integrated. The largest minority are the Swedish-speaking Finns, with 6 percent of the whole population. The rest of the Finns speak Finnish. The Lapps and Gypsies are small minorities. During recent years, increasing numbers of refugees and other foreigners have been immigrating into Finland, but their total number still remains below 50,000. Separate cultures are not very conspicuous within Finnish society.

The age distribution of the Finnish people is 0 to 14 years, 19.3 percent; 15 to 59 years, 62.9 percent; and 60 plus years, 17.8 percent. The birthrate in 1995 was twelve per 1,000, and the death rate ten per 1,000 population, giving an annual natural increase of 0.2 percent. Infant mortality was 5 per 1,000 live births in 1995. Literacy is 100 percent. Average live expectancy is 73 for males and 80 years for females. Finland has one hospital bed per 81 persons and one physician per 390 persons.

The per capita gross domestic product in 1995 was $16,100. Finland is counted among the countries of fair economic well-being, with an annual increase in the Gross National Product above the European average. The main exports are the products of paper and metal industries.

Social services are well developed in Finland. People receive free counseling in contraception for family planning at the communal health centers, expectant mothers have been given free guidance in child care centers for decades, mothers of small children have paid maternity leaves, and there are inexpensive communal day-care places for children, as well as child benefits until the age of 18. As a result, Finnish women play as active a part in paid employment as Finnish men.

In 1992, the sexual life of the Finns was studied using nationally representative data on the 18- to 74-year-old population in Finland (Kontula and Haavio-Mannila 1993). The response rate for the 2,250 Finns in this FINSEX survey was 76 percent. Each of the respondents was interviewed personally and asked to fill out a questionnaire about the most intimate sexual matters. The questionnaire responses were not shown to the interviewers. The results of this study have been compared with a corresponding 1971 study (Sievers et al. 1974) to provide a detailed picture of Finnish sexual attitudes and behaviors in recent decades. Worldwide, the 1971 study was only the second population survey based on nationally representative data of sexual matters. (The first nationally representative sexual study was done in Sweden in 1967.) The results of this most recent FINSEX study will be discussed in different sections of this chapter.

B. A Brief Historical Perspective

The early settlers of Finland probably arrived about two thousand years ago from the Ural area to the southeast. Swedish settlers brought the country into the Kingdom of Sweden in 1154, where it remained until 1809, when it became an autonomous grand duchy of the Russian Empire. A strong national spirit emerged, with Finland declaring its independence in 1917 and becoming a republic two years later. Finland was invaded by the Soviet Union in 1939, forcing the Finns to give up 16,173 square miles of territory. Further cessions were exacted by the Soviets after World War II. Finland became a member of the European Union in 1995.

1. Basic Sexological Premises

A. The Character of Gender Roles

Historically, Finland has a longer tradition of gender equality than most other countries of the world. This can be seen in the realm of politics, paid work, and in the division of labor at home.

In 1906, Finnish women gained parliamentary voting rights, second in the world after New Zealand. Finnish women also were the first in the world to gain the right to serve in parliament. These rights were immediately implemented. In 1907, nineteen women were elected to a parliament of two hundred members. At present, 39 percent of the MPs in Finland are women. In the 1994 presidential election, the female candidate got 46 percent of the votes. Even though she was not elected, her success indicates that a woman can reach the highest positions of power in this country.

Women in Finland are gainfully employed nearly as often as men. In 1991, some 72 percent of the women in the working-age population and 78 percent of the men respectively were part of the labor force. In Finland, both women and men work on a full-time basis. In 1991, the proportion of women working part-time was 10 percent and that of men 5 percent respectively.

The large proportion of gainfully employed women is also reflected in a high percentage of the entire labor force. In 1991, 48 percent of the labor force were women and women made up 51 percent of the salary and wage earners. Unlike most European countries in the 1980s, Finland had a lower rate of undisguised unemployment for women than for men. However, the rate of unemployment among women over 55 has been higher than the rate among men of the same age.

Public offices are equally open to women and men, and under the Equality Act no vacancy in the private sector can be announced exclusively for women or men on any other than weighty and acceptable grounds relating to the nature of the work. An exception to the rule of public offices open to both sexes are those offices at the Ministry of Defense, in the Armed Forces, and in the Border Guards, which require military training (Cedaw 1993).

The Finnish labor market remains somewhat gender-segregated. Women comprise approximately 60 percent of the labor force in the service sector, while the industrial and building sectors are dominated by men. The segregation extends to occupations and specific tasks. No dramatic change has taken place in the gender segregation of the labor market, although employees who have made nontraditional choices have entered practically every occupation dominated by the other sex. Another illustration of the gender-segregated labor market is the differences in the positions that women and men occupy in the official hierarchies. Men advance rapidly and attain higher positions than women (Haavio-Mannila and Kauppinen-Toropainen 1992).

Recent studies indicate that the quality of working life for women has deteriorated considerably in some respects. Time pressures and stress have become a more prevalent feature of jobs held by women.

The differences between women's and men's earnings diminished both proportionally and in real terms in the 1970s. In 1983, this development shifted, and the pay differentials between women and men began to grow in real terms in most sectors. In 1991, women's pay was 80 percent of men's pay.

Women are slightly more often unionized than men, and their daily working hours, as well as the time spent working during a lifetime, are nearly the same. The characteristics of women workers—unionization, rise in educational standards, full-time work, and very short absences from the labor force—have not served significantly to narrow the pay differentials between the sexes.

As most women work for pay, it is necessary that men share household work with them. In international comparison, gender equality in the division of housework is high (Gershuny 1990). Nevertheless, women still do more domestic work than men, even though their share of it has declined from 67 percent in 1979 to 64 percent in 1987 (Niemi and Pääkkönen 1989). In the United States, the percentage was 67 percent in 1987 (Robinson 1988).

B. Sociolegal Status of Males and Females

As the number of children in the families is small, children are valued as individuals. Even though there is a slight tendency to prefer boys when asked which gender one wishes the future child to be, girls are taken care of and loved as much as boys.

The provision of day care for children is a municipal responsibility. The Day Care Act of 1973 aims at providing communal day care for all children in need of it. Since 1985, parents have been able to choose between placing their child in communal day care or receiving a home-care allowance for taking care of their child at home. This allowance may also be used to cover some of the costs of private day care. Taking care of one's child at home with the help of a home-care allowance does not terminate employment or, since 1991, lower employee pension.

When the educational level of the entire population is examined, it is discovered that women and men are now at the same level. In 1989, half of those who had completed senior secondary school or vocational education or had a university degree were women. Women have reached a high level of general education. In the working-age population, women have a senior secondary school diploma more frequently than men, a circumstance that will prevail in the future, because 60 percent of senior secondary level students are women.

Men still have the majority of masters' degrees (60 percent), but women are quickly catching up; since 1986, the number of women graduating from universities has exceeded that of men. For example, in 1989, women represented 54 percent of students who obtained a master's degree and 34 percent of those with a higher degree. The proportion of women who have a doctorate has been steadily increasing since 1976. The percentage of women in the senior faculty of universities remains small.

The choice of fields is segregated by gender. The proportion of women is the largest in health care, and quite considerable in the fields of pharmacy and veterinary science. Similarly, students in teacher training are predominantly women. At the university level, clearly the smallest proportion of women can be found in the mathematical and technical fields.

The dropout rate at the basic level of education is very low nowadays. Law provides for compulsory education until the age of 16. The dropout rate at the upper secondary level was 7 percent in 1988. Somewhat fewer women leave school prematurely than men.

Leisure pursuits are differentiated according to gender. Girls are more interested in arts, boys in sports. Attempts to achieve equality in training are made by offering girls and boys the same opportunities to engage in various kinds of arts and sports.

Women are more active than men as consumers of cultural services. They go to the library, theater, concerts of classical music, museums, and art shows more frequently than men, and form the majority of students in voluntary adult education. Men go to sports competitions more often than women, and somewhat more often to the cinema and to concerts of popular music.

Gender differences in drinking alcoholic beverages have diminished; women have started to imitate the drinking habits of men. This applies particularly to women working with men (Haavio-Mannila 1992).

While men and women are in principle equal in Finland, the position of men in the public sphere, in politics, work, and economy, is still better than that of women. In the private sphere, at home, women have more power than men, but it also means a heavier work load there.

C. General Concepts of Sexuality and Love

Some general concepts of sexuality and love in the Finnish society will be discussed in Section 2B, where attitudes toward sexual relations before marriage, casual relationships, love as a precondition for sex, gender equality in initiating sexual intercourse, and attitudes toward homosexuality will be described. Here some other constructs of sexuality will be reported. They include opinions about health effects of sexuality, importance of sexual life in steady relationships, and double morals.

People in Finland have a positive attitude toward sexual behaviors as a health promoter—they do not see it as a threat to health. In 1992, 88 percent of Finnish men and 79 percent of women thought that sexual activity promotes health and well-being. A clear majority, 74 percent of men and 70 percent of women, believed that masturbation doesn't endanger one's health.

Sex is considered to be an important aspect of a steady relationship. In 1992, most Finns, 86 percent of men and 78 percent of women, considered sexual life very important or important for happiness in their relationship. Among women, the strength of this opinion had declined from 1971 to 1992. In 1971, 40 percent of women aged 18 to 54 considered sexual life very important for happiness in their relationship, while only 21 percent held this view in 1992, a development that reflects the strong public preoccupation with sexual liberation twenty years ago.

Traditional gender roles still include some double moralistic traits. Women are expected to be more restricted than men in their sexual behavior. These expectations are rationalized by referring to gender differences in sexual needs. In 1992, 51 percent of Finnish men and 61 percent of women thought that a grown-up man has a clearly or somewhat stronger sexual need than a woman. Forty-one percent of men and 33 percent of women considered the sexual needs of men and women as equally strong. Only 7 percent believed that the sexual needs of women are stronger.

In the case of marital fidelity, a double moral standard is not very strong. In 1971, 34 percent of men and 29 percent of women ages 18 to 54 said that one must be able to accept a husband's temporary infidelity, and 28 percent of men and 30 percent of women would accept a wife's temporary infidelity. In 1992, the corresponding liberal attitudes in regard to a husband's infidelity were 19 percent of men and 21 percent of women, and to a wife's infidelity by 22 percent and 23 percent, respectively.

Even though attitudes toward many aspects of sexuality, for example, adolescent and homosexual sex, have liberalized with the course of time, attitudes toward marital unfaithfulness have become more conservative in the last twenty years. This may be due to the fear of AIDS, or to a general increase in familism in the society. It is easier to be liberal in issues not directly tied to one's own life than in matters related to the personal relationship.

2. Religious and Cultural Factors Affecting Sexuality

A. Religious Factors

In terms of religiosity, Finland is a uniform country, for about 87 percent of the people belong to the Evangelical Lutheran Church of Finland and about fifty thousand people to the Orthodox Church. Both churches are considered state churches. Only a few thousand people at the most belong to each of a few other religious groups. About 8 percent of the Finns do not belong to any religious communities. The religiosity of the Evangelical Lutherans is in most cases rather passive; only a small percentage attend church services regularly. The influence of religion and religious values has declined significantly during the last few decades. Religious thinking does not have much meaning in the sexual lives of people, especially the younger generations.

Marriage is no longer considered a prerequisite to having a sexual life in Finland. The quality of the relationship has become more important than its religious or civil form. Sexual relations are accepted in steady dating relationships and most couples live together before marriage. A significant number of cohabiting people do not get married even after years of living together as a couple. The sexual life of single persons is also widely accepted. The percentage of single persons has gradually increased, with about 30 percent of the middle-aged not living with a sexual partner. One third of these single persons have a steady relationship with a person with whom they do not live.

B. Cultural Factors

It is an essential principle in recent Finnish legislation concerning sexual issues that people may and can do privately all they want when it does not involve forcing another person. In this regard, Finnish legislation aims to respect the individual's right of self-determination. This was a decisive principle in the reform of Finnish legislation around 1990. This principle is also strong in the general population where liberal sexual attitudes prevail among the secularized and independent-thinking majority. This liberalization of sexual attitudes is a significant change, because those with liberal attitudes on sexual issues are usually more satisfied with their sexual life than others.

The interval between publication of results from the 1971 national survey (Sievers et al. 1974) and the FINSEX survey (Kontula and Haavio-Mannila 1993) was marked by a great change in attitudes, values, and practices that began in the sexual revolution of the 1960s. Public discussion about the sexual revolution in the beginning of the 1970s in Finland concerned, to a great extent, the increased availability of sexual material and its commercial use in advertising and mass communication in general. The change could also be seen in legislation where the individuals' liberty to decide about their own sexual matters was increasingly recognized. While increased open discussion about sexual issues in society continued the erosion of some of the still-existing old taboos, a clear step was taken towards more accepting attitudes to sexual issues as a whole. Today, the sexual life of unmarried people is almost as accepted as that of married couples.

A major factor in this shift to more liberal attitudes has been a rise in the level of education, but even without this, the changes would have been significant. More positive attitudes about the sexual rights of adolescents, women, and homosexuals have been matched by more liberal attitudes regarding the acceptability of casual sexual relationships that are not based on love.

In 1971, two women out of three set the promise of marriage as the condition for beginning a sexual relationship; in 1992, only 16 percent of Finnish women were of this opinion (Table 1). Among adolescents, the revolution is even more apparent. Dating has replaced marriage as an institution, with sexual intimacy almost as accepted during dating as it was earlier only within marriage. As a consequence, very few young people marry their first sexual partners any more. As late as thirty years ago, 60 percent of women married their first sexual partners.

Table 1

Think That Adolescents' Sexual Intercourse Is Acceptable in a Regular Relationship (in Percentages), 1971 and 1992

Age	Men 1971	Men 1992	Women 1971	Women 1992
18-24	75	91	59	91
25-34	64	94	40	93
35-44	52	88	20	86
45-54	38	80	14	71
55-64		72		49
65-74		56		43

1971: *N* = 2,139; with 738 men and 1,401 women
1992: *N* = 2,244, with 1,101 men and 1,143 women

Attitudes have also become more positive towards casual relationships (Table 2). About 70 percent of Finns think that even a casual sexual relationship can be happy and satisfying. The necessity of love as a premise for sexual intercourse has also diminished. Sexual intercourse without love was considered wrong by 42 percent of men and 64 percent of women in 1971. In 1992, the corresponding shares were 29 percent and 43 percent. Still, 70 percent hold that living in a steady relationship in which sexual fidelity prevails is most desirable, compared with 10 percent who believe that living apart is most desirable. Twenty percent of men and 4 percent of women would like to maintain several concurrent and continuous sexual relationships. So, as far as their hopes are concerned, women are more monogamous than men.

Finns also take a more liberal attitude than before toward sexual relationships that are outside their own steady relationships. This shift is linked with the greater acceptance of sexual relationships among unmarried and single persons. Attitudes toward homosexual relationships are also significantly more accepting than before. In 1971, close to half of all Finns, 44 percent of males and 45 percent of females, regarded homosexual behavior

Table 2

Think That an Entirely Casual Sexual Relationship Can Be Happy and Satisfying (in Percentages), 1971 and 1992

Age	Men 1971	Men 1992	Women 1971	Women 1992
18-24	77	74	52	73
25-34	66	82	44	73
35-44	50	73	35	63
45-54	51	68	24	56
55-64		65		34
65-74		48		35

1971: N = 2,132, with 741 men and 1,391 women
1992: N = 2,239, with 1,101 men and 1,138 women

between adults as a private affair, with which officials and legislation should in no way interfere (Table 3). In 1992, this opinion was supported by 59 percent of men and by 72 percent of women. On the other hand, attitudes toward extramarital relationships of spouses and pornography have become somewhat stricter, but only among women. Two thirds of the men and one third of the women considered watching pornography sexually arousing for themselves. The quite free sale and distribution of pornographic films and videos were supported by 51 percent of men and by 24 percent of women.

Based on attitudes towards sexuality, equality of gender has made remarkable progress in Finland. Women's right to be the initiators at sexual

Table 3

Think That Interference in Homosexual Behavior from Authorities and Law Is Wrong (in Percentages), 1971 and 1992

Age	Men 1971	Men 1992	Women 1971	Women 1992
18-24	49	60	54	74
25-34	53	66	54	77
35-44	37	59	33	75
45-54	31	52	25	62
55-64		52		55
65-74		44		40

1971: N = 2,126, with 742 men and 1,384 women
1992: N = 2,242, with 1,101 men and 1,141 women

intercourse when they want it so, was supported by 94 percent of men and by 90 percent of women in 1992. This is a significant increase, especially among women. Three out of four women were of the opinion that a respectable woman could openly show her interest in sex.

The cohort analyses show that part of the changes in attitudes do not concern the oldest people at all, especially not the women. Women aged 55 to 74 approve of women initiating a sexual relationship, casual relationships, and sex without love as rarely as they did twenty years ago when they were 35 to 54 years of age. On the other hand, the attitudes towards gays and the sexual relationships between steady-going adolescents have become more liberal in all the gender and age groups.

The differences in sexual behavior between Finland and the U.S.A. are not very big. However, Finns are significantly more liberal than Americans, at least, in their attitudes towards the beginning of sexual life with adolescents, homosexual relationships, and pornography (Smith 1990). A corresponding difference was observed twenty years ago between Denmark and the U.S.A. (Christensen and Gregg 1970).

3. Sexual Knowledge and Education

A. Government Policies and Programs for Sex Education

Legal restrictions designed to control sexarche, the beginning of sexual coitus, which prevailed in Finland until as late as the 1800s, was gradually replaced by the moral education given by the Church and the school. This education with its religious morals gradually changed, giving way to medical views of sexual matters. In sexuality education, the main attention gradually turned from teaching about what is immoral and a sin and focused on the prevention of pregnancies and the health ill effects caused by sexual relationships. Contrary to the custom in many other countries, giving information, advertising, or distributing contraceptives have never been officially prohibited in Finland.

In the 1920s and 1930s, sex education was considered a family responsibility. There was no sex education in the schools as yet. In 1944, the National Board of Education sent a letter concerning sex education to the schools, directing teachers of biology, hygienics, Finnish, and religion to give instruction in sexual matters.

In 1948, an expert board set up by the Ministry of Education produced a program for instruction and education in sexual morals. The program contained guidebooks both for teachers and students. These guidebooks were distributed to schools, colleges, municipal officers of health, church registry offices, and youth organizations at the public expense. Apart from information about personal relations and sexuality, the program, with the guidebook to accompany it, also contained moral views about conditions in which sexual life was considered appropriate for young people.

In the early 1960s, the first summer university courses were held for teachers on family education. In the schools, sex education was still very scarce. In the 1970s, the National Board of Education set up a working committee to make a curriculum for the education in personal relations and sexual matters for the comprehensive school. The work was finished in 1976, but it did not lead to any wider reform of teaching. Instruction in contraception was, however, given in most schools.

From the 1950s on, Finnish municipalities have arranged equal school health care for all students, and sex education was already a part of this care prior to the 1970s. In practice, however, sex education has—and continues to be—concentrated on the anatomy and physiology of sexuality, contraception, and sexually transmitted diseases. Its outcome has largely depended on the personal interest of those teachers of biology and health education, together with physicians and nurses, who are responsible for the planning and the implementing of the educational experiences, most of which are aimed at the from 15- to 16-year-old students in the ninth grade. However, in comparison with the 1960s, all young people have been included in this program, and other sources of information have also been available.

Since the early 1970s, the number of unwanted pregnancies and abortions among adolescents has decreased considerably. In part, the increased liberalization may have contributed to the decline in sex-related research efforts at the end of the decade.

Since 1972, the Primary Health Care Act has required municipalities to organize contraceptive counseling for all who want it, including school children who were given access either to public clinics or to school physicians and nurses. When a physician or school nurse has found it necessary, girls have been provided with contraceptive pills.

In 1996, a comprehensive national study of sex education was started at the upper stage of the comprehensive school (grades 7 to 9). The questionnaire was mailed to the biology teachers in all upper-stage schools in Finland ($N = 603$) in February 1996. A total of 421 acceptable responses were returned from 70 percent of the target population.

The survey came during a period of transition in school sex education, for, in many schools, significant reductions have been carried out in the lesson hours reserved for Health Education. Family Education is about to disappear altogether and new self-governed curricula of the schools have recently been implemented.

Prior to the survey, sex education had been included in the curricula of most of the schools. Only 6 percent of the teachers reported otherwise. It has been given by a filtering method in connection with several other school subjects.

In the ninth grade, the biology teachers usually discuss the subject in connection with biology and the home economics teachers in connection with family education. In the eighth grade, the boys' and the girls' physical education teachers take up the subject in connection with health education.

In addition, approximately half of the schools use school health nurses in sex education (as instructors in contraception) in each of the upper-stage grades.

In the seventh (aged 13 years) grade, half of the schools had given instruction in the development in puberty and menstruation. In the eight grade, new items were sexual intercourse, "first time," contraception, sexually transmitted diseases, dating, and emotions, which had been dealt with in every other school. In the ninth grade, in addition to the above subthemes, nearly all the schools' sex education dealt with genitals and their functioning, ejaculations, conception, pregnancy, birth, and abortion. Other generally discussed new subthemes were sex roles, sexual minorities, sexual morals, sexual terminology, and sex life in adulthood.

Almost all the schools had used video tapes or films in the ninth grades. Textbooks had been used by four out of five, brochures of different kinds had been distributed by two out of three, and condoms had been given at least for examination in every other school. In one third of the schools, visits had been arranged to contraception or family planning clinics; and every tenth school had made visits to youth offices and/or to the congregation. A special event or happening related to sex education had been arranged in 16 percent of the schools within the school year.

According the survey, the most important objectives of school sex education were directing the growth to responsibility, transmission of correct information, promoting the growth of personality, and learning easy attitudes towards sexuality. On the other hand, teaching abstinence, finding the sexual experience nice and stimulating, as well as learning the unsatisfactoriness of casual relationships were considered the least important objectives. The chosen objectives emphasized promoting adolescents' readiness for couple relationships and sexual life. The teachers wanted to avoid moralistically intervening in adolescents' own choices or "feeding" them their own moral values. The teachers did not want to warn against sex too much, neither did they want to advertize it.

One of the objectives of the survey was to explain the possible differences in sex education across the country. As a whole, these differences were not strikingly great or systematic between the provinces. The perceived differences were mainly explained by the local governments' activity in arranging further training in this field or various campaigns.

The greatest problem in the Finnish school sex education is its timing: it comes too late for the stage in the adolescents' development. The present sex education given to the ninth graders (aged 15 years) should be provided two years earlier. Both the students themselves and the experts in this field agree unanimously that sex education in its full extent should already be given to the 12- to 13-year-olds. According the latest news, the syllabi of biology will cover sex education for the eighth graders (aged 14 years).

The strength of school sex education in Finland comes from the school health care which brings out sexual matters in connection with annual physical examinations. Over a third of the girls and a fifth of the boys go to the school health nurse even at other times to talk about sexual matters. In most schools, they also give contraceptive pills. According to the survey, school health nurses also give proper lessons in sex education in at least every other school. Without the contribution of the school health care, the level of adolescents' knowledge of sexual matters would be significantly lower than what it is now.

No detailed and effective public program for the development of sex education or other public services related to contraception is to give credit for the quite effective system of school sex education and the low teenage pregnancy rates in Finland. Rather would we thank the liberal climate around adolescents and their sexuality for the teachers' natural willingness to teach the subject. Adolescents' need for information about sexual matters has been taken for granted. When sexual relationships between adolescents are accepted, it is clear that they are entitled to be prepared and well-informed about various matters related to sexual life.

Public health care plays a significant role in sex education and advising on contraception. The system of the maternity and child care of the public health centers covers the whole country with almost all the expectant mothers and families with children. In the maternity centers, sexual life during pregnancy and contraception are discussed, among other things, and mothers and fathers are psychologically prepared to welcome the baby.

A liberal attitude towards sexuality may be reflected in the condom advertising found in the mass media, especially during the summer months. Women's magazines have also contained numerous sex-related articles that are read by both sexes.

B. Informal Sources of Sexual Knowledge and Education

In the FINSEX study (Kontula and Haavio-Mannila 1993), people were asked if they had gotten information about sexual matters in their childhood homes in their youth or sex education at school. At the same time, the people were asked to evaluate the sufficiency of the information and education they had received and their willingness then to receive such information about sexual matters in general. Similar questions were asked both in 1971 and 1992.

Discussion of sexual matters has gradually increased both in the homes and in the schools. In their childhood home, information had been received about sexual matters by 39 percent of men and by 41 percent of women in 1971; in 1992, correspondingly, by 61 percent and by 64 percent. Ten percent of men and 14 percent of women in 1971 regarded the information received at home as sufficient. In 1992, the percentages were 29 percent and 32 percent respectively. Until recently, most people have thus not been getting very much information about sexual matters at home, even if these matters have been more talked about.

In 1971, 28 percent of men and 33 percent of women reported having received sex education at school; in 1992, 64 percent of males and 74 percent of females. In 1971, 7 percent of men and 8 percent of women considered this information sufficient; in 1992, the percentages were 25 percent and 32 percent. This shows that sex education in the school has clearly improved, although only less than one third of the respondents considered the education sufficient. Nearly one tenth of the people said that they would not even have wanted such education. Slightly more people would have wanted to receive more education from the school than from the home.

Young people report clearly more often than others of having received sufficient information concerning sexual matters from the school or home (Figure 1). This suggests that speaking and teaching about sexual matters has clearly become more common, at least with those people who lived their youth in the 1980s. During the past twenty years, there was an especially clear increase in dealing with sexual matters. After 1971, the share of those who had received sex education in the school increased nearly threefold. Only a few people in the oldest age groups reported they had talked enough about sexual matters in their homes or at school.

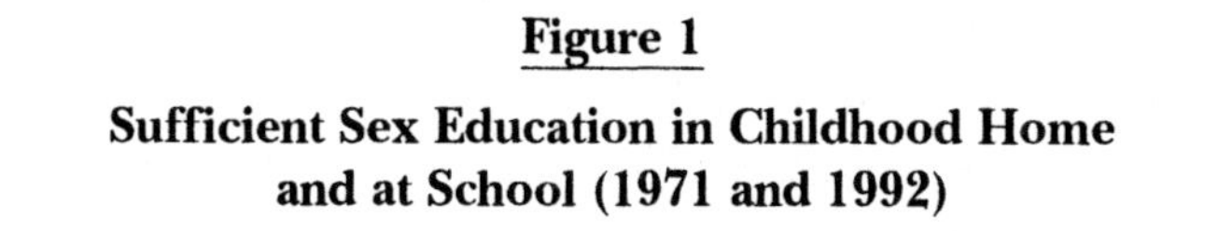

Figure 1

Sufficient Sex Education in Childhood Home and at School (1971 and 1992)

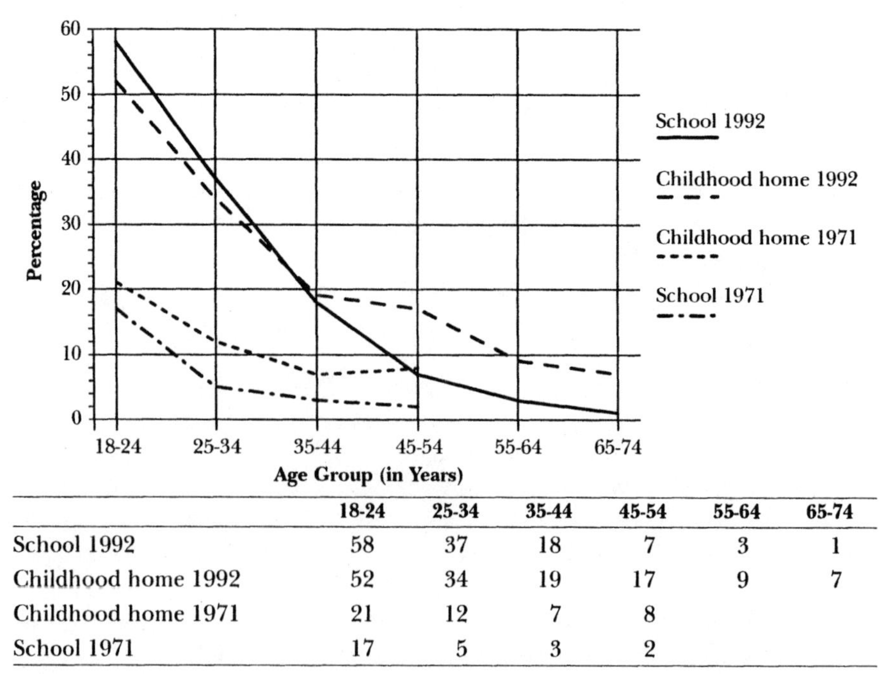

	18-24	25-34	35-44	45-54	55-64	65-74
School 1992	58	37	18	7	3	1
Childhood home 1992	52	34	19	17	9	7
Childhood home 1971	21	12	7	8		
School 1971	17	5	3	2		

The school has often tried to avoid taking the responsibility of giving sex education, maintaining that it is a question of family privacy with which the school should not interfere. This has been an attempt to cover the teachers' own feelings of insufficiency about the teaching of sexual matters. The homes again have shuffled off the responsibility upon the school. The young people in this awkward situation have had to find the information they needed from most diverse sources. Such sources have been the mass media and sex-related literature, from which the information received has been spread from one to the other in the circle of friends. Boys often use sex magazines as a source of information—often as their only source—where they have found actual information about sexual practices. The girls again have been more interested than the boys in the medical facts about becoming pregnant and contraception. This information has often been found in the readers' queries sections of magazines.

The attitudes about the school's sex education are fairly trusting in Finland nowadays, since at least 63 percent of the men and women reported that they did not think sex education in the schools would induce the young to start their sexual life too early. Only 19 percent of the men and 22 percent of the women feared that sex education would induce young people to have intercourse too early. Those who supported this opinion were strongly concentrated in the over 55-year-old group, where one in every two held this opinion. Since the people of this age group have had their say in the decision making of sex education in the schools up to now, it is no wonder there are still some deficiencies in the teaching.

4. Autoerotic Behaviors and Patterns

A. Children and Adolescents

According to Kontula and Meriläinen (1988), between 2 percent and 3 percent of both the boys and the girls reported having started masturbating already before age 10. In childhood, touching genitals to cause pleasure cannot very often be connected with masturbation. In addition, adolescents often dare not report it in a survey such as this. The researchers, therefore, believe that the percentage of children practicing masturbation at an early age is surely more than 2 percent or 3 percent.

In the follow-up of the same survey (Kosunen 1993), 13- to 17-year-olds were asked if they had ever practiced masturbation and if they had masturbated during the last month. Of the 13-year-olds, 36 percent of the boys and 23 percent of the girls reported that they had sometimes practiced masturbation; of the 15-year-olds, 67 percent and 45 percent reported this practice; and of the 17-year-olds, 79 percent and 59 percent. About 40 percent of the boys had masturbated during the last month and about 20 percent during the last week. With the girls, the corresponding figures were 20 percent and 5 percent. With age, the masturbation activity of the young increased.

B. Adults

The proportion of adults engaging in self-loving, clearly more common among men than women, has definitely increased during the last twenty years, according to the FINSEX study. There has been an increase in the practice of self-loving both during the previous month and during the past year. In 1971, 28 percent of the men and 16 percent of women reported masturbating during the previous month. In 1992, the corresponding shares were 42 percent and 25 percent. The strength of the change can be seen in the percentage of women who had masturbated during the previous year. In 1992, this figure for women was higher than the corresponding data for men in 1971.

With the spread of a more natural attitude towards self-loving, fewer and fewer people abstain from it entirely. In 1971, 49 percent of the women and 26 percent of the men had never tried this sexual outlet. In 1992, the corresponding figures were 23 percent and 10 percent. So, a large majority of both women and men have engaged in self-loving at least some time in their life.

Self-loving is considerably more common with the young than with older people (Figure 2). This, however, is not due so much to age differences as it is to changes in the times. People seem to keep the frequency pattern of self-loving they adopted in their youth throughout their lives. There are no obstacles to this, since masturbation is in no way dependent on the presence of a partner. With the aging of the present middle-aged people, the incidence of self-loving will increase further in the population.

The increase in self-pleasuring is explained by the fact that fewer and fewer people believe in the unfounded arguments that it entails health risks as booklets on sex education maintained as late as the 1950s. Two thirds of the women and over one third of the men who still believed in these risks, or were at least uncertain about them, had never engaged in this sexual activity. Very few of these women had masturbated during the last month. On the other hand, half of the men who had totally lost their belief in the health risks of masturbation, and nearly 30 percent of the women, had engaged in self-pleasuring during the last month. The spread of accurate information had been a major factor in encouraging people to feel free to enjoy their sexuality with self-pleasuring.

Having a steady sexual partner somewhat diminished the need for self-loving: the unmarried, the divorced, and the widowed engaged in self-pleasuring more regularly than did married people. The better educated people engaged in self-loving more often than others. Religiosity did not relate to the incidence of self-loving, but those who consumed more alcohol were more likely to masturbate than others. During the past twenty years, the differences in the incidence of self-loving among the different age groups has disappeared while the differences between the marital status groups and alcohol user groups had grown.

Figure 2

Masturbation During the Past Year (1971 and 1992)

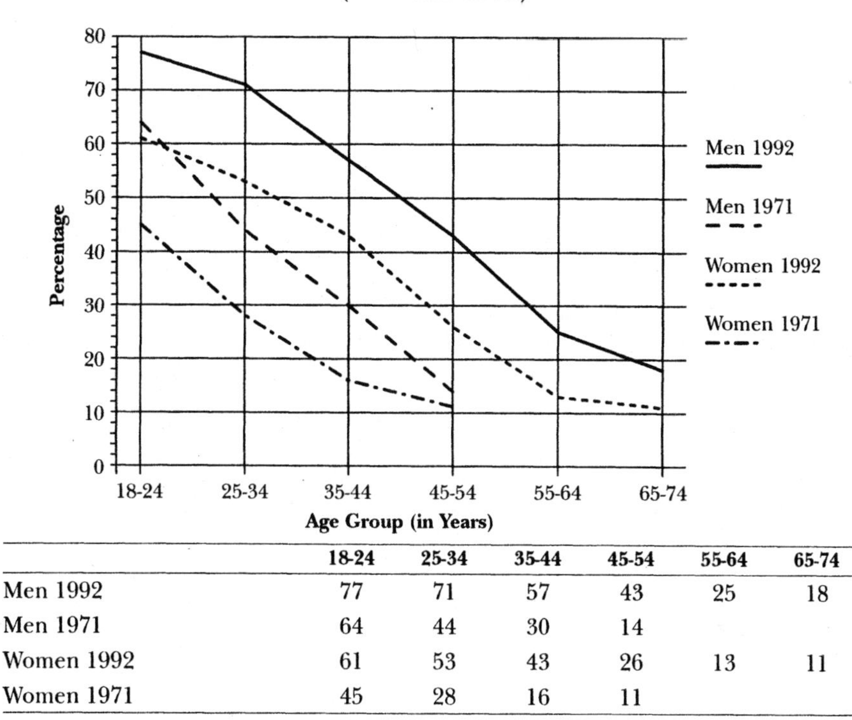

	18-24	25-34	35-44	45-54	55-64	65-74
Men 1992	77	71	57	43	25	18
Men 1971	64	44	30	14		
Women 1992	61	53	43	26	13	11
Women 1971	45	28	16	11		

Young low-income men and women engage in self-pleasuring more often than others. This relation of the masturbation frequency to low-income persists in middle-aged men. Further, this higher incidence of self-loving is related to the observation that low-income men enter into steady relationships less frequently than others. Masturbation thus serves them, at least in part, as a substitute for an intercourse-centered sexual life.

The use of pornographic materials has remained almost the same among men but decreased among women between 1970 and 1990. Even when sex videos were included in the printed publications in 1992, fewer people, on the average, had viewed such material during the previous year. During the past year, 50 percent to 60 percent of the men in different age groups and from 15 percent to 20 percent of the women had watched a sex video or read a sex magazine.

Obviously, interest in pornographic publications was exceptionally high in 1971, because open nakedness had come, for the first time, into the pictures of the sex magazines at the end of the 1960s in Finland. The charm of novelty and the taste of "the forbidden fruit" made this material especially attractive. More recently, this high excitement and attraction have settled down. Besides, the so-called soft pornography is now within everyone's reach, for example, in the pictures in the afternoon tabloids, although it is no longer referred to as pornography.

5. Interpersonal Heterosexual Behaviors

A. Children

Small children often play sexual games (doctor games) and masturbate, during which they examine the genitals of both their own and the other sex. According to the KISS study conducted in Finland (Kontula and Meriläinen 1988), sexual games have been played by at least 40 percent of the young adults in their childhood, half of them more frequent than one or two incidents. These games may also include imitating and trying the sex habits the children had seen adults using. This cannot, however, be regarded as an actual initiation of sexual life, because it is not yet conscious activity that could be interpreted as sexual. Sexual meanings are not generally understood before approaching adolescence and the effects of pubertal hormones on the brain. Puberty brings a quite new kind of interest in sexual matters.

B. Adolescents

Puberty

By age 13, about four out of five girls have had their first periods of menstruation and about 60 percent of the boys their first ejaculations. As a result, many young people show considerably more serious interest in the opposite sex than before. Over half of the boys of this age and one third of the girls have already viewed sex magazines and sex videos, and more than half of both boys and girls have kissed, according to the 1992 data. Many have experienced caressing over the clothing. Almost half of the 13-year-olds are ready to accept sexual intercourse in their peers' relationships. About as many report having already had a dating relationship with the opposite sex. Mostly, this means going around together with the dating partner as part of a group of young people. Sexual intercourse has been experienced by about 5 percent by the age of 13.

Between ages 14 and 15, most Finnish adolescents go to a confirmation class, a one-week church-sponsored camp, after which they are confirmed. This has become a kind of initiation rite for becoming a sexual adult.

Adolescence is a time of rapid changes, and, with age, sexual experience quickly grows. In Finland, the greatest changes in adolescent sexual behaviors occurred between 1960 and 1970. In 1992, Finns between ages 18 and 54 reported they had kissed for the first time, on the average, at the age of 14, had started dating at 17, and experienced their first sexual intercourse at the age of 18. Young people with a long education began sexual intercourse later than others.

Nowadays young people mature, both physically and mentally, earlier than before. Because of the increased economic well-being, they live in a more grown-up way at a fairly young age, when they build their sexual identity through a multinational youth culture. As a result, the age of sexual initiation has fallen. On the other hand, the time spent in education has lengthened and the age of entering into marriage has risen. This explains why young people have more relationships, both successive and casual, today, and why marriage has been displaced by cohabitation, at least before having children.

In the 1992 FINSEX survey, one third of the 18- to 74-year-old women and a quarter of the men reported dating (going steady) by age 15. About four out of five had experienced kissing, and two out of three caressing over the clothing. Petting under the clothing had been experienced by one of every two younger Finns. Sexual intercourse before the age of 16 had been experienced by 31 percent of the girls and 19 percent of the boys according to the 1992 data (Figure 3). On average, Finnish girls begin having intercourse somewhat younger than the boys. This is quite understandable, because girls often date boys from two to three years older than they themselves are. The boys are more eager to have intercourse than the girls, but the girls have better opportunities.

Early Noncoital Experiences

The sexual life of young Finns does not generally begin with sexual intercourse, but with kissing and caressing. These behaviors are often associated with first dating relationships. It has been observed in Finland that four

Figure 3

9th Grade Pupils (15-Year-Olds) Who Have Had the Indicated Experiences (1992)

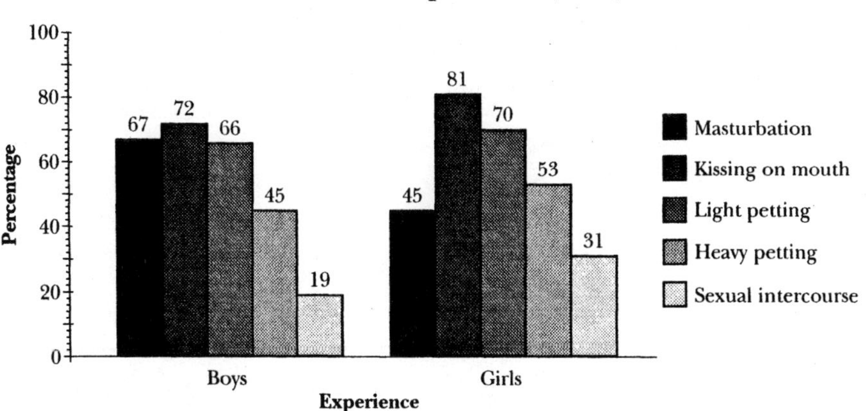

years, on the average, elapse from the first kisses and caresses of the young people to the first sexual intercourse (Kontula 1991). These experiences are surely as important to the young as the first intercourse. In the past, when a great number of people wanted or had to put off beginning sexual intercourse until marriage, kisses and caresses were the only forms of sexual life before entering matrimony.

A great number of people have already kissed before their first steady relationship, according to the 1992 FINSEX study. After the mid-1970s, about 60 percent of the men and 70 percent of the women were dating before the age of 18. About 40 percent of the present-day under-35-year-olds had had a steady dating relationship before the age of 16. Before the 1950s, it was quite unusual for women of this age to date. Nowadays, only 3 percent of the over-25-year-olds have never had a dating relationship. Since the 1980s, there have not been great changes in the onset of dating.

The age of sexual initiation has clearly fallen during the past few decades. Both first kisses and dating relationships are experienced at a younger age today than in the past. Four out of five have kissed before the age of 16, and two out of three have been going steady under the age of 18.

Characteristic of those adolescents who initiate a sexual life earlier than the others is a lifestyle that emphasizes a break with the norms of childhood and an orientation towards a freer social life. To these young people, free social life represents a means rather than a goal. The reverse is true for those who have less self-confidence and fewer sexual experiences. The acquired values and moral codes, such as associating love with family, lose their importance after sexual initiation.

Based on the KISS study (Kontula 1991), it can be said that the values associated with starting a sexual life early are today often connected with symbolic opposition or rebellion to authorities. Extended education with its upper-class values is ideal for arousing such opposition.

Sex is used to sell things and ideas to the young, but sex itself is rarely sold to them. Society and parents rarely provide adolescents with interpretations of sex (scripts) that would give a positive and an enjoyable picture of sexuality. Thus, adolescents, girls in particular, do not expect much good of their first sexual experiences, especially of sexual intercourse. Normally, organized education and instruction only provide warnings about the risks of getting pregnant, being infected with an STD or the HIV virus, getting a bad reputation, and similar dangers.

Moral values concerning reproduction and marriage have gradually been replaced by the values of satisfying one's social needs. This shift has contributed to a widening of interpretations relating to sexual interactions guided by strict Christian and conventional scripts towards "games," in which various tactics to achieve first sexual experiences are possible. The morals of satisfying social needs, which emphasize the importance of sexual life, give young people permission to initiate a sexual life in various practical situations. This widening of the sexual script towards "games" is one important reason for an earlier sexual initiation among Finnish adolescents during the last few decades (Kontula 1991). Tactics, interpretations, and values, which are all part of sexual interactions, are, however, still strongly regulated socially and culturally.

Dating

The age of first dating, like the age of first kisses, has lowered in recent years. In the 1930s, only half of the under-20-year-old people had dating relationships; currently, more than four fifths of the under-20-year-olds are dating. This increase stopped in the 1980s.

In the Finnish-Karelian culture area, "night courting or prowling" was a common way for young people to become acquainted until the early twentieth century. In rural areas, it was customary for groups of boys to visit several girls during a single outing, since the girls belonged to the same social group. In going to the girls' sleeping quarters, "night courting" constituted a formal social venture or endeavor, with identifying knocks, introductions, overtures, seductive lines, and poetry. The choice of a conversation partner was made with the help of night proposal rites. The many customary rules and norms in night courting were aimed at the preservation of morality (Sarmela 1967). In their classic study *Die Einleitung der Ehe* (*The Introduction to Marriage*) (1937), K. Rob and V. Wikman divided night prowling into two main types: organized group and individual courting. In group prowling, the boys watched, often very strictly, over each other's behavior. The girls could not refuse the visits of such groups. It was nevertheless in the power of the girls to decide which boys in the group would be allowed into their sleeping rooms in the storehouse or building where they were spending the summer.

Sexarche

Sexarche, first sexual intercourse, requires finding an appropriate partner and becoming sexually aroused. What a person defines as "appropriate" is closely associated with the interpretations given by society. "An appropriate partner" may be understood as a partner with whom one has a love relationship and a relationship in which both partners feel "ready" for sexual intercourse. The importance of these social conditions is emphasized by the fact that about 20 percent of the 15-year-olds with steady partners would have liked to have sexual intercourse, but, for some reason, they had not had that experience. They had had both the chance and the willingness; nevertheless, all the social conditions had not been fulfilled.

At the age of 15, adolescents usually accept the sexual intercourse of their peers on grounds of love. Thus, an important condition for starting a sexual relationship is that two people love each other enough. The importance of love in legitimating sexual relationships of the young people is somewhat greater among farmers and the upper-middle class. This applies to both youths and their parents. This emphasis on love is closely connected with the demand for faithfulness.

Girls tend to value sex less, to masturbate less frequently, and to report considerably less desire for sexual intercourse than boys of their age. Girls who have never had a steady relationship with a boy are less likely to report a strong sexual desire. A female culture that emphasizes love does not attach a high value to sexual enjoyment in the expectations of Finnish girls. The dating institution, however, diminishes the effect of this romantic value that delays sexarche. Among the girls, the importance of sex quickly increases with an increase in experience. Dating clearly brings the expectations of sexual life closer to each other in boys and girls.

Twenty percent of Finns currently experience sexual intercourse before the age of 16; approximately 50 percent by age 18. Seventy percent of the women and half of the men reported that they had had their first experience of sexual intercourse with a steady partner. Only 60 percent of the women and 50 percent of the men reported being in love with their first sexual partner (Figure 4).

Figure 4

First Sexual Intercourse by the Age of 18, in Different Decades, Based on the Cohort Analysis (1971 and 1992)

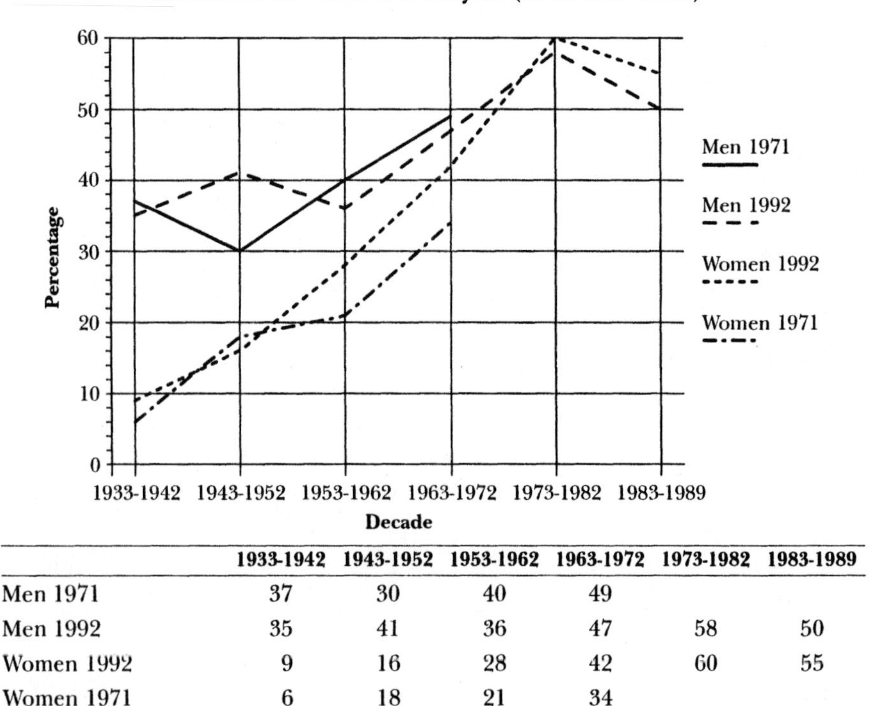

	1933-1942	1943-1952	1953-1962	1963-1972	1973-1982	1983-1989
Men 1971	37	30	40	49		
Men 1992	35	41	36	47	58	50
Women 1992	9	16	28	42	60	55
Women 1971	6	18	21	34		

Among the older Finns surveyed, nearly half of the women had their first sexual intercourse after the age of 20. With the men, the corresponding share was about one fifth. Among younger Finns, about 10 percent have their first intercourse after age 20. Two percent of the over-30-year-olds reported that they had never had sexual intercourse.

The age of first sexual intercourse does not differ significantly in the provinces of Finland. Nor is it related to population density, although people living in the rural areas start having sexual intercourse somewhat later than urban youth, probably because rural living provides less opportunities for making social contacts.

A significant change has also occurred in the extent to which sexual intercourse is involved in the first dating experiences. When ages of first dating relationship and first sexual intercourse are compared, it appears that, as late as the 1930s, sexual intercourse was not generally a part of a steady dating relationship. Less than a third of the women who had been dating at a particular age had had sexual intercourse at that age. After the 1930s, there was a continuous even growth in the proportion of the women who experienced sexual intercourse while dating. By the end of the 1970s, the proportion of women dating who had had sexual intercourse grew to nearly 90 percent. During the 1980s it dropped a little and is now about 80 percent.

Women's greater sexual initiative and willingness at the first intercourse has contributed to this change. However, for many women the first experience of sexual intercourse is still painful and a disappointment. Many women go through their first experience expecting it as a necessary routine in order to be able to start really enjoying their sexual life after this "puncturing."

The decreasing gap between the willingness of men and women to initiate sexual relations in the interval between the 1970s and 1990s is statistically very significant. In two decades, the share of the women who were reluctant at their first sexual intercourse fell from 40 percent to 10 percent. This increasing equality between women and men has been matched by an increase in equality in other sectors of life such as education, work, politics, family, and leisure time. Part of this change may be due to the more honest reporting of both men and women to these questions than before.

Early Contraceptive Use

The use of contraception at the first intercourse has increased considerably in recent decades (Table 4). Only a few percent of the over-55-year-olds had used contraception at the first time and about 70 percent had been entirely without contraception. Withdrawal was the most common contraceptive method. The use of the condom as a contraceptive method at the first intercourse increased significantly with the under-55-year-olds, espe-

Table 4

No Contraception at the First Sexual Intercourse (in Percentages), 1971 and 1992

Age	Men 1971	Men 1992	Women 1971	Women 1992
18-24	26	17	24	13
25-34	39	24	46	22
35-44	58	29	60	18
45-54	57	40	60	42
55-64		67		68
65-74		82		70

1971: *N* = 1,919, with 669 men and 1,250 women
1992: *N* = 2,048, with 1,002 men and 1,046 women

cially among the young after the middle of 1960s. In the 1970s, the use of the condom decreased slightly, according to age group comparisons, but increased again in the 1980s, obviously because of the condom campaigns against AIDS. In the recent years, 60 percent of the men and 65 percent of the women had used the condom at the first intercourse. About 15 percent used no contraception at all. These proportions correspond well with results of the most recent surveys among adolescents.

C. Adults

Single Adults

In 1992, 30 percent of Finnish men ages 18 to 74 and 34 percent of women were not married or cohabiting. One third of these had a steady sexual relationship. In the whole population covered by our survey, 11 percent of both men and women had a steady sex partner with whom they did not live.

The proportion of single adults, i.e., not having any steady sexual relationship, is highest in the youngest and oldest age groups (Table 5). A large proportion of people under 30 years have not yet started to live together with a partner but will probably do so later. Many of the women over 60 years are single because of widowhood and the shortage of older men. Among men, singlehood does not increase with age because they less often get widowed and have more potential partners available.

Singlehood in Finland does not mean celibacy. A large part of single people have a regular sex life: 40 percent of all single men and 28 percent of single women had not experienced periods of at least six months without sexual intercourse over the course of the previous five years. On the other hand, 8 percent of single men and 30 percent of single women had not engaged in sexual intercourse during the previous five years.

Table 5

Type of the Couple Relationship by Gender and Age (in Percentages, 1992)

Type of Relationship	Age, Years 18-24	25-34	35-44	45-54	55-64	65-74	Total
MEN							
No couple relationship	48	17	14	12	15	16	19
Steady sexual relationship without living together	29	12	4	5	7	8	11
Cohabitation	9	27	11	6	2	2	13
Marriage	4	44	71	77	76	74	57
(*N*)	(159)	(249)	(266)	(203)	(308)	(96)	(1103)
WOMEN							
No couple relationship	32	11	15	13	29	49	23
Steady sexual relationship without living together	32	11	8	9	6	3	11
Cohabitation	28	22	13	7	4	1	13
Marriage	8	56	64	71	61	47	53
(*N*)	(164)	(233)	(250)	(191)	(157)	(149)	(1114)

More single adults never had engaged in sexual intercourse, 14 percent compared with 3 percent of the total population. Single women started their sexual activity at a later age than other women, but for men singlehood was not connected to the age of initiating sexual intercourse.

Single men have a more varied sex life than single women. Forty-six percent of single men and 20 percent of single women reported sexual intercourse during the previous month. Thirteen percent of the single men and 3 percent of single women had engaged in sexual intercourse at least once a week during the previous month.

Measured by the number of partners, the sexual life of single adults is also more lively than that of married and cohabiting people. Close to half of all single men and more than a third of single women had had more than one sex partner during the previous year.

For single adults living without a steady sexual relationship, their last sexual partner was usually a sexually unaffiliated person. Fourteen percent of single women and 9 percent of the men said that their last partner was a spouse or steady partner of somebody else. Of single men, 2 percent said that their last partner was a prostitute. One tenth of single men had, during their lifetime, had intercourse with a prostitute. This is the same proportion as for married or cohabiting men. No single women reported contact with a paid sex partner.

Single people do not use as varied sex techniques as cohabiting couples and other people having a steady relationship. The positions used in last intercourse resemble those of married people: the missionary position with the man lying on top and the woman underneath. In the casual sexual relationships of single people, the love play and coital positions are fairly traditional: there is little oral sex and stimulating of a partner's genitals by hand.

For women, the incidence of orgasm in sexual intercourse varies according to having or not having a steady sexual relationship. However, 26 percent of single women did not recall whether they had an orgasm during their last intercourse, perhaps because this may have been several years ago.

Single adults reported less satisfaction with their last intercourse than other people. Single adults also reported less satisfaction with their sex life as a whole than people having a steady sexual partner. Single people have a lower sexual self-esteem than other people; this may be one reason for their lack of sexual partner. People not having sexual relationships do not receive positive sexual feedback, which might strengthen their self-esteem.

Slightly more single men have had some homosexual experiences during their lifetime than attached males, 7 percent compared with 4 percent. Single men also are more likely to have a homosexual identity or identify themselves as bisexuals than other men (see Section 6). Single women are not more often lesbians than other women.

Masturbation is more common among single adults than other adults. Half of single men and one fourth of single women reported self-loving during the last month, twice as high as married people. Self-loving is most common among single people living with their parents. Most of these are young people.

In addition to using self-loving to compensate for not having a steady sexual partner, singles watch sex videos. Forty percent of single men had watched sex videos at least a couple of times during the previous year. This is the same frequency as cohabiting men and more than married men. Only 5 percent of single women had watched sex videos during the year, less than cohabiting or married women had done. Similar differences were found in the use of pornographic books and magazines. Women with steady partners may get invitations from their partners to watch sex videos or read pornographic materials. Single women seem to be too shy to buy or borrow sex materials to use alone.

Sex toys and aids are generally not used as substitutes for sexual relations (see Section 8). Vibrators are not used more by single than by other women—about 5 percent of all women had ever used them.

Alcohol is associated with the sexual life of single adults more than it is for affiliated persons. As many as 58 percent of single men and 26 percent of single women reported drinking alcoholic beverages before their last intercourse. For single men, this proportion is almost double that of other men, perhaps because the casual relationships of single adults often begin in restaurants and other social situations where alcoholic beverages are served.

Even though single adults suffer from feelings of loneliness more than people living in a couple relationship, not all of them long for a sexual partner. Many deny the importance of having sex or living with somebody.

Cohabitating Adults

All over the world, families and couple relationships have changed in recent decades. In the developed countries, children move away from the parental home earlier than before, cohabitation has become a common form of starting a marriage, divorces have increased, and the number of children has declined.

Because of the higher standard of living, adult Finns today live less often with their parents than in earlier times and more often alone (Table 6). The increase in unmarried cohabitation has decreased the proportion of married people in the population. In 1971, 64 percent of the respondents ages 18 to 54 lived together with their spouse and only a few percent with their fiancées or steady partners. The rapid growth of cohabitation can be seen from the 1992 survey: 16 percent of the 18- to 54-year-olds were cohabiting and only 53 percent of the population in this age cohort was married.

Table 6

Change in Household Structure of People Aged 15 to 54 from 1971 to 1992 (in Percentages)

Living Companions	Men 1971	Men 1992	Women 1971	Women 1992
Parents or other kin	26	17	18	15.
Wife or husband	62	52	66	51
Cohabiting partner	3	17	2	18
Same sex companion	3	1	3	1
Other and no information	2	0	4	0
Lives alone	4	13	7	15
(*N*)	(744)	(877)	(1408)	(838)

The increase in cohabitation has not meant that there are more couples living together than earlier. When one adds the percentages of married and cohabiting people together, their proportion only grew from 66 percent in 1971 to 69 percent in 1992. The main change is that nowadays more people delay or do not enter a formal marriage, and maintain an official status as single. In the past twenty years, the proportion of never-married people among the 15- to 54-year-old Finns rose from 35 percent to 40 percent for men and from 27 percent to 36 percent for women.

The developmental cycle of the present union greatly varies by age in 1992 (Table 7). In the older age groups, 55 years and over, a large majority first moved together after the wedding. In the age category 25 to 44 years, half of the people first lived together and then married. Four fifths of the less-than-35-year-old people living together with someone were cohabiting without marriage. At present, most Finns start their marital life as a cohabiting couple.

Table 7

Developmental Cycle of the Present Union by Gender and Age (in Percentages, 1992)

	Age, Years						
Cycle of the Union	**18-24**	**25-34**	**35-44**	**45-54**	**55-64**	**65-74**	**Kaikki**
MEN							
From marriage to living together	6	10	36	80	87	93	50
From cohabitation to marriage	11	51	51	12	10	4	31
Cohabiting	83	39	13	8	3	3	19
(*N*)	(36)	(176)	(218)	(169)	(101)	(73)	(773)
WOMEN							
From marriage to living together	5	17	43	78	85	94	51
From cohabitation to marriage	15	52	39	13	8	3	28
Cohabiting	80	31	18	9	7	3	21
(*N*)	(59)	(182)	(193)	(150)	(101)	(72)	(757)

In 1992, the age at moving in together was for men aged 15 to 64 years on average 0.9 years lower than age at marriage in 1971, and among women 0.6. The increase in cohabitation thus made men, in particular, more inclined to move in together with their partner relatively early. Twenty years ago, the average age at first marriage was 24.6 for men and 22.3 for women—there is no data on when couples moved in together from that era. In 1992, men initiated cohabiting, or married for the first time, on average at age 23.7 years, women at age 21.8.

Of all the men interviewed in 1992, 79 percent and of the women 83 percent had lived in a matrimonial relationship. In the oldest age group,

65 to 74 years, there was a gender gap: 7 percent of men and 13 percent of women never had cohabited or married. This is partly explained by the fact that single men die young and single women live long.

A longer life expectancy and the growing divorce rate have contributed to the fact that people have time to enter several unions during their lives. According to the 1971 study, 5 percent of the ever married men and 6 percent of women had been married at least twice. In 1992, the proportions were 17 percent and 22 percent, respectively.

Cohabitation does not always lead to marriage, particularly among young people. One fourth of the 1992 respondents had been cohabiting without getting married to the partner. Among people under 35 years, the proportion was more than half.

Marital, Extramarital, and Postmarital Sexual Behaviors

(1) Sexual Intercourse. The frequency of sexual intercourse twenty years ago was almost as high as nowadays. Finns have sexual intercourse usually once or twice a week. The share of people who had had sexual intercourse during the last two days among the people ages 35 to 54 was higher in 1992 than in 1971 (Figure 5). Sexual relations seem nowadays to remain consistent and regular later in life than they did twenty years ago. The frequency of sexual intercourse does not decrease significantly until after the age of 55, especially among women. Even this change does not necessarily follow from aging but from generational differences.

Sexual intercourse has become more varied. While in 1971, as many as 68 percent of the most recent occurrences of sexual intercourse among 18- to 54-year-old people used the missionary position, in 1992 the proportion was 43 percent. The proportion of those who had used many different positions during their most recent sexual intercourse had increased in a very significant way, from 16 percent to 32 percent.

Twenty years ago, it was usual that the man was the sole initiator of sexual intercourse, in 49 percent of the incidents. In 1992, only 37 percent of the most recent experiences of sexual intercourse were initiated solely by the man. Fifteen percent of the male respondents said that the woman was the initiator of the last sexual intercourse, but this figure was only 10 percent according to the women's responses. Women were slightly more likely than men to report that both partners took an equal role in initiating intercourse, 51 percent compared with 45 percent. Women may find it more difficult to admit that they have taken an active role in coitus.

Alcohol consumption before the last sexual intercourse became slightly more frequent in the past twenty years. In 1971, alcohol had been used by 21 percent of the men and 11 percent of the women; in 1992, this figure was 25 percent and 16 percent respectively. This reflects an increased consumption of alcohol among Finns in general.

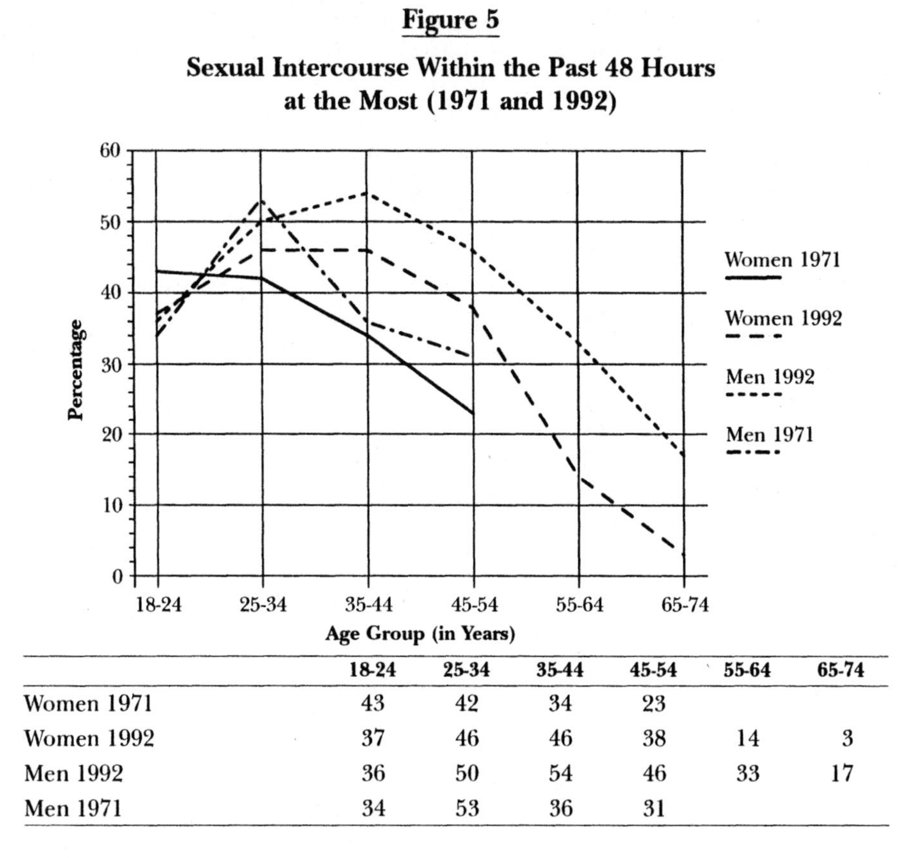

Figure 5

Sexual Intercourse Within the Past 48 Hours at the Most (1971 and 1992)

	18-24	25-34	35-44	45-54	55-64	65-74
Women 1971	43	42	34	23		
Women 1992	37	46	46	38	14	3
Men 1992	36	50	54	46	33	17
Men 1971	34	53	36	31		

(2) Sex Styles. Sexual satisfaction can be attained in many ways. Following factor analysis of the 1992 data to measure variables associated with different sexual habits and partners, three sex styles were identified:

1. Sex in a sexual-intercourse-centered steady relationship (frequent sexual intercourse with a steady partner);
2. sex in casual relationships (many sexual partners, including relationships with foreigners and prostitutes); and
3. alternative sexual habits (anal and oral sex, manually stimulated satisfaction, acquaintance with sexual aids, the use of different sex facilities, and masturbation).

The connection of the social background with these sex styles was examined by regression analyses. As explanatory variables in the simple linear regression model, there were gender, age, place of residence, type of marital relationship, years of education, income, days on working trips, religiosity, and two variables about alcohol consumption: the frequency of alcohol use and of getting intoxicated.

Sex in a steady relationship, meaning frequency of sexual intercourse and familiarity of the last sexual partner, relate naturally to living in a steady relationship, but also to youth and high income with a lower level of education. This sex style is typical of ambitious couples. The regression model explained 41 percent of the variation in the steady-relationship sex.

Those who practice casual sexual relationships, or people who have numerous sexual partners and/or sex with foreigners and paid partners are men, city residents, well-paid, who travel a lot for their work. They are indifferent to religion and often consume alcohol. The people cohabiting or in a steady noncohabiting relationship more often than other people had transient sexual relationships. The typical male practitioners of casual sexual relationships may well be called "rich good-time boys" for their social background even if they can be found in all age and gender groups. The regression model explained 18 percent of the variation in the casual sexual relationships.

Alternative sex was related to male gender, youth, frequency of alcohol consumption, and frequency of intoxication. The married and the single people did not engage in alternative sexual habits as much as the people living in cohabitation or in a steady sexual relationships. Alternative sexual habits are related to the lifestyle of young go-ahead men. As much as 43 percent of the variation in alternative sex was explained by these social factors.

(3) Sexual Partners. For Finns ages 18 to 54, the average number of sexual partners during the lifetime has risen from seven to ten during the last twenty years. In 1971, women of all ages had about three, men about eleven partners; in 1992, correspondingly, six and fourteen. In 1992, the male respondents between ages 25 and 44 years had the most partners, between 40 percent and 50 percent had at least ten partners; of the women in the same age cohorts, about 18 percent had at least ten partners (Figure 6).

In both surveys, the large number of sexual partners is related not only to gender and age, but also to marital status, according to a Multiple Classification (multivariant) analysis: the married people had fewer partners than the unmarried, widowed, and the divorced. Those alienated from religion, as well as the frequent consumers of alcohol, had more sexual partners than the religious and temperate people. Those who had passed the matriculation examination had fewer partners than the less educated; this difference, however, was no longer statistically significant in 1992.

Worldwide, in all the sex surveys, men claim to have had more sexual partners than women. This survey refined this general data by separating out data on Finnish men and women who had foreigners, homosexuals, or prostitutes as partners. When those who had, some time in their life, at least, one foreigner, one homosexual, and one prostitute as a sexual partner were separated from the data on under-56-year-old men and women, the men still had at least ten sexual partners—about twice as many as the

Figure 6

At Least 10 Sexual Partners During the Lifetime (1971 and 1992)

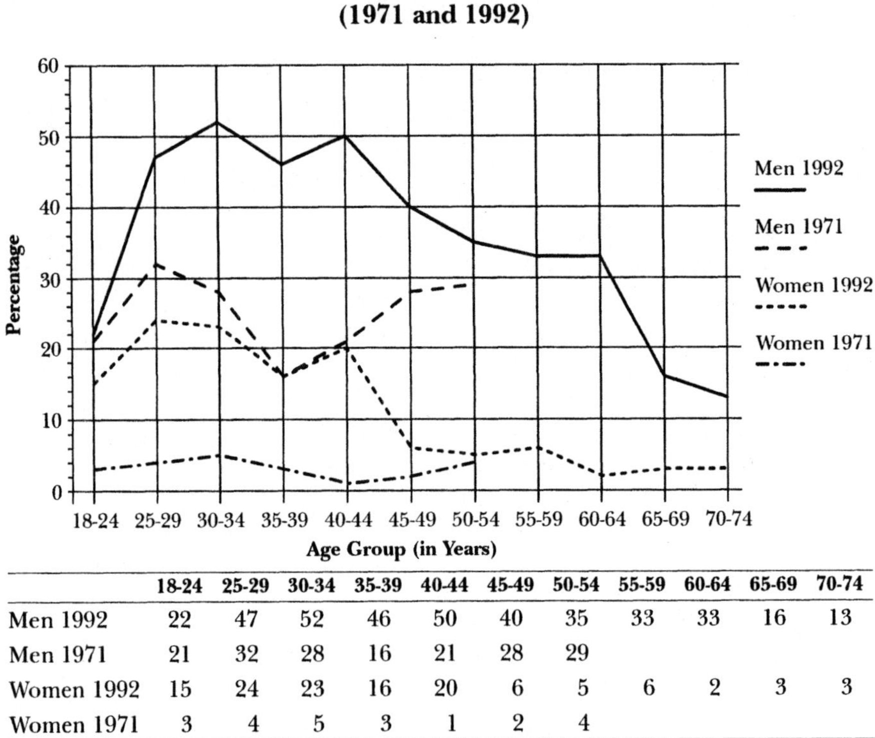

	18-24	25-29	30-34	35-39	40-44	45-49	50-54	55-59	60-64	65-69	70-74
Men 1992	22	47	52	46	50	40	35	33	33	16	13
Men 1971	21	32	28	16	21	28	29				
Women 1992	15	24	23	16	20	6	5	6	2	3	3
Women 1971	3	4	5	3	1	2	4				

women. One explanation of this might be that the Finnish men subconsciously overestimate the number of their partners, while the women underestimate their contacts. Another possibility is that many of the men with multiple sexual partners who responded to the survey have as sexual partners a small group of women who, for the main part, were left outside the survey and were among the nonrespondents of the questionnaire.

Finns report a somewhat higher number of sexual partners than Americans (Laumann et al. 1994). This may partly be explained by the fact that in the United States, a greater proportion of survey respondents left the question concerning the number of partners during the lifetime unanswered.

In addition, during the prior twelve months, the Finns more often than the Americans had more than one partner. During the previous year, 21 percent of the Finnish men and 11 percent of the women had had two or more partners; the corresponding figure for Americans was 17 percent and 7 percent respectively. Only 4 percent of the Finnish men and 7 percent of the women reported that they had had no partners at all during the prior year; in the United States, the proportions were 13 percent and 24 percent (Figures 7, 8, 9, and 10).

Figure 7

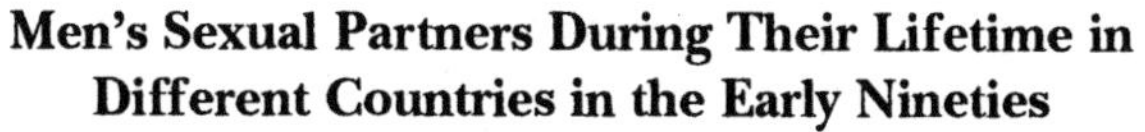

Men's Sexual Partners During Their Lifetime in Different Countries in the Early Nineties

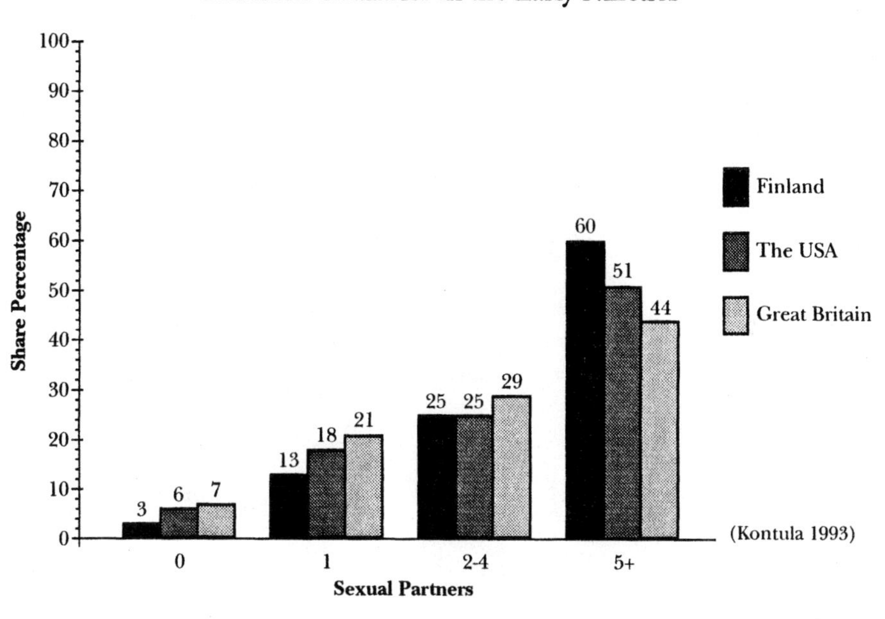

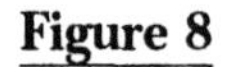

Figure 8

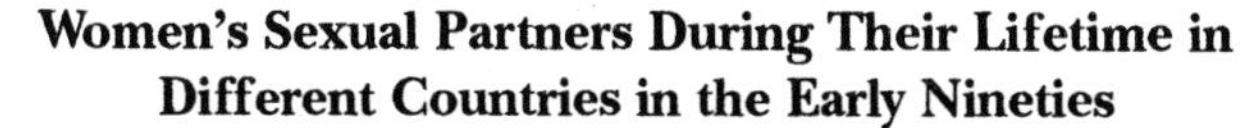

Women's Sexual Partners During Their Lifetime in Different Countries in the Early Nineties

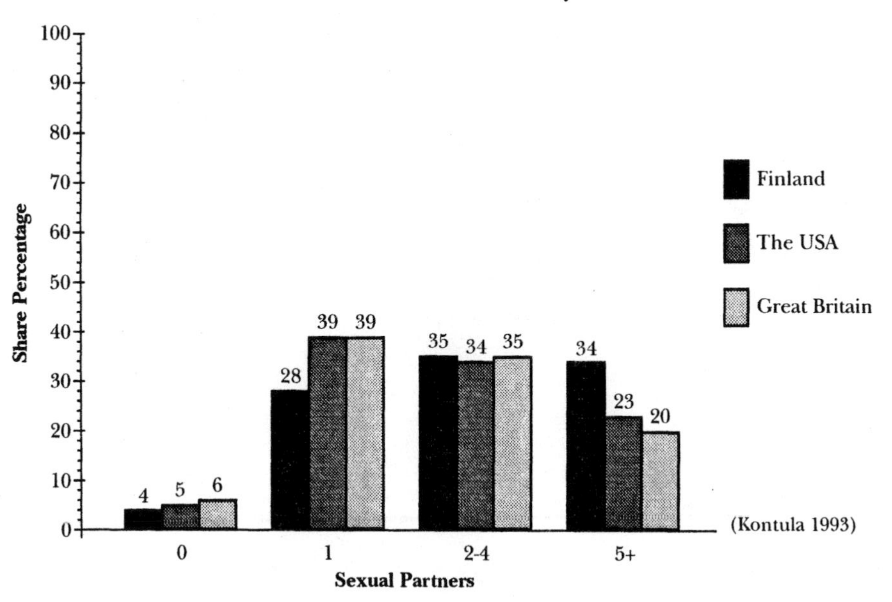

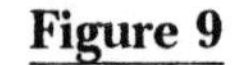

Figure 9

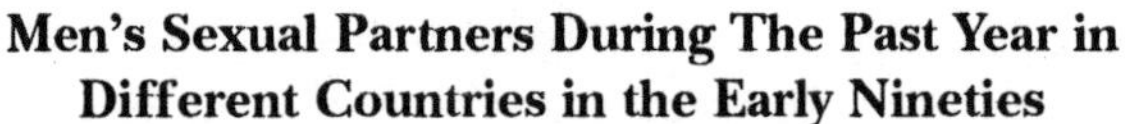

Men's Sexual Partners During The Past Year in Different Countries in the Early Nineties

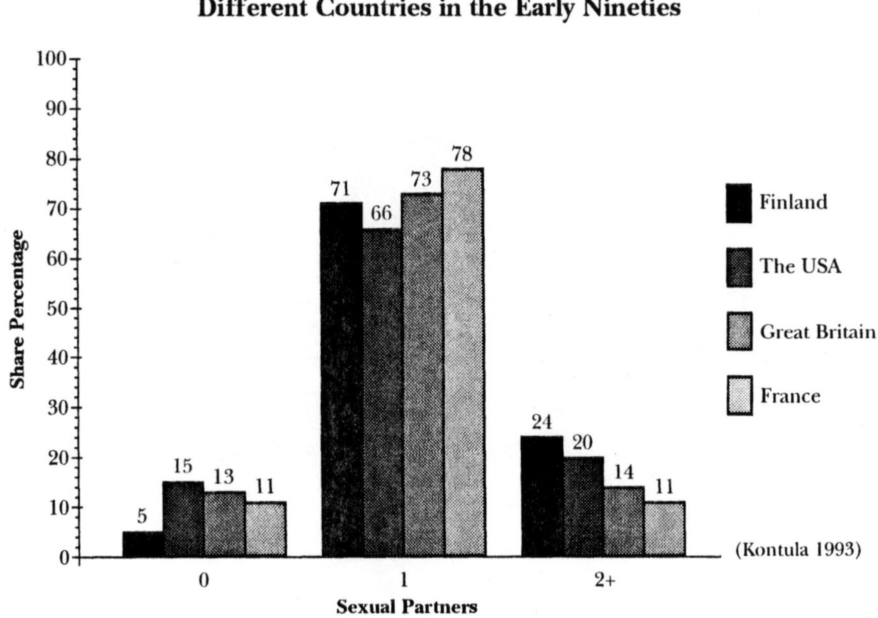

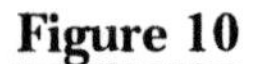

Figure 10

Women's Sexual Partners During The Past Year in Different Countries in the Early Nineties

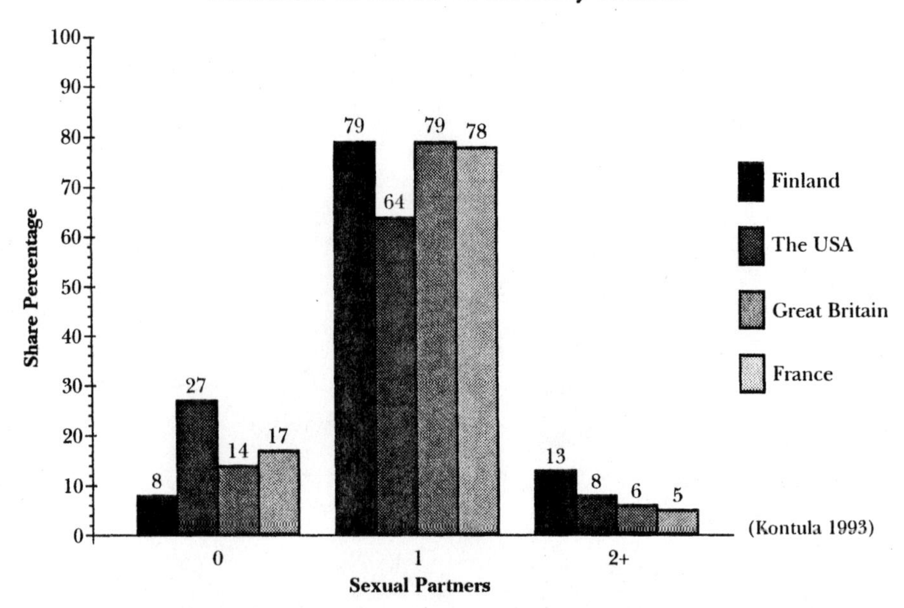

These results suggest that the sexual life of the Finns is at least as active as that of the Americans. Indeed, fear of AIDS and traditional sexual attitudes may restrict the number of sexual partners in the United States more than in Finland.

(4) Extra or Concurrent Sexual Relationships. The partners in the most recent sexual intercourse have mostly been steady partners or spouses in marriage or cohabitation. In 1992, only 6 percent of the men and 4 percent of the women in a steady sexual relationship had had someone other than the steady partner as the last partner. However, a greater and greater share of people have experiences of sexual relationships alongside their steady sexual relationships. Sexual relationships of this kind, including extramarital relationships, are called extra or parallel sexual relationships in the study.

The number of extra sexual relationships has approximately doubled during the twenty years among the Finns between 18 and 54 years old. In 1971, 24 percent of the men and 9 percent of the women who were married at the time of the survey stated that they had had sexual intercourse with some persons other than their spouses during their marriage. In 1992, 44 percent of the men and 19 percent of the women who were living in cohabitation or marriage had experiences of parallel sexual relationships during their cohabitation or marriage (Figure 11).

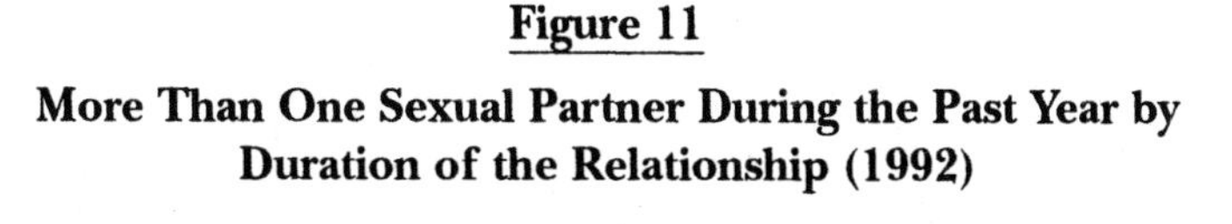

Figure 11

More Than One Sexual Partner During the Past Year by Duration of the Relationship (1992)

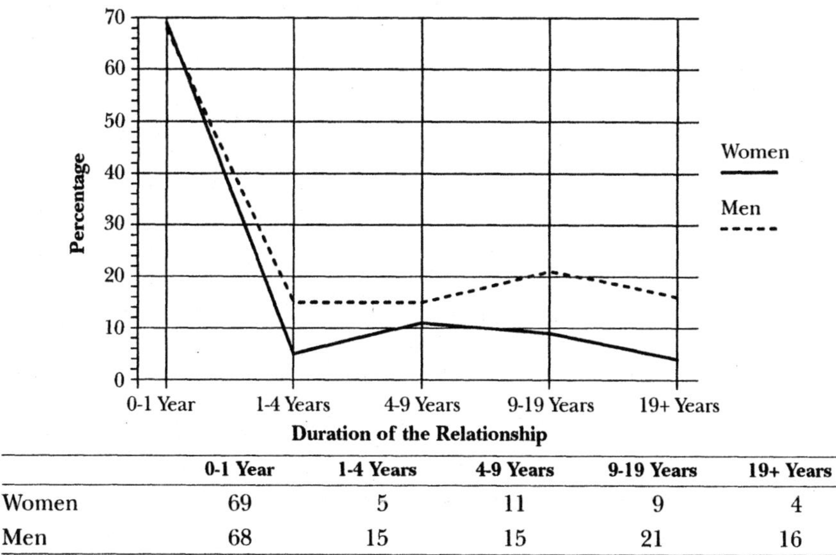

	0-1 Year	1-4 Years	4-9 Years	9-19 Years	19+ Years
Women	69	5	11	9	4
Men	68	15	15	21	16

In 1992, the respondents were also asked how many parallel sexual relationships they had had while in their steady relationship with their then or earlier partner. Of all the people aged 18 to 74 years who had sometimes lived in a steady relationship, 52 percent of the men and 29 percent of the women admitted having experienced at least one relationship of this kind. Even if the incidence of parallel sexual relationships has increased, attitudes to parallel sexual relationships have become stricter during the past twenty years. This discrepancy between liberated actual behavior and tightening attitudes may be related to the fear of AIDS and the growing conservatism in the society in general.

(5) Incidence of Oral and Anal Sex. In the 1992 data, stimulation of the partner's genitals (e.g., fondling and stimulating by hand) in order to give him/her satisfaction without sexual intercourse is a common form of petting and love play. It may or may not be linked to vaginal intercourse. A large majority, 86 percent of men and 76 percent of women, had at least sometimes during their lifetime stimulated a partner's genitals. During the last month, this had been done by half of men and more than a third of women. More than one year had gone since the last incidence of stimulation by hand for 26 percent of men and 42 percent of women. Women thus have been less active than men in giving satisfaction to a partner without sexual intercourse. Maybe some men offer fondling and stimulating by hand to their partners who otherwise do not have an orgasm in intercourse.

Young people stimulate partner's genitals by fondling much more commonly than older people. Of women aged 55 and over, half, and of men 30 to 40 percent, have never done it, whereas the proportion among 25- to 34-year-olds is only 5 percent. This huge age gap indicates that fondling the genitals was not considered a part of "normal" sex life to satisfy one's partner when today's older generation was in their youth. Vaginal intercourse was then the main sex technique.

Anal sex (sodomy) has been practiced throughout history for pleasure, birth control, and to avoid breaking a virgin's hymen. Including the anus in sexual activity is taboo in some cultures.

> Clinically there is no difference between stimulation of the mouth, ears, nipples, feet, or anus in the production of pleasure sensations to the brain. None of these activities have a direct role in reproduction so it seems inconsistent for people to accept some and not all points of arousal in sexual activity. (Love 1992, 10)

In Finland, anal intercourse is not illegal. Nevertheless, it seems not to have been an acceptable sex technique in earlier generations, as older people rarely admit having practiced it. According to the 1992 survey, only 20 percent of men and 17 percent of women reported having ever practiced anal intercourse. Eight percent of men and 6 percent of women had done it several times. It had most often been practiced by 25- to 34-year-old persons, 31 percent of the men and 29 percent of the women. In this age group, one in ten had had anal sex several times. Only 2 percent of the women over 55, and 5 percent of the older men, had ever tried this sex technique.

Cunnilingus and fellatio are very common sexual practices throughout cultures and history. In the Finnish questionnaire, experiences of oral sex were inquired by the following question: "In the last five years, how often have you had oral sex in your sexual relations, that is, fondling a man's penis or a woman's genitals by mouth?" Men reported to have done cunnilingus to their partner more often, 78 percent, than women had done fellatio, 67 percent (Table 8). More than half of the men and 42 percent of the women had done it often or sometimes. Men also had received oral sex more often, 73 percent, than women, 64 percent.

Oral sex was much more common among younger than older Finns. In the age group 18 to 34 years, almost all had done and received oral sex, whereas in the age group 55 to 74, only 35 percent of men had received it from and 46 percent had done it to the partner. Only one in five women admitted it either way. The discrepancy in older men's and women's reports of oral sex may be due to the more common experiences of extra sexual relations with prostitutes and perhaps a less-inhibited extra partner.

The wide age differences in the practice of oral sex are connected to the varied sex practices of young people in general. Young people use more varied positions in sexual intercourse, satisfy each other more often by hand and mouth, and have more often experimented with anal sex than older people. The liberated sexual behavior of younger people may be one explanation for their greater sexual satisfaction.

(6) Sexual Satisfaction. Perhaps the most positive result of the Finnish sex survey is the observation that young Finns are more satisfied with their sexual lives than their elders are. Sexual intercourse was more generally regarded as pleasant in 1992 than it was in 1971. The amount of love play was considered more adequate, the steady relationship was experienced as happier, discussing sexual matters with the partner was more open and easier, and sexual life as a whole was estimated to be more satisfying than in 1971. Women had experienced orgasm somewhat more often in their last sexual intercourse, and men had had less problems with getting erections during the prior year.

From the viewpoint of sexual equality, it was remarkable that women considered their experiences of sexual intercourse clearly more pleasant than twenty years ago and nearly as pleasant as men. The gender gap in experiencing sexual intercourse as pleasant or as unpleasant decreased significantly. Men enjoyed their sexual life as a whole more than women, but in the pleasantness of the last sexual intercourse, there was no difference between the genders.

Table 8

Oral Sex by Gender and Age (in Percentages, 1992)

	Age, Years			
Partner has done oral sex to me	**18-34**	**35-54**	**55-74**	**Total**
MEN				
Mostly	20	9	2	12
Sometimes	43	34	12	34
Seldom	22	34	21	26
Not at all	15	23	65	27
(*N*)	(371)	(395)	(163)	(929)
WOMEN				
Mostly	22	9	—	12
Sometimes	45	28	7	29
Seldom	20	32	12	23
Not at all	14	31	81	36
(*N*)	(377)	(408)	(241)	(1026)
I have done oral sex to partner				
MEN				
Mostly	23	12	5	15
Sometimes	46	41	14	39
Seldom	18	28	27	24
Not at all	3	18	54	22
(*N*)	(370)	(395)	(136)	(901)
WOMEN				
Mostly	18	6	1	10
Sometimes	45	30	5	32
Seldom	23	32	12	25
Not at all	15	31	81	33
(*N*)	(378)	(368)	(159)	(905)

Women are now able to enjoy sex partly because there is practically no fear of an unwanted pregnancy. Only a quarter of the women reported that they had been pregnant when entering into marriage or cohabitation; twenty years ago the share had been 45 percent. The number of marriages of necessity has decreased as sexual education and contraception became more common.

Sexual satisfaction as a whole is a combination of emotional and physical satisfaction. According to our 1992 survey results, the two aspects are equally important. Among women, the correlation between general sexual satisfaction and finding intercourse pleasant—measured by sum of finding them in general pleasant and considering the last intercourse as pleasant—was 0.47 and 0.40 for men. Happiness in the present steady relationship, meaning emotional satisfaction, correlated with sexual satisfaction as a whole for women at 0.44 and for men at 0.36.

Happiness of life was more strongly connected to emotional sexual satisfaction—for men 0.52 and women 0.59—than to physical satisfaction—0.23 and 0.20 respectively. Emotional satisfaction prevents feelings of loneliness—for men 0.27 and women 0.30—more than physical satisfaction—0.16 and 0.15 respectively.

Sexual satisfaction is a socially constructed phenomenon. It is related to emotions, sexual practices, and relationships. In Table 9, correlation coefficients between emotional, physical, and overall sexual satisfaction and a number of variables related to sexual feelings, practices, and partners are presented. Perhaps this analysis gives hints as to how to improve sexual life so that it will be more happy and enjoyable.

Loving and being loved is important for emotional, physical, and overall satisfaction in sexual life. Women in particular need love in order to be happy in their steady relationship. A loving relationship greatly increases satisfaction with sexual life as a whole. The quality of the present steady sexual relationship also has an impact on sexual satisfaction. People for whom talking about sex with their partner is not difficult at all, but open and easy, are emotionally, physically, and generally satisfied with their sexual life.

The number of persons one has really fallen in love with only correlates with the unhappiness of men's but not women's steady relationships; that is, men who have fallen in love often are not very happy in their present relationship. Perhaps they have known too many women with whom they can compare their present partner in order to feel totally happy with her. Or maybe falling in love very many times in life is an indicator of problems in getting really attached to anyone.

Sexual self-esteem is also more important for women's than men's sexual satisfaction. Women who consider themselves as sexually active, having great sexual skills, and being sexually attractive are happy in their steady relationships and especially satisfied with sexual intercourse and sex life as a whole. Men can consider their steady relationship quite happy irrespective of their own opinion of their sexual capacity. But for men's physical and overall sexual satisfaction, it is important to have a high sexual self-esteem.

The role of sexuality in life is connected more to women's than to men's sexual satisfaction. Considering sexual life as an important part of life is associated with emotional sexual satisfaction to the same extent for both sexes. Valuing sexuality counts more for women's than men's satisfaction

Table 9

Correlations Between Sexual Satisfaction and Sexual Feelings, Practices, and Partners (r) for Men and Women (1992)

	Sexual Satisfaction					
	Emotional		Physical		General	
Sexual Feelings and Behavior	**Men**	**Women**	**Men**	**Women**	**Men**	**Women**
FEELINGS	(Correlation Coefficients)					
Love:						
Loves somebody right now	0.26	0.38	0.23	0.26	0.32	0.38
Receives love	0.24	0.36	0.22	0.26	0.31	0.36
Talking about sex with one's partner is easy	0.16	0.22	0.23	0.23	0.23	0.28
Number of objects of love during lifetime	–0.10	ns	ns	ns	ns	ns
Sexual self esteem:						
I have great sexual skills	ns	0.16	0.26	0.30	0.26	0.31
I am sexually active	ns	0.28	0.21	0.35	0.27	0.35
I am sexually attractive	ns	0.18	0.16	0.24	0.19	0.21
Role of sex in life:						
Considers sexual life to be an important part of life	0.17	0.19	0.25	0.37	0.23	0.28
Sexual desire has increased in the last five years	ns	0.24	0.17	0.35	0.11	0.20
Happiness:						
Considers one's life happy	0.52	0.59	0.23	0.20	0.31	0.38
Is not lonely	0.27	0.30	0.16	0.15	0.30	0.29
PRACTICES						
Intercourse:						
Frequency of intercourse (in general and during the last month)	0.10	0.23	0.28	0.29	0.39	0.37
Both took initiative to last intercourse	0.12	0.12	0.11	0.25	0.13	0.16
Considers the amount of foreplay in intercourse suitable	0.11	0.24	0.11	0.29	0.18	0.33
Several positions in last intercourse	ns	0.14	ns	0.22	ns	ns

continued

Table 9 continued

Sexual Feelings and Behavior	Sexual Satisfaction					
	Emotional		Physical		General	
	Men	Women	Men	Women	Men	Women
PRACTICES continued	(Correlation Coefficients)					
Other sex practices:						
Stimulated recently partner's genitals without intercourse	ns	0.19	0.13	0.26	0.18	0.21
Partner gives oral sex	ns	0.20	0.16	0.25	0.16	0.19
Gives oral sex to partner	ns	0.18	0.19	0.25	0.18	0.18
Has had anal intercourse	ns	ns	ns	ns	ns	ns
Masturbates often	ns	ns	ns	ns	–0.20	–0.12
Has used sex materials (videos, movies, magazines etc.) during last year	ns	ns	ns	0.11	ns	ns
Has ever used sex facilities (vibrators, lubricants, erection rings, sexy underwear etc.)	ns	ns	ns	ns	ns	ns
PHYSIOLOGICAL REACTIONS						
Orgasm in intercourse in general	0.07	0.20	0.62	0.79	0.14	0.41
Orgasm in last intercourse	0.07	0.15	0.74	0.87	0.21	0.29
Experienced own or partner's impotence during last year	ns	–0.22	–0.22	–0.28	–0.15	–0.27
PARTNERS						
Number of sexual partners	ns	ns	ns	ns	ns	–0.10
Number of extra sexual relations during present or previous steady relations	–0.20	–0.16	ns	ns	ns	ns

with intercourse and, to some extent, sex life in general. Denial of sexuality in life may prevent women from enjoying sexual intercourse, or vice versa; women who do not like physical sex, may undervalue sexual life as part of their whole life. The subjective experience of an increase in sexual desire in the last five years is more closely correlated with women's than men's sexual satisfaction.

Happy peoplė enjoy their steady relations and also sexual intercourse. The relationship between happiness and sexual satisfaction is probably reciprocal: satisfactory sexual life contributes to feelings of happiness, and happy people are likely to find joy also in sexuality. Sexual partners are often good social companions. Thus it is understandable that sexual satisfaction diminishes feelings of loneliness.

Sexual habits or practices have a stronger effect on physical than emotional sexual satisfaction. Most of them correlate more with women's than men's satisfaction. From the point of view of sexual satisfaction, the following sexual habits have a positive outcome: frequent sexual intercourse, equal activeness in initiating it, a suitable amount of kissing, petting, or other love play in connection with coitus, and use several positions in intercourse (applies to men only).

In addition to practices related to sexual intercourse, the study also investigated other techniques aiming at sexual satisfaction. Stimulation by hand and oral sex clearly increase women's emotional, physical, and overall sexual satisfaction, and also to some degree, men's physical and general but not emotional satisfaction. Anal sex, masturbation, use of sex materials and aids are only to a small degree related to sexual satisfaction. People, particularly men, who masturbate often, are not satisfied with their sexual life as a whole. Women who use sex materials—sex movies and programs on TV, videos, magazines, and wall calendars with naked pictures—are somewhat more satisfied with intercourse than women who do not use them. Perhaps sex materials help women to adopt new, more rewarding sex techniques.

Orgasm during sexual intercourse is very strongly connected to finding sexual intercourse pleasant. The correlations are higher for women than for men. Also general sexual satisfaction, and to some degree, happiness of the steady relationship, correlate with experiencing an orgasm during intercourse.

It is not uncommon that a man cannot enter into sexual intercourse because he cannot get an erection or his penis becomes flaccid when sexual intercourse is started. One's own or one's partner's erectile problem decreases physical sexual satisfaction for both sexes. It is also connected to the emotional dissatisfaction of women in their steady relationships.

The number of sexual partners during a lifetime does not correlate with sexual satisfaction except at one point: women who have had many sexual partners report more dissatisfaction with their sexual lives as a whole than other women. Traditional gender roles may make women uncomfortable with a life in which sexual partners change frequently. This lifestyle probably includes a lot of short-time casual relationships that women do not take as lightheartedly as men have been socialized to take them.

The number of extra sexual relations during present or previous steady relations is connected to unhappiness of the present steady relationship, but not to physical nor overall sexual satisfaction. Parallel relations indicate a wish to escape the unhappiness of the steady relationship, or they may cause jealousy on the part of the steady partner that might deteriorate the relationship.

Determinants of physical sexual satisfaction have earlier been analyzed by using path analysis (Haavio-Mannila 1993). In the path models developed for explaining satisfaction with intercourse for men and women, some more general social factors than those presented in Table 9 were included.

Some of them only had an indirect influence on sexual satisfaction, but some also had direct effects on it. The social factors studied contributing to physical sexual satisfaction were: irreligious and sexually open childhood home, early age at starting sexual life, liberal attitudes toward sexual issues, short duration of the present steady relationship, and young age. These social background factors correlated with the sexual variables increasing sexual satisfaction: the value of sexuality in life, sexual assertiveness, love, use of sex materials, frequency and variety of intercourse, and orgasm.

Divorce and Remarriage

In 1986-89, there were 11.6 officially recorded divorces per 1,000 mean population of married women, compared with 5.3 in 1966-70. In 1989, 47 percent of marriages ended in divorce. The increase in divorces can also be seen in the survey data. In 1971, only 3 percent of the respondents were divorced or separated from their spouse; twenty years later the figure was 8 percent. Even changes in the structure of families with children reflect the increased incidence of divorces. In 1971, 90 percent of the respondents reported that their parents had lived together throughout their childhood; twenty years later the figure was 88 percent.

Cohabitation does not always lead to marriage; separation of cohabiting partners is relatively common, especially in the younger age groups. One in four respondents interviewed for the 1992 study had had a cohabitation relationship that had not continued as a marriage. This share was more than one in two in the age groups 35 or younger.

The increased life span and increasing occurrence of divorce allows people time to marry several times. According to the 1971 study, 5 percent of married men and women had been married at least twice. Two decades later, 17 percent of presently or formerly married or cohabiting men and 22 percent of the corresponding women had had at least two such relationships. Women had had a higher number of such relationships before age 54. In older age groups, men had been married more times than women.

Sexuality, Disability, and Aging

There are no serious obstacles concerning values and attitudes in dealing with the sexual needs and activities. In 1992, only 5 percent of the respondents believed that elderly people should not establish sexual relationships. Most Finns, 75 percent, held that people in residential facilities ought to have a privacy room for intimate meetings. Although the majority also approve of sexual relationships for physically and mentally challenged persons, no actual studies have been carried out on sexual issues and the disabled.

There is currently some kind of generation gap between elderly and young Finns in sexual issues. Elderly people, especially women, are more conservative in their attitudes to adolescents' sexual relationships, casual relationships, relationships without love, and women's right to take sexual initiatives. Elderly people have lived their childhood in the world where restrictions against free sexual pleasure were enormous. They have learned that sexual issues are not really important and that they have to be careful in order to avoid the problems and risks associated with fulfilling their sexual images and fantasies. They never had any knowledge and education, for instance, how to satisfy the needs of their partners such as young Finns have nowadays. They initiated their dating and sex life much older than the younger generations because sexual activities were interpreted to be as a part of marriage only. Many of them were, in practice, forced to abstain while married because there were almost no contraceptives available.

The frequency of sexual intercourse is increasing among older Finns. Most retired men have had intercourse during last month, and they report their experiences to be as pleasurable as the younger ones. Elderly people are still not as actively engaging in sexual relationships as the younger people. More than half of retired women abstain from sexual intercourse because they are widowed and are not able or willing to engage to some new relationship—there is also a lack of older men. Old women are many times sexually quite inactive because they have learned that sexual initiatives are men's duty.

The coital positions of elderly people do not vary very much and they quite seldom engage in oral sex, anal sex, or manual stimulation. They even abstain quite often from masturbation and pornographic products. Only 18 percent of men and 11 percent of women over 65 years have masturbated during last year. The sexual inactivity is explained only partly by aging and illness; the education and generation gap is the more important reason for this finding. This can be seen, for example, in data on the number of sexual partners during a lifetime that are much lower among elderly people. Elderly Finns have had much more time to engage in sexual relationships than younger Finns, but they seldom have experienced multiple relationships.

Because of their health status, elderly people have more sexual dysfunctions—lack of desire, problems with having vaginal lubrication, erections, and orgasms—than younger generations. These problems will be discussed later in this chapter.

6. Homoerotic, Homosexual, and Ambisexual Behaviors

Finnish homosexuals were studied by the snowball method in 1982 (Grönfors et al. 1984). More than one thousand homosexuals answered a relatively extensive questionnaire. Two thirds of the respondents were men and one third were women. About 60 percent of the respondents reported that they were exclusively homosexual in their feelings and about 70 percent in their behavior. Finnish homosexuals were quite similarly distributed into

Kinsey's categories (Kinsey et al. 1948; 1953). Feelings and behavior were in most cases consistent. However, it is not always possible to combine feelings with practice in real life. There were people who identified themselves as only or mostly homosexual but behaved only or mostly heterosexually.

In the Finnish sex survey of 1992, there were ten questions about sex with same-sex persons. They refer to sexual identity, sexual experiences with persons of one's own sex, age at first homosexual experience, type and frequency of these experiences, number of same-sex partners, and orgasm in homosexual intercourse.

Homosexual identity was measured by a five-point scale ranging from exclusive homosexuality to exclusive heterosexuality (cf. Kinsey et al. 1948). The question was phrased as follows: "Besides being sexually interested in the opposite sex, people are sometimes also interested in their own sex. Are you at the moment sexually interested in only the male sex, mainly the male sex, both sexes equally, mainly the female sex, or only the female sex?"

In the population aged 18 to 54 years, the proportion of persons interested only or mainly in people of the same sex was 0.8 percent in 1971, in 1992 only 0.6 percent. When one takes into consideration all people who have at least some interest in people of the same sex, the proportions were 7.6 percent and 6.5 percent respectively. When all people aged 55 to 74 years studied in 1992 are included, the proportion of the exclusively or mainly homosexually oriented persons was 0.7 percent and that of at least partly bisexually oriented 6.4 percent. Men more often than women identified themselves as homosexuals, whereas there was no gender gap in the proportion of bisexually oriented people. Same-gendered experiences are more common than homosexual identity. According to the 1992 survey, 4.0 percent of the Finnish men and 3.8 percent of the women had had same-sex partners during their life. In the United States, in 1991, the proportions were 5.0 percent for men and 2.7 percent for women (Laumann et al. 1994). The gender difference is thus larger in the United States than in Finland where there is hardly any gender gap. American women may be shyer than Finnish women in admitting their lesbian behavior, or they may avoid lesbian practices deliberately in order to avoid the social stigma attached to them. In Finland, the liberalization of attitudes toward homosexuality in the last twenty years may have helped lesbians acknowledge and report on their homosexual experiences.

The number of homosexual partners during one's lifetime was on the average of 7.4 for men and 1.6 for women. Compared with the number of sexual partners in the whole population (10.6), these figures are small. This is due to the fact that most homosexual encounters only have taken place with one person: 53 percent of men and 72 percent of women had had only one same-sex partner. Many homosexual contacts took place a long time ago. Only 29 percent of the same-sex contacts of people ever having had one had happened during the last twelve months. During the last year, 1.3 percent of the Finns and 1.6 percent of the Americans had had a homosexual relationship. This question had been left unanswered by a significantly greater proportion (23 percent) of the Americans than of the Finns (8 percent). This again suggests that there are more social taboos regarding homosexuality in the United States than in Finland.

The first homosexual experiences took place at the same age as first sexual intercourse—that is, on the average at the age of 18.3 years. Men started somewhat earlier than women. Eight percent of these experiences were probably sexual play of children, since they took place when the respondent was less than ten years old.

The most common type of homosexual experiences were arousing fondling without touching genitals (54 percent of people having had homosexual experiences), stimulation of genitals by hand or rubbing genitals against partner's genitals (also 54 percent), and oral stimulation of the genitals (29 percent). Only 19 percent of men with homosexual relations had been engaged in anal intercourse.

Thirty-eight percent of men and 26 percent of women had had orgasm in homosexual intercourse. This is less than the proportion of orgasm in heterosexual intercourse (see Table 13 below). Homosexually oriented and/or experienced men considered their sexual life as a whole somewhat less often very or quite satisfying (75 percent) than bisexually or mostly heterosexually oriented men without homosexual experiences (87 percent) and exclusively heterosexual men (85 percent). For women, the percentages were 77 percent, 61 percent, and 83 percent respectively.

The lower sexual satisfaction of homosexuals may be related to the prevailing conceptions about the superiority of heterosexual love and sex (Jeffreys 1990). It may be more difficult to enjoy homosexual experiences as freely as heterosexual experiences because of their ambivalent status in sexual culture. This can be concluded on the basis of the fact that 28 percent of men and 38 percent of women interested in their own sex have sometimes been bothered personally by or fearful and worried about their own sexual deviation. This is three times as common as in the population on the average. Of men with homosexual experiences, 38 percent, and of women 19 percent, have felt that kind of fear. This fear still prevails even though the attitudes toward homosexuality have liberalized during the last twenty years (see Table 3 above).

7. *Gender Conflicted Persons*

A. Sociological Status, Behaviors, and Treatment

In Finland, the most conspicuous gender minority group have been the transsexuals, because their situation requires both therapeutical and juridical measures to be resolved. Since 1991, Finland has taken specific steps to draft legislation and develop health care to meet this need. Following reports in 1992 and 1994, the National Research and Development Center for Welfare and Health (STAKES) has moved to secure health-care services for transsexuals and provide juridical protection for their gender reassignment and privacy.

In Finland, there are an estimated three hundred people who would benefit from sex-reassignment surgery. A 1994 Social Affairs and Health directive enables staff at university-hospital polyclinics to examine patients seeking sex reassignment and apply for a castration permission from the National Board of Medicolegal Affairs. Once approved, the corrective surgery is paid for by public health care. Since 1997, this surgical treatment has been centralized in Tampere University Hospital. Although the Castration Act was not drafted to deal with transsexuals, it is used as a prerequisite for national insurance coverage. In effect, Finland functions without specific legislation for transsexuals. If the medical treatment and legal problems of transsexuals can be settled by directives and recommendations without a separate law, no new law will be passed. However, if some municipalities decide to provide their own coverage of this treatment and others deny this, a new law may be needed.

SETA (Sexual Equality), originally a national organization for homosexuals and lesbians, has in recent years begun working actively on behalf of other sexual minorities. SETA now arranges group evenings for transsexuals and transvestites, where other sexual minorities have been welcomed. In addition, SETA has vigorously promoted some juridical changes for sexual minorities, such as allowing a change of one's name and an identity number as part of gender reassignment. A 1993 change in the system of population data collection has also made it easier for the transsexuals to change their names and identity numbers. This can now be done if a person has had hormonal treatment for a year and has a physician's certificate of transsexualism.

On the recommendation of the "Trans" Working Group of STAKES, the Trans-Support Center has provided social services, psychological counseling, advice on the medical-treatment process, and information from the transsexuals who have already been through the treatment process. This effort, begun in 1994, has been financed by RAY (Finland's Slot Machine Association). The political activity of sexual-minority groups has been coordinated by TRASEK, the association of transsexuals which now includes other sexual-minority groups such as hermaphrodites. Other new cross-gendered organizations formed in recent years include Postgender, which is open to all genders and tries to fade out the restrictive dichotomy of the gender system. The transvestites' own organization, Dreamwear Club, plans to be officially registered and active in 1997. Female-to-male transsexuals are also forming a group of their own.

B. Specially Gendered Persons

There are actually no hijra or berdache communities in Finland, but a so-called gender community that includes people from different gender groups such as transsexuals, transvestites, transgenderists, and gender-blending people does exist. There are so few people of each of the groups that they have not formed any subgroups of their own.

8. Significant Unconventional Sexual Behaviors

A. Coercive Sex

Sexual Abuse, Incest, and Pedophilia

Finnish women have been sexually abused as children more often than men: under the age of 18, 17 percent of women and 8 percent of men had been sexually harassed by peers, other boys or girls, parents, or other adults. There was no clear age difference in the incidence of child abuse. Women most often were harassed by male peers and men, and men by female peers and women. Two percent of women had been sexually abused by their fathers. No reports of sexual abuse by a mother have been made.

Sexual Harassment and Rape

Incidence of sexual harassment was studied by using the following question: "In the last five years, has anyone laid hands on you or touched you in an offensive way (with a sexual purpose) either in your apartment or elsewhere, e.g., in a restaurant, workplace or at school?" Affirmative answers were given by 3 percent of men and 9 percent of women. Younger women reported more sexual harassment than older women. For men, age made no difference. Sexual harassment in most cases was described as approaches (men 88 percent and women 69 percent), but 0.4 percent of all women described the incidence as rape, and 1.1 percent of all women defined it as attempted rape. Of all men, 0.2 percent described the harassment as attempted rape; no men reported actual rape. Regression analysis showed that becoming an object of sexual harassment was connected with being sexually abused as a child, young age, and female gender. Persons who were sexually harassed were more likely than other persons not to have steady sexual relationships and to have had extra sexual relations and homosexual experiences. Drinking to intoxication and having many sexual partners was also related to having been sexually harassed.

The harassers were mostly men. About half of the respondents knew the harasser before the incidence. Very few of the harassed—6 percent of the harassed men and 7 percent of women—had informed the police about the incident. The most common reason for not reporting sexual harassment to the police was that it was considered to be of minor importance. The second reason was that the respondent personally resolved the matter.

Becoming an object of sexual harassment increased sexual fears and worries. Other social factors influencing sexual fears were female gender, young age, lack of steady relationship, stress symptoms, casual and extra sexual relations, and sexual practices alternative to intercourse. One third of the variation of sexual fears was explained by these factors. In order to diminish sexual anxiety, it is worthwhile to discuss and control sexual harassment publicly.

Prostitution

Prostitution itself is not illegal in Finland, but it is against the law to organize prostitutes' services, for example, by maintaining a brothel. Until the beginning of the 1990s, prostitution was scarce (Järvinen 1990). One of the consequences of the fall of the Soviet Union was that many Estonian and Russian women came to Finland to earn money as prostitutes.

Attitudes toward prostitution differ greatly by gender. In 1992, men more often (51 percent) than women (21 percent) had nothing against people earning money by selling sexual services in Finland. This activity was opposed by 34 percent of men and 65 percent of women. People over 50 years were most negative toward prostitution.

There has been recurrent public discussion about establishing brothels under the control of the state as there were in the beginning of this century in Finland. Brothels might be a means to fight problems connected with prostitution: i.e., liability of clients and prostitutes to venereal diseases and connections to criminality, particularly drug dealing. Approval of state-controlled brothels was greater among men than women: 42 percent of men but only 17 percent of women approved public brothels while 41 percent and 67 percent respectively opposed them. Middle-aged people were most favorable to brothels. Support for public brothels has clearly increased since a 1972 survey. At that time only 20 percent approved establishing state-controlled brothels (Markkula 1981).

There is a certain amount of demand for paid sexual services in Finland. Twenty percent of women and 8 percent of men had during their lifetime been persuaded to intercourse by being offered money or similar economic advantages. Women under 35 years of age most often reported having received these kinds of offers. This indicates that they have increased with time. Only 0.2 percent of Finnish women and 1.5 percent of men admitted that they had complied with the request.

Men use paid sexual services more than women. Eleven percent of Finnish men and 0.3 percent of women had offered money or similar economic advantages for intercourse. One percent of all men and women said that their initiatives had not led to sexual activity.

For Finnish men, traditionally, buying sexual services starts at about age 40 when men begin to have the economic resources for it. Having sex with prostitutes was connected with having many sexual partners, extra relationships, sex with foreigners, high sexual self-esteem, and few homosexual experiences. Using paid sexual services was not related to sexual satisfaction nor sexual fears.

Pornography and Erotica

In Finland, between 1971 and 1992, women's attitudes to pornography became somewhat more negative, whereas men's attitudes have remained unchanged. This may be related to the contents of pornography becoming "harder" and less satisfying to women's expectations than before. The consumption of pornographic products has remained almost the same among men but has decreased among women. Even when sex videos are included with the printed publications, fewer women, on the average, used pornographic materials during the year in 1992 than in 1971.

Interest in pornographic publications was exceptionally great in 1971 because open nudity had only recently become available in pictures in sex magazines. The charm of novelty and the taste of the forbidden fruit made people anxious to have and use them. Since this initial interest, the greatest excitement and attraction have settled. Besides, the so-called soft pornography has come within everyone's reach—for example, in the pictures of the afternoon tabloids. Such material, however, is no longer referred to as pornography. There are legal restrictions against hard pornography in Finland, but soft pornography and erotica are shown even on public television.

Sex magazines published in Finland are forbidden by the Ministry of Justice to present pictures of anal and oral sex, sexual violence, sadomasochism, sex with children, sperm, paraphilias with sex models, and close-up pictures of genitals. All movies and video films are inspected by state authorities and hard-core pornography, as listed above, is not allowed to be presented in cinemas or to be rented in video markets. However, in practice, hard-core videos can be bought or leased from specific sex shops. Films presented on TV are not under any legal regulations.

Paraphilias

In Finland, the use of sexual aids and toys such as a vibrator or vibrating penis, lubricants, pills or substances increasing potency, erection rings, a penis enlarger with pump, ropes or gags, an artificial vagina, sexy underwear, sex dolls, and whips or handcuffs or fetters in masturbation or in sexual intercourse by the respondent or his/her partner is fairly rare.

Sexy underwear was the most commonly used aid: one fifth of people told about using it. In the younger age groups, under 35 years, the proportion was about one third, in the oldest age groups only a few percent.

Lubricant was the next popular aid: 17 percent of men and 15 percent of women had used it. Lubricant use increases with age because it lessens problems connected with vaginal lubrication during intercourse.

Vibrators or vibrating dildos were used by the respondent or a partner according to the replies of 7 percent of men and 6 percent of women. These were most popular among those around 30 years old (10 percent). The interest of young people in vibrators indicates that their use will increase in the future. The other sexual aids listed above were each used by less than 2 percent of the respondents.

Use of sex aids did not correlate with sexual satisfaction except in one case: use of a pump penis enlarger and sex dolls was related to women's unhappiness in steady relationships. These devices are meant for fighting impotency or for compensating for lack of a human sexual partner. As mentioned in the section of sexual satisfaction, impotency and lack of partner indicate an unhappy steady relationship as was mentioned above.

9. Contraception, Abortion, and Population Planning

A. Contraception

A decline in birthrate has been a common phenomenon in most west European countries and in all the Nordic countries during the past several decades. In Finland, the birthrate was at its highest after World War II; for instance, in 1947, as many as 108,000 children were born. After this, there was an even decline, so that, after 1968, the birthrate has been lower than the replacement birthrate, which would be about 70,000 births per year. At its lowest, in 1973, the birth rate was 56,787 births. In the 1990s, it has been about 65,000 children per year. Unless immigration increases, the population is estimated to grow until 1999, after which it will begin to decrease.

Contraception has been well taken care of in Finland. Young people may obtain contraceptives from their school health care services. The law or other regulations require that those who have given birth or had an abortion be given counseling in contraception. Generally, counseling and even the contraceptive methods themselves are easily available. There is also a variety to choose from, thanks to the development in the research and production of contraceptive methods. From an international viewpoint, Finland is considered a model country in organizing contraception.

In 1988, contraceptive use among 13- to 17-year-olds was surveyed (Kontula and Rimpelä 1988). No contraception had been used at the first intercourse by 27 percent of the 15-year-olds. Most of them, 66 percent of boys and 71 percent of the girls, had used the condom during the first intercourse. A few percent had used the pill. At the most recent intercourse, use of the pill was reported by 17 percent of the girls and 7 percent of the boys. At the same time, the proportion of those who used the condom had diminished to 59 percent with the girls. The share of those with no contraception had remained almost the same as at the first intercourse, about one in four.

Use of the contraceptive pill quickly becomes more common among the young as they settle into a relationship. As many as 44 percent of the 17-year-old girls in Helsinki had used the pill at their most recent sexual intercourse; the proportion using condoms remained at 45 percent. Nationwide, the proportion of 17-year-old boys relying on the pill was 25 percent; for girls, 56 percent. The differences in these responses stems from the fact that the girls usually have intercourse with boys some years older than themselves.

According to the 1971 sex survey, only about 3 percent of those who needed contraception did not use any method. According to a study conducted in 1977, one in ten women who needed contraception did not use any method (Riihinen et al. 1980).

In 1992, 29 percent of the men and 18 percent of the women did not need contraception at their last intercourse (Erkkola and Kontula 1993). About one fifth of the middle-aged people reported that they did not need contraception. A very important reason is that about 12 percent of the 35- to 54-year-old women had undergone hysterectomy which becomes more common with age.

The prevalence of contraceptive methods was surveyed by a question about the method used at last intercourse. Slightly over 3 percent of the men who had thought they needed contraception in their steady relationship had not used any method at their last sexual intercourse. No method had been used at the last intercourse by 5 percent of the 18- to 54-year-old women who thought they needed contraception.

The condom and contraceptive pill are popular with young people (Figures 12 and 13). After the age of 30, the pill loses most of its users although about one tenth of the women still use it after that age. This is due in part to the health officers' recommendations. The condom, however, holds its popularity fairly steady among users of all ages. This may be due to the protection the condom affords against diseases.

Use of the intrauterine device (IUD) increases considerably around the age of 30, at the same time as the popularity of the pill wanes. The IUD maintains its popularity until the age of menopause, after which it is naturally no longer needed. The IUD is used by about one third of women. The use of sterilization as a contraceptive method increases a little later than the use of the IUD. Sterilization is mostly used around age 40 years, with about 25 percent of middle-aged women using this method. Based on generation comparisons, it seems likely that the use of sterilization will clearly increase in the coming years.

The pill, IUD, and sterilization had been used by 59 percent of women; 27 percent had used the condom. Only slightly over 3 percent had used

Figure 12

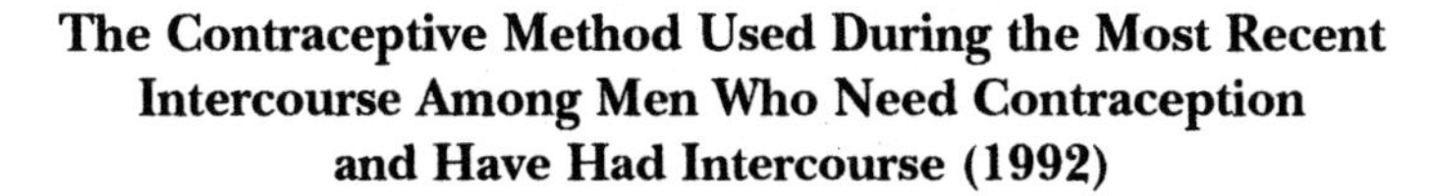

The Contraceptive Method Used During the Most Recent Intercourse Among Men Who Need Contraception and Have Had Intercourse (1992)

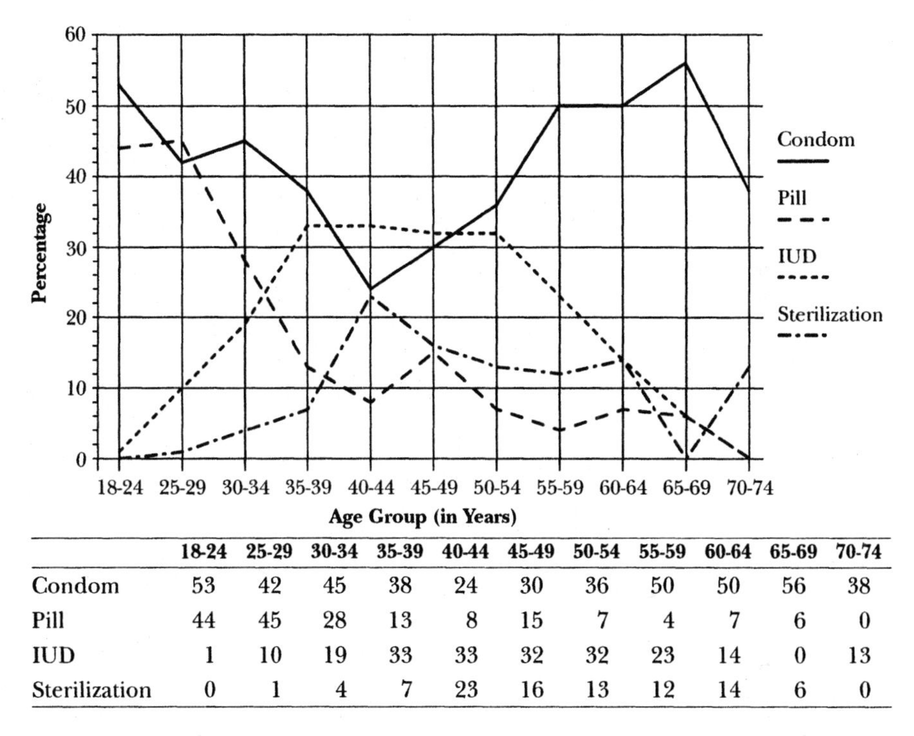

	18-24	25-29	30-34	35-39	40-44	45-49	50-54	55-59	60-64	65-69	70-74
Condom	53	42	45	38	24	30	36	50	50	56	38
Pill	44	45	28	13	8	15	7	4	7	6	0
IUD	1	10	19	33	33	32	32	23	14	0	13
Sterilization	0	1	4	7	23	16	13	12	14	6	0

withdrawal or the rhythm method ("safe period"); the latter had been used by only a few women. About 4 percent of the female respondents had used two methods at their last intercourse, mostly the condom with some other method.

Laws relating to sterilization were enacted in 1970 and 1985. The spirit of the latter law is quite liberal, for, in practice, any person over age 30 may be sterilized if he or she so wishes. This law caused sterilization to rise threefold compared to previous years.

Regional differences in contraceptive methods used are fairly insignificant. There are hardly any regional differences in the use of the pill and the IUD, but the condom has been more used in the big towns than in the smaller localities according to the women's responses.

Finns who had their last intercourse with a steady cohabitation partner or spouse and needed contraception had used the condom less frequently than others, 32 percent of the men and 27 percent of the women, compared with 46 percent and 28 percent respectively for those who had had their

Figure 13

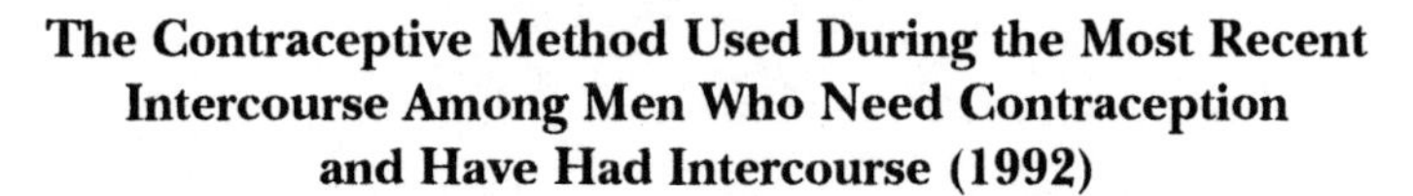

The Contraceptive Method Used During the Most Recent Intercourse Among Men Who Need Contraception and Have Had Intercourse (1992)

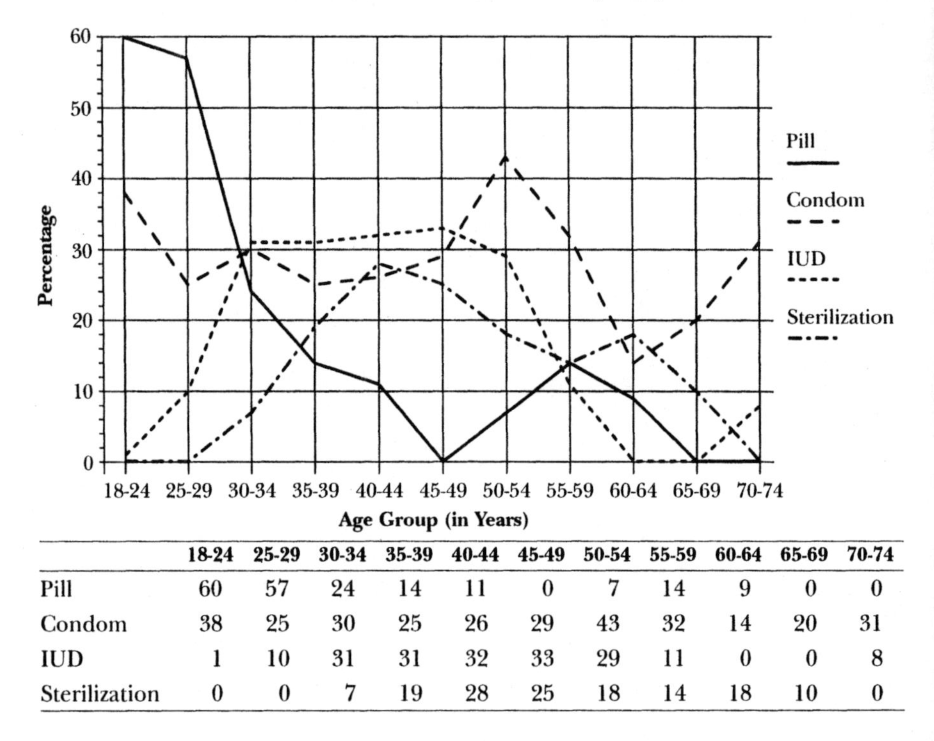

	18-24	25-29	30-34	35-39	40-44	45-49	50-54	55-59	60-64	65-69	70-74
Pill	60	57	24	14	11	0	7	14	9	0	0
Condom	38	25	30	25	26	29	43	32	14	20	31
IUD	1	10	31	31	32	33	29	11	0	0	8
Sterilization	0	0	7	19	28	25	18	14	18	10	0

last intercourse with some other steady partner, and 68 percent and 45 percent of those with someone other than a steady partner. The condom was most often used at the most recent intercourse by men, 71 percent, and women, 39 percent, who had no steady partners. No contraception had been used by 5 percent of men and 10 percent of the women with the latest not-steady partner, although they reported that they needed contraception. The pill had been used by 28 percent and the IUD by 10 percent of the women with their latest not-steady partners. Slightly over 40 percent of those men and women who had had their last intercourse with somebody else's spouse or steady partner had then used the condom.

Having children changes quite decisively the type of contraceptive method used. This is most apparent in the shift away from the pill, the most common contraceptive method before having children. In many cases, the pill is replaced by the IUD, which is almost solely used by women who have given birth to a child. As the number of children rises, the percentage of those who have undergone sterilization considerably increases, and the share of the condom users decreases.

B. Teenage Unmarried Pregnancies

Women under age 20 account for about 2,000 pregnancies each year, about 3 percent of the total number of 65,000 pregnancies. Teenage pregnancy and live births have been relatively one of the lowest of the whole world. The number of live births to unmarried women has been growing fast and is nowadays about 20,000 a year. The proportion of unmarried women giving birth is about 30 percent, a share that has doubled during last twenty years. There are no separate statistics of unmarried, noncohabiting couples. The estimated figure has been, according to surveys, about 5 percent of annual live births.

C. Abortion

In the earlier decades when prevention of pregnancies was poor and abortions illegal, the women in their despair resorted to infanticide in Finland. Nowadays, the situation is considerably better in this respect, but there is still discussion of the justification of abortions. In Finland, the situation is exceptionally good, for abortions had clearly decreased due to the improved contraception during the last twenty years, and abortions are exceptionally few by international comparison.

The current law regarding termination of pregnancies, which was preceded by a fierce debate, was enacted in 1970. As a result of this liberal law, abortion became practically free, and illegal abortions were believed to have almost entirely ceased. With the new Primary Health Care Act instituted in 1972, the cost of abortions was essentially paid by the municipalities.

A 1978 amendment to the abortion law required permission of the Central Administrative Board for termination of a pregnancy after twelve weeks. The latest law concerning abortions came into force in 1985, making it possible to terminate pregnancy prior to the twenty-fourth week of pregnancy on the grounds of the illness of the fetus, instead of the earlier twentieth week. If the mother's life or health is at stake, termination of pregnancy is permitted at any stage of pregnancy, even after the twenty-fourth week. In practice, termination of pregnancy has been without restriction, at least prior to the twelfth week of pregnancy, for the past over twenty years.

In the 1992 FINSEX survey, 57 percent of the men and 53 percent of the women supported free abortion, disagreeing with the statement, "I do not approve of free abortion (termination of pregnancy)." Agreement with this statement was expressed by 28 percent of the men and 34 percent of the women. Most abortion opponents were in the older age groups. Opinions on abortion did not vary much in the other age groups, or between men and women.

There are hardly any opponents of abortion in Finland when the pregnancy would seriously endanger the woman's health or the child would probably be born abnormal. Mostly, people understand free abortion as the right of the married people or sexual partners to decide about having the child when the pregnancy is unwanted.

Men's attitudes on abortion mainly reflect their religious views and their general sexual liberality. With women, the acceptance of abortion relates to the modern urban lifestyle, which emphasizes women's right to self-determination in sexual matters. Free abortion is generally accepted by women with a long education and a white-collar background who live in big population centers. Again, free abortion is opposed by religious and conservative women who have had only one sexual partner in their lifetime. These women connect sexual intercourse with a faithful marital relationship that they had entered young; they do not regard women's sexual initiative as proper and they often use unsafe contraception. Becoming pregnant is generally not experienced as a problem when it happens in a steady marital relationship (Kontula 1993).

In 1992, 18 percent of the women of fertile age thought that they would terminate their pregnancy if they just then found out that they were pregnant. One in two woman thought that they would not want to terminate their pregnancy. If a pregnancy had been a current problem, 16 percent of the men would have supported their partner's abortion and 69 percent would have opposed it. Women want to have abortions clearly more often than men, especially after the age of 35. Women's desire to have children is clearly concentrated within narrower age limits than with men—around the early 30s. With women, wanting to have an abortion is most centrally related to their age. Almost half of the young women under 25 and women over 40 years of age want to have their pregnancy terminated.

As a result of the 1970 law, the number of abortions rose quickly, reaching its peak of over 23,300 abortions, about 41 percent of the births, in 1973. After that, the number of abortions declined evenly to 11,200 abortions, about 17 percent of the births, in 1992. Since the early 1980s, the relative number of abortions has been about 30 percent lower in Finland than in the other Nordic countries (Ritamies 1994). With young people under 20, abortions have also decreased after the early 1970s. Abortion is more than twice as common among young women in the United States than it is in Finland, 44 per 1000 compared with 9 per 1,000.

Twenty percent of the women who had at some time been pregnant reported having had an abortion, 80 percent of these women having had only one. Thirteen percent had had two abortions; 4 percent, three abortions; and 2 percent, four abortions. Twelve percent of the men reported that a pregnancy resulting from their sexual relationship had been terminated. Sixteen percent of these men reported two or four abortions. The data suggests that in nearly half of the cases, the woman had an abortion without the man's knowledge.

In the big towns, about one third of the pregnant women had undergone an abortion. In smaller localities, only one in five pregnant women had an abortion.

Concerning the possible effect of abortions on the degree of gratification gained in sexual life, women who had had an abortion experienced orgasm at their last intercourse more often than women who had not had an abortion. Age was not a factor in this. The sexual life of the women who have experienced abortion is quite satisfying according to these results.

D. Population Control Efforts

Due to the low birthrate, Finnish population policies are directed to support families with children, not to limit the number of children. Child allowances, paid parental leaves, parents' right to stay at home for child care without losing their job or pension benefits, high-quality municipal day-care service for children, and other family policies aim at encouraging childbirth. The birthrate has remained relatively stable, and in the future, the population will decrease if fertility does not grow. There is some discussion about the compensation for the lack of births by loosening the strict immigration laws in order to avoid a population decline.

10. Sexually Transmitted Diseases

The 1992 FINSEX study shows that 15 percent of the men and 11.5 percent of the women surveyed had contracted gonorrhea, syphilis, chlamydia, condyloma, or the HPV, and/or genital herpes during their lifetime. Three percent of the men and 2.8 percent of the women had experienced at least two of these diseases. During the prior year, 0.7 percent of the men and 1.5 percent of the women had an STD infection. Based on the total population, these numbers suggest that 450,000 Finns had sometimes suffered from an STD, more than one STD had been contracted by about 100,000 people, and during the year about 38,000 people had been infected.

For the time being, the STDs have been somewhat more common with men than with women. Based on the under-35-year-old women's responses, women's morbidity is likely to surpass that of men's in the future. This change is due to the considerable spread of chlamydia and condyloma among young women. Among men, those who have had an STD appear rather evenly distributed in the different age groups because of gonorrhea, which has been prevalent among men since World War II. However, other STDs have replaced gonorrhea as the leading infections.

Compared to the corresponding study of the year 1971, morbidity among men only slightly rose; with women, the rise was fivefold. This can be explained by the fact that in 1971, only gonorrhea and syphilis were surveyed and diagnosed. In 1992, reports of chlamydia and condyloma greatly enlarged the share of the women who had experienced an STD.

One in ten middle-aged and older man has had gonorrhea. In the younger age groups, especially the under-25-year-olds, gonorrhea is significantly decreasing; none of these men had contracted gonorrhea during the prior year, and only 0.2 percent of the women. Earlier, gonorrhea had been relatively infrequent among women, but it has become more common in the younger age groups with the spread of other STDs. Genital herpes remains less frequent than gonorrhea. The responses to the survey suggest that only a few thousand Finns had suffered from herpes during the prior year (Table 10).

Table 10

The Shares of Those Men and Women of Two Age Groups Who Had Sometime in Their Life Been Infected with Different STDs (in Percentages)

	Gonorrhea		Chlamydia		Condyloma		Herpes	
Age	Men	Women	Men	Women	Men	Women	Men	Women
18-34	2.8	4.1	9.6	10.3	6.9	7.7	0.8	2.8
35 plus	11.5	2.0	2.3	1.5	1.9	3.1	11.9	1.0

While data on chlamydia are not available for older Finns, one in ten of the under-35-year-olds has had this infection. During 1991, 1.3 percent of both men and women had been infected by chlamydia. This share very well corresponds to the statistical observation of about 12,000 chlamydia infections per year.

Condyloma is also mainly a young adults' problem. It is more common among women than among men. Only a few of the older Finns have had it during their life. Among the under-35-year-old women, one in ten has suffered from condyloma. During the prior year, condyloma has centered on men around 30 years of age and on women under 40. Of all the women, almost 1 percent had been infected by the HPV during the prior year; 0.5 percent of the men. This means about 25,000 infections for the year in the total population.

Of those who had at some time suffered from an STD, 8.3 percent had had an infection during the year prior to the survey. All men who had been infected by an STD, excepting herpes, during the prior year were under age 35. With women, there were infected women in all age groups under the age of 55, with the highest incidence among 18- to 24-year-olds and 35- to 44-year-olds. Condyloma and chlamydia were clearly the most frequently contracted diseases.

Those men who had had at least ten sexual partners during their lifetime had had 81 percent of the men's infections. The women of the corresponding group had 43 percent of the STDs. The women's lower number comes from the fact that only 15 percent of all the women had had more than ten partners, while 44 percent of the men had had that many partners. About 2 percent of the people had contracted an STD, although they had had only one partner during their lifetime. Keeping to one sexual relationship only does not always guarantee safety against the STDs.

Of the men who had had sexual intercourse with at least ten partners during their life, 29 percent had sometimes had an STD and 7 percent had had more than one STD. With women who had more than five sexual partners, the corresponding figures are 35 percent and 14 percent. Half of those who had had twenty or more partners had been infected with an STD. Thus, in reality, most Finns have been spared an infection in spite of multiple partners.

Still, the number of sexual partners is directly linked with the risk of contracting an STD. The probability of the men's being infected by chlamydia or condyloma clearly increases after five partners; after ten partners for gonorrhea; and after as many as over fifty partners for herpes (Table 11). In the group with over fifty partners, one half had had gonorrhea. Yet, even in this group, most of the people had escaped the other STDs.

Table 11

The Shares of the Men Who Had Been Subjected to Different STDs During Lifetime According to the Numbers of Sexual Partners During Lifetime (in Percentages)

Partners during lifetime	Gonorrhea	Chlamydia	Herpes	Condyloma	(*N*)
1-3	1.6	0.3	0.3	1.0	(307)
4-9	2.3	3.3	0.5	3.3	(214)
10 or more	17.4	10.9	2.7	6.7	(403)

With women, the risk of contracting chlamydia, condyloma, or gonorrhea grew significantly already with those who had had more than five partners (Table 12). Almost one fifth of those who had had more than ten partners had had all the above mentioned STDs.

About 40 percent of those who contracted an STD during the last year had had only one partner during this time. Only one in ten had had more than five partners. This suggests that a great part of the STD infections still come from the steady partner and only a small share from people who continuously have many sexual relationships.

Table 12

The Shares of the Women Who Had Been Subjected to Different STDs During Lifetime According to the Numbers of Sexual Partners During Lifetime (in Percentages)

Partners during lifetime	Gonorrhea	Chlamydia	Herpes	Condyloma	(*N*)
1-3	—	1.1	0.4	1.8	(541)
4-9	2.7	8.1	2.4	7.5	(295)
10 or more	14.1	16.2	5.6	20.4	(142)

The reports of the men and the women on the sources of infection differ from each other greatly. The women suspect, more often than the men, that they had gotten the infection from the steady partner. The men estimate, more often than the women, that they got the infection from a casual partner or a prostitute. It seems obvious that a significant share of the infections the women got from their partners came from prostitutes. The number of prostitutes is not very great, but they often have infections. The large number of their partners offers them many occasions for spreading infections.

With women's sexual liberation and willingness to initiate, the sources of infection have been "equalized." More and more women are infected by casual partners or friends/acquaintances and men by their steady partners. Almost half of the under-30-year-old women have been infected by casual partners. One third of the under-30-year-old men, again, have been infected by their steady partners. This reflects a change particularly in women's sexual behavior.

In earlier times, a significant part of the men's infections were contracted from foreign women. During the past few years these infections have increased also with women. Twenty-nine percent of men and 27 percent of women who had at some time had sexual intercourse with a foreigner while in another country had had an STD. Seven percent of these men and 11 percent of these women had contracted more than one disease.

Fourteen percent of middle-aged men who reported an STD said they had been infected by a foreign woman, either by an acquaintance on a vacation or a prostitute. A foreign prostitute was the source of infection for 29 percent of the men who had had sexual intercourse with more than fifty partners during their life and had sometimes undergone an STD.

The anxiety about AIDS had caused about one tenth of all the people to decrease the number of sexual partners, and a little more than one tenth reported that they would find out more about the people they were going to have sexual intercourse with. This opinion was supported by 34 percent of the men and by 39 percent of the women who had had several partners during the year. The risk of HIV influences people's sexual life even if they did not restrict the number of their partners. One tenth of the people had felt fear of AIDS during the last year. Even the people who have no actual risk of becoming infected are often afraid of AIDS.

One fifth of the people reported that they had kept to only one partner more strictly than before. These people were, however, not always those with only one sexual relationship. One third of these men and women had had several partners during the year. Certain sex practices, obviously most often anal intercourse, was avoided by 8 percent of all the men and 5 percent of the women.

The use of the condom had, as reported, increased with 20 percent of men and 12 percent of women. An increase in condom use was reported by 30 percent of those under age 25 years. Among those who increased their use of the condom because of AIDS, not all use it regularly. Only 46 percent of the men and 40 percent of the women who reported they had increased their condom use actually used a condom in their last intercourse.

About 30 percent of men and women under age 35 who had experienced an STD reported having decreased the number of their partners for the fear of HIV infection. Every other man and one third of the women reported increasing their use of the condom for the same reason. The condom had been used as the contraceptive method in the most recent sexual intercourse by 25 percent of the men and 20 percent of the women who had at some time undergone an STD. With the other men and women, the corresponding shares were 32 percent and 24 percent.

Of the men who had never been infected with an STD and whose sexual partner in the most recent intercourse had not been a steady partner, 67 percent had used the condom on this occasion. The corresponding share was 57 percent with the men who had at some time had an STD. Of the corresponding groups of women, 45 percent and 38 percent reported using a condom. Those who had at some time had a STD did not much deviate from others in their habits of condom use in casual relationships. A previous infection did not seem to "teach" anyone the use of the condom.

About half the men and women who had experienced an STD reported that a physician had advised them in connection with the treatment on how to avoid STD infection. One third had been left completely without counseling. About one tenth had been given a brochure, and about 5 percent had received counseling from a public-health nurse or a nurse. So, there is still much to improve within the public health care system on STD prevention.

11. HIV/AIDS

The first public statements about AIDS in Finland were issued in 1983, with a general discussion following in 1985 and 1986. Health officials were immediately involved, concentrating their efforts on general information about AIDS and its transmission and about other sexually transmitted diseases, strongly recommending the use of condoms in casual sexual contacts. At the same time, together with communal health organizations, health officials also directed an effective information and support campaign for groups at special risk of AIDS. In schools, the AIDS issue was—and continues to be—associated with general sex education and the prevention of sexually transmitted diseases.

Public discussion and education concerning AIDS was at its strongest from 1986 to 1988, but the tone was considerably calmer than, for example, in the United States or the United Kingdom. By September 1990, the cumulative AIDS incidence rate per million of population was 14.3, compared with 66.3 in the United Kingdom.

By 1994, about 600 HIV infections had been diagnosed, and about a hundred people had died of AIDS. The proportion of the HIV-infected in Finland has remained fairly small in international comparison. This is mainly due to the scarcity of prostitution and intravenous drug use in Finland.

In the FINSEX study, 6.4 percent of the men and 7 percent of the women reported having taken the HIV test on their own initiative by the beginning of 1992. Multiple tests were reported by 30 percent of these men (1.9 percent of all men) and by 16 percent of the women tested (1.1 percent of all women). At the beginning of 1992, about 250,000 Finns had been tested for HIV, and about 50,000 of those who had had themselves tested several times. Multiple tests were most common among 30-year-old women. The young age groups had had themselves tested more frequently than older Finns. One tenth of young adults had taken the test.

Some of the HIV-tested had not had very many partners during their lives. One fifth of the men and one fourth of the women tested had had three partners at the most. About half of all the males tested had had at least twenty partners. Of the women tested, 40 percent had had at least ten partners. Eleven percent of the men and 17 percent of the women with more than one partner were tested during the prior year. This shows that, with the risk of infection rising, women were quicker to have themselves tested.

Seven percent of current or past intravenous drug users and 16 percent of men and 19 percent of women with a previous STD infection of the women had taken the HIV test on their own initiative. Of the other men and women, the test had been taken by 6 percent. Of those who had reduced the number of their sexual partners or increased their use of the condom because of anxiety experienced for AIDS or HIV, from 16 percent to 18 percent had taken the HIV test. Of the people who had sometimes used drugs intravenously, 7 percent had themselves tested for HIV.

12. Sexual Dysfunction, Counseling, and Therapies

In Finland, sexual dysfunction can be treated—depending on its causes—using sexual counseling, sexual short therapy, intensive therapy, medicines, and/or surgery. Sexual advice is given both in communal health-care centers and in medical and therapeutical service centers specializing in counseling. It is possible to get sex therapy all over the country.

In the FINSEX study, the prevalence of different kinds of sexual problems was surveyed, as well as the help sought to resolve these problems. Half of the men and 26 percent of the women in a steady relationship reported no lack of sexual desire during the prior year. Fifteen to 55 percent of women in a steady relationship in different age groups experienced a lack of sexual desire fairly often. The women had succeeded in concealing this lack of desire in many cases, since clearly fewer men than this, when asked about their partners' lack of desire, had experienced their partners' lack of desire as a problem in each of the age groups. The men's reports on their own lack of desire and the women's opinions about their partners' lack of desire fit well together. Five to 20 percent of the men had experienced a lack of sexual desire at least fairly often.

Married women clearly suffered from a lack of sexual desire more often than the women in other steady relationships. According to their own responses, 35 percent of the married women had experienced a lack of sexual desire at least fairly often during the prior year. For women in cohabitation and other steady sexual relationships the corresponding share was 15 percent. A similar perception, though slighter, could be found in the men's responses, where 18 percent of the husbands, 13 percent of cohabitors, and 8 percent of the men in some other steady relationship reported that their partners had had a lack of sexual desire at least fairly often during the past year. Partly, these differences are due to the fact that the married people are older, on the average, than those in other relationships, and a lack of sexual desire is noticeably frequent in over-55-year-old women.

In sexual therapy, it is presumed that love, trust, and security are generally needed as essential elements in the creation of sexual desire. Anxiety has been observed to inhibit sexual arousal from taking place (Kaplan 1987). Why then was there less desire in marriages that would appear more secure than other relationships? Important causes are certainly found in the effects of aging on sexual desire, the facilitation of marital relationships, and, in some cases, a sexual life changing into an obligation. Many speak about marital relationships' turning into boring routine. Most passion has been observed in new and, in some respect, insecure relationships. Particularly long-standing marital relationships may be regarded as already too secure, thereby lessening the sexual excitement (Hatfield and Rapson 1987).

During the prior year, 58 percent of the women and 52 percent of their male partners reported some problem with vaginal lubrication. In this respect, the women's and the men's responses corresponded very well to each other. On the other hand, 15 percent of the women reported suffering fairly often, often, or regularly from insufficient vaginal lubrication, while only 5 percent of the men reported this problem. This suggests that it is sometimes difficult for men to notice the woman's problems with vaginal lubrication. Men notice only what affects the insertion of the penis, but, obviously, they do not actually know how much pain and discomfort insufficient vaginal lubrication may cause the partner during sexual intercourse.

With women, vaginal lubrication problems increased considerably with age. About one tenth of the middle-aged women reported fairly frequent problems with vaginal lubrication; after age 50 this rose to about a third with hormonal changes a prime factor.

Many of the women who suffer from problems with vaginal lubrication experience intercourse as painful. Intercourse had fairly often been experienced as painful by 29 percent of the women who had suffered from vaginal dryness at least fairly often during the year. The corresponding proportion is 16 percent with the middle-aged and 40 percent with the aging. Of the same women, two out of three had experienced their sexual intercourse as painful at least sometimes during the year.

Almost half of the women who had suffered from problems with vaginal lubrication, at least fairly often during the year, had obtained lubricant cream to facilitate intercourse and to remove the possibility of pain, according to both the women's and the men's responses. Lubricants had been of evident help, for a greater number of the women who used lubricants experienced orgasm during the last intercourse than those who did not use lubricants.

On the average, 3 percent of the under-45-year-old women had consulted a physician for problems of lubrication; of the older women, more than 10 percent. About nine out of ten seekers felt they had been helped. The problem is thus quite easily resolved in most cases with the help of a lubricant.

Problems with vaginal lubrication have a strong connection with sexual desire and its possible deficiency. Half of the women who had experienced a lack of sexual desire at least fairly often during the year had also at least fairly often had problems with vaginal lubrication.

For the 1992 survey, 49 percent of the men who had intercourse during the prior year reported that they themselves had had at least some problems with having an erection during that year; 47 percent of the women reported the same about their partners. Six percent by the men and 9 percent by the women reported this a fairly frequent problem, a fairly good convergent appraisal, although men obviously tend to conceal their more difficult erectile problems. Comparatively, it seems that men's erectile problems are slightly less frequent than women's problems with vaginal lubrication.

Two clear observations emerge when the results of the years 1971 and 1992 are compared: on the one hand, erectile problems seem to have diminished during the twenty years and, on the other hand, they are very much age-bound. In 1971, 4.3 percent of the under-55-year-old men reported having experienced erectile problems during the last year; in 1992, 2.2 percent. The corresponding figures with women about their partners were 6.2 percent and 4.4 percent. Both vaginal lubrication and erectile problems become clearly more common after the age of 50. In the age group of the 70-year-olds, almost one third of the couples had at least fairly often suffered from them.

According to the 1992 survey, men's erectile ability is strongest around the age of 30, when two men out of three have no problems having erections, as reported by both the men and women. With the 50-year-olds, the corresponding share is about 40 percent; with the 70-year-olds, about one fifth. So, a significant number of men live throughout their life without experiencing any problems with having erections. Here, it may be of great importance what kind of partners men have intercourse with, among other things, and how healthy they themselves are.

Men were also asked about their experience with continuous erectile dysfunction during their life. The continuity was not defined except by options of varying spans of time, the shortest of which was the option of "a few weeks' time." Fifteen percent of the male respondents reported experiencing a continuous erectile dysfunction for a span of at least a few weeks at least once (Figure 14). The incidence of erectile problems increased significantly for those over age 50. Half of the 70-year-olds had experienced continuous erectile dysfunction. While erectile dysfunction remains a very common problem, it did decrease slightly between 1971 and 1992.

Figure 14

Men Who Have Sometimes Experienced Continuous Erectile Dysfunction (1971 and 1992)

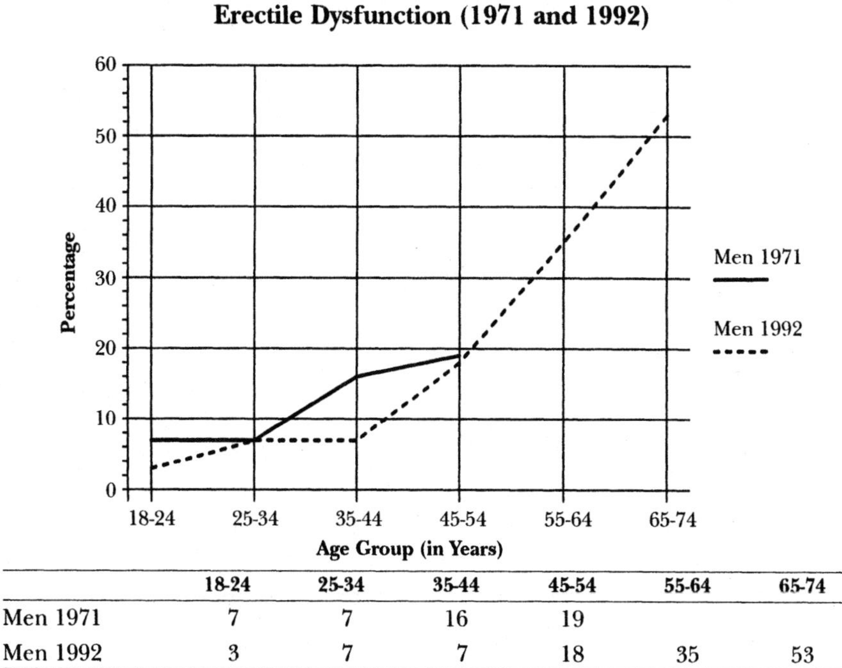

	18-24	25-34	35-44	45-54	55-64	65-74
Men 1971	7	7	16	19		
Men 1992	3	7	7	18	35	53

Fifty percent of all Finnish men had experienced no erectile problems during the prior year, nor a few weeks' continuous dysfunction prior to that. On the other hand, 5 percent of the men had fairly often had erectile problems during the past year as well as at least a few weeks' continuous erectile dysfunction during or prior to that time. About 9 percent of the men had had no erectile problems during the last year although they had suffered periods of erectile dysfunction prior to that time.

Slightly under 4 percent of all men in 1992 had consulted a physician for erectile problems, about one third of the men who had reported having sometimes experienced continuous erectile dysfunction. Nearly half of the men who had suffered from at least half a year's continuous erectile dysfunction had sought a physician for help. In 1971, fewer men than at present, 16 percent, had talked about the matter to a physician. More than half of the men who sought help in 1992 and about one fifth of the men who sought help in 1971 felt that they had been helped. So, seeking treatment and the efficiency of this treatment improved during the twenty years.

Of the men whose partners had had problems with vaginal lubrication at least fairly often during the last year, 31 percent had themselves had problems with obtaining or maintaining an erection at least fairly often. Twenty-three percent of the women who had had problems with vaginal lubrication reported that their partners had fairly often had problems having an erection during the same time. So, one's partner's sexual problems had obviously had an effect on the other's sexual responses. If the partner does not seem really eager to have intercourse, one's own excitement may easily die halfway.

About 5 percent of the men who had at least occasionally suffered from erectile dysfunction told that they had sometimes used some substances or pills that increase potency. Rings to maintain erection or penis enlargers with pumps, on the other hand, had not been much used by the men who had erectile problems. Neither had vibrators or vibrating dildos been used by these men with their partners more often than by the others. These devices had not been sought to substitute for deficiency in obtaining an erection.

Experiencing orgasm is a focal matter in view of the gratification of sexual life. This is true even though the FINSEX study shows that many women reported enjoying their sexual life although they had not experienced orgasm or had seldom experienced it during intercourse. However, those who had experienced orgasm more regularly were clearly more satisfied with their sexual life and their partners than the others.

About half of the men and from 6 percent to 7 percent of the women reported, irrespective of age, that they always experienced orgasm at sexual intercourse. This shows that only a small share of women experience orgasm very easily and that orgasm is not a self-evident matter even to men, for instance, if—from their point of view—their coitus is interrupted. With women, having no orgasm is often a consequence of the quickness of their partner's "coming" after which the love play ceases.

Most men have orgasm during sexual intercourse, either always, almost always, or, at least, mostly. Less frequently than this, orgasm had been experienced by 8 percent of the 18- to 24-year-old men and 19 percent of the 65- to 74-year-old men. In the other age groups, from 1 percent to 2 percent of the men obtain orgasm during intercourse less frequently than "mostly." Thus, men remain without orgasm during intercourse mostly at the beginning of their sexual life and at retirement age when their physical condition is declining.

With women, experiencing orgasm is much more occasional than with men. Orgasm is experienced at least mostly during sexual intercourse by slightly over half of the women; by about 60 percent of the middle-aged women. When the incidences of women's orgasms by the 1971 and the 1992 surveys are compared, the regularity of experiencing orgasm had slightly increased with the over-35-year-olds. With women younger than this, no change had happened. At least mostly, orgasm had been experienced during intercourse by 53 percent of the under-55-year-old women in 1971; in 1992, by 58 percent.

Comparing orgasm data in 50-year-olds of 1971 with the 70-year-olds twenty years later in 1992, experiencing orgasm had not decreased in spite of aging and the increased morbidity (Table 13). So, the preconditions for sexual satisfaction seem to have improved in this respect. On the other hand, since a considerable number of women do not experience orgasm during intercourse, it is a clear sign of the many restraints there still are obstructing women on their way to enjoyment. And if the woman does not find real satisfaction in sexual intercourse, the man cannot enjoy himself to the full either.

Table 13

Women Who Have at Least, Mostly, or at the Most "Seldom" Experienced Orgasm During Intercourse (in Percentages), 1971 and 1992

Age	Mostly 1971	Mostly 1992	Seldom 1971	Seldom 1992
18-24	52	50	16	12
25-34	58	59	8	10
35-44	51	64	9	9
45-54	44	56	17	5
55-64		44		8
65-74		45		16

1971: *N* = 1,231; 1992: *N* = 1,031

A third of a percent of the men had not experienced orgasm during intercourse; of the women, 4.4 percent. This is a relatively small percentage when one looks at the United States, for instance, where about 10 percent of women do not have orgasm during intercourse (Darling et al. 1991).

Orgasm during intercourse had been experienced seldom or never by 0.7 percent of the men and 10 percent of the women according to the 1992 data on 18- to 74-year-old Finns. In 1972, 12 percent of the women under 55 years old had experienced orgasm seldom or never. In 1992, 9 percent of the women under age 55 reported orgasm never or seldom; quite seldom orgasm had been experienced by 30 percent of the women between the ages 18 and 74 years. Thus, sexual satisfaction has remained significantly deficient for a large number of women and little improvement has been observed in this regard between 1971 and 1992.

Achieving orgasm reportedly is decisively important to finding sexual intercourse pleasant. Of the men who report that they always experience orgasm at intercourse, half consider sexual intercourse very pleasant; while only 18 percent of the men who have orgasm approximately on every other occasion or less frequently regard intercourse as very pleasant. With women, the corresponding shares are 65 percent and 15 percent. Some women considered intercourse very pleasant, although they had never experienced orgasm.

Ninety-two percent of the men and 56 percent of the women reported having experienced orgasm in the latest intercourse (Figure 15). There was a rise in this level of experiencing orgasm for all the women's age groups between 1971 and 1992. In 1971, 56 percent of the under-55-year-old women had experienced orgasm at their last intercourse; in 1992, 63 percent. The possible change concerning men is not known, for, in 1971, only the women had been asked questions about experiencing orgasm. With women, the level of experiencing orgasm had stayed at 60 percent until the age of 50, after which it had fallen to about one third.

Fifty-five percent of the married women, 71 percent of the cohabiting women, 64 percent of the women in other steady relationships, and 41 percent of the women with no steady relationship experienced orgasm in their latest intercourse. Perhaps it is surprising that orgasms are experienced less frequently within marriages than in other steady relationships, for it has been presented that having orgasm is in an important connection with the feeling of security experienced in a relationship (Kaplan 1987).

The regularity of the orgasms experienced by women at sexual intercourse is clearly related to their sexual desire and to the quickness of the partner's "coming" (Table 14). The women who had reported having themselves suffered from a lack of sexual desire during the last year experienced orgasm less frequently than the other women. Also a great number of the women who feel that their partner "comes too fast" are usually left without orgasm.

Figure 15

Orgasm at the Most Recent Intercourse (1971 and 1992)

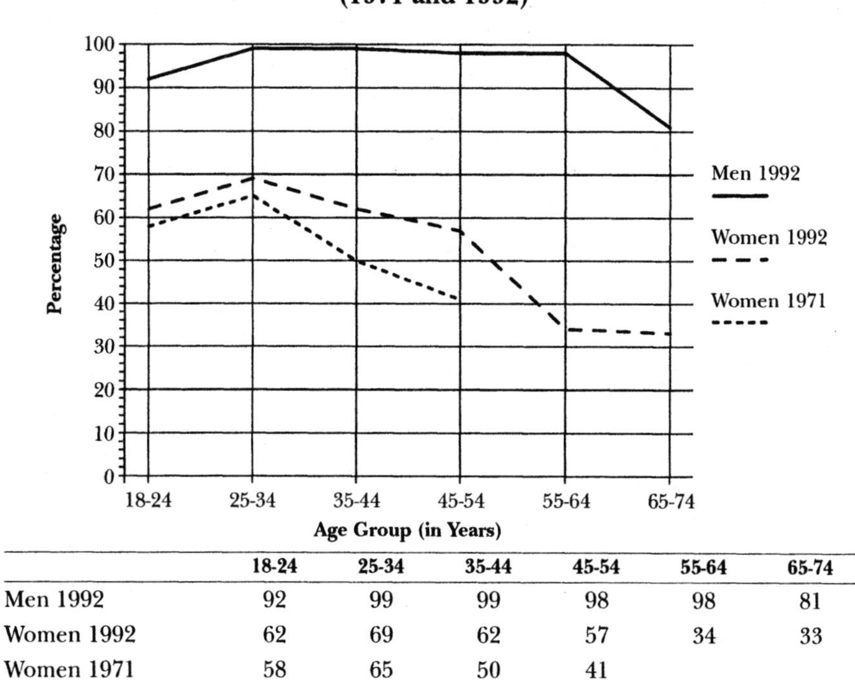

	18-24	25-34	35-44	45-54	55-64	65-74
Men 1992	92	99	99	98	98	81
Women 1992	62	69	62	57	34	33
Women 1971	58	65	50	41		

Table 14

Women's Orgasms During Intercourse by Their Sexual Desire and the Quickness of Partner's Coming (1992)

	Orgasm at least mostly	Orgasm every other time	Orgasm at the most quite seldom	(*N*)
Lack of sexual desire				
Very often	26	14	60	(62)
Quite often	45	18	37	(161)
Quite seldom	62	17	21	(370)
Never	73	13	14	(205)
Partner comes too soon				
Very often	28	11	61	(36)
Quite often	35	23	42	(141)
Quite seldom	62	17	21	(350)
Never	73	12	15	(250)

The orgasm experienced in the most recent intercourse was about as strongly related to a person's own sexual desire as to the quickness of the partner's "coming." An orgasm had been experienced by 24 percent of the women who had very often felt a lack of sexual desire during the year; and by 73 percent of the women who had not had any lack of sexual desire at all. If the partner's "coming" was not felt to be too soon, 70 percent of the women reached orgasm in their most recent intercourse. If the woman herself is desirous and the partner "considerate" in his speed, the woman mostly achieves orgasm.

The partner's sexual desire is also connected with the woman's orgasm. Only 38 percent of the women whose partners had at least fairly often suffered from a lack of sexual desire during the last year had experienced orgasm during intercourse at least mostly. That is clearly fewer women than average.

The orgasms experienced by women during their most recent intercourse has a clear connection with the sexual practices applied. The best practice at sexual intercourse, in this respect, had been using two or three positions; the second best had been the "woman-on-top" position. The shares of the women who had experienced orgasm in these cases was 72 percent and 67 percent respectively. In the "man-on-top" position, 49 percent of the women had experienced orgasm. Practicing varying positions at intercourse and the woman's own activity thus greatly increase the probability of her experiencing orgasm.

A number of people experience their first orgasms before their first sexual intercourse during various kinds of petting experiences. Most of the men, however, have their first intercourse-related orgasm at the same time they have their first sexual intercourse. Less than a third of the women reported achieving an orgasm in their first intercourse. Half of the women and one tenth of the men had not experienced their first orgasm until a few years after their first experience of sexual intercourse. There has not been much change in this timing even in the younger age groups. With one tenth of the women, more than ten years had elapsed between their first intercourse and their first orgasm. Four percent of the women reported no orgasm at all.

There has been some informal courses for sexual therapists in order to provide those who work as sex therapists with some professional skills. However, anyone can start working as a sex therapists without any special training, certification, or licensing.

13. Research and Advanced Education

A. Institutes and Programs for Sexological Research

In Finland, sexological research is conducted by individual scholars working at universities and research institutes or projects financed mainly by the state. A bibliography of sex literature for the time period 1549-1989 includes over 2,000 authors (Turpeinen 1991). Most of the articles and books listed are written by medical doctors, but some important sociological studies on sexual behavior have also been published in this century.

B/C. Post-College Sexuality Programs and Sexological Publications

None currently exists in Finland.

D. Sexological Organizations

Two sexological organizations are active in Finland:

Seksuaalipoliittinen Yhdistys Sexpo Ry (Sexual Policy Association). Address: Nilsiänkatu 11-13, SF-00510 Helsinki, Finland

Seksuaalinen Tasavertaisuus SETA Ry (Sexual Equality Association). Address: Oikokatu 3, SF-00170 Helsinki, Finland

References and Suggested Reading

CEDAW Convention. 1993. *Second Periodic Report by Finland.* Helsinki: Ministry of Foreign Affairs.

Christensen, H.T. and C.F. Gregg. 1970. "Changing Sex Norms in America and Scandinavia." *Journal of Marriage and Family*, 32:616-27.

Darling, C. Anderson, J. K. Davidson, and R. P. Cox. 1991. "Female Sexual Response and the Timing of Partner Orgasm." *Journal of Sex and Marital Therapy*, 17(1):3-21.

Erkkola, Risto, and Osmo Kontula. 1993. "Syntyvyyden Säännostely" (Birth Control). In *Suomalainen Seksi* (Finnish Sex). Osmo Kontula and Elina Haavio-Mannila, eds. Helsinki: WSOY, pp. 343-370.

Gershuny, J. 1990. "International Comparisons of Time Budgets—Methods and Opportunities." In: R. von Schweitzer, M. Ehling, and D. Schäfer, eds. *Zeitbudgeterhebungen—Ziele, Methoden und Neue Konzepte.* Stuttgart: Metzler Poeschel.

Grönfors, M., E. Haavio-Mannila, K. Mustola, and O. Stålström. 1984. Esitietoja Homo-ja Biseksuaalisten Ihmisten Elämäntavasta ja Syrjinnästä (Preliminary Data on Lifestyle and Discrimination of Homo- and Bisexual People). In: K. Sievers and O. Stålström, eds. *Rakkauden Monet Kasvot.* Espoo: Weilin+Göös.

Haavio-Mannila, E. 1991. "Impact of Coworkers on Female Alcohol Use." *Contemporary Drug Problems*, 18(4):597-627.

Haavio-Mannila, E., and K. Kauppinen-Toropainen. 1992. "Women and the Welfare State in the Nordic Countries." In: H. Kahne and J. Giele, eds. *Women's Work and Women's Lives—The Continuing Struggle Worldwide.* Boulder, Colorado: Westview Press.

Haavio-Mannila, E., T. R. Harris, A. D. Klassen, R. W. Wilsnack, and S. C. Wilsnack. 1996. "Alcohol and Sexuality Among American and Finnish Women." *Nordisk Sexologi*, 4(3):129-146.

Haavio-Mannila, E., J. P. Roos, and O. Kontula 1997. "Repression, Revolution and Ambivalence: The Sexual Life of Three Generations." *Acta Sociologica*, 40(1):2-22 (in press).

Haavio-Mannila, E., and O. Kontula 1997. "What Increases Sexual Satisfaction?" *Archives of Sexual Behavior*, 26 (in press).

Hatfield, E., and R. L. Rapson. 1987. "Passionate Love/Sexual Desire: Can the Same Paradigm Explain Both?" *Archives of Sexual Behavior,* 16(3):259-78.

Järvinen, M. 1990. *Prostitution i Helsingfors—En Studie i Kvinnokontroll* (*Prostitution in Helsinki—A Study on Control of Women*). Åbo: Åbo Academy Press.

Jeffreys, S. 1990. *Anticlimax: A Feminist Perspective on the Sexual Revolution.* New York: New York University Press.

Kaplan, H. S. 1987. *The Illustrated Manual of Sex Therapy.* 2nd ed. New York: Brunner/Mazel.

Kinsey, A. C., W. B. Pomeroy, and C. E. Martin. 1948. *Sexual Behavior in the Human Male.* Philadelphia: Saunders.

Kinsey, A. C., W. B. Pomeroy, C. E. Martin, and P. H. Gebhard. 1953. *Sexual Behavior in the Human Female.* Philadelphia: Saunders.

Kontula, Osmo. 1991. "Sukupuolielämän Aloittamisen Yhteiskunnallisista Ehdoista" (Cultural Terms of Sexual Initiation). *Sosiaali-ja Terveyshallitus. Tutkimuksia* 14/1991. Valtion Painatuskeskus. Helsinki.

Kontula, Osmo. 1993. "Ketkä Hyväksyvät Vapaan Abortin (Who Approves a Free Abortion)?" In: Suomalaisia Mielipiteitä Raskauden Keskeytyksestä. *STAKES. Julkaisusarja Aiheita* 34/1993. Helsinki, p. 23-39.

Kontula, O. 1996. "Sex Education in Finland." Paper presented in the 39th Annual Meeting of The Society for the Scientific Study of Sexuality (SSSS) held in Houston, November 14-17, 1996.

Kontula, Osmo, and J. Meriläinen. 1988. "Nuorten Kypsyminen Seurusteluun ja Seksuaalisuuteen" (Adolescents' Maturation for Social Intercourse and Sexuality). Lääkintöhallituksen Julkaisuja. *Sarja Tutkimukset* 9/1988. Valtion Painatuskeskus. Helsinki.

Kontula, O., and M. Rimpelä. 1988. "Onko AIDS-Valistus Vaikuttanut Nuorten Seksuaalisuuteen 1986-1988" (Has AIDS Education Influenced the Adolescents' Sexuality 1986-1988)? *Suomen Lääkärilehti,* 43:3493-3500.

Kontula, Osmo, and E. Haavio-Mannila, eds. 1993. *Suomalainen Seksi: Tietoa Suomalaisten Sukupuolielämän Muutoksesta* (*Finnish Sex: Information of Changes in Sexual Life in Finland*). Juva: WSOY.

Kontula, O., and E. Haavio-Mannila 1994. "Sexual Behavior Changes in Finland in the Past 20 Years." *Nordisk Sexologi,* 12(3):196214.

Kontula, O. and E. Haavio-Mannila 1995. *Matkalla Intohimoon: Nuoruuden Hurma Ja Käsimys Seksuaalielämäkertojen Kuvaamana* (*Along the Way to Passion: The Joy and Suffering of Youth Revealed in Sexual Autobiographies*). WSOY. Juva.

Kontula, Osmo, and Elina Haavio-Mannila. 1995. *Sexual Pleasures: Enhancement of Sex Life in Finland, 1971-1992.* Aldershot, Brookfield USA, Signapore, and Sidney: Dartmouth.

Kontula, O., and K. Kosonen 1996. "Sexuality Changing from Privacy to the Open—A Study of the Finnish Press over the Years from 1961 to 1991." *Nordisk Sexologi,* 14(1):34-47.

Kosunen, E. 1993. "Teini-ikäisten Raskaudet ja Ehkäisy" (Teen-age Pregnancies and Contraception). *STAKES.* Helsinki: Raportteja, 99.

Laumann, E. O., J. Gagnon, R. T. Michael, and S. Michaels. 1994. *The Social Organization of Sexuality.* Chicago, Illinois: University of Chicago Press.

Love, B. 1992. *Encyclopedia of Unusual Sex Practices.* Fort Lee, New Jersey: Barricade Books.

Markkula, H. 1981. *Maksettu Nainen* (*Paid Woman*). Hämeenlinna:Kustannus-Mäkelä Oy.

Niemi, I., and H. Pääkkönen. 1989. Ajankäytön Muutokset ("Changes in the Appropriation of Time in the 1980s"). *Tutkimuksia* (*Research Reports*), 153. Helsinki: Tilastokeskus (Statistics Finland).

Riihinen O., A. Pulkkinen, and M. Ritamies. 1980. *Suomalaisen Perheen Lapsiluku* (*The Number of Children in the Finnish Family*). Helsinki: Väestöntutkimuslaitos D.7.

Ritamies, M. 1994. *Finland: A Comparative Handbook.* Westport, CT: Greenwood Press, pp. 85-99.

Robinson, J. 1988. "Who Is Doing the Housework?" *American Demographics,* 10(12):24-28.

Sarmela, M. 1969. *Reciprocity Systems of the Rural Society in the Finnish-Karelian Culture Area.* Helsinki: Academia Scientiarum Fennica. FF Communications No. 207.

Sievers, K., O. Koskelainen, and K. Leppo. 1974. *Suomalaisten Sukupuolielämä* (*Sex Life in Finland*). WSOY, Porvoo.

Smith, T.W. 1990. "The Sexual Revolution?" *Public Opinion Quarterly,* 1990:54:415-35.

Turpeinen, T. 1991. *Suomalaisen Seksuaalikirjallisuuden Bibliografia 1549-1989* (*Bibliography of the Finnish Sexual Literature 1549-1989*). *Kellokosken Sairaala, Mariefors Sjukhus And Sexpo Ry.* Jyväskylä.

Wikman, K, and V. Rob. 1937. Die Einleitung der Ehe. *Åbo: Acta Academiae Åboensis. Humaniora,* Xi, 1.

Germany
(*Bundesrepublik Deutschland*)

Rudiger Lautmann, Ph.D., and Kurt Starke, Ph.D.

Contents

Demographics and a Historical Perspective

A. Demographics

Located in central Europe, Germany has 137,838 square miles. It is bordered by Denmark and the Baltic Sea on the north, the Netherlands, Belgium, Luxembourg, and France on the west, Austria and Switzerland in the south, and Poland and the Czech Republic on the east.

Germany's 81.3 million population is 85 percent urban. The age distribution is 16 percent under age 15; 69 percent 15 to 65; and 15 percent over age 65. Life expectancy is 73 for males and 80 for females. The birthrate and death rate are both 11 per 1,000 population. The 1995 infant mortality rate is 6 per 1,000 live births. The natural growth rate is a negative 0.1 percent. Germany has one hospital bed per 126 persons, one physycian per 313 persons. Literacy is 100 percent with 100 percent attendance in nine or ten years of compulsory schooling. The per capita Gross Domestic Product in 1993 was $16,500.

Germany, as well as the predominantly German-speaking countries of Austria and Switzerland, has always received large numbers of immigrants. For many centuries, its geographic situation in the middle of Europe meant that the country functioned as a transit land and clearinghouse for people of other nations. The Iron Curtain only interrupted this mobility for four decades. And fascist rule with its tenet of Aryan purification was effective for just a dozen years. Apart from these historic peculiarities, the German-speaking countries have always fulfilled the paradox of a "cosmopolitan province." Exportation and importation of ideas and persons created a melting pot. Diverse cultural traditions and ethnic backgrounds currently form a contradictory mixture, apparently productive as well as unstable.

In this region, the following events occurred within this century: the invention of sexology, a sexual repression of extreme cruelty, and most recently a fundamental sexual liberation. The leadership in sexual reasoning was suddenly lost when the Nazi government annihilated the symbiosis with the Jews who until then had fruitfully and uniquely assimilated themselves into German culture. The leaders of German sexual science included Albert Moll (1862-1939), Iwan Bloch (1872-1922), Magnus Hirschfeld (1868-1935), and Albert Eulenburg (1840-1917). The German-speaking sexual science has never recovered from this loss of genius.

B. A Brief Historical Perspective

Julius Caesar defeated Germanic tribes in 55 and 53 B.C.E., but Roman expansion north of the Rhine River was stopped in 9 of the Common Era. After Charlemagne, ruler of the Franks from 768 to 814, had consolidated Saxon, Bavarian, Rhenish, Frankish, and other lands, the eastern part became the German Empire. The Thirty Years' War (1618-1648) split Germany into several small principalities and kingdoms. After Napoleon, Austria challenged Prussia's dominance in the area, but Prussia prevailed. In 1867, Otto von Bismarck, Prussian Chancellor, formed the North German Confederation. After Bismarck managed the defeat of Napoleon III, he formed the German Empire in 1871 with King Wilhelm I as Prussian German emperor or kaiser. The German Empire and its colonial possessions reached its peak just before World War I. The Republic of Germany (1919-1933) faced a disastrous economic collapse brought on by war reparations to France and its allies. The National Socialist German Workers' (Nazi) Party came to power with Adolph Hitler in 1933, and started World War II. In the aftermath of the war, Germany was split into an eastern portion under Communist control, and a western democratic republic.

The unification of the Federal Republic of Germany (West Germany) and the German Democratic Republic (East Germany) in 1990 caused serious economic problems for the whole population. The long-lasting tension between richer and poorer regions will mask the remarkable differences that have developed in sexual habits. Possibly the unexpected unification, together with the increasing immigration, will lead to new turbulences on the sexual front.

1. Basic Sexological Premises

A. Character of Gender Roles

The structure of and changes in gender differentiation in Germany resembles that of other Western countries. The long-term trend since the first feminist movement in the 1880s exhibits an egalitarian tendency with regard to political, economic, as well as sexual participation. The trend was interrupted by the Nazi regime, which tried to push women back into household and nursing activities. The policy of "a child as a donation to the Fuehrer" was a remarkable failure. World War II brought women back into the industrial workplaces and to autonomous decision making in all social domains.

Today there are many endeavors to emancipate women (and, possibly, men). Political rights and the wording of laws and official texts are strictly gender neutral. Affirmative action, quotas, governmental subsidies, and similar programs support and proclaim an egalitarian policy. But there are numerous barriers to putting these incentives into everyday practice (Lautmann 1990). Equality remains a task for generations to come. Still, the actual progress—sometimes in the economic, but mainly in the private sphere—is noteworthy.

B. Sociolegal Status of Males and Females

Jurisprudence says that every human being from birth on is granted a status as a person with their own rights. Attention is even paid to children's decision making, according to their level of maturity. Family jurisdiction has to orientate itself around the child's welfare, as its highest principle. Corporal punishment is strictly forbidden, abrogating a traditional customary right of adults. In practice, the children's autonomy contradicts their factual dependency and older ideas of "parents' property" and parental rights.

Formal education is gender neutral. Girls and boys are given equal opportunities at schools. The principle of coeducation has been implemented thoroughly. Some feminists are currently recommending a partial return to gender-specific classes in order to overcome certain problems in the learning of mathematics and technical subjects.

After puberty, men and women enjoy a high level of sexual autonomy. Some youngsters leave the parental house before majority (18) to share a flat with other adolescents.

The perception of gender roles is clear for many adolescents. They fixate on these roles, while other factors and, above all, their individuality, are neglected as one-sided. The actual or intended relationship between men and women is partly seen as threatening, especially in the west. The proportion of women with a habitual feeling of disadvantage on account of their sex is much greater in the west. At the same time—and this only appears to be a contradiction—girls in the west also reflect the advantages of their sex more than girls in the east.

Adolescents in the east see themselves to a lesser extent than in the west as men or women, and experience relations between the sexes as less conflict-ridden. Feminist thinking was hardly disseminated in East Germany and did not influence girls as they grew up to develop a critical perception of men, who in turn did not experience a resulting feeling of insecurity. They attribute events in their lives, their success and failure, less to their membership of one of the sexes and more to their overall personality.

C. General Concepts of Sexuality and Love

In Germany, the basic ideologies and configurations of the erotic world do not differ very much from those found in western and northern Europe and in the WASP population of the United States of America. With respect to sexual behaviors, the most important cleavage runs between the two principles of Romantic Love versus Hedonism. Romanticism binds together personal love and sexual attraction. Without a "harmony of hearts," no orgastic fulfillment is possible. This principle is founded in the Christian idea that the spiritual community dignifies the genital encounter. The prosaic concept of hedonism emphasizes the erotic quality of the body and the satisfaction of desires. The sexual drive is a natural need. One may give way to it without making many preconditions, calculating only costs and gratifications.

Similarly there are two ideal types of intimate partnership. Affective solidarity is the principle of a stable and universal relationship between two human beings whose individual disparities are balanced through a mutually complementary performance. On the other hand, contractual partnership is based on a calculation of mutual benefits. The relationship lasts as long as the balance remains positive for both participants. The contractual element allows for negotiations about sexual relations.

Sexual phenomena are generally conceptualized from a naturalistic point of view developed in the nineteenth century. The average person and most experts—outside sexology, of course—follow a version of naive biologism that reflects this naturalistic view point. In this view, innate programs, hormones, and so on direct the sexual response. Psychoanalytic and sociological approaches are not prominent, with the exception of a behavioristic learning theory.

2. Religious and Ethnic Factors Affecting Sexuality

A. Source and Character of Religious Values

Since the Reformation in the sixteenth century, Germany has been the arena of fierce conflicts between the two main religious denominations, including long wars. Not until the twentieth century could the two churches find an arrangement for coexistence—today 45 percent of the population are Protestant and 35 percent Catholic. A growing proportion of the population has left the Church—roughly 18 percent—and even more are only nominal members without much belief (but still paying the not-so-insignificant Church tax).

Thus the sexual morals of Protestantism and Catholicism exist side by side with all their differences and similarities. Many surveys show that the sexual teachings of the churches do not effectively direct the behaviors of the sexually active population, although they may have some effect on the attitudes. Instead the churches exert a considerable influence on sexual politics. They are accepted as an expert voice in moral debates, but to a diminishing extent. In the new, controversial legislation since 1970, no-fault divorce, liberalization of abortion, and sexual autonomy, the ecclesiastical positions were overruled.

B. Source and Character of Ethnic Values

The current growing immigration rate, which includes, for example, 1.7 million Turks now resident in Germany, may lead to new conflicts. The Islamic and paternalistic view of family values, gender differentiation, same-sex relations, and the like is opposed to the secularized Western view. Immigrants of the second generation experience tensions between intra- and extrafamilial worlds. Moreover, in combination with low social prestige, an explosive mixture arises, bursting with violence against women, gays, and other persons defined as weak.

3. Sexual Knowledge and Education

A. Government Policies and Programs

The parental family and the school have the mandate to give the necessary instructions about sexuality. To a certain degree, both institutions are reluctant to perform that task. They mutually suspect each other of being inefficient in advising and/or of being dangerous with respect to the contents. Sex education, if publicly discussed, immediately becomes a political controversy where the right-left continuum corresponds to the poles of repressive versus emancipative doctrines.

School curricula provide for the instruction of sexual issues from the first elementary class onwards. Since there is no special course, the matter can be addressed in various fields such as biology, religion, politics, and so on. The outcome, in spite of existing detailed syllabi, is a sporadic sex education. The teachers think of themselves as not being competent enough. As a matter of fact, the academic training is entirely insufficient; only a tenth of the pedagogic students are offered suitable courses. The parents' attitudes are of a similar uncertainty. They hesitate to speak frankly to their children; and many parents wish that teachers would refrain from doing so (Glueck 1990).

B. Informal Sources of Sexual Knowledge

As in other Western countries, the mass media and peer group conversation are the primary sources for spreading sexual knowledge. The censoring of magazines, books, and films does not occur except for pornographic material. There are laws to prevent minors from being exposed to sexual matters, but the general media are full of instructive articles and illustrated stories. Public television has developed a high standard of feature programs dealing with sexual issues. Sex-related problems and questions are presented to audiences and discussed by experts. Presumably these widely watched features and talk shows have raised the level of knowledge and value consciousness about most variants of sexuality.

4. Autoerotic Behaviors and Patterns

Nine out of ten men and seven out of ten women in Germany admit to having performed masturbation. Female activity in this field has been rising rapidly within the last decades (Clement 1986). Boys start mostly during puberty, girls during adolescence. Today, the majority of parents and teachers accept masturbation of young people as a normal and important experience (Glueck 1990).

The social construction of masturbation has undergone a radical change during this century. Around 1900, the meaning of masturbation was associated with ideas of pollution, removing sexual tensions, depletion, risks for health, and moral dangers. Today the meaning of masturbation is principally satisfaction, to work out sexual phantasies, to maintain inner balance; it bears no risks for physical and moral development. What has been considered to be a surrogate is now appreciated as a sexual expression in its own right.

5. Interpersonal Heterosexual Behaviors

The following findings are derived from various investigations of a social-scientific and sociosexual nature—in particular the relationship studies headed by Kurt Starke among 11,313 people aged between 16 and 48, and an east-west comparative survey of youth sexuality (Starke et al. 1984-89; Starke 1991; Starke et al. 1993).

A. Children

Children explore each other's intimate parts in games like doctor/nurse-patient. Even if informed parents know what their children are doing, these games are surrounded by a certain suspicion that they may be too early or the fear that the children may become oversexualized. Picking up on these silent messages, the children tend to hide their encounters and games from their parents. Since there is no discussion of the morality of these activities and their expressions not subjected to empirical investigation, one knows very little about their reality.

B. Adolescents

Puberty Rituals

No significant rituals mark the passage from childhood to adolescent or young adult.

Premarital Sexual Activities and Relationships

Nowadays, young people become sexually mature on an average of three years earlier than at the beginning of this century; menarche occurs at approximately the age of 12.8 years while the ejacularche takes place at around the age of 13.9 years. This physical acceleration has been accompanied by a mental acceleration marked by the earlier inclusion of adolescents in adult society in terms of consumption and information. Young people now have a more dynamic lifestyle; their plans for life are becoming more diverse and open and, at the same time, more short-term and unpredictable. The perspectives of life are expanding with the increase of not only opportunities and alternatives, but also risks and imponderables. Sexual behavior, which is an integrated part of a personality's all-round behavior, is thus social behavior, and is learned in the same way. Sexual self-discovery, the search for a partner, and partner relationships represent important socialization factors and promote the personal development of adolescents.

Ninety percent of Germans at the age of 16 have already been in love. This feeling of being in love quickly brings with it an urge for reciprocation and the establishment of a pairbond. Infatuation without trying to organize further contact or vigorous efforts to achieve interaction are no longer characteristic. Being in love is not suppressed, hidden away, or enjoyed secretly, but is institutionalized (as long as mutuality is present).

Adolescents in Germany enter into steady relationships at an early age. About 80 percent of 16-year-olds have experience of a relationship, and at any one time a quarter of the males and half the females aged 16 have a steady boyfriend or girlfriend. This proportion used to be higher in East Germany. These days, young males in particular want to live without firm ties for the present, preferring to wait a while so that they can be open and flexible when planning their lives and careers. They do not necessarily long for the joys of having a partner and would rather avoid any risks, hassle, or pressure. However, even among those not currently involved with a long-term partner, the majority yearn for love and desire a steady relationship.

This is not merely the case among youngsters, but also true of older unattached people. The main reasons for being involuntarily single are that Mr. or Miss Right has not yet been found, or that one has not yet gotten over a recent broken relationship. People often hold themselves responsible for this; they expect too much or have contact problems and are less likely to see the causes in the objective circumstances of life. Those who are voluntarily single explain their lifestyle particularly by a shortage of time and the pressure to achieve good results at school or work. A good quarter of the males and exactly half of the females with no fixed partner say that they do not want to give up their sexual freedom, or even their freedom as a whole.

Emotional bonds in steady relationships are close. Even at the beginning, phrases like "I don't know" or "a feeling of ambivalence" are almost never used to describe emotional ties, and "we like each other" only occurs rarely; "being in love" or more commonly "love" are the order of the day. Most young Germans only enter into a bond and seek closeness and intimacy when they can classify the relationship as "love." Both males and females have a mental attitude of expectation and then a feeling of certainty that their partner is also at least as equally committed as they are. Finding a partner purely out of boredom or loneliness, in order to bolster one's own self-confidence or prestige, or for other reasons, sexual, for instance, has become completely untypical.

Relationships among adolescents are as a rule romantic attachments of a high standard and of very definite qualities. The dominating and overriding criterion and simultaneously the chief motive for the establishment of a pair group is mutual trust. This includes being able to trust one other, mutual empathy, harmony of the heart, mental and physical communication, and affection—all connected with mutual respect for the other person, recognition of her/him as an individual, and the acceptance of the other's need for personal freedom. By contrast, differences in desires, quarreling, fear of the other, the domination of one partner by the other, latent or actual interference in the other's affairs, and chiefly sexual liaisons are immediately regarded as negative and detached from love, and are rejected as unbearable.

It is not "any old relationship" but love that characterizes young couples. Love is also verbalized: around 90 percent have already told their partner they love them and have in turn themselves heard the phrase "I love you."

Young love in modern Germany, both in the east and in the west, is not silent, but rather a communicative relationship.

The romantic question, "Do you wish to spend your whole life with your partner?" was answered by half of the males and females asked in both eastern and western Germany with a hearty "Yes." However, a difference is to be observed among the other half. Whereas in western Germany the more common answer is "No," those asked in eastern Germany give the answer "Undecided." This corresponds completely to a general strategic concept of life in the eastern regions—most youngsters, around 80 percent, want to remain with one and the same partner as long as possible, while the remaining 20 percent plan partner mobility. Hardly anybody wants to abstain from having a relationship their whole life long.

Love as Condition for Sexual Intercourse

Throughout Germany and equally among the sexes, love is not only the most important motive for a relationship, but also the decisive condition for sexual intercourse. Sexual intercourse without love is, particularly among females, just as much of an exception as anonymous sex. The major sexual experiences are not exotic and anonymous (although such do occur), but are shared by young people with a chosen partner. A steady romantic attachment is regarded as the ideal setting for sexual activity. In this sense, love and sex closely belong together in the thoughts and feelings of German adolescents. Despite the variety of lifestyles and current exceptions, their real behavior and sexual experience, their hopes and fears, the prospective meaning of life and probable disappointments, are also determined by it.

A renaissance of romantic love is currently to be observed in Germany. In both east and west, the ideal of the one great love, exclusive and lasting a lifetime, is predominant. Adolescents do not fall in love temporarily or in order to try it out—they search for a steady, lasting relationship and devote themselves completely and unconditionally to their chosen partner, to whom they also intend to remain faithful. The ideal of eternal love is supplemented by the ideal of current fidelity. Partner mobility consequently does not represent a rupture of the idea of love and faithfulness, but a consequence of it (see the second subsection under Section C below for discussion of partner mobility). Similarly, the modern unwillingness to form close ties cannot be regarded as a countertendency. It too is a consequence of the ideal to allow oneself to get involved with just one particular beloved and loving partner.

First Coitus

Romantic attachments quickly lead to sexual contact, including sexual intercourse. Longer-term phases of petting for its own sake are uncharacteristic, especially in eastern Germany. The first instance of sexual intercourse occurs among approximately half of males and females within the first three months of their going out together. Almost all adolescents tolerate premarital coitus and also practice it. Virginity is not regarded as a stigma, a success, nor as something special to be preserved. Sex has freed itself from the institution of marriage, but not however from a romantic attachment.

The first instance of sexual intercourse is based on love or being in love and 75 to 85 percent of the time takes place within a steady relationship. It is only rarely that sexual intercourse first takes place anonymously, by chance, or casually. Although the general tendency is for partners to be of the same age, the first coitus partner (especially among the girls in eastern Germany, who also start earlier) is usually a little older. The older partner, usually male, in many cases is equally sexually inexperienced.

Eight percent of 17-year-old males with experience of coitus from western Germany have had sex with a prostitute; the corresponding figure for males from East Germany is 0 percent. But experience with a prostitute is almost never the first experience of sexual intercourse. Ideally the intimate partner is the object of one's love, making the first instance of sexual intercourse an event that is mutually striven for and desired by both parties. If this is not the case, then young people would rather abstain from sexual intercourse.

The average age at which young males and females have sexual intercourse for the first time, about 17, has remained constant for about a decade. One difference that is to be observed is that boys in western Germany and girls in eastern Germany start somewhat earlier; in fact, one third of the latter have their first experience of coitus before their 16th birthday. Members of the lower classes start particularly early in western Germany, whereas the upper classes and future intellectuals are somewhat slower.

In both eastern and western Germany, young people have a place where they can be with each other undisturbed, exchange affection, and sleep together; this is nearly always their own room in the parental home, or else their partner's home. Adolescents usually enjoy a close emotional relationship with their parents. The mother, and to a lesser extent the father, is the chief person in whom young people confide and the preferred communication partner, including in matters of love. Two thirds of young males and females say that they can often talk to their mother openly about sex. By contrast, communication between father and daughter is often either disrupted or only rarely touches on intimate topics, and only one quarter of daughters can talk openly with their fathers about sex. Most parents accept their children's partner relationships, allow them to sleep together, and know about their sexual contact. Sex does not take place somewhere outside in secret, but cosily in one's own bed.

C. Adults

Premarital Courtship, Dating, and Relationships

Men and women aged 22 have sexual intercourse around nine times a month; the frequency among 17-year-olds is six or seven times (six times for males, eight times for females). The figure falls only marginally among the over-30s and over-40s. Psychological and social factors are mainly responsible for intrapersonal and interpersonal differences in the frequency of sexual intercourse, especially the nature of the relationship, as well as external circumstances such as separation from one's partner and living conditions. People who are happily in love have sexual intercourse more often.

The proportion of women experiencing orgasm increased sharply in the 1970s. About 75 percent of 16-year-olds, 90 percent of 18-year-olds, 95 percent of 22-year-olds, and 99 percent of 27-year-olds have experienced orgasm. The rate of orgasm during sexual intercourse and other intimate behavior has also increased. The sexual satisfaction of both men and women is judged as an invariant component of sex within a relationship. Affection is the most common aspect associated with love and sex, and sexual sensitivity is expected and appreciated. Sexual contact without a feeling of desire is generally not even undertaken by women.

Young women and men have partnership concepts of sexual relations and want their partners to be desirous of sex as well. People still experience being forced or pestered, and this is regarded as harassment; however, pestering or force have since come to contradict the morals of most young men. The initiative for sexual intercourse hardly ever comes from the man alone, and in fact it is now more common for the woman's desire to be decisive. Sexual interaction in a relationship among young people is rarely controlled by the male, but quite often by the female.

One in ten acts of coitus takes place outside a steady relationship. Four out of ten adults have had sexual intercourse with somebody else during their current relationship. In the 1980s, sexual contact outside the main relationship became more common, this increase being especially true of women, and the number of females experiencing sex outside their steady relationship quadrupled in this decade (whereas the figure for men merely doubled). There are no differences in this respect between married and unmarried people. Men have had an average of seven sex partners; women have had five on average, with a fifth having had only one and another fifth having had more than five. Apart from sex, other factors that affect the various number of previous sexual partners include conditions of origin and development, as well as of age. Furthermore, partner mobility is higher in an urban environment than in rural areas. In the past year, three out of ten men and two out of ten women have had more than one sex partner. Younger women are more mobile than older men.

The frequency of orgasm has not changed in keeping with sexual liberalization, but the attitude towards it, its experience, and its function within a relationship have changed. The sexist emphasis on male and female potency measured in terms of orgasm has become fragile, and the compulsion to have orgasm is being resisted. There is a growing aversion to orgasm achieved with all manner of tricks, and used as a measure of male or female performance, celebrated as a victory in joint conflict, and feared as a stress-obsessed prestige event. Instead, the individual quality of a steady relationship is sought, linked with closeness, trust, warmth, carefree pleasure, and unpredictable, uncalculating, uncalculated affection within the total erotic form. Cuddling is back in fashion; compulsive or cheap commonplace sex is out.

There are many common aspects in partner and sexual behavior between western and eastern Germans. However, noticeable differences continue to exist. These differences are not so much on the level of behavior as on the level of desire, the experience of sex, and sexual attitudes. More eastern than western German females look forward to their first sexual intercourse and they start somewhat earlier. Sexually inexperienced boys and girls in eastern Germany clearly want to have more sexual experiences than those in the west. Females from eastern Germany begin sexual relations earlier than those of the same age in the west. Western German males, on the other hand, link sexual intercourse more firmly than males from eastern Germany to a steady relationship; then again, twice as many have sex with occasional partners. It is possible that they are quicker than eastern German males to detach sexuality from a person or relationship, at least occasionally.

More adolescent females in eastern Germany regard their sexual activity to be gratifying and enjoyable. This refers both to masturbation, which they experience with more pleasure, and especially to sexual intercourse. About 30 percent more young females in the east say that their latest incidence of sexual intercourse was enjoyable, was sexually satisfying, was a great experience, and that they were happy. The differences are not the frequency of orgasm, but rather the sexual experience, the joy of sexual arousal, the subjective quality of the entire erotic form, and the feelings of happiness experienced during intimacy. In both eastern and western Germany, young females are less appreciative of their latest incidence of sex if they did not achieve orgasm; however, the experience of eastern girls not experiencing orgasm is hardly less positive than that of western girls who do experience orgasm. In the west, some adolescent females feel sexually unsatisfied during sexual intercourse and are not happy, even though they had an orgasm. In eastern Germany, on the other hand, women are also sexually satisfied and happy, even if (on the last occasion) they did not experience orgasm. They are apparently less "fixated" on the orgasm, but are by no means less able to achieve orgasm. On the one hand, female adolescents in eastern Germany are more "conservative" in the sense that they (without disregarding other forms) are more strongly centered on sexual intercourse and orgasm with their lover. By contrast, they are not so strongly centered on the "autonomous" orgasm. At the same time, they are more "liberal," as they begin earlier than their western German counterparts. In addition, it can be seen that among eastern German adolescents, virtually all the differences between the sexes as regards the experience of sex is concerned have been dispelled, whereas they continue to exist among western German adolescents.

Partner Mobility in Lifestyles

Four tendencies in the pattern of relationship that individuals adopt are to be observed:

1. Serial Monogamy—having a succession of steady relationships, especially at a young age. This is part of learning exercised by young people as they mature. It is connected with practicing partnership and sexual behavior, the search for the optimal liaison with high demands being made on its quality. The high demands also lead to the end of one relationship and the commencement of the next. This succession of relationships is an expression of increased sovereignty in the treatment of sexuality as the basis of social developments, which have led to a liberalization of sexual norms. Changing one's partner one or more times during the course of one's life is connected to the ideal of the unity of love and sex. Such a romantic love morality adheres less and less to the traditional model of lifelong marital monogamy, even though, or precisely because, great importance is attached to faithfulness within each relationship.
2. Sexual Nonexclusivity—sexual relations are entered into outside a steady relationship, either occasionally or continually. One reason for this—along with a thirst for adventure, an urge to undergo new experience, curiosity, and many other factors—is an unsatisfactory sex and emotional life in the primary relationship. This behavior has increased in the past ten to twenty years, something that should be neither celebrated as an expression of libertarian norms, nor condemned as a violation of the traditional command of exclusive monogamy. It is self-contradictory and above all a product of the problems of long-term relationships. Having sex outside a relationship has traditionally been a male privilege. However, in modern society, where women enjoy a considerable amount of emancipation and independence, particularly in the professional sphere, the situation has been balanced out. Sexual contact outside the primary relationship almost always takes place with close acquaintances or friends. Anonymous sexual contact is a rare exception and is usually rejected.

   By and large, a moral assessment of either (1) or (2) cannot be based on the number of partners. Neither large nor small quantities of partners can provide a general expression of quality, performance, stability, satisfaction, or happiness. In addition, people's personalities and their activity in life's various situations are too different. If one follows these findings, then the appeal for fidelity in view of AIDS is just as justified as it is out of touch and repressive. Partner mobility alone does not constitute a risk in terms of AIDS, especially when the comarital relationships involves outercourse more than intercourse as frequently occurs in such responsibly nonmonogamous relationships as couples move beyond the raging hormones of youth. Hardly anybody sacrifices happiness in life for the sake of abstract faithfulness.

3. Commercial Sex—new partners can easily be obtained in the form of disposable items without the assumption of mutual responsibility, and lust can be quickly satisfied without any complications. Although forms of male prostitution exist, mainly for homosexuals, but also for women, female prostitution is the predominating form. The entire sex industry, including pornography, is chiefly aimed at men, and as a result these sexual relationships, including long-term relationships and regular clients, are far more common among men than among women.

   In terms of prostitution, men can be divided into three habitual groups. The first group has no contact whatsoever with prostitutes, the second visits prostitutes occasionally, while for the third group, prostitution is an integral part of their lives. These groups are clearly separated from each other in terms of their sociological and psychological profile, and the borders dividing them are not fluid. The size of the groups varies among the various social subgroups, and also geographically.
4. Promiscuity. This refers to the very frequent change of sexual partners and the lack of a steady relationship. Further forms of partner mobility within a steady, long-term relationship include partner swapping and group sex.

Cohabitation Patterns

Most people who maintain a steady sexual relationship will live together in one residence, although not all men and women who share a residence are necessarily having sex with each other. The housing situation in Germany allows living together. Frequently, occupational mobility may lead to a separation of partners.

Marriage and the Family

As regards the current family, the following model is preferred: "Man and wife both pursue their own profession and are equally responsible for housework and bringing up the children, so that both have the same amount of time for their career." Having one's own family with children remains a high aim in life, and only a few do not wish to have any children at all. Since unification, however, both the number of marriages in eastern Germany and the number of newborn children has drastically declined—within three years the birthrate has fallen by 60 percent. Adolescent mothers and female students with children have suddenly disappeared as if by magic. The once-low marriage age has rapidly risen and is set to reach that prevalent in western Germany, with the result that the establishment of families is being delayed. What remains unchanged are the attitudes coordinating parenthood/family with career/employment.

Female and male adolescents in eastern Germany are more likely to have grown up with both parents employed full-time than their counterparts in western Germany, and this is thus the model on which they base their own lives. (Before unification, the number of women working full-time in East Germany was over 90 percent, compared to over 50 percent in West Germany.) Men and women have become accustomed to their respective partner's professional activity and regard it as an important aspect of life. The compatibility of parenthood and work does not at all only mean for them the adaptation of family necessities to the parents' work, but also the consideration of the family at work and the repudiation of the complete dominance of the job. Work and family are not seen as alternative, mutually exclusive values, but are only acceptable when organized in conjunction with each other. This is a demand being made on both society and the relationship.

Incidence of Oral and Anal Sex

Oral stimulation of the genitals, both fellatio and cunnilingus, has become a customary practice. Since hygienic standards and opportunities are high, there are no longer aesthetic scruples. For example, at least 60 percent of German students have practiced fellatio or cunnilingus. Anal intercourse has remained quite rare; less than 20 percent report this experience, most of them only occasionally. Personal hygiene education in early childhood blocks the unaffected dealing with this aperture of the body.

6. Homoerotic, Homosexual, and Ambisexual Behaviors

A. History and Legal Status

Same-sex genitality as an institution is rooted in a changeable history. Before the advent of Christianity, German tribes repressed such acts with capital punishment. From the Middle Ages on, there were meeting places in some metropolitan cities such as Cologne, which, however, were not large enough, compared with London or Paris, to develop an urbanity suitable for a real subculture. From the early nineteenth century, Swiss and German writers gave expression to the voice of love between men. The term homosexual was created, interpretations of same-sex relations were published, and civil liberties for homosexuals were demanded.

The foundations for the modern concepts, lesbian and gay, were laid in Germany. In 1933, this hopeful development was suddenly interrupted by the Nazi government. The persecution was based on racial-biological and demographic beliefs. Enforced with jail and concentration camps, it was the fiercest ever seen in modern times. It was not until the 1970s that the gay and lesbian existence could recover from this knockout blow.

Today homosexuality is societally established as never before in history. Not even the menace of AIDS has reversed the trend. Despite the numerous victims of HIV, one may say that the life chances of homosexual and bisexual people continue to be enhanced. Same-sex relations between consenting adult men were completely depenalized some twenty years ago. Same-sex relations among women were only criminalized in Austria in earlier decades. Currently, any differentiation between homosexual and heterosexual has been removed from the penal code, as is the case in Switzerland since 1992 and in the former East Germany since 1988. Contemporary political demands include an antidiscrimination amendment to the constitution and the legalization of marriages of same-sex couples.

The state has long since abstained from open denial of rights and privileges, e.g., against teachers or civil servants, in the judiciary, public administration, social security, and the like. Many politicians, even conservatives, hasten to confirm that they won't "discriminate." That does not mean that the politicians are willing to grant equal rights to homosexuals. They are given as much equality, meaning tolerance, as necessary, but not as much equality as possible in terms of integration.

Residual discrimination remains in niches like the military and the Church. And it is difficult to intervene in the antihomosexual policies of the private sector of the economy. Homosexual lifestyles are possible even here, as long as they are restricted to the private sphere.

B. Children

Children, before they "discover" the other sex during or after puberty, naturally look for friends and intimacy within their own sex. So there are many occasions for homoerotic feelings, even for sexual encounters between friends. The passage through such a temporary "youngster homosexuality" is no predictor of adult homosexuality. Most youngsters with homoerotic experiences will follow the path of "normalcy," with the sole difference that their antihomosexual prejudices are less negative than those of the general population. The same-gender contact of youngsters has been reduced, but has not disappeared, in the last decades due to coeducational schools and acceleration, including the earlier start of heterosexual coitus (cohabitarche). Moreover, the age of coming out for homosexuals has been getting ever lower so that today this often occurs during adolescence.

C. Adult Psychology and Lifestyles

Turning to gender roles, the theory of the third sex proposed by Magnus Hirschfeld has faded away. Today gays are thoroughly masculine, lesbians quite feminine. Sometimes they play with the possibilities of cross-gender behavior, onstage or in subculture situations. But their personal identity is confined to their biological sex. One is a faggot for fun, for provocative purposes, i.e., in a voluntarily chosen role. In lesbian subculture, the rigid separation into butch or femme has diminished.

Uncertainties of gender, intergenerational longings, and love relations between the social classes are no longer the prerequisites of a homosexual preference. Transgression of class, generation, and gender frontiers contributed to earlier sex scandals, and even constituted their kernel. Today the only and really subversive moment in homosexuality is its negation of compulsory heterosexuality.

The homosexual desire as it has crystallized throughout the twentieth century signifies precisely the same-sex relationship. By this, homosexuals were confronted with the possibility and necessity of forming lasting partnerships. Meanwhile a considerable portion of this population follows a quasi-conjugal lifestyle. Two men, two women establish one household, share income, leisure time, and friends. Their descent families consider them as a pair; the partner of one's own offspring, after a certain time, will be treated as child-in-law and vice versa. The couple, especially a lesbian one, may enlarge to a family with children from a former marriage, sometimes from adoption or fostering.

There is no separation of rights, duties, and prestige according to the traditional roles of husbands and wives. Gay and lesbian couples attach great value to egalitarian decisions. On the other hand, their stability is endangered by the lack of institutionalization and public recognition. Too many details of daily life have to be negotiated. Most couples admit some form of sexual contacts with third parties. This sort of "legitimate infidelity" gives rise to erotic flexibility as well as a certain burden of jealousy.

Homosexuality as an accessible form of erotic preference enjoys a high degree of social visibility that was increased but not generated by the public reaction to AIDS. There are more occasions than ever before to learn about homosexuality, to discuss it, and to confront oneself with such experiences. In many sectors of everyday life, the questions of homosexuality are addressed, at school, in the family and peer group, at work, and during leisure activities. So a latent desire can quite easily manifest itself, and one can look for possible partners.

Many doors open to the homosexual world. A lot of newspapers—public or subculture—have a rubric for contact ads. Special guides list the commercial and the hidden places where homosexuals meet. Today, each city with more that 50,000 inhabitants has at least a gay bar and an anonymous meeting point in a public park or lavatory ("tea room"). Bigger cities have baths, numerous bars for special interests, book shops, voluntary groups, and a "gay switchboard." The opportunity structure for a lesbian/gay lifestyle has an extraordinary density.

Nationwide associations address cultural and professional interests for Christians, adolescents, teachers, medical people, writers, and the like. On the one hand, only a tiny minority of this minority affiliates with such an organization. On the other hand, these few people operate as a real avant-garde to improve homosexuals' life chances.

Homosexuals have conducted numerous experiments with gender roles, forms of coupling, and techniques of sexual outlet. Some of their inventions have gained significance for nonhomosexuals: the social autonomy of women explored in the economically independent existence of lesbians; body image and sensitivity of men explored via some feminine components in gay performance; the remasculinization of men in the 1980s experienced in the so-called clone style. Homosexual relations, of course, are not a model for the general public; nevertheless they give a striking example for the plasticity of erotic configurations.

D. Bisexuality

Bisexuality, in the narrow sense of having homosexual and heterosexual relations during the same phase of a sexual biography, occurs quite often, presumably more often than exclusive homosexuality. Nevertheless the concept is obscure and psychologically underdeveloped.

Most experts agree with the thesis that they have never seen a genuine bisexual, i.e., someone who reacts with equal sexual appetite to women and to men. Since this judgment refers mostly to a population of therapy clients and since the universe of bisexual people has not yet been empirically investigated, the question of what types of bisexuality really exist remains open.

There are quite a few sexual biographies where phases of intimate relations with a woman alternate with relations with a man. Such a "successive bisexuality" is frequently reported by women, and there is no reason to suggest a "latency" of either homosexuality or heterosexuality.

7. *Gender Conflicted Persons*

For transvestites there are no institutionalized roles in German society. The dichotomy of two and only two sexes is highly crystallized. So transvestites very seldom gain public attention. They are generally considered deviants but do not constitute a social problem. The phenomena of transvestism, transsexuality, and homosexuality are today clearly separated. Behaviors of cross-dressing and making-up as the other gender do not irritate public opinion, and the individual reaction contains a greater degree of amusement than of worry. Furthermore, since the 1980s, some transvestites have won high prominence as entertainers in stage shows.

For some people, transgressions of the valid definitions of gender leads to a considerable amount of hostility. Transgenderists and transsexuals are therefore marginalized even today when legislation, medicine, and the mass media have acknowledged their right to live as they are and accommodate their outward appearance to their gender identity.

German law provides some procedures for people who wish to change the sex designation ascribed to them shortly after birth. They may choose between officially changing their name or also altering their sex status. The second step presupposes the surgical adaptation of the genitals. In addition, the surgery presupposes expert evidence given by a psychologist or physician testifying that the person is able to live in the long term in the chosen gender role. Several hospitals in the country have specialized in this sort of medical support and are quite willing to deliver it.

At present, several juridical initiatives are being directed towards normalizing transsexuality. Support groups have been organized and receive state subsidies. New sociological research describes the life world of gender changing people (Hirschauer 1993; Lindemann 1993). The leading German sexologist is pleading for depathologizing the phenomenon (Sigusch 1992). But this will remain a utopia as long as transsexuals themselves apply for medical help, psychotherapy, hormonal treatment, and surgery to gain a healthy condition.

8. Significant Unconventional Sexual Behaviors

A. Coercive Sex

Sexual Abuse of Children and Incest

The criminal law prohibits sexual acts with young people under age 14 and under age 16 if the acts are exploitative. Moral crusades initiated by some feminist groups argue with increasing numbers of child sexual abuse cases. With some lag, the figures in the official statistics rose after decreasing for three decades. Actually, it is only the public and private awareness that has changed, and child abuse is a more or less stable phenomenon—about 60,000 cases per year. The common construction and terminology throws together three distinguishable interactions: parent-daughter (incest), men-children (abuse), and intergenerational love (pedophilia) (Lautmann 1994). These forms vary in ingredients and consequences.

Rape

Sexual violence against women is the other big topic exciting the public opinion during recent years. The punishment of rape in the roughly 2,000 convictions per year is quite severe. But many women do not go to the police even though officers have recently been taught sensitivity in dealing with victims.

Legislation has hesitated to criminalize marital rape.

Many young people are afraid of sexual violence. A quarter of the 16- to 17-year-old males in western Germany, compared to a tenth of those in the east, and more than half of adolescent females in the west, compared to a third in the east, reported that they had personally experienced sexual violence, sexual molestation, or sexual interference. In the east, 4 percent of women said they were forced to engage in sexual intercourse against their will the first time they experienced coitus. The figure among homosexual men is 2 percent. A fifth of women in eastern Germany have experienced rape or attempted rape.

Sexual Harassment

There are many cases of verbal and bodily molestation of women. Some women train in techniques of self-defense. The majority of men have not yet learned to pay complete respect to a woman's NO.

Sexual molestation in the workplace or elsewhere is penalized as an insult, but seldom prosecuted. Some feminists are campaigning for legal recognition of a special offense of sexual harassment. However, the German legislature usually resists the demands to adapt the penal code to social problems addressed by moral crusades.

B. Prostitution

More than 100,000 women offer sexual services to men either as a professional, casual job, or to obtain money to buy drugs. The organization of the activity varies. The most respected form is to use an apartment with a telephone and to receive the visitors there after having advertised in a paper. Working in a brothel provides less autonomy for the women, but perhaps equal comfort. Other women wait in bars or hotels for clients. Dangerous, hard, and least profitable in comparison with the other forms is soliciting on the streets.

Male homosexual prostitution is not as common but organized in quite similar ways. Some call boys offer their services equally to men and women. The demand from lesbians is extremely small, if any.

The social prestige of prostitutes has improved to a certain extent since they founded interest groups for "whores." They argue that, if they have to pay income tax (and they do), then they may claim social security and recognition for their vocation.

The law forbids prostitution only under special circumstances, in certain areas, in the neighborhood of schools, and the like. It is also forbidden to further prostitution and to recruit minors. These statutes are enforced in a very incomplete and selective way.

C. Pornography and Erotica

All forms of sexual, pornographic, and/or obscene material are easily available in Germany, the soft variety from newsstands and television, the harder types in numerous shops where even the most extreme examples are available under the counter. The law forbids hard-core pornography that includes violence, children, or animals and the sale of all sorts of sexual materials to minors. The debate about the character and danger of pornography has also taken place in Germany (Lautmann and Schetsche 1990).

9. Contraception, Abortion, and Population Planning

A. Contraception

Contraception is regarded positively and for the most part is correctly practiced throughout Germany. All but 1 percent of Germans accept the prevention of unwanted pregnancy, without any differentiation as regards age, sex, origin, qualifications, or profession. Around 80 percent of women used contraception the first time they had sexual intercourse, and at least 90 percent used some method of birth control during the last incidence of coitus. Three quarters of 16-year-olds and nine tenths of 18-year-olds have experience with the contraceptive pill. Some sexually inexperienced females take the pill as a precautionary measure, while others prefer to refrain from sexual intercourse because they are not on the pill. Similarly, many male adolescents also avoid sexual intercourse if a condom is not available. Only 5 percent of those who have experienced sexual intercourse have never used contraception. Almost everybody regards contraception as a joint responsibility. The current types of contraception are well known among adolescents.

The most popular contraceptive is the pill, favored by 99 percent. The IUD and diaphragm are less popular. Ninety-four percent of eastern German women aged between 30 and 44 have taken the pill, usually over a protracted period of time, and 52 percent continuously. (The pill was easily accessible and free of charge in East Germany; it was prescribed by doctors, even to 14-year-old girls.) Two thirds have used condoms; one fifth have used the IUD. Another fifth prefer the rhythm method, a method half of all women have never exercised.

Although hormonal contraception is not decreasing in significance and acceptance of the pill has actually increased among both men and women, the condom, which was completely out of fashion in East Germany, has been rediscovered as a result of AIDS. However, the condom has not become a rival to the pill or the IUD. It is normally used as an additional means of contraception, and also as a means of protection. The condom is in fact the preferred method in certain situations, but regular users are rare. What are sometimes referred to as "natural methods" such as the rhythm method have decreased in popularity. Coitus interruptus is also widely shunned.

Safe contraception these days, even more than a decade ago, is regarded as an indispensable condition for sexual intercourse. The degree of care exercised, especially in eastern Germany, has actually increased as a result of the changes in values and the social risks, and a significant number of men and women in eastern Germany have taken the opportunity to be sterilized, something that has only been possible since German unification.

B. Teenage Unmarried Pregnancies

Not more than about 1 percent of all live births are to minor mothers (under age 18), and half of these are unmarried. A considerable number of teenage pregnancies are terminated by abortion.

C. Abortion

The acceptance of contraception contains a critical, negative assessment of abortion as a method of birth control, although the principle of the legal option of the termination of pregnancy is supported. Only 2 percent are in favor of the complete prohibition of abortion, and the majority of Germans are in favor of at least allowing abortion within the first three months. A quarter of eastern German adolescents and a tenth of their western German counterparts are totally against any form of criminal legislation governing abortion. Most German youngsters support the concept of self-determined pregnancy and liberal legislation. Planned childbirth remains the ideal.

D. Population Control Efforts

A negative population growth holds only for "native" Germans. The secular trend of a sinking birth rate began here at the end of the nineteenth century. It has various causes, many of them grounded in the rationalization of the social structure and private life. Many children born in Germany do not become German citizens because their parents are immigrants. The laws of citizenship follows the principle of jus sanguinis instead of that of jus soli.

Unification of Germany has unexpectedly resulted in the sharpest drop in birthrates in modern world history. Birthrates have been very low in west Germany for many years. In the last several years, slightly more west Germans have died than have been born. Birthrates in all five states of east Germany have fallen sharply. In Brandenburg, births have fallen by more than two thirds, from nearly 38,000 in 1989 to barely 12,000 in 1993. Birthrates are down by more than half in the other four states in the same period. In late 1994, Brandenburg announced it would begin immediately to pay parents $650 for every new child they have. This is in addition to both the national health insurance, which covers obstetric and other medical expenses and a monthly allowance, called *Kindergeld* that is awarded on a sliding scale based on income. *Kindergeld*, which has been distributed in western Germany since 1955, can reach a monthly cap of $420 for a family of four (Kinzer 1994).

War, famine, and plague are the usual factors triggering such a precipitous drop in the birth rate. In Germany today, the rising rate of unemployment increasing the threat of poverty is the cause for the free-falling birthrate, which is accompanied by a drop in the rate of marriage and a more than tenfold increase in sterilizations. "Young people in east Germany used to think that the most important conditions for marriage were love and a good partnership," a recent report noted, "Now they are seeing that the crucial condition is a secure job." Prior to unification, the Communist system provided jobs and day care for all and a strong social safety net prevented anyone from falling into poverty. If the current trend continues to 2010, there could well be fewer than half as many children in eastern Germany as there are today.

Nearly all the former Communist countries in Europe have experienced drops in their birthrates, though none match the drop in east Germany. Some countries, including Hungary and Poland, provide payments to the families of newborn babies, but they are much smaller than those initiated in Brandenburg. In the West, Belgium, Luxembourg, and Portugal pay the parents of new babies.

10. Sexually Transmitted Diseases

The incidence of STDS is incompletely known since there is a legal obligation to report only four of the twenty-some diseases. Presumably the incidence of STDs equals that observed in other Western countries. That means it has remained quite high in spite of medical and hygienic progress. Within the medical profession, venereology is associated with dermatology. National and private health insurance pays for the cost of treatment.

11. HIV/AIDS

Among the people diagnosed as HIV-positive, men with homosexual experiences constitute the biggest category, about 70 percent, followed by IV drug users, about 15 percent. Consequently, in Germany, AIDS is essentially understood as a venereal disease. The prevalence up to 1993—about 10,000 cases of AIDS—is lower than in some other European countries, not to mention the United States. Women constitute 10 percent of the cases. Eastern Germany is as yet a sort of developing country for HIV infection following the fall of the Iron Curtain, which served as a preventive measure.

The comparatively low incidence is a result of a policy that emphasized rational recognition instead of repression and denial. Campaigns in the mass media, at schools, and by street workers delivered preventative messages. Homosexual men changed some of their practices (Bochow 1993;

Dannecker 1990). Since the rules of safer sex are not observed completely, some new infections still occur.

Because the official information applies to the whole population, instead of just to special risk groups, it is understood that sexuality in general will be affected by the AIDS crisis. It may be that the recently identified return of young people to the ideal of Romantic Love results partly from official condemnation of promiscuity.

Approximately one tenth of adolescents with experience in sexual intercourse say they have on at least one occasion shunned some sort of sexual activity for fear of being infected with the HIV virus. For most young people, sexual contact is not normally connected with a current fear of being infected with AIDS, and when it is, there is some obvious reason, such as a suspected at-risk partner or unprotected intercourse. Despite the very different epidemiological situations reigning in eastern and western Germany—there are hardly any AIDS patients in eastern Germany and most of these are in Berlin, AIDS has produced equal degrees of consternation. This anxiety is rarely fear for one's own health or behavior, but rather a more general sense of concern, including sympathy for those infected by HIV and PWAs (persons with AIDS). Somewhat older and more experienced young people in particular do not see themselves in danger as a result of their partnership activity and sexual behavior and know how to protect themselves in doubtful cases. The fear of AIDS among younger adolescents results from uncertainty, ignorance, and a lack of experience. It represents a sort of "mental barrier" to the adoption of sociosexual contact, which is subsequently dissipated during the relationship. The real dangers are often suppressed in daily sexual life.

Autistic concepts of safer sex are out of fashion, especially among younger people and in particular in eastern Germany. Sexuality is not idealized as aseptic sex without contact if at all possible (with the "enemy"), or as an anonymous service, or as isolated desire, but rather as firmly linked with the (beloved) partner. Both heterosexuals and homosexuals love a concrete person, enter into a relationship, and have sexual contact with them. The rates of masturbation are comparatively low. Although masturbation is accepted as a sexual activity, and inhibitions in this respect have been dispelled, partnership sex is still preferred.

12. Sexual Dysfunctions, Counseling, and Therapies

A. Concepts of Sexual Dysfunction

Real fears of sexual joys exist. The most common fear in connection with sex among males and females and throughout Germany is that of unwanted pregnancy. Sexual diseases and AIDS are by contrast currently regarded as worry factors of lesser importance. Other fears refer to the anticipation of sex and the experience of sexuality.

Only one quarter of 16- to 17-year-old, sexually inexperienced females in western Germany have a desire for more sex, and only 10 percent of them want to have their first experience of sexual intercourse. They are afraid of disappointment, they are fearful of not finding the right partner who will meet their expectations, they are occasionally conscious of an aversion to men in general, not wanting to become a man's sexual plaything, and they are rather wary of both abstract and direct involvement in sex.

Male adolescents, especially those from western Germany, often abstain from sexual contact: their sex drive is not that great. During their first incidence of sexual intercourse, only a good half of males from western Germany, compared to 80 percent from eastern Germany, said that a strong sex drive was a motive. They link sexual intercourse with a steady relationship and having a faithful girlfriend, and certainly do not want to get involved in something "wishy-washy," unpredictable, restrictive, or vexing only in order to establish a close bond or for reasons of sex.

Sexual experience: by no means all females experience their sexual activity to be pleasant and enjoyable, especially those from western Germany. This refers both to masturbation, which they often do not find gratifying, and above all to intimacy with their partner and sexual intercourse. Half are sexually unsatisfied after sexual intercourse, and only the remaining half derive any pleasure from it at all. It is only a great experience for a quarter, and only a quarter have the wish to repeat it soon. Among eastern German females, almost two thirds find sex a great experience. This appraisal is acted on as girls from eastern Germany have sexual intercourse more often than their counterparts from the west.

Men in the west suffer in particular from mental problems connected with sexual competence, sexual performance, their own attractiveness, and frustrations in love and sex, and these are connected with failure to cope with the pressure of norms or a fear of not being accepted without bias, but rather having to first fight as a man against a barrage of devaluation, mistrust, and prejudice.

B. Availability of Counseling, Diagnosis, and Treatment

Counseling and therapy in sexual matters is offered by a range of public institutions and private practitioners, most of them psychologists. However, this scene is not as widespread as it is in the U.S.A. Special certifications and licenses for sexual therapists do not exist. National and private health insurance pays a considerable portion of the costs.

13. Sexual Research and Advanced Education

A. Advanced Education and Research Institutes

Funding and support for sexological research in Germany are deplorably low considering the public demand for knowledge and the gravity of social and individual problems with sexuality. The funds available are far less proportionately than in the U.S.A. Consequently, Germany is throwing away its great tradition in sexology.

There are some small institutes within the medical departments of the universities of Frankfurt/Main, Hamburg, and Kiel. Empirical sex research is mainly conducted in Leipzig, pedagogical in Landau, and sociological in Bremen. Ideological cleavages cause controversies, which means that researchers do not cooperate very much. Frequently they ignore and despise each other. The small sexological community is split into five organizations—which, in turn, contributes to the political weakness of the profession.

Postgraduate training exists at only one or two medical faculties. Graduate-level programs for the advanced study of human sexuality are unknown. Some private institutes for family counseling and birth planning offer courses for interested adults, that is, at college level. What the Federal Bureau for Health Information (offices in Cologne) can do depends on the ruling party. The conservative government, in power since 1982, had an information pack destroyed soon after it had been developed by their liberal predecessors. This symbolizes how the evolution of sexology in Germany is impeded by the public moralization of sexual matters, even in the time of AIDS.

B. Sexological Publications and Organizations

Only one sexological journal, a quarterly founded in 1988, is published in Germany: *Zeitschrift für Sexualforschung.* Address: Enke, Box 101254, Stuttgart.

National sexological organizations include:

Deutsche Gesellschaft für Sexualforschung, based at the Universities of Hamburg and Frankfurt/Main. Address: Martinistr. 52, 20251 Hamburg, Germany.

Gesellschaft für Sexualwissenschaft (Leipzig) Address: Bernhard-Goering-Str. 152, 04277 Leipzig, Germany.

Gesellschaft für praktische Sexualmedizin (Kiel) Address: Hospitalstr. 17-19. 24105 Kiel, Germany.

Deutsche Gesellschaft für Geschlechtserziehung (Bonn/Landau) Address: Westring 10A, 76829 Landau, Germany.

Deutsche Gesellschaft für sozialwissenschaftliche Sexualforschung (Düsseldorf) Address: Gerresheimer Str. 20, 40211 Düsseldorf, Germany.

References and Suggested Readings

Bochow, M. 1993. "Einstellungen und Werthaltungen zu Homosexuellen Maennern." In C. Lange, ed. *AIDS—Eine Forschungsbilanz.* Berlin: Bohn.

Clement, U. 1986. *Sexualitaet im Sozialen Wandel.* Stuttgart: Enke.

Dannecker, M. 1990. *Homosexuelle Maenner und AIDS.* Stuttgart: Kohlhammer.

Glueck, G. 1990. *Heisse Eisen in der Sexualerziehung.* Weinheim: Deutscher Studien Verlag.

Hirschauer, S. 1993. *Die soziale Konstruktion der Transsexualitaet.* Frankfurt/M: Suhrkamp.

Kinzer, S. 1994 (November 25). $650 a Baby: Germany to Pay to Stem Decline in Births. *The New York Times,* p. A3.

Lautmann, R. 1977. *Seminar: Gesellschaft und Homosexualitaet.* Frankfurt/M.: Suhrkamp.

Lautmann, R. 1994. *Die Lust am Kind.* Hamburg: Klein.

Lautmann, R., and M. Schetsche, 1990. *Das Pornographierte Begehren.* Frankfurt/M.: Suhrkamp.

Lindemann, G. 1993. Das Paradoxw Geschlecht. Frankfurt/M.: Fischer.

Sigusch, V. 1992. *Geschlechtswechsel.* Hamburg: Klein.

Starke, K. 1991. "Jugend und Sexualitaet." In: W. Friedrich, and H. Griese, eds. *Jugend und Jugendforschung in der DDR.* Opladen: Leske.

Starke, K., and W. Friedrich. 1984-1991. *Liebe und Sexualitaet bis 30.* Berlin: Deutscher Verlag der Wissenschaften.

Starke, K., and K. Weller. 1993. "West-und Ostdeutsche Jugendliche." In: G. Schmidt, ed. *Jugendsexualitaet.* Stuttgart: Enke.

Winawer-Steiner, H., and N. A. Wetzer. 1982. "German Families." In M. McGoldrick, J. K. Pearce, and J. Giordano, eds. *Ethnicity and Family Therapy.* New York: Guilford Press.

Ghana

Augustine Ankomah, Ph.D.

Contents

Demographics and a Historical Perspective

A. Demographics

Ghana, on the southern coast of West Africa, is a land of 92,098 square miles, slightly smaller than the state of Oregon or about the size of the United Kingdom. Ghana has fertile plains of luxuriant vegetation in the forest zone in the south and much sparser savanna, woodland, and scrub land in the north. The south supports the growing of cash crops like cocoa—the main export commodity—rubber, coffee, kola nuts, and coconut, and food crops such as maize, cassava, and plantain. The north is particularly suited for cereal cultivation and cattle rearing. Although the official language is English, Ghana's neighbors are all French-speaking nations: Burkina Faso on the north, Togo on the east, and Côte d'Ivoire (the Ivory Coast) on the west.

Slightly under two thirds of 17.7 million Ghanaians lived in rural areas of the country. Ghana has a young population with 45 percent under age

15, 52 percent between ages 15 and 64, and 3 percent 65 and older. The 1995 birthrate was 44 per 1,000 population, and the death rate 12 per 1,000, giving an annual population growth rate of 3.0 percent. The average life expectancy for newborns in 1995 was 54 years for males and 58 for females. Infant mortality is 82 per 1,000 live births. Ghana has one physician per 22,452 persons. The per capita gross domestic product in 1995 was $1,500.

B. A Brief Historical Perspective

Ghana was named for an African empire that existed along the Niger River between 400 and 1240 of the Common Era. The country was ruled by Britain for 113 years as the Gold Coast. In 1956, the United Nations approved the merger of the Gold Coast with the British Togoland trust territory. In 1957, it emerged as the first country in black Africa to achieve independence from a European power. Since that time, Ghana has witnessed a seesaw of political power shared between military and elected governments.

In the years immediately following independence, schools, hospitals, and roads were built, along with hydroelectric power plants and aluminum plants by President Nkrumah, but the economic situation deteriorated between the 1970s and late 1980s. J. J. Rawlings, a flight lieutenant who took over the administration of the country through a military coup in 1979 and again in 1981, won the national election and was sworn in as president in 1993.

1. Basic Sexological Premises

A. Character of Gender Roles

In Ghana, the human world is basically a "man's world." Women are in a subordinate position in terms of decision making within the household. Women work both inside and outside the home. At home, they are responsible for mothering, cooking, washing, food storage, and processing. Outside, they participate in agricultural activities and farm different crops, but few hold titles to land. It is in the sphere of trading that the ingenuity of Ghanaian women is most displayed and apparent. Traditionally they have maintained an autonomous economic role as market traders, and some of them in Accra and Kumasi are perhaps among the most independent women in Africa. Although women who work in the informal sectors may support themselves, their children, and sometimes the husband, decision making on sex and reproduction is still regarded as a man's prerogative. In 1988, three in ten households were female-headed, yet these heads have to refer issues relating to their children to the male kin. It can be said that in Ghana, women can achieve considerable economic autonomy, but the female power and prestige accruing from her economic independence at the societal level is unable to affect, to any considerable extent, the power relations within marriage.

B. Sociolegal Status of Males and Females

Children

On the whole, Ghana is a pronatalist country and the value of children inestimable. To suggest that children are the *raison d'etre* of marriage is an underestimation: they are the *raison d'etre* of life. The specter of childlessness is indescribable, and it is felt by both men and women as the greatest of all tragedies and humiliations. Children are the sign of a woman's normality, femininity, and healthiness. Among some Akan groups in the not distant past, a public ceremony of congratulation was performed for a couple when they had ten living children. A woman who has no children is open to various suspicions. The two most common are that she or a relative is a witch who has "killed" all her children or that she led an immoral life when she was young. The changing social and economic conditions have not diminished the traditional desire for children, although the number of children women consider as an ideal family size has been considerably reduced. For example, the ideal family size was found to be 6.1 children in 1979/80, but had dropped to 5.3 by 1988, both of which are still higher than actual current fertility. Today, the status of a family, to a very large extent, depends on how well they are able to support their children rather than on the absolute number of children.

Unlike in some developing countries where sex preference is very strong with dire consequences for the "unwanted sex," Ghanaians do not appear to have any strongly held bias for a particular sex. Ideally, every parent would like to have boys and girls in certain proportions depending on whether the society is matrilineal or patrilineal. For example, among the matrilineal Akan, since descent and inheritance are reckoned through the mother's side, women provide the continuity of the lineage. A man without sisters is haunted by a sense of frustration.

There is no evidence of sex bias in the feeding or mothering of infants. A government survey in 1988 based on anthropometric measures found no differences between males and females. However, male children under the age of 5 years were more prone to illness and injury than their female counterparts.

An increasing number of school-age children roam the streets and lorry parks of Accra and other cities. This is gradually becoming a social problem. Children at risk include those from broken or extremely poor homes and migrants. Very little has been done in terms of research on these street children. The Ghana National Commission on Children (GNCC) was established in 1977 in response to the United Nation General Assembly's Declaration of 1976, which set 1979 as the International Year of the Child.

The GNCC is the sole coordinator of issues relating to the development of children. In order to support such children, GNCC in 1987 established the Child Education Trust to enable needy dropouts to continue their education. Sustaining breast feeding and promoting the use of locally produced weaning food products has also been one of the commission's achievement, as well as putting on the public agenda issues relating to child labor.

Adults

Although there are no legal barriers to female education, employment, and other formal public sectors, situational factors put females in a disadvantageous position. Parents are more likely to educate boys beyond basic education than girls who, it is thought, will soon get married or can earn a living through trading. Consequently, the proportion of females in secondary schools is about 30 percent; and in the universities, the percentage has always been around 18 percent. Through education, many women have been able to embark on careers that were considered to be for men.

In Ghana, professional women—doctors, lawyers, administrators, headmistresses, and judges—are highly respected, and in their societies serve as role models. Parents are proud of such daughters and may boast to colleagues and friends about them. Women earn the same salary and have the same conditions of service in employment as their male counterparts, although there is a tendency for men (and some women as well) to feel reluctant to work under a woman boss. In general, women occupy subordinate positions in the Ghanaian society and are not regarded as equals of men, who still monopolize most positions of influence.

Given that the early socialization process is modeled along distinct sex roles, every Ghanaian grows up with the knowledge that it is the woman who cooks, does the washing up and the laundry, and indeed is responsible for all household chores. Notwithstanding her level of education, profession, or schedule of work, a woman does not expect her husband to share in household chores. A few men in highly educated homes may occasionally assist their wives in the kitchen, but many will abandon whatever they are doing when there is a knock at the door, for it is considered disgraceful for outsiders, especially from the man's family, to find a man engrossed in feminine roles such as cooking or washing up. Yet it is the man who always has the lion's share. There is unequal allocation of food between husband and wife in the home, especially in the rural areas. Men are given the prime cut of meat, for example. The patriarchal nature of the Ghanaian society also has negative implications for the health of women.

C. General Concepts of Sexuality and Love

The sexual culture of Ghana can be described as a paradox. Sexual matters are among the popular topics for conversation and gossip, but there is less evidence for serious societal debate about sexual issues. Though many cultural artifacts, Ghanaian traditional and "high life" music, dances, jokes, and gibes are frequently woven around sex, the topic hardly comes into the forefront of any formal discussion, and blunt questions about sexual matters may encounter opposition. It must be stated that Ghanaian sexual mores, as elsewhere in Africa, can be well understood if one keeps in mind that sexual facts are significant since they affect other spheres of life. In most traditional societies, there was a seemingly inseparable link between the sexual and the social.

In Ghana, public exhibition of emotions by lovers through kissing is frowned at. This does not imply that there is no love in Ghanaian sexual relationships as some foreign writers claim; however, love alone is not enough to persuade parents to approve of a relationship.

2. Religious and Ethnic Factors Affecting Sexuality

A. Source and Character of Religious Values

There are three main forms of religious practice in Ghana: Christianity (50 percent), traditional indigenous (22 percent), and Muslim (14 percent). In terms of religion, Ghana is a very tolerant country. There is little or no evidence of religious intolerance and fanaticism as are known in some African countries. As with most African countries, Ghanaians believe in the existence of one Supreme Deity, known by different names, whom they regard as far greater than any other being. Atheists are very rare.

In every Ghanaian town there are churches everywhere. The largest Christian denomination is the Catholics. There are Protestant churches like the Methodists and Anglicans, and also a growing number of Pentecostal and charismatic churches. Many members, especially those of the orthodox churches, still maintain some traditional practices that are unacceptable to their churches—such as polygyny—although more and more churches are becoming tolerant. Since it lacks literary document, traditional religion is not systematic in doctrine. However, one basic characteristic is the belief in the spirits of the ancestors who influence the living in every conceivable sphere of life, and apply rewards and sanctions where appropriate. There are also lesser gods or deities with different powers who represent the Almighty God on earth. Compared with other West African countries, the proportion of Muslims in Ghana is low. Most of Ghana's Muslims are Sunnis, although there is a substantial group of Ahmadi Mission who are well established in Saltpond in southern Ghana. Apart from northern Ghana, the biggest concentration of Muslims is to be found in the two largest cities of Accra and Kumasi.

In a recent study in an urban center in southern Ghana, it was observed that religion has no relationship with female sexual behavior in terms of number of sexual partners and age at first sexual intercourse, although

Catholics are more likely than other religious groups to have first sexual intercourse late in life.

B. Source and Character of Ethnic Values

With over ninety ethnic groups, there is relative diversity not only in language but also in customs including sexual norms. The Akan, consisting of several tribes with closely related languages, are by far the largest. Inhabiting most of central and southern Ghana, they form 44 percent of the total population. The southeast is inhabited by the Ewes (13 percent). In northern Ghana, the ethnic situation is more diverse and relatively few groups have been extensively studied. Other ethnic groups include the Moshi-Dagomba (16 percent) and Ga (8 percent).

One basic difference with significant implications for sexual values exists between the Akan and other ethnic groups. The Akan is a matrilineal group and the others patrilineal. In matrilineal societies, descent is traced through the mother's line and a person is therefore legally identified with his or her matrikin. A person inherits from the mother's line and thus children hold no claim whatsoever to their father's estate. As in many matrilineal groups, conjugal ties are weak and considered less important than blood ties. Conversely, in patrilineal societies, descent is traced from the father's line and children inherit from their fathers. The "luckiest" Ghanaian children are from intertribal marriages where the father comes from a patrilineal group and the mother from a matrilineal society. The reverse (father from a matrilineal and mother from a patrilineal) is the "worst" match, since children cannot inherit from either side. While all the matrilineal Akan groups generally share similar sexual values and norms, within the patrilineal societies there are striking variation in premarital, marital, and extramarital sexual ethos. Generalizations on "Ghanaian sexuality" is therefore very hazardous. As far as possible, where differences are striking, attention is drawn to them in this chapter.

3. Sexual Knowledge and Education

A. Government Policies and Programs for Sex Education

The government's attitude toward sex education in Ghana, as in several other subSaharan African countries, can be described as ambivalent. In a survey in 1987, it was found that all the teachers agreed that there was a need for sex education in schools. When surveyed in 1991, secondary schools in Accra revealed some disturbing findings showing a high degree of ignorance, especially on questions relating to menstrual cycle and pregnancy. In a study by the Health Education Division of the Ministry of Health conducted in 1990, when Junior Secondary School (JSS) students were asked whether one can get pregnant the first time one had sex, 47 percent thought it was not possible. The situation is expected to be worse in rural schools. Yet, some people have argued that the Ghanaian society is open and that the children are not ignorant of human sexuality, and hence, it is unnecessary to handle the subject matter in the formal school setting. Others from a religious point of view are worried that sex education is likely to encourage sexual experimentation among sexually quiescent adolescents.

Theoretically, sex education should be covered, but in practice few schools have a comprehensive program on family life education. Policy makers, perhaps for the fear of arousing religious opposition, are ambivalent on issues concerning sex education. On the one hand, sex education is part of the school curricula in order to acknowledge official interest, yet on the other hand, most officials feel unconcerned that it is not effectively taught, thus pacifying the moral and religious critics. The establishment of junior secondary schools, which marks a radical change in Ghana's educational system, may result in a new approach towards the teaching of sex education. With the new educational structure, family life education at both junior and senior secondary school levels is to be covered in a new subject called Life Skills and again at the senior level within Home Economics.

B. Informal Sources of Sexual Knowledge

Though a child's own relatives (mostly grandmothers, in the case of females) were responsible for his or her upbringing, they did not have exclusive right in the traditional society. The society as an entity had a system of preparing and training the young children for every aspect of future life, including sexual life. The training was given by traditionally recognized instructors, usually the elders. In most Ghanaian societies, the initiation or puberty rites were occasions where guidelines and instructions were provided. This was the traditional approach to sex education.

Rapid urbanization, increased mobility, education, and other agents of change have together undermined the traditional channels of sex education. With very limited access to sex education both at home and in the schools, coupled with long periods of schooling in an unmarried state, the gap between sexual and social adulthood has widened, and the modern Ghanaian adolescent faces a sexual dilemma. When in 1991, students in two secondary schools in Accra were asked to state their sources of knowledge on reproduction, the most frequently mentioned source was teachers—apparently as part of biology lessons. On the broad issue of sexual knowledge, students most frequently get their first information on sex from friends, and further from their teachers and relatives. According to Bleek's study in 1976, girls more than boys tend to rely on relatives, especially their mothers, for their first knowledge on sex education. Boys generally receive this information from male friends. The role of teachers appears to be equal for both sexes. In the urban centers, students also report magazines and books as an important source of sex information.

4. Autoerotic Behavior and Patterns

Information on self-pleasuring is hard to come by in Ghana. Kaye, in his impressionistic survey in the 1960s on how Ghanaian children are brought up, noted that parents strongly disapproved of their children engaging in self-pleasuring. They are sternly scolded or severely beaten. Even small boys who play with their genitals are warned to cease. Rattray, who wrote extensively in the 1920s on the Ashanti, an Akan subgroup, described the phenomenon with a phrase, *owo ne kote afeko* (he makes a pestle of his penis). In Ghana, self-pleasuring is not considered an alternative means of sexual expression and is abandoned or forgotten after childhood. This is supported by Bleek's study of school children in the 1970s, during which he did not observe the slightest hint of self-pleasuring. Adult male self-pleasuring is extremely rare, and local terms for this sexual behavior are hard to find.

5. Interpersonal Heterosexual Behaviors

A. Children

The genitals of children, especially females, are not referred to directly. Special attention is given to children's genitals during bathing. The penis and vagina are washed clean to avoid sores. This is almost universal in Ghana. Warm water is dribbled into the girl's genitals (the opened vulva) and sometimes ground ginger is applied in some traditional homes to prevent disease, or sometimes as punishment for misbehavior.

Sex games in which children play the role of mothers and fathers are commonly practiced in Ghana. The games are not forbidden, but sexual exploration in the form of mutual examination of genitals may not go unpunished. Until puberty, boys and girls play together freely, and in towns and villages, especially in moonlit nights, clandestine affairs are sometimes reported.

B. Adolescents

In traditional Ghana, as in most other African countries, the sexual transition from infancy to adulthood was not only a physiological phenomenon, such as onset of menarche, but also social. Adolescence as a reality, where a person is neither a child nor an adult, did not exist. Puberty in girls is a sign of approaching womanhood and special nubility rites for girls are performed after the first menstruation. The sociological function of initiation rites and ceremonies is to usher the child to adulthood without the period now called adolescence. In Ghana as a whole, girls' initiation ceremonies are culturally more widespread, interesting, and complex than boys' initiation. Girls' entry into womanhood, especially among the Krobo, are marked with complex ceremonies involving elaborate preparation and rituals. Generally speaking, Ghanaian boys enter manhood quietly: there are no initiation ceremonies or public ceremonies for boys.

At the end of the girl's initiation, she is gorgeously dressed and beautifully decorated. The initiate sets out with her retinue to thank all people in her village or town. She is now regarded as marriageable. If she is betrothed, her "husband" (fiancé) is formally informed to perform the marriage rites and take her as his wife as soon as practicable. If she is not already "engaged," then bachelors have a chance to have a closer look at her. During the initiation period, "sex education" lessons were provided by recognized older women who serve as custodians of instructions on motherhood. The sexual instructions given included: how to "sleep" with the husband, menstrual taboos, how to recognize pregnancy, and personal hygiene, especially of the genitals.

Unlike parts of East Africa where there are cycles of initiation periods, and ceremonies are performed for groups of persons, in Ghana with few exceptions, initiation ceremonies are mainly individual affairs, although two or three girls may begin their rites on the same day in one village. But even here, the ceremonies are often separate, except where the neophytes are either closely related or are close friends. While puberty rites are still performed in some rural areas, they have lost a great deal of their pomp and pageantry, perhaps with the exception of the Krobo, the rural Ga, and the Adangbe, where it is still popular.

Circumcision

Female circumcision is ritually unknown among all Akan groups in Ghana. On the whole, the practice is fairly common among the Frafra and other groups that inhabit the regions of northern Ghana. The practice is also reported in the areas in the city of Accra, such as Nima and Madina, with a large concentration of migrants from the north. In these societies, it performs a social function as a puberty rite. It is claimed by the local people that it is a precondition for marriage and a test of virginity. Most doctors are of the view that circumcised females stand a higher chance of experiencing problems during childbirth, and female circumcision has always been cited as one of the cultural practices negatively affecting women's health in Ghana.

There are significant differences in the practice of male circumcision among the various ethnic groups in Ghana. For example, the Ga of Accra and the Krobo have traditionally been practicing circumcision. A Krobo parent will not give her daughter in marriage to an uncircumcised man (apparently from an Akan tribe). Traditionally, among the Akan groups, however, male circumcision was not practiced, since it was considered as mutilation of the human body. The Akan have a rule that no one who has a scar can be elected a chief, and one already selected can be "destooled" (deselected) as soon as it is found that he has been circumcised—apparently because his body has been maimed in a way that disfigures him.

In spite of the traditional mores, male circumcision has become very popular. In boarding schools, uncircumcised boys feel shy and are unable to join others in the bathrooms, as they are constantly ridiculed and called *koteboto* (uncircumcised penis). They lack the confidence to profess love since girls are known to shun them. The pressure may be so great that many young men are compelled to undergo a painful adult circumcision. These days, however, a great number of boys are circumcised shortly after birth.

C. Adults

Premarital Courtship, Dating, and Relationships

In Ghana, traditional norms involving attitudes to and acceptance of premarital sexual relationships differ from society to society. Among the Kwahu (a subgroup of the Akan), girls were not to engage in sex before they were married, and certainly not before their first menstruation. Rattray, who wrote in the 1920s, also stated that among the Ashanti, premarital coitus was forbidden. The official code on prenubility sexuality was rather strict. In olden times among the Akan, a girl was killed, or both parties banished, when she engaged in sexual intercourse prior to her puberty and initiation. In most societies in southern Ghana, since girls were usually married shortly after their initiation, many entered the conjugal union as virgins.

Among the communities in northern Ghana, the situation was different. Prenuptial chastity was not particularly valued. It is reported that among the Kokomba, for example, many women were already pregnant before marriage. The Tallensi, also of northern Ghana, explain that copulation and marriage are not the same thing. It can be said that while premarital sexual relationships have been permitted in most societies in northern Ghana, it arrived in the south as an influence of modernization. Chastity can mean two things in Ghanaian sexual mores: chastity before puberty rites and chastity after initiation, but before marriage. In olden days, both were thought important among most ethnic groups of southern Ghana. The attitude towards postpubertal but premarital chastity, however, has undergone substantial changes in many parts of Ghana.

The force of social change in Ghana resulting from education, increasing urbanization, and monetization of traditional economic systems, among others, have blended to produce changes in sexual culture. In Ghana today, it is clear that even in societies where premarital relationships were not openly permitted, they are now at least condoned. In Ghana as a whole, the onset of sexual activity is fairly early. The median age at first sexual intercourse for females is 17 to 18 years, although one survey puts the mean age at 15. Although a substantial minority have multiple partners, for females premarital serial monogamy with frequent partner switching is the norm. Durations of sexual relationships are generally short and women do not appear to be worried about frequent partner switching. In a study in one town in 1991, mean duration of relationship was thirteen months.

The underlying issue that shapes the duration of sexual relationships is basically pecuniary in nature. For many single women, especially in the urban areas, sexual relationships are means of additional income. A recent study in a town in southern Ghana has shown that personal sociodemographic variables are not significantly associated with parameters of sexual behavior, including the number of sexual partners and duration of sexual relationships. The strongest predictor of sexual behavior is women's attitude to material recompense for sex. Several anthropological studies in southern Ghana, especially, have shown that for women, economic pressures, among others, provide the background for most premarital sexual relationships. At present, the consumerist nature of premarital sexual relationships (but not formal prostitution) is generally acceptable, and it is its absence, rather than its presence, that is strange. It is interesting that most Western researchers mistakenly label this phenomenon as prostitution, apparently because some women obtain money and other gains from sexual relationships.

Premarital sexual relationships are essentially secretive in nature, although secrecy is always a matter of degree. Public show of love and affection through kissing and holding of hands while walking is hardly seen among lovers. This often misleads researchers from other cultures to misinterpret this to mean lack of love in Ghanaian "lover relationships." In Europe or America, dating couples may agree on the nature and extent of their relationships: for example, whether it is to be sexual or not. In most premarital relationships in Ghana, there is no such decision to be made. In both traditional and modern societies, premarital relationships are primarily sexual. Implicitly, male-female relationships are never nonsexual.

Sexual Behavior and Relationships of Single Adults

Until recently, the term "single adult" was a misnomer in the Ghanaian sense. The puberty rites marked a graduation from youth to adulthood, and a woman was usually married out soon after into a relationship sometimes contracted by the couple's families prior to the initiation. The transition from childhood to adulthood was therefore definite and clear-cut.

The modern young adult is in a different social milieu. Modern schooling keeps boys and girls longer in an unmarried state. Some people after school spend some years looking for decent jobs. This has widened the gap between sexual maturity and married life. However, since the social position of a person, especially a woman, is often dependent on marital status, single adulthood as a chosen option is hardly acceptable. The normal pattern of Ghanaian life is to marry and have children. Any alternative lifestyle is highly questionable. Within the past few years however, an increasing number of women do not conform to social norms and remain single.

It is worth noting that most of the few voluntarily single women are not without children. Some had unwelcome pregnancies at early ages, while others with experience from previous unions find married life distasteful and men untrustworthy. The fact that most single women choose to do so after having had children underscores the importance Ghanaian women attach to their reproductive roles.

The position of a male single adult, compared with the female, is perhaps even more untenable. While a single female adult can have children, and in the process, exhibit her fecundity to her family and indeed the entire community, the single man has no way of demonstrating his virility. Men who continue as single right up to late ages are viewed with suspicion, and may even be thought to be impotent. A middle-aged man who cooks on his own, or eats outside his home, is in an awkward position, because society does not tolerate his position as a single adult. In villages, children may refuse to go on his errands—a Ghanaian child is trained to go on errands—and some impertinent children can boldly tell him to have children of his own if he requires the services of those younger. He is normally regarded as irresponsible: he cannot assume responsibility of a wife and children. This may impair his social esteem, and can become an issue for gossip at his workplace, especially if he holds a responsible position.

Marriage and Family

Marriage, perhaps the most important social institution in Ghana, is almost universal. Age-specific marital rates are very high and increase rapidly through successive cohorts. According to the Ghana Demographic and Health Survey of 1988, 98 percent of all women aged between 30 and 40 years were in marital unions. The median age at first marriage is around 8 years, and there has been no significant change since the 1970s. The national figure, however, conceals regional variations. The northern regions of Ghana together exhibit the highest rates, with over 84 percent of all women aged 15 to 19 in marital unions.

As elsewhere in Africa, marriage is not an individual affair, but rather a union between two families. Even today, highly educated urbanized men and women will go to great lengths to persuade an unwilling mother, but especially the father, to agree to their marriage. Costs involved in marriage differ from society to society and between families, depending on the status of the couple or their parents. On the whole, marriage among the matrilineal peoples is far cheaper. Bride wealth is considerably smaller, compared with the patrilineal groups where husbands may be asked to pay dozens of fowls or cattle, which in terms of money is quite substantial.

In Ghana, there is legal pluralism of marriages. There are four basic ones: customary marriage; marriage under the ordinance; Christian marriage; and Muslim marriage. Eight out of every ten marriages are under customary law, under which a man can marry many wives (polygyny). Marriage under the ordinance is a British colonial legacy, which introduces attributes of legitimacy, monogamy, and inheritance into the Ghanaian context. To many, this has caused ambiguity in Ghanaian marriage law. For example, it precludes the husband from the practice of polygyny. In fact, only a small minority of Ghanaian marriages are contracted this way. Marriage types are not necessarily mutually exclusive. Persons who marry in church or in a registrar's office under ordinance do so only after they have performed the necessary customary rites.

In Ghana, as in other parts of Africa, a man, his wife or wives, and children do not constitute a family. Although the Western concept of the nuclear family can be distinguished, it is not the basis of social organization and community living. The extended family network consists of a long list of kinsmen who are matrilineally or patrilineally delineated.

In Ghana, cohabitation as a practice may be better referred to as a consensual union. In very many instances, marriages under customary practice do not take place as a single, definite event. It is rather a process that involves a series of presentations by the man's family to the family into which he proposes to marry. These presentations may be made at once as among the Kokomba, or over a period of several years as among the Akan. After the first presentation, a marriage may begin as a consensual union approved by parents of both partners and accepted as a proper marriage for all practical purposes. However, such unions have some drawbacks: for example, under customary law, the husband cannot claim damages if his wife commits adultery. This type of marriage is called *mpenawadie* (concubine marriage), and is less respected, and wives will put pressure on husbands to perform the final rites.

Polygyny

In almost all Ghanaian societies, polygyny (where the husband has two or more wives) is socially accepted, and was even desirable. It is practiced in all the different customary marriage patterns. Although there are some variations, it is practiced in both urban and rural areas, and by literate and nonliterate.

Many reasons are put forward to explain, if not to justify, polygynous marriages. These include long periods of postpartum sexual abstinence from anywhere between three months and two-and-a-half years. It is common for the pregnant wife to leave the husband's home in order to deliver among her kinsmen; she does not return until the baby is able to walk. To satisfy his sexual desires, a man is allowed to marry more than one wife. In the not-too-distant past, social status and economic prestige were the motivating factors. The large number of children from the different wives was useful in the husband's occupation, which was basically farming.

Polygyny demands some domestic residential arrangements. The most uncommon arrangement is the situation where all wives live separately from the husband who arranges periods for visits. Another solution is that in which the husband lives with all his wives in one house. This is not highly desirable, given the embedded rivalry and tension among cowives, which not infrequently results in brawling. The most favored option is that one wife (usually the first) resides with the husband, and the other(s) live on their own or with kinsmen. Cooking, "sleeping," and other wifely duties are arranged by the husband.

Polygyny is commonly practiced. Ghana's 1960 Population Census showed that 26 percent of all married men had more than one wife; in 1979-80, according to the Ghana Fertility Survey, 35 percent of all married women were in polygynous homes. The figure for 1988 was 33 percent. Younger women are less likely to be in polygynous unions than older women. Given that in Ghana an unmarried woman is an anomaly, polygyny affords all women (who desire) the opportunity of being attached in marriage to a man (who, unlike in the past, may not be necessarily supporting her in full). Ironically, polyandrous marriages (where one wife is legally married to more than one husband) is not practiced in Ghana or any studied society in Africa.

Divorce

Marriages among the matrilineal groups in Ghana, strictly speaking, do not promote stability. The children and their mother are considered "outsiders" by the man's matrilineage. After the husband's death, the wife and the children are allowed up to one year to live in the deceased's property after which they can be forcefully ejected—and many are. The man's children, until the introduction of the Intestate Succession Law in 1985, had no claim to their father's property. Given that the woman and her children are always welcomed back into their lineage after divorce, and the bride wealth, even where refundable, is fairly small, the incidence of divorce in matrilineal societies is higher than in patrilineal societies.

Under customary law, divorce is common, simple, and easily obtained. Both husband and wife can initiate divorce. Divorce in Ghana can result from several causes: the key culprit being infertility on the part of either partner. Other frequent reasons to merit divorce are: bad conduct, neglect of marital duties (such as a man's failure to provide money for food and family upkeep, popularly called "chop-money"), gossiping and tale bearing (usually on the part of the woman), laziness, accusation or suspicion of witchcraft, and interference in lineage affairs or lack of respect for in-laws. Adultery of a woman is grounds for divorce, but in customary law, the wife cannot enforce divorce on the grounds of her husband's adultery or his marrying more wives. The practice is that before an additional wife is married, the first wife is informed by the husband who pacifies her with money or in kind. There is usually a small and simple ceremony or ritual performed to legalize divorce. Among the Akan, it consists of the sprinkling of white clay before the woman's feet, thus formally loosening her from her former matrimonial bonds.

Although it cannot be exaggerated how easily and rapidly marriages dissolve with little trouble, it must be pointed out that because marriage is a union between families, most divorces are preceded by family "arbitration." The aggrieved party will have to state his or her case before responsible men. The arbitrators deliver their finding after hearing each party, and then attempts are made to reconcile the couple. Unlike the matrilineal groups, traditionally among the patrilineal groups, especially the Ewe, there usually was stability of marriage. However, there have been significant changes due largely to the curtailment of the power of traditional authorities, which used to enforce the sexual morality of the people. Now divorce is common among the Ewe, but perhaps not as frequent as it is among the Akan.

It appears the proportion of divorced persons is on the decline. In 1960, up to 20 percent of women aged over 44 years were divorced, compared with 13 percent in 1988. It is difficult, however, to obtain any useful idea of the frequency of divorce by examining the proportion of divorced persons in the population. Studies have shown that few women spend long intervals between marriages. They are usually in the process of contracting another marriage before the previous one has been formally terminated. Remarriage rates are therefore high, given that the society looks down upon single women.

Extramarital Sexual Behavior

Among the Akan, extramarital relationships have been very common traditionally, and today are still practiced by married adults of both sexes and by people of all socioeconomic groups. There are some circumstances that are especially conducive to this phenomenon. Differences in status or age may demand different sexual or social habits that the partner is unable to provide. Given the high cost of living in Ghana today, some women engage in extramarital liaisons for material recompense, especially if the husband is unable to provide support. In a society where procreation is the main reason for marriage, the husband or wife may indulge in extramarital sex in the hope of having children when the other is infertile. Broadly speaking, women engage in extramarital relationships less than men.

An extramarital relationship by a married woman is regarded as adultery and both males and females; culprits are liable to punishment and ridicule. Among the traditional Ga, for example, a man caught in the act of adultery with a married woman is severely beaten there and then by the family of the injured husband, their friends, and helpers. In villages, the distinctive sound of an adultery-hoot may be heard all over. A crowd gathers around the house where the adulterous act is claimed to be taking place. People begin hooting—*huu huu huu*—to emphasize the shameful behavior of the woman. The guilty man sensing danger may jump out the window. If he is lucky enough to avoid a severe beating by escaping into the bush, his family has to pacify the aggrieved husband in his absence. For his own safety, the male adulterer may avoid any public appearance until his family has completed all necessary rites to pacify the husband.

A wife's adultery, especially among the Ewe, is believed to cause not only her own death but even that of her husband. Among the Anlo Ewe, for example, husbands, including highly educated ones, know well the risk to their lives of the infidelity of their wives. To prevent these misfortunes, many men have charms which help to strike terror in wives with adulterous intentions. Sometimes adultery is believed to make childbirth difficult, and unless confession is made before or during childbirth—and some women do so in the rural areas—the adulteress may die with the child.

In Akan customary marriage, where a married woman is seduced, her seducer is bound to pay the husband, as damages, an amount which is fixed by law (called *ayefare* by the Akan), although one could seek divorce outright. Today, *ayefare* is not routinely claimed by men because of the shame attached to its acceptance. Many prefer that their wives' extramarital affairs are kept secret, but once it comes out in the open, divorce is sought rather than the claim of damages that may be considered embarrassing. The societal attitude to extramarital affairs of men can be described as a double standard. The philandering of married men is generally accepted until a point is reached at which a wife feels she is suffering a grievous hardship; then she may ask her husband's family to restrain him. A woman who seeks divorce because her husband has an affair with another woman is considered to be overreacting, and she cannot expect much sympathy, let alone support, from her relatives, unless there is compelling evidence that the man is financially not supporting her and the children.

Levirate

Levirate marriage, in the strict sense of a man marrying his deceased brother's wife and bearing children with her for the dead person, is practiced in very few ethnic groups in Ghana, among the traditional Ga, for instance. As a rule, levirate does not exist among the Anlo Ewe where the husband's sexual rights are personal, nontransferable, and end with his death. His widow is then free to remarry any man of her choice including the deceased's agnates. What is customary among the Akan groups, and is currently practiced in a few instances, is widow inheritance. Here, the brother of the dead man becomes the real husband of the widow, but the children by that marriage belong to him and not the deceased brother. Sororal polygyny, where a man marries two sisters of a family, is unheard of in Ghana.

Sexuality and the Disabled and Aged

Ghana's 1984 population census recorded that about 3 percent of all the population aged 15 years and over were disabled, with the number of women twice that of men. No studies on the sexual adaptations of this segment of the population have been undertaken.

Very little, if at all, is known about the sexuality of the aged in Ghana. It is not uncommon to find an old man married to a young woman, although many of such women may still have sex with their former lovers or with other young men. In most villages, however, some situational factors may inhibit sexual relations of aged couples. As they grow old, children may be asked to sleep with the grandparents to give privacy for the young couple. This makes it difficult for the aged couple to have sexual intercourse and they therefore slowly drift apart. While young widows normally remarry, remarriage for women over 50 years is rare. They are unlikely to find marriageable single men and many at this age are unwilling to be married as second or third wives to polygynous men. Secretive sexual exploits at this stage is very rare: it is considered disgraceful not only to the aged person, but also to the children and grandchildren.

Incidence of Oral and Anal Sex

Penile-vaginal penetrative sex with little foreplay is the normal sexual style in Ghana. Although among the well-educated youth some form of foreplay is introduced, fellatio or cunnilingus is abhorrent. Even among prostitutes vaginal sex is the norm; very few practice oral sex. Genital manipulation is hardly accepted and traditionally women feel shy to touch the penis, and most men are not interested in having their genitals manipulated anyway. Anal sex is considered a sexual depravity and is reserved for animals. It is abhorrent even to prostitutes. In a recent study in Accra, the capital city, only one respondent reported that she would engage in anal intercourse if the price was right.

6. Homoerotic, Homosexual, and Ambisexual Behaviors

Any form of same-sex activities is hardly mentioned in Ghanaian society. Homosexual activities among boys is exceedingly rare. Even where homosexual activities are practiced by boys, they are considered basically "presexual" and are quickly abandoned as they mature. The situation may be different for female homosexuality. It is practiced by a few students in girls' boarding schools "who want to release tension," but are either afraid of getting pregnant or have no access to male partners, given the strict rules regarding male visits to girls' schools. But here too, it is basically situational and not an alternative means of sexual expression. It is quickly forgotten once the girls leave school. In Bleek's study in the 1970s, he observed that no reference whatsoever was made to homosexuality and no word gave a hint of its occurrence. It is the impression that homosexuality is so rare in Ghana that people hardly have any idea of it, even on university campuses. Young male adults may dance together at night clubs, and may even imitate a couple, without any inhibition. If there existed a secret or clandestine practice of homosexuality, this would not be possible and boys would be too embarrassed to behave in such a way. It is virtually impossible to prove that homosexuality does not exist: what can be said is that homosexuality as a means of adult sexual expression hardly exists in Ghana, and it is not listed as a sexual offense because self-identified gay men are virtually unheard of.

7. Gender Conflicted Persons

There is no knowledge of gender conflicted persons. Adult homosexuality is so rare that the sociolegal status of a homosexual is unthinkable. Transsexuals are virtually unheard of in the Ghanaian society.

8. Significant Unconventional Sexual Behaviors

A. Coercive Sex

Sexual Abuse

Child sexual abuse is very rare in Ghanaian society. Those who engage in it may be regarded as perverts. Even in societies where daughters could be given in marriage at a very tender age in a form of betrothal, sexual intercourse is precluded until after the girl has undergone the initiation rites. Domestic maids often brought into the cities by middle-class families may in some instances be sexually abused by unscrupulous husbands, especially if there develops a marital discord or the maid becomes more and more beautiful as she grows up in the city.

Incest

Incest, sexual intercourse between parents and children or between full siblings, is abhorred, extremely rare, and culprits are severely punished. An incestuous act may be wider than imagined, depending on whether the society is endogamous (the Dagaaba of Upper West and the Ewe, for instance) or exogamous (the Akan) where sexual relationships within the large clan is prohibited.

The sexual mores on what relationships are incestuous may appear strange to an outsider. For example, among the matrilineal Akan, while it is incestuous for a man to have sexual intercourse with his mother's sister's daughter, he is enjoined to marry his mother's brother's daughter or father's sister's daughter. Among the Ga of southern Ghana, it is so repugnant that in the early days, an incestuous man was punished by drowning and the woman driven away into the bush. To make sure that the practice is not condoned by the family, none of the relatives of the offenders was allowed to hold any post of importance for one generation. Today, it still is a family calamity. An offender is denied from using the family name, and is forbidden to attend public festivals.

Sexual Harassment

Traditionally, a woman's body is considered special, and care should be taken in the way a man handles it. To pull or play with a woman' nose, ear, or any other part of the body, or tickle the palm of a woman's hand is considered highly indecent and immoral. If this is done to a married woman, it could be likened to adultery and the aggrieved husband may claim damages. In contemporary Ghana, few single women will consider any of these as sexual harassment. Rather they are signs of a man showing interest, but lacking the courage to say so because "he has a mouth that is sewn."

It is, however, common to hear reports of young women, especially typists and secretaries, being sexually harassed by their bosses, or student girls by their teachers. Given the subordinate role of women, coupled with the fear of losing their jobs or being denied promotion when they tell others or decline the sexual advances, women are put under tremendous pressure. Some women are compelled to give in or blow the matter up by exposing the boss, who may become a reference point for public ridicule. It must be stated that sometimes the advances may also be made by women who think they can materially gain from a sexual relationship with the boss.

Rape

In Ghana, as elsewhere, indecent assault and rape are criminal offenses. Rape is defined in Ghana's Criminal Code as an unlawful carnal knowledge against any female, and when the assaulted woman is physically incapable of resistance to force, rape does not have to be proved. Its occurrence in Ghana is very rare, and a woman walking alone in a city late in the night may be afraid of mugging, but would hardly think of rape.

Very little research has been done on the issue. In 1977, 273 cases of assault and rape were reported. The victims were mostly house girls, babysitters, and were, like the offenders, mainly in the lower social class. The minimum sentence for rape is twelve months, which is considered too lenient by women activists. An attempt in 1993 by female members of parliament to increase the minimum sentence to three years was opposed. The main national newspaper, the *People's Daily Graphic*, described the men's behavior as "sheer display of male chauvinism and lack of respect and understanding of women's sensitivity."

There is a variant of unconventional sexual behavior that is fairly common in the villages. This is an attempt to seduce a woman while she is sleeping in the night, not infrequently with the connivance of the woman, especially if she is married. Consent of the woman is immaterial if they are caught. The man can be so ridiculed that he may be compelled to move out of the village.

[*Female Ritual Slavery*

[In the isolated farming villages along the Volta River in southeastern Ghana, several thousand young women are caught in a religious tradition that condemns them to a form of perpetual ritual slavery. The *trocosi* as they are known in the Ewe language, or "slaves of the gods," work in local religious shrines to appease the fetish gods for crimes committed by their relatives. In the local culture, justice and punishment are viewed in communal rather than individual terms. Thus, a young female who has no connection with a crime, and may not even know what it was, may be sent by her family to atone for a (male) relative's crime by serving the local fetish priest. Because the priest is a spiritual intermediary between worshipers and deities of the area's traditional Ju-ju religion, the *trocosi* can appease the fetish and keep them from punishing her whole family. Her life becomes one of unquestioned service to the priest, cooking, cleaning, weeding the shrine's farm, growing yams, manioc, and corn, and providing sexual favors to the shrine's priest. The *trocosi* gain nothing personally from their service; their families must even provide them with food. The people are convinced that without the protection provided by the *trocosi*, the gods may wreak vengeance on their entire extended family or community (French 1997).

[The *trocosi*, who must begin their service as virgins, can only be freed by the priest. A *trocosi* usually gains her freedom only when she is middle-aged, has borne the priest many children, and has lost her sex appeal. But freedom for one *trocosi* means enslavement of another virgin from the same family who must replace her. Thus, the slavery continues generation after generation in perpetual atonement.

[This form of ritual slavery, which is also found in neighboring Togo, Benin, and southwestern Nigeria, is deep-rooted in a very powerful superstition that will be difficult to eradicate. A government law banning the practice would have no effect, since the whole community is in agreement with the custom and firmly believe their survival depends on their freely sending a "scapegoat" *trocosi* to serve the local fetish priest when someone commits a crime. Recently, there has been increasing criticism from international human rights advocacy groups and from women's rights groups within Ghana. Individual women's rights advocates and private groups within Ghana have had some success in stopping the practice by negotiating with paramount chiefs and other prominent local leaders. One local group,

International Needs, has persuaded several fetish priests and their shrines to abandon the custom in return for a gift of ten cows, a bull, a corral for the priest's new cattle, and cash given to the surrounding villages (French 1997). (Editor)]

B. Prostitution

From the onset, it is necessary to distinguish between sexual exchange and prostitution in Ghanaian sexual culture. These two practices are often misunderstood by outsiders, who consider them as the same. Sexual exchange, a recent phenomenon, is a socially acceptable and pervasive practice in which sexual relationships, both premarital and extramarital, are contracted for material recompense. While implicit pecuniary gains underline the relationship, it is worth noting that in sexual exchange material rewards, especially money, are not given directly after sexual intercourse, as is the case with prostitution. The giving and receiving of gains is separate from the act of coitus. A girl is likely to be offended for being thought a prostitute, if she is given money immediately after sexual intercourse. Unlike prostitution, in sexual exchange it is not the sexual act that is rewarded, but the relationship.

Prostitution, the exchange of sexual acts for money, is illegal in Ghana, and women who practice it are often harassed by the police and other officials of city or local councils. Nevertheless, it is openly practiced in many cities and towns. In Accra, for example, an area called Korle Wokon is noted for its prostitutes. Unlike sexual exchange, prostitution is unacceptable to the Ghanaian society—the only exception being perhaps among the Krobo—and constitutes an infraction of Ghanaian sexual mores. Those who engage in it often conceal their identities by working in suburbs where they are not likely to be recognized by familiar faces, and some may even change their names altogether.

Ghanaian prostitutes generally operate without pimps. At least two main groups of prostitutes can be identified: home-based prostitutes and hotel-based prostitutes. The former usually work in rented rooms or brothels and are of low class with little or no education. They are usually old, with an average age of around 40 years, divorced, and are heads of households with four or more children to support. They all cite acute financial problems as reasons for prostitution. They charge around $1 per client per sexual act or "round," and report an average of two or three clients a day.

Hotel-based prostitutes operate from hotels, night clubs, and discos. They are sophisticated, are of high class, much younger, highly educated, and serve an equally high-class clientele. Their prices, which are generally higher, depend on the class of the hotel where they operate.

Tema is the major port and industrial complex of Ghana, and the visiting seamen, both Ghanaian and foreign, attract many prostitutes. With the scourge of HIV/AIDS infection, intervention programs, with support from

Family Health International (FHI) and other international agencies, are being implemented to encourage prostitutes to use condoms, given that in 1986, about 60 percent of all prostitutes surveyed in Accra had never used condoms before.

C. Pornography

Nudity is culturally repugnant. It is considered inappropriate for parents to undress in the presence of their children. Societal attitudes to nudity are severer towards females than males. Women are expected to cover their breasts and thighs in public. In the Muslim areas, the rules are tighter. Even in Ghana's large cities, a lady wearing a pair of shorts in public is considered immoral. Any explicit display of erotic materials is highly unacceptable and magazines on erotica are not available. Television programs never include sexual material likely to be offensive. With the growing number of video rentals and show spots, there is an increasing concern about the sexually offensive nature of some films, although they come nowhere near the soft pornographic materials available in the Western countries.

D. Sexual Taboos

Apart from incest, there are other sexual taboos worth mentioning. These include sexual intercourse while a woman is in her menstrual period, with a widow less than a year after her husband's death, and sexual intercourse with a woman in the bush. The latter is called by the Akan *ahahantwe* (sexual intercourse in the leaves), and is considered antisocial because it threatens the life of the society. By being performed in the bush, sexual intercourse, upon which society depends for its perpetuation and hence is regarded as sacred, is reduced to the level of an act that is performed without regard to the environment. If it was done without the connivance of the woman, it could lead to death in the olden days. Today, however, if reported, it is treated as rape. But whether there is consent or connivance on the woman's part, the man is asked to provide a live sheep, which is sacrificed upon the spot where the adulterous act had taken place. This is currently practiced in most rural settings among the Akan.

9. Contraception, Abortion and Population Planning

A. Contraception

The present high level of Ghana's population is the result of persistent high birthrates and declining mortality rates over the years, leading to a high rate of natural increase. For a variety of social, economic, and cultural reasons, large families are attractive to many Ghanaians. The average Ghanaian woman in the 1990s is expected to have 6.4 children in her lifetime. Knowledge about contraception is high. According to the Ghana Demographic and Health Survey in 1988, 79 percent of currently married and 79 percent of all husbands have heard about contraception, but only 13 percent of the women were using any method of contraception (5 percent if restricted to modern methods). The pill and postpartum abstinence are the most popular modern and traditional contraceptive methods respectively. For adolescents and young adults, however, the condom is the most popular.

There are some differentials in contraceptive knowledge and use by educational level, type of residence, age, and reproductive intentions. Modern contraceptives are available at several service delivery points owned by the Ministry of Health, the Planned Parenthood Association of Ghana (PPAG; an affiliate of International Planned Parenthood Federation), the Christian Council of Ghana, private maternity homes, contraceptive social marketing outlets, and pharmacies. However, about one in every five users obtained their supplies from friends or relatives. With the scourge of HIV/AIDS infection, condom promotion has been intensified through social marketing and community-based distribution.

B. Teenage Unmarried Pregnancies

Births to adolescents accounted for 11 percent of Ghana's births in 1978-80. Teenage premarital pregnancy is becoming an increasing social and health problem. One reason for low teenage (unmarried) pregnancies in the traditional societies was the observance of puberty rites after which marriage followed almost immediately. Increased education and other forces of social change have eroded the traditional constraints. Unfortunately, no replacement has been found for these rites and the sex education it provided. Modern counseling is inadequate for teenagers, and access to family planning is limited.

When sexual relations between teenagers result in pregnancy, the boy's parents are informed. Pressure is exerted on the man to marry her, unless the girl's lineage does not want him as an in-law. In a few instances, a pregnancy can be used to persuade the elders of a lineage to approve of a relationship to which they would not have normally consented.

C. Abortion

Abortion is illegal unless for medical reasons, and very few Ghanaians would want this changed. Yet many pregnant student girls procure abortions in order to complete school or because their partners are not yet ready to father a child. While these are the official reasons women give, it appears that it is the fear of shame that is the dominant factor. Statistics of induced abortion are hard to come by and, even where they exist, are grossly defective. In a 1990/91 study among secondary school students, 10 percent of male students who have had intercourse admitted having impregnated a girl, and for 61 percent of these, the girl concerned resorted to abortion. Induced abortion is reprehensible and always remains hidden. Although the official rules for procuring an abortion are not liberal, it is well known that, provided the client is able to pay, most hospitals will undertake it.

Many abortions, however, are performed outside of hospital premises by unqualified back-street abortionists, quack doctors, and self or friends. In the last category, herbs and other incredible combinations of concoctions form the largest method. The knowledge of alleged abortifacients among young men and women is amazing. Bleek, in his study among the Kwahu in the 1970s, listed at least fifty-three different methods for procuring self-induced abortion, which included "modern" methods involving the use of assorted pills and herbs, such as the insertion of the twig of *nkrangyedua* (*Jathropa curcas*) or *menyenemen-yeneme* (*Thevetia peruviana*) into the uterus. Many of these amazing methods are still in use. In a study in 1990/91 among secondary school students, respondents' lists of abortifacients included: a mixture of sugar and lemon, *akpeteshie* (a very strong local gin), and Guinness ale.

The life-threatening risk arising from induced abortions is all too obvious. In 1973, for example, between 60 percent and 80 percent of all minor operations at Korle Bu Teaching Hospital, Ghana's largest hospital, involved abortion-related complications.

D. Population Control Efforts

Currently, Ghana's population growth rate is 3.0 percent per annum, with 45 percent of the population below 15 years of age, thus epitomizing a high dependency burden. In 1969, Ghana was among the first countries in Africa to declare an explicit population policy. The Ghana National Family Planning Programme was established in 1970 to offer individual citizens the freedom to choose family planning and eventually slow down the rapid population growth. Not very much has been achieved, partly due to inadequate support from subsequent governments. Since the mid-1980s, however, Rawlings' government has reinforced Ghana's commitment to its population policy through the collaborative participation of international donor agencies. A National Population Council has been established, and it is likely that some decline in the fertility measures will be observed in the near future.

10. Sexually Transmitted Diseases

Very little is known about STDs in Ghana, but given that it is considered a cofactor of HIV infection, considerable attention is now being focused on its prevalence, prevention, and treatment. Although no reliable data are available, there is the consensus among experts that STDs are fairly common in Ghana, the most common being gonorrhea. There is a greater incidence of STDs among the 15- to 19-year-olds than among other age groups. This may be partly explained by the fact that STDs are considered as part of normal growing up when one begins sexual exploits.

Antibiotic treatment is available in hospitals and health centers, and there are also a few STD clinics, such as the Adabraka STD clinic. Still-infected persons, especially adolescents, are particularly slow to seek medical attention. Many tend to resort to traditional medicine or self-medication.

The government through the National AIDS Control Programme (NACP) has intensified efforts in STD control as part of the national HIV/AIDS control program. The European Economic Community (EEC) Task Force on AIDS is supporting the procurement of material, equipment, and reagents for a project on STD control.

11. HIV/AIDS

Until recently, it was widely assumed that West Africa has been spared the social, economic, and health burdens of AIDS. Sadly, this optimistic view can no longer be justified. The first reported case of AIDS in Ghana was in 1986. At the beginning of 1995, there were some 12,500 reported AIDS cases. This is likely to be an underestimation since many cases are unreported. Over 80 percent of all cases of HIV infection involve persons infected through heterosexual intercourse. No other particular sexual practice has been implicated in the sexual transmission. As noted earlier in the chapter, homosexual practice and anal sex are unacceptable and extremely rare. The early phase of HIV transmission was among prostitutes with a history of outside travel. As in many other countries, this led to finger pointing at other countries. The current trend indicates that the diffusion has gone beyond the so-called risk group. There has been almost a fourfold increase between 1986 and 1990 in the number of AIDS patients without any history of foreign travel. It can be stated that the future spread of HIV in Ghana may largely depend not on formal prostitution, but on the socially acceptable and pervasive phenomenon of sexual exchange in which women constantly switch sexual partners in order to maximize material gains accruing from sexual relationships.

In Ghana, as elsewhere, AIDS is primarily a disease that affects the economically active group. For both sexes, adults in the age group 20 to 29 account for 70 percent of the cases. The pattern, however, shows female preponderance over males. At the early stage of the epidemic in Ghana, there was one male to every eight females, although this has narrowed down to a current level of 1:2. Ghanaian epidemiologists agree that the sex ratio is changing to the direction of 1:1, which is consistent with heterosexual transmission in most countries.

Another pattern of HIV/AIDS infection in Ghana is that the majority of cases were initially not reported from major cities. Recent data on seropositives, however, show a tremendous increase in the number of cases in Ghana's main cities of Accra and Kumasi, thus supporting the generalization that in Africa AIDS is primarily an urban disease. Three regions out of ten, Ashanti, Eastern, and Greater Accra, account for over 70 percent of all reported HIV cases. It is not clear, however, whether the regional variation results from level of reporting, although the general impression is that certain sociosexual practices in these regions may facilitate HIV transmission.

No nationwide HIV seropositive studies have been conducted yet, apart from a few using convenience samples. However, a study conducted in 1989-90 among patients of Ghana's second largest hospital, the Okomfo Anokye Hospital in Kumasi, found a prevalence rate of 12.6 percent. Although this apparently high figure should not be extrapolated to the rest of the country, it definitely indicates a serious problem for the immediate future. Up to June 1991, only 25 out of 2,474 reported AIDS cases were under five years. Given that a substantial and fast-growing number of women of childbearing ages may be infected, perinatal transmission will soon become an issue of grave concern in Ghana.

There is a National AIDS Control Program (NACP) within the Ministry of Health. NACP, through information and education campaigns, is attempting to reinforce HIV risk-reduction sexual behaviors by discouraging casual sexual relationships or having multiple partners, and encouraging relationships with one faithful partner (or partners in polygynous homes). Condom promotion has also been intensified through social marketing and community-based distribution. The care of AIDS patients is generally home-based, given the lack of trained counselors, a task now being addressed by the Counseling Unit of the NACP. The best organized counseling program has been developed at St. Martin's Hospital in Agomanya by the Catholic Mission. Other international, nongovernmental organizations, such as the World Vision, are also involved in providing physical and economic support for AIDS patients.

12. Sexual Dysfunctions and Therapies

The most obvious sexual disorder is sterility. A barren woman is always in despair. The desire for children makes impotence in men even more disgraceful and pitiful. A childless couple is scorned and despised. Among the Akan, the man's penis is ridiculed as being flabby, and is nicknamed *kote kra* (wax penis). In the olden, days it is reported that an impotent man, after his death, had great thorns driven into his soles, and the corpse addressed: *woanwo ba, mma no saa bio* (you have not borne children; do not return again like that). Although family planning centers and general hospitals may provide some advice and counseling, professional therapy is almost nonexistent. Given the embarrassment associated with impotence, very few men may accompany their wives to seek treatment from professionals in modern medicine. The source of childlessness is usually attributed to the wife, rather than the husband.

Traditional healers in Ghana, while conceding the superiority of Western biomedical medicine for certain diseases, have insisted that infertility and sexually transmitted diseases are believed to be more effectively treated by traditional medicine than modern medicine. The secret and highly confidential nature of their practice makes traditional medicine men, herbalists, Mallams, fetish priests, and others the main source of treatment. They are visited by people of different educational and economic status. Men who claim to have medicines potent enough to induce pregnancy soon become rich.

13. Research and Advanced Education

Studies on sexuality in Ghana are particularly scanty. Until the onset of HIV/AIDS, all that was known was based on anthropological evidence gleaned from discussions on family, initiation rites, and other rites of passage. Although there are no special centers or institutes devoted to sex research, there has been a gradual interest in the subject, and surveys on sex have been undertaken. Specific groups surveyed in addition to the general population include; adolescents, young adults, return migrants, long-distance truck drivers, and secondary school students. The Departments of Sociology and Geography at the University of Cape Coast; the Institute of Statistical, Social, and Economic Research; and the Institute of African Studies, both at the University of Ghana, are all involved in sex research. The Institute of Population Studies, University of Exeter (U.K.), is also engaged in collaborative research with local investigators on sexual behavior and HIV risk-reduction strategies in Ghana. One key methodological finding on sex research in Ghana is that, on the whole, respondents are more willing to discuss sexual matters and provide frank answers than it was first thought.

There is no professional association, nor are there journals for sexuality. Graduate programs devoted to sexuality are nonexistent. However, there is a Department of Guidance and Counseling at the University of Cape Coast that offers graduate programs. Perhaps the only major book of academic significance that deals exclusively with sexuality in Ghana is Bleek's (1976) *Sexual Relationships and Birth Control in Ghana: A Case Study in a Rural Town.* A well-written book based on participant observation and field survey, the study was done among only one group (the Kwahu), and therefore will not satisfy the needs of a student who wants a handbook on Ghanaian sexuality.

References and Suggested Readings

Akuffo, F. O. 1987. "Teenage Pregnancies and School Dropouts: The Relevance of Family Life Education and Vocational Training to Girls' Employment Opportunities." In C. Oppong, ed. *Sex Role, Population and Development in West Africa*. Portsmouth: Heineman, pp. 154-64.

Anarfi, J. 1992. "Sexual Networking in Selected Communities in Ghana and the Sexual Behavior of Ghanaian Female Migrants in Abidjan, Cote d'Ivoire." In T. Dyson, ed. *Sexual Behavior and Networking: Anthropological and Sociocultural Studies on the Transmission of HIV*. Liege: Derouaux-Ordina, pp. 233-48.

Ankomah, A. 1992. "Premarital Sexual Behavior in Ghana in the Era of AIDS." *Health Policy and Planning*, 7(2):135-43.

Ankomah, A. 1992. *The Sexual Behavior of Young Women in Cape Coast, Ghana: The Pecuniary Considerations Involved and Implications for AIDS*. Ph.D. Thesis. Institute of Population Studies, University of Exeter (U.K).

Bleek, W. 1976. *Sexual Relationships and Birth Control in Ghana: A Case Study of a Rural Town*. Amsterdam: Centre for Social Anthropology, University of Amsterdam.

French, H. W. 1997 (January 20). "The Ritual Slaves of Ghana: Young, Female, Paying for Another's Crime." *The New York Times*, A1, A5.

Neequaye, A. 1990. "Prostitution in Accra." In M. Plant, ed. *AIDS, Drugs and Prostitution*. London: Tavistock/Routledge, pp. 175-85.

Greece
(*Elliniki Dimokratia*)

Dimosthenis Agrafiotis, Ph.D., and Panagiota Mandi, Ph.D.

Contents

Demographics and a Historical Perspective

A. Demographics

The Greek peninsula projects into the Mediterranean Sea from south of the Balkans. The mountainous, mostly nonarable land of the Greek peninsula is deeply indented by long sea inlets and surrounded by over 2,000 islands, of which only 169 are inhabited; these include Delos, Lesbos, Samos, Kerika (Corfu), Crete, and Rhodes. Greece's neighbors in southeastern Europe are Albania, Yugoslavia, and Bulgaria on the north borders and Turkey on the east. With an area of 51,146 square miles, Greece is about the size of the state of Alabama.

Since sexual identity, attitudes, and behavior are in a large part formed in a nation's sociocultural environment, it is important to sketch out the general ethnic, racial, and socioeconomic character of Greece.

In the past century, Greece has been a country searching for its national boundaries and identity, as well as its economic survival. Being a backward agrarian society, its economy has oscillated between self-subsistence and dependency on external markets. Since the advent of the twentith century, constant territorial and, consequently, demographic expansion has provided the foundations for a rapid development. Greece finally embarked on the process of industrialization, though considerably later than the rest of Europe, and under rather violent and short-lived stimuli. However, this rapid development has produced an imbalance between its economic and sociocultural level. This lack of correspondence is a common aspect of societies that are in a stage of development that is neither well articulated nor well defined, and of societies where coexisting economic, social, and cultural structures correspond to different modes of production. Thus it can be said that Greek economy is characterized by heterogeneity due to the coexistence of "traditional" and "modern" components of technoeconomic activity. The social structure of institutions, groups, and relations is still in a state of inertia imposed by the past. Social groups and/or classes cannot easily and creatively articulate their role in the context of prevailing conditions and available opportunities. The cultural environment is under the pressure of imported models, while the traditional characteristics do not show any signs of endurance. The confusion between the old and the new, the Greek and the foreign, could paralyze the existing forces and resources.

Nearly two thirds of the 10.6 million Greeks live in urban areas, with more than 4 million in the two cities of Athens and Piraeus. Life expectancy at birth in 1995 was 75 for males and 81 for females. Infant mortality decreased from eleven per 1,000 live births in 1991 to eight per 1,000 live births in 1995. The birthrate has fallen appreciably during the last two or three decades and appears to be on a definite downward trend. While remarkable reductions have taken place in most of the European countries, Greece has the highest reduction in fertility among Eastern European countries. Thus the fertility indicator has been reduced from 2.3 children per woman in 1975 to 1.4 children in 1990, which is 30 percent below the lowest limit necessary for the renewal of the Greek population. The 1995 birthrate was 11 per 1,000 population; the death rate nine per 1,000 population, giving a natural annual increase of 0.1 percent. Greece has one hospital bed per 199 persons and one physician per 303 persons. The literacy rate is 96 percent for men and 89 percent for women. The 1993 overall literacy rate was 93 percent. Nine years of schooling are compulsory. The per capita gross domestic product in 1993 was $8,900.

Out of its labor force of nearly 4 million, about 26.6 percent are employed in agriculture, 27.7 percent in industry and construction, and the remaining 46.2 percent in other activities, mainly services. In 1990, the gross national product (GNP) per capita was U.S. $5,990.

B. A Brief Historical Perspective

The achievements of ancient Greece in art, architecture, science, mathematics, drama, literature, philosophy, and democracy are acknowledged by all as the foundation of Western civilization. Classical Greece reached its apex in Athens during the fourth century B.C.E. In 336, the kingdom of Macedonia, which under Philip II dominated the Greek world and Egypt, passed to his son Alexander. Tutored by Aristotle in the Greek ideals, Alexander the Great conquered Egypt, all the Persian domains, and reached India in 13 years. After his death in 323, his empire was divided into three parts: Egypt under the Ptolemaies, Macedon, and the Seleucid Empire. During the ensuing 300 years, the Hellenic Era, a cosmopolitan Greek-oriented culture permeated the ancient world from the borders of India to western Europe. The sciences thrived, especially in Alexandria, where the pharaohs financed a great library and museum. Major advances were made in the fields of medicine, chemistry, hydraulics, geography, astronomy, and Euclidian and non-Euclidean geometry.

Greece fell under the domination of Roman rule in the second and first centuries B.C.E. In the fourth century C.E., Greece became part of the Byzantine Empire, and, after the fall of Constantinople in 1453 to the Turks, a part of the Ottoman Empire. Greece gained its freedom from Turkey between 1821 and 1829, and became a kingdom. A republic was established in 1924, followed by restoration of the monarchy in 1935. In 1940, Greece was occupied by Germans, Italians, and Bulgarians troops. In the late 1940s, the Communist's guerrilla warfare ended with restoration of the monarchy; the monarchy was abolished in 1975.

Greece has experienced, although with some chronological differences, about the same population growth as most advanced countries have, despite the mass immigration during the two periods from 1900 to 1922 and from 1951 to 1973. Ever since, immigration has given way to repatriation and the entrance of refugees of Greek origins (*Pontioi*) as well as of foreign refugees and immigrants who came mainly from Asia and Africa.

1. Basic Sexological Premises

A. Character of Gender Roles

Greek society was mainly a masculine-based society. With its transformation from a predominantly agricultural to a semi-industrial society, men's work moved out from the home, leaving women isolated from the economic mainstream and utterly dependent on their menfolk for the essentials of life. In this environment, the inferior status of women was widely accepted as an unalterable fact of life. The idea that females could contribute significantly to public life, or even benefit from higher education, was considered preposterous. In fact, women were not allowed to vote, to make contracts, or even to own property.

Much of this has been progressively changed because of three factors: the active participation of women in the ethnic and social movements of modern history, the increasing number of educated women in the last forty years, and the imported Western influences on the equality of the two sexes. In addition, the contribution of the state with its legislative regulations cannot be ignored.

However, despite the fact that gender roles and the law have changed in recent decades, there are distinct gender-role differences in Greece, which are reflected in the personalities, interpersonal relationships, and workplace experiences of men and women. For instance, women have recently made some inroads into occupations defined as "men's jobs," but so far only to a limited degree. Women are poorly represented in the electorate of the national government. Women still retain the primary responsibility for care of the home and children.

B. Sociolegal Status of Males and Females

From the legal viewpoint, Greek men and women now enjoy the same rights as children, adolescents, and adults. Men and women have the same right to vote and equal rights for education and employment. However, because the legal equality between the sexes was enacted only in 1983, it remains to be seen when and how far the law will be implemented in reality.

C. General Concepts of Sexuality and Love

In Greek society, the expression of sexuality and "romantic" love are interdependent. Many people believe that sexual pleasure is realized only in a relationship governed by love (Apostolodis 1992; Ioannidis et al. 1991; Mandi et al. 1993). The ability to love is regarded as something special, and individuals who are indifferent to or unable to feel it are held in contempt. Some believe that although the sexual act is possible with someone else besides the "one and only," true passion and completeness become real only when there is mutual care and devotion.

2. Religious and Ethnic Factors Affecting Sexuality

A. Source and Character of Religious Values

In Greece, the majority of the population (98 percent) declares to be Greek Orthodox by religion. There are also some Catholics, a few Jews and Protestants, and a number of Moslems, mainly from Thrace. The Greek Orthodox Church is much more liberal than the Roman Catholic Church in some aspects, allowing divorce (up to three times normally) and remarriage in church. Although archbishops are not allowed to get married, the majority of parish priests are married.

Influenced by the Platonic and Stoic dualism and the Persian Gnostic tradition (Francoeur 1992), Christianity is governed by a dualistic opposition between the soul and the body, with the soul and mind seeking liberation from the prison of the flesh. Christian faith provides "a special kind of knowledge, gnosis, which the soul can use to transcend this earth and rise to the divine heavenly sphere." Thus, Christianity has awakened in each person the worry of saving one's soul, with this salvation depending on the value of one's personal actions, particularly in the sexual sphere. If the flesh is somehow the source of evil, all sexual practices that are not procreative in character are condemned.

However, there is no correspondence between the official teachings and daily practices, at least in present-day Greece. Greeks regard love and sex as a main part of their existence, as evidenced by the incidence of extramarital relations and abortion, both of which are condemned by the Church. Greece's abortion rate is among the highest in Europe. In reality, Greeks often indicate that they do not consider themselves particularly religious; however, there are the "faithful" who follow the Church's teachings, and the latter does intervene in the sexual life of couples.

B. Source and Character of Ethnic Values

With 98.5 percent of the population ethnic Greek, the country has no influential ethnic minorities. Apart from the Moslems, who comprise about 1 percent of the population, live in a particular area, and follow their own religious and cultural patterns, there is an ethnic homogeneity. It is obvious that the differences in Greece are more of a sociological than of an ethnic nature.

3. Sexual Knowledge and Education

A. Government Policies and Programs for Sex Education

It is not an exaggeration to say that in Greece, sexual education is not the target of any systematic and well-planned governmental program. Even today, sexual education is not included in the school curriculum, although sporadic knowledge is given as part of lessons in such subjects as anthropology. However, this knowledge concerns more elements of physiology and anatomy than references to the external genital organs, the sexual relationship, or the search for and existence of pleasure in connection with the body and sexuality.

Currently, there is an effort and movement to include sexual education in the schools, although two Ministries, that of Health and Social Welfare and that of Education, have not made clear which one will be responsible for these matters. In recognizing the need for sex education, the government has taken some steps, starting in the early 1980s, by bringing Family Planning under the auspices of the Ministry of Health and Social Welfare. Prior to this move, contraceptive education was mainly handled by the Family Planning Association, a nongovernmental organization. The Ministry established forty-six Family Planning Centers all over Greece to provide genetic counseling, sexual education, information about AIDS and sexually transmitted and gynecological diseases, contraceptives, etc.

However, a 1991 evaluation of the efficiency and effectiveness of these centers made by the Family Planning Association has shown that the Family Centers in Greece meet the needs of only a very limited number of people. Their geographic distribution is not sufficient and there does not appear to be any strategy for a systematic operation. A large number of the centers have departed from the initial aim of their operation and now focus their interest more on medical matters, such as Pap-test and gynecological pathology, rather than on sexual education.

B. Informal Sources of Sexual Knowledge

The inadequacy of formal sexual education programs and the resultant lack of sexual knowledge in the population have been detected in a small number of studies carried out by the Department of Sociology of the Athens School of Public Health (Pantzou et al. 1991). Four different research projects, focusing on the general population and on pupils (a pilot study) using quantitative and qualitative methods, have indicated that: (1) the mass media as a whole and television in particular seem to be the main sources of information for both the general population and young people on matters concerning health and AIDS, (2) high school pupils receive no kind of information on sexuality and AIDS at school, and (3) there is a need both for intensification of information on sexual contraception, sexually transmitted diseases and AIDS, and improvement of the quality and specialization of this information.

4. Autoerotic Behaviors and Patterns

The data on autoerotic behaviors in Greece are very limited. The only available information is that which is derived from the K.A.B.P. study in relation to AIDS in the city of Athens (Agrafiotis et al. 1990). A section of this study was devoted to sexual practices, but only one question, in the section on sexual practices that someone follows with his or her sexual partner, referred to autoerotic behaviors. According to the results, men reported twice the percentage of self-pleasuring than that of women (10.6 percent and 5.1 percent respectively) when they were with their partner.

Otherwise, the frequency or the attitudes towards self-pleasuring, both of children, adolescents, and adults have not been examined.

5. *Interpersonal Heterosexual Behaviors*

A. Children

Sexual exploration by children in nursery school between ages 3 to 5 has been observed. The first discoveries are connected with gender and take place mainly among peers. Different kinds of games (playing doctor and nurse, mother and father, king and queen) imitate adult roles, sometimes producing specific pleasure connected with stimulation of the genitals.

Later on, at the age of 10 or 11 years, children's interest is focused on details and confirmation of earlier knowledge on gender differences. At the prepubertal age, they are usually engaged in self-pleasuring activities that occur either in pairs or in groups of peers of the same and other gender, as well as alone.

B. Adolescents

Puberty Rituals and Adolescent Sexual Activities

In the pubertal period, children are more interested in matters related to emotional/sentimental relations and sexuality. Usually the parent of the same sex assumes the responsibility of preparing the child for its physical maturation. Although there are no particular puberty rituals, the occurrence of the first menstruation and the first nocturnal emission or ejaculation are the signs of sexual maturation. These events, however, are not celebrated in any particular formal way in the family or among relatives.

Premarital sexual activities, especially in large cities, are not any longer socially condemned, and sexual intercourse begins between the ages of 14 to 17. Research showed that the most frequent types of contact are through hugging, deep (open mouth) kissing, petting above and below the waist, sleeping together (without sexual intercourse), and oral and vaginal sex.

C. Adults

Premarital Courtship, Dating, and Relationships

In a society in which major social and cultural transformation are taking place, it would be misleading to present facts and opinions that seem definite and absolute. However, it seems definite that there are great differences concerning premarital relations and courtship among urban and rural settings.

In today's predominantly urban and anonymous setting, young people often have access to automobiles that allow an exceptional degree of privacy in their courting. The practice of dating enables young Greeks to find out about one another, to improve their own interpersonal skills, to experiment sexually if they wish to, and finally to select a marriage partner. The courtship period usually varies between one to about six or seven years, with attendance at a college or university being a factor in longer engagements. Beyond all the economic and financial constraints, it is very difficult for an unmarried couple to find an apartment and live together because of the strong opposition of the majority of Greek society.

In more "closed" rural communities and small villages, premarital relations and courtship are not yet the norm before marriage. Although freer than in the past, young adults and especially women do not have the opportunity of dating their future spouse. The idea of arranged marriages and matchmaking (*proksenio*) is still present; the difference is that now women have the right to chose which matchmaking will end in marriage. In some areas a dowry (*prika*) is still required.

Single Adults

Up until the last two decades or so, a large proportion of Greek men and women found their primary identification in their family, and moral approval was given to those who fulfilled traditional expectations of being "good" husbands and "housewives." The proportion of those who were remaining single was very low, and, as a result, data on their sexual behavior and relationships are limited.

However, certain groups, mainly the younger and more educated people, are adopting more contemporary attitudes towards family and marriage, giving greater priority to their personal rights and self-fulfillment as individuals. Nonetheless, the numbers of children born to unmarried women is the lowest in Europe; between 1926 and 1980, the rate changed from 1.1 percent to 1.5 percent of all births.

Marriage and the Family

According to the 1993 statistical data of a Parliamentary Committee responsible for the study of the demographic problem, the Greek family seems to be going through a period of transformation, following the patterns of all other industrial societies. The number of marriages decreased from 7.78 per 1,000 people in 1953 to 6.41 in 1985 and to 5.77 in 1990. On the other hand, the number of divorces is rising.

The typical Greek family unit is monogamous: Greeks may marry only one person at a time. Second, it is increasingly nuclear, although occasionally a grandparent or other relative may live with a family group. Third, it is increasingly egalitarian, with wives becoming much more assertive and husbands more flexible than they were even a decade ago.

Divorce and Remarriage

The divorce rate, although low compared to other European countries, has been rising steadily in the last decade. In 1978, the courts granted 4,322 divorces; in 1989, this number increased by 47 percent to 6,360 cases. According to the statistical data on the culpability of a divorce, it is evident that there has been a great change in the mentality and structure of the Greek family. In a total of 5,684 divorces reported in 1980, men were held culpable for the breakdown of 2,162 marriages and women for 1,144. In a total of 6,360 divorces reported in 1989, after amendment of the divorce law, culpability numbers were 280 and 294 respectively. In addition, the above numbers indicate that the "no-fault" divorces are on an upward trend, reaching about 75 percent of all divorces.

The majority of divorces are obtained after five to ten years of marriage. Also, the majority of divorcing couples have no children or only one child. In 1989, 1,730 divorced couples had no children and 1,520 had only one. Although both divorced parties may experience difficult times, ex-wives in particular may face severe economic problems, especially if they have to raise young children. In the past, when most wives were not expected to work outside the home, courts frequently awarded alimony to divorced women. Now, after adoption of a new Family Law in 1983 that considers women capable of earning their own living, they receive alimony only for a period of three years. After this period, the alimony is automatically interrupted, without considering the possibility that a woman may not find a job. Courts award child custody to mothers rather than to fathers in most cases; however, the courts usually require that the fathers provide child support. A mother cannot retain the children's custody if she is a drug or alcohol addict, mentally or physically disabled, or psychopathic.

The Greek Orthodox Church allows a person to get married up to three times in his/her lifespan. Although there are no statistical data, it is estimated that 90 percent of those who obtain divorce will marry again—especially now that divorces are easier to get and provoke less social disapproval than ever before.

Marital and Extramarital Sexual Behaviors

Although some scientific studies have been undertaken in relation to sexual practices and behaviors of Greeks, no study was concerned with married couples in particular. According to some opinion polls however, both men and women, although satisfied with their sexual life, express their desire for even greater sexual activity. In addition, men in higher percentages than women report extramarital relationships at least with one partner. In addition, it can be said that there is a kind of tolerance on this matter. For instance, the extramarital relationships of important political persons do not constitute a cause for political disgrace or resignation, as is common in other European countries.

Incidence of Oral and Anal Sex

The survey conducted by the Department of Sociology of the Athens School of Public Health (Agrafiotis et al. 1990) has revealed some interesting results in relation to the sexual practices of the general population. The representative sample drawn from the general population of Athens, which really covers one third of the total Greek population, consisted of 1,200 people aged 16 to 65. Generally, for all practices, men reported higher percentages than women. This included vaginal sex (97.3 percent of men versus 94.5 percent of women), oral sex (36.3 percent versus 19.3 percent), and oral sex with body fluids transmission (8.2 percent versus 3.5 percent). Anal sex was also reported at double the rate to that of women (10.8 percent versus 5.1 percent).

Women were less likely to respond to questions concerning sexual practices, (37 percent versus 9 percent). Age groups also showed a considerable variation in sexual practices, with younger groups mentioning a wider variety of practices and a higher rate of them. Those who were 16 to 22 years old were less likely to practice vaginal sex (92.6 percent versus 96 percent) and more likely to practice anal sex (14.9 percent versus 8 percent). Oral sex was over 40 percent for the age groups 16 to 30, but declined to 5.3 percent in age groups 51 to 64. Of course, whether this difference is related to age, to religious and moral objections, or simply to an unwillingness by the older generation to admit to such practices is open to debate.

The above results were more or less confirmed by another research study (Malliori et al. 1991) with a representative sample of 1,980 Athenians of both sexes, 15 to 49 years old. According to these results, 95.5 percent of the females and 96.5 percent of the males employ ordinary intercourse, 35.6 percent of the females and 45.5 percent of the males use additional fellatio practices, 32 percent of the females and 40.5 percent of the males employ cunnilingus, and 10 percent of the females and 17 percent of the males use anal intercourse. Greek law contains no legal restrictions on fellatio, cunnilingus, or anal sex.

6. Homoerotic, Homosexual, and Ambisexual Behaviors

According to the first scientific research conducted by the Athens Medical School (Hantzakis 1992) in an unrepresentative sample of homosexual men, about half of the sample of 213 men were single without ever being married, and either lived alone or with a parent or relative. The majority of these gay men's sexual activity is taken up in the three behaviors of self-pleasuring, fellatio, and anal intercourse. In addition, the majority claimed to have heterosexual contacts as well. This can be partly attributed to the fact that in Greek society there are different kinds of homosexuals (i.e., gays and bisexuals), and a mixture of tolerance and taboos coexist. As a result, many gay men are forced to get married and pass as heterosexuals, whereas in reality, they are ambisexual or psychologically and emotionally exclusively homosexual although engaging in some heterosexual relations.

The legal age of consent for homosexual men is 17 years. The legislation of 1981 can force STD testing of homosexual men. The gay community is visible in the Greek social scene, principally in Athens, Mykonos, and Thessaloniki, and has formed a small political action organization.

7. Gender Conflicted Persons

There is no official data on this matter. According to the opinion of Dr. D. Papoutsakis, who works at the Ministry of Health and Social Welfare, there are forty to fifty transsexuals who had their surgery abroad, mainly at Casablanca and Morocco, who work among the female registered prostitutes.

Greek law does not allow for the change of gender, nor does Greek society provide for any special gender roles, such as the *hijra* of India or the *berdache* among Native Americans.

8. Significant Unconventional Sexual Behaviors

A. Coercive Sex

Child Sexual Abuse and Incest

The phenomenon of child sexual abuse has only recently been surfacing in Greece as an issue of concern among professionals, researchers, and the public, following a long period of denial that continues to exist in many settings. This change can be partly attributed to changes in society's general attitudes towards sexuality as well as to the appearance of AIDS. The term "child sexual abuse" does not exist in Greek criminal law; there are, however, many provisions that specify offenses that infringe upon a child's purity. These offenses are rape, seduction of a minor, indecent assault, incest, and pimping. When the person culpable of such an offense is a parent, a teacher, or a minor's guardian, the punishment is particularly severe. In the seduction of a minor, the younger the child, the harsher the punishment. If the child is less than 10 years old, the penalty can be at least ten years imprisonment; if the child is between 10 to 13 years, the penalty can be between five to ten years; the penalty is five years imprisonment for children 13 to 15 years of age. For the offenses of rape, incest, and pimping the prosecution is automatic, ex officio, while for the rest of the offenses, the prosecution continues only if the sufferer or his/her legal representative brings a charge against the perpetrator.

In cases of child sexual abuse, it is not possible to ascertain the incidence of pedophilia, since this category is not included as such in the offenses that infringe upon a child's purity.

All types of sexual offenses are socially condemned. Although there is no statistical evidence, a study of child sexual abuse among an unrepresentative sample of Greek college students conducted by the Department of Family Relations of the Institute of Child Health (Agathonos et al. 1992) has shown that the phenomenon in Greece is unexplored and its magnitude very likely underestimated. Among the 743 respondents, 96 students (13 men and 83 women), or 13 percent, had experiences of sexual victimization, while 230, or 31 percent, had sexual experiences that did not contain the element of victimization. In one third of the group with the sexual victimization cases, the abuse has been intrafamilial; in one third of the cases, the perpetrator was known to the child. The remaining perpetrators were strangers. In men, perpetrators were on average 12 years older, while women were abused by offenders who were on average 22 years older than them.

Sexual Harassment

Although Greek legislation does not distinguish this category of behavior, sexual harassment, especially by males in the workplace, is not uncommon.

Rape

Although Greece, according to the statistical data of the United Nation's Report, had the lowest number of rapes per 100,000 women in 1992 (only 2 rapes compared to New Zealand with 254 rapes), scientific studies have shown that only 15 percent of rapes are reported to the authorities. Greek society shows an inexcusable tolerance to a criminal behavior that insults human beings. It is not accidental that ten years ago, rape was the only felony for which prosecution was not automatic, ex officio. The public regards the victims of this form of sexual assault as being responsible for their own rapes: they asked for it, flaunted their sexuality, enjoyed it although they pretended not to, started something they could not stop, were out alone at night, or dressed provocatively. According to the new legislation, the penalty for rape is between five and twenty years' imprisonment. However, this new legislation still leaves out the concept of marital rape.

B. Prostitution

Prostitution has for many years been a socially accepted practice, especially for young Greek men. Given traditional rules of virginity for women and the expectation of masculine behavior including sexual prowess for men, prostitutes were both an outlet and a schooling for many men. Nowadays, particularly in the urban centers, young men are more likely to have a girl friend with whom they have sex. In the rest of the country, the situation has not changed dramatically.

In Greece, professional prostitutes, who are officially estimated to be around 200 to 270, are registered with the local police, have a health book, and are obliged to report twice a week for health inspection at a special clinic of the Ministry of Health and Welfare. In order to monitor and control the further spread of HIV infection among registered prostitutes, an intense educational program was implemented in December 1985 (Papaevangelou et al. 1988). As a result, there was a considerable reduction of the incidence of HIV infection and other STDS among prostitutes.

In addition to officially registered prostitutes, there are an estimated ten times as many unregistered prostitutes for whom there is no adequate information about their practices. The number and extent of unregistered prostitutes can only be roughly estimated, because many prostitutes are now being "imported" from former communist countries and the Philippines to work the market unofficially. Alongside the unregistered female prostitutes, there is also an unknown number of male and adolescent prostitutes, mainly in Athens and Thessaloniki.

C. Pornography and Erotica

Despite legislation that prohibits the production and distribution of pornography and erotica, both hard- and soft-core pornography are easily accessible in Greece. In addition, during the last three or four years, there have been a few telephone "hot lines" which, however, are based abroad and their charge is extremely expensive. Many kiosks sell pornographic magazines, and pornographic videotapes are unofficially available to anyone over age 18. However, these tapes are not openly displayed and there is an unwritten code of communications between the customer and the shop owner.

9. Contraception, Abortion, and Population Planning

A. Contraception

Unlike other countries where a considerable amount of social research has been carried out on attitudes of the population towards contraceptive methods, in Greece, until the appearance of AIDS, there were only a few studies on such issues.

In a statistical survey conducted in the context of the Family Planning Center in Thessaloniki, it was found that, among the women visiting the Center, 6.5 percent used the pill, 15 percent the IUD, and most had had some experience with condoms. However, 90 percent of the women never bought condoms, leaving this to their male partners. The latest research concerning the attitudes toward and the use of contraceptive methods by the population of Athens have shown that 46.7 percent of the population use condoms (although it was not clear whether this use was systematic and consistent), 6.6 percent of the women use the pill, and 4 percent the IUD. The preferences of different contraceptive methods depended on age, knowledge of AIDS, educational level, and religiosity. Women did not perceive the condom as their responsibility and were hesitant to propose or promote its use. Young people, on the other hand, were less negative in their attitudes towards condom use, and many have adopted it both as a contraceptive method and a prophylactic against AIDS. The same findings were evident in the pretest study of the K.A.B.P. survey on young people in Athens (Agrafiotis et al. 1990). Sixty-one percent of the pupils did not consider condom use to be against their religion and 84 percent did not consider it contrary to their "traditional beliefs."

What is evident in comparison with other European countries is two particularities of the Greek situation in regard to the attitudes towards contraceptive methods. First, Greek society has not fully adopted the use of modern methods of contraception. According to the statistical data provided by the pharmaceutical companies (Margaritidou et al. 1991), such methods are not easily available and their use is relatively low (i.e., IUD sales are 20,000 annually). Thus, the condom, which is available through pharmacies, supermarkets, and kiosks, is still the most widely used method of contraception. Second, there is a tendency for many Greek couples to prove their fertility by not using contraception and resorting to frequent abortion. It is worth noting that while many countries reported that abortion concerns a very small percentage of women and is considered "marginal" behavior from a psychosocial point of view, in Greece repeated abortion and withdrawal are the most widespread methods of birth control (Agrafiotis et al. 1990).

As for education in the contraceptive methods, it can be said that little systematic information was provided by the state or medical practitioners until the founding of the Family Planning Centers after 1982. Some of these centers provide contraceptive methods free of charge to persons who are not insured, while the National Health Insurance organization does not cover the costs of contraception.

B. Teenage Unmarried Pregnancies

The latest epidemiological figures indicate a marked increase in the incidence of teenage pregnancies. In 1974, teenagers accounted for 5.3 percent of the pregnancies in Greece; in 1988, they accounted for 10.3 percent of the total number of pregnancies. According to the statistical data of the Adolescent Gynecology Department of the Alexandras Hospital (Creatsas et al. 1991), during 1987 and 1988, the ratio of adolescent childbirths, compared to the overall number of childbirths of the clinic, was 10.65

percent, with 88.7 percent of these teenagers 17 to 19 years of age. Half of the pregnant teenagers (49.8 percent) were of low socioeconomic status. Unmarried pregnancies were higher among teenagers than in older age groups. (Greek law allows marriage at the age of 18; girls or boys who wish to marry before that age must obtain a special license with the consent of their parents.)

The doubling of the teenage pregnancy rate and its continued increase can be mainly attributed to several reasons. First, the lack of information on ways to avoid an undesirable pregnancy. It has been estimated that in countries where adolescent sexual education is put into practice, the percentage of undesirable pregnancies is kept relatively low. Second, biological maturation of girls now comes earlier than in the past. And third, premarital sexual activities start at a younger age now than they did in the 1940s and 1950s. Many of the expectant teenage mothers, however, decide to terminate their pregnancies, being fearful of both the medical and social consequences. Thus, parallel to the teenage pregnancies, teenage abortions are increasing.

C. Abortion

Greece possesses the highest percentage of abortions among the European countries. Although the data from the National Statistical Service indicate that only 200 legal abortions are registered every year, the actual number of abortions is estimated to be around 150,000 per year. In research carried out by The National Center for Social Research (E.K.K.E.) in 1988, it was found that the ratio between abortions and live births was nearly one to three. Forty-three percent of all Greek women in the sample reported at least one abortion or miscarriage. In the study conducted by the Family Center in Thessaloniki (Anapliotis 1985), it was found that a large number of women,around 64 percent aged 16 to 46 (and over), had an abortion with the ratio between abortion and live births being 1:8 to 1:3 per woman respectively. Thus,it can be said that repeated abortion is a "norm," a traditional form of birth control, especially for Greek women who have already acquired the desirable number of children.

The above evidence indicates that abortion in Greece is not considered a moral issue of any dimension, and there is a general lack of guilt about the subject. One explanation provided for this behavior is that the traditional importance of the mother role and the constraints concerning the expression of female sexuality come into conflict with the symbolic and real meaning of modern contraceptives (Naziri 1988). The "unwanted" pregnancy that usually ends up in abortion is used as evidence by both men and women of their continuing fertility, whereas modern contraception would create doubts about this.

Abortion was legalized in 1986, although no prosecutions were ever brought against those performing or having abortions under prior laws.

The law allows for abortion until twelve weeks of pregnancy. The National Health System covers the expenses and provides the right of three days' full-pay leave. Despite this, only a few women use the National Health System and their insurance fund for abortion, while there is still a substantive use of private gynecologists for unreported abortions. This can be partly attributed to the fact that private abortions are usually performed immediately, in contrast to the state system that requires some bureaucratic procedures and therefore involves delays. Finally, it must be stressed that only a vocal minority associated with the Orthodox Church was against the legalization of abortion, though in general the Orthodox Church, unlike the Catholic, is not so absolute in its teachings and is more tolerant in its attitudes towards people's practices such as birth control, abortion, and so on.

D. Population Control Efforts

In the last decade, Greece's population growth rate was 1 percent annually compared to the rate of 12 to 13 percent before the World War II. Thus, the government's aim is to promote population growth. However, the birthrate still remains very low, because the government so far has employed only financial incentives, such as allowances, houses, and reduced military service. It seems that the government is content to rely on Greek immigrants who show a tendency of repatriation as the main way of increasing the nation's population.

10. Sexually Transmitted Diseases

A. Incidence, Patterns, and Trends of STDs

The data do not provide reliable indications, or even close estimates, of the actual incidence of STDs in Greece, because the requested notifications are not always made to the authorities. Also, many cases treated by doctors in private practice are not reported. However, a study made by using data from the National Statistical Service, the University Hospital for STDs, and the special clinic for STDs of the Ministry of Health (Kaklamani et al. 1981) has shown that between 1962 and 1976, the frequency of both syphilis and gonorrhea declined among men as well as among women, with the decline more evident among women and among the older age groups. Among men, the highest incidence was in the age group 20 to 29 years, whereas among women the peak incidence was a little earlier. The rates for both syphilis and gonorrhea were higher in men than in women, higher in the greater Athens area than in the rest of Greece, and higher in single persons than in married ones. There was also a marked seasonal variation of STDs with peak incidence at late summer.

From the latest figures, it is evident that there has been a stabilization in the incidence of STDs infection at a relatively low rate. A possible explanation lies in the preventive measures against AIDS and the greater usage of condoms, particularly by prostitutes.

B. Availability of Treatment and Prevention Efforts

In Greece, there are two public dermatological hospitals for the treatment of STDs, with 200 beds in Athens and 60 beds in Salonica.

The considerable reduction in STDs should be attributed to the increasing use of condoms, especially by prostitutes. This was the result of an educational campaign implemented by the Ministry of Health in order to control the spread of HIV infection among registered prostitutes. Indeed, the use of condoms has been considerably increased, from 66 percent in 1985 to 98.5 percent in 1989. As a result, the incidence of syphilis and gonococcal infections has been substantially reduced: for syphilis from 17.1 percent in 1985 to 2 percent in 1989 and for gonococcal infection from 14 percent in 1985 to 1.2 percent in 1989 (Roumeliotou et al. 1990).

11. HIV/AIDS

Greece continues to remain among the European countries with the lowest rates of AIDS. Of the 721 cases of HIV infection detected by December 1992, 366 were homosexual or bisexual males, 153 were heterosexuals, 49 had multiple plasma transfusions, 44 had blood transfusion, 30 were drug addicts, and 5 homosexual drug addicts. The remaining 74 could not be categorized. The overall number of pediatric cases, ages 0 to 12 years, was 12. From the above data, it is evident that, although homosexuals comprise the greatest percentage of people with AIDS, the rate of heterosexual cases is relatively high. This rate may be fictitious due to the fact that homosexual men sometimes hide their sexual identity and pass as heterosexuals.

According to Agrafiotis et al. (1990), the Greek Ministry of Health has used three strategies of preventative intervention: information, laboratory infrastructure, and control measures for the disease. The information campaign, begun in February 1983, was focused primarily at health services and hospitals. The campaign continued through 1985 with special emphasis on "high risk groups," while at the same time providing information pamphlets for health personnel, dentists, the general public, and travelers. In 1988, pamphlets were also produced for certain professions, e.g., hairdressers and earring sellers. At the same time, there were television and radio discussions and public debates all over the country. At that time, six national reference centers for AIDS were operating and approximately ten hospitals offered HIV testing and treatment of AIDS patients. In addition to the Blood Donation Centers where HIV-antibody screening was performed on a routine basis, prevention efforts were supplemented by control measures implemented by the Ministry of Health, such as the HIV-antibody blood screening for transfusions and use of heat-sterilized products for blood testing.

In September 1992, two new services began to operate in Greece, an "Open Phone Line" and an Information Center for AIDS. These services aimed both at reducing the spread of HIV infection and at solving the various psychological problems deriving from the increasing incidence of the disease. These services resulted mainly from a proposal to the Ministry of Health made by the "Psychological Problems" Subcommittee of the National Committee of AIDS. Responsibility for running these services rests with the Department of Psychology at the Psychiatric Clinic of the University of Athens. In addition, a Hostel for psychological support was established to provide support for those who face difficulties with their close family and social environment.

At the level of prevention, the Ministry of Health created a video concerning issues related to the spread of HIV, sexual behavior, and psychosocial problems as a basis for launching an education campaign in the schools. Finally, the Ministry of Health, working with the Greek General Trade Union and the Greek Army, decided to broaden its educational campaign in two specific populations, workers and those in the military.

However, the information campaign that began in the mid-1980s appears to have been curtailed, and television campaigns or public discussions have decreased. In 1993, public debate focused on numerous issues. The import of blood products from Europe has raised concern among hospitals and other healthcare organizations about mechanisms of quality control. Due to the fact that some hospitals refused to accept and treat AIDS patients, there has been a controversy as to whether there should be special units for the treatment of AIDS patients and to the precautions that should be taken.

The situation in Greece, at the beginning at least, can be characterized as "AIDS information epidemic," that is to say, before the virus had arrived in Greece, the media had already created a situation of panic. On the other hand, the mass media has played an important role in the exchange of views. In most cases, AIDS patients are treated in the Department of Infectious Diseases. However, because Greek journalists are not expert on AIDS issues, discourse is often reduced to journalistic rhetoric. More recently, the Ministry of Education has initiated a number of interventions, by preparing a program for prevention and health promotion in schools, as well as initiating a special project on AIDS and drug use. However, prevention programs have no kind of continuity and the policies are not very well established. One explanation for this is that the epidemic is very limited, in comparison with other European countries, and there is an absence of nongovernmental organizations that could push for cooperation. In addition, Greek bureaucracy has no long-term views.

12. Sexual Dysfunction, Counseling, and Therapies

A/B. Concepts of Sexual Dysfunction and the Availability of Treatment

Even at the end of the twentieth century, the sexual act in Greece seems to be shrouded by myths and antiscientific attitudes and approaches that lead to the superficial management of sexual dysfunctions.

It was only at the end of the last decade that some private institutions, both in Athens and Salonica, began to deal with sexual therapy. Having a better mechanism for preserving a patient's privacy, they brought the problem up for open discussion, recognized it, and helped in its demystification. The acceptable methodology for the diagnosis and therapy of sexual dysfunctions is based on the protocol I.S.I.R (International Society of Impotence Research). Impotence is regarded as a symptom of both psychological and organic problems. According to the statistical data of the Andrological Institute, which specializes in male impotence, from a sample of 5,000 patients treated, 25.1 percent of impotence was due to psychogenic causes, 24.6 percent to organic causes, and 50.3 percent resulted from combined causes. The distribution of cases according to age has shown that problems exist in all age groups, with more cases between the ages of 40 and 50. In addition, the analysis of cases according to profession and social class has shown that the problem is present in all social classes with more or less the same frequency. From the same data, it is evident that one in four men in Greece has some kind of sexual dysfunction. (The name "Andrological" reveals the distinction of science into two specialities related to sex. From a sociological and cultural point of view, it is interesting to see how this will operate in Greece.)

13. Research and Advanced Education

The need for sexual research in Greece was pointed out in the early 1980s by D. Agrafiotis. But it was the advent of AIDS that forced these matters to emerge somewhat into the public consciousness and policy. In Greece, there are no institutions engaged in sexological research on a regular basis. Research on sexual matters is conducted occasionally and by different research teams without any national coordination. Among the teams engaged in various kinds of sexological research are:

University of Athens, Department of Psychiatry. Director: C. Stefanis. Address: 74 Vas. Sophias Avenue, Athens, Greece

Athens School of Public Health, Department of Sociology. Director: Demosthenis Agrafiotis. Address: 196 Alexandras Avenue, Athens, Greece

Athens School of Public Health, Department of Epidemiology. Director: G. Papaevangelou. Address: 196 Alexandras Avenue, Athens, Greece

A Syngros Hospital. Director: G. Stratigos. Address: 6 Dragoumi, Athens, Greece

Family Planning Association (FPA). Address: 121 Solonos, Athens, Greece

Athens Medical School. Department of Epidemiology and Hygiene, Director: D. Trixopoulos, Address: Athens, Greece

Hellenic Society of Paediatric and Adolescent Gyaecology (HSPAG). Director: C. Kreatsas. Address: 9 Kanarie str, Athens, Greece

The Department of Psychiatry, the FPA, and the HSPAG offer sex education programs for parents.

Undergraduate courses are provided to doctors by the Medical School but only as part of the general curriculum (knowledge of organic systems), and are not intended to be a study of human sexuality as such. There is no medical specialization in sexology, and the psychiatrists or gynecologists who wish to specialize in this field should go abroad. The question of sexology as a scientific field is not fully recognized and there is always a controversy on this matter. As a result, psychologists, sexologists, psychiatrists, and psychoanalysts try to determine their domains of competence. On the other hand, the Department of Sociology of the Athens School of Public Health explores various issues related to sexuality, and in general, the social sciences includes sexuality and sexual issues in their area of research.

There are no Greek journals or periodicals on sexuality.

A Final Remark

The issues of sexuality in Greece have yet to be adequately studied. Over all, there is an urgent need for a more systematic investigation of the coexistence of traditional and modern values due to the social particularities of the Greek society and their influence on current sexual attitudes and behaviors.

References and Suggested Readings

Agathonos, H., et al. 1992. "Retrospective Study of Child Sexual Abuse. Experiences Among Greek College Students." Paper presented at the ISPCAN Conference Chicago, USA. August 30 to September 2, 1992.

Agrafiotis, D. 1981. *Social and Cultural Development in Greece.* Scientific Report Ministry of Health. Athens.

Agrafiotis, D., et al. 1990. *Knowledge, Attitudes, Beliefs and Practices of Young People. Pre-Test WHO/GPA/SBR (World Health Organization; Global Programme on AIDS; Social and Behavioural Research).* Research Monograph No. 26. Sociology of Health and Illness.

Agrafiotis, D., et al. 1991. *Knowledge, Attitudes, Beliefs and Practices in Relation to HIV Infection and AIDS. The Case of the City of Athens.* Department of Sociology. Athens School of Public Health.

Apostolodis, T. 1992. *A Cross-Cultural Investigation of Socio-Cultural Models on Sexuality and Love, Between Students in France and in Greece.* Unpublished Thesis. University of Paris, France.

Creatsas, O., et al. 1991. "Teenage Pregnacy: Comparison with Two Groups of Older Women." *Journal of Adolescent Health Care,* 15-17:77-81.

Francoeur, Robert T. 1992. "The Religious Supression of Eros." In: *The Erotic Impulse.* David Steinberg, ed. New York: Tarcher/Perigee.

Hantzakis, A. 1992. "Homosexuality in Greece." In: *Homosexual Response Studies. International Report.* Anthony P. M. Coxon, ed. World Health Organization.

Ioannidis, E., et al. 1991. *Sexual Behavior in the Years of AIDS in Greece.* Lisbon Workshop. ECCA.

Kaklamani, E., et al. 1981. "Syphilis and Gonorrhea: Epidemiology Update." *Paediatrician,* 10:207-215.

Malliori, M., et al. 1991. *Sexual Behavior and Knowledge about AIDS in a Representative Sample of Athens Area.* Department of Psychiatry, University of Athens.

Madianos, M., et al. 1988. *Health and Greek Society.* Athens: EKKE.

Mandi, P., et al. 1993. *Sexual Patterns in Contemporary Greece A Pilot Study.* Research Monograph No.9. Athens School of Public Health/Andrological Institute.

Naziri, D. 1988. *Greek Women and Abortion. Clinical Study of Repeated Abortion.* Unpublished Thesis. University of Paris.

Pantzou, P., et al. 1991. "The Demand for Health Education on Sexuality and AIDS Based on Sociopsychological Research." Second European Conference on Effectiveness of Health Promotion and Education.

Papaevangelou, G., et al. 1988. "Education in Preventing HIV Infection in Greek Registered Prostitutes." *Journal of Aquired Immune Deficiency Syndromes,* 1:386-89.

Primpas Welts, Eve. 1982. "Greek Families." In M. McGoldrick, J. K. Pearce, and J. Giordano, eds. *Ethnicity and Family Therapy.* New York: Guilford Press.

Roumeliotou, A., et al. 1990. "Prevention of HIV Infection in Greek Registered Prostitutes. A Five-Year Study." 6th International Conference on AIDS, San Francisco, USA. June 20-24, 1990.